Lecture Notes in Computer Science 3815

Commenced Publication in 1973
Founding and Former Series Editors:
Gerhard Goos, Juris Hartmanis, and Jan van Leeuwen

Editorial Board

David Hutchison
  Lancaster University, UK
Takeo Kanade
  Carnegie Mellon University, Pittsburgh, PA, USA
Josef Kittler
  University of Surrey, Guildford, UK
Jon M. Kleinberg
  Cornell University, Ithaca, NY, USA
Friedemann Mattern
  ETH Zurich, Switzerland
John C. Mitchell
  Stanford University, CA, USA
Moni Naor
  Weizmann Institute of Science, Rehovot, Israel
Oscar Nierstrasz
  University of Bern, Switzerland
C. Pandu Rangan
  Indian Institute of Technology, Madras, India
Bernhard Steffen
  University of Dortmund, Germany
Madhu Sudan
  Massachusetts Institute of Technology, MA, USA
Demetri Terzopoulos
  New York University, NY, USA
Doug Tygar
  University of California, Berkeley, CA, USA
Moshe Y. Vardi
  Rice University, Houston, TX, USA
Gerhard Weikum
  Max-Planck Institute of Computer Science, Saarbruecken, Germany

T0223703

Edward A. Fox   Erich J. Neuhold
Pimrumpai Premsmit   Vilas Wuwongse (Eds.)

Digital Libraries: Implementing Strategies and Sharing Experiences

8th International Conference on
Asian Digital Libraries, ICADL 2005
Bangkok, Thailand, December 12-15, 2005
Proceedings

 Springer

Volume Editors

Edward A. Fox
Virginia Tech, Department of Computer Science
660 McBryde Hall, M/C 0106, Blacksburg, VA 24061, USA
E-mail: fox@vt.edu

Erich J. Neuhold
Fraunhofer IPSI
Dolivostr. 15, 64293 Darmstadt, Germany
E-mail: neuhold@ipsi.fhg.de

Pimrumpai Premsmit
Chulalongkorn University, Department of Library Science
Bangkok 10330, Thailand
E-mail: pimrumpai.p@chula.ac.th

Vilas Wuwongse
Asian Institute of Technology
Km. 42 Paholyothin Highway, Klong Luang, Pathumthani 12120, Thailand
E-mail: vw@cs.ait.ac.th

Library of Congress Control Number: 2005937123

CR Subject Classification (1998): H.3, H.2, H.4.3, H.5, J.7, D.2, J.1, I.7

ISSN   0302-9743
ISBN-10   3-540-30850-4 Springer Berlin Heidelberg New York
ISBN-13   978-3-540-30850-8 Springer Berlin Heidelberg New York

This work is subject to copyright. All rights are reserved, whether the whole or part of the material is concerned, specifically the rights of translation, reprinting, re-use of illustrations, recitation, broadcasting, reproduction on microfilms or in any other way, and storage in data banks. Duplication of this publication or parts thereof is permitted only under the provisions of the German Copyright Law of September 9, 1965, in its current version, and permission for use must always be obtained from Springer. Violations are liable to prosecution under the German Copyright Law.

Springer is a part of Springer Science+Business Media

springer.com

© Springer-Verlag Berlin Heidelberg 2005
Printed in Germany

Typesetting: Camera-ready by author, data conversion by Scientific Publishing Services, Chennai, India
Printed on acid-free paper   SPIN: 11599517   06/3142   5 4 3 2 1 0

Preface

The International Conference on Asian Digital Libraries 2005 (ICADL 2005), held in Bangkok, Thailand, 12–15 December 2005, was the 8th in a series of annual international conferences organized by digital library researchers in Asia. ICADL was set up to facilitate and stimulate the exchange of digital library research, information, and technology in the Asian region while also functioning as a sister conference to its North American and European counterparts, i.e., JCDL and ECDL. The theme of ICADL 2005 was "Digital Libraries: Implementing Strategies and Sharing Experiences," covering strategies, implementation experiences, systems, techniques, management, and applications. ICADL 2005 provided a forum for sharing experiences and exchanging research results, innovative ideas, and state-of-the-art developments among researchers, educators, practitioners, and policy makers from a variety of disciplines such as computer science, library and information science, archival and museum studies, and knowledge management.

ICADL 2005 also marked the special occasion of the 50th birthday anniversary of Her Royal Highness Princess Maha Chakri Sirindhorn, Patron of the Thai Library Association.

ICADL 2005 received 164 paper submissions from 17 countries, including a good number from outside the Asian region. From these, 40 full papers, 15 short papers, and 15 poster papers were accepted and are included in these proceedings. Each paper was reviewed by the Program Committee members and additional co-reviewers. The technical program comprised one day of tutorials, followed by keynote and invited speeches, paper and poster sessions as well as a post-conference workshop on metadata and Dublin Core.

The 14 technical paper sessions are: "Concepts and Models for Digital Library Systems," "Case Studies in Digital Libraries," "Digital Archives and Museums," "Multimedia Digital Libraries," "Information Processing in Asian Digital Libraries," "Digital Libraries for Community Building," "Information Retrieval Techniques," "Ontologies and Content Management in Digital Libraries," "Information Integration and Retrieval Technologies in Digital Libraries," "Information Mining Technologies in Digital Libraries," "Digital Library System Architecture and Implementations," "Information Processing in Digital Libraries," "Human–Computer Interfaces," and "Metadata Issues in Digital Libraries."

Many people have contributed to the organization of this conference. We would like to express our sincere thanks to the members of the Program Committee for their continuous advice and help in reviewing and selecting papers. We thank the sponsors, members of the Steering Committee, and all individuals for their support in making the conference a success. We also thank all authors and delegates for participating in the conference.

Finally, we would like to express our gratitude to the Organizing Committee Chair, Khunying Maenmas Chavalit, and the Organizing Committee for their excellent work.

December 2005

Edward Fox
Erich Neuhold
Pimrumpai Premsmit
Vilas Wuwongse

Organization

Steering Committee Chair

Khunying Maenmas Chavalit (The Thai Library Association, Thailand)

Steering Committee Co-chairs

Ching-chih Chen (Simmons College, USA)
Hsinchun Chen (The University of Arizona, USA)
Ee Peng Lim (Nanyang Technological University, Singapore)

Program Committee Co-chairs

Edward Fox (Virginia Tech, USA)
Erich Neuhold (University of Vienna, Austria)
Pimrumpai Premsmit (Chulalongkorn University, Thailand)
Vilas Wuwongse (Asian Institute of Technology, Thailand)

Program Committee

Jun Adachi (NII, Japan)
Robert Allen (Drexel, USA)
Toshiyuki Amagasa (Nara Institute of Science and Technology, Japan)
Chutiporn Anutariya (Shinawatra University, Thailand)
Thomas Baker (Goettingen State and University Library, Germany)
Jose Borbinha (National Library of Portugal, Portugal)
Donatella Castelli (Italian National Research Council (IEI-CNR), Italy)
Chao-chen Chen (National Taiwan Normal University, Taiwan)
Hsinchun Chen (The University of Arizona, USA)
Hsueh-hua Chen (NTU, Taiwan)
Key-Sun Choi (KAIST, Korea)
Gobinda Chowdhury (University of Strathclyde, UK)
Weiguo Fan (Virginia Tech, USA)
Schubert Foo (NTU, Singapore)
James French (University of Virginia, USA)
Maruf Hasan (Shinawatra University, Thailand)

Jieh Hsiang (National Chi-nan University, Taiwan)
San-Yih Hwang (NSYSU, Taiwan)
Peter Jacso (University of Hawaii, USA)
Paul Janecek (Asian Institute of Technology, Thailand)
Noriko Kando (NII, Japan)
Ji-Hoon Kang (Chungnam National University, Korea)
Wai Lam (CUHK, Hong Kong SAR)
Carl Lagoze (Cornell University, USA)
Jianzhong Li (Harbin Institute of Technology, China)
Yan Quan Liu (Southern Connecticut State University, USA)
Dion Goh Hoe Lian (NTU, Singapore)
Ee Peng Lim (NTU, Singapore)
Gary Marchionini (University of North Carolina, USA)
Cliff McKnight (Loughborough University, UK)
Takeshi Nagatsuka (Tsurumi University, Japan)
Marc Nanard (Laboratoire d'Informatique de Robotique et de Microélectronique
    de Montpellier (LIRMM), France)
Ekawit Nantajeewarawat (Sirindhorn International Institute of Technology,
    Thailand)
Claudia Niederee (Fraunhofer IPSI, Germany)
Paul Nieuwenhuysen (Vrije Universiteit Brussel, Belgium)
Doug Oard (University of Maryland, USA)
Somporn Puttapithakporn (Sukhothai Thammathirat Open University,
    Thailand)
Edie Rasmussen (University of British Columbia, Canada)
Andreas Rauber (Vienna University of Technology, Austria)
Tetsuo Sakaguchi (Tsukaba University, Japan)
Hideyasu Sasaki (Ritsumeikan University, Japan)
Michael Seadle (Michigan State University, USA)
Praditta Siripan (National Science and Technology Development Agency,
    Thailand)
Ingeborg Solvberg (Norwegian University of Science and Technology, Norway)
Shigeo Sugimoto (ULIS, Japan)
Katsumi Tanaka (Kyoto University, Japan)
Yin-Leng Theng (NTU, Singapore)
James Z. Wang (Penn State University, USA)
Ian Witten (Waikato University, New Zealand)
Christopher C. Yang (CUHK, Hong Kong SAR)
Jerome Yen (Chinese University of Hong Kong, China)
Masatoshi Yoshikawa (Nagoya University, Japan)
Marcia Lei Zeng (Kent State University, USA)
Li-zhu Zhou (Tsinghua University, China)

Co-reviewers

Pengbo Liu (Virginia Tech, USA)
Rao Shen (Virginia Tech, USA)
Teerapat Sanguankotchakorn (Asian Institute of Technology, Thailand)
Xiaoyan Yu (Virginia Tech, USA)

Organizing Committee Chair

Khunying Maenmas Chavalit (The Thai Library Association, Thailand)

Organizing Committee Co-chairs

Vatcharaporn Esichaikul (Asian Institute of Technology, Thailand)
Pimrumpai Premsmit (Chulalongkorn University, Thailand)

Organizing Committee

Chindarat Burpan (Chulalongkorn University, Thailand)
Suphalak Chantharaksri (Chulalongkorn University, Thailand)
Lapapan Choovong (UNESCO, Thailand)
Suwakhon Siriwongworawat (Dhurakijpundit University, Thailand)
Suchit Suvaphab (The Thai Library Association, Thailand)
Duangnate Vongpradhip (Chulalongkorn University, Thailand)
Prachak Wattananusit (National Library, Thailand)

Local Organizing Chair

Jaffee Yee (InfoMedia Asia, Ltd. Thailand)

Secretariat

Secretary General: Daruna Somboonkun (The Thai Library Association, Thailand)
Deputy Secretary General: Suwadee Vichetpan (The Thai Library Association, Thailand)
Assistant to Secretary General: Wanpen Kongpoon (SPAFA, Thailand)

Table of Contents

Concepts and Models for Digital Library Systems

Case Studies in Digital Libraries

Digital Archives and Museums

Multimedia Digital Libraries

Information Processing in Asian Digial Libraries

Digital Libraries for Community Building

Information Retrieval Techniques

Ontologies and Content Management in Digital Libraries

Information Integration and Retrieval Technologies in Digital Libraries

Information Mining Technologies in Digital Libraries

Digital Library System Architecture and Implementations

Information Processing in Digital Libraries

Human-Computer Interfaces

Metadata Issues in Digital Libraries

Posters

Keynote and Invited Papers

A Model of ITS Using Cold Standby Cluster

Khin Mi Mi Aung[1], Kiejin Park[2], and Jong Sou Park[1]

[1] Computer Engineering Dept., Hankuk Aviation University
{maung, jspark}@hau.ac.kr
[2] Division of Industrial and Information System Engineering, Ajou University
kiejin@ajou.ac.kr

Abstract. Current intrusion detection mechanisms have quite low detection and high false alarm rates. Thus we propose a model of intrusion tolerant system (ITS) to increase the survivability level from the successful attacks. In this paper, we present the cluster recovery model using cold standby cluster with a software rejuvenation methodology, which is applicable in security field and also less expensive. Firstly, we perform the steady state analysis of a cluster system and then consider an ITS with cold standby cluster. The basic idea is investigate the consequences for the exact responses in face of attacks and rejuvenate the running service or/and reconfigure it. It shows that the system operates through intrusions and provides continued the critical functions, and gracefully degrades non-critical system functionality in the face of intrusions.

Keywords: Security, Concepts and Models, Intrusion Tolerant System, Rejuvenation, Cluster System.

1 Introduction

After intrusion protection and detection mechanisms, the next security mechanism is the intrusion tolerant system (ITS). Current intrusion detection mechanisms have quite low detection and high false alarm rates, and their progress has reached to unacceptable levels.[1]. Thus we propose a ITS model to increase the cluster system survivability level by maintaining the essential functionality. In this paper, we present the cluster recovery model with a software rejuvenation methodology, which is applicable in security field and also less expensive. The nature of attacks is very dynamic because attackers have the specific intention to attack and well prepare their steps in advance. So far no respond technique able to cope with all types of attacks has been found. In most attacks, attackers overwhelm the target system with a continuous flood of traffic designed to consume all system resources, such as CPU cycles, memory, network bandwidth, and packet buffers. These attacks degrade service and can eventually lead to a complete shutdown. In this work, we address attacks mainly related to CPU usage, physical memory and swap space usage, running processes, network flows and packets. It will automatically detect potential weaknesses and reconfigure with attack patterns, which are characterizing an individual type of attack and attack profiles. We had analyzed the attack datasets and injected the attacks

E.A. Fox et al. (Eds.): ICADL 2005, LNCS 3815, pp. 1–10, 2005.
© Springer-Verlag Berlin Heidelberg 2005

events into a system, and learned the prior knowledge. The next step is to restore the system to a healthy state within a set time following the predictive alerts [2].

Software rejuvenation is a proactive fault management technique aimed at cleaning up the internal system state to prevent the occurrence of more severe future crash failures. It involves occasionally terminating an application or a system, cleaning its internal state and restarting it. IBM Software Rejuvenation is a tool to help increase server availability by proactively addressing software and operation system aging [3]. The effect of aging is captured as crush/hang failures [4].

Survivability is the ability of a system to continue operating in the presence of acci-dental failures or malicious attacks [5]. We illustrate our abstract model for the survivability from the malicious attacks. We evaluate the survivability of systems and services as well as the impact of any proposed changes on the overall survivability of systems. The paper has also presented aspects of the operational requirements for information systems such as the ability to operate through attacks and graceful degradation. In the current literature, there are significant numbers of researches, which are mainly concerned with survivability analysis. Jha et. al. and Nikolopoulos et. al. [6, 7, 8] have studied reliability, latency and cost benefit model. Jha et. al. [7] have analyzed survivability of network systems, which are service dependent; therefore a system architect should focus on the design of the system by analyzing only the service required of that system. Liew et. al. [9] had presented a survivability function model. In their study, a survivability function is used as the measure instead of a single value for survivability. Newport [10] built node and link connectivity models. The terms connectivity and survivability are used interchangeably in their research. Moitra et. al. [11, 12] simulated the model for managing survivability of network information systems. They propose a model to assess the survivability of a net-work system. Different parameters affect survivability such as the frequency and impact of attacks on a network system.

In this paper, we present a model to increase the cluster system survivability level using software rejuvenation. The organization of the paper is as follows. In Section 1, we define the problem and address related research. Section 2 presents a proposed model which can be used to analyze and proactively manage the effects of cluster network faults and attacks, and recover accordingly and in the following section, the model is analyzed and experiment results are given to validate the model solution. Finally, we conclude that software rejuvenation is a viable method and present further research issues.

2   Proposed Model

Significant features of various system resources may differ between specific attacks. And the response and restore methods would differ as well. In this work, the system has divided into three stages; healthy stage, restoration stage and failure stage (refer to Figure. 1). The model consists of five states, such as healthy state (H), infected state (I), rejuvenation state (R_j), reconfiguration state (R_c) and failure state (F). The healthy state represents the functioning and service providing phases. In the healthy stages, the systems aware to resist by various policies and offer proactive managements which are periodic diagnostics and automatic error log analysis, scheduled tasks (checking routine) based on experiences to assess the approximate frequency of unplanned outages due to resources exhaustion, monitoring server subsystems and software processes to ascertain common trends accompanying regular failures, error logging and alerts (error logging controls).

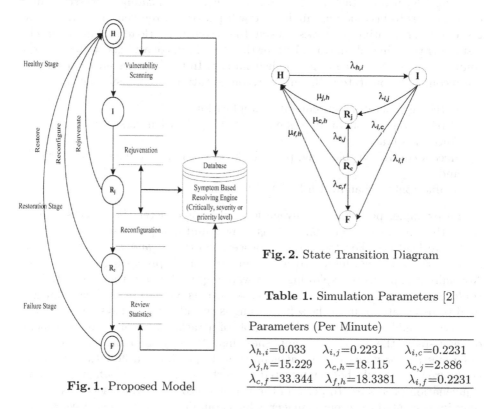

Fig. 2. State Transition Diagram

Table 1. Simulation Parameters [2]

Parameters (Per Minute)		
$\lambda_{h,i}$=0.033	$\lambda_{i,j}$=0.2231	$\lambda_{i,c}$=0.2231
$\lambda_{j,h}$=15.229	$\lambda_{c,h}$=18.115	$\lambda_{c,j}$=2.886
$\lambda_{c,f}$=33.344	$\lambda_{f,h}$=18.3381	$\lambda_{i,f}$=0.2231

Fig. 1. Proposed Model

At the rejuvenation performing state, we need to be able to weigh the risk of policy with further damage against the policy of shutting the system in an emergency stage. In this case, the tools not only detect an attacker's presence but also support to get the information containments. The events are preconditions and are related to compromised system states. Susceptible to attack is an action or series of actions that lead to a compromise. Multiple defense mechanisms are the set of actions that may be taken to correct vulnerable conditions existing on the system or to move the system from a more compromised state to a less compromised state. To this end, software rejuvenation methodologies are reviewed and synthesized by the policies. The main strategies are occasionally stopping the executing software, cleaning the internal state and restarting by means of effectiveness of proactive managements, degrading mechanism, service stop, service restart, reboot and halt.

At the restoration stage, they may be decomposed into three types according to their specific attacks such as

- Performing rejuvenation only
- Performing reconfiguration only and
- Performing both rejuvenation and reconfiguration

For example, if an attacker carries out attack by overloading processes, causing resources to become unavailable, we will perform a rejuvenation process by gracefully terminating processes causing the resource overload and immediately restarting them in a clean state. But for the other kinds of attacks, we have to reconfigure the system according per their impact. In this case we have considered the reconfiguration state with various reconfiguration mechanisms, such as

- Patching (operating system patch, application patch),
- Version control (operating system version, application version),
- Anti virus (vaccine),
- Access control (IP blocking, port blocking, session drop, contents filtering), and
- Traffic control (bandwidth limit)

As an example, performing rejuvenation only could deter the attacks, which cause the process degradation such as spawn multiple processes, fork bombs, CPU overload etc. For the cases of process shutdown and system shutdown attacks, the attackers intend to halt a process or all processing on a system. Normally it happens by exploiting a software bug that causes the system to halt could cause system shutdown. In this case, just as with software bugs that are used to penetrate, so until the software bug is reconfigured, all systems of a certain type would be vulnerable. An example of attacks called mail bombardment or mail spam, the attacker accomplishes this attack by flooding the user with huge message or with very big attachments. Depending on how the system is configured, this could be counteracted by performing both reconfiguration and rejuvenation processes. To perform the various reconfiguration mechanisms, we have implemented the event manager, which contains the various strategies with respect to the various impact levels of the specific infected cases. Each type of event has its own routine, to be run when the attack takes place [2].

3 ITS with Cold Standby Cluster

3.1 Steady-State Analysis on a Single Node Through Markov Process

According to the state transition diagram of Figure. 2 We denote as,

$\lambda_{h,i}$ = infected rate from the healthy state
$\lambda_{i,j}$ = rejuvenation rate from the infected state
$\mu_{j,h}$ = rejuvenation service rate to the healthy state

$\lambda_{i,c}$ = reconfiguration rate from the infected state
$\mu_{c,j}$ = reconfiguration service rate to the rejuvenation state
$\lambda_{c,f}$ = failure rate from the reconfiguration state
$\mu_{c,h}$ = reconfiguration service rate to the healthy state
$\lambda_{i,f}$ = failure rate from the infected state
$\mu_{f,h}$ = service rate from the failure state

And let the steady-state probabilities of the state of the system be

π_h = the probability that the system is in Healthy State
π_i = the probability that the system is in Infected State
π_j = the probability that the system is in Rejuvenation State
π_c = the probability that the system is in Reconfiguration State
π_f = the probability that the system is in Failure State

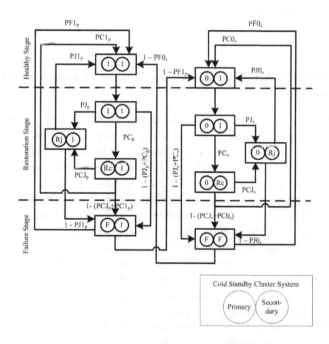

Fig. 3. ITS with cold standby cluster

Using principle of the rate at which the process enters each state with the rate at which the process leaves can derive the balance equations for the system (refer to Figure 3).

$$\lambda_{h,i}\pi_h = \mu_{j,h}\pi_j + \mu_{c,h}\pi_c + \mu_{f,h}\pi_f \tag{1}$$

$$\pi_i = E\pi_h \tag{2}$$

$$\pi_c = \frac{\lambda_{i,c}}{F}E\pi_h \tag{3}$$

$$\pi_j = \left(\lambda_{i,j} + \frac{\lambda_{c,j}\lambda_{i,c}}{F} \right) E \frac{1}{\mu_{j,h}} \pi_h \tag{4}$$

$$\pi_f = \left(\lambda_{i,f} + \frac{\lambda_{c,f}\lambda_{i,c}}{F} \right) E \frac{1}{\mu_{j,h}} \pi_h \tag{5}$$

By solving above equation in terms of π_h and the condition $\pi_h + \pi_i + \pi_r + \pi_c + \pi_f$, we get

$$\pi_h = \frac{1}{1 + E + \frac{\lambda_{i,c}}{F}E} + \frac{1}{\left(\lambda_{i,j} + \frac{\lambda_{c,j}\lambda_{i,c}}{F} \right)} E \frac{1}{\mu_{j,h}} + \frac{1}{\left(\lambda_{i,f} + \frac{\lambda_{c,f}\lambda_{i,c}}{F} \right)} E \frac{1}{\mu_{j,h}} \tag{6}$$

Where $E = \frac{\lambda_{h,i}}{\lambda_{i,j}+\lambda_{i,c}+\lambda_{i,f}}$ and $F = \lambda_{c,f} + \lambda_{c,j} + \mu_{c,h}$

The availability for the steady-state analysis on a single node through Markov Process can be expressed as:

$$A = 1 - (\pi_f + \pi_j + \pi_c) \tag{7}$$

3.2   Steady-State Analysis with Two Nodes Through Semi-markov Process

Semi-Markov models contain a Markov chain, which describes the stochastic transitions from state to state, and transition or 'sojourn' times, which describe the duration that the process takes to transition from state to state. We address the survivability model with semi-Markov process. We consider a cold standby cluster with two nodes through Semi-Markov process. One node is as an active (primary) and other as a standby (secondary) unit. The failure rate of the primary node and secondary node are different, and also the effect of failure of the primary node is different from that of secondary node. The state transition diagram is shown in Figure. 3. Initially the system is in state $(1,1)$. When the primary is infected by active attacks, the system enters state $(I, 1)$. In the infected state, the system has to figure out whether rejuvenate or reconfigure to recover or limit the damage that may happen by an attack. If the primary node has to reconfigure, the system enters state $(R_c, 1)$ otherwise enters state $(R_j, 1)$. If both strategies fail then the primary system enters the fail state. When the primary node fails a protection switch successfully restores service by switching in the secondary unit, and the system enters state $(0,1)$. If the node failure occurs when the system is in one of the states : $(0,I)$ or $(0, R_c)$, the system fails and enters state (F,F). To calculate the steady-state availability of the proposed model, the stochastic process of equation 8 was defined. Through SMP (Semi-Markov Process) analysis applying M/G/1, whose service time is general distribution; we calculated the steady-state probability in each state.

$$X(t) : t > 0 \tag{8}$$

$$X_S = (1,1), (I,1), (R_j,1), (R_c,1), (F,1), (0,1), (0,I), (0,R_j), (0,R_c), (F,F)$$

As all the states shown in Figure 3 are attainable to each other, they are irreducible. Additionally, as they do not have a cycle and can return to a certain state, they satisfy the ergodicity (Aperiodic, Recurrent, and Nonnull) characteristics. Therefore, there is a probability in the steady-state of SMP for each state and each corresponding SMP can be induced by embedded DTMC (Discrete-time Markov Chain) using transition probability in each state. If we define the mean sojourn times in each state of SMP as hi's and define DTMC steady-state probability as di's, the steady-state probability in each state of SMP (pi) can be calculated by equation 9 [14].

$$\pi = \frac{d_i h_i}{\sum_j d_j h_j}, i, j \in X_S \tag{9}$$

Whereas, steady-state probability of DTMC di's will have the following relationship as shown in equation 10 and equation 11.

$$\vec{d} = \vec{d} \cdot P \tag{10}$$

$$\sum_i d_i = 1 i \in X_S \tag{11}$$

Where $\vec{d} = \{d_{(1,1)} d_{(I,1)} d_{(R_j,1)} d_{(R_c,1)} d_{(F,1)} d_{(0,1)} d_{(0,I)} d_{(0,R_j)} d_{(0,R_c)} d_{(F,F)}\}$ and P is the transition probability matrix of DTMC expressed by the transition probability in each state of XS in Figure 3 $(P_{(i,j)})$. The system availability in the steady-state is defined as equation 12, which is the same as the exclusion of the probability of being in (F, 1) and (F, F) in each state of XS in the state transition diagram.

$$A = 1 - (\pi_{F,1} + \pi_{F,F}) \tag{12}$$

When D* indicates the deadline of the mean sojourn time ratio (dihi) for determining whether the system survives in case either of the primary server or the secondary server is in the attack state $((R_j, 1), (R_c, 1), (0, R_j), (0, R_c)), Y_i(i = (R_j, 1), (R_c, 1), (0, R_j), (0, R_c))$, the indicator variable for determining the survivability of the system in the corresponding state is decided as follows.

$$d_i h_i \leq D^* Y_i = 0, d_i h_i > D^* Y_i = 1 \tag{13}$$

Using the indicator variable decided above, the survivability measure of a restore system is defined as equation 14.

$$S = A - \left[Y_{(R_j,1)} \pi_{(R_j,1)} + Y_{(R_c,1)} \pi_{(R_c,1)} + Y_{(0,R_j)} \pi_{(0,R_j)} + Y_{(0,R_c)} \pi_{(0,R_c)} \right] \tag{14}$$

4   Numerical Results

In this section, we illustrate the evaluation of model with numerical results. To evaluate our SMP model, we need to set parameters for the transition probability and the mean sojourn time in each state. The accurate model parameter values are unknown and we assume the relative differences for various model parameters [2]. The use of various model parameters makes it relevant to get the sensitivity level of different measures to variations in the model parameter values.

Figure 4 shows that infected rate from the healthy state and rejuvenation rate from the infected state are more sensitive to decrease the steady state availability.

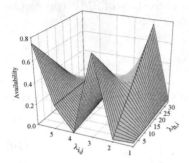

Fig. 4. Steady-state analysis of non-cluster system

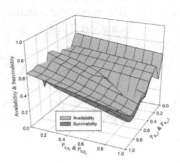

Fig. 5. Analysis of availability and survivability according to the change of the transition probabilities of the primary-secondary servers

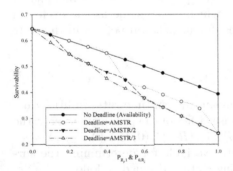

Fig. 6. Analysis of survivability according to early coping ability and the change of deadline

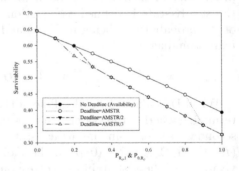

Fig. 7. Analysis of survivability according to the ability to cope with attacks and the change of deadline

Table 2. Simulation Parameters for SMP

Mean Sojourn Time	$h_{(1,1)}{=}50$ $h_{(I,1)}{=}30$ $h_{(R_j,1)}{=}25$ $h_{(R_c,1)}{=}50$ $h_{(F,1)}{=}50$
	$h_{(0,1)}{=}50$ $h_{(0,I)}{=}30$ $h_{(0,R_j)}{=}25$ $h_{0,(R_c)}{=}50$ $h_{F,F}{=}50$
Transition Probability	$0 \prec P_{(R_j,1)}, P_{(R_c,1)}, P_{(0,1)}, P_{(0,R_j)}, P_{(0,R_c)} \succ 1$
Deadline	$AMSTR/3 \prec D* \prec AMSTR$

As we expected, the steady-state availability decreases as the proportion of time, which is spending in every state, is increased. Because the mean sojourn time in each state has a general distribution, values are meaningful only as relative differences. On the other hand, deadline (D*) for analyzing survivability was set based on $\left(d_{R_j,1} d_{R_c,1} + d_{0,R_j} d_{0,R_c}\right)/2$, which is the average of mean sojourn time ratio (AMSTR) in the attack state.

Figure 5 shows the change of system availability and survivability with the decrease of system performance. As transition probabilities for the primary server $(R_j, 1)$ and $(R_c, 1)$ or $(0, R_j)$ and $(0, R_c)$ related to the secondary server increase at the same time, availability and survivability gradually decrease. To prevent the decrease of survivability, it is necessary to diagnose the system in order to lower the sojourn time ratio in the state of and while attacks from outside are going on. Figure 6 shows the changes the level of system survivability according to the changes in rejuvenation probability when the servers are attacked. The difference between no deadline and deadline is insignificant in the section where transition probability is less than 0.4. It means that the affect of performing rejuvenation is not sensitive up to that section but after this section the coping ability of restore system is decreasing and by using this graph we can analyze the effectiveness of applying our approach. Figure 7, which is used to determine the coping ability of a system when the system is exposed to attacks shows the change of survivability according to the change of the probabilities $(R_c, 1)$ and $(0, R_c)$. The cold-standby restore system suggested in Figure 6 and Figure 7 shows that survivability is maximized when the primary-secondary servers detect abnormal behaviors as early as possible when each of them is exposed to attacks and vulnerable situations.

5   Conclusion

In this paper, we have presented a model of ITS with cold standby system. This study defined ten states for a cold-standby cluster system, computed DTMC steady-state probability and SMP steady-state probability using the transition probability and the mean sojourn time in each state and based on the results, defined the availability of general systems. We have demonstrated the model can be used to analyze and proactively manage the effects of cluster network faults and attacks, and restore accordingly. According to the system operating parameters, we have modeled and analyzed steady-state probability and survivability level of cluster systems under DoS attacks by adopting a software rejuvenation technique. The result shows that the system operates through intrusions and provides continued the criticalfunctions, and gracefully degrades non-critical system functionality in the face of intrusions. As an ongoing work, we are performing our model with the real sojourn times of specific attacks in order to generalize it with various attacks. We are analyzing a variety of probability distributions in the real attack data, which is, described the attackers' transitions and the sojourn time that they spend in every state. The integration of response time and throughput with downtime cost will provide a more accurate evaluation measure.

Acknowledgment

This research is granted by Ajou University and Regional Research Center(RRC) Program, a research program of Korea Science and Engineering Foundation.

References

1. J. Lala: Introduction to the Proceedings of Foundations of Intrusions Tolerant Systems (OASIS 03), Dec. 2003.
2. J. Park and K. Aung: Transient Time Analysis of Network Security Survivability Using DEVS, Lecture Notes in Computer Science, Springer, Vol. 3397, ISBN 3-540-24476, pp.607-616, 2005.
3. Y. Huang, C. Kintala, N. Kolettis and N. Fulton: Software Rejuvenation: Analysis, Module and Applications, Proc. of FTCS-25 Pasadena, CA pp.381-390, 1995.
4. S. Garg, A. Puliafito, M. Telek and K. S. Trivedi: Analysis of Software Rejuvenation Using Markov Regenerative Stochastic Petri Nets, International Symposium on Software Reliability Engineering, Oct. 1995.
5. R. Ellison, D. Fisher, R. Linger, H. Lipson, T. Longstaff, and N. Mead: Survivable Network Systems: An Emerging Discipline, Technical Report CMU/SEI-97-153, Software Engineering Institute, Carnegie Mellon University, Pittsburgh, PA 15213, Nov. 1997.
6. S. Jha, J. Wing, R. Linger and T. Longstaff: Survivability Analysis of Network Specifications, International Conference on Dependable Systems and Networks, IEEE, pp.53-58, 2000.
7. S. Jha and J. Wing: Survivability Analysis of Networked Systems, Proc. of the 23rd International Conference on Software Engineering, IEEE, pp.872-874, 2001.
8. S. Nikolopoulos, A. Pitsillides and D. Tipper: Addressing Network Survivability Issues by Finding the Kbest Paths through a Trellis Graph, 16th Annual Joint Conference of the IEEE Computer and Communications Societies, Vol. 1, pp.370-377, 1997.
9. S. Liew and K. Lu: A Framework for Network Survivability Characterization, IEEE International Conference on Communications, pp.441-451, 1992.
10. K. Newport: Incorporating Survivability Considerations Directly into the Network Design Process, 9th Annual Joint Conference of the IEEE Computer and Communication Societies, pp.1963-1970, 1990.
11. Moitra, D. Soumyo and S. Konda: Survivability of Network Systems: An Empirical Analysis, SEI, Dec 2000.
12. Moitra, D. Soumyo and S. Konda: A Simulation Model for Managing Survivability of Networked Information Systems, SEI, Dec 2002.
13. A. Moore, R. Ellison and R. Linger: Attack Modeling for Information Security and Survivability, Technical Note CMU/SEI-2001-TN-001, Mar. 2001.
14. K. Trivedi: Probability and Statistics with Reliability Queueing and Computer Science Applications, John Wiley and Sons, Inc. 2003.

From Heterogeneous Information Spaces to Virtual Documents

Leonardo Candela, Donatella Castelli, Pasquale Pagano, and Manuele Simi

Istituto di Scienza e Tecnologie dell'Informazione "Alessandro Faedo" - CNR,
Via G. Moruzzi, 1 - 56124 PISA - Italy
{candela, castelli, pagano, simi}@isti.cnr.it

Abstract. This paper introduces DoMDL, a powerful and flexible document model capable to represent multi-edition, structured, multimedia documents that can be disseminated in multiple manifestation formats. This model also allows any document to be associated with multiple metadata descriptions in different formats and to include semantic relationships with other documents and parts of them. The paper discusses also how the OpenDLib Digital Library Management System exploits this model to abstract from the specific organization and structure of the documents that are imported from different heterogeneous information sources in order to provide virtual documents that fulfill the needs of the different DL user communities.

1 Introduction

Digital Library Management Systems (DLMSs) [1] are complex systems whose main role is to mediate between content providers and content consumers in order to fulfill information and functionality needs of the DL users.

In particular, DLMSs must support the storage and management of documents collected from heterogeneous information sources. These documents may vary in their structure, format, media, and physical representation. They may be described by different metadata formats and their access may be regulated by different policies. The documents may either be copied from proprietary repositories into the digital library (DL) own repositories or they may be accessed on demand following the link stored into the corresponding metadata records.

The DLMSs must also satisfy the demand of the DL users that want to search, retrieve, access and manipulate documents semantically meaningful in their application domain. Some users for example, may want to see the information space as composed of journals structured in articles, while others may want to work with collections of articles of the same author or with composite documents made by a text and all the images that illustrate that text. Such documents may not correspond to documents submitted to the DL or collected from existing sources, rather they may be virtual documents created by reusing or by processing real documents or parts of them.

Reconciling these two diverse requirements in a complex and application independent framework is one of the most important challenges of a DLMS. In

E.A. Fox et al. (Eds.): ICADL 2005, LNCS 3815, pp. 11–22, 2005.
© Springer-Verlag Berlin Heidelberg 2005

order to fulfill these requirements a DLMS must be able to abstract from the organization and structuring of the concrete underlying information space and make it accessible through collections of virtual documents tailored to the needs of the DL audience.

This paper focuses on the document model as one of the major factors that influences the level of abstraction provided by a DLMS. In particular, the paper introduces the *Document Model for Digital Library* (DoMDL), a document model which has been successfully exploited in the OpenDLib system [2]. DoMDL can represent multi-edition, structured, multimedia documents that can be disseminated in multiple manifestation formats. This model also allows any document to be associated with multiple metadata descriptions in different formats and to include semantic relationships with other documents and parts of them.

In OpenDLib, DoMDL plays the role of the logical document model that is shared by all the services. Documents harvested from different sources are logically represented to and known by all the OpenDLib services as DoMDL documents. The services provide functionalities that act at the level of abstraction specified by this model. For instance, the storage service is able to accept multiple editions of the same document and automatically generate additional new metadata formats, whereas the index service can index any of the metadata formats associated with an edition. By exploiting the richness and flexibility of the DoMDL model, OpenDLib is thus able to provide the DL users

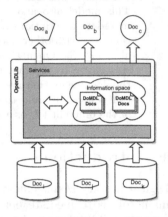

Fig. 1. DoMDL in a DLMS

with different views of the information space as this space is populated by virtual documents that fulfill the needs of different application frameworks.

The rest of this paper is organized as follows: Section 2 presents the DoMDL document Model; Section 3 illustrates how this model has been implemented in the OpenDLib system and how it impacts on the provided functionalities; Section 4 presents two examples, extracted from real OpenDLib DL applications, that show how DomDL has been instantiated to represent specific types of documents; Section 5 compares DoMDL with the document models supported by two other well known DL systems; and finally, Section 6 concludes.

2   The Document Model for Digital Library

DoMDL has been designed to represent structured, multilingual and multimedia documents and can be customized according to the DL content to be handled. For example, it can be used to describe a lecture as the composition of the teacher presentation together with the slides, the video recording and the summary of the talk transcript. However, the same lecture can be disseminated as the MPEG3 format of the video or the SMIL document synchronizing its parts.

In order to be able to represent documents with completely different structures, DoMDL distinguishes four main aspects of document modeling and, using terms and definitions very similar to the IFLA FRBR model [3], represents these aspects through the following entities: Document, Edition, View, and Manifestation (see Figure 2).

The *Document* entity, representing the document as a distinct intellectual creation, captures the more general aspect of it. For example, the book "Digital Libraries and Electronic Publishing" by W. Arms or the lecture "Introduction to Mixed Media Digital Libraries", by C. Lagoze, can all be modeled as Document entities. Each entity of this type is identified via the *Handle* attribute.

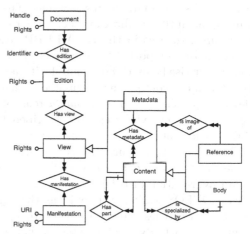

Fig. 2. Document Model for Digital Library

The *Edition*, representing a specific expression of the distinct intellectual creation, models a document instance along the time dimension. The preliminary version of this paper, the version submitted to a conference, the version published in the proceedings, are examples of editions of the same document. These Editions are related to the appropriate Document with an *Identifier* whose value is linear and numbered.

The *View*, modeling a specific intellectual expression, is the way through which an edition is perceived. A view excludes physical aspects that are not related to how a document is to be perceived. For example, the original edition of the proceedings of a DELOS workshop might be disseminated under three different views: *a)* a "structured textual view" containing a "Preface" created by the conference chairs, and the list of thematic sessions containing the accepted papers, *b)* a "presentation view", containing the list of the ppt slides used in the presentations, and *c)* a "metadata view", containing a structured description of the proceedings.

The *Manifestation* models the physical formats by which a document is disseminated. Examples of manifestations are: the MPEG file containing the video recording of the lecture made by C. Lagoze at a certain summer school, the AVI file of the same video, the poscript file of a lecture given by another teacher at the same school, etc. Physical formats are accessible via *URIs*, used to associate local or networked file locations.

These entities are semantically connected by means of a set of relationships. The relationships *Has edition*, *Has view*, and *Has manifestation* link the different aspects of a document. Note that these relationships are multiple, i.e. there can be several objects in the range associated with the same object in the domain. This means that there can be multiple editions of the same document, multiple views of the same edition and multiple manifestations of the same view.

The View entity is specialized in two sub-entities: *Metadata* and *Content*. The former allows a document edition be perceived through the conceptualization given by its metadata representations. These may be a flat list of pairs (fields, values), as in the Dublin Core metadata records [4], or more complex conceptual structures, such as in the IFLA-FRBR records. Typically, this metadata view is indexed to support attribute-based querying and browsing operations, but it may otherwise be used. For example, it may be disseminated free of charge while the document contents are regulated by fee access, or disseminated on a mobile device. By using the *Has metadata* relationship it is possible to model the fact that also content views can be described by one or more metadata records in different formats.

The Content view has two sub-entities: *Body*, and *Reference*. The former is a view of the document content when it is to be perceived either as a whole or as an aggregation of other views. For example, a textual view of the proceedings a DELOS workshop is built as the aggregation of the textual views of its component articles. The relationship *Has part* links a Body view with its component views. A Body view may be specialized by other views that represent more detailed perceptions of the same content. For example, an article of the cited proceedings may be specialized by two views related to the French and English version of that document, respectively. A view is related to all its specializations through the relationship *Is specialized by*.

The Reference entity represents a view that does not have associated manifestations because it is linked with an already registered manifestation. This entity has been introduced to represent the relationship between views of different document editions. Articles presented at the same workshop, for example, can be modeled as single documents and grouped together by the workshop proceedings document that contains only the references to them. It is worth noting that this entity, bringing together parts of real or virtual documents, makes it possible to manage virtual documents that are not explicitly maintained by the storage system. For example complex reports, or training lectures, can easily be modeled as composition of parts extracted from real documents. A reference view is linked with another view via the relationship *Is image of*.

Each of the entities described above has a set of attributes that specify the rights on the modeled document aspects. This makes it possible, for example, to model possibly different rights on different editions, different access policies on different views or on different parts of the same view, and so on.

3   The OpenDLib Implementation

The document model we have presented has been successfully validated by the OpenDLib experience. OpenDLib [2] is DLMS developed at ISTI-CNR; at present, this system is running in a number of instances serving different institutions. OpenDLib flexibility and customizability are mainly due to the adoption of the DoMDL as logical model to represent both the physical and semantic structure of the documents.

The four ways to think of relationship between a DLMS and its document model are in the following patterns: *(i)* document storage, *(ii)* document discovery, *(iii)* document access, and *(iv)* document visualization. In the following, we first describe the OpenDLib representation of DoMDL and then we address some issues that affect the system from the point of view of the patterns above.

3.1 DoMDL Representation

The representation of a document model usually deals with *(i)* the description of the internal relations among document entities, and *(ii)* the management of the related physical parts of each entity. The OpenDLib solution to these problems is to decouple the definition of the document model instance from its real data. With this approach a document is really composed by several files. The instance of the document model for a given document is described in a separate file, named *Structure file*, which is the only mandatory element that must be provided. The goal of this file is to explain the composition and the relations among the other files that compose the document.

The natural way to express such structured data is through an XML document. Therefore, a major design issue was to define an appropriate XML Schema, able to cover all the DoMDL features. XML Schemas provide a standard means to specify which elements may occur in an XML document and in which order, and to constrain certain aspects of these elements. The result of this effort is the DoMDL XML Schema [5]. An XML document validated against this Schema describes a particular edition of a document; main entities (views and manifestations) belonging to a document are represented with tags while relationships among them are expressed by nesting these tags. As well, a number of attributes on the entity tags allows their type and the related behavior be specified. In this way, a Structure file can put together different physical components to form an unique and coherent structured document. Different editions of the same document are not physically linked together, rather they are logically grouped by the storage model in order to obtain a higher flexibility of the system. The storage model, in fact, is able to manage editions as a single entity since they share the same document identifier.

Finally, according to the document model specification, it is also possible to express a set of rules that regulate the rights on the document views via the properties child tag; in this implementation the rights to download, deliver, transcode or display a view may be, or not be, granted.

In the next section we analyze how the DoMDL model impacts on the OpenDLib system design and how OpenDLib exploits the model to offer new functionalities.

3.2 Related System Issues

The adoption of a particular document model involves the system design and implementation at various levels.

Document Storage. The heart of any DLMS is its storage model, that is how the information is maintained in the system. Here we do not argue about the physical storage manager implemented by OpenDLib since, traditionally, a storage model decouples the document model adopted from the underlying technologies used to store documents. Rather we present both the constraints and opportunities that the utilization of DoMDL has introduced in the system.

Primarily, according to the DoMDL specification, the storage model must be able to manage multiple metadata formats for the same document and multiple physical manifestations for the same view of a document. This allows OpenDLib to be enriched with the capability to: *(i)* automatically move from one metadata format to another one using the provided XSLT stylesheet, and *(ii)* automatically migrate from one physical manifestation (e.g. a pdf file) to another one using a provided transformation procedure or configuring the system to use a 3rd party tool. Among the others, two major advantages that rise from these functionalities are *(i)* to make it easy to create new Digital Libraries starting from existing heterogeneous information sources and *(ii)* to preserve documents from the technological obsolescence. Regarding manifestations, they are identified by URIs. A manifestation can be stored inside or outside the system, depending on the time in which the URI is dereferenced. When a new document is submitted, a number of solutions is offered in order to support a range of different needs. In fact, a manifestations can be: *(i)* directly uploaded with the document, *(ii)* automatically retrieved from an external location and locally stored, *(iii)* maintained as an external manifestation and dynamically retrieved at the access time, or *(iv)* maintained as an external manifestation and displayed through its original location at the access time. These options are made available by properly combining the values of the attributes of the manifestation tags in the document Structure file. The combination of these options at document level makes it possible to build new structured documents that enrich the original ones by aggregating multiple parts of different documents from different heterogeneous information sources. Moreover, these choices promote an optimal utilization of the storage resources. For instance, if an manifestation requires too many storage resources to be stored internally, it can simply be referred to its external original location. This optimization is also supported by the reference view mechanism. Following the model specification, a view can be a reference to another view of a different document; by implementing this mechanism, data duplication is avoided.

The last advantage we mention here is the possibility to submit and manage documents that are modeled in very different fashions in the same OpenDLib instance, if they are compliant with the DoMDL XML Schema. This introduces a high level of flexibility and promotes a full integration among heterogeneous information sources with different types of documents or metadata.

Finally, let us mention addressability, i.e. the granularity of documents that can be directly addressed or referenced. The basic addressable unit is the single manifestation. Moreover, the list of all views or manifestations as well as the list of editions of a document can also be addressed.

Document Access. The access granularity, i.e. how a document or its components can be accessed, is closely tied to the storage model. Possible options include: *(i)* to expose data according to the document model representation, and *(ii)* to hide the representation and provide an interface to query the model in order to obtain the document parts. OpenDLib implements both solutions by providing direct access to the Structure file and also an interface to query a given document. This design choice allows users to select the option that fulfils their needs at best. For instance, to speed up the operations, other OpenDLib modules retrieve from the storage subsystem the Structure files and then manage the corresponding documents. External applications should instead request the document entities (e.g. all the editions of a document, all the manifestations, etc.) in order to be independent from the DoMDL representation.

Document Discovering. Documents discovering is a crucial component of any distributed Digital Library system. This feature is usually achieved through indexing and search mechanisms. OpenDLib provides these functionalities both on the document metadata and, when possible, on the documents themselves (full-text indexing) via its search subsystem. The adoption of DoMDL had a great impact during the design of this subsystem because documents can be expressed in any format and thus no assumptions could be made about the presence of any field or structure of the indexed information. The result is a highly customizable search subsystem based on: *(i)* a complete configuration of any index concerning the metadata or manifestation format, the elements to be indexed and the set of elements to be return after a query, *(ii)* an abstraction layer between the query engine and the format-independent query language supported, and *(iii)* inspection mechanisms that support the discovery of which indexed format, which query operators and which result sets are supported by a particular instance of an index. Therefore, thanks to the document model, an OpenDLib instance can have multiple indexes able to index any format independently of their number or location. Also the graphical user interface provided to interact with the search subsystem has the capability to configure itself, depending on which index it currently interacts with, by automatically adding, removing or changing both its components and look and feel. In addition, the search subsystem offers the very new possibility to execute queries across documents handled by different information sources and expressed in different formats.

Document Visualization. The visualization of documents is the last main issue strictly related with the document model. DoMDL gives a great number of opportunities for the presentation of complex documents. For instance, it allows document visualization be personalized by deciding who has the rights to view what.

OpenDLib provides two kinds of document visualization, one tab-based and one window-based, both able to display documents compliant with the DoMDL model. In either mode, a graphical rendering of the document structure is visualized and manifestations are retrieved on demand next to the user requests. As well, OpenDLib can easily be extended with additional visualization features;

this is specially useful for OpenDLib instances that manage classes of documents with the same structure, e.g. papers or talks, to better exploit the specific structure of those documents. The mechanisms above make it possible to present the same document in different ways by making the concept of *virtual document* concrete.

4   DoMDL Exploitation

In this section we present two successful stories of exploitation of the DoMDL features in the context of digital library instances that are powered by OpenDLib. We do not want to show these examples to validate the design choices made by these digital libraries to represent their documents; rather we want to demonstrate that DoMDL is suitable to accommodate the needs of different user communities.

The first example we report is extracted from the DELOS DL [6]. This DL handles documents published by the homonymous Network of Excellence on Digital Libraries. It stores, maintains, and disseminates, among the others, the proceedings of several DELOS events like the ECDL conferences, a number of thematic and brainstorming workshops, and the international summer schools.

These documents are characterized by a large number of inter-relationships that are emphasized to improve the accessibility and readability of semantically related documents.

Figure 3 depicts a typical edition of an ARTICLE maintained in this DL. Each edition has the following views: *Metadata*, *Abstract*, and *Content* which are expressions of the article related to manifestations in different formats; *Related Talk*, which links with the presentation of the article made by its author during the related event; and *In Proceedings*, which links with the document that represents the proceedings where the article has been published. Reference views are also used to link a TALK document with the content of the edition of the respective article. It is also important to point out that in the DELOS DL different metadata formats are used to represent the description of an article, that multiple manifestations in different content types are associated with the same view, and that the video manifestations are stored on video streaming servers able to improve their fruition. Finally, we highlight that the end-user perceives an intellectual creation via the homogeneous and coherent presentation of a virtual document

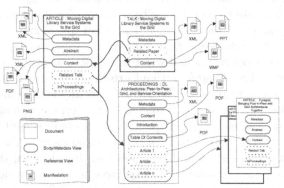

Fig. 3. DELOS Digital Library documents

that, instead, is obtained collecting parts of different and heterogenous stored documents.

The second example is extracted from the ARTE DL [7]. This DL stores, maintains, and disseminates the digitized versions of ancient texts and images linked by relationships that express semantic associations among them, such as the *contains, is contained in, is related to,* and *has authored by* relationships. The original documents are collected from very heterogeneous information sources: *(i)* ranging from different types of database to file-system based storage systems, and *(ii)* based on proprietary content representations. A typical edition of an ICONOGRAPHY is represented by its metadata and related picture. The value added by using DoMDL is perceived by analyzing the document relationships. Using reference views, it has been possible to model virtual documents allowing end-users to navigate the relationship from an iconographic document to the book that contains it, analyze the textual part before and after the mentioned picture, browse the book to see other similar documents, and also immediately access to the other related iconographic documents.

Finally, it is important to note other specific characteristics of the documents managed by this digital library, namely: the wide heterogeneity of the representation and description formats; the existence of access policies regarding many parts of the documents; and the variety of new documents that are created by the members of the digital library by composing parts of existing documents.

5   Related Works

Most of DLMSs are designed to manage *simple* documents, i.e. documents composed by a single entity having a fixed metadata format. In this section we present a comparison between DoMDL and two rich document models that have been designed to fulfill requirements arising from different contexts, the DSpace data model and the Fedora digital object model.

5.1   The DSpace Data Model

DSpace[1] [8, 9] is an open source digital library system designed to operate as a centralized system for capturing, storing, indexing, preserving, and redistributing documents in digital formats. It has been designed to fulfill the requirements of a university research faculty for managing its intellectual outputs.

Item is the basic archival element in DSpace and thus it corresponds to the DoMDL Document entity. An item is organized into bundles of bitstreams, where a *bundle* is a set of somehow closely related bitstreams corresponding in part to our View entity, while a *bitstream* is a stream of bits, usually is a computer file and it is thus close to the physical part of our Manifestation entity. For example, a document having two different manifestations, a PDF and an HTML one, is

---
[1] http://www.dspace.org

modeled in DSpace with an item having two bundles: *(i)* the PDF manifestation that has a bitstream representing the PDF file, and *(ii)* the HTML manifestation with a set of bitstreams representing HTML files and images that compose the main HTML manifestation.

The ordered sequence is the only type of relationship that can be expressed between bitstreams of the same bundle. Moreover, the concept of edition is not explicit within this model, even if it may be modeled via particular structural metadata by adapting some DSpace components. Further, references, that make it possible to build documents by aggregating already existing ones, are not modeled explicitly.

DSpace manages descriptive, administrative and structural metadata. Regarding descriptive metadata, each item has one qualified Dublin Core metadata record. This schema can be changed but the system search and submission functionalities are not capable to automatically react to these changes and thus they must be updated. Moreover, it is possible to manage just one metadata record for each item, i.e. if there are two or more descriptive metadata records about an item, only one is considered as the metadata record while the others can only be stored into the system by using the bundle concept and thus they will not be used in the discovery phase. Administrative metadata include (a) preservation metadata and (b) authorization policy metadata in a sort of proprietary format. DSpace structural metadata can be considered as being fairly basic, i.e. bitstreams of an item can be arranged into separate bundles as described above, and this probably will be an area of future development as DSpace designers state.

5.2   The Fedora Object Model

Fedora[2][10, 11] is a repository service for storing and managing complex objects. At its core there is a powerful document model and thanks to the richness and flexibility of this model the system is nowadays used by many institutions.

A Fedora digital object is composed by i) a *unique identifier*, ii) a set of *descriptive properties*, iii) a set of *datastreams*, and iv) a set of *disseminators*. Descriptive properties are the information needed for the management of the objects within the repository, i.e. the object type, its state, its creation, and last update date. The type is used to distinguish among the primitive Fedora objects while the state is used to distinguish among active, inactive and deleted objects.

Datastreams are containers used to maintain both data and metadata belonging to an object. Thus, the same concept is used to model bytestreams representing the document, as well as metadata to express relationships with other objects, policies and audit data. Moreover, a datastream is either used to encapsulate any type of bytestream internally as well reference to it externally. In this way, on the one hand it is possible to aggregate local content with exter-

---

[2] http://www.fedora.info

nal content, on the other hand there is not a complete decoupling between the document structure and its content. This broad concept of datastream, equivalent to the DoMDL view, uses reserved datastreams to differentiate between its types. For instance, a datastream of type DC is used to express the DC Metadata record [12], while a datastream of type REL-EXT is used to express object to object relationships following a well established ontology of relationships[3].

Disseminators are components capable to associate an external service with the object in order to supply a virtual view of the object itself, or of its datastream content. The Fedora repository, interoperating with the service, is in charge to produce this view. As a consequence this approach is object centric, i.e. in order to create a new view over a set of documents it is needed both to create a service capable to offer it and to update all the objects that this service must act on.

Fedora object model covers also versioning related to components, i.e. datastreams and disseminators. The system automatically creates a new version of them whenever they are modified, while maintaining also the former representation without changing the document structure. Thus, within the same component identified by its identifier, all the versions are maintained and identifiable via their own identifier.

DoMDL and Fedora digital object model have many commonalities and both aim at managing complex structured documents. Main differences are related with the mechanisms for offering virtual views as well as with how they decouple structural information from content information.

6   Conclusion

This paper has illustrated the DoMDL model and discussed how it has been exploited by the OpenDLib system to achieve the ability of abstracting from the specific organization and structure of the documents whether they have been submitted or harvested from exiting heterogeneous information sources. The paper has also shown how the proposed model has been used to support the document representation requirements of two different OpenDLib empowered DLs. The reported examples have highlighted the DoMDL capability of representing complex documents built by aggregating related parts, where each part, in turn, may be shared with other documents. These characteristics, together with the ability to distinguish different aspects of a document and associate multiple matadata formats, are the major distinguishing features of DoMDL with respect to other DLs document models.

We strongly believe that these features will also be important in the future DLs which will support the construction of documents which have no analogous in the traditional physical world. In this framework models like DoMDL will provide the necessary substrate for the semantic layer of a DL information model [13].

---

[3] http://www.fedora.info/definitions/1/0/fedora-relsext-ontology.rdfs

References

1. DELOS-NSF Working Group on Digital Library Information-Technology Infrastructures: Final report. Technical report, DELOS NoE and NSF (2003)
2. Castelli, D., Pagano, P.: OpenDLib: A Digital Library Service System. In Agosti, M., Thanos, C., eds.: Research and Advanced Technology for Digital Libraries, 6th European Conference, ECDL 2002, Rome, Italy, September 2002, Proceedings. Lecture Notes in Computer Science, Springer-Verlag (2002) 292–308
3. IFLA Study Group on the Functional Requirements for Bibliographic Records.: Functional Requirements for Bibliographic Records: Final Report. (http://www.ifla.org/VII/s13/frbr/frbr.htm)
4. Dublin Core Metadata Initiative: Dublin Core Metadata element set, version 1.1: Reference description. (http://dublincore.org/documents/dces/)
5. OpenDLib: DoMDL XML Schema.   (http://www.opendlib.com/resources/-schemas/domdl.xsd)
6. OpenDLib: The DELOS Digital Library. (http://delos-dl.isti.cnr.it)
7. OpenDLib: The ARTE Digital Library. (http://arte-sns.isti.cnr.it)
8. Tansley, R., Bass, M., Stuve, D., Branschofsky, M., Chudnov, D., McClellan, G., Smith, M.: The DSpace Institutional Digital Repository System: current functionality. In: Proceedings of the third ACM/IEEE-CS joint conference on Digital libraries, IEEE Computer Society (2003) 87–97
9. Tansley, R., Bass, M., Smith, M.: DSpace as an Open Archival Information System: Current Status and Future Directions. In Koch, T., Sølvberg, I., eds.: Research and Advanced Technology for Digital Libraries, 7th European Conference, ECDL 2003, Trondheim, Norway, August 17-22, 2003, Proceedings. Lecture Notes in Computer Science, Springer-Verlag (2003) 446–460
10. Payette, S., Thornton, S.: The Mellon Fedora Project: Digital Library Architecture Meets XML and Web Services. In Agosti, M., Thanos, C., eds.: Research and Advanced Technology for Digital Libraries, 6th European Conference, ECDL 2002, Rome, Italy, September 2002, Proceedings. Lecture Notes in Computer Science, Springer-Verlag (2002) 406 – 421
11. Lagoze, C., Payette, S., Shin, E., Wilper, C.: Fedora: An Architecture for Complex Objects and their Relationships. Journal of Digital Libraries, Special Issue on Complex Objects (2005)
12. DC Team: Dublin Core Metadata Initiative. (http://dublincore.org)
13. Del Bimbo, A., Gradmann, S., Ioannidis, Y.: Towards a Long Term Agenda for Digital Library Research. Third Delos Brainstorming Meeting Report - Corvara - Italy, DELOS NoE (2004)

Traveling in Digital Archive World: Sightseeing Metaphor Framework for Enhancing User Experiences in Digital Libraries

Taro Tezuka and Katsumi Tanaka

Graduate School of Informatics,
Kyoto University
{tezuka, tanaka}@dl.kuis.kyoto-u.ac.jp

Abstract. Digital libraries are currently growing rapidly in number and size, covering various fields. However, despite the great deal of intellectual effort and large budgets necessary for their construction, digital libraries are often limited to use by specialists. We describe a framework that will attract more users to digital libraries through enhancing the presentation layers. We propose the guiding principle to such enhancement, the Sightseeing Metaphor Framework (SF), which is a structure based on user activities during sightseeing. We exemplify it in a Web-based regional information presentation system. The evaluation we did for an elementary school classroom revealed that the system created a better impression on the students compared to an existing presentation scheme.

1 Introduction

A common problem with many digital libraries is that users are often limited to specialists from specific fields. Despite the great deal of intellectual efforts and large budget necessary for their constructions, those who can benefit are limited. It would be preferable for more users to benefit, to maintain extensive public support for the construction and maintenance of digital libraries. To attract more users, the presentation layer must be enhanced. Ordinary directory structures and search interfaces are often insufficient to create an attractive presentation mechanism for digital libraries.

Many proposals have already been made to improve the presentation layer of digital libraries. However, these proposals all involved separate techniques under different operating principles.

We present the Sightseeing Metaphor Framework (SMF), a framework for enhancing user experiences based on metaphorical mapping for sightseeing activities in the real world. The SMF provides an easy-to-apply guiding principle to expand digital libraries and enhance user experiences.

We built an application example based on the SMF, a Web-based regional information search system. We evaluated the system in an elementary school classroom, to see its usability among students.

The rest of the paper is organized as follows. Section 2 discusses related work. Section 3 describes the Sightseeing Metaphor Framework. Section 4 presents an application example. Section 5 discusses the evaluation of the application. Section 6 is the conclusion.

E.A. Fox et al. (Eds.): ICADL 2005, LNCS 3815, pp. 23–32, 2005.
© Springer-Verlag Berlin Heidelberg 2005

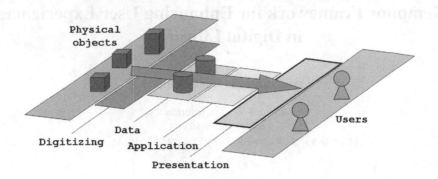

Fig. 1. Elements of digital library

2   Related Work

Many researchers consider the low rate of usage of digital libraries to be a problem. Without extensive public support, it is difficult to construct a digital library [1]. Procrastination in the construction of digital libraries often results in the loss of valuable cultural heritage.

The presentation layer has been attracting a great deal of attention as a method of attracting more users [2][3][4]. However, these have been separate proposals and a more general scheme has not been discussed.

There have been discussions on metaphors being helpful in planning digitized systems [5]. The spatial metaphor has also been said to play a crucial role in the cognition of abstract concepts. Cognitive linguistics researchers have argued that many abstract expressions are based on spatial relationships in the physical world [6]. The SMF is an extension of the spatial metaphor.

The travel metaphor discussed by Hammond and Allison is similar to the SMF [12]. It was a design principle aimed at making a complex system easily understandable and navigable. Consequently, their metaphorical mapping was simple, and limited to three minimum aspects in traveling. These were 1) *go-it-alone travel and guided tours*, 2) *a map*, and 3) *guidebooks, or an index*.

The aim of our system was not to make the system easily understood, but to improve user experiences and draw more user attention to digital libraries. Consequently, SMF covers wider aspects of traveling than Hammond and Allison's travel metaphor did.

There is also the tour metaphor, which is actually a synonym for the travel metaphor. This metaphor is also sometimes used in digital libraries [15][16].

3   Sightseeing Metaphor Framework

Activities in the digital environment resemble those during sightseeing in the real world. Since sightseeing has created enjoyable experiences for tourists for centuries, we presume that designers of digital libraries can learn from different aspects of sightseeing.

The aim of the SMF was to set metaphors that could be used to enhance the presentation layer of a digital library. Figure 2 outlines the overall structure for the SMF.

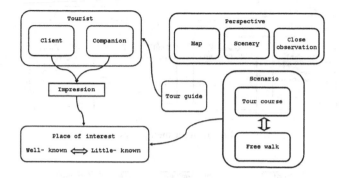

Fig. 2. Elements of Sightseeing Metaphor Framework

We will describe elements of the SMF in detail in the following subsections. Each element is a function that digital libraries are encouraged to implement, to enhance user experiences.

3.1   Actors: Tour Guide and Companion Metaphors

Digital libraries are encouraged to provide elements that correspond to tour guides and companions in sightseeing.

A tour guide gives directions to a tourist, recommends sightseeing spots, and provides background information at each spot. He or she acts as an *annotator* to the sightseeing. *Annotation* has been attracting a great deal of attention recently as a key concept in content analysis [9]. It is also a function encouraged in digital libraries.

It is more enjoyable in the real world sightseeing if the tourist has a companion. He or she can share experiences and exchange impressions. Digital library users often have to confront content along by themselves. Although it may satisfy the purpose of searching for information, the experience itself is not as exciting. Users of digital libraries should be encouraged to interact with others, either in real time or by leaving comments on the content that they encountered. The companion metaphor does not necessary involve face-to-face contacts. The user can interact with other users through shared comments on the content.

3.2   Scenarios: Tour Course and Free Walk Metaphors

Digital libraries are encouraged to provide both tour courses and free walks .

In sightseeing, tourists either travel along a tour course or stroll around. Although tourists using a tour course will not miss popular places of interest, they have less of a

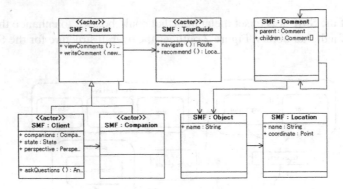

Fig. 3. Actor metaphors

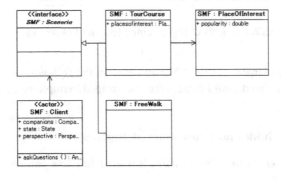

Fig. 4. Scenario and place of interest metaphors

chance of finding unexpected spots. In contrast, strolling tourists have more chances to encounter unexpected spots or events. In a same manner, tour courses and free walks are encouraged in digital libraries. Different scenarios must be provided to meet user demands.

3.3   Perspectives: Map, Scenery, and Close Observation Metaphors

Digital libraries are encouraged to provide various perspectives to view content, such as maps, scenery, and close observation, depending on user's requests.

Sightseeing tourists are able to change perspectives; they can check maps, view scenery, or make close observations of the place of interest. Such diversity in perspectives enriches the sightseeing activity. Users of digital libraries would also like to change their perspectives. The map and scenery metaphor provides an overview of the user's surrounding environment. It gives the *context* to the content. The context enriches his or her experience, by extending his or her interest and relating different topics. Digital libraries are encouraged to provide various views to the content, depending on user requests.

3.4 Places of Interest: Well-Known and Little-Known Places of Interest Metaphors

Digital libraries must be able to recommend both well-known and little-known content.

Sightseeing involves both well-known and little-known places of interest. Tourists on a regular course can visit well-known spots efficiently, while unguided tourists can also check out little-known places.

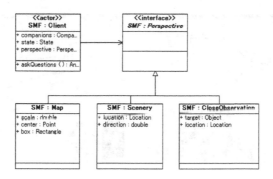

Fig. 5. Perspective metaphors

Such significant content provides orientation to the user while browsing. Digital libraries are encouraged to recommend both well-known and little-known content, depending on user requests.

4   Application Example

We implemented an application example based on SMF, the Train Window system. Some of, though not all, the SMF elements were applied in its implementation. The system is a presentation layer of the regional information on the Web. The Web today contains vast amounts of regional information, provided free to the public.

Like many privately owned digital libraries, regional information on the Web is a set of digitized content under a certain topic, and is structured based on the location attribute. The difference from privately owned digital libraries is that it is created and maintained by a number of groups and individuals distributed over the globe.

In the Train Window system, web pages are searched using the Google Web API [18]. Geographic data originates from a digitized residential map provided by Zenrin Ltd [19]. The system was implemented in Java. It has a client-server architecture over the Internet, consisting of a Web browser, a servlet, and a database. The user interface is a regular Web browser.

4.1   Map Interface, Based on Map Metaphor

The map metaphor was implemented as a map-based user interface. The map interface is the most straightforward implementation of the map metaphor and is located at the upper half of the user interface, which is the Web browser. The map can be dragged, turned, and zoomed in/out with the mouse. When the area on the map changes, a message is sent to the servlet, which sends the (visible) place name located closest to the map center to the Google Web API. The Google Web API then returns the (putative) most relevant Web page, which is shown in the lower half of the user interface. The user can also make the map jump to an arbitrary destination, by typing in a location name into the text search field.

Fig. 6. Train Window system: application example

4.2   Landmark Presentation, Based on Places of Interest Metaphor

The place of interest metaphor was implemented as a landmark presentation function. The map interface for the Train Window system presents significant landmarks. Names of landmarks shown on the map interface are actually links to the regional content on the Web. In our application, the links are acting as recommendations for the content.

4.3   Path Recommendation, Based on Tour Course Metaphor

The tour course metaphor was implemented as a path recommendation function. The user is provided with different paths recommended by the system. Once a path is chosen, the map automatically moves along the path. The system continuously displays Web pages related to the landmark closest to the map center, as the map moves. It is a mechanism to recommend the most significant places of interest along a given route. Like a recommended course, the user can browse the most significant content, without the need for actions such as typing in search keywords or clicking on hyperlinks.

4.4   Local Landmark Selection, Based on Free Walk Metaphor

The free walk metaphor was implemented as a local landmark selection mechanism. When the map interface is showing an arbitrary area, the most significant landmarks within the area will be presented. This is corresponding to the real world in the following manner. When discussing a small area, even a traffic sign or a grocery store can act as a landmark. On the other hand, there are significant landmarks that symbolize a city or even a state. In free walk, the user has chances to meet less significant landmarks. In our implementation also, the user can zoom in and move around the map by his or her will to find less popular contents.

We described a concrete algorithm for evaluating landmark significance based on Web documents in our previous paper [17].

5 Evaluation

The system was evaluated by an elementary school class. The class was for the "Period for Integrated Studies", a curriculum aimed at bridging different subjects such as information technology and social studies.

5.1 Experiment Setup

The target class consisted of 5th and 6th grade students, aged 10-12. A total of 56 students attended. They were divided into small groups of 3 to 9 members. Each group chose a specific area of interest in their neighborhood, and was asked to create a plan for their field research with computers. The students had to gather information on their target region, choose places to visit, and check bus or train timetables, through the Internet. By the end of the class, they had to fill in the route plan with suitable means of transportation. They could use either our Train Window system or regular Web search engines to gather information about their target regions.

Fig. 7. Evaluation at elementary school

The class was two hours. Two teachers and two assistants supported the students and taught them how to use the Train Window system. The teachers and assistants also provided hints on preparing route plans. A questionnaire was passed around at the end of the class.

5.2 Results

After the classroom experiment, we obtained 33 effective answers from a total of 38 answer sheets. This was because some of the students were unable to try the Train Window system, due to the group-based style of the assignment. Some students gathered using the Train Window system, while others worked on arranging the travel schedule. Out of the 33, 22 were from 5th grade students, and 11 were from 6th grade students. Figures 8-9 are pie charts of the results. The students' impressions are listed in Fig. 10-11.

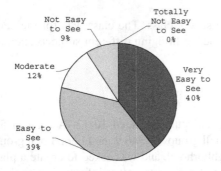

Fig. 8. Impressions of map interface with landmarks, in comparison to ordinary map

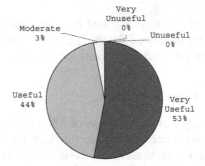

Fig. 9. Impressions of automatic presentation of Web content, in comparison to static presentation

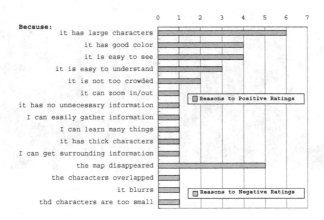

Fig. 10. Impressions of map interface with landmarks, in comparison to ordinary map

The results were favorable for the extensions based on SMF, apart from some technical shortcomings with the implementations. In this case, our automatic presentation based on the recommended course metaphor was more attractive for children, when

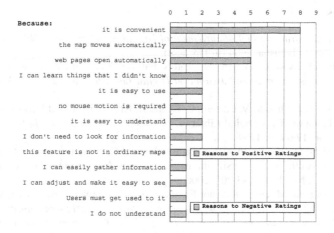

Fig. 11. Impressions of automatic presentation of Web content, in comparison to static presentation

compared to the traditional static presentation based on the map metaphor and the point of interest metaphor, as indicated in Figure 9 and 11.

6   Conclusion

This paper described the SMF (Sightseeing Metaphor Framework), the guiding principle for enhancing user experiences in digital libraries. It can be applied to different variations of digital libraries.

An application example was implemented, using three metaphors contained in the SMF. The application enabled regional content to be searched and browsed on the Web. We evaluated the SMF in an elementary school classroom. We found that the presentation of regional Web content based on the SMF received favorable comments from students.

Acknowledgments

We would like to thank the staff and students of the Kyoto City Municipal Inari Elementary School for their cooperation in the evaluation of our application.

This work was supported in part by the Japanese Ministry of Education, Culture, Sports, Science and Technology under a Grant-in-Aid for Software Technologies for Search and Integration across Heterogeneous-Media Archives, a Special Research Area Grant-In-Aid For Scientific Research (2) for the year 2005 under a project titled Research for New Search Service Methods Based on the Web's Semantic Structure (Project No, 16016247; Representative, Katsumi Tanaka), and the Informatics Research Center for Development of Knowledge Society Infrastructure (COE program by Japan's Ministry of Education, Culture, Sports, Science and Technology).

References

1. H. Kasaba, *Construction and Management of Digital Archives - from Museum to Regional Development* , Suiyousha, 2004 (in Japanese).
2. M. Costabile, F. Esposito, G. Semeraro and N. Fanizzi, An Adaptive Visual Environment for Digital Libraries, *International Journal on Digital Libraries*, Vol. 2, No. 2-3, pp. 124-143, 1999.
3. L. D. Bergman, J. Shoudt, V. Castelli, C. Li and L. Knapp, Drag-and-Drop Multimedia: An Interface Framework for Digital Libraries, *International Journal on Digital Libraries*, Vol. 2, No. 2-3, pp. 178-189, 1999.
4. C. Stephanidis, D. Akoumianakis, A. Paramythis and C. Nikolaou, User interaction in digital libraries: coping with diversity through adaptation, *International Journal on Digital Libraries*, Vol. 3, No. 2, pp. 185-205, 2000.
5. M. Rauterberg and M. Hof, Metaphor Engineering: a Participatory Approach, W. Schuler, J. Hannemann and N. Streitz (Eds.), *Designing User Interfaces for Hypermedia*, pp. 58-67, 1995.
6. G. Lakoff, *Woman, Fire, and Dangerous Things: What Categories Reveal about the Mind*, University of Chicago Press, Chicago, 1987.
7. P. Baird and M. Percival, Glasgow Online: Database Development using Apple's HyperCard, R. McAleese (Eds.), *Hypertext: Theory Into Practice*, Ablex Publishing Corporation, New Jersey, 1989.
8. K. Stathis and M. J. Sergot, Games as a metaphor for interactive systems, M. A. Sasse, R. J. Cunningham, and R. L. Winder (Eds.), *People and Computers XI (Proceedings of the HCI'96)*, pp. 19-33, BCS Conference Series, Springer-Verlag, 1996.
9. K. Zettsu, Y. Kidawara and K. Tanaka, Discovering Aspects of Web Pages from Their Referential Contexts in the Web, *Proceedings of the 9th International Conference on Database Systems for Advanced Applications (DASFAA 2004)*, pp.618-629, Jeju, Korea, 2004.
10. S. Ransom, X. Wu and H. Schmidt, Disorientation and Cognitive Overhead in Hypertext Systems, *International Journal on Artificial Intelligence Tools*, Vol. 6, No. 2, pp. 227-253, 1997.
11. V. Balasubramanian, State of the Art Review on Hypermedia Issues and Applications, *Workshop on Information Technologies and Systems*, 1993.
12. N. Hammond and L. Allinson, The travel metaphor as design principle and training aid for navigating around complex systems, D. Diaper and R. Winder (Eds.), *People and Computers III, (Proceedings of the Third Conference of the British Computer Society Human-Interaction)*, pp. 75-90, 1988.
13. S. Shum, Real and Virtual Spaces: Mapping from Spatial Cognition to Hypertext, *Proceedings of the Workshop on Spatial User Interface Metaphors in Hypermedia Systems*, Edinburgh, Scotland, 1994.
14. C. McKnight, A. Dillon and J. Richardson, Space – the Final Chapter or Why Physical Representations Are Not Semantic Intentions, C. McKnight, A. Dillon and John Richardson (Eds.), *Hypertext: A Psychological Perspective*, Ellis Horwood, New York, 1993.
15. D. M. Zorich, Beyond bitslag: Integrating museum resources on the internet, K. Jones-Garmil (Eds.), *The Wired Museum: Emerging Technology and Changing Paradigms*, pp. 171-201, American Association of Museums, 1997.
16. R. Davies and M. Jefsioutine, 3-D or not 3-D? Putting theory into practice in a virtual gallery of contemporary jewellery, *Exchange Online: Research Papers in Art, Media and Design*, Issue 1, 2000.
17. T. Tezuka and K. Tanaka, Landmark Extraction: a Web Mining Approach, *Spatial Information Theory*, Lecture Notes in Computer Science 3693, pp. 379-396, Springer-Verlag, 2005.
18. Google Web API, http://www.google.com/apis/
19. Zenrin Co.,Ltd, http://www.zenrin.co.jp/

Flexing Digital Library Systems

Hussein Suleman, Kevin Feng, Siyabonga Mhlongo, and Muammar Omar

Department of Computer Science, University of Cape Town,
Private Bag, Rondebosch, 7701, South Africa
{hussein, ffeng, smhlongo, momar}@cs.uct.ac.za

Abstract. Digital library systems with monolithic architectures are rapidly facing extinction as the discipline adopts new practices in software engineering, such as component-based architectures and Web Services. Past projects have attempted to demonstrate and justify the use of components through the construction of systems such as NCSTRL and ScholNet. This paper describes current work to push the boundaries of digital library research and investigate a range of projects made feasible by the availability of suitable components. These projects include: the ability to assemble component-based digital libraries using a visual interface; the design of customisable user interfaces and workflows; the packaging and installation of systems based on formal descriptions; and the shift to a component farm for cluster-like scalability. Each of these sub-projects makes a potential individual contribution to research in architectures, while sharing a common underlying framework. Together, all of these projects support the hypothesis that a consistent component architecture and suite of components can provide the basis for advanced research into flexible digital library architectures.

1   Introduction

It is fast becoming recognised that current models in software engineering need to be integrated and applied to digital libraries. Most important among these models are the pivotal role of simplicity of design and the construction of larger systems from components [5, 3].

Some component frameworks have emerged in recent years to attempt to model systems as networks of loosely connected components instead of the traditional monolithic model. The Open Digital Library project (ODL) [7] generalised the well-understood syntax and semantics of the OAI-PMH to support general inter-component communication. This generalisation was then used as the basis for designing a suite of simple protocols to support search engines, category-based browsing, recommendation systems, annotation engines and other typical services expected by users of a digital library. Components, corresponding to each of these protocols, were created and connected together to test the performance of such systems and the ability of the model to elaborate various different types of digital library systems. The results of such tests [8] showed that the model has much promise. At the same time, feedback from users and developers has indicated that while simplicity of the individual components is useful, much work

E.A. Fox et al. (Eds.): ICADL 2005, LNCS 3815, pp. 33–37, 2005.
© Springer-Verlag Berlin Heidelberg 2005

still needs to be done in order to simplify the process of going from a set of components to a fully-fledged and seamless digital library.

Concurrent with the development of the ODL model, similar efforts were underway on the OpenDLib project [2]. The aims of both projects are similar, but the approach differs in that OpenDLib uses a transport layer that is composed of custom protocols layered over SOAP. Lessons learnt from both projects can ultimately lead to the creation of a standardised component model.

These models were proposed to support flexible digital libraries, and simplicity of components has proven to be popular. The natural next step is to investigate higher level techniques to support the creation of complete digital libraries from components in a simple and flexible manner. This paper thus provides an overview of a series of experiments conducted with components in the ODL family, to demonstrate higher level functionality in creating systems, while discovering some of the requirements for component frameworks in order to support such higher level functionality. Details of the ODL framework are omitted for brevity but can be found in referenced publications [7, 8].

2   Experiments

The main aim of these experiments was to investigate techniques, models and tools for constructing flexible digital libraries based on simple components arranged into a network of services. To this end, a number of questions were asked and tackled relatively independently:

- How do we create visual interfaces to compose components into complete systems and how do we specify the connections between components?
- How can the user interface and workflow be designed and specified to create a customisable front-end to back-end components?
- How can systems made up of components be packaged for use at remote sites, maintaining flexibility while promoting rapid deployment?
- Since these components are largely independent of one another, can they be run on a cluster of computers instead of a single system, thereby gaining the advantages of robustness and scalability?

2.1   Visual Component Composition

The BLOX system [4] was developed to demonstrate that a digital library could be constructed using a visual IDE, similar to those used in conjunction with popular programming languages. A suite of services corresponding to the abstract model of a digital library could be created and clicking on a "Publish" button instantly created and configured all component instances on a live server!

Extensive testing was conducted on the usability and utility of BLOX as compared to older methods of manually installing and configuring digital library components. The overwhelming results of the evaluation indicate that users would far rather prefer a graphical interface because of the familiarity and flexibility that it affords. This is not atypical but confirms that digital library systems and Web-based information management systems in general need to move towards simpler and more customisable configuration procedures.

A major contribution of this study was the development of a simple descriptive language (similar to the 5SL project [6], but simpler and more specific to ODL) for specifying the interconnections among components, and a standardised interface for the remote management of components and component instances (creating, listing, editing, listing types, etc.).

2.2   Interface Customisation

In addition to customising the collection of component instances, it is also necessary to build different user interfaces for varying system configurations and user requirements. In a typical Web design environment, this would correspond to the design of individual pages and their sequencing or workflow management, with the additional complication that the pages are dynamically-generated by the back-end of a digital library system.

Fig. 1. User interface workflow editing

Figure 1 illustrates one view of the prototype system that was developed to design user interfaces for flexible digital libraries. In this prototype, the designer can lay out page elements as well as specify which services are to be incorporated and how the workflow among the pages of the interface will be effected, all through a Web-based interface. Formative evaluations were conducted through a series of participatory design sessions with stakeholders from different communities (e.g., digital library students, librarians).

2.3 Flexible Component Packaging

As a final step in the process of making components appear as a cohesive whole, it should be possible to package a set of components, along with a description of their interconnections and a specification of the user interface(s) and workflows, into a single redistributable package.

A prototype packager and installer were developed to bundle a suite of components into a package for subsequent installation at a remote location. The packaging process allows a system designer to load a specification file, as output by the BLOX system, and then enter parameters and default values particular to the installation process.

Formal pilot studies have been conducted on the packaging and installing system and the feedback indicates that the system is preferable to one where individual components are installed and configured in isolation. Minor improvements have been made to the tools and further evaluation is planned for the near future. Like the first experiment, this study reinforces the need for components/instances to have a well-defined and standardised machine interface for configuration from an external source.

3 Conclusions

It is now widely accepted in the DL and Web Services communities that systems should be built as collections of loosely-connected communicating components. Much effort has already been expended on demonstration projects where components are used in innovative ways to build systems with different base requirements. It is time to move on to a higher level of design.

This paper reports on various studies that have built on earlier work in component technologies for digital libraries. These studies have all demonstrated the utility of and need for high level tools for the construction of digital libraries. In addition, they have uncovered the need for standard machine interfaces for the configuration and maintenance of components/instances.

In general, these experiments support the basic notion that components are an enabling technology to expand the boundaries of what is possible with information management and digital library systems.

4 Future Work

A study on scalability based on component farms is in its design phase and will test whether or not components provide an effective choice in granularity. There are still many unanswered questions and it is anticipated that much research will need to be done on how the component interfaces/protocols need to evolve and how services must be cast to get maximal benefit from cluster computing.

Existing production DL projects are, at the same time, gradually adopting component technologies and service-oriented architectures. The next version of Greenstone (v3) is being designed and developed according to a service-oriented architecture for increased extensibility [1]. Similarly, DSpace is considering a far more modularised approach for its next generation [9].

Eventually, it is hoped that the higher level experiments with components discussed in this paper will contribute to an understanding of the pertinent issues in developing component frameworks so that production frameworks, such as the ones mentioned above, will be more robust and support a broad range of possible use cases.

5 Acknowledgements

This project was made possible by funding from UCT, NRF (Grant number: 2054030), NRF-THRIP, Telkom and Siemens.

References

1. Bainbridge, David, Katherine J. Don, George R. Buchanan, Ian H. Witten, Steve Jones, Matt Jones and Malcolm I. Barr (2004), "Dynamic Digital Library Construction and Configuration", in Heery, R., and L. Lyon (eds), Research and Advanced Technology for Digital Libraries: 8th European Conference (ECDL2004), 12-17 September, Bath, UK, LNCS 3232, Springer.
2. Castelli, Donatella, and Pasquale Pagano (2002), "OpenDLib: A Digital Library Service System", in Research and Advanced Technology for Digital Libraries, Proceedings of the 6th European Conference, ECDL 2002, Rome, Italy, September 2002, pp. 292-308.
3. DELOS (2001) Digital Libraries: Future Directions for a European Research Programme, San Cassiano, Alta Badia, Italy, 13-15 June 2001. Available http://delos-noe.iei.pi.cnr.it/activities/researchforum/Brainstorming/brainstorming-report.pdf
4. Eyambe, Linda K., and Hussein Suleman (2004), A Digital Library Component Assembly Environment. Proceedings of SAICSIT 2004, Stellenbosch, South Africa, pp.15-22.
5. Gladney, H., Z. Ahmed, R. Ashany, N. J. Belkin, E. A. Fox and M. Zemankova (1994), "Digital Library: Gross Structure and Requirements", Workshop on On-line Access to Digital Libraries, June 1994.
6. Kelapure, Rohit, Marcos André Gonçalves, Edward A. Fox (2003), Scenario-Based "Generation of Digital Library Services", in Proceedings of 7th European Conference on Digital Libraries (ECDL 2003), 17-22 August, Trondheim, Norway, Springer-Verlag GmbH, Lecture Notes in Computer Science, vol. 2769, pp. 263-275.
7. Suleman, Hussein, and Edward A. Fox (2001), "A Framework for Building Open Digital Libraries", in D-Lib Magazine, Vol. 7, No. 12, December 2001. Available http://www.dlib.org/dlib/december01/suleman/12suleman.html
8. Suleman, H. (2002), Open Digital Libraries, Ph.D. dissertation, Virginia Tech. Available http://scholar.lib.vt.edu/theses/available/etd-11222002-155624/
9. Tansley, Rob (2004), DSpace 2.0 Design Proposal, presented at DSpace User Group Meeting, 10-11 March, Cambridge, USA. Available http://wiki.dspace.org/DspaceTwo

An Ontology-Based Model of Digital Libraries

László Kovács and András Micsik

MTA SZTAKI,
Computer and Automation Research Institute,
of the Hungarian Academy of Sciences,
Department of Distributed Systems,
H-1111 Budapest XI. Lágymányosi u. 11. Hungary
{laszlo.kovacs, micsik}@sztaki.hu

Abstract. In this paper a new unifying model is suggested for digital libraries which contains four conceptual layers, and defines the concepts of each layer as an OWL ontology. Instances of the ontology can be used to define an overall view of a digital library in terms of the four layers and the relationships between them. Such a model has the advantage that the methodology is formalized and extensible, thus models are comparable and manageable.

Keywords: digital library concepts, ontologies, reference models, OWL.

1 Introduction

Digital libraries represent a truly interdisciplinary research domain; modeling activities in this area thus have very complex requirements. Models related to digital libraries published so far can be grouped as follows:

- External models have some overlap with the digital library research area, but these models are widely used outside the area as well [3,4],
- Partial models are restricted to certain views or services of digital libraries [5,6,7,9]. Models for digital library evaluation form a subset of partial models, for example [2,10],
- Generalized models: the 5S model [8] is a formal model for digital libraries, while the DELOS model can be seen as a conceptual model [1].

The single general model applicable for digital libraries is the 5S model [8]. According to this model a digital library consists of a repository, metadata catalogs, services and a society of users. The 5S refers to *streams* and *structures* for the construction of digital objects, *spaces* for the description of digital object collections and their interrelations, *scenarios* for the definition of how services and activities change the state of the system, and finally *societies* for the interconnection of roles and activities within the user community. The 5S model is based on mathematical formalism, and has been used in various case studies, including the generation of a taxonomy of DL terms. 5SL is a declarative language based on this model for the generation of DL applications.

Another holistic view of digital library is given by the DELOS working group for digital library testbeds and evaluation [1]. Although the model focuses on evaluation,

E.A. Fox et al. (Eds.): ICADL 2005, LNCS 3815, pp. 38–43, 2005.
© Springer-Verlag Berlin Heidelberg 2005

its view can be generalized. The model emerges from three non-orthogonal components of digital libraries: the users, the data/collection and the technology used. The
interaction of these three defines the fourth component: usage. Each component connects the DL domain to different fields of research, with different interests and
evaluation 'culture'. This model is less formal than the 5S model.

2 Suggestion of a Holistic Model for Digital Libraries

In this section we outline a model that covers all possible aspects of digital libraries
on the conceptual level, and provides means for relating modeled aspects on the formal level. Our work is rooted in the DELOS model [1], and starts from the basic aspects of a digital library identified as: Collection/Content, Services, Inter-
faces/Infrastructure and Community.

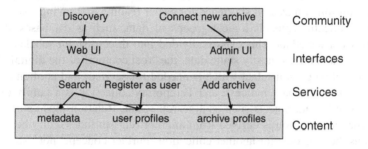

Fig. 1. Layered approach for digital library modeling

These components can be illustrated as a layered model (Figure 1), with the content as the bottom layer, and the community as the top layer. Layers provide access to
lower layers, and combine individual capabilities of lower layers into more complex
functionalities. On the topmost layer we reach complex work patterns such as discovering new relevant documents or inserting a new document collection into the digital
library.

The traditional goals of reference models are to establish a common basic terminology and to provide a generic architecture or structural modal for the area. Digital
libraries are very different in their aims, services and architecture. Still the goal of establishing a common basic terminology remains necessary, and the emerging use of
ontologies in connection with the Semantic Web effort offers new and valuable tools
for that purpose.

An ontology describes concepts and relationships within the investigated area or
phenomena [11]. OWL (the Web Ontology Language) was selected as the format of
this new ontology [12]. Each layer in our model defines its key concepts and their relationships. Relationships exist also between layers. First, each layer is introduced in a
bottom-up order, and then the overview of the whole ontology is presented. The main
concepts and relationships in the content layer are:

```
Class(Concept owl:Thing)
Class(Collection Concept)
Class(PersistentCollection Collection)
Class(DataCollection PersistentCollection)
Class(MetadataCollection PersistentCollection)
Class(DynamicCollection Collection)
Class(TemporaryCollection Collection)
DisjointClasses(PersistentCollection DynamicCollection
                TemporaryCollection)
ObjectProperty(has_metadata domain(DataCollection)
               range(MetadataCollection))
ObjectProperty(derived_from range(Collection)
               domain(Collection))
ObjectProperty(refers_to range(Collection)
               domain(Collection))
```

The class Concept is used as a common root for all classes defined in our ontology. Definitions are sometimes a bit shortened for easier reading and saving space. The basic concept Collection models logical groups of data, such as databases, document stores, indices or metadata. This class is divided into three disjoint subclasses: a PersistentCollection contains mostly static data, the 'real content' of the digital library, a DynamicCollection contains data which is needed for services and is often actualized (e.g. user profiles, database indices), and TemporaryCollection is a family of temporary, reproducible data objects such as a search result. Relationships can be used to describe when a collection is derived from another (e.g. an index), or when a collection contains the metadata for another collection. Further concepts not listed here describe data formats, internal structures, etc. The characteristic elements of the next layer are:

```
Class(Service Concept)
Class(AtomicService Service)
Class(CompositeService Service)
Class(ServiceGroup Concept)
ObjectProperty(has_service domain(ServiceGroup)
               range(Service))
ObjectProperty(composed_of domain(CompositeService)
               range(Service))
ObjectProperty(uses domain(Service) range(Collection))
ObjectProperty(reads uses domain(Service)
range(Collection))
ObjectProperty(updates uses domain(Service)
               range(Collection))
ObjectProperty(produces uses domain(Service)
               range(Collection))
```

In the service layer services can be atomic or composed, and services can be grouped together for easier reference. Services are usually modeled by their pre- and postcondition; the requirements for deploying the service and the effect of service deployment. Here, the 'uses' properties can be applied to connect the required input and the output to a service. It should be noted that services are abstract on this layer: they are accessible only through interfaces provided by the next layer:

```
Class(Interface Concept)
Class(MachineInterface Interface)
Class(HumanInterface Interface)
Class(Node Concept)
ObjectProperty(provides domain(Interface)
                range(ServiceGroup))
ObjectProperty(has_interface domain(Node)
                range(Interface))
ObjectProperty(communicatesWith
    domain(MachineInterface) range(MachineInterface))
```

The interface layer defines the infrastructure of the digital library system with respect to service deployment and communication. Services are accessible through interfaces, where human interfaces communicate with users (upper layer), and machine interfaces communicate with each other. Nodes may be used to represent the various separate hardware elements of the system, and their roles in the system are indicated by the interfaces they provide. Interfaces may also be characterized by their availability (PDAs, touchscreen kiosks, etc.).

```
Class(Role Concept)
Class(WorkPattern Concept)
Class(Actor Concept)
Class(User Actor)
Class(Professional Actor)
Class(Agent Actor)
ObjectProperty(has_access domain(Role)
range(HumanInterface))
ObjectProperty(responsible_for domain(Role)
range(Role))
ObjectProperty(participator domain(WorkPattern)
range(Role))
ObjectProperty(has_role domain(Actor) range(Role))
```

The community layer represents the use of the system. Roles define which interfaces are accessible for which users, and the organizational structure of the digital library can also be illustrated by responsibilities between roles. Work patterns collect the roles needed to perform that work. Actors can be used to describe the user community. The subclasses of actors are defined as in [9].

Figure 2 provides an overview of the main classes and their relationships in the ontology. It can be seen that the layers are connected in a simple, hierarchical way. The ontology can be enhanced with more classes and properties in order to provide richer or finer conceptualization. When the required level of conceptualization is reached, instances are created to represent aspects of the modeled digital library, and relations are used to define connections between these instances.

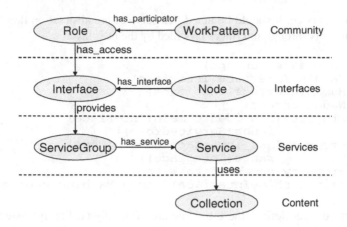

Fig. 2. The main concepts in the layers and their connections

3 Summary

A new modeling technique is suggested for digital libraries in which layers provide the separation of main aspects of digital libraries such as content and organization. The concepts and their relationships of each layer are defined as an ontology. This results in a formal way of capturing the essence of a digital library which is extensible to model high-level details as well.

The presented approach is very general, and it is not limited to digital libraries, but can be applied to other complex networked information systems (CNIS) such as web portals or organizational memory applications. As the borders of the digital library field are still blurred, this generality may also help to find the "differentia specifica" of digital libraries, and to give more contour to borders.

Acknowledgement. This work was supported in part by the DELOS Network of Excellence on Digital Libraries funded by the European Commission.

References

1. Norbert Fuhr, Preben Hansen, Michael Mabe, András Micsik, Ingeborg Sølvberg: Digital Libraries: A Generic Classification and Evaluation Scheme. ECDL 2001, September 4-9 2001, Darmstadt, Germany, Springer LNCS 2163, pp. 187-199
2. László Kovács and András Micsik. The Evaluation Computer: a Model for Structuring Evaluation Activities. DELOS Workshop on the Evaluation of Digital Libraries, Padova, 2004, http://dlib.ionio.gr/wp7/workshop2004_program.html
3. A Reference Model for an Open Archival Information System, Document Number: ISO 14721:2003
4. Tefko Saracevic. Relevance: a review and a framework for thinking on the notion in information science. Journal of the American Society for Information Science, 26:321-343, 1975

5. Functional Requirements for Bibliographic Records,   http://www.ifla.org/VII/s13/frbr/frbr.pdf
6. Bing Wang. A hybrid system approach for supporting digital libraries. International Journal on Digital Libraries, 2(2-3):91-110, 1999.
7. Donatella Castelli, Carlo Meghini, Pasquale Pagano. Foundations of multidimensional query language for digital libraries. ECDL 2002, Springer LNCS 2458, pp. 251-265.
8. M. A. Goncalves, E. A. Fox, L. T. Watson and N. A. Kipp. Streams, Structures, Spaces, Scenarios, Societies (5S): A Formal Model for Digital Libraries, ACM Transactions on Information Systems, 22(2), 2004, pp. 270-312
9. Final Report of DELOS/NSF Working Group on 'Reference Models for Digital Libraries: Actors and Roles', 23 July 2003, http://www.delos-nsf.actorswg.cdlib.org/finalreport.pdf
10. Tefko Saracevic. Digital Library Evaluation: Toward Evolution of Concepts. Library Trends 49(2): (2000)
11. O. Olsson. Two Uses of Ontologies in Digital Libraries. Second DELOS Workshop: Metadata and Interoperability in Digital Library Related Fields, Bonn, 7-8 October 1996, ERCIM Workshop Reports No.97/W002
12. D. L. McGuinness, F. van Harmelen (eds.). OWL Web Ontology Language Overview. W3C Recommendation 10 February 2004, http://www.w3.org/TR/owl-features/

The Impact of ICT on Library Services for the Visually Impaired

Young Sook Lee

The National Library of Korea,
San 60-1, Banpo-dong, Seocho-gu,
137-702 Seoul, Korea
ysooklee@nl.go.kr

Abstract. ICT gives visually impaired people two fundamental freedoms – Independence and Choice in library services. Before electronic information and on-line catalogues became available visually impaired people required assistance with reading and had limited choice of reading material. But now visually impaired people are no longer disabled in searching and surfing information on digital libraries. This study examines the ICT impact on library services for the visually impaired in mainstream libraries. New opportunities for mainstream libraries to integrate visually impaired people are discussed as well as the problems facing the mainstream libraries.

1 Introduction

Does the Information Communication Technology (ICT) give an opportunity to general libraries to open their doors to the blind and visually impaired people? Unlike other disabled people, visually impaired people have not been recognized as users by the librarians of local libraries in most countries mainly due to their inability to read printed materials. Instead, visually impaired people have been left on the hands of social workers or volunteers who produce Braille and talking books—alternative formats—for the blind. However, the production of these materials in alternative formats for the visually impaired amounts only up to 2% of the total reading materials published per year even in the most developed countries. Even in Canada, the visually impaired receive much less opportunity to access library materials compared to the rest of the general populations. For example, Calgary Public Library in Albert, Canada, has 14,000 items in alternative formats for the visually impaired, while there are more than 2 million items for the rest of the populations[1].

Attempts spearheaded by governments in many countries have been made to level the disparity in access to information between the haves and have-nots. Korean government is not an exception. Minimizing digital divide the Korean government has been financially supporting public or private sectors which developed programs or services designed for the disadvantaged in society. The programs include helping

---

[1] Rosemary Griebel: Partnering services between public libraries and library services for the blind: a Canadian experience. PNLA Quarterly, Vol.65 (2000). 17.

E.A. Fox et al. (Eds.): ICADL 2005, LNCS 3815, pp. 44–51, 2005.
© Springer-Verlag Berlin Heidelberg 2005

disabled people to get the IT literacy, etc. Nevertheless, majority of disabled people in Korea are still marginalized in the mainstreams of library services. They have to sorely rely on private sectors with very limited resources for reading. Some public libraries in Korea have attempted to provide the visually impaired with talking books and Braille by installing production facilities for materials in alternative formats within their premise. But this could not be an appropriate solution to solve the shortage of reading materials for the visually impaired. Considering the financial situation of the most of the public libraries in Korea, for an individual library to set up such production unit is not practical. Generally the cost for installing the production unit is about US$100,000 which is higher than their annual budget for purchasing library materials. In addition to this, the production cost of materials in alternative reading formats is 10 times higher than that of printed sources. Moreover, since the production of materials in alternative formats is very time consuming, some items take more than 2 years to be placed on the shelf. And even if public libraries can afford the expenses in producing materials in alternative formats, they cannot overcome the imbalance in the accessibilities for reading materials between the print disabled and their peers without disabilities. New strategies should be sought for the disabled, such that they, in this era of digital library services, will not be fallen into the disadvantaged group, unlike the previous era in which electronic materials did not exist and over 90 % of the materials housed by public libraries were in printed format.

This paper discusses the impact of ICT on lives of disabled people and the attempts of general libraries to integrate the disabled into the mainstream of their library services. Also the most common problems of mainstream libraries, when they implement new services for the print disabled, are pointed out by analyzing the practices done by the National Library of Korea.

2   The Impact of ICT on Lives of Disabled People

The development of library services for the disabled has been paralleled with the development of new technology which has played a significant role in the increase of library membership, particularly in the print disabled[2]. In the 1930s, the advent of talking books served as a milestone in the progress of library services for the visually impaired. The talking books are voice recordings of printed materials, which are used as a means of compensating people with reading difficulties. Before the production of talking books, Braille had been used as a major reading format for the blind. Braille is a system of six-dot cells invented by Louis Braille in 1829. Braille is read by using fingertips, thus requires the sensitivity in the fingertips. Therefore, the people who have lost eyesight at their latter stages of life find great difficulty in reading Braille because they may have lost the sensitivity in their fingertips already. Consequently they need another alternative format for reading. So the talking books have become an invaluable reading method for visually impaired people and also for those who cannot hold books or turn pages because of their physical limitation. Beside this, in some countries people with mental problems have benefited from talking books as well.

---

[2] Young Sook Lee: Accessible Library Services for People with Disabilities: A Model for Korean Libraries. A Ph.D thesis in the School of Library, Archive and Information Studies at University College London (2001) 69.

Since the introduction of the talking books, the readership in many countries has been increased. For instance, when the Royal National Institute for the Blind in Britain first introduced talking books in 1935, the readership of the talking books grew from 6,600 in 1950s to 22,000 in 1960, 40,000 in 1970s and over 66,000 in 1980s[3]. In the United States, as soon as talking books were introduced, legislation was passed by Congress to include talking books in the National Library Service (NLS) for the Blind at the Library of Congress (LC) and increased its annual appropriations to the LC to be used for talking books in 1935. The budget was increased from US$100,000 to $175,000 for the first talking book production in 1935, and later in 1959 the appropriation was $1,350,000, and in 1965 it was $2,446,000[4].

In Korea the first talking book services started in 1970s by Canes Club. One of the noticeable changes that happened since the introduction of the talking books was the increased number of services centers for the visually impaired. Before the introduction of talking books, there were few libraries for the blind in Korea. However, because talking books, compared Braille, were much easier to produce and also available in mass production with low cost, the advent of talking books initiated a number of services centers to spring up in order to meet the reading needs of visually impaired people.

The advent of talking books has contributed greatly to the increase of library membership of not only the visually impaired and but also people with other disabilities who cannot access print materials. Despite the great contribution of talking books, however, visually impaired people are still left poor in reading and information resources compared to sighted people. For instance, in the total stocks of the two largest libraries in Braille and talking books in Korea account for less than 10,000 titles. This number will be much lowered if duplication number is subtracted from it, and also the same titles are normally produced both in Braille and talking books. Even in developed countries, the situation is not much better than that in Korea. The holding of the Union Catalogue of alternative format materials in five English speaking countries including Australia, Canada, and USA lists approximately 250,000 titles[5]. This number is no more than that of a medium-seized public library in any developed countries. This was mentioned at the 63rd International Federation of Library Associations and Institutions (IFLA) General Conference in 1997 to raise the awareness of the library and information professionals worldwide for information needs of the disabled.

Although the development of talking book technology has increased the library memberships, the major services providers of the visually impaired were still the libraries for the blind, not the general libraries. Main reason is that the production of talking books still requires much human involvement: somebody has to read the printed materials for recording. But visually impaired people are now able to access

---

[3] Allan Leach: Library services in the United Kingdom. Paper to the Expert Meeting of Libraries for the Blind, prior to the IFLA General Conference, Brighton, the United Kingdom (1987).

[4] The National Library Service for the Blind and Physically Handicapped (NLSBPH) Library of Congress: A History of the National Library of Service for Blind and Handicapped Individuals, Library of Congress. That all may read: Library of Service for Blind and Physically Handicapped People (1983) 83-141.

[5] Rosemary Kavanagh, Barbara Freeze: VISUNET: A Vision of Virtual Library Services for the Blind. Paper to the 63rd IFLA General Conference, Copenhagen, Denmark (1997).

reading and information materials in the same way as their sighted counterparts. They can directly access the original text by using assistive technology. As a result, human involvement is no longer necessity. These days even a totally blind person can search the Internet when the computer is equipped with assistive technology such as a screen reader. "A friend of mine recently said to me that if she didn't know better she'd have thought that the Internet was made for blind people," said Damon Rose in his article, *The Internet: made for blind people*[6]. Visually impaired people who use various Internet services feel a great sense of independence. Moreover, the visually impaired are able to browse the up-to-date online catalogues and choose what they want to read, not what others think they want to read. Therefore, technology provides disabled people two fundamental rights: independence and choice. Probably the dream of a world where visually impaired people can independently access magazines, books, newspapers, documents and even private mails has come true. Thus, technology helps enhance the self-esteem and self-reliance of the disabled as they work and study independently and even feel normal. In fact, information technology may be more revolutionary for disabled people than for the rest of the population.

Another feature of electronic materials is that the same document could be converted into varying formats such as Braille, speech or large print by using assistive technology. Therefore, the visually impaired can choose their preferred formats of output, whether that be speech, Braille, large print for themselves or ink print for their sighted peers. In addition, multiple copies of the same format can be made within a short time; otherwise it would take several days or months if it is done by manually intensive methods. In the matter of storage of bulk Braille that has always been a headache in libraries, Braille materials in digitized format solve this storage problem. All these issues show the possibilities of general libraries to play a significant role in minimizing the dearth of reading and information resources for the visually impaired. Besides, these days more libraries in turn are increasingly moving into producing and providing electronic document through their digital library services. All these features of electronic materials could be a great opportunity to general libraries to open their doors to the visually impaired who have been lost customers for so long in general libraries.

3 Assistive Technology

Assistive computer technology means any modification made to standard computer software and hardware to enable people with disabilities to work independently. This is often called adaptive, access or enabling technology. In the US federal law, the definition of assistive technology comes from the Individuals with Disabilities Education Act (IDEA), stating "as used in this chapter, assistive technology device means any item, piece of equipment, or product system, whether acquired commercially off the shelf, modified, or customized, that is used to increase, maintain, or improve the functional capabilities of a child with disabilities" (Individuals with Disabilities Education Act, 1999, §300.5, from IDEA Practices, 2003)[7]. Assistive technology has

---

[6] Damon Rose: The Internet: made for Blind people. New Beacon, Vol.944. (1996) 7.
[7] School Library Accessibility: The Role of Assistive Technology. Teacher Librarian, Vol.31(2004) 15.

been developed along with the development of general computer technology. For instance, screen reading software is used to convert the text on the computer screen into speech. By using this software, the blind can access OPAC, electronic books, newspapers and various information resources through the Internet.

Assistive technology devices are often more expensive than the standard ones because of the high research and development costs and the small market. But more and more, the assistive technology is becoming the mainstream. For instance, when the first Kurzweil in the United States came out in the mid of 1970s, it cost about US$ 45,000. Also it was the size of a large washing machine. However, now the scanning equipment can be purchased for as little as US$120 and it is the size of a laptop. The early reading machine could only read certain types of quality print on good quality paper, but nowadays even the cheapest scanner can read more styles of print than the first reading machine. The reduction in price of assistive technology devices is rendering a great deal of opportunity for general libraries to meet the needs of the visually impaired without spending a large amount of money.

Among the access technology the following are the most popular:

Screen Readers
The screen readers or speech access software are the most common forms of assistive technology which are used with speech synthesis hardware to convert the text on the computer screen into speech. Some screen readers work two-ways, both reading and writing. People who cannot use a keyboard or mouse because of limited mobility may use this two-way software. There are numerous screen reader products available and the software price ranges from US$200 to US$250 for read-only station.

Screen Magnifiers
Screen magnifiers help partially sighted people to view the contents on a computer screen at various levels of magnification. They are able to magnify a line, a word, or an icon as large as the computer screen allows. It can also change the background color and textual color to help those having trouble distinguishing a certain color combination. The price of screen magnifiers ranges from US$400 to US$2,000. In addition, some computer operating systems, such as Microsoft Windows 98 and above, offer built-in accessibility options, including a magnifier.

Braille Displayer
It is also called a Braille display or softBraille. A series of dots can be raised to form Braille characters. Braille displays are usually augmented to standard keyboards. Blind people use the keyboard as an input device and the Braille displayer to read what is on the screen. The range of price is from US$1,500 to US$15,000.

Braille Embossers
Braille embossers are the printers that punch out Braille. In most cases, these printers only print the Braille on one side of the paper. But there are double sides Braille embossers which line up the Braille dots so that the dots punched on the one side of the paper do not interfere with the dots punched on the other. The price ranges from US$600 to US$7,500.

Braille Translators
Braille translators translate text to Braille. Non-text information such as charts, graphs or mathematical formulas cannot be accessed. There are several packages which are based on DOS, Windows and MAC. The range of price is from US$150 to US$1,000.

4 Opportunity for General Libraries

As mentioned earlier, various factors in technological environment affect general libraries in their accessibility by the disabled. In fact, accessibility has already become a legal matter since disability discrimination acts are already in effect in some countries such as the United States and the United Kingdom. No person with disability shall be excluded from the participation in, be denied the benefit of, or be subjected to discrimination under any services or programs that is supported by public fund. In Korea, a disability discrimination act is under preparation and will come out within this year.

Whether or not such laws exist, in ethical aspect, the library professional should recognize their disabled users by integrating them into the rest of the users. Therefore, the library services must offer equitable access to information resources to the disabled, as much as to their non-disabled counterparts.

In pursuance of this, the National Library of Korea, like many other libraries, is very committed to serving the visually impaired since the Internet and web open the digital library services in 2001. The staff at the National Library of Korea understands that the right to know is a fundamental citizenship issue in the democratic society in any countries. Therefore, they recognize that the visually impaired also have the same right as the rest of the populations to gain access to publicly funded general libraries such as schools, universities and public libraries. Unlike libraries for the blind, the National Library of Korea moves forward to the digital future. In 2003, the NLK began producing universities' textbook titles in digital format, and it has distributed them through the NLK's web site to the students with visual impairments from 2004. At the end of 2004, the total of titles of textbooks accounted for 2,276 (827,542 pages). This web based service reflects the NLK's commitment to integrate the visually impaired into the mainstream of library services by making its collections more useful and accessible to them. Before initiating this new service, the NLK, using the standard MAchine Readable Cataloging system (MARC), had already developed a union catalogue of alternative format materials, comprising 90,000 records that were housed by 32 libraries for the visually impaired. The major purpose of building the union catalogue is to minimize the duplication of alternative format materials housed by different libraries for the visually impaired. These libraries for the visually impaired offer limited amount of resources, and they are run by private sectors. In fact, most of them are hard to be called libraries because of both the quality and quantity in their holdings, and also because they are run by social workers or volunteers, not by professional librarians. The more the duplicates are, the less the resources to the visually impaired. The union catalogue can be accessed at the KOLISNET, Korean Library Information System Network (www.nl.go.kr/kolisnet), and also at the NLK's visually impaired website (sigak.nl.go.kr/kn). Improvement in the services for the disabled are going to be accelerated since the responsibility of implementing library policies at national level has been transferred from the Minister of Culture and Tourism to the NLK in the late 2004. Taking over the responsibility for implementing the national library policy, the NLK recommends to the government to install a library support center at the NLK in order to help the general libraries integrate the services for the disabled into the mainstream of their services. The center will be assumed a leadership role in the development and delivery of service to the visually impaired by making partnership with the libraries for the visually impaired. The center will also train library practitioners on the sensitivity of disabilities and assistive technology.

5 Common Problems Faced by General Libraries

Thanks to the ICT, the NLK has initiated new services for the visually impaired in Korea. Before developing new services, the NLK had invited the representatives from associations and agencies of the disabled to hear what they want. When a new service was initiated, the NLK has received ideas and recommendations from those who used the service from its beginning stage. But the service did not always satisfy the clients. For instance, the Full-text universities' textbooks in digital format, which is mentioned above, have not been used much by university students with disabilities. One of main reasons is that the students could not download the texts but should read them in front of computer. Unlike leisure reads, textbooks are read frequently, and therefore, the service had to be modified so that the textbooks could be downloaded to individuals' devices for later use. In addition to this, the textbooks could not meet the time when new semester started; they usually came out in the middle of the semester. These are the factors that dissatisfied the university students with disabilities. In order to provide this service, the NLK had spent a great sum of money, digitizing textbooks. The NLK learned a lesson from the above case. The NLK recognized what university students with disabilities needed but did not know how to make the product accessible and appropriate to the users.

Another common problem is that, when librarians develop a new service, they think that the services will be used sorely by those who have good sights, hearing and mobility. However, the truth is that there are many people with disabilities who try to make a use of it. For instance, nowadays web based services are becoming more available and the number of services is growing in many countries. Unfortunately, many of library websites cannot be accessed in particular by people with visual impairments due to their highly graphical and visual contents. Technology can be double-edged unless careful consideration is given to it. When Microsoft Window 95 came out, Windows became much easier to use than the previous versions of Windows. However, many visually impaired computer users immediately faced tremendous challenges. The information on the computer screen was represented graphically and not in a text format. Therefore, the graphics could not be read to those who used a screen reader. Neither speech nor Braille can interpret graphics. To overcome the graphical user interface, the NLK like other libraries has designed a text-only website for the visually impaired. But the disabled want to be treated the same as the others without disabilities. They want to use the same building, devices, programs, services, and websites as their able bodied peers do. They do not want to receive a special treatment. Unfortunately most librarians in general libraries do not have much knowledge and experience on the characteristics of disabilities and the disabled. As a result, librarians are likely to develop what they thought the disabled wanted instead of what the disabled really wanted. Therefore, a universal design is the most crucial issue when a website is developed, since websites are the gateways to gain access to information and reading materials in the era of digital library services. In well-designed buildings, facilities or websites, disabled people do not need assistance at all, and they can even feel as normal as any other people by using them independently.

6 Conclusion

The ICT provides general libraries with an opportunity to integrate the services for the disabled into the mainstream of their services. This means that any individual with a disability should be able to visit any local library and receive access, directly or indirectly, to information and reading resources in accessible formats. Cost of ignoring the needs of the disabled can be higher than the cost of the solution. Generally, it is estimated that one in every ten of the population is disabled. On the economic front, as long as disabled people are excluded or discriminated from education, employment, programs, activities, or services, they remain unproductive and dependent. The cost of lifelong support to disabled people is costly and even wasteful.

References

1. Griebel, Rosemary: Partnering services between public libraries and library services for the blind: a Canadian experience. PNLA Quarterly, Vol.65 (2000). 17
2. Kavanagh, Rosemary, Freeze, Barbara: VISUNET: A Vision of Virtual Library Services for the Blind. Paper to the 63rd IFLA General Conference, Copenhagen, Denmark (1997)
3. Leach, Allan: Library services in the United Kingdom. Paper to the Expert Meeting of Libraries for the Blind, prior to the IFLA General Conference, Brighton, the United Kingdom (1987)
4. Lee, Young Sook: Accessible Library Services for People with Disabilities : A Model for Korean Libraries. A Ph.D thesis in the School of Library, Archive and Information Studies at University College London (2001) 69
5. The National Library Service for the Blind and Physically Handicapped (NLSBPH) Library of Congress: A History of the National Library of Service for Blind and Handicapped Individuals, Library of Congress. That all may read: Library of Service for Blind and Physically Handicapped People (1983) 83-141
6. Rose, Damon: The Internet: made for Blind people. New Beacon, Vol.944. (1996) 7
7. School Library Accessibility: The Role of Assistive Technology. Teacher Librarian, Vol.31(2004) 15

An Asian Study of Healthcare Web Portals: Implications for Healthcare Digital Libraries

Yin-Leng Theng and Eng-Soon Soh

Division of Information Studies,
School of Communication and Information,
Nanyang Technological University,
Singapore 637718
{tyltheng, SOHE0001}@ntu.edu.sg

Abstract. In contrast to most studies conducted in the West, this study investigated online trust of healthcare Web portals from Asian countries. A Web-based survey was conducted through the Internet for about two weeks and achieved 127 responses. The respondents assessed two healthcare Web portals based on task completion before answering questions in a Web-based questionnaire. Congruent to related studies carried in the West, this study also suggested a significant relationship between usability and perceived credibility of healthcare Web portals. Findings from this pilot study seemed to indicate that the "error prevention" usability heuristic was most severely violated in two healthcare Web portals. The paper then concludes with implications on design of user-centred healthcare digital libraries.

1 Introduction

Emergence of Web portals delivering information, services, products and advertisements to consumers on the Internet has changed the nature of consumer buying. Due to the many advantages of healthcare Web portals, many people are going online to search for healthcare information, products and services (for example, Eastin, 2001; Goldstein, 2000; Young, 2000). More people are surfing the Internet for healthcare and financial information and they are facing important decisions about determining which sites to be trusted (Fogg et al., 2002). Goldstein (2000) defined healthcare Web portals as advertising channels that deliver information, services, products and advertisements to consumers in the Internet. Not only do they provide high standard search capability, they also contain complete information on healthcare, symptoms and diseases that enable consumers and patients to educate themselves anywhere and at anytime of the day.

Besides being excellent advertising tools and information databases, healthcare Web portals could also reduce costs and improve healthcare quality (Young, 2000). There are many kinds of healthcare sites on the Internet. Some serve the general public while some more subject-specific ones serve healthcare professionals or users of particular groups, such as women and children.

In this paper, "Web portal/site" is used to denote single-point-access information systems intended to provide easy and timely access to information and support communities of knowledge workers who share common goals.

E.A. Fox et al. (Eds.): ICADL 2005, LNCS 3815, pp. 52–61, 2005.
© Springer-Verlag Berlin Heidelberg 2005

2 Problems Facing Healthcare Portals and Related Studies

However, the quality of healthcare Web portals has become a cause for concern as they vary greatly in terms of accuracy, completeness and consistency, and inaccurate or misleading information can potentially harm Web users (Purcell, Wilson & Delamothe, 2002). For example, Eastin (2001) mentioned that although a large proportion of Internet users in America seek health information online, many of the health information is not provided by medical professionals and there are no government or ethical regulations controlling most of the online information. As a result, many people may be misled and turned away from proper treatment. In addition, Stanford et al. (2002) found that consumers tend to use visual appeal as a marker of credibility so usability may have influenced the perception of credibility of the consumers.

From the study conducted by Eysenbach and Köhler (2002), some respondents expressed that the Internet had allowed them to assess the quality of information more easily because they could verify and cross-check the information with different sites. In general, the respondents favoured the Internet as a source of health information because they could verify and countercheck what the doctors told them. However, they also maintained that they would always confirm the information found online with their doctors (Eysenbach & Köhler, 2002). Therefore, due to the advantages of healthcare web portals, more people are going online for healthcare and medical information, products and services. Determining which site is credible and which one to trust might still be a problem for the general public.

Responding to this concern, a group of researchers from Sliced Bread Design, Consumer WebWatch and Stanford University's Persuasive Technology Lab studied how consumers (general public) determine the credibility of healthcare Web portals, and whether they did it correctly (Stanford et al, 2002). Credibility in the study was defined as "believability and is a perceived quality". The study found that the criteria used by the consumers to evaluate the credibility of healthcare Web portals greatly differed from that of the healthcare professionals. The consumers were relatively influenced more by the overall visual appeal of the sites while the healthcare experts emphasized more on the name reputation of the sites, site operators or affiliates, information source and company motives. Thus, it seems to suggest that in the absence of expertise, the consumers tend to evaluate a site's credibility based on looks and ease of use (Fogg et al., 2002; Stanford et al., 2002).

3 The Study

When one judges the credibility of Web portals, particularly healthcare portals, one would naturally be concerned about factors such as the reputation and authority of the organisation or site owner, seals of approval, accuracy, completeness, currency of the information content, and so on (Eysenbach & Köhler, 2002; Fogg et al. n.d.; Stanford et al., 2002; etc.).

While this study acknowledges the importance of those factors to healthcare portal credibility assessment, the main focus of this study was on Web portal credibility and usability. In contrast to few studies carried out mostly in the West to evaluate credibility of healthcare portals, this study had three objectives :

- *Objective 1* : To find out important criteria determining perceived credibility;
- *Objective 2* : To determine severity of Nielsen's usability heuristics violated in two well-known healthcare portals; and
- *Objective 3* : To find whether there was a significant relationship between perceived credibility and usability of healthcare Web portals' among Asian consumers, when compared with Western consumers.

Before describing the study, we briefly define two important concepts identified in the objectives used in this study :

1   *Credibility*. It is defined as perceived credibility that does not reside in any object, person or piece of information and is made up of multiple dimensions, based on Fogg and Tseng (1999)'s definition. The "perception" of credibility is believed to be contributed by two key components, namely, trustworthiness and expertise :

- "Trustworthiness" is defined by terms such as well-intentioned, truthful, unbiased and so on. It is a dimension of credibility that captures the perceived goodness or morality of the source.
- "Expertise" is referred by terms such as knowledgeable, experienced, competent, and so on. It is also a dimension of credibility but it captures the perceived knowledge and skill of the source.

As such, the evaluation of credibility will be measured by the overall assessment of the *trustworthiness* and *expertise* dimensions of the Web portal. We believe that since most consumers do not have the medical expertise to assess healthcare Web portals, they would usually judge credibility based on their perceptions of such sites (Fogg et al., 2002; Stanford et al., 2002). In this study, we used "credibility" and "trust" interchangeably in order not to confuse the respondents because it is believed that most lay persons would not distinguish between the two words.

2   *Usability*. Following "ISO 9241-11: Guidance on Usability (1998)", usability is defined as "the extent to which a product can be used by specific users to achieve specified goals with effectiveness, efficiency and satisfaction in a specified context of use" (Bevan, 2001, p. 536), and "ISO/IEC FDIS 9126-1: Software Engineering —Product Quality—Part 1: Quality Model (2000)" defines usability as "the capability of the software product to be understood, learned, used and attractive to the user, when used under specified conditions" (Bevan, 2001, p. 537).

Protocol

The on-line survey was conducted from 3rd to 19th August 2004 for a period of about two weeks, including a three-day extension because one of the respondents who missed the deadline had asked to be allowed to participate. As a result, a few more data were collected after the extension. The potential respondents were invited to respond to the survey through emails. One day after the last day of the survey, a message was put up on the introduction page to inform visitors that the survey collection period had ended.

Profiles of Target Respondents

The target respondents were 15 years old and above, and had not been healthcare professionals or medical students. Since the healthcare Web portals under study were designed for the general public, respondents with strong medical backgrounds were not invited to minimize biases and from the data. The respondents also needed to have at least six months of Internet experience, a duration suggested by a survey carried out by the Health On the Net Foundation ("Health," 2003) to differentiate novice and non-novice Internet users.

Selected Healthcare Web Portals for Evaluation

Initially, four well-known healthcare Web portals were chosen based on rankings of the portals made by both medical professionals and consumers in the Stanford et al (2002) study. The portals were ranked according to perceptions of the credibility and usability of the sites instead of the sites' actual credibility. Since they were U.S. sites rated by residents in the U.S., one would argue there could possibly be some biases. However, Jarvenpaa, Tractinsky and Saarinen (1999) found that cultural differences had little effect on online trust. Moreover, in terms of content, the U.S. based sites used for the study were more or less general in their description of the illnesses. Although they might contain statistical information of U.S. relevance and biases, users should not be affected by such information as they could always check them out at Asia's official Web sites for health statistics. In addition, using healthcare portals that were well-known or that contained logos of authority, such as Ministry of Health, might downplay all other influencing factors as the brand name or logo alone might exert an overpowering influence on the users' judgement.

Survey Instrument Design

The survey form was implemented by an online survey application developed in Active Server Page.NET (ASP.NET) and the data updated into a Microsoft Access database (see http://islab2.sci.ntu.edu.sg/projects/eref/sessurvey/).

A pilot study was carried out to verify survey instrument and estimate the time needed for completion. Two male and two female pilot testers were recruited. On average, each pilot tester took about 40 minutes to complete the online survey, excluding the time taken to jot down the comments and suggestions about the online survey itself. The online survey form was later improved based on feedback from pilot study. They also felt that reducing the number of portals to two or three would reduce the strain on the respondents. Hence, in the actual study, only MDChoice (http://www.mdchoice.com/) and WebMD (http://www.webmd.com/); were used, as MDChoice was supposed to be more usable but less credible than WebMD.

The revised online survey instrument consisted of :

- *Introduction* Page. It informed the respondents about the purpose and running period of the survey, pre-requisites and expectations of the respondents, privacy policy, copyright statement, disclaimer and contact person of the survey. The respondents would click on the "Start" button to go to the "survey" page.
- *Survey Page.* It included the demographic section which asked for respondents' personal particulars as well as criteria used to judge credibility of healthcare portals (Fogg et al., 2002; Stanford et al., 2002).: (i) accuracy

of the information; (ii) name and reputation of the portal; (iii) completeness of the information; (iv) owner or sponsor(s) of the portal; (v) currency of the information; (vi) usability of portal (ease of use, design look, navigability, etc.); (vii) motive of the owner or sponsor(s); and (viii) others.

Respondents were also asked to complete "Task 1" and "Task 2". "Task 1" required the respondents to perform some pre-determined tasks as guidelines to browse the pre-selected healthcare Web portals (see Figure 1). The respondents would click on the links of the Web portals and evaluate the Web portals for their Web site usability and perceived credibility.

After the evaluation, the respondents would continue to "Task 2" to rate the severity of heuristics violated by the healthcare portals based on Nielsen (1994b)'s usability heuristics/criteria (see Figure 2). Each question had an accompanying example to allow the respondents to understand the question better. This survey used a 5-point Likert scale from "-2" (strongly disagree), "-1" (disagree), "0" (neutral), "1" (agree) to "2" (strongly agree) to measure severity of heuristics violated, as suggested by Nielsen (1994a). Negative values were used to give a sense of direction in the choices made by the respondents.

Other pages included :

- *Thank You Page*. After the data was submitted to the database, a "Thank you" Web page was shown to thank the respondents for taking part in the study.
- *Update Error Page*. This page allowed the respondents to continue to submit their data through the email without the need to redo the survey.
- *Survey Form Validation*. Basic checks could be performed on the online survey form after the respondents pressed the "Submit" button to ensure that all the fields were answered.

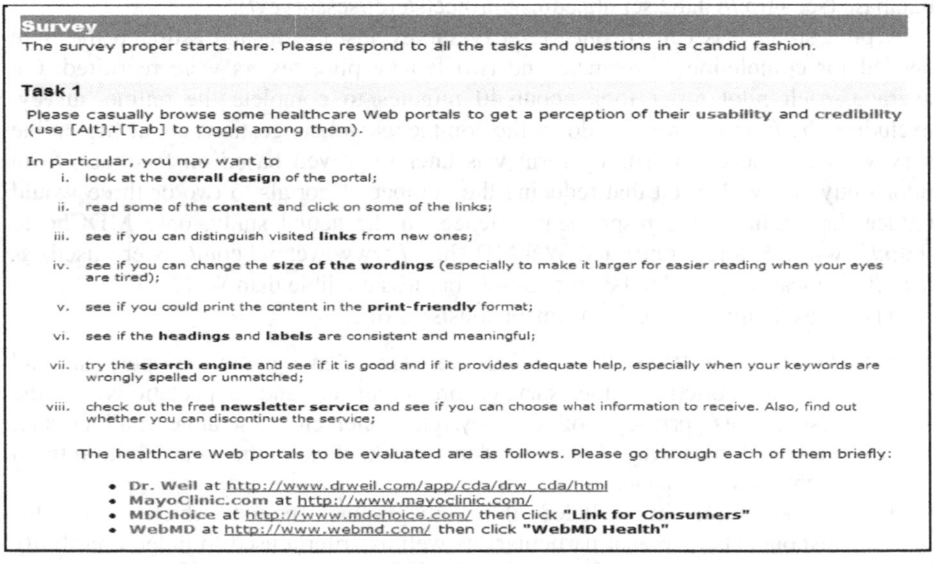

Survey

The survey proper starts here. Please respond to all the tasks and questions in a candid fashion.

Task 1

Please casually browse some healthcare Web portals to get a perception of their usability and credibility (use [Alt]+[Tab] to toggle among them).

In particular, you may want to
  i.   look at the **overall design** of the portal;
  ii. read some of the **content** and click on some of the links;
  iii. see if you can distinguish visited **links** from new ones;
  iv. see if you can change the **size of the wordings** (especially to make it larger for easier reading when your eyes are tired);
  v.   see if you could print the content in the **print-friendly** format;
  vi. see if the **headings** and labels are consistent and meaningful;
  vii. try the **search engine** and see if it is good and if it provides adequate help, especially when your keywords are wrongly spelled or unmatched;
  viii. check out the free **newsletter service** and see if you can choose what information to receive. Also, find out whether you can discontinue the service;

The healthcare Web portals to be evaluated are as follows. Please go through each of them briefly:

- Dr. Weil at http://www.drweil.com/app/cda/drw_cda/html
- MayoClinic.com at http://www.mayoclinic.com/
- MDChoice at http://www.mdchoice.com/ then click **"Link for Consumers"**
- WebMD at http://www.webmd.com/ then click **"WebMD Health"**

Fig. 1. Web Page Showing Task 1

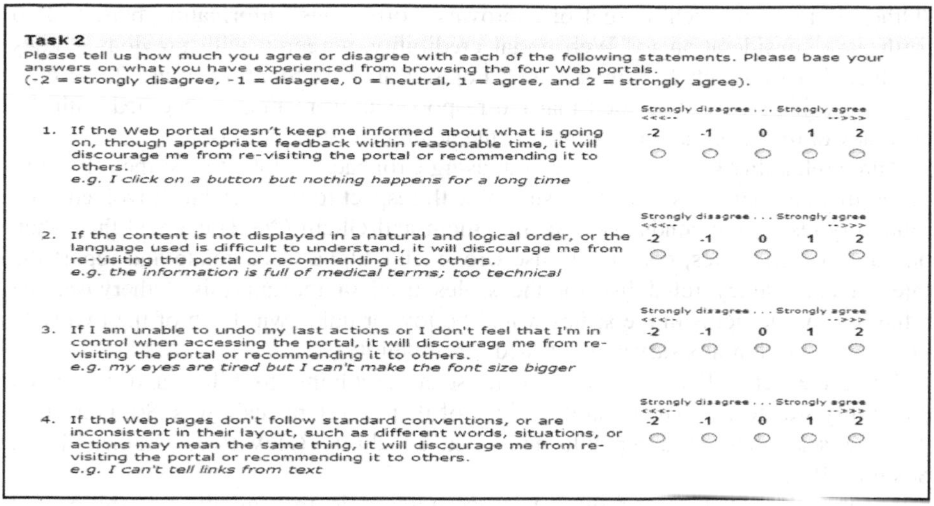

```
Task 2
Please tell us how much you agree or disagree with each of the following statements. Please base your
answers on what you have experienced from browsing the four Web portals.
(-2 = strongly disagree, -1 = disagree, 0 = neutral, 1 = agree, and 2 = strongly agree).

                                                              Strongly disagree . . . Strongly agree
                                                              <<<--                        -->>>
 1.  If the Web portal doesn't keep me informed about what is going    -2    -1     0     1     2
     on, through appropriate feedback within reasonable time, it will
     discourage me from re-visiting the portal or recommending it to    O     O     O     O     O
     others.
     e.g. I click on a button but nothing happens for a long time

                                                              Strongly disagree . . . Strongly agree
                                                              <<<--                        -->>>
 2.  If the content is not displayed in a natural and logical order, or the   -2    -1     0     1     2
     language used is difficult to understand, it will discourage me from
     re-visiting the portal or recommending it to others.             O     O     O     O     O
     e.g. the information is full of medical terms; too technical

                                                              Strongly disagree . . . Strongly agree
                                                              <<<--                        -->>>
 3.  If I am unable to undo my last actions or I don't feel that I'm in   -2    -1     0     1     2
     control when accessing the portal, it will discourage me from re-
     visiting the portal or recommending it to others.               O     O     O     O     O
     e.g. my eyes are tired but I can't make the font size bigger

                                                              Strongly disagree . . . Strongly agree
                                                              <<<--                        -->>>
 4.  If the Web pages don't follow standard conventions, or are        -2    -1     0     1     2
     inconsistent in their layout, such as different words, situations, or
     actions may mean the same thing, it will discourage me from re-   O     O     O     O     O
     visiting the portal or recommending it to others.
     e.g. I can't tell links from text
```

Fig. 2. Web Page Showing Task 2 : Ranking Usability Criteria Based on Nielsen's Heuristics

4   Findings and Analyses

4.1   Profiles of Respondents

There were a total of 133 respondents of which 48% were male and 52% were female. Almost all of the respondents (98%) belonged to the Asia continent except for two who (1%) came from the Australia/Oceania and North America continents, which were not considered in the analyses.

Majority of the respondents were aged between 15 and 34 and very few were from the other age groups. As indicated earlier, most Internet users likely to make use of online healthcare Web portals were from the age group of 15 to 39 years old. Hence, the samples were suitable for the purpose of this study.

Likewise, most of the respondents were university students with the rest made up of students of other educational levels, and members of the general public whose occupation was indicated by "Others". And as stated earlier, university students were representative of the profile of the Internet community who were also most likely to make use of healthcare information online.

4.2   Objective 1: Factors Determining Credibility

"Accuracy of the information" criterion with 133 counts (100%) was the most considered criterion in determining the credibility of the healthcare site, followed by other criteria in the descending order: "Completeness of the information" (70%), "Currency of the information" (68%), "Name and reputation of the portal" (64%) and "Usability of the portal (ease of use, design look, navigability, etc.)" (55%).

The other stated criteria were considered by less than 50% of the 133 respondents. Only 2% of the respondents included other non-stated criteria (as indicated under the

"Others" criterion) such as seal of approvals, corrections, information bias, and so forth as a consideration for Web portal credibility, agreeing with previous studies conducted (Eysenbach & Köhler, 2002; Fogg et al. n.d.; Stanford et al., 2002; etc). Hence, in this study, it seemed that the respondents were most concerned with the accuracy of the information presented in the healthcare Web portals.

Three reliability tests were carried out using Cronbach's alpha to test the reliability of the measurement or scale of the survey with respect to the variables involved. The reliability tests were conducted because Gliem and Gliem (2003) claimed that when one uses Likert-scales, one should use Cronbach's alpha to calculate and report the internal consistency reliability for the scales used in the analysis. Otherwise, the reliability of the items in the scales would be low or unknown. Each of the two two-item scales used in this survey was tested for reliability.

First, the reliability of the two-item scale involving usability and perceived credibility was tested. The reliability alpha of that two-item scale was .80, indicating that the scale has an acceptable and good reliability (Howitt & Cramer, 1999; Sekaran, 1992).

Second, the reliability of the other two-item scale that involved usability and gender was tested. The alpha reliability of that two-item scale was .00, indicating that the scale is not acceptable for reliability (Howitt & Cramer, 1999; Sekaran, 1992). Because of that, another reliability test was done with a three-item scale that involved usability, perceived credibility and gender. The reliability alpha of that three-item scale was only .47, indicating that the scale was also weak and not acceptable for reliability (Howitt & Cramer, 1999; Sekaran, 1992). It was also found that by removing gender from the scale, it would help to improve the reliability to .80, which was the same as that of the first two-item scale. Hence, it seemed that gender was not highly correlated to the other two items in the scale.

4.3   Objective 2: Severity of Usability Heuristics Violation

The data for analysis were provided by Questions 1 to 10 in the Task 2 subsection. It was found that the "Error prevention" (5th) heuristic was most severe when violated because it received the highest count of 133. This finding was in agreement to what Fogg et al. (2000) found in their study. The next in line were the "Visibility of system status" (1st), "Help and documentation" (10th), "Match between system and the real world" (2nd), "Consistency and standards" (4th), "Flexibility and efficiency of use" (7th), "Help users recognize, diagnose, and recover from errors" (9th), "Aesthetic and minimalist design" (8th), "Recognition rather than recall" (6th) and "User control and freedom" (3rd) heuristics.

4.4   Objective 3: Relationship Between Usability and Perceived Credibility

The result of the usability rankings of the two healthcare Web portals shows that WebMD received higher number of counts for rank 1 (57%) than MDChoice (43%). Hence, in terms of usability, WedMD seemed more usable than MDChoice. On the other hand, the perceived credibility rankings of the two healthcare Web portals show that WedMD also received higher number of counts for rank 1 (60%) than MDChoice (40%). Hence, in terms of perceived credibility, WedMD was seen as more credible than MDChoice.

By comparing rankings of the two portals, it is found that WedMD was both more usable and credible than MDChoice. This seemed to contrast with findings from study by Stanford et al. (2002) because the consumers in their study ranked MDChoice better than WedMD. One explanation could be that WebMD had changed and improved its Web site design to become better than that of MDChoice at the time of our study, hence resulting in the difference. Another reason why MDChoice was seen as less credible in this study might be because it was a portal that comprised content of several medical websites assembled by their editorial board (MDchoice.com, Inc., 2000).

To determine the statistical significance of our finding, a Chi-square test of independence and Spearman Correlation were performed to examine the relationship between *usability* and *perceived credibility*. The relationship between these variables was significant, $\chi^2(1, N = 133) = 58.03$, $p < .001$. Likewise, the Spearman correlation also reported that there was a statistically significant positive correlation between *usability* and *perceived credibility*, $r(131) = .661$, $p < 0.01$.

Hence, it seemed that healthcare Web portals that were more usable were perceived to be more credible, hence attracting more visits and re-visits. This result also concurred with some other earlier studies (Eastin, 2001; Eysenbach & Khler, 2002; Fogg et al., 2000).

Yet, only about half of the respondents (55%) indicated that they would look at usability when they assessed the credibility of healthcare Web portals (as obtained from factors affecting credibility). It seemed to suggest that most users would judge the credibility of a healthcare site based on the credibility of the information it provided rather than its usability. It could be that most respondents did not realise they were affected by usability, hence they did not select usability as one of the credibility assessment criteria.

5   Implications for Design of Healthcare Digital Libraries

This study highlighted the top three criteria considered by respondents were "information accuracy", "completeness" and "currency". This finding differed from that of Stanford et al. (2002) study in that the top three criteria considered by the *health experts* were "name reputation and affiliation", "information source" and "company motive", while the top three criteria considered by the *consumers* of that same study were "design look", "information focus" and "information design". The "name reputation of the owner and affiliation", and "design look" (presented by usability) criteria in this study, however, only ranked 5th or 6th respectively, indicating that they were not as important as the accuracy of the information on healthcare sites.

It seemed that health experts in the Stanford et al.(2002) study based more on the source of and organization behind healthcare portals to judge the credibility of the sites, while the consumers based on the ability to make use of or find information on healthcare portals to judge their credibility. On the other hand, this study seemed to indicate that the respondents were more concerned with the credibility of the information presented on healthcare portals, rather than the credibility of the portals themselves or the ability to find the right information.

Nevertheless, the differences might be because the findings from the study of Stanford et al. (2001) were deduced from the comments made by the health experts and consumers (qualitative) but the findings of this study were obtained by asking respondents questions (quantitative) directly. Or, perhaps it could be that this survey concentrated on information credibility and excluded transactional (sale of products and services) credibility that might have led to the differences.

In objective 2, we looked at usability of the two healthcare sites using Nielsen's heuristics. The respondents were concerned about the design violations detected. Building good, user-centred healthcare portals is a challenge to designers/developers in that "design" of any system is seen as both a science and an art. It is a *science* in that it realises an emphasis towards a principled, systematic approach to the creation and production of a portal. It is an *art* in the creative conceptualisation, expression and communication of the design ideas with a touch of aestheticism for the intended community of audience or users. For portals to satisfy users' needs, they have to be useful and usable. By "usefulness", we mean portals should support users' tasks with a good understanding of models of task completion. "Usability" refers to how information is organized "behind the scenes", and this is especially important in healthcare Web portals where wrong or inaccurate information and services provided could be detrimental.

Results of Objective 3 seemed to confirm previous studies that usability affects users' perception of credibility of healthcare portals. In addition, according to Roberts and Copeland (2001), portals that are ill-defined in their purposes could decrease confidence as a medium for healthcare advice and knowledge. Usability of Web sites seems to be influential to users' faith (or trust) in the information presented in the Web sites or portals, which in turn might affect the credibility of those sites.

Mandel (1997) mentions in one of Nielsen's 1996 findings, based on a user's comment that *"The more well-organized a page is, the more faith I will have in the information."* Gefen and Straub (2003) also advocate that trust, in a broad sense, is the belief that other people will react in predictable ways. This trust is crucial because people need to control, or at least feel that they understand, the social environment in which they live and interact.

In recent years, the distinction between portals and digital libraries is blurring as digital libraries are becoming more sophisticated. Not only are digital libraries just digital collections for specific purposes with powerful search strategies that are clearly defined, they are also becoming single-point-access information portals intended to provide easy and timely access to information and support communities of users who share common goals. Therefore, the issues surrounding credibility and usability of healthcare portals discussed in this paper also apply to digital libraries. Hence, if designers were to build *credible* healthcare portals/digital libraries, they need to ensure that they are *usable*.

6 Conclusion and On-Going Work

This study investigated online trust of healthcare Web portals from Asian countries. Findings from this pilot study seemed to suggest that "error prevention" usability heuristic was most severely violated in these two healthcare Web portals.

Congruent to related studies carried in the West, this study also confirmed there is a significant relationship between usability and perceived credibility of healthcare Web portals.

On-going work involves more studies carried out with more respondents and portals/digital libraries.

References

1. Bevan, N. (2001, October). International standards for HCI and usability. *International Journal of Human-Computer Studies, 55*(4), 533-552. Retrieved September 26, 2003, from ScienceDirect database.
2. Eastin, M. S. (2001, July). Credibility assessments of online health information: The effects of source expertise and knowledge of content. *Journal of Computer-Mediated Communication, 6*(4), Retrieved September 28, 2003, from http://www.ascusc.org/jcmc/vol6/issue4/eastin.html
3. Eysenbach, G., & Köhler, C. (2002, March 9). How do consumers search for and appraise health information on the World Wide Web?: Qualitative study using focus groups, usability tests, and in-depth interviews. *British Medical Journal, 324*, 573-577. Retrieved November 25, 2003, from http://bmj.bmjjournals.com/cgi/reprint/324/7337/573.pdf
4. Fogg, B. J., Soohoo, C., Danielson, D., Marable, L., Stanford, J., & Tauer, E. R. (2002, November 11). *How do people evaluate a Web site's credibility?: Results from a large study.* Retrieved November 25, 2003, from the Consumer WebWatch Web site: http://www.consumerWebwatch.org/news/report3_credibilityresearch/stanfordPTL.pdf
5. Gefen, D., & Straub, D. (2003, Winter). Managing user trust in B2C e-services. *e-Service Journal, 2*(2), 7-24. Retrieved September 26, 2003, from Computer Source database.
6. Gliem, J. A., & Gliem, R. R. (2003, October 8-10). *Calculating, interpreting, and reporting Cronbach's alpha reliability coefficient for Likert-type scales.* Paper presented at the Midwest Research-to-Practice Conference in Adult, Continuing, and Community Education, The Ohio State University, Columbus, OH. Retrieved August 23, 2004, from http://www.alumni-osu.org/midwest/midwest%20papers/Gliem%20&%20Gliem--Done.pdf
7. Goldstein, D. E. (2000). *E-healthcare: Harness the power of Internet e-commerce & e-care.* United States of America: Aspen Publishers, Inc.
8. Health On the Net Foundation. (2003, January 21). *Raw data for the survey May/June 2002.* Retrieved January 2, 2004, from http://www.hon.ch/Survey/Spring2002/res.html
9. Howitt, D., & Cramer, D. (1999). *A guide to computing statistics with SPSS™ release 8 for Windows.* London: Prentice Hall.
10. Jarvenpaa, S. L., Tractinsky, N., & Saarinen L. (1999, December). Customer trust in an Internet store: A cross-cultural validation. *Journal of Computer Mediated Communication, 5*(2). Retrieved November 21, 2003, from http://www.ascusc.org/jcmc/vol5/issue2/jarvenpaa.html
11. Mandel, T. (1997). *The elements of user interface design.* United States of America: John Wiley & Sons, Inc.
12. Nielsen, J. (1999a, March 7). *Trust or bust: Communicating trustworthiness in Web design.* Retrieved November 28, 2003, from http://www.useit.com/alertbox/990307.html
13. Nielsen, J. (1999b, May 2). *"Top Ten Mistakes" Revisited Three Years Later.* Retrieved November 27, 2003, from http://www.useit.com/alertbox/990502.html
14. Purcell, G. P., Wilson, P., & Delamothe, T. (Ed.). (2002, March). The quality of health information on the Internet. *British Medical Journal, 324*, 557-558. Retrieved November 25, 2003, from http://bmj.bmjjournals.com/cgi/reprint/324/7337/557.pdf
15. Young, K. M. (2000). *Informatics for healthcare professionals.* United States of America: F. A. Davis Company.

Annotations in an Academic Digital Library:
The Case of Conference Note-Taking and Annotation

Sally Jo Cunningham[1] and Chris Knowles[2]

[1] Department of Computer Science
[2] School of Education,
University of Waikato, Hamilton, New Zealand
{sallyjo, chrisk} @waikato.ac.nz

Abstract. This paper explores the potential usefulness and acceptability of annotation facilities by prospective users of an IT research digital library. We studied current annotation and note-taking behavior of IT researchers (academic and commercial), as exhibited at IT conferences. Here, we examine the implications of this information behavior for the design of annotation tools in a research-oriented digital library.

1 Introduction

The digital libraries and hypertext document construction research communities have shown strong interest over the past decade in supporting annotation by users of a digital library or hypertext document collection. Within these communities it has been noted that, from the user's point of view, annotation can serve many purposes: an annotation can serve "as link making, as path building, as commentary, as marking in or around existing text, as decentering of authority, as a record of reading and interpretation, or as community memory" [5]. When designing tools to support annotation, it then becomes imperative to first come to an understanding of which of the many potential annotation behaviors are important for the target user community.

The study reported in this paper is in the spirit of earlier digital library work by Cathy Marshall [4], who examined annotation artifacts (in that case, used university textbooks) to elicit annotation practice of those potential digital library users (university students) and to considered how those behaviors should affect the design of annotation tools within a digital library. A naïve view of annotation is that it is a uniform practice—that all motivations for annotation can be supported by a single facility. A closer look at actual annotation behavior suggests, however, that this in not the case. For example, typically people draw firm distinctions between annotations that are strictly personal and annotations that are suitable for sharing with other digital library users [7].

We studied the annotation and note-taking behaviors of IT researchers—both commercial and academic—as these behaviors were exhibited at IT conferences (Section 3). The note-taking media (Section 4), 'physical' features of individual notes (Section 5), and motivations for taking notes (Sections 6 and 7) are characterized. We then explore the implications of these observed behaviors for incorporating annotation support within a digital library for IT researchers (Section 8).

E.A. Fox et al. (Eds.): ICADL 2005, LNCS 3815, pp. 62–71, 2005.
© Springer-Verlag Berlin Heidelberg 2005

2 Previous Work

The digital library and hypertext communities have evinced a strong interest in supporting users of document collections through all phases of information behavior—not limiting system support to information seeking, but extending system facilities to include document 'use' (including active reading, comprehension, and summarization by the user) and the creation of new documents. One significant behavior crossing seeking, use, and creation is annotation: we make notes and marks to indicate promising trails when we look for new documents, to aid in maintaining attention when reading, to remind ourselves of important points to consider on re-reading a text, to give pointers to other readers of interesting or problematic sections, to create links to related documents, and for a host of other reasons.

Digital library tools supporting annotation exist to support interaction with web-based collections [7] and on a personal reading appliance [6]. Some annotation tools focus on supporting an individual user in working with personal copies of documents, where the annotations are not shared or even necessarily saved within the digital library [3]. Other tools are intended to support communities of users in some way: for example, to augment existing metadata with user-specified annotations [10], to identify passages within a document that may be particularly effective in supporting relevance feedback [2], or to help digital libraries 'get a social life' [8] by supporting annotation sharing [9].

The IT and Computer Science research community has been well-supported by digital libraries since the inception of the DL field—in fact, the earliest digital libraries focused on computing research documents. Grass-roots interest by computing researchers in conference annotation is growing, as conferences experiment in supporting annotation, note-taking, and commentary through Wikis and Blogging (see, for example, OOPSL '04; http://www.socialtext.net/oosla2004/) and IRC (for example, CSCW'04; [1]). An examination of note-taking motivations and behaviors by computing researchers is timely, to investigate how digital libraries can formally support this significant, long-existing user base.

3 Methodology

Three data gathering techniques were employed in this study: participant observation, semi-structured interviews, and examination of paper and electronic notes.

Participant observation provides the opportunity to gain a broad brush understanding of behavior in its natural context; in this study, literally hundreds of academic researchers were observed as they made the decision on what, when, and how to take notes. The researchers attended five conferences with an Information Technology or Information Systems focus, spending an estimated 50 hours observing conference attendees in conference sessions. The observations were fully anonymous; the researchers observed only the circumstances surrounding the attendees' acts of note-taking, and not the contents of the notes.

Participant observation is generally complemented by interviews and document analysis, to tease out the motivations behind observed behavior and issues with the embedding of the behavior in other, unobserved activities (in this case, how the note-taking is incorporated into research and other professional work). Twenty interviews were conducted. The participant was encouraged to 'walk' through the notes, explaining its meaning, form, and the motivation for making that note. All participants had a notably high level of self-awareness of their strategies, goals, and motivations for taking notes; it required very little prompting to elicit reflective, detailed, and in many cases eloquent descriptions of their note-taking habits. Note-taking (or in some cases, the deliberate abstention from note-taking) is not a minor behavior incidental to attendance at conferences. It is seen as an important professional tool for the support of research and other professional activities.

Eight participants provided physical or electronic copies of notes. These notes provide tangible examples of note-taking behaviors discovered in the participant observations and described in the interviews.

4 Note-Taking Media

We first consider the media used by conference attendees to take notes, then examine the contents of those notes—the signs and marks they comprise (Section 5)—and their meanings and the motivations for taking notes (Section 6).

4.1 Paper: The Preferred Medium

Paper is overwhelmingly the preferred primary (18 participants) or a backup medium (1) for note-taking. Notes are recorded on official conference, hotel, or personal notepads; conference programmes; loose pieces or scraps; Post-It notes; copies of papers; and the proceedings themselves.

Conference programmes play a significant role in note-taking. The schedules are commonly annotated to indicate which presentation one wishes to attend, will definitely not attend, or has attended and liked/disliked. At conference end, an annotated programme is a history of how an individual spent her time. The potential amount of annotation possible on the schedule is usually severely limited by the small size of the margins and the lack of available white space near the titles or abstracts of the presentations. Despite these limitations, annotating the programme remains popular, mainly because the programme is usually much more compact and lightweight than other options (such as the proceedings) and can usually be folded into a pocket or handbag. The schedule also provides temporal cues when reviewing the annotations after the conference—a person may not remember the title of an interesting presentation, but may recall that it was delivered early in the morning, or in a lengthy session of other interesting talks.

If the conference proceedings is not too bulky—in one volume, not too heavy, and can fit easily into a handbag—then it is likely to be carried into the presentations by a substantial minority of attendees. Most participants had strong, negative reactions to the suggestion of directly annotating conference proceedings: "It's immoral!" [R]. At the same time, they recognized the utility of having their notes with the papers. One solution is to make copies of the papers for note-taking, leaving the proceedings pristine. Two participants adopted this strategy, despite the obvious inconvenience of creating copies at a conference.

Four participants reported writing on proceedings, one strictly as a last resort if no other paper was available. Three participants viewed their proceedings as simply another research 'resource', although two of these reported having had to go to significant effort to overcome early training to respect books. One reason to persist in these struggles is that it is now much easier to acquire additional, pristine, copies of a paper or proceedings: "Proceedings aren't so replaceable, often you can't get them easily, but that's changing too with online" [P].

4.2 Digital Note-Taking

Interview participants use, or had used in the past, a variety of digital devices to take notes: PDA, Tablet PC, cellphone, and laptop. The PDA and cellphone have the advantage of being lightweight and small, particularly in comparison to a laptop or the conference proceedings. Participant A found the cellphone particularly attractive because, "My mobile phone is always there", whereas one has to remember to tote other note-taking paraphernalia.

Input is an issue for the PDA and Tablet PC. The speed of entry and error rate for graffiti input can be an issue ("It's probably half, three quarters of the speed of writing on paper, but some parts of it are faster because of word completion." [P]). The sole participant who experimented with a Tablet PC reported spending much of his time at the conference attempting to train himself to write "clearly enough for that to recognize", but could not create what he felt were "coherent" notes on the Tablet [C]. The sole participant who used a cellphone for note-taking, A, had originally used paper, then moved to a PDA, then abandoned that for the cellphone; she prefers the cellphone for its relative ease of input: "I'm quicker at texting than at using graffiti, the error rate is smaller with texting than with graffiti."

None of the interview participants currently used a laptop to take notes—an interesting statistic, given the large and increasing number of conference attendees seen sporting laptops. Interviewees reported that clicking keys ("you get a little bit of noise on a laptop" [P]) and other laptop noise is distracting to other conference attendees and calls unwanted attention to the laptop user.

Laptops are seen as "too inconvenient, too heavy, too bulky" (B), too unwieldy ("I don't want to carry around a laptop bag" [A]), too slow for those who don't touch type ("I'm faster putting notes on paper" [B]), unreliable ("the battery keeps dying out" [N]), and "just too complicated, to boot up and start up and what" (M). Word processors also force notes to be linear and textual, limiting the expressive power of the notes and by extension the types of ideas that the note-taker can bring away from a presentation: "...the chances of drawing a diagram or formula are near zero. With paper, whatever they put up I can draw it. ... I feel that they're [the laptop user] already shutting off a part of what is going to be talked about." [P]

Given these significant drawbacks, why are so many people bringing laptops to conferences? Interviewees doubt that laptop users are engaging with the presentations: "you wonder is that person playing solitaire [P]"; "I assume they're not reading, they're blogging, reading their email, surfing the web [S]"; these speculations were borne out by the participant observations.

4.3 Recordings

Two attendees at one conference were observed using hand-held video recorders to record the entirety of keynote presentations. These attendees had not asked permission of the speakers or the conference organizers to make the recordings, and obviously felt that they might not have a right to record—they were seated well off to the side and were attempting to be unobtrusive. Video recording raises intellectual property issues, and also may violate social protocols: Participant P pointed out that recordings make people self-conscious, and can stifle the free discussion of ideas that makes a conference more than is recorded in the proceedings: "...at a conference I can speak my mind and make things up on the spot, correct it, backtrack, put something out there that's a little exaggerated, like 'Windows is the worst thing that's happened to the world'—but your body language is saying I don't really mean that, if it's recorded it could be quoted out of context."

5   'Physical' Characteristics of Notes

Conference notes tend to be brief: the largest set of notes from this study summarized a four day conference and two associated workshops in approximately 13 pages of a steno pad, while the shortest was a single sheet torn from a hotel notepad. Digital notes were of similar length, perhaps amounting to a page or two when printed out.

For some attendees, this pithiness is a deliberate strategy: participant T declared the goal of his note-taking to be notes that are "short, actionable, and understandable". Further, the primary motivation for most notes is as a reminder rather than a summary—for after all, if a summary is later required for a literature review or work-mandated report, then it can be generated later by consulting the proceedings ("Obviously I've got the proceedings so I don't need to take notes." [M]). One participant [N] reported summarizing presentations, but even she was quite selective about which to summarize, and her summaries were two or three sentence reflections on how they related to her own research. Two interview participants responded that they did not take 'real' or 'full' notes (that is, notes that in themselves could form a summary, without recourse to the proceedings), associating that form of note with students or as a relic of a previous era when proceedings might not be included with a conference.

Note sets varied in their degree of 'tidiness'. Some attendees were observed carefully lining up text on the margins, indenting consistently for sub-notes, and working strictly linearly down the page. Others scribbled in margins, wrote slant-wise wherever there was a bit of white space, and in general adopted a style one interviewee described as: "nonlinear document, impressionistic if I'm being posh. Another way of putting it is shoddy." [R]

In some cases this non-linear arrangement allowed note-takers to group notes with similar content together, regardless of the chronology of the note-taking. In other cases, the groupings appeared random, and the interviewees could not recall their motivation in placing specific notes.

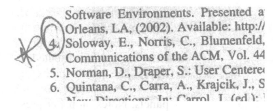

Software Environments. Presented a
Orleans, LA, (2002). Available: http://
4. Soloway, E., Norris, C., Blumenfeld,
Communications of the ACM, Vol. 44
5. Norman, D., Draper, S.: User Centere(
6. Quintana, C., Carra, A., Krajcik, J., S
Now Directions In: Carrol I (ed):

Fig. 1. Indicating importance, giving emphasis

Paper notes included a striking number of non-textual marks, including arrows, to show relatedness between notes or to emphasize bits of text; circles and asterisks, again for emphasis or to indicate importance (Figure 1); exclamation points, to indicate surprise, agreement, or importance; and various types of doodles. Figures, diagrams, and equations are copied from presentation slides only if they do not appear in the proceedings. Novel drawings may also be included in notes to illustrate or explore an idea that has occurred to the note-taker during a presentation: "I tend to draw, sometimes there are little pictures that go with ideas, like what the screen would look like if I do this." [R]

Digital note-takers acknowledged the awkwardness, relative to paper, of recording equations and figures. The cellphone user was not working in an area that might require equations ("For a start, I don't do formulas, I don't do math" [A]. Drawing facilities in a PDA support crude diagrams, and simple mathematical notation is more or less readable.

Text included in notes—both paper and digital—is typically brief, just a few words or phrases. The sole exception occurs with direct quotes from a presentation, when the attendee feels that the speaker has made a particularly eloquent or significant statement; otherwise, few or no complete sentences occur in notes. Text is intended as a reminder, and points are noted in an idiosyncratic manner ("Usually it's written in a way to only be legible [that is, understandable] to me." [S]). Sometimes the intention or meaning of a note is no longer clear even to its author; it was not uncommon for interviewees to be puzzled as they explained their notes to the researchers ("Weird! That is strange. Why [did I write that]? [S]).

6 Meanings and Motivations

The content of notes and the motivation for taking them was neatly summed up by one of the interview participants [P]: "Just cool stuff I want to remember." In this section we categorize the different types of 'cool stuff' described in the interviews. Interview participants characterized the content of, and motivations for taking, individual notes in the following ways:

References. Occasionally a full bibliographic reference was recorded, but more frequently interviewees used this term to indicate a URL, or an identifying name or phrase sufficient to allow that person, research group, or concept to be 'googled' later. The intention here is to "keep an eye" [I] on individuals or groups conducting interesting research, or to identify new research areas "to start educating myself in" [I].

Reminders. Notes may include 'to-do' items, frequently reminders to pass on references, ideas, and contact information to colleagues (Figure 2). Typically these are brief—just a jotting in the programme schedule.

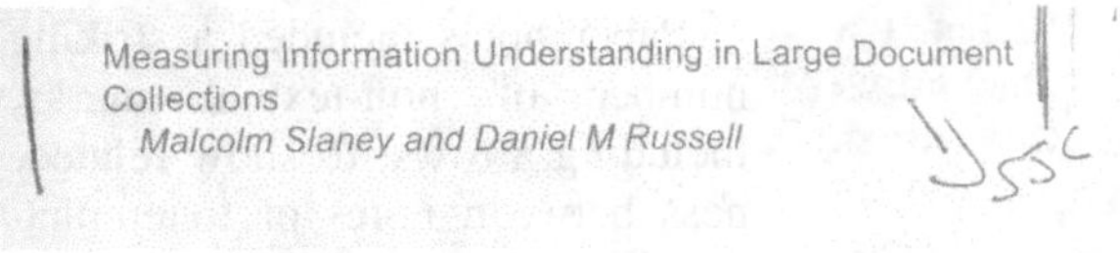

Measuring Information Understanding in Large Document Collections
Malcolm Slaney and Daniel M Russell

Fig. 2. Schedule notes (vertical lines), and arrow indicating reminder to send this reference to SJC

Supplements to proceedings. Attendees were more likely to take notes on presentations not represented in the proceedings—for example, keynote addresses and panels. Notes on paper presentations might include additional figures and data not included in the proceedings, and particularly resonant statements or phrases on slides: "Sometimes the speaker will phrase things a different way. I'm very word oriented so having something restated in a different way reinforces it for me." [G]

Ideas, or more usually fragments, outlines, and 'seeds of ideas' [H], are noted for possible exploration later. Ideas can be on-topic or off-topic, and off-topic ideas can be productive or non-productive. On-topic ideas are directly sparked by the presentation, and generally entail ways to incorporate that research into one's own research, teaching, or other aspects of one's work. Off-topic ideas can be productive—that is, they are also ideas and plans to support aspects of the attendee's professional activities, but they are wholly unrelated to the content of the presentation. The appearance of these off-topic inspirations may be a product of the opportunity to sit anonymously in an audience without possibility of interruption ("It isn't what they said, it's having the space to think. [Q]). These off-topic, productive ideas are sometimes perceived to be the most valuable outcomes from conference attendance ("It's an interesting thing, what you actually achieve at a conference isn't actually related to what you hear." [K]). Unproductive off-topic ideas are the intellectual equivalent of doodling—exploring hobbies ("I was thinking about making a square for a quilt project, so I was trying to scribble out some ideas for my square." [D]) or mental puzzles.

Paper Conversations. Academics, like schoolchildren, pass notes during presentations; participant R termed these 'paper conversations', and interviewees reported these as being conducted on conference programmes, notepads, and even conference proceedings. Sometimes they may include a critique of the contents of the presenter, but generally they are off topic and a response to boredom ("Like, how boring is this guy and how bad is his shirt?" [D]).

Questions. Publicly asking questions during the formal question-and-answer period at the end of a presentation can be daunting; writing down one's question (in brief, or in its entirety) can be helpful "so if I do stick up my hand I know what I'm talking about". [R]

Negative notes. Sometimes the noteworthy aspect of a presentation is that the technique presented is not applicable to the reader's research, or that the work presented is seriously. A negative note indicates that the work being presented does not require further consideration ("A lot of the annotations are negative, don't bother pursuing these, they're of no use." [E]).

Boredom notes. One reaction to difficulty in attending to a talk is to take notes on it, to make brief summaries or take down questions for the presenter. This activity can be useful in maintaining a professional appearance ("It was so boring, I decided that I had to take notes to keep from falling asleep." [L]).

Doodles. When boredom sets in, another common response is to amuse oneself by drawing or doodling—for example, filling in characters in handouts. 'Mindless' doodling is really only possible with paper ("The last time I checked, Word didn't have a doodling feature. [D]). Doodling is enjoyable, and the doodler has the advantage of looking as though s/he is attending to and engaging with the presentation.

Miscellaneous. The interviews and document (note) analysis revealed a smattering of other content types: related to social aspects of a conference (for example, dinner restaurant possibilities), expense records for travel claim forms, and last minute notes on what to say in one's own presentation.

7 Notes, Motivation, and Remembering

The act of note-taking affects the listening experience: "I don't know if you just think differently, it spurs some thought processes." (A). Note-taking is a formal technique to compel oneself to engage: "It stops my mind from wandering, makes me concentrate" [G]; "This is my way of taking part when I'm not presenting." [S]

A consequence of this engaging process is an aid to memory; things written down are reported as being more likely to be remembered ("When I write that down, 'it could be useful for', it goes bang into your head." [S]). One interview participant described how she used to worry about losing notes, but then six months after one conference she found a set of lost notes and realized that she had remembered all of the reminders, references, and ideas contained in them—so now the notes themselves are not as important to her as the act of making them [F]. The process is not perfect, of course; as described in Section 5, as interview participants re-examined their conference notes they sometimes were puzzled by their content or motivation.

Not all presentations are literally note-worthy—conference attendees are seen to take notes on a small proportion of presentations, an observation confirmed by interview participants ("At a conference generally there's maybe 10 or 20 percent of the talks that are interesting enough to take relevant notes on." [D]). An absence of notes does not necessarily imply that nothing is being taken away from the presentation, however; several interview participants reported that the hallmark of a truly important or useful idea is that it does not have to be written down ("I didn't take any notes…if I didn't remember it in my head it wasn't worth knowing about." [O]).

8 Conclusions

Examination of the media (Section 4) and format (Section 5) of notes indicates that the physical device and software facilities for annotation should be, both literally and figuratively, lightweight. If annotations are to be made in the context of use—whether at a conference or when later examining research papers—then the facilities must support fluid, natural annotations. At the conference itself, this indicates that the physical device must be small, light, silent in operation, and quick to turn on or off. The note-taking facilities must also recognize that annotation styles are highly idiosyncratic. It is difficult to imagine a more flexible and personalizable system than the simple pen and pad of paper. The advantages cited for using a digital device are that the notes are searchable, can be stored with other digital work material, and can be more easily integrated into one's workflow. These first two potential advantages do not appear to be fully realized. It's unclear how useful the ability to search actually is in practice, given that interviewees report spending the most time looking through notes either at the conference or shortly thereafter, and rarely or never deliberately consulting their notes long after the conference has ended (Section 7). Workflow integration (Section 7) occurs as the material in notes is 'processed' and incorporated into a digital 'to-do' list, date book, or projects file (a list of ideas for future research or student projects), rather than by direct searching of stored, 'raw' conference notes.

Intellectual 'processing' of presentations and papers is the key benefit of note-taking and annotation. Simple video-recording of a presentation is not only intrusive, but leaves no space for annotation. Similar disadvantages hold with voice recordings or photography. One participant used a digital camera to photograph slides at keynote presentations. Two others reported wanting to take photographs at conferences, but felt constrained because there were 'social and private things going on' [P], and picture-taking might make other attendees uncomfortable. Further, video and photographs are too close to the raw experience of attending a conference, and lack the interpretive value of notes.

The ability to keep notes in the context of use is important for many participants— here, the context is the history of the conference as recorded through, for example, the schedule, but also by associated the annotated paper with the work for which it is being read. This study provides evidence of the utility of a digital library that supports the user in tying together notes, documents, work in progress, and social context (e.g., a conference schedule, contact details, URLs, etc.).

As far as encouraging notes relating to on-topic matters, a fully connected digital note-taking appliance may be counter-productive in that it supports numerous sources of distractions. During one participant observation, a researcher was seated directly behind three people who had adopted Blackberry wireless handhelds just days before the conference. The attendees could not resist checking the Blackberries every few minutes, and immediately responded to all incoming email—which of course then stimulated still more email. One of the attendees appeared to be developing an addict's twitch, reflexively turning the Blackberry over to glance at the screen.

Evidence is mixed on the usefulness or acceptability of a system that would make annotations publicly available. As an experiment, try leaning over towards a colleague at a conference as though you will read his notes. In most cases, his arm will move around reflexively to protect his work. Interview participants appeared diffident about the 'quality' of their notes, deprecatingly referring to their annotations as 'scribbles' [B], 'ravings' [D], or 'stupid notes' [M]. Further, notes are taken for a variety of reasons (Section 6); some types of notes are suitable for sharing, others are only for personal use, and some notes are not even useful or usable by the original note-taker. An earlier study indicates that most users will not make annotations public unless the original private note has been 'cleaned up' [7]. It is difficult to imagine a scenario whereby a digital library would incorporate a reward structure encouraging users to go to the (often significant) extra effort of clarifying their notes.

An interesting exception to this diffidence about sharing notes lies in the subset of annotations that involve reminders to share a reference or paper with colleagues (Figure 2). This sharing is essentially 'clipping' [8], a significant behavior involving the reinforcement of social and intellectual networks by sharing encountered information. Copyright issues may restrict the ability of users to freely pass 'clippings' to colleagues, and there is room for innovation in supporting a more casual and sociable mechanism for clipping exchange than simple email [8].

Digital annotations have an advantage in supporting sharing in that the notes do not permanently mark the document, as happens with physical notes on paper. The ability to easily create a pristine, annotation-free copy is important: it allows the digital library user to share the document without concern that others will view their 'ravings', and so may free users to annotate more fully. Additionally, the electronic document seems liberated from the strongly-held inhibitions that many people feel about making marks in a formally printed document ("I guess it's my nominal Presbyterian upbringing that I won't damage a book. I just don't." [N])—again, indicating that an annotation facility may encourage annotation behavior in digital library users.

References

1. Cohen, D. Digital note-passing gains respect among adults. USA Today, 26 Nov 2004. http://www.usatoday.com/tech/products/services/2004-11-26-im-gains-cred_x.htm
2. Golovchinsky, G., Price, M.N., Schilit, B.N. From reading to retrieval: freeform ink annotations as queries. In; Proceedings of the 22nd ACM SIGIR Conference on Research and Retrieval. ACM Press: New York (1999) 19-25.
3. Jones, S., Staveley, M. Phrasier: A system for interactive document retrieval using keyphrases. In: Proceesings of the 22nd ACM SIGIR Conference on Research and Information Retrieval. ACM Press: New York (1999) 160-167.
4. Marshall, C.C. Annotation: From paper books to the digital library. In: Proceedings of the ACM Conference on Digital Libraries '97. ACM Press: New York (1997) 131-140.
5. Marshall, C.C. Toward an ecology of hypertext annotation. In: Proceedings of HyperText '98. ACM Press: New York (1998) 40-49
6. Marshall, C.C., Price, M.N., Golovchinsky, G., Schilit, B.N. Introducing a digital library reading appliance into a reading group. In: Proceedings of the ACM Conference on Digital Libraries '99. ACM Press: New York (1999) 77-84.
7. Marshall, C.C., Bernheim Brush, A.J. From personal to shared annotations. In: Proceedings of CHI 2002. ACM Press: New York (2002) 812-813.
8. Marshall, C.C., Bly, S. Sharing encountered information: Digital libraries get a social life. IN: Proceedings of the Joint ACM/IEEE Conference on Digital Libraries '04. ACM Press: New York (2004) 218-227.
9. Phelps, T.A., Wilensky, R. Multivalent Annotations. In: Proceedings of the European Conference on Research and Advanced Technology for Digital Libraries. Springer: London (2004) 287-303.
10. Rosenstock, B., Gertz, M. Web-based scholarship: Annotating the digital library. In: Proceedings of the Joint ACM/IEEE Conference on Digital Libraries '01. ACM Press: New York (2001) 104-105.

Relevance Judgments for Image Retrieval in the Field of Journalism: A Pilot Study

Tsai-Youn Hung[1], Chuck Zoeller[2], and Santiago Lyon[2]

[1] School of Communication, Information and Library Studies, Rutgers University,
4 Huntington St., New Brunswick, NJ 08901, USA
Transworld Institute of Technology, Yunlin, Taiwan
tyhung@scils.rutgers.edu
[2] The Associated Press, W 450 33rd St., New York, NY 10001, USA
{czoeller,slyon}@ap.org

Abstract. The objective of this pilot study is to investigate relevance judgments made by end-users when searching for image information. The pilot study involved 10 undergraduate students from the Department of Journalism and Media Studies at Rutgers University using the AccuNet/AP Photo Archive to retrieve specific, general, and subjective photos. The study identified core relevance criteria used across the three different image searches, and found that the participants in the general and subjective image searches relied more on personal feelings and textual information of photos to make relevance judgments, while the participants in the specific image search depended more on the features of objects in photos. Four textual representations--caption, object name, location, and creation date, were chosen to see how useful they were for the participants making relevance judgments. The results show that location was the most useful information among the four textual representations.

1 Introduction

The notion of relevance is a fundamental concept of information science and has played a major role in the evaluation of information retrieval (IR) since the 1950s. Since then interest in the concept of relevance has waxed and waned. Numerous theorists and researchers have explored the conceptual properties of relevance and have constructed theories or frameworks for relevance research [1, 2]. Over the recent five decades, this field has gained consistent knowledge about relevance factors and their effects. However, it has mainly focused on traditional textual information retrieval. With today's digital imaging technology, many holders of image collections have digitized their collections and made them accessible online. Users' accesses to digitized images and interests in image retrieval have increased. However, research on users' relevance judgments in visual information seeking process is still sparse. The research to investigate how people determine relevant images is desirable, because relevance is a necessary part of understanding human information behaviors [3]. Similarly, Shatford [4] also points out that relevance criteria suggested from empirical user studies can be regarded as possible access points to images and can provide valuable information as to users' information needs for image retrieval systems.

E.A. Fox et al. (Eds.): ICADL 2005, LNCS 3815, pp. 72–80, 2005.
© Springer-Verlag Berlin Heidelberg 2005

2 Literature Review

In the 1990s, there was a new wave of empirical work on users' perceptions of relevance. Many researchers have explored users' relevance by identifying the relevance criteria applied by users performing searches on their own information problems [5, 6, 7, 8]. Many of the relevance criteria found in those studies show that there is a finite range of relevance criteria shared across users and situations [7]. However, due to the basic difference between text and image information, users' criteria for image relevance judgments may be very different from textual document relevance judgments. Thus those relevance criteria found in textual IR environments might not be applicable to visual IR environments. Relevance research on image context has not received extensive investigation. There is only a small body of literature discussing how people make relevance judgments when searching for image information.

Hirsh [9] interviewed and observed ten fifth-grade students who were motivated information seekers working on a school research project. The project had students find three sources of information on a sports figure. She identified elementary school children's relevance criteria for graphical materials on the Web which are something that struck the students as interesting, the picture showed complete picture of the athlete, pictures that were of interest to their peers, and authority of resources. Her analysis indicated that criteria applied for pictorial information differed from those for textual materials.

Choi and Rasmussen [10] studied thirty-eight faculty and graduate students of American history and found that the user's perception of topicality was the most important factor among nine criteria. They also found that the ranking of the criteria changed between the stage of defining information problem and seeing the images. The authors claimed that their study was the first research on users' image relevance judgment. However, in their study nine criteria identified from previous textual relevance studies were chosen as target criteria in the questionnaire. These criteria were not elicited directly from the subjects' image searching.

Markkula & Sormunen [11] observed journalists' photo selection by using a photo archive at Aamulehti, the second largest newspaper in Finland. The first criterion journalists employed during a search session was topicality. Among others, technical, biographical, impressive, expressive and aesthetic criteria were also important. Topicality was always the first criteria to start their searches and aesthetic attributes, e.g., color and composition, were applied in the final selection phase.

The results of previous research show that topicality is the most important and often the first criteria people use in both image visual and textual information searching. However, there are some other criteria which only apply to images, such as emotion and visual attributes.

3 Research Questions

Enser and McGregor [12] analyzed image requests at the Hulton Deutsch Collection Ltd., and found that almost 70% of the requests were for a unique person, object or event. Based on Enser and McGregor's classification, Chen [13] examined twenty-nine participants' image queries and found that in addition to unique queries, nonunique queries were used as well. Some researchers also suggested the importance of the subjective meaning of images [14, 15, 16]. Fidel [17] proposed that image retrieval tasks might affect searching behavior. To address issues related to validity, this study observed searchers' relevance judgments by assigning them three different tasks---finding unique (specific), nonunique (general), and subjective images. The research questions are as follows:

1. What criteria do searchers employ to judge relevant images in searching for specific, general, and subjective images? Are the relevance criteria in these three types of searches different?
2. What textual representations are useful for users in making relevance judgments? Is the usefulness of textual representations in these three types of searches different?

4 Methodology

The data of the pilot study were collected through interviews and questionnaires. Content analysis and quantitative methods were used to analyze the verbal and questionnaire data.

4.1 Participants

Ten students from the Department of Journalism and Media Studies at Rutgers University were recruited to participate in this pilot study. To entice students to participate in the study, each participant received fifteen dollars for their participation.

4.2 Database System

This study used AccuNet/AP Photo Archive database system. The photo archive is a carefully selected collection of photographs from the vast holding of the Associated Press (AP). It contains over 700,000 photos and dates back over 150 years. Each picture is accompanied by a 50-to-75-word caption that fully describes the person or event in its surrounding context. The search interface has three free text search boxes labeled "What," "When," and "Where." Search results can be ranked by date or relevance (based on caption words), and can be displayed with thumbnails or in a faster loading, text-only title list. Searchers can use this database not only to search for factual photos but also subjective and emotional photos. The photo archive is available through the Rutgers University Library System.

4.3 Setting

The experiment of this study was conducted in the Observation Laboratory at the School of Communication, Information, and Library Studies at Rutgers University.

4.4 Procedures

Three types of search tasks-- specific, general, and subjective, were created based on Shatford's image analysis [15].

Table 1. Shatford's Image Analysis

Specific	General	Subjective
Images of individually named person, group, thing, event, location, or action.	Images of kind of person, group, thing, event, place, condition, or action.	Images of having emotional or abstract concepts.

Task 1--Specific

You are photo editing a story on Tiger Woods for a sports magazine. For this story, you need to find some photos of Tiger Woods as illustrations.

Task 2--General

You are photo editing a report on the crisis in the Middle East for a newspaper. For this report, you need to find some photos regarding this topic to be used as illustrations.

Task 3--Subjective

You are photo editing a special report on the topic of "Peace" and you need to find some photos to illustrate the meaning of "peace".

A tutoring class of how to use the photo archive was provided prior to the experiment. A user guide of Accunet/AP Photo Archive was also available for participants' reference. During the searching, participants had to save selected photos for later evaluation. An interview followed after the participants had completed each search. In each interview session, the participants described what relevance criteria they had used to select the photos. At the end of each search, the participants answered a Likert seven- point scale questionnaire to collect the usefulness of text representations in making relevance judgments. The search time for each task is ten minutes.

5 Results and Discussions

Comparing the relevance criteria used in the three search tasks, several common relevance criteria were identified (Table 2, 3, 4). They were typicality, emotion, action, aesthetic, text, familiarity, context, impression, preference, posture, facial feature, and appearance. Among them, "typicality", "emotion" and "aesthetic" were the most common relevance criteria and were used across these three searches.

Table 2. Relevance criteria for specific task

Relevance criteria	Example
Typicality	Holding trophy/ Winning something/Winning and wearing a green jack/ Showing who he is and wins something/ Trophy
Emotion	Hugging his mother/ Showing emotion/ Hugging a guy / Hugging a looser/ Showing human interests
Facial feature	Close-up of Tiger Woods/ Facial feature showing his effort/ Smiling, happy, confident and enthusiastic/ Triumphant / Showing aggressiveness/ Concentration
Aesthetic	Shot angle of the picture, photo color/ Artistic/Pretty view of the golf course/ Bright color to catch your attention/ View of the mountain and camera angle make him taller
Action	Action shot; good sand shot/ Hitting ball and dust going up
Posture	A good posture of Tiger Woods/ Swinging, portraying golf
Appearance	He looks good in white T shirt/ He is in red all the time/
Affection	Family relationship/ Big inspiration of his father on him/ Showing soft side of Tiger Woods

Table 3. Relevance criteria for general task

Relevance criteria	Example
Typicality	This is a political image/ It's obvious important when you talk about crisis in the Middle East
Emotion	A lot of actions, showing what is going on/ Crying/He was happy about the capture of Saddam Hussein/ Emotional side of what is going on in Iraq/ To show how many people die/ Appeal to other people's emotional side
Aesthetic	Black and white picture, it's cool
Action	Action shot, holding guns that would draw attention
Impression	Pretty powerful/ Soldiers in Iraq showing image really stand out
Familiarity	I have seen this in The New York Time
Preference	Just like the picture/ I like Yasser Arafat
Text	Caption shows supporting for the war

Table 4. Relevance criteria for subjective task

Relevance criteria	Example
Typicality	Universal representation/Peace sign, no war sign, peace protest/ Shaking hands showing peace/Peace pole/ Peace demonstration/ Holding sign for peace/ Girl is selling peace T-shirts/ Peace rally
Emotion	Showing how happy people are in Iraq/ Kids are around with candles showing emotional side
Aesthetic	That was nice lanterns; I think it was pretty
Impression	Pop, looks peaceful to me/ Marching outside, that was impressed
Familiarity	I remember this in high school/ I know the people in the picture
Context	Two women in a church/ The scene makes the picture very peaceful
Text	Caption shows the achievement of World War II/ Object name is peace treaty sign agreement

"Typicality" was the most mentioned relevance criterion in this study. "Typicality" is a criterion that can exhibit universal representation of an object in a photo. In the specific image search, most participants selected photos of Tiger Woods describing that the photos show Tiger Woods is "holding a trophy", "winning something", and "winning and wearing a green jacket"; in the general image search, some participants selected photos indicting that "This is a typical political image", and "It's obviously important when you talk about crisis in the Middle East"; in the subjective image search, the participants selected photos in which there are "peace" marks such as peace signs, and connotations of peace such as shaking hands. Because of their obvious universal representation, these selected photos easily caught the participants' attention. This may explain the reason that why some of these photos were selected several times by different participants.

"Emotion" is the second frequently used relevance criteria across these three searches. A photo contains the emotional context telling what is happing in the photo. This kind of photo stands out among other photos and more likely to be selected as a relevant photo. Interestingly, when the participants described the criteria they used, they seemed to narrate a story. However, what they described did not quite correspond to the description in the caption. This might explain why "caption" is not the most useful textual information for making relevance judgments found in the research question two.

Aesthetic criterion was not used as frequently as other core criteria. In this study, only female participants used this criterion. This might suggest that there could be a gender difference in relevance judgments in image retrieval. This assumption needs further study to verify if such a gender pattern exists.

In addition to the three core criteria, the results also show that there was a difference when using relevant criteria among these three search tasks. For example, in the specific image search, the outward characteristics of objects in a photo is an important factor affecting the participants' relevance decisions, such as objects' facial feature, posture, and appearance. This might be because the retrieval sets were so large and the similarity among the retrieved photos was very high. Thus, if a photo can exhibit the characteristics or features of the objects and has an artistic attribute, the participants are more likely to choose such a photo. This also explains why the aesthetic criterion was used more in the specific image search, which has larger retrieved sets. In the general image search, because the participants were not familiar with the topic, they had to base decisions on the text, familiarity, or personal feelings such as impression or preference.

Basically, the participants used similar criteria for selecting relevant photos in both the general and subjective image searches, except the "context" criteria. The "context" could be an important relevance criterion for selecting photos containing abstract or subjective meanings.

In summary, the participants in the general and subjective image searches relied more on personal feelings and textual information of photos to make relevance judgments, while the participants depended more on the features of objects in photos in the specific image search.

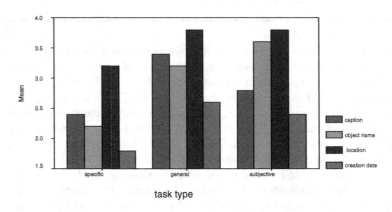

Fig. 1. The usefulness of textual information—caption, object name, location, and creation date, for judging relevant photos

Four textual representations-- caption, object name, location, and creation date, were chosen to see how useful they were for users when making relevance judgments. The results show that location had the highest mean of usefulness among the four textual representations (Fig. 1). This may be because in the general search task the participants chose photos taken in the Middle East, and in the subjective search task the participants chose photos related to Iraq's peace issue. Most photos chosen from these two searches have to do with location. However, in the specific image search, the participants also considered that location was very useful when making relevance judgments. This might be so because journalists know the location of each event occurring and its importance. The object name had the second highest means of usefulness. It shows that the object name plays an important role for helping the participants making relevance judgments. The role of object name in image retrieval is analogous to the role of title in textual information retrieval, a very important criterion for relevance decision-making. Previous studies have shown that in textual information retrieval, the abstract plays a major role in relevance decision-making. In image retrieval, the role of caption in visual representations is similar to the abstract in documentation representations. However, it is surprising that the caption of a photo is not the most useful textual representation when making relevance judgments in this study. The participants' search moves show that they did read captions before selecting photos, especially for the general and subjective image searches. The low means of the usefulness of the caption could be that the textual information provided by the database system did not give sufficient information to users for relevance decision-making. The indexers need to include more diverse terms and terms related to concepts, moods, and feelings, etc., not just indexing terms from the captions and other descriptions associated with photos. The creation date is the least useful textual representation in making relevance judgment. In general, when searching for specific images, the participants relied less on the textual representations, whereas in the general and subjective image searches, the participants relied more on textual information when making in relevance judgments.

6 Conclusions

The results indicate that search tasks affect users' relevance judgments for image retrieval. It supports Fidel's [17] proposition that image retrieval tasks might affect searching behavior. In this study, the participants relied more on personal feelings and textual information of photos to make relevance judgments in the general and subjective image searches, while the participants depended more on outward characteristics of objects in photos in the specific image search. The findings show that both internal context criteria, e.g., emotion, impression, and familiarity, and external context criteria, e.g., facial feature, aesthetic, and appearance, are applied for making relevance judgments during image searching. Since users' relevance criteria for image information are determined by their search tasks, interfaces for relevance feedback should be developed to capitalize on this aspect of use. To date, some image retrieval systems employ users' relevance feedback to modify retrieved sets as the search progress. However, the most common relevance criteria applied to the relevance feedback function focus primarily on external context such as color, shape, and texture. Internal context criteria, such as related users' subjective feelings are still not implemented in image retrieval systems. In order to allow users to have more control when using relevance feedback features to support them to search different types of images, an integration of concept and content-based approaches for designing more powerful relevance feedback interface is needed.

The pilot study used a specific group of undergraduate students. Images of different kinds or from different disciplines will have their own particular attributes that appear to be different for different users. This study focuses on the journalism field, thus the results of this study cannot be generalized to other groups of users or the examination of different types of images. Additionally, only a small number of participants were tested in this study, further research on more participants and other types of tasks are needed. A follow-up study will be continued after the pilot study.

References

1. Saracevic, T.: Relevance: A review of and a framework for the thinking on the notion in information science. Journal of the American Society for Information Science, 26 (1975) 321-43.
2. Saracevic, T: Modeling interaction in information retrieval (IR): A review and proposal. Proceedings of the 59th Annual Meeting of the American Society for Information Science, 33 (1996) 3-9.
3. Schamber, L.: (1994). Relevance and information behavior. Annual Review of Information Science and Technology, 29 (1984) 3-48.
4. Shatford, L. S.: (1994). Some issues in the indexing of images. Journal of the American Society for Information Science, 4 (1994) 583-588.
5. Schamber, L.: User's criteria for evaluation in a multimedia environment. Proceedings of the American Society of Information Science, 28 (1991) 126-133.
6. Barry. C. L.: User-defined relevance criteria: An exploratory study. Journal of the American Society for Information Society, 45 (1994) 149-159.
7. Park, T. K.: The natural of relevance in information retrieval: An empirical study. Library Quarterly, 63 (1993) 318-351.
8. Wang, P.: A cognitive model of document selection of real users of information retrieval systems. Doctoral dissertation, University of Maryland, College Park, MD. (1994).
9. Hirsh, S. G.: Relevance determination in children's use of electronic resources: A case study. Proceedings of the American Society for Information Science, 35 (1998) 63-72.
10. Choi, Y. & Rasmussen, E.: Users' relevance criteria in image retrieval in American history. Information Processing and Management, 38 (2002) 695-726.
11. Markkula, M., & Sormunen, E.: End-user searching challenges indexing practices in the digital newspaper photo archive. Information Retrieval, 1 (2000) 259-285.
12. Enser, P., & McGregor, C.: Analysis of visual information retrieval queries._ Report on Project G16412 to the British Library Research and Development Department. London: British Library (1992).
13. Chen, H.-L.: An analysis of image queries in the field of art history. Journal of the American Society for Information Science and Technology, 52 (2001) 260-273.
14. Shatford, S.: Analyzing the subject of a picture: A theoretical approach. Cataloging & Classification Quarterly, 6 (1986) 39-62.
15. Ornager, S.: The newspaper image database: Empirical supported analysis of users' topology and word association clusters. Proceedings of the 19th Annual Conference on Research and Development in Information Retrieval, SIGIR (1995) 190-197.
16. Jorgensen, C.: Indexing images: Testing an image description template. Proceedings of the 59th Annual Meeting of the American Society for Information Science, 33 (1996) 209-213.
17. Fidel, R.: Image retrieval task: Implications for the design and evaluation of image databases. The New Review of Hypermedia and Multimedia, 3 (1997) 181-199.

Image Classification for Digital Archive Management

Cheng-Hung Li, Chih-Yi Chiu, and Hsiang-An Wang

Institute of Information Science, Academia Sinica,
128. Sec. 2. Academia Road, Nankang, Taipei 115, Taiwan
{chli, cychiu, sawang}@iis.sinica.edu.tw

Abstract. As tools and systems for producing and disseminating image data have improved significantly in recent years, the volume of digital images has grown rapidly. An efficient mechanism for managing such images in a digital archive system is therefore needed. In this study, we propose an image classification technique that meets this need. The technique can be employed to annotate and verify image categories when gathering images. The proposed method segments each image into non-overlapping blocks from which color and texture features can be extracted. Support Vector Machine (SVM) classifiers are then applied to train and classify the images. Our experimental results show that the proposed classification mechanism is feasible for digital archive management systems.

1 Introduction

There has been an enormous growth in the number of digital image files in digital libraries in recent years; however managing these files has become increasingly difficult. To reduce the cost of digital image management, an automatic tool for digital libraries is required. In digital image management, research activities include image retrieval [1], digital rights management [2], and image annotation [3]. These research activities are very much related to image classification techniques. In addition, if there is a large volume of images, an efficient classification technique is very useful for maintaining the quality and correctness of the digital library. Take, for example, a set of naïve images in which no metadata has been embedded. An image classification technique can be applied to annotate the images and store them in appropriate categories. Furthermore, we can use the classification technique to verify the correctness of manually labeled image categories and dubious images can be identified and double-checked to maintain the quality of the digital library.

In this paper, we integrate an image classification technique with a digital archive management system. Image classification in our system comprises two components: off-line image training and on-line image classification. In the first component, each image is segmented into non-overlapping blocks. A color and texture histogram of each image block is then extracted as its feature representation, and the Support Vector Machine (SVM) technique is applied to train several image category classifiers. In on-line classification, we extract the features of the image and use the trained SVM classifiers to store gathered images in appropriate categories.

E.A. Fox et al. (Eds.): ICADL 2005, LNCS 3815, pp. 81–89, 2005.
© Springer-Verlag Berlin Heidelberg 2005

The remainder of this paper is organized as follows. In the next section, we discuss related works. In Section 3, we address SVM training and classification, together with image feature extraction. Section 4 describes the implementation platform and experimental results. Finally, we present our conclusions and discuss future research directions in Section 5.

2   Related Work

Many content-based image retrieval (CBIR) systems have been developed since the early 1990s. CBIR for large image databases [5] has been studied extensively in relation to image processing, information retrieval, pattern recognition, and database management. Most CBIR research efforts have focused on finding effective feature representations for images. First, the histogram method has been widely used for various image categorization problems. Szummer and Picard [4] and Vailaya et al. [6] use color histograms to classify indoor and outdoor images. Chapelle et al. [7] apply SVM to classify images containing a generic set of objects based on color histogram features. The above works show that histograms can be computed at a low cost and are effective for certain classification cases. However, a major shortcoming of general histogram representation is that spatial structural information is missed. Hence, other features such as texture and shape have been proposed to solve this problem [8-11].

A number of methods that extract features by dividing an image into blocks have been proposed. Gorkani and Picard [12] first divide an image into 16 non-overlapping, equal-sized blocks, and then compute the dominant orientations for each block. Finally, the image is classified as a city or suburb scene by the major orientations of the blocks. Wang et al. [13] develop an algorithm for classifying graphs or photographs. The classifier divides an image into blocks, and classifies each block into one of two categories based on the wavelet coefficients in high frequency channels. If the percentage of blocks classified as photograph is higher than a pre-defined threshold, the image is marked as a photograph; otherwise, it is marked as a graph. Yu and Wolf [14] propose a Hidden Markov Model (HMM) classifier for indoor/outdoor scene classification that is trained on vector quantized (VQ) color histograms of image blocks. Li and Wang [15] suggest that a particular category of images can be captured by a two-dimensional multi-resolution HMM trained on the color and texture features of the image blocks. Yanai [16] describe a generic image classification system that uses images gathered automatically from the World Wide Web as training images for generic image classification, instead of using image collections gathered manually. Murphy et al. [17] propose four graph models that associate the features of image blocks with objects and perform joint scene and object recognition.

3   Image Classification

Image classification in our system comprises two components: off-line image training and on-line image classification. In the training component, we extract features from images sourced by the archive system and link them to categories through SVM training. Next, in the classification component, we classify unknown images into one of the categories using SVM classifiers. Figure 1 shows the workflow of the image training and classification modules in our digital archive management system.

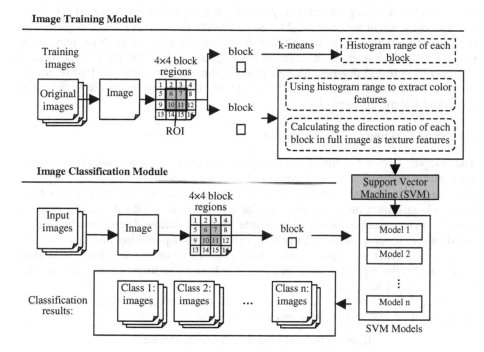

Fig. 1. An overview of the image training and classification components

3.1 Feature Extraction

Since archive images in the same category have similar characteristics, an image's content, such as its color and texture, can be used to represent the characteristics of the category. For example, an image of Archaeological Data usually has an ancient object in the center of the image, while a Han Wooden Slip image usually exhibits natural wood colors, but the use of ultra red rays may reveal detail not visible in the chromatic image. In the following, we describe the color and texture feature extraction process.

To obtain color features, we first normalize the size of a training image into 96×120 pixels, and segment them into 4×4 non-overlapping blocks (see Figure 1). Next a color histogram vector for each block is computed. A mean vector is also computed by averaging the color histogram vectors of the sixteen blocks. We then calculate the color histogram intersection between each block's histogram vector and the mean vector. Finally we have sixteen similarity values as our color feature representation.

For texture feature extraction, we apply Canny's edge detection algorithm [18] to each block. First, we use a Gaussian mask to smoothing the image's noise, and use a pair of 3x3 Sobel convolution masks to estimate the gradient in the x-direction (Gx)

and y-direction (Gy). Then we use the gradient of Gx and Gy to compute the pixel direction as follows:

$$Direct = 180 - ((\tan^{-1}(Gy/Gx)) * (180/\pi)); \tag{1}$$

For quantization, an edge direction is given a setting based on the range it falls within. An edge direction in the range (0~22.5 & 157.5~180 degrees) is set to 0 degrees. Any edge direction falling in the range (22.5~67.5 degrees) it is set to 45 degrees; in the range (67.5~112.5 degrees) it is set to 90 degrees; and in the range (112.5~157.5 degrees) is set to 135 degrees. We calculate the direction histogram of four region-of-interest (ROI) blocks (blocks 6, 7, 10, and 11 in Figure 1) in the image to determine its texture feature representation.

3.2 SVM Training and Classification

The Support Vector Machine (SVM) technique utilizes the minimal structured risk principle in machine learning theory, and generally performs effectively on pattern classification problems without incorporating domain knowledge [19]. It is based on a binary classification method, and looks for a hyper-plane to divide objects into two classes. It can ensure the minimal error rate of classification. The main advantage of SVM is that it can process linearly inseparable cases by training and analyzing the given data to generate support vectors. After removing extreme data from the training data, it builds the support vectors into a model. It then classifies any existing test data into the appropriate classes.

The color and texture features are used for training and classification. We normalize the features of training images as follows:

[Label] [Index1]:[Value1] [Index2]:[Value2] ...

For example, a feature vector of the first image could be:

1 1:0.268169 2:0.332564 3:0.246752 4:0.101631 5:0.202088 6:...etc

where [Label] is the correct category number of the image, and [Index] is series of feature values of the image. In this study, we employ the radial basis function as the kernel function.

4 Experimental Results

Our image collections contain Archaeological Data, Buddhist Rubbings, Han Dynasty Stone Relief Rubbings, Fu-Ssu Nien Ancient Books, and Han Wooden Slips. An image database, built by Redhat Linux 7.3, is divided into two components: the multimedia center web system (MMC) and the image processing daemon (IPD). These two components share the kernel function module layer and the database and file storage layer. The MMC executes the Servlet through JavaBeans invoked and compiled by the Application Server. The IPD uses the API through the kernel function module layer to communicate with the database and file storage layer. The classification module was developed by Java-Servlet and SVM tools [20]. Figure 2 shows some of the class images from the digital archive management system.

Archaeo-
logical Data

Buddhist
Rubbings

Han Dynasty
Stone Relief
Rubbings

Fu-Ssu Nien
Ancient
Books

Wooden slips
(chromatic)

Wooden slips
(ultra red
rays)

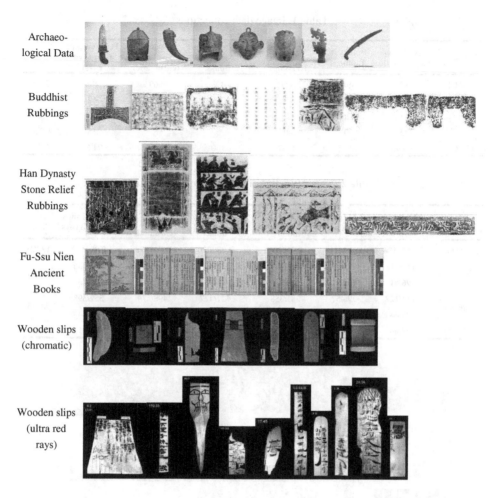

Fig. 2. Part of each class of images from the digital archive management system

Table 1 lists the image collections. There are 2716 collected images (# CI) 385 training images (# TRI), and 2331 testing images (# TI). In the training stage, we use a different cross-validation parameter (# CV) in each class to increase the accuracy ((%) CVA). The recall rate, precision rate, and   F-measure are used to evaluate the classification performance. Table 2 shows the accuracy rates derived from experiments that evaluated the proposed classification technique. The recall rate (Rec. (%)) is denoted by TI_R / TI_T, the precision rate (Pre. (%)) is defined by $TI_R / (TIr + TIw)$, and the F-measure is the harmonic mean of the recall and the precision rates. TI_R, TIw, and TI_T are the number of correctly clustered images, the number of incorrectly clustered images, and the number of test images for each class, respectively. All values are represented in percentages. A test image estimated by each SVM classifier returns a decision value, and the classifier with the highest decision values is assigned as the category of the test image. ADV is average of the decision values in the classifier. We obtained an average F-measure of 86.67%, as shown in Table 2.

Table 1. Image data collections

Class	Archaeo-logical Data	Buddhist Rubbings	Han Dynasty Stone Relief Rubbings	Fu-Ssu Nien Ancient Books	Wooden slips (chromatic)	Wooden slips (ultra red rays)	total / avg
# CI	154	498	499	498	569	498	2716
# TRI	36	72	72	72	71	62	385
# TI	118	426	427	426	498	436	2331
# CV	5	50	40	5	5	15	
(%) CVA	98.96	90.65	89.87	100	98.96	94.55	

Table 2. Experimental results of image classification

Class	Archaeo-logical Data	Buddhist Rubbings	Han Dynasty Stone Relief Rubbings	Fu-Ssu Nien Ancient Books	Wooden slips (chromatic)	Wooden slips (ultra red rays)	total / avg
ADV	1.571186	1.007611	0.958000	0.989020	0.903878	0.982123	1.0728
Rec. (%)	114/118	339/426	281/427	421/426	498/498	352/436	86.93
	96.61	79.58	65.81	98.83	100.00	80.73	
Pre. (%)	114/122	339/457	281/358	421/422	498/574	352/398	86.85
	93.44	74.18	78.49	99.76	86.76	88.44	
F (%)	95.00	76.78	71.59	99.29	92.91	84.41	86.67

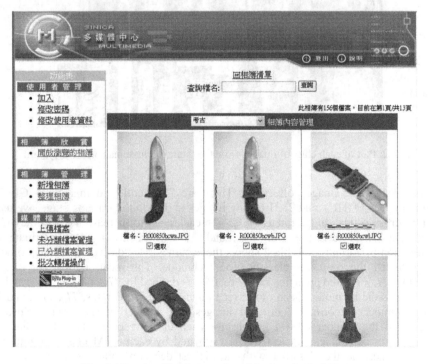

Fig. 3. The classification results of Archaeological Data

Figures 3 and 4 show the classification results of Archaeological Data and Fu-Ssu Nien Ancient Books in the digital archive management system. The results of Archaeological Data, Fu-Ssu Nien Ancient Books, and Han Wooden Slips (ultra red rays) are superior to the Buddhist Rubbing, Han Dynasty Stone Relief Rubbings, and Han Wooden Slips (chromatic). We assume that the color tones of the first three categories are similar. The image sizes in the last three categories are irregular so that the images have different textures. From our experimental results, it is clear that the average F-measure is extremely effective for image classification.

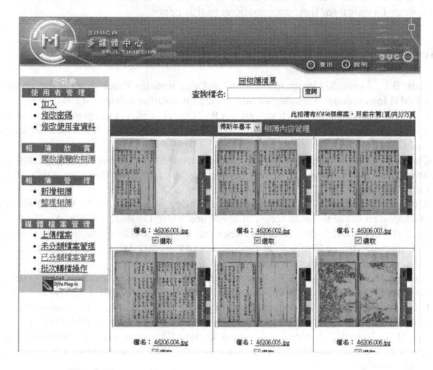

Fig. 4. The classification result of Fu-Ssu Nien Ancient Books

5   Conclusions and Future Work

In this paper, we have integrated an image classification technique with a digital archive management system. Images are segmented into blocks to extract their color and texture histograms as their feature representations, which are then trained to generate Support Vector Machine (SVM) classifiers. Our experiments show very promising results for the proposed technique. We believe the proposed image classification technique would be very useful for automatic annotation and validation in large image databases.

In our future work, we will investigate and compare the effectiveness of other image features (shape, spatial layout, etc.) and classification techniques (Bayesian networks, decision trees, etc.). In addition, we will build a multi-level semantic annotation mechanism to facilitate image management and searching.

Acknowledgements

This work was partially supported by the following grants: NSC 94-2422-H-001-006, 94-2422-H-001-007, and 94-2422-H-001-008. The authors would like to thank Dr. L. F. Chien and various professional parties in the NDAP Research & Development of Technology Division for their contributions to this paper.

References

1. Saux, B.L., Amato, G.: Image recognition for digital libraries. Proceedings of the 6th ACM SIGMM International Workshop on Multimedia Information Retrieval, (2004) 91-98
2. Liu, Q., Safavi-Naini, R., Sheppard, N.P.: Digital rights management for content distribution. Proceedings of the Australasian Information Security Workshop Conference on ACSW Frontiers, 2 (2003)
3. Cheng, P.-J., Chien, L.-F.: Effective Image Annotation for Search Using Multi-Level Semantics. International Journal of Digital Libraries: Special Issue on Asian Digital Libraries, (2004) 258-271
4. Szummer, M., Picard, R.W.: Indoor-outdoor image classification. In Proc. IEEE Int'l Workshop on Content-Based Access of Image and Video Databases, (1998) 42–51
5. Kim, D.-H., Chung, C.-W.: QCluster: Relevance Feedback Using Adaptive Clustering for Content-based Image Retrieval. In Proceedings of the 2003 ACM SIGMOD International Conference on Management of Data, (2003) 599-610
6. Vailaya, A., Figueiredo, M.A.T., Jain, A.K., Zhang, H.-J.: Image classification for content-based indexing. IEEE Transaction on Image Processing, Vol. 10, No. 1, (2001) 117-130
7. Chapelle, O., Haffner, P., Vapnik, V.N.: Support vector machines for histogram-based image classification. IEEE Transactions on Neural Networks, 10(5) (1999) 1055–1064
8. Do, M.N., Vetterli, M.: Rotation Invariant Texture Characterization and Retrieval Using Steerable Wavelet-Domain Hidden Markov Models. IEEE Transactions on Multimedia, 4 (2002) 517-527
9. Jing, F., Li, M., Zhang, H.-J., Zhang, B.: An Effective Region-based Image Retrieval Framework. In Proceedings of the 10th ACM International Conference on Multimedia, (2002) 456-465
10. Safar, M., Shahabi, C., Sun, X.: Image Retrieval by Shape: A Comparative Study. In Proceedings of IEEE International Conference on Multimedia and Expo (ICME'00), (2000) 141-144
11. Zhang, D., Lu, G.: Generic Fourier Descriptors for Shape-based Image Retrieval. In Proceedings of IEEE International Conference on Multimedia and Expo (ICME'02), 1 (2002) 425-428
12. Gorkani, M.M., Picard, R.W.: Texture orientation for sorting photos "at a glance". In Proceedings of the 12th IAPR International Conference on Pattern Recognition,, (1994) 459-464
13. Wang, J.Z., Li, J., Wiederhold, G.: SIMPLIcity: Semantics-sensitive integrated matching for picture libraries. IEEE Transactions on Pattern Analysis and Machine Intelligence, 23(9) (2001) 947–963

14. Yu, H.H., Wolf, W.H.: Scenic classification methods for image and video databases. In Proc. SPIE Int'l Conf. on Digital Image Storage and archiving systems, 2606 (1995) 363-371

15. Li, J., Wang, J.Z.: Automatic linguistic indexing of pictures by a statistical modeling approach. IEEE Transactions on Pattern Analysis and Machine Intelligence, 25(9) (2003) 1075-1088

16. Yanai, K.: Generic Image Classification Using Visual Knowledge on the Web. In Proceedings of the Eleventh ACM International Conference on Multimedia, (2003) 167-176.

17. Murphy, K., Torralb, A., Freeman, W.T.: Using the forest to see the trees: a graphical model relating features, objects, and scenes. In Advances in Neural Information Processing Systems 16. Cambridge, MA:MIT Press, (2004)

18. Canny, J.: A computational approach to edge detection. IEEE Transactions on Pattern Analysis and Machine Intelligence, 8(6) (1986) 679-698

19. Moghaddam, B., Yang, M.-H.: Gender Classification with Support Vector Machines. IEEE Int. Conf. on Automatic Face and Gesture Recognition (FG), (2000) 306-311

20. Chang, C.-C., Lin, C.-J.: LIBSVM: a library for support vector machines. (2001). Software available at http://www.csie.ntu.edu.tw/~cjlin/libsvm

Digital Content Development of Taiwanese Folklore Artifacts

Po-Chou Chan[1,2], Yung-Fu Chen[3,*], Kuo-Hsien Huang[1], and Hsuan-Hung Lin[1]

[1] Department of Management Information Systems,
Central Taiwan University of Science and Technology, Taichung 411, Taiwan, ROC
{bjjem, kshuang, shlin}@chtai.ctust.edu.tw
[2] Taichung Folklore Park, Taichung 411, Taiwan, ROC
[3] Department of Computer Science and Information Engineering,
Dayeh University,Changhua County 515, Taiwan, ROC
yfbchen@mail.dyu.edu.tw

Abstract. Folklore artifacts hold strong cultural meaning for a people. Taiwan Folklore Museum (TFM) is Taiwan's first official folklore museum which aims at providing the people of Taiwan with a place where they can reflect about the past and experience how the pioneers lived. There are a great variety of artifacts, which were classified into ten categories according to their life styles and functions, collected in the museum and it attracts a great number of oversea tourists each year. The museum is also the most popular place for students from kindergartens and primary schools and for general citizens to learn what their tradition is and how their ancestors lived. In this paper, we report our current progress in digitization and content development of the artifacts. Totally 1412 collected artifacts have been digitized so far. The originality and function of each collected artifact was described in three different languages, including Chinese, Japanese, and English, in which detailed information of the artifacts were examined and studied by several Taiwanese folklore specialists. To facilitate inter-museum communication, metadata based on Dublin core and its extensions were provided as well. A website (http://www.folkpark.org.tw) dedicated to demonstrate the digital contents of the artifacts and to support digital surrogates for the folklore researchers was also constructed. It allows people from all over the world to surrogate the information about the collected artifacts so that studies regarding Taiwanese folklore artifacts can be done without territory constraint. Future works will focus on the construction of 3D models for the artifacts on demonstrating their global views. E-learning contents for Taiwanese folklore courses will also be authored for providing general publics and children an interactive way of learning on the Internet.

1 Introduction

Taiwan Folklore Museum (TFM) is Taiwan's first official folklore museum which aims at providing the people of Taiwan with recreation and with a place where they can reflect about the past and experience how the pioneers lived. The park hosts seminars about folk customs and provides a space for folk art exhibitions or performances, so as to raise the quality of people's lives and allow them to see first-hand traditional Southern Fujianese-style architecture and taste Taiwan's down-home country flavor.

---

* Corresponding author.

E.A. Fox et al. (Eds.): ICADL 2005, LNCS 3815, pp. 90–99, 2005.
© Springer-Verlag Berlin Heidelberg 2005

In recent years, Taiwanese government has focused on promoting digital content development and reservation of the artifacts regarding to arts, languages, ecology, living styles, etc. [1,2]. Although a number of digital contents with great variety have been done or partially finished, a digital content concerning Taiwanese folklore artifacts which reflects people's life styles in various ways is still not found. TFM reserves a great variety of artifacts donated by general citizens and charity clubs that the functions and originalities of many artifacts are not clear for general publics.

In this paper, we report the current progress in digitization and content development of the folklore artifacts collected in this museum. The originality and function of each collected artifact were described in three different languages, including Chinese, Japanese, and English, in which detailed information of the artifacts were examined and studied by several Taiwanese folklore specialists. A website which dedicates to demonstrate digital contents of the artifacts and to support digital surrogates for researchers was also constructed.

1.1 Meaning and Merits of Folklore Artifacts

The word "artifact" refers to a physical object or a primary record. An artifact is an information resource in which the information is recorded on a physical medium [3]. The term "folklore artifacts" refers to artifacts connected to people's lives including those related to food, clothing, shelter, transportation, ancestor worship, religion, festivals, leisure activities and other customs. As such, they refer to objects people use in their customs or general cultural lives. To take this a step further, it can be stated that folk customs take shape within a definite area, among a group of people in a collective environment. After a long period of settling and accumulation, during which the people can make their own choices and spur each other on a certain way of life, and then a certain mindset gradually emerge, which in turn lead to folk customs, religious beliefs, and value systems. People growing up in the same circle of folklore and customs will mutually understand each other, and will have the similar beliefs and share a worldview and a tacit understanding about many practices.

Furthermore, in general folklore refers to the society and culture tradition of the common people (serving as a concrete display of the common people's culture) and the customs practiced and beliefs held by the vast majority of people in the cultural mainstream that they have inherited from their ancestors, including legends, stories, religious beliefs, festivals, ancestor worship, taboos, ceremonies, leisure activities, music, singing, dance and so forth [4]. As a result, the value of folk artifacts lies in their demonstration of popular conceptions, life wisdom and the ancestral legacy hidden within the culture. Their basic value lies in their tight intermeshing of spirituality, psychology, and social mores; and their social functions and symbolic cultural meanings lie largely in their artistic and historical worth.

In accordance with the above discussion, folk artifacts can be put in the following functional categories: social and political cultural artifacts; artifacts from everyday life; tools of production; artifacts related to transportation, shipping and communications; artifacts related to trade; artifacts related to folk knowledge; artifacts connected to religious and secular ceremonies, architectural ornamentation; artifacts relating to music, theater, and entertainment; toys and other recreational artifacts (including those connected to gambling); as well as certificates and deeds.

1.2 Categories of Collected Artifacts

The artifacts can be classified into ten categories according to their life styles and functions. Table 1 summarizes the categories and numbers of the artifacts collected in this museum. Figure 1 shows examples of the representative artifacts for ten categories.

Table 1. Categories and Numbers of Collected Folklore Artifacts

Item	Category	Number
1	Clothing and Jewelry	353
2	Kitchenware and Dinnerware	242
3	Furnishings	232
4	Transportation	67
5	Arts and Recreation	81
6	Machinery and Tools	14
7	Religion and Religious Ceremonies	264
8	Study	96
9	Aborigines	31
10	Documents and Deeds	32
	Total	1412

Clothing and Jewelry. Traditional Taiwanese clothing is very similar to traditional clothing found on mainland China, although showing some natural variations due to time and place and differences in climate. Most of Taiwan's early Han Chinese setters came from the provinces of Fujian or Guangdong in order to make a living in Taiwan, and as a result they were diligent and frugal and strived to accumulate wealth. They only showed extravagance in the silk and satin clothing they would wear during festivals and ceremonies.

In Taiwan, red clothing was used to express auspiciousness. At normal times people would wear simple clothing, but at times of ceremonies and celebrations, the women would wear red clothing or red flowers in their hair. The clothing of adults and children would alike be embroidered with various detailing and beautiful auspicious designs and might even be made out of silk and satin. Most women's jewelry was made out of silver and gold, and the affluent preferred jade. There were a great variety of hair ornaments, anklets, bracelets, rings and earrings with intricate carving and exquisite workmanship. Men wore their hair in braids, and city gentlemen would wear guaban (melon petal) skullcaps. From head to foot, people of different sexes, age groups and professions would wear different kinds of clothes. Apart from matters of taste, clothing also expressed position in society.

Kitchenware and Dinnerware. In Taiwan, farmers can grow two crops of rice a year. The glutinous rice grown in Taiwan is sweet in flavor and is therefore quite suitable for brewing sweet wine and making cakes and pastries. Red turtle cakes and red peach buns are symbols of good fortune. They are but a few examples of Taiwanese desserts made with wheat flour or glutinous rice flour. People eat these desserts as symbols of reunion and for good luck on every festive occasion. In olden times, people in Taiwan would eat simply most of the time, but for special occasions, such as New Year's, festivals or religious ceremonies, they would make extravagant offerings to the gods and put out sumptuous feasts for their guests. Banquets would have eight appetizers and 16, 18 or sometimes even 24 courses. During banquets, betel nuts, which were believed to be potent in preventing miasma, were often offered. For a marriage proposal or when friends had an argument, betel nuts would be offered as a friendly gesture to dispel suspicion or ill will.

Furnishings. A family centers around their home for daily activities. More than just providing shelter, a house must be comfortable, beautiful, in tune with nature, and possess good fengshui. Therefore, traditional Taiwanese residential architecture put great emphasis on craftsmanship, garden and pathway layout, living space layout, and interior decor. Decorative features on the roof, as well as on lintels, doorframes, and pillars were believed to be important for allowing the family to live in peace and prosperity.

Transportation. Ox carts were an important means of transportation during the early days of Taiwan, and they were used to carry both people and goods. Sedan chairs were a means of transportation for the middle and upper classes. Rickshaws were introduced at the end of the Qing Dynasty, and their numbers continued to increase after Taiwan was ceded to Japan. Their speed and lower cost quickly made sedan chairs obsolete. In 1887, Liu Ming-chuan submitted a report asking the emperor to build a railroad in Taiwan. He then purchased rails, iron bridges, locomotives and passenger cars from Great Britain and Germany. In 1891, the stretch between Keelung and Taipei was finished. In 1893, the line was extended to Hsinchu. In 1908, Japan finished Taiwan's north-south railway.

In 1904, the first bicycles appeared in Taiwan. During the twenties, bicycles and rickshaws were the most numerous transportation devices in Taiwan. After the return of Chinese rule, tricycle rickshaws introduced from the mainland replaced man-pulled rickshaws. For river crossings, there were bamboo and wooden bridges, ferries, and ropeways. Walkers used carrying poles, back racks, back frames and knapsacks to transport goods. Railroads and buses, introduced during the end of the Qing Dynasty and the start of the Republic of China, gradually replaced all other vehicles with the exception of bicycles.

Religion and Religious Ceremonies. Folk religion in Taiwan is a mixture of Confucianism, Buddhism and Taoism, with Taoism having the most influence. One salient feature of its practice in Taiwan is that people do not differentiate between Taoist deities and Buddhist bodhisattvas. For example, in Buddhism, General Guan Yu is referred to as Wenheng Shengdi (the Sacred Emperor Wenheng) or Gaitian Gufo (the Heavenly Buddha), whereas in Taoism, he is referred to as Yihan Tianzun (the Supreme Minister), Xietian Dadi (the Heaven's Aide Emperor) or Shanxi Fuzu (Master of Shanxi). In Confucianism, Lu Dongbin is referred to as Fuyu Dijun (the God of Trust) or Chunyang Tianzi (the Pure Yang Emperor), in Taoism he is Miaodao Tianzun (the Wonderous Tao Supreme) or Lu Xianzu (Lu, the Elder), and in Buddhism he is Wenni Zhenfo (the True Buddha Wenni). In Taiwan, Taoism gives the largest number of names to its deities. This is partly because Taoism is the most influential religion. Religion often conducts rituals connected to the time of year or season, and Taoist rituals are mostly performed during New Year's, festivals, coming-of-age ceremonies, weddings or funerals. The artifacts used in these rituals are among the most important for demonstrating folk customs and practices.

Aborigines. Most Taiwanese aborigines live in the mountains. There are ten major tribes: the Atayal, Saisiyat, Bunun, Tsou, Paiwan, Rukai, Amis, Puyuma, Tao (Yami) and Thao. Although the techniques vary somewhat from tribe to tribe, all of their artifacts possess a simple beauty, including ceremonial objects, carvings, weapons, embroidery, objects used in everyday life, handicrafts, etc. Most of these objects are decorated with primitive designs such as human figures or snakes, which are simple, elegant and powerful. Most tribal villages are found in remote areas deep in the mountains, where the living environment and conditions are not good. As a result, most of their objects are hand-made and relatively primitive.

Documents and Deeds. Documents are important for researching history, and in particular social, economic and legal history. Currently, examination of Taiwan's ancient documents has yielded some of the best research into the history of the island. Ancient documents include government announcements, law suit papers, official seals, bulletins, deeds, laws, regulations, provincial regulations, records of regulations and systems, inscriptions, news of victory; and private sector's deeds, licenses, account books, letters, bills, family pedigrees, clan organizations, adoption papers, special adoption papers for adopting one's own brother's son, papers dividing family property, as well as wooden tablets with inscription of a clan's origin, clan banners, personal seals and lanterns decorated with the character of a family's surname. Among the most valuable of documents are those connected to land transactions, including deeds, transaction tax papers and leases.

Machinery and Tools. Taiwanese machinery and tools were aimed at practicality. Most of them lacked ornamentation and were simple, sturdy and durable. The techniques used in making these tools reflected the political and economic situations of Taiwan during their eras. At the end of the Ming Dynasty and the beginning of the Qing Dynasty, the tools of both immigrants and aborigines were simple and rough. Most of them were homemade from the materials found in the region. The styles reflected the origins of the early Han settlers (Fujian and Guangdong).

Study. During the Qing Dynasty, educational institutions in Taiwan included county and city schools, community schools, free private schools, private schools and village private schools. Private schools and village private schools were more common than on the mainland. As for the stationery, the most famous inkstones in Taiwan were Luohsi inkstones made in Ershui. Ink came easily and quietly, like polishing jade. Both on cold winter days and hot summer days, it would perform well. It was really among the best of all inkstones. In the past, the residents of Taiwan respected scholars, and as a result, they also treasured paper. All used or discarded papers would be collected and burned in a special "paper burner." This special custom arose out of Confucian respect for education. Other stationery supplies or study furnishings included brush holders, ink boxes, paper weights, water containers, inks, water holders, inkstone screens, baskets for holding scrolls, bookcases, chaise longs, etc.

Arts and Recreation. In their leisure time, people enjoyed festivals and group entertainments, such as by holding lanterns during the Lantern Festival, performing lion dancing during the Chinese New Year, racing dragon boats during the Dragon Boat Festival, worshiping the gods, giving banquets, performing operas for deities, as well as gambling and watching vaudeville performances during temple fairs. Although these are all activities connected to religious ceremonies, they are nonetheless pleasurable for both the deities and the people. Folk arts can generally be divided into the following categories: music, drama, dance and handicrafts.

| (a) | (b) | (c) | (d) | (e) |
| (f) | (g) | (h) | (i) | (j) |

Fig. 1. Examples of the Taiwanese folklore artifacts, which were classified into ten categories including (a) clothing and jewelry, (b) kitchenware and dinnerware, (c) furnishings, (d) transportation, (e) religion and religious ceremonies, (f) aborigines, (g) documents and deeds, (h) machinery and tools, (i) study, and (j) arts and recreation

2   Materials and Methods

The task force is consisted of multi-discipline scholars, including folklore specialists, archivists, and academic researchers majored in computer and information sciences [3]. Currently, there are totally 1412 artifacts have been digitized. Their dimensions, originalities, functions, and other detailed descriptions were examined, investigated, and recorded by folklore specialists. Metadata based on the Dublin core were also constructed for compatible with international standard. Finally, a database system and a website were designed for providing general publics and researchers to browse and surrogate the digital contents.

2.1   Digitization and Artifacts Descriptions

The dimensionality, originality, category, and function of each artifact were studied, examined, and recorded by several Taiwanese folklore specialists recruited to participate in this project. For each artifact piece, at lease 50 Chinese characters were written to describe its originality, function, and its folklore and cultural significance. In order to meet the needs for oversea visitors and folklore researchers, the Chinese descriptions were translated into Japanese and English. The translators closely interacted with the folklore specialists for discussion on the details of artifacts, so that the translation can best describe their embedded contents.

Pictures of the artifacts were taken by a professional photographer using a professional Hasselblad camera with 120mm positive films. Three infrared-synchronized spotted lamps, one was placed above the artifact and the other two at its left and right sides, were used to eliminate the shadow effect. The pictures were then digitized by a high-quality scanner with resolution as high as 600 dpi and stored in true-color format (TIFF) for further processing and future references. A commercial software package (Adobe Photoshop) was used to calibrate the color saturation and hue deviation caused by over- or under-exposure caused by differences in exposure characteristics among artifacts with great variety.

In addition to the digital contents, paper-based documents were also prepared for supporting on-site demonstration and back-up. Pamphlets for all artifacts were printed out on non-acid paper using high-quality color inject printer for long-term reservation.

2.2 Database and Metadata Design

Metadata designed based on the examples demonstrated in [1] for the Taiwanese folklore artifacts are shown in Table 2, in which the field names are consistent to Dublin core for compatibility with international standard [5]. Database of the digital contents were stored in tables designed using Microsoft Access. A SQL server and a Web server constructed by using MYSQL and PHP, respectively, were applied for handling database management and query and for generating XML web pages [6].

3   Results

Folklore artifacts hold strong cultural meaning for a people. In preserving and exalting our artifacts and artistry, we have finished digitization and content development of 1421 artifacts. The dimensions, originalities, functions, and other information

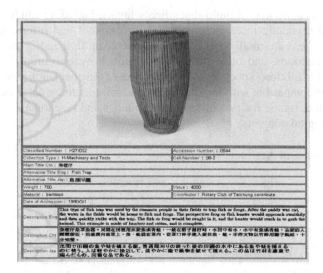

Fig. 2. An example of the collected artifacts with its relevant information is shown

Table 2. Metadata of the Taiwanese Folklore Artifacts

Element			Qualifier
Type			Collection Type
Type			Aggregation Level
Type			Original Level
Title	Main/Sub Title		Main Title-Chinese.
Title	Main/Sub Title		Alternative Title-Japanese
Title	Main/Sub Title		Alternative Title-English
Subject			Classified Number
Subject			Content
Subject			Situation and Function
Format	Generally format		Media Type
Format	Generally format		Quantity
Format	Generally format	Size/weight	Length
Format	Generally format	Size/weight	Width
Format	Generally format	Size/weight	Height
Format	Generally format	Size/weight	Diameter
Format	Generally format	Size/weight	Perimeter
Format	Generally format	Size/weight	Weight
Format	Generally format		Material
Format	Digital format		Digital Format
Format	Digital format		File Type
Format	Digital format		File Name
Format	Digital format		File Description
Format	Digital format		Authorization
Format	Digital format		File Size
Format	Digital format		Version
Format	Digital format		Doc Type
Format	Digital format		Resolution
Format	Digital format		Pixel Number
Format	Digital format		Image Size
Format	Digital format		Comp. Ratio
Format	Digital format		Audio Sampling Rate
Format	Digital format		Channel Nos.
Format	Digital format		Quantization
Format	Digital format		Video Frame Size
Format	Digital format		Frame Rate
Format	Digital format		Other Spec.

Element			Qualifier
Description			Chinese
Description			Japanese
Description			English
Description			Way of Acquisition
Description			Date of Acquisition
Description			Value
			Creator
			Contributor
			Publisher
Date			Creation Date
Date			Fabrication Year
			Language
Identifier	Standard Number		ISBN
Identifier	Standard Number		ISSN
Identifier	URL		UIN
Identifier	URL		URL
Identifier	URL		Digital Identifier
Identifier	Local Number		File Name
Identifier	Local Number		Catalog Number
Identifier	Local Number		Accession Number
			Source
Relation			Has Part
Relation			Is Part Of
Relation			Reference Source
Coverage	Spatial class		Repository Area
Coverage	Spatial class		Call Number
Coverage	Spatial class		Place of Origin
Rights	Copyright Use and Limitation		Copyright Owner
Rights	Copyright Use and Limitation		Copyright Duration
Rights	Copyright Use and Limitation		Copyright Status
Rights	Copyright Use and Limitation		Use Limitation
Rights	Owner		Owner Country
Rights	Owner		Owner Institute

regarding to all the collected folklore artifacts were studied and recorded by Taiwanese folklore experts. Figure 2 shows an example of the collected artifacts, in which the Chinese, Japanese, and English titles and descriptions are included.

A website (http://www.folkpark.org.tw) which serves as an Internet entry for browsing the digital artifact contents was supported, as demonstrated in Fig. 3(a). As illustrated in the figure, visitors can directly click on the category icons to look up the digital contents of the artifacts, as shown in Fig. 3(b).

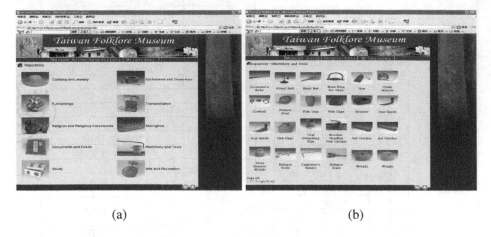

(a)   (b)

Fig. 3. (a) Home page of the Taiwanese folklore museum and (b) examples of the artifacts classified as the machinery and tools category shown on a web page

4 Discussion and Conclusion

There are many kinds of folklore artifacts, and collectively they reflect the culture of the people. From the angle of the relationship between humans, folklore artifacts concretely display the customs of people's life. From the angle of the relationship between humans and supernatural forces, folklore artifacts bring a concrete form to the abstract religious beliefs and ideas. Folklore artifacts are crystallizations of our ancestors' wisdom.

Although a short description for an artifact has been supplemented to partially clarify its function and originality, the connections among these artifacts have not yet been clarified. The contributions and impacts of the digitized contents are manifested in two aspects. First, the contents supply rich resources which motivate a serious of investigations regarding the Taiwanese folklore. For example, the artifacts classified as the Religion and Religious Ceremonies category are currently studied by a group of researchers from authors' institute to further classify the items into more sub-categories and to picture the scene of religious ceremonies and the role of each artifact item. Secondly, the contents enrich the materials for tutoring of multimedia design and education of Taiwanese folklore in general universities.

In conclusion, we have developed the digital contents of 1412 artifacts collected in this museum. Additionally, English and Japanese translation of the artifact descriptions, design of the metadata and database system, and design of a website for contents demonstration have also been done. Future works will focus on (1) the construction of 3D models of the artifacts, (2) the development of folklore E-learning courses for general citizens, (3) the design of interactive materials for attracting children learning, and (4) the introduction of virtual reality for recovering the living scenes and environments of our ancestors.

Acknowledgments

This project was funded by Council for Culture Affair of Executive Yuan, Taichung City Cultural Affairs Bureau, and Central Taiwan University of Science and Technology (CTUST). It was also supported in part by National Science Council of Taiwan under Grant No. NSC92-2622-E-212-024-CC3. The authors would like to express their appreciation to Prof. T.Y. Zwen, Mr. W.H. Chen, Mr. H.T. Lin, Mr. Y.H. Shih, Miss H.Z. Chang, and Miss F.C. Lin for their assistances. Special thanks also go to Prof. P.H. Hsu and Mr. W.R. Wang of CTUST for their encouragements and to M. Findler of National Taiwan Normal University for his endeavor in translating the materials into English.

References

1. National Digital Archives Program, Taiwan: http://www.ndap.org.tw/
2. Digital Treasure Island: http://dlm.ntu.edu.tw/dlm/land/index.html
3. Nichols, S.G., et al.: The Evidence in Hand: Report of the Task Force on the Artifact in Library Collections. Available at http://www.clir.org/pub/reports/pub103/contents.html (2002).
4. Bronner, S.J.: The Meanings of Tradition: An Introduction. Western Folklore 59 (2000) 87-104.
5. Day, M.: Metadata-Mapping between Metadata Formats. Available at: http://ukolon.ac.uk/metadata/
6. Powell, A.: Guideline for Implementing Dublin Core in XML. Available at: http://dublincore.org/documents/2003/04/02/dc-xml-guidelines/ (2003)

Electronic Restoration: Eliminating the Ravages of Time on Historical Maps

German Diaz[1] and Patricia Seed[2]

[1] Rice University, Fondren Library MS 225,
P.O. Box 1892, Houston, TX 77251-1892
gdiaz@rice.edu
[2] Stanford University Center for Latin American Studies,
Bolivar House, 582 Alvarado Row, Stanford, CA 94305
seed@rice.edu

Abstract. Geographic and mathematic analyses of historical maps require highly accurate adjustments to manuscripts in order to eliminate distortions caused by time and use. Earlier proposals for electronic restoration only offered effective solutions when compensating for tightly bound or straightly creased books. Applying a different solution, we have encountered a way of electronically restoring the map to its original shape, producing not only a more beautiful map, but also one suitable for further geographical analyses.

Keywords: Electronic restoration, digital preservation, digital archives and museums, historical maps, geographic analysis, and mathematic analysis.

Time and nature have not been kind to many of the world's most important and beautiful historical maps. Stored either folded or tightly rolled, maps can be damaged by being opened, examined, and then stored. Edges fray along the folds, or the curled map refuses to lay flat. Exposure to rain, seawater or moisture in any form causes the previously flat surface of maps to ripple, distorting the flat face of the original drawing into a series of peaks and depressions. Surviving charts thus contain characteristics that significantly distort the original drawing or engraving.

In an era of digital photography, high-end digital back scanners or cameras can capture the image of the original and transform the paper or vellum into pixels. With wavy and damaged maps, photographers most often electronically eliminate distortion with editing software such as Photoshop because maps are usually scanned or photographed for purposes of illustration. Editing out the ripples and tears transforms the map into an appealing image for presentation in books, postcards, publicity brochures, and calendars. However eye-catching these images seem, they remain useless beyond their visual impact.

However, in the last ten years a digital revolution has occurred in map-making. Highly sophisticated geographic software such as ArcGIS, and ERDAS Imagine has replaced pen and paper as the basic tool for constructing and analyzing maps in many countries around the globe.

More can be accomplished with digital images of maps than ever before. For example, census and voting information can be overlaid on maps to discover how groups of people voted, and locations of crimes can be plotted to help police find the perpetrators.

E.A. Fox et al. (Eds.): ICADL 2005, LNCS 3815, pp. 100–108, 2005.
© Springer-Verlag Berlin Heidelberg 2005

While images produced for illustration obviously cannot be used for geographic analysis, the original unretouched digital images can be employed. However, without taking the ripples, folds, and frayings upon the map into account, any resulting analysis is flawed. Eliminating the distortions caused by time and nature remain essential to answering important geographical questions.

With such digital corrections we could begin to answer previously asked but irresolvable questions: the accuracy of scales, uniformity of measures of distance, and the type of projection or underlying model upon which early cartographers drew their maps. Since Mediterranean nautical charts marked the first stages in the development of modern scientific cartography, we considered rectifying these maps crucial to understanding how mathematical and geometrical construction of maps unfolded between the thirteenth and sixteenth centuries when Mercator drew his now famous world map. As a result we considered medieval and early modern maps one of the more important artifacts to restore electronically as well as one of the most technically challenging.

Because no library would allow its patrons or conservators to physically alter the map by steaming or taping it together, the process of correcting the ravages of time has to be accomplished electronically.

Others have proposed useful techniques for modifying digital images or scans to compensate for shadows in too-tightly bound books or paper that has been creased in a single vertical line. [1] However, all these methods of correction rely upon industrially manufactured rectangles that define the sheet of paper or page of a book. Rectifying distortion of pre-industrial books and papers remains a different task. Medieval vellum and early modern paper rarely form perfect geometric shapes; somewhat flawed, misaligned sheets prevail. Damage on these surfaces also often presents itself as oddly shaped waves or curves.

Maurizio Pilu still proposed a process for altering warped documents, but his corrected images remained far too flawed to be suitable for the additional mathematical analyses needed to answer questions about early map-making. [2] We agree with Pilu that a polygonal mesh (such as the one shown in Fig. 6) constitutes the best geometric starting point for correction, but we drew upon a different procedure to create a mesh and applied other mathematical formulae to rectify present-day distortions. In short, to subject historical maps to newer sophisticated analyses, we needed to restore the maps to the condition in which they were originally created.

The basic principle of the triangular mesh has been introduced into cartography (for adjusting contemporary maps) under the rubric of "rubber sheeting," so called for its virtual stretching of the underlying image. Both of the major map-making software packages, ArcGIS and ERDAS Imagine utilize a mesh as the foundation of their transformation of maps. While designed for contemporary maps, both tools could potentially electronically restore historical maps to their original condition. Both software programs employ the same mathematical formula (polynomial transformations) to the digital mesh in order to adjust a digital image into a known coordinate system, but they do so differently. Of the two, however, ERDAS Imagine's method proved to be more useful for historical maps because it can adjust to multiple misshapements.

Maps become distorted or destroyed in different parts or sections. Thus, the right hand edge of a map may have frayed, or water may have damaged the center left region. One corner of a map may have ripples while another corner does not. Put in other terms, distortions in historical charts are locally distributed. However one of the software packages, and the most widely used, ArcGIS turned out to be unsuitable for digital refurbishment. Even if you chose control points in just a small damaged area of the map, ArcGIS' technique distributes the error over all of the map's pixels, thus changing even those areas that have remained in their original (undamaged) condition. Thus this process introduces error in the already correct portions of the map even as it attempts to fix the error in a small region.

The other major software package, ERDAS Imagine, not only allows us to correct each of the damaged areas of the map separately, but also it keeps the undamaged sections of the map in their original form. (In geometric and mathematical terms, ERDAS Imagine's referencing tool constructs a local polynomial transformation by employing a triangular-based network generated using the nearest contiguous three points.) Employing the nearest three points to construct a triangle eliminates the problems that Pilu encountered in constructing the mesh. Using ERDAS Imagine we were able to select the damaged area to transform while leaving the unharmed areas intact. The resulting map is as beautiful as the retouched digital image, but has the additional advantage of being closer to the original.

If reconstructing a medieval map in the Mediterranean coastline tradition were as simple as applying ERDAS Imagine's procedures to create the triangular mesh, we would simply refer readers to the appropriate pages in ERDAS Imagine's manual [3] along with a few simple instructions on using general control points. Unfortunately, other issues complicate this process.

The foundation of this kind of map - as of every chart in this Mediterranean tradition - is a circle with thirty-two spokes or rhumbs, each corresponding to a sailing ship's direction. Research on several of these coastline charts in the British Library using microscopes and magnifying glasses confirmed that the rhumb lines of the compass were laid down first, and the map then drawn on top of them. [3] Therefore the underlying grid to which we would adjust the maps is not the more familiar right-angled grid, but rather a series of compass roses.

To illustrate the electronic restoration process, we chose an important historical map, Jorge de Aguiar's 1492 drawing of the entire coastline of Western Europe, the Mediterranean, and Africa almost to the Equator. The first large dated map to cover such an immense territory (including Portuguese voyages down the coast of Africa to the Equator), this map resides in the Rare Book Collection of Yale University. Like many older maps, it has suffered damage over the centuries. Drawn on vellum, the map

Fig. 1. Rosette generated using CAD software

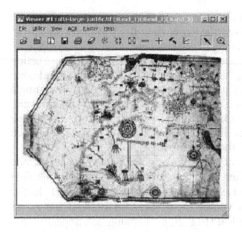

Fig. 2A. Original map loaded into Viewer 1

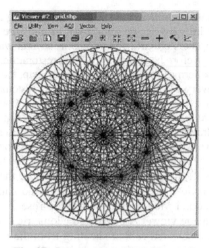

Fig. 2B. Rosette loaded into Viewer 2

Fig. 2C. Options in the raster image viewer

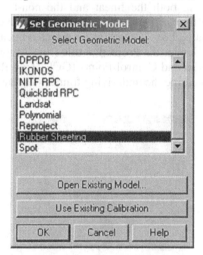

Fig. 2D. Geometric models dialog box

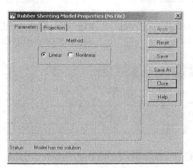

Fig. 2E. Rubber sheeting model parameters dialog box

has a significant rip at the bottom along a crucial part of the African coast. Exposure to rain, seawater or some form of moisture caused the previously flat surface of vellum to ripple. Aguiar's chart contains several wavy areas in different areas along the coastline.

Before beginning the digital restoration, we needed to precisely identify the construction pattern of the grid. In the Aguiar map, the map's foundation is a circle with lines radiating every 11.25 degrees. This circle is systematically repeated every 22.5 degrees generating a rosette shaped structure. Using AutoCAD, a Computer Aided Design (CAD) software, we were able to create a circuit of compass roses that corresponded to every rhumb line drawn upon the chart (Fig. 1). This rosette became our reference, the structure to which we would adjust the wavy and torn sections of the Aguiar map.

To start the restoration, we opened two "classic" viewers in ERDAS Imagine, one with the distorted original map and the other with the structural rosette. In the first viewer, we added the image of the nautical chart as a raster layer (Fig. 2A). In the second viewer, we loaded the rosette as a vector layer (Fig. 2B). Under the raster image viewer, we selected geometric correction (Fig. 2C). A dialog box appeared and we selected rubber sheeting from the menu (Fig. 2D). Under the parameters title, we were faced with two choices, linear and non-linear. After multiple transformations using both the linear and the non-linear method, we did not note any significant difference between linear and non-linear transformation options in the rubber sheeting dialog box. Therefore we selected linear transformation.

Under the Projection title (Fig. 3A) we selected Set Projection from GCP Tool, and a Ground Control Points (GCP) Tool Reference Setup dialog box appeared asking us to define the underlying framework that we would use to adjust the map (Fig. 3B).

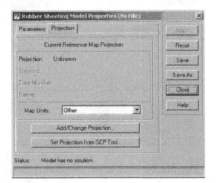   

Fig. 3A. Rubber sheeting model properties   **Fig. 3B.** Ground Control Points (GCP) Tool Reference Setup dialog box

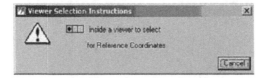

Fig. 3C. Viewer Selection Instructions dialog box

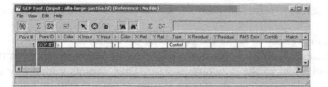

Fig. 4A. Ground control point tools table

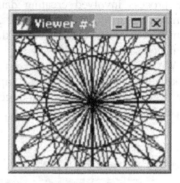

Fig. 4B. Chip extraction viewer from Viewer 1

Fig. 4C. Chip extraction viewer from Viewer 2

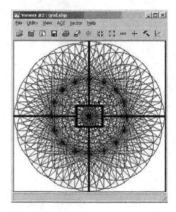

Fig. 4D. Selector box in Viewer 1

Fig. 4E. Selector box in Viewer 2

Since we already had the structural rosette in another window, we selected "Existing Viewer" by clicking on the viewer. A dialog box containing a table of input and reference data points (Fig. 4A) emerged at the bottom of the screen and two smaller viewers, viewer 3 (Fig. 4B) and Viewer 4 (Fig. 4C) appeared in addition to the two viewers containing the original image and the compass circuit. The selector box was dragged across the map image in Viewer 1 (Fig. 4D) and the corresponding selector box pulled across the rosette in Viewer 2 (Fig. 4E). The contents of the selector box Viewer 3 and Viewer 4 respectively displayed the close-up image of the area inside each of the two selector boxes. Using the rhumb lines as a guide, we aligned the selector boxes in each of the viewers so that they corresponded to the same areas.

We were then ready to begin the geometric correction.

The next step began the precise identification of common points in the map image and their equivalent in the structural rosette. These points commonly called Control Points link a place on an unreferenced image to a location on a structure with coordinates, in our example the lines of the rose. The next and most delicate step of the process involved creating data points first in Viewer 1 (Fig. 4D), and the corresponding location in Viewer 2 (Fig. 4E), by a mouse click. For each of the damaged areas we chose a set of three or four control points that included all of the damaged section.

We repeated the process, identifying each of the damaged sections on the map and linking them to the underlying compass rose circuit. With a large image as complex as the Aguiar map, we created three hundred such separate points, with the image appearing as it does in Figures 5A and B.

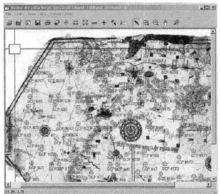

Fig. 5A Selected Ground Control Points (GCP) in the raster viewer

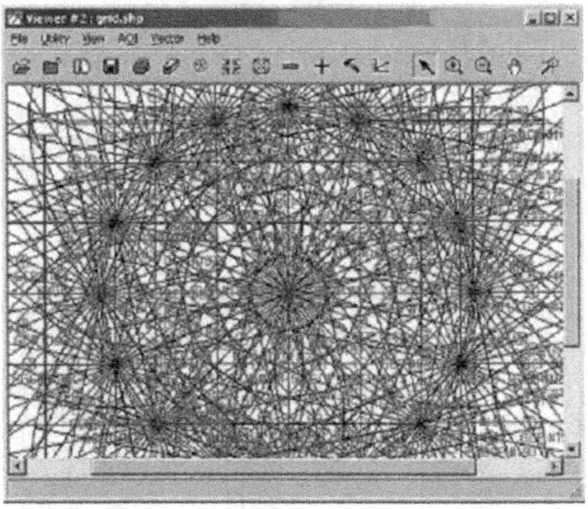

Fig. 5B. Selected Ground Control Points (GCP) in the vector viewer

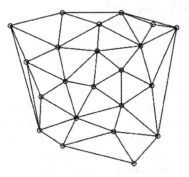

Fig. 6. Triangular Mesh

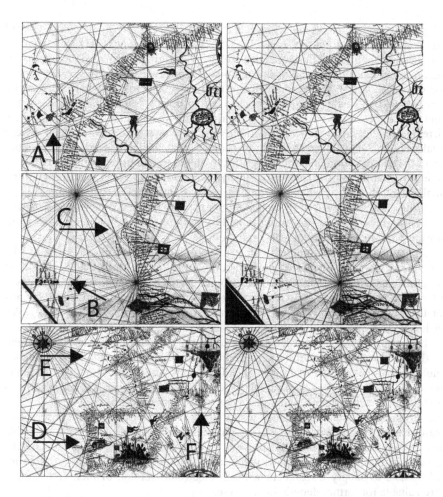

Fig. 7. Comparison between the original map (left) and the rectified (right)

Once we had control points distributed over the separate damaged sections, by pressing the calculation button, the computer began a process of taking the list control points and joining them into a mesh of triangles (Fig. 6), ERDAS Imagine uses the Delaunay Triangulation that creates the most equiangular triangles--those without any other point inside. Having created this mesh, the computer then solved a first order polynomial equation system in each triangle using the polynomials:

$$x'=a_0+a_1x+a_2y \qquad (1)$$
$$y'=b_0+b_1x+b_2y \qquad (2)$$

Where x' and y' refer to the coordinates in the original image, x and y to the coordinates in the rosette, and a_0, a_1, a_2, b_0, b_1, and b_2 are the Unknown values. To solve an n-order transformation, the computer requires a minimum of $(n+1)(n+2)/2$ points; in the case of the first order, the minimum of points are three (the ones in each triangle). Therefore, the problem is reduced to solving a system of six equations with six unknown values.

To go from the equation to a corrected image, we clicked in the multicolored square icon in a window on the screen labeled "Geo Correction." ERDAS Imagine's rubber sheeting tool then adjusted each pixel in the original (damaged) image using the solved equations and saved the adjusted pixels as a new file.

We compared the newly restored image to the original to see what changes the transformation had made. The easiest changes to detect visually are those in the alignment of the compass rose itself. In the damaged images, the compass rose lines are irregular, often located a considerable distance away from where they were originally drawn. On the corrected map, we can see how the spokes radiating from the center of the compass line up almost perfectly with the foundational compass rose.

To ensure that the rubber sheeting correctly transformed the map, we imported the original image, the corrected image, and the rosette into ArcGIS as separate layers. Next we georeferenced each of the separate layers using the first order transformation option. This option only rotates, rescales and moves the images, allowing us to align the images with the grid without distorting them.

In addition seeing realignment of the spokes of the compass wheel, the georeferenced map shows that many apparent errors on the map actually resulted from subsequent damage. Indeed the electronically restored version demonstrates a map far more accurate than first suspected. (Fig. 7) Aguiar drew the Canary Islands closer to where they actually lie relative to the African coast (near Cape Juby) (A). Other locations drawn more accurately include: the Cape Verde Islands (B) and Cape Blanc (C) in the North Atlantic coast of Africa, the Atlantic Coast of Portugal and Spain (D), the English Channel between England and France (E), and Hyeres Islands off the Mediterranean coast of France (F). The electronic refurbishment of the map allows us to appreciate the talent of this fifteenth century map-maker, but improved understanding of cartographic techniques is only one benefit of this technique.

The advantage of undertaking such restorations should not be lost on conservators and rare manuscript librarians. By having an electronic version of the map available for use by scholars, libraries could prevent further wear and tear generated by the same packing and unpacking process that damaged the original. In addition, libraries would be able to supply researchers with an electronic version of their rarest maps that are suitable for further geographic analyses.

Acknowledgements

Joseph Kellner, layout and Sarah Billington, research.

References

1. Brown, M. S. et al, "Document Restoration Using 3D Shape", *Int'l Conference on Computer Vision (ICCV'01)*, Vancouver, July 2001.
2. Pilu, M. "Undoing Paper Curl Distortion Using Applicable Surfaces", *Computer Vision and Pattern Recognition (CVPR'01)*, Hawaii, December 2001.
3. "Chapter 6: Polynomial Rectification" *ERDAS Imagine Tour Guides v8.5*. Atlanta, GA: 2001. 135-150.
4. Campbell, Tony. "Portolan Charts from the Late Thirteenth Century to 1500," in *The History of Cartography,* volume one, *Cartography in Prehistory, Ancient, and Medieval Europe and the Mediterranean*, eds. J.B. Harley and David Woodward. Chicago: University of Chicago Press, 1987, pp.371-463.

Automatic 3D Blogging to Support the Collaborative Experience of 3D Digital Archives

Rieko Kadobayashi

National Institute of Information and Communications Technology,
3-5 Hikaridai, Seika-cho, Soraku-gun, Kyoto 619-0289, Japan
rieko@nict.go.jp

Abstract. Digital archives that include 3D CG models of, for example, art works and archaeological sites are now commonly created for a wide range of purposes. Unlike traditional museums where people can visit in a group, access to digital archives and browsing of their contents are solitary activities. Thus, users cannot as easily gain a deep understanding of the contents and are less likely to truly enjoy the contents. We therefore propose a method to support collaborative experiencing of 3D digital archives related to cultural heritages. To achieve this goal, we developed a system that enables automatic blogging of annotations made to 3D content. The annotations a user makes to the 3D content of archives while "walking" through them are automatically converted into a blog on a web page. Users' experiences, through annotations expressing their impressions, opinions, suggestions, and so on, are converted into content, which can then be used by subsequent users as a reference or guide when browsing the archives.

1   Introduction

Digital archives are now commonly created for a wide range of purposes: study, school, social education, and regional development, as well as for recording, preserving, and restoring items of cultural heritage such as historical buildings, art works, and archaeological sites.

While the contents of most digital archives are mainly photographs and videos with text explanations, digital archives now include 3D CG models. Advances in the performance and reductions in the cost of 3D scanners and improvements in digital photogrammetry have made it practical to measure and record the shape of target objects directly in digital form.

One of us has conducted several 3D measurements of archaeological sites in Japan and abroad, and has created various 3D models such as Byzantine basilicas, burial stone chambers, pieces of pottery and digital archives [11, 12]. The 3D models can be of small objects which can be picked up, such as figurines and vases, or of huge objects which one can walk around, such as historical buildings and archaeological sites. In this paper, digital archives that include 3D models are referred to as 3D digital archives.

At many international conferences, such as those held by the CIPA [9] and ISPRS [10], many case studies reflecting the expansion of 3D digital archives

E.A. Fox et al. (Eds.): ICADL 2005, LNCS 3815, pp. 109–118, 2005.
© Springer-Verlag Berlin Heidelberg 2005

have been presented (e.g. [3]). The main focus of these conferences has been on ways to create 3D models and digital archives. Although there have been few studies on how these can be used, many museums in Japan and content holders are interested in creating or expanding digital archives [7].

Creating a digital archive requires a huge investment of time and money, so failure to add value through such projects will discourage their creation or expansion in the future. To prevent this, we need more discussion regarding the best ways to develop and use digital archives, systems for developing them, and case studies on actual usage.

While there may be several reasons digital archives are rarely used effectively in practical applications, such archives are still promising for use in a variety of areas such as education, research, and entertainment. Possible reasons for their limited use include

- limited public knowledge about the existence of digital archives and/or limited opportunities to find out about them,
- lack of a fully implemented environment that supports browsing and operating of 3D models via the Internet,
- contents not appealing to those who have little interest in a particular field or who are not knowledgeable enough to understand the content without an explanation, and
- poorly designed archives that do not support group use, making it hard for users to stimulate each other's interest and complement each other's knowledge.

When people visit a museum, they can usually share the experience with other people such as their family, friends, or schoolmates. They can watch how other people interact with exhibits, and this observational or social learning is thought to be very important [8]. The sharing of knowledge, interest, impressions, and experience can deepen each person's understanding and appreciation of the exhibits. Unfortunately, existing digital archives do not support such sharing.

To overcome this problem, we need to provide functions or environments that allow users to share their experience with others. By transforming someone's experience using digital archive content into a form that other users can refer to and share (i.e., experience-based content), we may be able to make the content more understandable to those with less initial interest or knowledge, and thereby increase their willingness to use it.

There have been many studies on Networked Virtual Environment (NVE) where multiple users can share a 3D virtual space and do many kind of tasks collaboratively [1]. Among promising applications of NVE are virtual 3D museums that provide on-line chat function so that users can communicate with other users [15] and they can obtain a help for deep understanding of content from those who may be more experienced. The main problem in virtue 3D museums from the viewpoint of communication and collaboration is that users need to be in a virtual museum simultaneously. In practical case, this could be too restrict requirement and other means should be provided [2].

We have therefore decided to choose a way that allows users to communicate with other users asynchronously while there are several possible ways to realize an environments that allow users to share their experience with others. Accordingly, we propose a method for automatically creating a blog from annotations a person makes regarding the 3D contents of an archive while "walking" through them. We have implemented this method in a prototype system. We think each person's experience should be transformed into content that is not closed to a certain community or to a certain system, is highly reusable, and that can be accessed using widely available tools or environments.

In this paper, we explain how our method enables a person to automatically create a blog from annotations made regarding the 3D contents of an archive while "walking" through them. We also discuss our prototype system.

2   Digital Archive Experience as Content

Digital archives basically present information (images, 3D models, explanations, etc.) organized by object. They are like an encyclopedia in that they give information about a subject rather than display an item as in a museum or discuss it as in an educational program. This means that users without specialized knowledge might find it difficult to grasp the relationships among objects while obtaining information about each object.

Some users might not clearly understand an explanation or might not be interested in particular contents because the explanation or level of detail is targeted at users of a different level. If a user could refer to the experience of other users, for instance, which part other users found interesting or how they interacted with the contents, the user would have a model for interacting with the contents. Visiting a museum accompanied by a knowledgeable person who can explain the various displays can stimulate a person's interest in the exhibits and enable a better understanding of them. Likewise, by using another person's experience as a reference, a user of digital contents can obtain a better understanding of the contents and achieve deeper satisfaction.

This can be done by transforming a digital archive experience into a form that enables it to be shared among users. By "digital archive experience", we mean not only the interaction between users and content, but also any intellectual experience such as gaining new information and knowledge, forming impressions, and experiencing a sense of satisfaction. This experience remains simply personal if it remains isolated, but we can transform it into a form that others can browse, refer to, experience vicariously, and record.

The key to this concept is making the transformed experiences (i.e., usage experience content) easily accessible for other users. By accessing such collected experiences, a single user can feel like part of a group of people browsing the content together. For example, a user who is having trouble understanding some item can refer to the experiences of others to gain a better understanding and/or see where to focus. Moreover, sharing the emotions of others (passion, surprise, sadness, and so on) can enrich a user's experience. Digital archives that

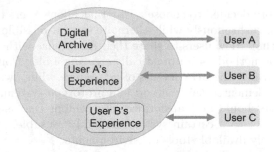

Fig. 1. Digital archive evolution model

incorporate "usage experience" content could even evolve in a beneficial way as they are browsed by users over time.

The relationship between a digital archive and user experiences that are transformed into content is illustrated in Fig. 1. Without any changes to the original content, the value of the digital archive can rise with each incremental user experience. Collectively, users can thus enhance a digital archive by adding value while using the archive.

3   Automatic Blogging from Annotation to 3D Content

3.1   System Design

Whatever methods are adopted for recording and editing experiences, the most critical step is publishing the experiences. Simply converting the experiences into content is not enough. The content should be easy to access and browse with commonly available tools such as web browsers. It should also be easy to cite and respond to the content since the convenient interchange of experiences among users will promote understanding. We thus use blogging to transform experiences into content since blogging is a convenient and increasingly popular way to publish opinions, comments, notes, and so on.

While it is difficult to strictly define "weblog" or "blog", we consider a blog to have the following features.

- The thoughts or opinions of the writer of a blog entry (i.e., the blogger) are recorded along with the date of posting.
- There is one blogger per site and the site is identified based on the blogger.
- The site has RSS ("Really Simple Syndication [16] or "RDF Site Summary [17]).
- The site has functions to support connections among users, enabling them to make comments and track back along links.

In short, we regard web content produced using blog tools such as Movable Type [14] and Blogger [4] to consist of blogs.

Annotations about 3D models are transformed automatically into content by blogging. Basically, a user annotates a particular part of a 3D model while "walking" through it, and the system automatically creates a web page containing the annotations in blog format. Users can then refer to a particular part of a 3D model in the digital archives while blog entries usually refer to web contents; e.g., the URL of a web page.

Automatically created blog entries and the updated blog can be viewed while browsing 3D content. When a user approaches a location where someone has added comments, the system visually indicates that there are comments available and displays them if requested. Automatic transformation of annotation into a blog and provision of the blog to users browsing the content will improve their browsing experience by giving them a better understanding of the content and making the experience more enjoyable.

The automatic blogging of annotations to digital archives has several advantages.

- Blogs are easy to publish on the web, facilitating the use of digital archives.
- Information complementing the annotations of other users can be easily added.
- It is easy to add functions, such as one for browsing related blog entries as a group.
- Participation is easy because the blogs are similar to conventional ones, making the process which decreases the mental burden on the user.

Accordingly, we believe that automatically transforming content-related annotations from a digital archive into blog entries is a worthwhile endeavor.

3.2 System Functions

The system has three major functions: an annotation function, an automatic blog generation function, and an annotated-part display function.

The annotation function allows a user to add annotation to any part of the 3D model while walking through the 3D virtual space. A small ball is attached to the part to indicate that an annotation has been added. This marker will let later users know which parts were of interest to former users.

The automatic blog generation function converts the annotation into the form of a blog entry, stores it in a blog entry database, and registers it to the user's blog site.

The annotated-part display function shows the markers on the 3D models at a user's request so that the user can see information about previously added annotations, such as how many annotations have been added and which parts are frequently annotated.

3.3 System Architecture

The system architecture is illustrated in Fig. 2.

3D Model Viewer. The 3D model viewer is realized through a web browser and a VRML viewer. The viewer shows the 3D model and lets users manipulate the 3D model or explore the 3D virtual space by providing three different interaction

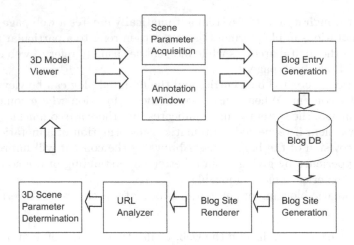

Fig. 2. System architecture

modes: walk through, fly through, and study. Users can select a particular area to annotate by clicking a mouse. When part of the 3D model is selected, a small ball will appear on the part to indicate the position of the annotated area.

Scene Parameter Acquisition. This module obtains the 3D coordinates of the position clicked with the mouse. It also obtains the position and direction of the virtual camera; i.e., the viewpoint information. This is because the annotations could differ depending on the viewpoint. The viewpoint is obtained every time the viewpoint is changed from the event issued by the VRML viewer.

Annotation Window. After the user clicks a position with a mouse, a new browser window opens and prompts the user to type the annotation text. The "user name" and "position of annotated area" parameters are automatically set by the system.

Blog Entry Generation and Blog Database. Along with information such as the position of the annotated area, the viewpoint of the virtual camera, and the date and time, the annotation (i.e., the title and comments) is converted into a blog entry and stored in the blog database. A blog entry is an html document. The position of the annotated area and the viewpoint information are embedded in a URL as shown in the first row of Table 1.

Blog Site Generation. Based on the current blog database conditions, the user's blog site (i.e., a collection of blog entries) is created and an html file is produced.

Blog Site Renderer. The web browser is used to render the user's blog site and a VRML viewer without operational functionality is used to display a snapshot of the 3D model from the viewpoint when annotated.

URL Analyzer. Each blog entry has a link to the annotated area of the 3D model. The position of the area and the viewpoint are encoded in a URL. An

Table 1. Example of viewpoint information embedded in URLs

(1) http:localhostcgi-bininput_blog.cgi?position=(-2.014,3.0302,88.1678) &camera=(0.928,10.682,92.403,0.011,0.5031,0.8642,3.103)
(2) http:localhost3dblog3d_blog.html?x=0.928&y=10.682&z=92.403 &rotX=0.011&rotY=0.5031&rotZ=0.8642&rotAngle=3.103

example is shown in the second row of Table 1. When a user clicks the link, the system analyzes the URL and sends it to the 3D scene parameter determination module.

3D Scene Parmeter Determination. This module sets the parameters needed for rendering the 3D scene based on the analyzed position and viewpoint information. According to the parameters, the 3D model viewer changes the viewpoint and renders the 3D scene.

3.4   Prototype System

We have created a prototype system using Lily[13] as a blogging tool and Cortona VRML Client [6] as a viewer for the 3D models. Lily is an implementation in ruby of blosxom [5] written in perl.

The automatic blogging in our prototype system works as follows.

1. When a user logs in, a 3D model is shown in the 3D model viewer (Fig. 3). The user browses and interacts with the model in either the walk-through, fly-through, or study mode.

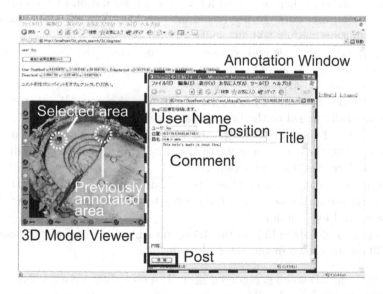

Fig. 3. System snapshot: 3D model viewer (left) and annotation window (right)

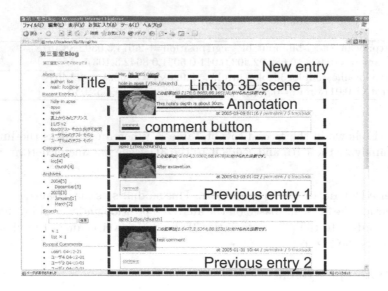

Fig. 4. Automatically generated Blog page

2. A user who finds an interesting spot and wants to make an annotation clicks on the spot. A new window (i.e., the annotation window) opens and the user types an appropriate title and a comment in this window as shown in Fig. 3. At the same time, a small ball appears that covers the spot in the 3D model viewer to indicate that an annotation has been made at that location. Although there is a field for location information in the annotation window, the user does not need to input anything. The 3D scene parameter determination module will automatically set the value.

3. After entering the title and comment, the user clicks the 'post' button. The system posts the title and comment to the blog site and adds it to the top of the site as the latest entry (Fig. 4).

4. The user can annotate a 3D model as often as desired. All annotations are automatically added to the blog site as separate entries.

5. All annotated spots are indicated by individual balls. These are not shown initially, but the user can activate them by clicking the 'view indications' button above the 3D model viewer.

6. Another user can add a comment to any annotation by clicking the 'comment' button at the bottom of each entry to open an input window. This is a standard blog function.

7. A user who clicks the link to the 3D scene embedded in the entry can view the 3D scene shown in the 3D model viewer.

Note that the 3D scene is rendered using the viewpoint information, so if the user selects the link to the 3D scene in the first entry, the system renders the 3D scene like that shown in Fig. 3.

In this prototype system, annotations represent the recorded experiences of previous visitors to the digital archives. That is, the system enables a user to share the experiences of previous visitors. In contrast, digital museums are designed to promote real-time communication among visitors logged in at the same time by using on-line chatting or an avatar metaphor.

4   Conclusion

Our primary objective has been to enrich the cultural activities of the general public by providing an environment allowing users to freely and enjoyably use detailed 3D content of the type increasingly found in digital archives. We believe the experiences and impressions accumulated from users of such digital archives can be used to promote greater use of these archives by increasing each user's sense of satisfaction. In this way, digital archives can beneficially evolve by incorporating user experiences as part of the content. We have implemented this method in a prototype system. We need further investigation on additional functions of the system to support users' communication and experience-sharing via 3D blogging.

Although we focused on digital archives in this paper, we believe 3D blogging has a greater potential and can be applicable to many domains. For example, when discussing preservation of a historical area or an archaeological site, it could be used as a tool to facilitate consensus-building efforts among general public as well as experts of cultural heritages and it encourages people who lives in a long distance from the area to join the discussion. In short, it can acquire wider audience than ever and make them involved in preserving valuable curltural heritages.

References

1. Barbieri, T.: Networked Virtual Environments for the Web: The WebTalk-I and WebTalk-II Architectures. In Proceedings of International Conference on Multimedia & Expo. IEEE (2000)
2. Barbieri, T., Paolini, P.: Cooperative Visits for Museum WWW Sites a Year Later: Evaluating the Effect. In Proceedings of Museums and the Web 2000, Archives & Museum Informatics (2000) 173–178
3. Beraldin, J.-A., Picard, M., El-Hakim, S., Godin, G., Valzano, A., Bandiera, A.: Carpiniana: A Virtualized Byzantine Crypt. In Proceedings of The e-Way into the Four Dimensions of Cultural Heritage Congress (2003)
4. blogger: http://www.blogger.com/
5. blosxom: http://www.blosxom.com/
6. Cortona VRML client: http://www.parallelgraphics.com/products/cortona/
7. Digital Archives White Paper 2004, Japan Digital Archives Association (2004)
8. Falk, John H. and Dierking, Lynn D.: Learning from Museums. AltaMira Press (2000)
9. International Committe for Architectural Photogrammetry (CIPA): http://cipa.icomos.org/.

10. International Society for Photogrammetry and Remote Sensing (ISPRS): http://www.isprs.org/.
11. Kadobayashi, R.: 3D digitizing and modeling of Japanese Stone Burial Chamber Using Two Types of 3D Laser Scanners. In Proceedings of First International Conference on Information Technology & Applications (ICITA 2002) (2002)
12. Kadobayashi, R., Furukawa, R., Kawai, Y., Kanjo, D., Yoshimoto, J.N.: Integrated Presentation System for 3D Models and Image Database for Byzantine Ruins. In Proceedings of the ISPRS Workshop on Vision Techniques for Digital Architectural and Archaeological Archives (2003) 187–192
13. lily: http://www.mikihoshi.com/lily/
14. movabletype: http://www.movabletype.org/
15. Paolini, P., Barbieri, T., Loiudice, P., Alonzo, F., Gaia, G., Zanti, M.: Visiting a Museum together: How to share a visit to a virtual world. In Proceedings of Museums and the Web 1999, Archives & Museum Informatics (1999) 27–35
16. RSS 2.0 Specification: http://blogs.law.harvard.edu/tech/rss
17. RDF Site Summary (RSS) 1.0: http://web.resource.org/rss/1.0/spec

Towards a Unified Framework for Context-Preserving Video Retrieval and Summarization

Nimit Pattanasri[1], Somchai Chatvichienchai[2], and Katsumi Tanaka[1]

[1] Department of Social Informatics, Kyoto University, Kyoto, Japan
{nimit, tanaka}@dl.kuis.kyoto-u.ac.jp
[2] Department of Info-Media, Siebold University of Nagasaki, Nagasaki, Japan
somchaic@sun.ac.jp

Abstract. Entirely watching separate video segments of interest or their summary might not be smooth enough nor comprehensible for viewers since contextual information between those segments may be lost. A unified framework for context-preserving video retrieval and summarization is proposed in order to solve this problem. Given a video database and ontologies specifying relationships among concepts used in MPEG-7 annotations, the objective is to identify according to a user query *relevant* segments together with summaries of *contextual* segments. Two types of contextual segments are defined: *intra-contextual* segments intended to form semantically coherent segments, and *inter-contextual* segments intended to semantically link together two separate segments. *Relationships among verbs* [3] are exploited to identify contextual segments as the relationships can provide the knowledge about events, causes and effects of actions over time. A query model and context-preserving video summarization are also presented.

1 Introduction

As one of the fundamental components in digital libraries, digital videos become increasingly important because of the availability of data and the ease of access. By today search engine technologies, videos can be *entirely* retrieved and ranked according to user queries (if relevant results exist). This is possible because of *metadata*, e.g. keywords, associated with each video as its content itself cannot be intuitively understood by machines. As intended for being a machine-processable language, XML is currently a key technology for representing and exchanging information on the Web. As a result, there are several attempts to provide a standard for describing multimedia content including videos in an XML format such as MPEG-7 [6] and TV-Anytime [11]. According to its temporal nature, a video as a single continuous segment can be decomposed to hierarchical subsegments, namely, *sequences*, *scenes*, *shots*, and *frames*. After the decomposition process, one can provide descriptions for these subsegments as *indexes* allowing fine-grained search *within* a video, that is, not only a whole video but also any (annotated) segment of that video can be retrieved with respect to user needs. Researches in this area are regarded as *video segment retrieval* [8, 7, 5, 4, 2, 10].

E.A. Fox et al. (Eds.): ICADL 2005, LNCS 3815, pp. 119–128, 2005.
© Springer-Verlag Berlin Heidelberg 2005

Video Segment Retrieval. Generally, the approach aims to answer a user query with relevant segments of a given video. Mostly, user queries are not precise since users usually have in mind only rough requirements; as a result, several segments are returned as the *expected* answer. A number of works thus show as the result these segments individually as a list ordered by ranking scores [8, 7, 5, 4]. Slightly different from the previous approach, *relevance feedback* [2] requires user effort to determine the relevance of some results in order to refine queries. This process, however, can take much time since users have to explore some of the results and justify whether they are relevant or irrelevant examples. The approach [7] uses an extended algebraic operation to calculate all possible expected answers by connecting relevant segments with irrelevant ones, which may lie between those relevant segments, in order to form answer segments. In the approaches [8, 5, 4, 2, 10], contextual information between those separate segments may be lost, which can be useful to understand the separate segments as a whole. Consuming separate video segments without contextual information can sometimes result in confusion, which might lead to additional searches required by users. Thus, context around scenes of interest can be very important as it can reduce repetitive searches from users. Although the approach [7] can produce relevant results including irrelevant segments through extended union operations, it provides no focus point for users as too much information can be obtained which may not be related to user interest.

Video Summarization. To provide overall understanding of video content is of the essence in *video summarization* [1, 9]. One of the conventional methods is to extract *key frames* as representatives of a specific video segment. Although the approach can take into account *user preferences* in order to provide a personalized overview of video content [9], parts of segments of user interest may be removed in the process of summarization. For example, only key frames (with text annotations) are selected and shown to users. More importantly, only video segments that are relevant to the user preferences are mainly concerned. (Although most summarization systems allow users to choose the segments of interest to be watched entirely, they have to watch wholly irrelevant segments which may lie between those segments of user interest.)

Out of focus on both of the research areas is the *context* around video segments of interest. For example, it might be a video segment that lies between any two separate segments which are of user interest. Although such a segment is considered *irrelevant* to a user query in the research area of video segment retrieval and to a user preference in the research area of video summarization, its context may be necessary in order to understand the two separate segments as a whole, especially in the context of movies. Therefore, there is a need to develop a unified framework that combines the approaches of video segment retrieval and summarization in order to solve the problem of previous work. In the proposed solution, two types of contextual segments are introduced: intra-contextual segments intended to form semantically coherent segments, and inter-contextual segments intended to semantically link together two separate segments. Relationships among verbs [3] are exploit to define contextual segments, and *XML*

Declarative Description (XDD) [12] is employed to define the knowledge about events, causes and effects of actions specified in video segments over time and to derive by a deduction technique implicit information, namely, relevant and contextual segments. Contributions of the paper can be summarized as follows:

1. Based on the knowledge defined by a declarative language (XDD), a query model that provides necessary information for identifying relevant and contextual segments is proposed.
2. A concept for providing different levels of summarization (LOS) on different kinds of video segments (identified from 1) is presented.
3. Based on 1 and 2, a unified framework for context-preserving video retrieval and summarization is proposed.

The rest of the paper is organized as follows. Section 2 gives the problem definition, Section 3 explains basic concepts of video segments and ontologies, Section 4 mainly gives definitions of a video database, relevant, irrelevant, and contextual video segments, and presents a unified framework for context-preserving video retrieval and summarization, and Section 5 presents conclusions and future work.

2   Problem Statements

Watching fascinating films again and again is not unusual for viewers. Fast-forward is usually used for searching scenes of interest; however, viewers may find it difficult to look for those scenes since ones might not remember all the scenes nor their sequence. Moreover, video scenes of interest may be separate, and this may require viewer effort for skipping some of the scenes. As a result, there is a need for a video scene retrieval system in order to satisfy user needs, which are normally expressed through queries. Figure 1 shows the chronicle excerpt of text annotations and corresponding RDF representations from *The Matrix*. Supposing viewers need to watch fight scenes between Neo and Smith, conventional approaches might be able to retrieve segments S1, S2, S3, S14, S18, S19, and S20 as the result by considering, e.g., *Smith shoots Neo* (S18) as a kind of *Neo fights Smith*. Watching only these segments sequentially may not, however, be smooth enough nor understandable for viewers. The segment S15 may not be retrieved as relevant segments when considering only its description alone since the semantics of *dead* is, in some degree, not similar to that of *fight*. Also, the segments S7, S9, and S11, namely *Neo runs away from Smith*, are closely related to the answer of the query although it is hard to explain a reason. These kinds of segments are considered *contextual segments*, which can enhance viewers understanding and reduce repetitive searches. In order to address the problem, definitions and classifications of video segments are proposed based on temporal relationships among verbs (actions), e.g., kill *implies* die and run away *indirectly relates* fight *through* meet. A query model is also proposed to identify relevant and contextual segments to which different levels of summarization are further applied in order to provide context-preserving yet concise results.

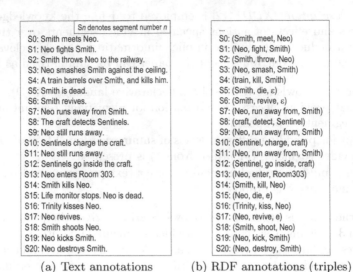

...	*Sn* denotes segment number *n*
S0: Smith meets Neo.
S1: Neo fights Smith.
S2: Smith throws Neo to the railway.
S3: Neo smashes Smith against the ceiling.
S4: A train barrels over Smith, and kills him.
S5: Smith is dead.
S6: Smith revives.
S7: Neo runs away from Smith.
S8: The craft detects Sentinels.
S9: Neo still runs away.
S10: Sentinels charge the craft.
S11: Neo still runs away.
S12: Sentinels go inside the craft.
S13: Neo enters Room 303.
S14: Smith kills Neo.
S15: Life monitor stops. Neo is dead.
S16: Trinity kisses Neo.
S17: Neo revives.
S18: Smith shoots Neo.
S19: Neo kicks Smith.
S20: Neo destroys Smith.

...
S0: (Smith, meet, Neo)
S1: (Neo, fight, Smith)
S2: (Smith, throw, Neo)
S3: (Neo, smash, Smith)
S4: (train, kill, Smith)
S5: (Smith, die, ε)
S6: (Smith, revive, ε)
S7: (Neo, run away from, Smith)
S8: (craft, detect, Sentinel)
S9: (Neo, run away from, Smith)
S10: (Sentinel, charge, craft)
S11: (Neo, run away from, Smith)
S12: (Sentinel, go inside, craft)
S13: (Neo, enter, Room303)
S14: (Smith, kill, Neo)
S15: (Neo, die, e)
S16: (Trinity, kiss, Neo)
S17: (Neo, revive, e)
S18: (Smith, shoot, Neo)
S19: (Neo, kick, Smith)
S20: (Neo, destroy, Smith)

(a) Text annotations   (b) RDF annotations (triples)

Fig. 1. An example of annotations from *The Matrix*

3   Basic Concepts

Terminologies as well as assumptions for context-preserving video retrieval and summarization are described.

Definition 1. *A video segment is a tuples* $\mathcal{S} = (\mathcal{L}, \mathcal{M}, \mathcal{D}, \mathcal{T})$ *where* $\mathcal{M} = (s, p, o)$ *is an RDF triple[1] representing a multimedia description,* $\mathcal{D}$ *is a temporal decomposition consisting of a set of video subsegments, each of which is* $\mathcal{S}$, $\mathcal{L}$ *is a media locator pointing to a referenced video segment source* $\mathcal{S}_s = (\mathcal{L}, \mathcal{M}_s, \emptyset, [0, t_s])$ *where* t_s *is the length of* $\mathcal{S}_s$, *and* $\mathcal{T} = [t_i, t_j]$ *is the time interval referenced to* $\mathcal{S}_s$ *where* $t_i \geq 0$ *and* $t_j \leq t_s$.

In the paper, MPEG-7 is chosen as a standardized framework for describing video segments by means of *descriptors (D)* and *description schemes (DS)* [6]. *VideoSegment DS* is a tool providing a variety of descriptions for a video such as the location of a video segment expressed by *MediaLocator DS*, the descriptions of video content using natural language text expressed by *TextAnnotation DS*, and the time point and time interval in a referenced video expressed by *MediaTime DS*. In addition, VideoSegment DS can incorporate with *TemporalDecomposition DS*, which is a tool for describing the decomposition of segments into subsegments with respect to a time interval. The simplified assumption of the paper includes the use of sequences of *FreeTextAnnotation DS* to form RDF triples through which (semantic) multimedia descriptions are described and user queries can be formulated. In this respect, the type of user queries of this paper is limited to an event form: *who* do *what* with *whom*. Below is an example of

---

[1] http://www.w3.org/TR/rdf-concepts/#dfn-rdf-triple

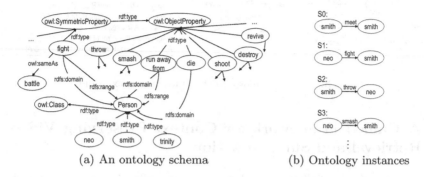

(a) An ontology schema   (b) Ontology instances

Fig. 2. A domain ontology for the motivating example

VideoSegment DS for describing the segment S1. Conforming to the semantics of RDF triples, *neo, fight,* and *smith* are *subject, predicate,* and *object,* respectively.

```
<VideoSegment>
  <MediaLocator><MediaUri> http://movies/matrix</MediaUri></MediaLocator>
  <TextAnnotation>
    <FreeTextAnnotation>neo</FreeTextAnnotation>
    <FreeTextAnnotation>fight</FreeTextAnnotation>
    <FreeTextAnnotation>smith</FreeTextAnnotation>
  </TextAnnotation>
    <MediaTime><MediaTimePoint>T:01:50:08</MediaTimePoint>
        <MediaDuration>PT14S</MediaDuration></MediaTime>
</VideoSegment>
```

Definition 2. *A domain ontology $\mathcal{OD}$ is a set of RDF triples, $\mathcal{OD} = \{(s, p, o)$ | each of s, p, o is a user-defined or OWL vocabularies}.*

Figure 2(a) shows a graph representation of $\mathcal{OD}$ describing relationships among concepts used in the annotation process. Figure 2(b) shows examples of multimedia annotations in terms of RDF triples. In addition, $\mathcal{OD}$ is used to identify video segments that are *relevant* to user queries. Annotators can also consult the ontology in the annotation process. In this paper, $\mathcal{OD}$ is represented by an XML document conforming to the specification of *Web Ontology Language (OWL)*[2].

Definition 3. *A verb ontology $\mathcal{OV}$ is a set of RDF triples, $\mathcal{OV} = \{(v_i, imply, v_j)$ | each of v_i, v_j is an English verb or phrasal verb}. Associated with $(v_i, imply, v_j)$ $\in \mathcal{OV}$ is a constraint $\mathcal{CT}_{(v_i, imply, v_j)}$ on domains and ranges of v_i and v_j that must be satisfied when taking into account the imply relation between v_i and v_j.*

For example, given a situation that A kills B, it can be implied that B must be died. This kind of knowledge is encoded in $\mathcal{OV}$ (Fig. 3), representing relationships among verbs [3]. As the constraint for kill implying die, $\mathcal{CT}_{(kill, imply, die)}$ is satisfied iff $range(\text{kill})=domain(\text{die})$, i.e., B must be C for the annotations $(A, kill, B)$ and (C, die, ε). In this paper, $\mathcal{OV}$, represented by an OWL document, is used to identify contextual video segments through the semantics of verb relationships and constraints $\mathcal{CT}$ defined by XML clauses (explained in Sect. 4.1). Note that constraints $\mathcal{CT}$ cannot be expressed and enforced by the ontology.

---

[2] http://www.w3.org/2004/OWL

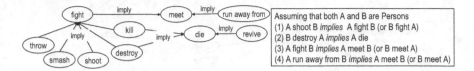

Fig. 3. A verb ontology for the motivating example

4   A Unified Framework for Context-Preserving Video Retrieval and Summarization

An overview of a unified framework for context-preserving video retrieval and summarization is shown in Fig. 4. The input of the framework is a user query formulated in terms of an XML clause. Based on the knowledge encoded in predefined XML clauses, the XDD query engine repetitively transforms the user query until relevant and contextual video segments are obtained. The video summarization components determine the levels of summarization and then execute a summarization process for each video segment using the derived information from the query engine. The output of relevant segments together with summaries of contextual segments is finally generated by XSLT.

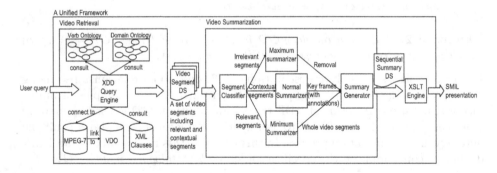

Fig. 4. A unified framework for context-preserving video retrieval and summarization

4.1   A Query Model for Context-Preserving Video Retrieval

Although MPEG-7 provides a framework for describing multimedia through descriptors and description schemes, it cannot explicitly express relationships among descriptors or description schemes, constraints, and rules. *XML Declarative Description (XDD)* [12] is an XML representational language for modeling XML databases, which can express explicit and implicit information through *XML expressions*, and relationships, constraints, and rules through *XML clauses*. XML expression is an XML element that can carry variables to represent implicit information and to enhance XML elements' expressive power. For example, E-variables represent sequences of XML expressions, I-variables represent parts of XML expressions, and S-variables represent character strings. XML elements without variables are called *ground XML expressions*. XML clause is of the form: $H \leftarrow B_1,...,B_n$. where $n \geq 0$, and H and B_i are XML expressions or constraints. When $n=0$, a clause is called *unit clause*, otherwise *non-unit clause*. A logical reading of the form is: H is true if $B_1,...,B_n$ are all true. The symbol $\leftarrow$ is often omitted in the case of unit clauses; thus, XML elements or documents such as MPEG-7 descriptions and ontology schemas and instances can immediately become ground XML unit clauses. Given a database XDB consisting of XML unit and non-unit clauses and a query Q formulated in terms of a non-unit clause, the answers Q' can be derived by semantics-preserving transforming Q repetitively using information in XDB [12]. The XML clauses in XDB can also be used as *formal specifications* in the implementation phase as they can provide the precise semantics of the relationships as well as constraints among relevant segments, contextual segments, ontologies, and user queries.

Definition 4. *A video database consists of videos, MPEG-7 documents describing a set of videos, OWL documents representing domain and verb ontologies, and XML non-unit clauses as rules specifying relationships and constraints among relevant segments, contextual segments, ontologies, and user queries. MPEG-7 and OWL documents are XML unit clauses.*

It is assumed that for each MPEG-7 document there are only two levels of video decomposition: one representing a whole video segment and another one representing non-overlapped, fine-grained subsegments (e.g. shots) in which semantic descriptions are annotated.

Definition 5. $\mathcal{S}_r$ *is a relevant segment to the user query iff one of the two conditions is satisfied: i). $s_i = s_q$, $p_i = p_q$, $o_i = o_q$ ii). $s_i = s_q$, $o_i = o_q$, and $(p_q,$ owl:sameAs, $p_i) \in \mathcal{OD}$ or $(p_i,$ owl:sameAs, $p_q) \in \mathcal{OD}$ where (s_i, p_i, o_i) and (s_q, p_q, o_q) representing the description of $\mathcal{S}_r$ and the user query, respectively.*

Due to space limitation, XML clauses are partially represented in terms of *Horn Clauses*. The clauses $\mathcal{C}_1$ and $\mathcal{C}_2$ below specify that $\mathcal{S}$ is a relevant segment for the query iff both descriptions are exactly the same. $\mathcal{C}_1$ and $\mathcal{C}_3$ specify that $\mathcal{S}$ is a relevant segment for the query iff both descriptions have the same meaning determined by owl:sameAs. By $\mathcal{C}_1$ and $\mathcal{C}_2$, it can be deduced that S1 (from Sect. 2) is a relevant segment for the query *find fight scenes between Neo and Smith*.

```
C1: relevant(L,M,D,T,Mq) <- S(L,M,D,T), sameAs(M,Mq).
C2: sameAs(M(s1,p1,o1),Mq(s2,p2,o2)) <- [s1=s2],[p1=p2],[o1=o2].
C3: sameAs(M(s1,p1,o1),Mq(s2,p2,o2)) <- [(p1,owl:sameAs,p2) or (p2,owl:sameAs,p1) ∈ OD],
                                         [s1=s2],[o1=o2].
where (based on Definition 1) S is S, L is L, M(s1,p1,o1) is M, D is D, T is T,
      Mq(s2,p2,o2) is M representing a user query, and inside a bracket is a constraint.
```

Temporal relationships around a verb (action) are used, in this paper, as *contextual information*. Consider the concept *fight* in Fig. 3 as an example. The concepts that are directly connected to *fight* in the ontology through the *imply* relation are regarded as the *direct-contexts* of *fight*, i.e., *throw, smash, shoot, destroy, kill*, and *meet* as they have *direct* relationships to the concept *fight*. In the same way, the concepts that are directly connected to the direct-contexts of *fight* (indirectly connected to *fight*) through the *imply* relation are regarded as the *indirect-contexts* of *fight*, i.e., *die* and *run away*. This kind of information is applied to identify contextual video segments around the segments of interest.

Definition 6. S_c *is a contextual segment of* S *iff* S_c *is* S_{direct} *or* $S_{indirect}$ *of* S. S_{direct} *is a direct-contextual segment of* S *iff the predicate (verb) of the description in* S_{direct} *implies the predicate (verb) of the description in* S *or vice versa, and the constraint* CT *of the imply relation is satisfied.* $S_{indirect}$ *is an indirect-contextual segment of* S *iff the predicate of the description in* $S_{indirect}$ *implies the predicate of the description in* S_{direct} *(of* S*) or vice versa, and the constraint* CT *of the imply relation is satisfied.*

The clauses C_4 and C_5 below specifies that S_{direct} is a direct-contextual segment for S iff the description of S_{direct} implies the description of S or vice versa. C_6 specifies that $S_{indirect}$ is an indirect-contextual segment for S iff $S_{indirect}$ is a direct-contextual segment of S_{direct} and S_{direct} is a direct-contextual segment of S. C_7 and C_8 specify the constraints CT for the concepts *shoot* and *fight*. XML clauses for identifying contextual segments through other verb relationships can be described in the same way (by considering the verb ontology) and are omitted due to space limitation. By C_4 and C_8, it can be deduced that S18 is a direct-contextual segment of S1 (a relevant segment).

```
C4: contextual(direct,Sdirect,S) <- Sdirect(L1,M1,D1,T1), S(L2,M2,D2,T2), imply(M1,M2).
C5: contextual(direct,Sdirect,S) <- Sdirect(L1,M1,D1,T1), S(L2,M2,D2,T2), imply(M2,M1).
C6: contextual(indirect,Sindirect,S) <- Sindirect(L1,M1,D1,T1), Sdirect(L3,M3,D3,T3),
         S(L2,M2,D2,T2), contextual(direct,Sindirect,Sdirect),contextual(direct,Sdirect,S).
C7: imply(M1(s1,p1,o1),M2(s2,p2,o2)) <- [p1=shoot], [p2=fight], [s1=s2], [o1=o2],
   [(s1,owl:type,Person),(s2,owl:type,Person),(o1,owl:type,Person),(o2,owl:type,Person)∈ OD].
C8: imply(M1(s1,p1,o1),M2(s2,p2,o2)) <- [p1=shoot], [p2=fight], [s1=o2], [o1=s2],
   [(s1,owl:type,Person),(s2,owl:type,Person),(o1,owl:type,Person),(o2,owl:type,Person)∈ OD].
      where S,Sdirect,Sindirect are S, L1,L2 are L, M1(s1,p1,o1),M2(s2,p2,o2) are M,
      D1,D2 are D, T1,T2 are T.
```

Definition 7. *Given a relevant segment* S_i *for a query* Q, *if* $S_{i-j},...,S_{i-2},S_{i-1},$ $S_{i+1},S_{i+2},...,S_{i+k}$ *are contextual segments of* S *(where* $S_{i-j},...,S_{i-2},S_{i-1},S_{i+1},$ $S_{i+2},...,S_{i+k}$ *are non-overlapped segments before or after* S_i*),* $S_{i-j},...,S_{i-2},S_{i-1},$ $S_{i+1},S_{i+2},...,S_{i+k}$ *are classified as intra-contextual segments, which are intended to form semantically coherent segments for* S.

Definition 8. *Given relevant segments* S_i *and* S_j *for a query* Q, *if* $S_{i+1},S_{i+2},...,$ S_{i+k} *are contextual segments of* S_i, *and* $S_{j-1},S_{j-2},...,S_{j-n}$ *are contextual segments of* S_j *(where* $S_{i+1},S_{i+2},...,S_{i+k}$ *and* $S_{j-1},S_{j-2},...,S_{j-n}$ *are non-overlapped segments lying between* S_i *and* S_j*),* $S_{i+1},S_{i+2},...,S_{i+k}$ *and* $S_{j-1},S_{j-2},...,S_{j-n}$ *are classified as inter-contextual segments, which are intended to semantically link together* S_i *and* S_j.

Definition 9. S_{ir} *is an irrelevant segment for the user query iff* S_{ir} *is not a relevant segment nor a contextual segment for the query.*

The query *find fight scenes between Neo and Smith* can be formulated in terms of a non-unit clause below. By semantic-preserving transformation of the query clause

[12], a set of relevant segments together with corresponding contextual segments is derived as unit answer clauses, each of which has the semantics: *which* segment is a contextual segment of *which* (relevant) segment. This result is further interpreted and processed by the summarization process explained in Sect. 4.2.

```
pair(Sr,Sc,t) <- relevant(Sr,(neo,fight,smith)), contextual(t,Sc,Sr).

where Sr is a relevant video segment, Sc is a contextual segment of Sr,
      t is a type of contextual segment, (neo,fight,smith) represents a user query
      find fight scenes between Neo and Smith.
```

4.2   Context-Preserving Video Summarization

The main idea is to apply different *levels of summarization (LOS)* to different kinds of video segments (determined by the proposed query model) in the way that less important segments will be more summarized. In order to preserve yet minimize contextual information, one of the possible solutions is to extract key frames and their annotations from only indirect-contextual video segments while leaving unchanged the relevant and direct-contextual video segments. After determining different LOS throughout a video and processing video summarization, *SequentialSummary DS* is employed to generate a video summary based on different LOS. SequentialSummary DS is extended so that not only key frames but also whole video segments are allowed in a summary. VideoSummaryComponent DS and VisualSummaryComponent DS are responsible for representing relevant and direct-contextual segments, and key frames of indirect-contextual segments, respectively. Finally, according to the summary information, a *Synchronized Multimedia Integration Language*[3] *(SMIL)* presentation can be easily created and shown to users by using XSLT. Figure 5 shows the temporal details of the output for the query *find fight scenes between Neo and Smith.*

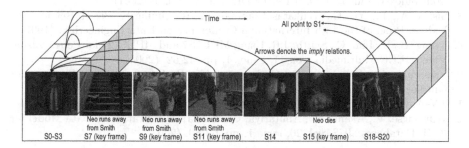

Fig. 5. Temporal details of the output for the example query

5   Conclusions and Future Work

A unified framework for context-preserving video retrieval and summarization is proposed to solve the problem of contextual information lost in video segment

---
[3] http://www.w3.org/AudioVideo/

retrieval and summarization of related previous work. In order to solve the problem, contextual video segments are classified into two types: intra-contextual and inter-contextual segments, both of which intend to enhance viewer understanding in video content by providing semantic contexts for video segments of interest. The proposed query model employs XDD as a language for knowledge management to represent relationships among actions specified in video segments over time and to deduce relevant and contextual segments as implicit information. Different levels of summarization are applied to different types of video segments to provide context-preserving yet concise results. Implementation of the proposed framework as well as experimental and evaluation results forms part of future work. Complex queries including logical operators such as *and*, *or*, and *not*, and temporal operators such as *before* and *after* will also be studied.

References

1. Bailer, W., et al. Content-based Video Retrieval and Summarization using MPEG-7. Proceedings of SPIE, vol. 5304, pp. 1-12. (2004)
2. Browne, P., Smeaton, A. F. Video Information Retrieval Using Objects and Ostensive Relevance Feedback. ACM Symposium on Applied Computing. (2004)
3. Fellbaum, C. A Semantic Network of English Verbs. WordNet: An Electronic Lexical Database, MIT Press, pp.69-104. (1998)
4. Gaughan., G., et al. Design, Implementation and Testing of an Interactive Video Retrieval System. MIR'03. (2003)
5. Graves, A. Lalmas, M. Video Retrieval using an MPEG-7 Based Inference Network. SIGIR'02 (2002)
6. Manjunath, B. S., Salembier, P., Sikora, T. Introduction to MPEG-7: Multimedia Content Description Interface. (2002)
7. Pradhan, S., Tajima, K., Tanaka, K. A Query Model to Synthesize Answer Intervals from Indexed Video Units. IEEE TKDE, vol. 13, no. 5. (2001)
8. Sistla, A., P., Yu, C., Venkatasubrahmanian, R. Similarity Based Retrieval of Videos. Proc. of the 13th International Conference on Data Engineering. (1997)
9. Tseng, B., L., Lin., C., Smith, J.R. Using MPEG-7 and MPEG-21 for Personalizing Video. IEEE Multimedia, vol. 11, issues 1, pp. 42-52. (2004)
10. Tsinaraki, C., Polydoros, P., Christodoulakis, S. Interoperability Support for Ontology-Based Video Retrieval Applications. CIVR'04. (2004)
11. TV-Anytime Forum. http://www.tv-anytime.org (2003)
12. Wuwongse, V., Akama, K., Anutariya, C., Nantajeewarawat, E. A Data Model for XML Databases. JIIS, vol. 20, issue 1, pp. 63-80. (2003)

Content Augmentation and Webification for Enhancing TV Viewing

Qiang Ma[1], Hisashi Miyamori[1], and Katsumi Tanaka[1,2]

[1] National Institute of Information and Communications Technology,
3-5 Hikaridai, Seika-cho, Soraku-gun, Kyoto 619-0289, Japan
{qiang, miya}@nict.go.jp
[2] Graduate School of Informatics, Kyoto University,
Yoshida Honmachi, Sakyo, Kyoto, 606-8501 Japan
tanaka@dl.kuis.kyoto-u.ac.jp

Abstract. A system is described for enhancing the viewing of programs on storage televisions. The content of a program is webified and augmented by analyzing the closed captions to structuralize the content online and by searching for Web pages that provide information complementary to the program. The structuralized content and related information are viewed using an intuitive, zooming user interface that enables the user to switch gradually from watching a program to browsing the program like a Web page and to change the level of detail. Prototype testing validated the concept of this "**WA-TV**" (**W**ebifying and **A**ugmenting **TV**-content) system.

1 Introduction

Constant advances in information technologies and the spread of these technologies have altered our daily lives considerably. For instance, digital broadcasting and storage television combining broadcasting and computer technologies are changing the way we watch television. While television programs can provide excellent quality and realism, they suffer from restrictions on time and an obligation to accommodate popular opinion, which limit the level of detail and the scope of information they can provide. In contrast, information published via the Internet is diverse and faces few restrictions. Thus, there is a great need for functions that can provide additional information about the TV programs in which we are interested.

In addition, the introduction of storage TV enables more than 1000 hours (about 600 GB) of programming to be recorded at a certain level of quality. This is changing the recording style from "searching-recording" to "recording-searching". In other words, instead of searching a program guide for programs to record, we can now record a great many programs and then later search for interesting ones to watch. However, since we do not have an unlimited amount of time to spend searching through a great amount of content, there is a great need for functions that enable particular video segments to be selected from a huge amount of recorded data, that present an overview of the segment content in a compact form, and that can provide a digest of the content in a limited amount of time.

E.A. Fox et al. (Eds.): ICADL 2005, LNCS 3815, pp. 129–138, 2005.
© Springer-Verlag Berlin Heidelberg 2005

We previously proposed a primitive version of an application system we call "WA-TV" (Webifying and Augmenting TV content) that works offline for browsing video content[6]. Actually, in Japanese, "WA" can mean "Japan", "fusion", "harmonious", and "smooth". We have now extended this system to work online and supplement viewing of storage television. We use online text stream segmentation and complementary information retrieval methods. In contrast to conventional TV viewing, our system provides additional information about a program being watched by online analyzing the text stream (closed captions, etc.) and retrieving information from the Internet. It enables gbrowsingh a TV program like a Web page and switching gradually from TV watching to TV browsing, enabling the user to explore video segments of interest.

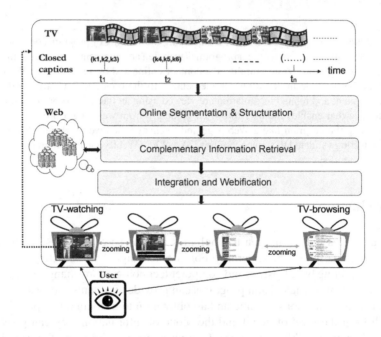

Fig. 1. Overview of WA-TV

In this paper, we assume that closed captions are broadcast continuously during a TV program via datacast. As illustrated in **Fig. 1**, WA-TV first analyzes the closed captions of a program and uses them to segment the scenes and to construct a hierarchical structure of the programfs topics. It then searches for Web pages complementary to each topic by using a complementary information retrieval method described elsewhere[4]. The segmented closed captions and corresponding scenes are grouped into pairs and laid out in the form of a storyboard. The retrieved complementary information is integrated at the corresponding positions in the storyboard. The display of this integrated information is controlled using a zooming interface. The sizes of the displayed images of the segmented scenes can be changed smoothly, and the storyboard can be switched to another one with a different level of detail. Users can thus seamlessly move back and forth between storyboard screens (TV browsing) with different levels of detail and the normal playback screen (TV watching), enabling them to easily explore for specific scenes. Moreover, hyperlinks to the related information are integrated into each storyboard, so users can efficiently access the related information.

In Sect. 2 we discuss related work. In Sect. 3 we describe the online segmentation methods used for structuring TV programs. The complementary information retrieval method is described in Sect. 4. In Sect. 5 we describe the zooming interface. In Sect. 6 we show some experiment results. We conclude with a brief summary and our plans for future research in Sect. 7.

2 Related Work

A lot of research has addressed the display of video overviews and the creation of video digests[1, 9, 11]. These methods improve browsability or comprehension of content in a limited time by spatially or temporally expanding key frames or video segments. They basically reduce the amount of information displayed to the user. In contrast, WA-TV augments the information displayed to users via hyperlinks, while at the same time improving browsability and content comprehension in a limited time.

Informedia[2, 3] introduced various methods for video segmentation based on analysis of closed captions. However, because these methods require scanning of the whole body of data, they cannot be applied to data streams, which are received continuously.

Henzinger et al. proposed methods for automatically generating queries from closed captions that can be used to find Web pages with content similar to that of the program being watched[7]. Unlike their approach, our mechanism does not search for Web pages with content merely similar to that of the program. It searches for pages that provide additional information.

3 Online Structuration of TV Programs

In contrast to conventional text stream segmentation methods[2, 3, 10], of which most are top-down approaches, we propose a bottom-up segmentation method that incrementally identifies the story boundary so that it does not need to scan all the data. The basic unit used for further processing is the closed captions received at a certain time. We call such unit block. In the closed captions for a Japanese news program, for example, one sentence generally straddles more than two blocks. Our method for online

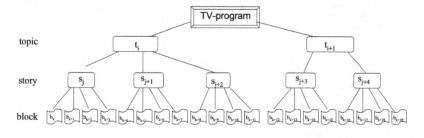

Fig. 2. Hierarchical Structure of TV Program

structuring of TV programs includes two phases: 1) story segmentation and 2) merging related adjacent stories into one topic. The result is a hierarchical structure of a program corresponding to its closed captions: topic, story, and block, as shown in **Fig. 2**.

3.1   Incremental Story Segmentation

The basic idea is that a high rate of keyword pairs with strong co-occurrence relationships among all keyword pairs within various closed captions suggests that these captions describe one story. Intuitively, we compute the co-occurrence relationships of keywords in the received closed captions data. If their co-occurrence relationships are strong, the corresponding closed captions may describe the same story. We then merge them with the next set of closed captions and recompute the keyword co-occurrence relationships. If they are weak, 'noisy' captions describing another story may have been received, so there should be a boundary identifying the story change.

When words w_1 and w_2 co-occur frequently within a text collection, we say that they have a strong co-occurrence relationship and that their co-occurrence rate is high. In this paper, we estimate the co-occurrence rate $cooc(w_i, w_j)$ between the words w_i and w_j as follows.

$$cooc(w_i, w_j) = \frac{df(\{w_i, w_j\})}{df(\{w_i\}) + df(\{w_j\}) - df(\{w_i, w_j\})} \tag{1}$$

where $df(\{w_i\})$ is the number of texts containing the word w_i within a pre-specified text collection, and $df(\{w_i, w_j\})$ is the number of texts containing both w_i and w_j.

The details of the procedure are as follows (see also **Fig. 3**). Here, CT_i is the keyword set used to detect a story at time point t_i. ST and ET, respectively, are the initial and terminal time points of an identified story.

1. Let $CT_0 = \emptyset, ST = 0, i = 1$.
2. Receive closed captions. If there are no other closed captions, stop.
3. After receiving the closed captions at time point t_i $(i \geq 1)$, extract keyword set K.

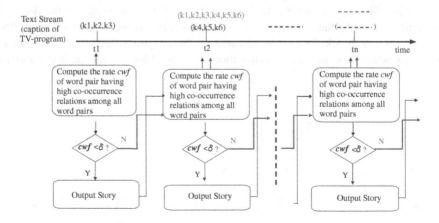

Fig. 3. Online Story Segmentation (t_i is the time point at which closed captions are received.)

4. Let $CT_i = CT_{i-1} \cup K$.
5. Compute rate $cwf(t_i)$ of keyword pairs with high co-occurrence rates ($\geq \theta$) among all keyword pairs within CT_i. Here, θ is a pre-specified threshold, and m is the number of keywords included in CT_i.

$$cwf(t_i) = \sum_{j=1,k=j+1}^{j=m-1,k=m} cr(w_j, w_k) / \frac{m \cdot (m-1)}{2} \tag{2}$$

$$cr(w_j, w_k) = \begin{cases} 1 \text{ if } cooc(w_j, w_k) \geq \theta \\ 0 \text{ if } cooc(w_j, w_k) < \theta \end{cases} \tag{3}$$

6. If $cwf(t_i) > \Theta$, go to 9. Θ is a pre-specified threshold.
7. Let $ET = t_i$. The initial and terminal time points of output $story_i$ are ST and ET, respectively. The keywords for the story are also output for further processing.
8. Let $CT_i = \emptyset, ST = t_i$.
9. $i = i + 1$. Receive closed captions. If there are no other closed captions and $CT_i = \emptyset$, stop. If there are no other closed captions, and $CT_i \neq \emptyset$, go to 7. Otherwise, go to 3.

3.2 Topic Segmentation by Incremental Joining of Stories

We try to merge the story identified using the above method with the next story and continue doing so until a merger can no longer be done. The merger of stories is based on join of their topic structures[?, 5]. Here, we give a brief overview of the topic structure model and its joining operation.

Intuitively, a topic structure consists of a pair of subject and content terms. The subject terms denote the dominant terms on a Web page or in a text stream (keyword sequence, e.g., closed captions for videos). A content term is a term that has strong co-occurrence relationships with the subject terms. In other words, subject terms are centric keywords that play a title role on a Web page (or video), and the content terms play a supporting (or describing) role. The subject and content terms are extracted by using the term frequency (tf) and the co-occurrence relationship between two terms. In short, if a keyword has high rates of co-occurrence with other keywords and its term frequency is higher than that of other keywords, it is considered to be a subject term. Of the remaining keywords, those that have a high co-occurrence relationship with the subject terms have a high probability of being content terms.

A topic structure is represented as a connected directed acyclic graph (DAG) called a topic graph. In a topic graph, a node denotes a keyword, subject term, or content term. A directed edge denotes the subject-content relationship between two keywords. The join of two topic structures, s and s', is defined as the union of their topic graphs.

$$s \bowtie s' = \begin{cases} G(s) \cup G(s'), \text{ if } G(s) \cup G(s') \text{ is a connected DAG.} \\ \phi, \text{ otherwise} \end{cases} \tag{4}$$

where $G(s)$ and $G(s')$ stand for the respective topic graphs of s and s', and ϕ stands for null. In addition, $s \bowtie \phi = \phi$.

If the result of joining the topic structures of two stories is not ϕ, they are merged. All stories that can be merged together are organized into one topic. In other words, a topic is a series of related stories that can be merged based on join of their topic structures.

$$topic = s_i \bowtie s_{i+1} \bowtie ... \bowtie s_j \tag{5}$$
$$s_i \bowtie s_{i+1} \bowtie ... \bowtie s_j \neq \phi$$
$$s_i \bowtie s_{i+1} \bowtie ... \bowtie s_j \bowtie s_{j+1} = \phi$$

where s_i is the initial story of this topic. Obviously, s_{j+1} is the initial story of the next topic, in the given definition.

4   Structured Queries for Complementary Information Retrieval

We defined four types of queries for finding Web pages related to the given story and topic: 1) CD (content-deepening), 2) SD (subject-deepening), 3) SB (subject-broadening), and 4) CB (content-broadening) queries[4].

CD and SD queries are based on a join such that the subject terms in one topic structure appear as the content terms in the other. Such joins add more detail to the original information. SB and CB queries are based on a join such that two topic structures have the same subject or content terms. Such joins provide broader coverage of the information.

A previous report [8] showed the feasibility of extracting the topic structures of a Web page by using the "title" and "body" tags. Based on this work, we assume that the keywords appearing in the title and body of a Web page are its subject and content terms, respectively. Thus, we can use the structure option of Google, intitle, intext, etc., to search for Web pages complementary to the TV program.

Hereafter, let topic structure t of the segmented story be $(\{s_1, s_2\}, \{c_1, c_2, c_3\})$, where s_i and c_i stand for a subject term and content term, respectively. "intitle" and "intext" indicate that the following terms are the respective subject and content terms of a topic structure contained in the retrieved Web page. "∧" and "∨" stand for "logical AND" and "logical OR", respectively. "¬" means "logical NOT".

1. Content-Deepening Queries:

$$(intitle : c_1 \wedge c_2 \wedge c_3) \wedge (\neg(intext : s_1 \vee s_2)) \tag{6}$$

2. Subject-Deepening Queries:

$$(intext : s_1 \wedge s_2) \wedge (\neg(intitle : c_1 \vee c_2 \vee c_3)) \tag{7}$$

3. Subject-Broadening Queries:

$$(intext : c_1 \wedge c_2 \wedge c_3) \wedge (\neg(intitle : s_1 \wedge s_2)) \tag{8}$$

4. Content-Broadening Queries:

$$(intitle : s_1 \wedge s_2) \wedge (\neg(intext : c_1 \wedge c_2 \wedge c_3)) \tag{9}$$

We issue these queries to Google. The top result of each query is regarded as the complementary Web page and will be integrated with the corresponding story (or topic).

5   Zooming User Interface

The structured program data (topic, story, and block) is integrated with the retrieved related information into Web content for display. An example snapshot displayed on WA-TV is shown in **Fig. 4**. The segmented caption texts and videos are displayed vertically in the form of a storyboard. Hyperlinks to the complementary information are located below the caption texts, enabling users to access more detailed or broader information than provided by the broadcast program. The transformation of the screen appearance is illustrated in **Fig. 5**. The zooming feature can be used to smoothly change the size of the thumbnails as well as to switch from one storyboard to another with a different level of detail.

For example, suppose that we are watching on TV. Zooming-out smoothly switches the watching (playback) scene to a storyboard including one block. Further zooming-out smoothly change the size of TV-viewer on the storyboard, and when the size reaches a certain level, the storyboard switches to one containing thumbnails of stories (current story and previous stories) of TV-program. The corresponding closed captions and hyperlinks to complementary Web pages are also displayed. Further zooming out will smoothly changes the size of the thumbnails on the storyboard, and when their size reaches another certain level, the storyboard switches to one including thumbnails of topics (current topic and its previous topics) and related information (closed captions and links to complementary Web pages). Zooming-in produces the opposite effect.

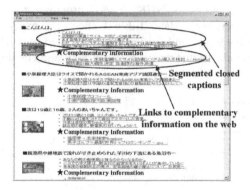

Fig. 4. Example Snapshot Displayed on WA-TV

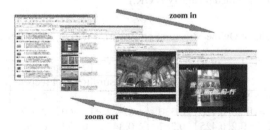

Fig. 5. Gradual Changing of TV Viewing On WA-TV

During the zooming operation, it is also possible to change the focus onto specific scene (story or topic). As a result, users can seamlessly move back and forth between story-board screens showing different levels of detail and the normal playback (watching) screen, enabling them to easily explore for specific scenes.

6   Evaluation

6.1   Online Structuration Experiment

We used closed captions (in Japanese) from NHK News 7 (a well-regarded news program in Japan) collected over a 28-month period to build a co-occurrence relationship dictionary. We used ChaSen (chasen.aist-nara.ac.jp/) for Japanese morphology analysis and only nouns as keywords for further processing. To exclude stop words, we built a stop-word dictionary containing 593 terms in English and 347 terms in Japanese.

A boundary is defined as correct if and only if it is a true boundary. However, due to our use of topic-structure-based complementary information retrieval in WA-TV, one segmentation method usually produces satisfactory results because it always comes close to the true boundary. Here, we relax our correctness criteria to accept all boundaries that are one block off the true boundary. The distance between the identified boundary and the closest true boundary is defined as the degree of relaxation. **Fig. 6** illustrates the relaxed failure model for our block-based segmentation method adapted from Hauptmann et al. [3].

We used the closed captions for NHK News 7 programs collected over two days (821 blocks) as the experimental data. **Table 1** shows the experimental results. The reference boundaries for topics and stories were specified by evaluators beforehand. The *F-measure values* indicate that the proposed structuration method performed better

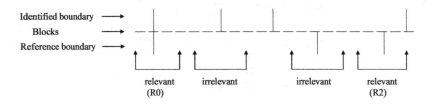

Fig. 6. Relaxed Failure Model of Block-based Text Segmentation Method (Rx means under the degree of relaxation x, identified boundary is OK.)

Table 1. Results of Online Structuration Experiment (Degree of Relaxation is 1)

	Story Segmentation			Topic Segmentation		
	Recall	Precision	F-measure	Recall	Precision	F-measure
$\theta = 0.2, \Theta = 0.2$	0.286	0.395	0.332	0.301	0.446	0.360
$\theta = 0.2, \Theta = 0.25$	0.426	0.330	0.372	0.360	0.387	0.373
$\theta = 0.25, \Theta = 0.2$	0.425	0.287	0.343	0.342	0.333	0.338

than the topic change detection method used in Informedia whose best F-measure value is 0.367[3].

6.2 Structured Query for Complementary Information Retrieval Experiment

We used 88 topic structures extracted from the closed captions collected over three days for NHK News 7 programs. Each one consisted of two subject terms and three content terms.

For the CD, SD, CB, and SB queries, we used the top-ranked result from a Google search as the complementary Web page. Based on human assessment of the relevance of these complementary Web pages, the calculated precision ratios were 0.489, 0.625, 0.511, and 0.705, respectively. Details of the experimental results are shown in **Table 2**. When the query was based on a topic structure containing proper nouns, the search results were better. This suggests that proper nouns play an important role in using topic structures to retrieve information from the Web. We will examine this feature further in future work.

Table 2. Results of Complementary Information Retrieval Experiment

	topic structure	relevant pages	precision ratio
SB	88	62	0.705
SD	88	55	0.625
CB	88	45	0.511
CD	88	43	0.489

6.3 User Interface Evaluation

Simple experiments were conducted to evaluate the user interface, especially the zoom operation. Most of the participants (8 out of 11) found the ability to search for scenes by looking through a list of closed captions and thumbnails on the storyboard "useful" compared to a conventional interface based on fast-forwarding and rewinding. They also found the ability to control the different levels of detail "intuitive". Evaluation tests using more participants will be conducted to better evaluate usability, understandability, etc.

An important advantage of WA-TV is that it enables active browsing of TV programs, which are conventionally viewed by passive watching, by converting them into Web content. WA-TV enables active browsing by hyperlinking various positions in the program to external related information with greater detail or from different perspectives.

7   Conclusion

We have described an application system for augmenting and webifying TV content to enhance viewing of storage televisions. WA-TV segments and structures a TV program into different levels of detail online and then generates hyperlinks between various positions in the program and complementary Web pages it retrieves to provide additional information about the program. The retrieved information and the original TV content are integrated into a Web form for browsing. In addition, a zooming feature enables the user to switch gradually from TV watching to TV browsing. Experimental results valided the proposed methods.

We plan to improve the proposed methods used in WA-TV, particularly the online topic segmentation and complementary information retrieval. Further experiments with a larger number of participants are also planned.

References

[1] Christel, M.G. and Huang, C. Enhanced access to digital video through visually rich inter-faces, *Proc. of ICME 2003*, 2003.

[2] H. D. Wactlar. Informedia - search and summarization in the video medium. In *Proceedings of Imagina 2000 Conference*, 2000.

[3] Huauptmann A., Chang J.C., Hu N.N., and Wang Z.R. Text Segmentation in the Informedia Project, *http://www-2.cs.cmu.edu/ hnn/project/ML-project/ml-report.htm*.

[4] Ma Q. and Tanaka K. Topic-structure-based Complementary Information Retrieval and Its Application, *ACM Transactions on Asian Language Information Processing (to appear)*, 2005.

[5] Ma Q. and Tanaka K. Topic-structure-based complementary information retrieval for in-formation augmentation, *Proc. of APWeb2004, LNCS3007*, pp. 608-619, 2004.

[6] Miyamori, H., Ma, Q., and Tanaka K. WA-TV: Webifying and Augmenting Broadcast Con-tent for Next-generation Storage TV, *Proc. of ICME2005*, 2005.

[7] Henzinger M., Chang B.-W., Milch B., and Brin S. Query-free news search. *Proc. of WWW2003*, 2003.

[8] Oyama S. and Tanaka K. Exploiting document structures for comparing and exploring topics on the Web. *Proc. of WWW2003 (poster tracks)*, 2003.

[9] Sumiya, K., Munisamy, M., and Tanaka, K. TV2Web: generating and browsing Web with multiple LOD from video streams and their metadata, *Proc. of ICKS2004*, pp. 158- 167, 2004.

[10] TDT site. http://www.itl.nist.gov/iaui/894.01/tests/tdt/index.htm, 2005.

[11] Uchihashi, S., Foote, J., Girgensohn, A., and Boreczky, J. Video Manga: generating seman-tically meaningful video summaries, *Proc. of ACM Multimedia 99*, 1999.

CLOVER: A Mobile Content-Based Leaf Image Retrieval System

Yunyoung Nam[1], Eenjun Hwang[2,*], and Dongyoon Kim[1]

[1] Graduate School of Information and Communication,
Ajou University, Suwon, Korea
{youngman, dykim}@ajou.ac.kr
[2] Department of Electronics and Computer Engineering,
Korea University, Seoul, Korea
Tel. +82-2-3290-3256
ehwang04@korea.ac.kr

Abstract. In this paper, we present an effective and robust leaf image retrieval system called CLOVER that works especially in the mobile environment. For the inquiry, users sketch or photograph a leaf using a PDA equipped with a digital camera, and then send it to a server. Most leaves tend to have similar color and texture, which makes shape-based image retrieval more effective than color-based image retrieval. In order to improve retrieval performance, we proposed a new shape representation scheme based on the well-known MPP algorithm. The new scheme can reduce the number of points to consider for matching. In addition, we proposed a new dynamic matching algorithm based on the Nearest Neighbor search to reduce the matching time. We implemented a prototype system that supports adaptive transmission of images over 802.11b wireless networks to mobile devices and demonstrate its effectiveness and scalability through various experimental results.

1 Introduction

There are many kinds of plants and trees on earth. When you take a walk on the wild side, you may want to know the name of plants or trees. In this case, you might take note of their attributes such as color, shape, texture for searching. Whereas leaves of most plants are green or brown, the leaf shapes are distinctive and thus can be used for identification. That is, shape-based retrieval can be more effective than any other methods.

Another issue is the searching performance. If you want to know the name of a plant, you should look up its information in an illustrated book of plants or take their pictures and search them on the WWW. However, we want to know immediately what they are. For the real-time retrieval, we extended our system to the mobile environment

Like typical content-based image retrieval, shape-based image retrieval consists of three steps. The first step is to detect edge points. Among the existing edge detection methods [1] [2], we use Canny Edge Detection method [3]. The next step is to

---

* Corresponding author.

E.A. Fox et al. (Eds.): ICADL 2005, LNCS 3815, pp. 139–148, 2005.
© Springer-Verlag Berlin Heidelberg 2005

represent shapes in such a way that it is invariant to translation, rotation, scale, and viewing angle changes. The last step is shape matching that determines how similar shapes are to a given query.

In general, shape representations are classified into two categories: boundary-based and region-based. The former describes a region of interest using its external characteristics [4] (i.e. the pixels along the object boundary) while the latter represents a region of interest using its internal characteristics [1] (i.e. the pixels contained in the region). We choose the external representation since the primary focus is on shape characteristics such as length of boundary, orientation of straight line, joining the extreme points, or number of concaves. For the internal representation, we use a methodology based on the "skeleton" of a shape. In this paper, we use MPP (Minimum Perimeter Polygons) [5-7] for shape representation. MPP is a polygonal approximation method to identify curvature descriptions [8] [9], but it only uses outside boundary of the strip of cells. Nevertheless, it takes long time to retrieve images due to many unnecessary points to consider. In order to solve this problem, we propose a new shape representation method that is based on our improved MPP.

Another important issue of shape-based image retrieval is the effective shape matching method on which the retrieval performance heavily depends. There are several approaches to solving the matching problem. In this paper, we develop a dynamic shape-matching algorithm with the intention to reduce matching time.

The rest of this paper is organized as follows. Section 2 describes the outline of our system. In section 3, we introduce how to segment images and section 4 presents image matching and retrieval. In section 5, some of the experimental results are presented and finally the last section concludes the paper and discusses future work.

2 System Overview

In this chapter, we describe our prototype retrieval system called "CLOVER" in detail. To access the system, we first photograph or sketch a plant using a PDA equipped with a digital camera. Next, we record several simple characteristics of the plant on the PDA. Then, we send the image and the characteristics of plants to the server. In the server, several shape relevant characteristics are extracted from the received image. Those characteristics combined with user-specified characteristics are used to retrieve images from the database and the matched results are displayed on the server web page or screen of the PDA. Figure 1 shows overall architecture of our CLOVER system. As was described before, the system has components for noise filtering, edge detection, shape representation and shape matching.

3 Image Segmentation

Image segmentation decomposes images into regions that correspond to independent objects. It is an essential preliminary step in most automatic pattern recognition and image analysis process. Successful shape feature extraction depends on good image segmentation. In this paper, we segment images using boundaries between regions based on discontinuities in gray levels.

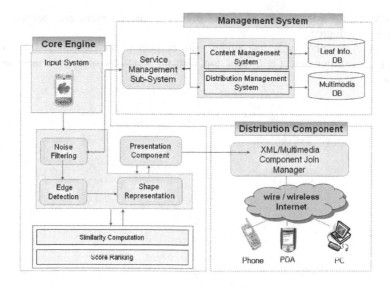

Fig. 1. Overview of CLOVER

3.1 Shape Representation

A boundary can be approximated with arbitrary accuracy by a polygon. In case of a closed curve, the approximation is exact when the number of segments in the polygon is equal to the number of points in the boundary, so that each pair of adjacent points defines a segment in the polygon. MPP is a method for defining curvatures when a change of the slope occurs with the control points approximately uniformly spaced along the curvatures. However, since MPP may include unnecessary points, there is a chance of unnecessary computation for shape matching, which results in longer search time. In this paper, we improve the MPP algorithm for more effective representation.

MPP algorithm produces convex points and concave points depending on the angle between two points. Therefore, when an image contains plenty of straight lines along the boundary, segmentation result may include useless points. To condense these points, we have merged points along boundary if the angle exceeds some threshold.

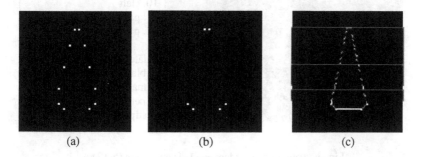

| (a) | (b) | (c) |

Fig. 2. Image segmentation using point merging

Figure 2 shows the result when the points of the segment are merged with the threshold 160 degree.

For the invariance, we adjust angles with respect to the longest distance between two points, and then detect left, right, top, bottom points for scale invariance as shown in Figure 3.

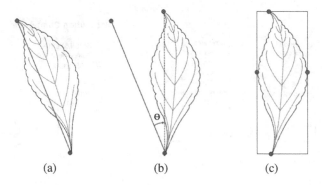

(a)   (b)   (c)

Fig. 3. Image adjustment based on viewing angle and scale. (a) Original image, (b) Rotational adjustment, and (c) 4-edge points detection for scale invariance.

3.2 Vein Representation

In order to improve the search performance, we used a hybrid-search scheme that uses not only leaf shape, but also arrangement of leaves and veins. Fig. 4 shows the

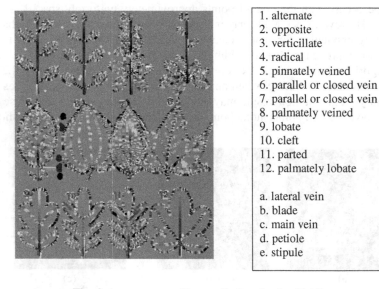

1. alternate
2. opposite
3. verticillate
4. radical
5. pinnately veined
6. parallel or closed vein
7. parallel or closed vein
8. palmately veined
9. lobate
10. cleft
11. parted
12. palmately lobate

a. lateral vein
b. blade
c. main vein
d. petiole
e. stipule

Fig. 4. Arrangement of leaves (1-4) and veins (5-12)

arrangement of leaves and veins. The arrangement of leaves can be classified into alternate, opposite, verticillate, radical. While the alternate arrangement has one leaf per node, the opposite arrangement has two leaves per node and the verticillate has three or more per node. On the other hand, the arrangement of veins can be classified into 5-12 as shown blow.

The arrangement of leaves and veins is extracted from user-sketched images, which is identified by leaf base and the number of leaf per node. The leaf base indicates the shape of the leaf base where it attaches to the stem.

To represent the arrangement of veins, we construct a weighted graph $G(V, E)$ with weight function w (see Figure 5). The weight $w(u, v)$ of the edge $(u, v) \in E$ is simply stored with vertex v in u's adjacency list. In Figure 5-(b)(c), we compute the circumference C of an ellipse to calculate the length of lateral vein.

$$C = 2\pi \sqrt{\frac{a^2 + b^2}{2}} \tag{1}$$

where the x-axis along the major axis, whose length is $2a$, and the y-axis along the minor axis, whose length is $2b$.

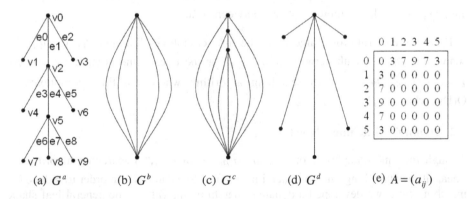

	0	1	2	3	4	5
0	0	3	7	9	7	3
1	3	0	0	0	0	0
2	7	0	0	0	0	0
3	9	0	0	0	0	0
4	7	0	0	0	0	0
5	3	0	0	0	0	0

(a) G^a (b) G^b (c) G^c (d) G^d (e) $A = (a_{ij})$

Fig. 5. Different representations of vein. (a) An undirected graph G^a of pinnately veined. (b) and (c) Two undirected graph G^b and G^c of parallel or closed vein. (d) An undirected graph G^d of palmately veined. (e) The adjacency-matrix representation of G^d.

4 Image Matching and Retrieval

The final step of image retrieval is image matching and browsing. In this section, we present an efficient dynamic matching method for obtaining ranks of all database objects in approximate order of similarity to the query object. Typically, a similarity query is defined as finding the most similar data object. In the case of image databases, a similarity query is to find out the most similar images to a given image with respect to the given features.

4.1 Similarity Measure

After extracting points of interest from images, we perform shape matching to measure the similarity between images. Generally, similarity between two objects is measured by simply evaluating the Euclidean distance [10] between each object's points. Accordingly, the distance between two images can be calculated by the following equation.

$$D(U,V) = \sqrt{\sum_{i=1}^{k} (u_i - v_i)^2}$$ (2)

where U and V are the query and database image, respectively, and u_i and v_i are their i_{th} features, respectively, and k is dimension of the feature space.

According to the Euclidean distance, we can also evaluate similarity between query and database image using the following equation.

$$S(U,V) = \frac{1}{|u|} \sum_{i=1}^{|u|} \min(D_i(u,v))$$ (3)

where $|u|$ is the number of points of interest extracted from the query image and $\min(D_i(u,v))$ is the minimum distance between u_i and v_i.

If we use the brute-force algorithm, the time complexity T is $O(|u \| v|) = O(n^2)$ to search the shortest path between u_i and v_i. For the linear time complexity, we use $\varepsilon - nearest\ neighbor(\varepsilon - NN)$ searching algorithm where the time complexity is $O(Dpolylog(N))$ [11].

4.2 Dynamic Matching Algorithm

Though the time complexity of $\varepsilon - nearest\ neighbor(\varepsilon - NN)$ searching algorithm is linear, it may take long time to match images for large database. In order to reduce the matching time, we developed a dynamic matching algorithm. The general leaf shape of distribution has roughly symmetric distribution. Symmetry can occur in any orientation as long as the image is the same on either side of the central axis. The axis of symmetry is vertical and this makes a good model for symmetry in visual information. Using this property, the matching scope on the shape can be reduced by $1/2 \times 1/2 = 1/4$ times with respect to full matching. Moreover, the matching process may stop when the accumulated similarity value is beyond the threshold.

Even the improved MPP algorithm can produce many points of interest for complicated images. To solve this problem, we created a function called SMP based on the sampling methodology. Let $|u|$ and $|v|$ be the number of points of interest extracted from the query image and database image, respectively. If $|u|$ is less than $|v|$, the number of interest points can be reduced by $|v|/|u|$ when we use $SMP(v)$ function. The dynamic matching algorithm is described as below.

```
Dynamic_matching(input_image, db_image, N, threshold){
  input_point=condensing_point(input_image);
  db_point=condensing_point(db_image);
  if(sizeof(input_point) < sizeof(db_point))
    SMP(db_point);
  for (i=0; i<N/2; i++){
    NN_point=NN_search(input_point[i], db_point);
    Sim = S(input_point[i], NN_point, N/2);
    if(Sim > threshold) { Sim = -1; break; }
  } return result;
}
```

Algorithm 3. Dynamic matching algorithm

5 Experiments

We have implemented a prototype shape-based leaf image retrieval system as part of a nationwide project that aims to develop an information bank for all domestic aqua-plants in Korea. In the experiments, we used as IPAQ HX-4700 for mobile device and hardware platform PCs with Dual 2.8 GHz Xeon Processors and 1GB of RAM and MS SQL Server 2000 as underlying DBMS.

In order to show the effectiveness of our proposed algorithm, we collected 1032 leaf images from "The Korea Plant Picture Book" [12] and compare it with other methods including Centroid Contour Distance (CCD), Fourier Descriptor, Curvature Scale Space Descriptor (CSSD), Moment Invariants, and MPP.

The representation must be invariant to viewing angle change. For this reason, we adjust the viewing angle.

Fig. 7 shows the recalls and precisions of the revised MPP, MPP, Fourier Descriptor, CSSD, CCD, and Moment Invariants. Precision is the fraction of retrieved images

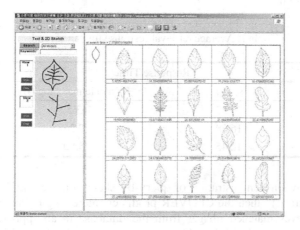

Fig. 6. User Interface on the web

that is relevant to a query. In contrast, recall measures the fraction of the relevant images that have been retrieved. Recall is a non-decreasing function of rank, while precision can be regarded as a function of recall rather than rank. In general, the curve closest to the top of the chart indicates the best performance. In this figure, our proposed algorithm achieves approximately 25% better precision and recall than MPP. In addition, precision and recall of the proposed algorithm are 2.11 times better than that of Fourier Descriptor.

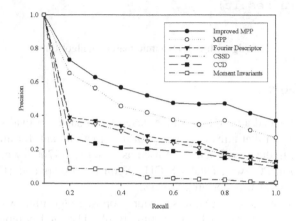

Fig. 7. Precision and recall curve

Table 1 illustrates the average response time of the NN-search and Dynamic matching with different cell sizes. From the table, we can observe that regardless of matching method used, the response time is decreased as the cell size is increased. Overall, our proposed method achieved approximately 2.2 times faster response time than the NN-search.

Table 1. Average retrieval response time in seconds

Cell size	Response Time		A / B
	NN-search (A)	Dynamic matching (B)	
5	29.57	13.57	2.18
7	16.58	7.26	2.28
9	12.45	5.80	2.15

Figure 8 shows a demonstration of query-by-sketch on the CLOVER. First, you can sketch a leaf, and then the CLOVER produces interesting points using improved MPP and retrieves matched images from the database in an approximate order of similarity to the query object. Finally, you can recognize its detailed information and habitat by the GPS coordinates.

(a) Query by Sketch

(b) Query by Photograph

Fig. 8. Demo scenes of CLOVER

6   Conclusions and Future Work

In this paper, we have presented an effective and robust leaf image retrieval system for mobile devices. To improve the efficiency of leaf representation, we revised the MPP algorithm to reduce the number of points to consider for matching. For the matching, we proposed a dynamic matching algorithm that reduces the matching time. In addition, by using a hybrid-search scheme that considers both leaf shape and leaf arrangement as well, we further improved the overall system performance. To evaluate its effectiveness, we have compared our proposed scheme with Fourier Descriptor and Moment Invariants. Experimental results show that the proposed algorithm is more efficient than other methods.

Acknowledgments

This research was supported by the MIC (Ministry of Information and Communication), Korea, under the ITRC support program supervised by the IITA and a grant (no. BDM0100211) to JRL from the Strategic National R&D Program through the Genetic Resources and Information Network Center funded by the Korean Ministry of Science and Technology.

References

1. Gonzalez, Rafel C., et al.: Digital Image Processing. Addison-Wesley. (1992)
2. Lin, H., et al.: A prompt contour detection method. Seventh International Conference on Distributed Multimedia Systems (2001)
3. Michael Heath, et al.: A Robust Visual Method for Assessing the Relative Performance of Edge Detection Algorithms. IEEE Transactions on Pattern Analysis and Machine Intelligence, Vol.19. No.12. (1997) 1338-1359,.
4. Sundar, H., Silver, D., Gagvani, N., Dickinson, S.: Skeleton based shape matching and retrieval. Shape Modeling International. (2003) 130
5. Kurozumi Y., Davis W.A.: Polygonal approximation by the minimax method. Computer Vision, Graphics and Image Processing. (1982) 248-264
6. Sklansky, Chazin et al.: Minimum perimeter polygons of digitized silhouetts. (1972)
7. Sklansky J.: Finding the Convex Hull of a Simple Polygon. Pattern Recognition Letters, Vol.1 No.2. (1982) 79-84
8. Nishida, H.: Structural feature indexing for retrieval of partially visible shapes. Pattern Recognition, Vol.35. No.1. (2002) 55-67
9. Loncaeic, S.: A survey of shape analysis techniques. Pattern Recognition, Vol.31. No.8. (1998) 983-1001
10. Veltkamp, R.: Shape matching: similarity measures and algorithms. Technical Report UU-CS-2001-03, Netherlands (2001)
11. Indyk, P., Motwani, R.: Approximate nearest neighbors: towards removing the curse of dimensionality. The 30 annual ACM symposium on Theory of computing, (1998) 604-613
12. Lee, C.B.: Illustrated flora of Korea. ISBN-8971871954, Hangmoonsa, (1999).
13. Petrakis, E., Diplaros, A. and Milios, E.: Matching and Retrieval of Distorted and Occluded Shapes Using Dynamic Programming. IEEE Transactions on Pattern Analysis and Machine Intelligence, Vol.24. No.11. (2002) 1501-1516
14. Choi, W., Lam K. and Siu, W.: An adaptive active contour model for highly irregular boundaries. Pattern Recognition, Vol.34. (2001) 323-331

Global Memory Net Offers New Innovative Access to Tsurumi's Old Japanese Waka Poems and Tales, and Maps

Takashi Nagatsuka[1] and Ching-chih Chen[2]

[1] Tsurumi University, Dept. of Library, Archival and Information Studies,
Tsurumi 2-1-3, Tsurumi-ku, Yokohama 230-8501, Japan
nagatsuka-t@tsurumi-u.ac.jp
[2] Simmons College, Graduate School of Library and Information Science,
Boston, MA 02115, USA
chen@simmons.edu

Abstract. This paper describes how *Global Memory Net (GMNet)* has been able to provide new kind of innovative access to the invaluable content of the classical Japanese ancient poems and maps at Tsurumi University that was not available for public access before. The collaboration began with the development of a prototype collection, based on images included in two publications of the Tsurumi University Library - the *Eighty Selections of Waka Poems and Tales from the Classical Japanese Literature* and the *Japanese Maps in the Old Age*. As the project developed, coinciding with the technology development of *GMNet* in bilingual retrieval as well as with sound presentations, the inclusion of sound files for each of the Waka selection was considered a very desirable feature since Waka poems are generally only readable by very small number of specialists.

The paper will present a bird's eye view of how Tsurumi's rare collection is organized, presented with much enhanced access in *GMNet* system. Through this project, the Tsurumi team has gained considerable important experiences. The overall process for them was very time consuming even though the technology of *GMNet* was already in place. These valuable experiences will be discussed and shared.

1 Introduction

This paper is to describe how by taking part in the *Global Memory Net (GMNet)*, one can gain new innovative access to the invaluable content of the rare classical Japanese ancient Waka poems and maps at Tsurumi University that was not available for public access before.

The possibility to participate at the *GMNet* became a reality after Ching-chih Chen's visit to the Tsurumi University as the first invited speaker at the University's initial *Digital Library Symposium* in late December 2004 [1]. At that symposium, Chen stated that *GMNet* aims to be an effective gateway or digital portal to the world culture and heritage. It can also be viewed as a comprehensive multimedia digital library which can offer the global culture, history, and heritage instantly to the

E.A. Fox et al. (Eds.): ICADL 2005, LNCS 3815, pp. 149–157, 2005.
© Springer-Verlag Berlin Heidelberg 2005

information seekers [2]. She indicated that Japanese contents are not yet sufficiently accessible by people in the world due to language and other factors, and that *GMNet* can provides a platform to make it possible for global sharing and distribution of some selective Japanese resources. She also pointed out *GMNet*'s great potential for "real" collaboration with different countries in the world not only in the "content" areas, but also the needs for involving subject specialists in those countries in order for *GMNet* to provide more in-depth knowledge on the significant cultural and historical "memories" of those countries [1].

With this impetus, Tsurumi group led by T. Nagatsuka welcome the opportunity to join *GMNet* by benefiting from its cutting-edge technology to develop a prototype for resource sharing and for promoting universal access.

2   Development of a Prototype Tsurumi Collection

Tsurumi's collaboration with *GMNet* began in early 2005 with the development of a prototype collection related to the rare Waka poems and tales, as well as ancient maps on Japan. The value of ancient maps on Japan is clear, however, why Waka poems and tales?

Waka poems and tales are rare and important classical Japanese literature, thus an invaluable part of Japanese cultural heritage. Hundreds of original texts, translations, studies, and electronic texts of classical Japanese literature are available on the Web, and many are in Japanese only. As to the Waka literature, there are several useful Web sites as well, such as the *Japan 2001 Waka* Website by the University of Sheffield which translates some Japanese texts of the imperial waka anthologies to English (http://www.shef.ac.uk/japan2001/), and the site of the Japanese Text Initiative of the University of Virginia Library's Electronic Text Center which displays classical Japanese literature including Waka poems in Japanese characters (http://etext.virginia.edu/ japanese/). Yet, none has introduced the original look of the handwritings of the poems, presented sound files of the contemporary Japanese reading, and permitted bilingual retrieval capabilities. These are the features of our prototype in *GMNet*.

The Tsurumi collection includes images chosen to be included in two publications of the Tsurumi University Library -- the *Eighty Selections of Waka Poems and Tales from the Classical Japanese Literature* and the *Japanese Maps in the Old Age*. The first book, *Eighty Selections of Waka Poems and Tales from the Classical Japanese Literature,* includes images taken from detached segments of Waka poems and Tales selected from royal anthologies, poetic anthologies, prose narratives, tales of war, panels of screens, and Japanese backgammon and playing cards. These were handwritten or printed from the end of 11th to 19th centuries. Each image represents a part or the whole writings, and Japanese description of this portion is included in the back part of the book, which form a good base of the metadata of the image. The second book, the *Japanese Maps in the Old Age*, is composed of thirty-seven ancient maps on Japan published in Europe and three in Japan. Each map image comes with descriptive title and associated bibliographic information in both English and Japanese.

The reasons for selecting these two books were:

- The cultural contents of the two books were considered to be the best of the Tsurumi University Library's rare collection. They are unique, rare, and appropriate for meeting the criteria for inclusion in *GMNet*.
- The prototype development will need the involvement of the subject specialists in Japan.
- The contents of the books are made up of images with Japanese descriptions. Without English descriptions, it will be of lesser use to non-Japanese people. In handling both English and Japanese, this offers new challenges to *GMNet* for demonstrating its bilingual capabilities.
- The rare Waka poems and tales are not readable by most Japanese, and thus, the need for currently reading by experts in the field is great, and this allows the *GMNet* to explore the retrieval of sounds in addition to images.

3 Developmental Process

As the developmental work starts, all images were scanned by Chen's research group at Simmons College in the US. Also, the baseline database information in English, when possible, was completed by Chen's research staff as well using the *GMNet*'s existing metadata structure.

3.1 Metadata and Descriptive Information

After the creation of the initial baseline database, it was found that several metadata elements will need to have the Japanese translated by the Tsurumi University staff. Specifically, the descriptive information on each image of the handwriting page of the Waka poem or tale has to be prepared in English for the "Description" field of the metadata. This has proven to be a very difficult task, because most Japanese descriptions could not be translated to English directly, otherwise they would not be understandable by readers without possessing the basic knowledge of the classical Japanese literature. Thus, the Tsurumi staff had to create new modified descriptive information in English for every image.

To complete this job, it was necessary to consult and discuss with subject specialists at the Tsurumi University for each description. Although the descriptive information for each record is short, yet it is a very labor-intensive process. It is also a difficult one because there is an obvious cultural difference between the staff in information science and that in classical Japanese literature studies. Each has his/her own emphasis. For example, the kind of English description needed for *GMNet* does not correspondent to that considered to be important by the classical Japanese literature specialists at Tsurumi University.

To prepare for the use of bilingual retrieval functions, the metadata in Japanese language is also prepared for the 80 Waka Poems and Tales. Except the "description" field, all other metadata fields in Japanese are created using the same content as those in the English version using the *GMNet*'s existing database structure. The Japanese description follows the same contents as published in the book.

3.2 Tsurumi Collection in *GMNet*

In this section, we shall provide a bird's eye view on how one can access Tsurumi Collection via the web-base *GMNet*. Figure 1 is the introductory page of the Tsurumi Collection. As indicated there, "The process in developing this digital collection is a perfect example of both difficulties -- distance, cultural differences between the subject and the technology specialists, language difficulties, ability to interpret ancient contents, etc. -- and exciting results of international collaboration. In meeting the challenges, *GMNet* has extended its image retrieval capabilities to include the retrieval of sound files, and also begun to experiment bilingual retrieval. To explore bilingual retrieval capabilities, we have included the metadata in both English and Japanese in UNICODE. The Japanese version is produced by the Tsurumi team using our metadata structure. Users can thus search in both languages if they have the Japanese input capabilities on the browser.

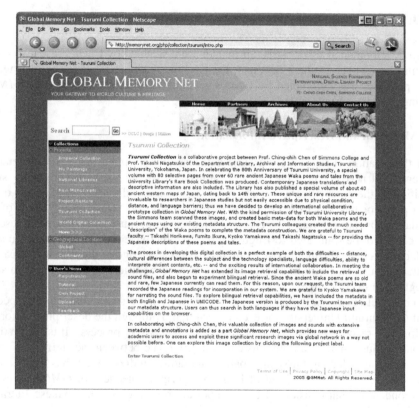

Fig. 1. Introductory page of the Tsurumi Collection in *GMNet*

When one enters the Tsurumi "image collection," the screen as shown in Figure 2 will show up. Where a user can decide to find what they want by searching in any of the metadata field or all. It can also search by using the cutting-edge content-based image retrieval technique, SIMPLIcity of the Penn State University. Here, one can browse images of the collection, or can randomly access the image collection. When the images are displayed, simple titles of these are also shown (Figure 2).

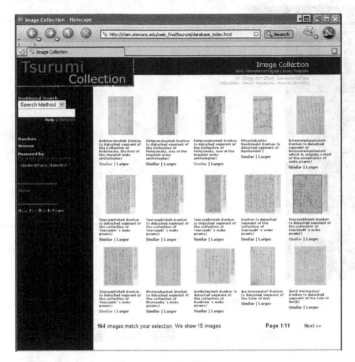

Fig. 2. Images of Tsurumi's Waka poems with English titles

When a specific image of the Waka poem is chosen, additional descriptive information of that poem can further be obtained by clicking on the image, as shown in the left panel of Figure 3. In addition, if one would like to see the current Japanese translation of the ancient writing, one can go the pdf file directly (Fig. 4). When "larger" is clicked, the image can be zoomed and enlarged several times to enable the seeker to view the details of the handwriting of the Waka poem. To protect the ownership of the image, dynamically generated digital watermark can be seen in the lower right corner of the enlarged image (Figure 5).

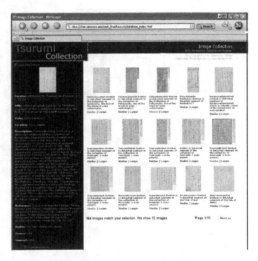

Fig. 3. Metadata with detailed descriptive information

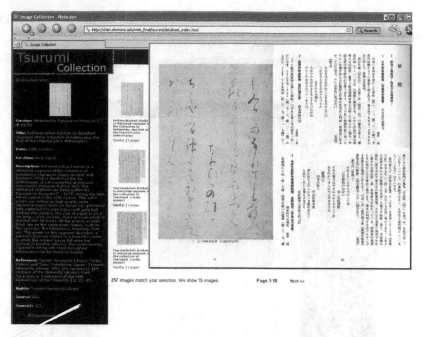

Fig. 4. The pdf file of the Japanese translation and transcription of the Waka poem

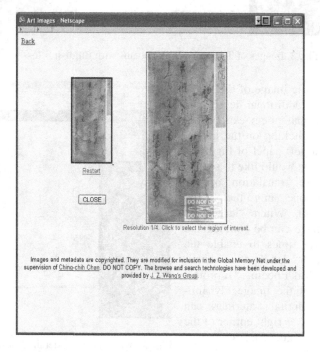

Fig. 5. The chosen image can be enlarged several times depending on the image resolution. Note the dynamically gene-rated digital watermark in the lower right corner.

3.3 Bilingual Retrieval

As the project developed, coinciding with the technology development of *GMNet* in bilingual retrieval, *GMNet* naturally explore the retrieval of the Tsurumi collection in both English and Japanese. If a user can input the Japanese characters from his/her PC with a bilingual wordprocessing software, it will be able to access to the Tsurumi Collection by Japanese. After the user retrieved in English and received the output in English, he/she would like to read more detailed description in Japanese. In this case, he/she can retrieve the descriptive information in Japanese. Figure 6 shows the database information in Japanese on the front screen, while the English is on the back.

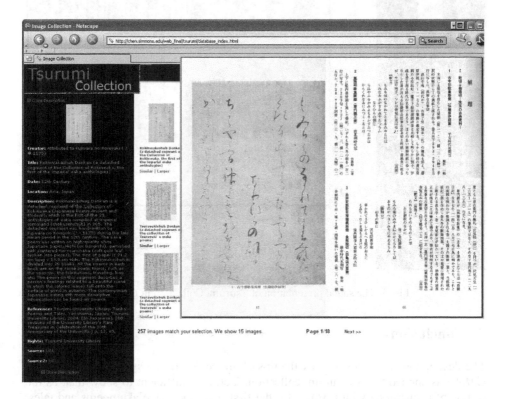

Fig. 6. The bilingual retrieval of images in the Tsurumi Collection in *GMNet*

3.4 Sound Presentations

As *GMNet* is developong bilingual retrieval capabilities, it is also exploring the use of sound presentations. It was considered that the inclusion of sound files for the Waka selection is truly a desirable feature since few people, even Japanese, are able to read the old and ancient Japanese poem. Thus, the sound files for most writings were created by recording the readings digitally and then converted to Winamp (Windows Audio MPEG Player) media files for the web presentation.

As shown in Figure 7, when a user retrieved the Japanese transcription in pdf file shown in the upper right panel, the sound file narrating that transcript can also be retrieved as shown in the lower right panel.

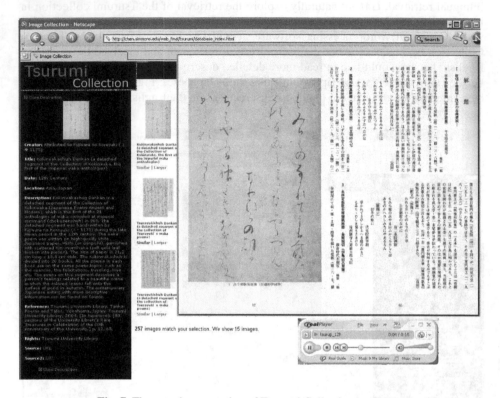

Fig. 7. The sound presentation of Tsurumi Collection in *GMNet*

4   Conclusions

The description above covers only the tips of an iceberg of the system capabilities of *GMNet* as applied to the Tsurumi collection. Yet, it is sufficient to show that, as the results of cooperating with *GMNet*, for the first time, the old Waka poems and tales, as well as ancient maps of the Tsurumi University not only can be shared with those scholars and learners who are interested in classical Japanese culture and heritage, but also greatly enhanced their capabilities in obtained needed multimedia information quickly and effectively in a way not possible before.

With the cutting-edge technology of *GMNet*, Tsurumi's collection is now available for universal access with many attractive features as an exciting part of the global gateway. However, the seemingly small number of records with only the provision of limited metadata information have consumed lot more time and effort than originally anticipated by the Tsurumi staff, even though the technology-related work has been handled and completed by Chen's *GMNet* group.

Through this project, we have gained considerable important experiences. The overall process was very time consuming, especially there was much difficulty in the process of preparing the raw English descriptive data. One of the major reasons is the information science specialist's lack the subject knowledge to the classical Japanese literature. This kind of difficulty will be experienced by any other similar types of projects. The other reason is the subject expert's understanding and knowledge on the purpose as well as use of digital library applications. Basically two group's purpose and focus are not similar. "What we should do next?" will be a significant question for us to consider.

There are numerous digital library projects for preserving cultural heritage in Japan, but great majority of them are mainly targeting to the Japanese audience or the Japanese information seeker. Clearly to create the English access capability is essential for international sharing and information distribution, but it is also of great difficulty at the moment. Tsurumi's participation in *GMNet* not only confirms this problem, but also suggests that there is a great and urgent need to explore possibilities in meeting these challenges.

This pilot project is an important step for Tsurumi in international collaboration for introducing the Japanese cultural heritage, especially the classical Japanese Literature, to the world. We now know that we have much work ahead of us if we are serious in pushing our digital library initiatives.

Acknowledgements

We are grateful to Tsurumi University's Faculty - Takashi Horikawa, Fumito Ikura, Kyoko Yamakawa - for their effort and advice in our creation of the English descriptions of the Waka poems and teles. Special thanks goes to Kyoko Yamakawa for narrating the sound files.

We greatly appreciate the efforts of several research staff of the Chen's *GMNet* group at Simmons College. Specifically, Annie Cain did all images scanning, Peishan Tsai completed the much needed metadata work. Shengqiang Zhang of Sichuwan University in Chengdu, China and visiting researcher with Chen's group developed the bilingual capabilities in addition to the current PHP-based system under Chen's overall direction.

References

1. Chen, Ching-chih, *"Global Memory Net* offers the world instantly: Potentials for universal access to invaluable Japanese contents," *Journal of Information Processing and Management* (in Japanese) 47 (11): 751-760 (2005). Translated to Japanese by Takashi Nagatsuka.
2. Chen, Ching-chih, *"Global Memory Net*: New Collaboration, New Activities and new Potentials," in *Proceedings of ICADL 2004*, Shanghai, December 14-16, 2005. Edited by Z. Chen et al. pp. 73-83.

Keyword Spotting on Korean Document Images by Matching the Keyword Image

Soo Hyung Kim[1], Sang Cheol Park[1], Chang Bu Jeong[2], Ji Soo Kim[1], Hyuk Ro Park[1], and Guee Sang Lee[1]

[1] Department of Computer Science, Chonnam National University, 300 Yongbong-dong, Buk-gu, Kwangju 500-700, Korea
{shkim, sanchun, jskim}@iip.chonnam.ac.kr,
{hyukro, gslee}@chonnam.ac.kr
[2] Department of Internet Software, Honam University, 59-1 Sebong-dong, Gwangsan-gu, Kwangju 506-714, Korea
cbjeong@honam.ac.kr

Abstract. In this paper, we propose a keyword spotting system for Korean document images and compare the proposed system with an OCR-based document retrieval system. The system is composed of character segmentation, feature extraction for the query keyword, and word-to-word matching. In the character segmentation step, we propose an effective method to resolve the connection between adjacent characters. In the query creation step, feature vector for the query is constructed by a combination of the features for the constituent characters. In the matching step, word-to-word matching is applied based on a character matching. We demonstrated that the proposed keyword spotting system is more efficient than the OCR-based one to search a keyword on Korean document images, especially when the quality of documents is quite poor.

1 Introduction

Methods of searching document image with a keyword can be classified into one of OCR (Optical Character Recognition)-based or image-based (keyword spotting or keyword detection). An OCR-based method uses a text-to-text matching approach, that is, it transforms the document image into a machine-readable form by applying appropriate recognition process and then examines the document with a keyword. This method depends on recognition process and suffers from low recognition accuracy for low quality images. [1, 2]

The image-based method searches the document by comparing the similarity between the keyword image and every word image in the document. It generally consists of a pre-processing step and a searching step. In the former, a document image is segmented into word images and then the word images are stored in a database along with their feature. This helps to reduce the feature extraction time in the next step. In the latter, a similarity between the keyword image and the word image is calculated by comparing their features [3].

Some keyword spotting approaches on the English document images have been reported in the past few years [4-9]. As a representative among them, Lu et al. [5]

E.A. Fox et al. (Eds.): ICADL 2005, LNCS 3815, pp. 158–166, 2005.
© Springer-Verlag Berlin Heidelberg 2005

represents each word as a string of feature codes and therefore each document image can be represented as a series of strings. To match a query word with the words in a document, an inexact string matching technique is used.

There are some studies on the image-based keyword spotting on Korean document images. Oh et al. [10, 11] segments a document image into word images by using Kwak's algorithm [12], and constructs a database of word images. To make query images, they generated a character sets using a text-editing tool with the same font used in document image. Two-stage retrieval scheme is used to reduce processing time, where a profile feature and wavelet feature are used in each stage respectively. Furthermore wavelet feature is obtained by selecting the largest 30 coefficients using the Haar wavelet transform.

Fig. 1 describes a block-diagram for the proposed keyword spotting system. We assume that word images, which are segmented by using Jeong's system [13], are already stored in a database. First, a word image is split into character images and each character image is normalized into a designated size. Secondly, a mesh feature is extracted from the normalized character image and then stored in the database along with the image. When the user inputs a keyword, the system searches the similar words from the database.

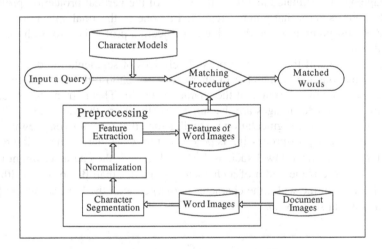

Fig. 1. A block diagram of the proposed system using character feature models

2   Character Segmentation

In Korean document, there exists a small gap between two adjacent characters. All the character widths are the same, and the ratio between width and height of a character is 1. Based on these general observations, we devise a character segmentation algorithm composed of the four stages.

In the first stage, we guess the number of characters in the word. The word length l is easily estimated by dividing the height of the word image into the width of vertical projection profile - refer to Fig. 2. If $\lfloor l \rfloor + \gamma \le l \le \lceil l \rceil - \gamma$, then the estimate number

160   S.H. Kim et al.

is $\lfloor l \rfloor$. In case $\lfloor l \rfloor + \gamma > l$ and $\lceil l \rceil - \gamma < l$, the number is $\lfloor l \rfloor -1$ or $\lfloor l \rfloor$ and $\lfloor l \rfloor$ or $\lceil l \rceil$, respectively, where γ is a small value in $0 < \gamma < 0.2$, and $\lfloor l \rfloor$ and $\lceil l \rceil$ is the floor and the ceiling of l, respectively.

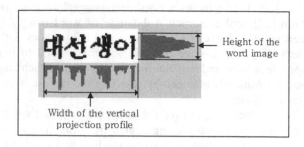

Fig. 2. Projection profiles for a word image

In the second stage, we search the split points to segment the word image using the estimated length. Candidates of split points are first obtained by equally dividing the word image by the estimated length. If the value of the vertical projection profile at a candidate point is zero, that point is regarded as one of the final split points. Otherwise, the nearest point at which the value of projection profile is zero is chosen as the final split point.

In the third stage, if there are two possible choices of segmentation due to the two possible estimations for the number of characters, we choose the better segmentation result that has a smaller variance of the character widths. This is from the observation that widths of character images are the same, and therefore the variance of character widths from an accurate segmentation is smaller than that from a wrong segmentation.

In the last stage, a post-processing is performed to revise the segmentation result. If a character has a vertical vowel such as " ㅏ ", " ㅔ ", " ㅣ ", the character might be split into two. Therefore if the width of a character is smaller than $\beta\%$ of the width of the biggest character in the word, the character is merged with the left one, where β is an empirical constant set to 30%.

Fig. 3. Revision of the character segmentation result by post-processing

In case where adjacent characters are connected as in Fig. 4(a), the above algorithm fails to segment the word. In these cases, we remove some portion of the vertical projection profile to make it easy to find the candidate split points in the second stage of the algorithm. We call it as "α-cut" in which the value of projection profile is set to zero whose value is less than α. In Fig. 4(b), the α-cut produces four candidate split points marked as ①, ②, ③ and ④. The two arrows →← in ① express a zone between two neighboring segments, and the split point is the center of it. Here α is an empirical constant set as 7% of the average of the vertical projection profile values.

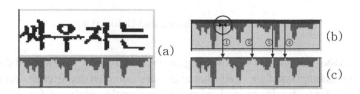

Fig. 4. Resolving the connection between adjacent characters

Fig. 5(a) shows the input word image. The downward arrows are the target split points. Fig. 5(b) shows the segmentation results without α-cut and Fig. 5(c) is the results with α-cut.

Fig. 5. The result of the character segmentation

3 Feature Extraction

Two groups of the typefaces, Myungjo and Gothic, are generally used in Korean documents, but the shapes of characters printed in the typefaces of the groups are quite different. There is no doubt that the image-based keyword spotting system has poor performance on the document in different typefaces. Thus classifying the typefaces in advance is more efficient to improve the retrieving performance. In this paper, we assume that the typeface of the document is already discriminated [12]. Fig. 6(a) shows a part of document image in Batang typeface, which is a representative for Myungjo group. Fig. 6(b) is an image having the same characters as in Fig. 6(a) but printed in Gullim typeface, which is a representative for Gothic group. As can be seen from these examples, the location and the width of strokes are quite different according to the typeface.

A number of photocopying and/or scanning of a document can produce some noises or distortions of character strokes. The skew correction might also give additional distortions to the image. Therefore we need a feature minimizing the effect of noises and distortions. In our system, a number of samples for each character class have been used to train the model.

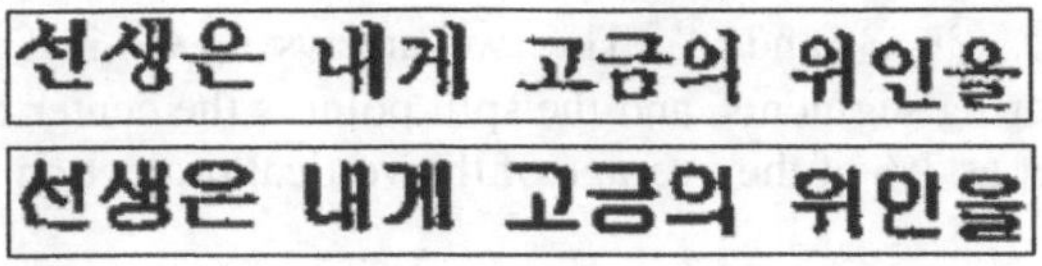

선생은 내게 고급의 위인을 (a)

선생은 내게 고급의 위인을 (b)

Fig. 6. Korean images in Batang and Gullim typefaces

Fig. 7 describes the process of extracting an average feature vector for the character class "각" in Batang typeface. Ten characters are sampled from each training data according to a fonts, finally total sixty character samples are used for the character class. All samples are normalized to $i \times j$ size. An $m \times n$ grid feature is computed from each sample, and the averages of the sixty features of each grid are taken as the model of that character class. In our system, i and j are 36, and m and n are 6. So 36-dimensional feature vector is used.

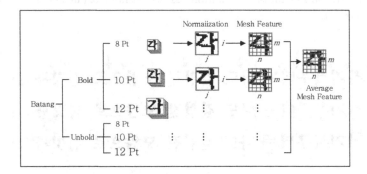

Fig. 7. Character model for "각 " in Batang typeface

4 Word Matching

Let $Q(C_1^q, C_2^q, ..., C_k^q)$ and $T(C_1^t, C_2^t, ..., C_k^t)$ be a keyword image and word image in the document respectively, where C_i represents v-dimensional feature vector extracted from $i\text{-}th$ character. Each of them consists of k characters. The similarity between $i\text{-}th$ characters of the query and word image is defined in the equation (1). Here T_c is a threshold for character matching.

$$
\begin{cases}
if \quad Dist\left(C_i^q, C_i^t\right) \leq T_c , \quad then \quad C_i^q \equiv C_i^t \\
else \hspace{4.5cm} C_i^q \neq C_i^t
\end{cases}
\tag{1}
$$

$$
where \quad Dist\left(C_i^q, C_i^t\right) = \sum_{j=1}^{v} \left| c_{i,j}^q - c_{i,j}^t \right|
\tag{2}
$$

Given the similarities for k character pairs are computed by the equation (1), the word-level similarity is calculated using the equation (3). Here T_w is a threshold for word matching.

$$\begin{cases} if & Dist(Q,T) \le T_w, & then & Q \equiv T \\ else & & & Q \ne T \end{cases} \tag{3}$$

$$where \quad Dist(Q,T) = \frac{1}{k}\sum_{i=1}^{k} Dist\left(C_i^q, C_i^t\right) \tag{4}$$

Fig. 8 shows the process of matching the keyword image with a word image. In this figure, ① represents the word image and ② indicates that the first two characters are not matched to the query image. ③ shows a successful matching. All of the characters in the query and word images satisfy both the equation (1) in character-level and equation (3) in word-level. The matching process continues to the next position as in ④.

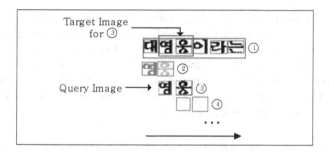

Fig. 8. Matching process

5 Experimental Results

5.1 Experimental Environment

We typed a part of the autobiography, "Baek-Bum Il Ji", to make a text file of 20 A4 pages. They are formatted by using a Microsoft word processor in 12 different combinations of fonts – two typefaces (Batang and Gullim), three types of point sizes (8, 10, and 12), and two kinds of font styles (bold and regular). They are printed by a SAMSUNG ML_8065 printer, and then copied iteratively by 8 times using a XEROX Document Centre 285 PLUS G copier, and finally scanned by an EPSON GT-30000 scanner at 200 DPI.

All the document images are partitioned into word images using the system of [13]. Every word is in turn segmented by our segmentation method in Section 2, and each character is normalized into 36 by 36 size. A 36-D feature is extracted by applying a 6×6 mesh as described in Section 3. One half of the data is used for training, and the other half is used for testing. The system has been implemented in a C/C++ language on a personal computer with a Pentium-4 2.80 GHz CPU and 1 GB RAM.

Words of two characters and words of three characters appear most frequently in Korean document. Therefore we prepared 30 query keywords of length 2 or 3. To do this, we counted the frequencies of every word in the training data and select 20 most frequent words among length 2 and 10 most frequent words among length 3.

5.2 Performance Evaluation

Table 1 compares the performance of our system with an OCR-based one. The OCR-based system first converts the input document image into a machine-readable form using a commercial OCR software ARMI 6.0 [14], and then examine each word whether it is the same as the user keyword. Note that the precision of OCR-based system is 100% since there is no false accepting error in our experimental data. The F-measure, which is described like the equation 5, combines recall and precision in a single efficiency measure [15].

$$F - measure = \frac{2 \times \text{Re } call \times \text{Pr } ecision}{\text{Re } call + \text{Pr } ecision} \tag{5}$$

The proposed keyword spotting system shows better performance for Gullim rather than Batang, better for bold rather than regular, better for large size rather than small size fonts. Note that the performance of OCR-based system, in case of Gullim typeface and small font sizes, is remarkably worse than that of our system. In a conclusion, the proposed system has better performance than the OCR-based one, especially when the quality of documents is quite poor or the point size is small. Fig. 9 shows an example of keyword spotting with a keyword "선생".

Table 1. Performance of the OCR-based system and the proposed one

Font			OCR-based system			Proposed system		
Typeface	Bold	Size	Recall (%)	Precision (%)	F-measure (%)	Recall (%)	Precision (%)	F-measure (%)
Batang	On	8	39.21	100	56.33	67.84	67.84	67.84
		10	77.53	100	87.34	80.34	80.34	80.34
		12	87.22	100	93.17	79.74	79.74	79.74
	Off	8	55.95	100	71.75	70.80	70.80	70.80
		10	81.94	100	90.07	71.68	71.68	71.68
		12	92.51	100	96.11	76.21	76.21	76.21
Gullim	On	8	25.11	100	40.14	78.76	78.76	78.76
		10	55.51	100	71.39	85.02	85.02	85.02
		12	75.33	100	85.93	83.41	83.41	83.41
	Off	8	21.15	100	34.92	69.16	69.16	69.16
		10	59.03	100	74.24	74.01	74.01	74.01
		12	70.07	100	82.40	81.06	81.06	81.06
Average			61.71	100	76.32	76.50	76.50	76.50

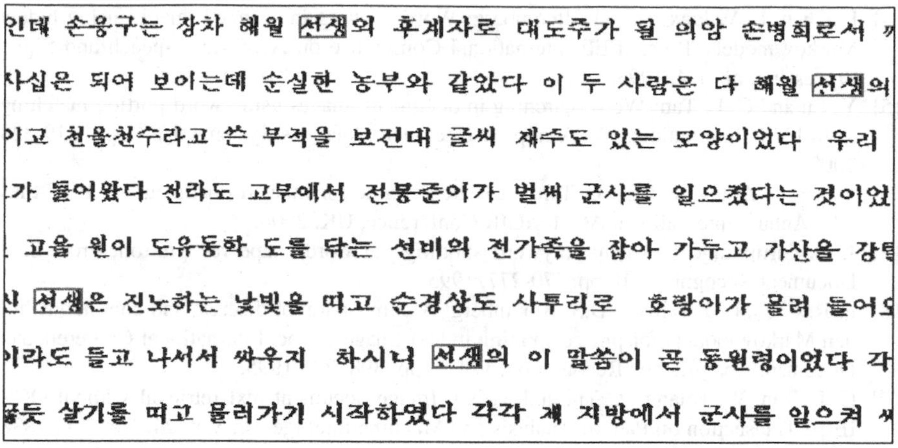

인대 손웅구는 장차 해월 전쟁의 후계자로 대도주가 될 의암 손병희로서 갸

사십은 되어 보이는데 순실한 농부와 같았다 이 두 사람은 다 해월 전쟁의

이고 천물천수라고 쓴 무적을 보건대 글씨 재주도 있는 모양이었다 우리

가 물어왔다 전라도 고무에서 전봉준이가 벌써 군사를 일으켰다는 것이었

고을 원이 도유동학 도를 닦는 선비의 전가족을 잡아 가두고 가산을 강

선생은 진노하는 낯빛을 띠고 순경상도 사투리로 호랑이가 몰려 들어

라도 들고 나서서 싸우지 하시니 전쟁의 이 말씀이 곧 동원령이었다 각

굶듯 살기를 띠고 물러가기 시작하였다 각각 제 지방에서 군사를 일으켜 써

Fig. 9. Part of a result searched document image for " 선생 "

6 Conclusion

We have proposed a keyword spotting system for the full-text retrieval for Korean documents and proved that the performance of our system is better than that of OCR-based one, especially when the quality of documents is quite poor.

Our system is composed of character segmentation, feature extraction, and word-to-word matching. In the character segmentation step, we proposed an effective method to split touching characters. One of major distinguished characteristics of our system is to generate an image for the keyword and utilize the keyword image for keyword spotting. Our system can be further improved by incorporating the capabilities for font recognition, the discrimination of Korean and English texts, and the generation of similar-looking keyword images.

Acknowledgement

This work was supported by the Korea Research Foundation Grant (2004-041-D00631).

References

[1] M. Ohta, A. Takasu, and J. Adach: Retrieval methods for English-text width missrecognized OCR characters, Proceedings of 4th International Conference on Document Analysis and Recognition, Vol. 2, pp. 950-955, 1997.

[2] K. Marukawa, T. Hu, H. Fujisawa, and Y. Shima: Document retrieval tolerating character recognition errors-evaluation and application, Pattern Recognition, Vol. 30, No. 8, pp. 1361-1371, 1997.

[3] D. Doermann: The indexing and retrieval of document images: a survey, Computer Vision and Image Understanding, Vol. 70, No. 3, pp. 287-298, 1998.

[4] F. Chen, L. Wilcox, and D. Bloomberg: Word spotting in scanned images using hidden Markov models, Proc. IEEE International Conference on Acoustics, Speech and Signal Processing, pp. 1-4, 1993.

[5] Y. Lu and C. L. Tan: Word searching in document images using word portion matching, Fifth IAPR International Workshop on Document Analysis Systems, USA, pp. 319-328, 2002.

[6] Y. Lu, L. Zhang, and C . L. Tan: A search engine for imaged documents in PDF files, 27th Annual International ACM SIGIR Conference, UK, 2004.

[7] J. DeCurtins and E. Chen: Keyword spotting via word shape recognition, Proc. SPIE Document Recognition II, pp. 270-277, 1995.

[8] F. R. Chen, L.D. Wilcox, D.S. Bloomberg: A comparison of discrete and continuous hidden Markov models for phrase spotting in text images, Proc. International Conference on Document Analysis and Recognition, Vol. 1, pp. 398-402, 1995.

[9] C. L. Tan, W. Huang, Z. Yu, and Y. Xu: Image document text retrieval without OCR, IEEE Transaction on Pattern Analysis and Machine Intelligence, Vol. 24, No. 7, pp. 838-844, July 2002.

[10] H. G. Kim, J. H. Yang, J. S. Lee, and I. S. Oh: Image-based retrieval of printed Korean words using wavelets, Journal of Korea Information Science Society, Vol. 28, No. 2, pp. 91-103, Feb. 2001.

[11] I. S. Oh, Y. S. Choi, J. H. Yang, and S. H. Kim: A Keyword spotting system of Korean document images, Proc. 5th International Conference on Asian Digital Libraries, Singapore, p. 530, Dec. 2002.

[12] H. K. Kwag: A Study on Word Segmentation and Attribute Extraction from Document Images, Ph.D. dissertation, Chonnam National University, Korea, 2001.

[13] C. B. Jeong and S. H. Kim: A document image preprocessing system for keyword spotting, Proc. International Conference on Asian Digital Libraries, China, pp. 440-443, Dec. 2004.

[14] http://www.perceptcom.com/.

[15] R. B. Yates and B. R. Neto: Modern Information Retrieval, ACM press, pp. 75-82, 1999.

Robust Feature Extraction for Automatic Classification of Korean Traditional Music in Digital Library

Kang-Kue Lee and Kyu-Sik Park

Dankook University,
Division of Information and Computer Science,
San 8, Hannam-Dong, Yongsan-Ku, Seoul, 140-714 Korea
{fitz, kspark}@dankook.ac.kr

Abstract. In this paper, we propose an automatic classification system that classifies the Korean traditional music in digital library. In contrast to previous works, this paper focuses on the following issues of music classification. Firstly, the proposed system accepts query sound and automatically classifies input query into one of the six Korean traditional music categories such as "Court music", "Classical chamber music", "Folk song", "Folk music", "Buddhist music", and "Shamanist music". Secondly, in order to overcome system uncertainty due to the different query patterns, a robust feature extraction method called multi-feature clustering (MFC) combined with SFS feature selection is proposed. Finally, several pattern classification algorithms such as k-NN, Gaussian, GMM and SVM are tested and compared in terms of the classification accuracy. The experimental results indicate that the proposed MFC-SFS method shows more stable and higher classification performance than the one without the MFC-SFS.

1 Introduction

This paper is motivated from the observation that for the music digital library (MDL) to develop the advanced tools to support new ways to classify and retrieve with the music content. This paper is developed as a part of the research fulfillment in The National Library of Korea to set up the automatic classification system for Korean traditional music.

Most of content-based classification and retrieval of audio sound has three common stages of a pattern recognition problem: *feature extraction*, *classification* based on the selected feature, and *retrieval* based on the similarity measure. Depending on the different combinations of these stages, several strategies are employed. Good accounts are described in [1-4].

In contrast to previous works, this paper focuses on the following issues on music classification. Firstly, the proposed system accepts query sound and automatically classifies a query into one of the six Korean traditional music categories such as "Court music", "Classical chamber music", "Folk song", "Folk music", "Buddhist music", and "Shamanist music" which are defined in National Center for Korean Traditional Music. Secondly, a robust feature extraction method called MFC (multi-feature clustering) combined with SFS (sequential forward selection) is proposed to

E.A. Fox et al. (Eds.): ICADL 2005, LNCS 3815, pp. 167–170, 2005.
© Springer-Verlag Berlin Heidelberg 2005

overcome system uncertainty problem due to the different query patterns. Finally, several pattern classification algorithms including k-NN, Gaussian, GMM and SVM [5] are tested and compared in terms of the system stability and classification accuracy. This paper is organized as follows. In section 2, the feature extraction, selection and a new feature optimization method MFC-SFS is introduced in detail. In section 3, we compare the performance of the proposed system with extensive experimental results on genre classification. Finally, section 4 is our conclusion.

2 Robust Feature Extraction for Classification

Two types of features are computed from each 23ms frame with 50% overlapped hamming window. One is the timbral features such as spectral centroid, spectral rolloff, spectral flux and zero crossing rates. The other is coefficient domain features of thirteen mel-frequency cepstral coefficients (MFCC) and twelve linear predictive coefficients (LPC). The mean and standard deviation of these six original features are computed over each frame for each music file to form a total of 58-dimensional feature vector. At this moment, an efficient feature selection method is required to reduce the computational burden and so speed up the search process. As in ref. [6], we used a sequential forward selection (SFS) method for feature selection to reduce dimensionality of the features and to enhance the classification accuracy.

The classification results corresponding to different input query patterns within the same music file may be much different. It may cause serious uncertainty of the system performance. In order to overcome this problem, a robust feature extraction method called multi-feature clustering (MFC) combined with SFS is implemented based on VQ. Key idea is to extract features over the full-length music signal in a step of 15 sec large window and then cluster these features in four disjoint subsets (centroids) using LBG-VQ technique .

3 Experimental Results

For experimental setup, 180 music files of Korean traditional music were formed to DB. 30 music samples were collected for each of the six categories in "Court music", "Classical chamber music", "Folk song", "Folk music", "Buddhist music", and "Shamanist music" resulting in resulting in 180 music files in database.

Fig. 1 demonstrates the usefulness of MFC-SFS feature optimization method as described in section 2. It shows average classification accuracy with 15 sec query sound. As seen from the figure, among the k-NN, Gaussian, GMM and SVM classifiers, k(1)-NN and SVM classifier shows fast convergence speed with higher classification accuracy while Gaussian and GMM model shows somewhat insufficient performance. From the figure 1, for the case of k-NN and SVM classifier, we see that the classification performance increases with the increase of features up to certain number of features, while it remains almost constant after that. Thus based on the observation of these boundaries, we can select first 20 features up to the boundary and ignore the rest of them. In this way, we can determine the number of best feature sets for each classifier.

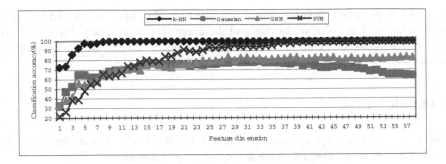

Fig. 1. Average classification accuracy rate using MFC-SFS method

As pointed out earlier, the classification results corresponding to different input query patterns (or portions) may be much different. To see the improvement of the proposed algorithm MFC-SFS, six excerpts with duration of 15 sec were extracted from every other position in a same query music file. Fig. 2 shows the classification results with proposed MFC-SFS and without MFC-SFS for the case of k-NN and SVM classifiers.

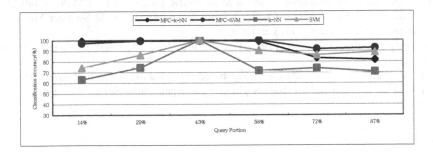

Fig. 2. Average Classification results with proposed MFC-VQ and without MFC-VQ

As we expected, the classification results without MFC-VQ greatly depends on the query positions and its performance is getting worse as query portion towards to two extreme cases of beginning and ending position of the music signal. On the other hand with the proposed MFC-SFS method, we can find quite stable classification performance and it even yields higher accuracy rate in the range of 83% ~ 98%. Even at the two extreme cases of beginning and ending position, the system with proposed MFC-SFS can achieves classification accuracy as high as 83% which is more than 20% improvement.

4 Conclusion

In this paper, we propose an automatic classification system that classifies the Korean traditional music into one of six categories. In order to overcome system uncertainty due to the different query patterns, a robust feature optimization method called

MFC-SFS is proposed. Several pattern classification algorithms are tested and compared in terms of the system stability and the classification accuracy. From the comparison statistics on genre classification, we verify the stable and successful classification performance of the proposed algorithm.

Acknowledgment

This work was supported by grant No. R01-2004-000-10122-0 from the Basic Research Program of the Korea Science & Engineering Foundation.

References

1. E. Wold, T. Blum, D. Keislar, and J. Wheaton, "Content-based classification, search, and retrieval of audio," IEEE Multimedia, vol.3, no. 2, 1996.
2. G. Tzanetakis and P. Cook, "Musical genre classification of audio signals," IEEE Trans. on Speech and Audio Processing, vol. 10, no. 5, pp. 293-302, July 2002.
3. T. Li, M. Ogihara and Q. Li, "A comparative study on content-based music genre classification," in Proc. of the 26th annual internal ACM SIGIR, pp. 282-289, ACM Press, July 2003.
4. J. Foote et al, "An overview of audio information retrieval," ACM-Springer Multimedia Systems, vol. 7, no. 1, pp. 2-11, Jan. 1999.
5. R. Duda, P. Hart and D. Stork, Pattern Classification, 2nd Ed., Wiley-Interscience Publication, 2001
6. M. Liu and C. Wan, "A study on content-based classification retrieval of audio database," Proc. of the International Database Engineering & Applications Symposium, pp. 339 - 345. 2001.

A New Re-ranking Method for Generic Chinese Text Summarization and Its Evaluation

Xiaojun Wan and Yuxin Peng[*]

Institute of Computer Science and Technology,
Peking University, Beijing 100871, China
{wanxiaojun, pengyuxin}@icst.pku.edu.cn

Abstract. In this paper a new EMD-MMR (EMD: earth mover's distance; MMR: maximal marginal relevance) re-ranking method is proposed for generic Chinese text summarization. Our extraction-based summarization approach first ranks the sentences in a document by their weight calculated based on word frequency and position, and then re-ranks a few highly weighted sentences by the EMD-MMR method for sentence extraction. The proposed re-ranking method adopts a novel EMD-based similarity metric instead of the Cosine metric into the MMR approach. The EMD-based similarity metric can naturally take into account the semantic relatedness between words and compute the semantic similarity between texts with a many-to-many matching among words. We evaluate the performance of the proposed approach with a novel *nk-blind* method and the results demonstrate its effectiveness.

1 Introduction

Automated generic text summarization has drawn much attention in recent years and a generic summary should contain the main topics of the document while keeping redundancy to a minimum. The summarization methods can be categorized into two categories: extraction-based methods and abstraction-based methods. Extraction is much easier than abstraction because extraction is just to select existing sentences while abstraction needs understanding and rewriting sentences. Extraction-based methods usually assign each sentence a score and then rank the sentences in the document. Statistical and linguistic features, including word frequency, position, cue words, stigma words, topic signature, etc., have been employed for scoring sentence.

Our summarization approach takes two steps to extract summary sentences. In the first step, sentences are ranked by their weight calculated based on word frequency and position, and then a few salient sentences (10 sentences in the experiments) are reserved as candidate sentences. The weight based on word frequency is computed as the sum of the *tf*idf* weights of words in the sentence. The weight based on position is computed with *1-((i-1)/n)*, where *i* is the sequence of the sentence and *n* is the total number of sentences in the document After the above weights are calculated for each sentence, we linearly combine the weights and normalize the sum by the length of the sentence to get the final score. The normalization aims to avoid favoring long sentences.

---

[*] Contact author.

E.A. Fox et al. (Eds.): ICADL 2005, LNCS 3815, pp. 171–175, 2005.
© Springer-Verlag Berlin Heidelberg 2005

The second step is a redundancy-removing process and in this step those candidate salient sentences are re-ranked by the proposed EMD-MMR (EMD: earth mover's distance; MMR: maximal marginal relevance) method and the summary is produced by extracting several top sentences. The EMD-MMR re-ranking method adopts a novel EMD-based similarity metric instead of the Cosine metric into the popular MMR approach [1]. The EMD-based similarity metric can naturally take into account the semantic relatedness between words and get the semantic similarity between texts with a many-to-many matching among words. The EMD-MMR method is described in detail in next section.

2   The EMD-MMR Re-ranking Method

The maximal marginal relevance (MMR) method strives to maximize relevant novelty in summarization. A sentence is selected into the summary as follows:

$$
\text{MMR} \underset{\text{def}}{=} \text{Arg} \max_{s_i \in D \setminus S} \left[\lambda (\text{sim}_1 (s_i, q) - (1 - \lambda) \max_{s_j \in S} \text{sim}_2 (s_i, s_j)) \right], \tag{1}
$$

where q is a query representation; D is the set of sentences in the document; S is the set of sentences in the summary, which is a sub set of D; $D \setminus S$ is the set difference, i.e. the set of as yet unselected sentences in D; sim_1 is the similarity metric for calculating the similarity between the query q and a sentence s_i. sim_2 is the similarity metric for calculating the similarity between two sentences s_i and s_j. λ is a weighting parameter. In the experiments, we use all the occurrences of top 50 words with the largest tf^*idf values in the document as the query representation. The parameter λ is set to 0.7.

The similarity metrics *sim1* and *sim2* are usually the widely-used standard Cosine measure and the terms are weighted by tf^*idf value. Texts are usually represented by a bag of words (or phrase) and then the similarity is calculated between the lists of words. In the Cosine metric, different words are usually assumed to be semantically independent and in the similarity calculation process one word in a text can only be matched to the same word in another text. However, different words could express the same or similar meanings due to the synonym phenomenon. An example of synonyms is the words "cat" and "feline". In Chinese language, "战斗" and "战役" represent almost the same meaning. There is also other semantic relatedness between different words, such as hypernymy/hyponymy, and all these phenomena in natural language argue that words are not independent with each other in reality. Extremely, a text containing one set of words might be semantically similar to another text containing a different set of words. The proposed EMD-based similarity metric can naturally consider the semantic relatedness between words and adopt it into the MMR method for re-ranking. We denote the MMR method with the EMD-based similarity metric as EMD-MMR.

In the EMD-based similarity metric, the semantic distance (the contrary metric of semantic relatedness) between words is required to be calculated and then EMD is employed to measure text similarity with a many-to-many matching among words. In this study, we extracts sense explanation of each word from a Chinese dictionary and builds a feature vector for the word, and then the semantic relatedness s of two words is calculated by applying the Cosine metric on the two vectors. In the feature vector, each word is weighted by *tf*idf*. The semantic distance between the two words is gotten by 1-*s*, which is between 0 and 1. The more "similar" two words are, the smaller the semantic distance is. The semantic distances of all pairs of words in the test document set are calculated beforehand. For example, the semantic distance between "战斗" and "战役" is 0.257, and 0.455 for "战斗" and "战火".

The Earth Mover's Distance (EMD) [2] is a method to evaluate dissimilarity between two multi-dimensional distributions in some feature space where a distance measure between single features, which we call the *ground distance* is given. The EMD "lifts" this distance from individual features to full distributions. Computing the EMD is based on a solution to the well-known transportation problem. In our context, the distributions are the word distributions of texts, and a weighted graph is constructed to model the similarity between two texts, and then the EMD is employed to compute the minimum cost of the weighted graph as the similarity value between two texts. The problem is formalized as follows:

In our context, the distributions are the word distributions of texts, and a weighted graph is constructed to model the similarity between two texts, and then EMD is employed to compute the minimum cost of the weighted graph as the similarity value between two texts. The problem is formalized as follows:

Given two texts *A* and *B*, a weighted graph *G* is constructed as follows:

- Let $A=\{(t_{a1},w_{a1}),(t_{a2},w_{a2}),...,(t_{am},w_{am})\}$ as the representation of text *A*, t_{ai} represents a unique word in text *A* and w_{ai} is the word's *tf*idf* value.
- Let $B=\{(t_{b1},w_{b1}),(t_{b2},w_{b2}),...,(t_{bn},w_{bn})\}$ as the representation of text *B*, t_{bj} represents a unique word in text *B* and w_{bj} is the word's *tf*idf* value.
- Let $D=\{d_{ij}\}$ as the distance matrix where d_{ij} is the semantic distance between words t_{ai} and t_{bj}. In our case, d_{ij} has been computed beforehand.
- Let $G=\{A, B, D\}$ as a weighted graph constructed by *A, B* and *D*. $V=A \cup B$ is the vertex set while $D=\{d_{ij}\}$ is the edge set.

In the weighted graph *G*, we want to find a flow $F=\{f_{ij}\}$, where f_{ij} is the flow between t_{ai} and t_{bj}, that minimizes the overall cost

$$WORK \ (A, B, F) = \sum_{i=1}^{m} \sum_{j=1}^{n} f_{ij} d_{ij} ,$$ (2)

subject to the following constraints:

$$f_{ij} \geq 0 \quad 1 \leq i \leq m \ 1 \leq j \leq n \quad (3) \qquad \sum_{j=1}^{n} f_{ij} \leq w_{ai} \qquad 1 \leq i \leq m \qquad (4)$$

$$\sum_{i=1}^{m} f_{ij} \leq w_{bj} \quad 1 \leq j \leq n \quad (5) \qquad \sum_{i=1}^{m} \sum_{j=1}^{n} f_{ij} = \min\left(\sum_{i=1}^{m} w_{ai}, \sum_{j=1}^{n} w_{bj}\right) \quad (6)$$

Constraint (3) allows moving words from *A* to *B* and not vice versa. Constraint (4) limits the amount of words that can be sent by the words in *A* to their weights. Constraint (5) limits the words in *B* to receive no more words than their weights. Constraint (6) forces to move the maximum amount of words possible. We call this amount the *total flow*. Once the transportation problem is solved, and we have found the optimal flow F, the earth mover's distance is defined as the resulting work normalized by the total flow:

$$EMD\ (A,B) = \frac{\sum_{i=1}^{m} \sum_{j=1}^{n} f_{ij} d_{ij}}{\sum_{i=1}^{m} \sum_{j=1}^{n} f_{ij}} \cdot \qquad (7)$$

The normalization factor is introduced in order to avoid favoring shorter text in the case of partial matching. Finally, the similarity between texts A and B is defined as

$$Sim_{EMD}\ (A,B) = 1 - EMD\ (A,B) \cdot \qquad (8)$$

$Sim_{EMD}(A,B)$ is normalized in the range of [0,1]. The higher the value of $Sim_{EMD}(A,B)$, the more similar the texts A and B.

The above EMD-based similarity metric allows for many-to-many matches among words according to their semantic relatedness. For example, the word "战斗" in text A can match both the words "战役" and "战火" in text B.

Efficient algorithms for the transportation problem are available, which are important to compute EMD efficiently.

4   Evaluation with the *nk-blind* Method

For Chinese document summarization, there are no gold standard data set for evaluation. So we downloaded 30 Chinese news articles from *news.sina.com.cn,* one of the most famous news portals in China, and those articles include political news, sports news and recreational news. Then eight students are employed to extract five sentences from each article and produce a summary for that article. The inter-human agreement between students is low by our analysis. So in fact there is no ideal summary for each document and we cannot evaluate system summaries based on any single annotated summary. The traditional metric for evaluating extraction-based summaries, such as precision and recall, can not be applied directly.

To resolve the issue of low inter-human agreement, we introduce a so-called *nk-blind* method which has been used to evaluate Chinese word segmentation systems [3]. This method is based on an intuitive idea of "majority win". Given a document, n human-annotated summaries (or n judges) were created independently. Then, the system-generated summary is compared against the annotated ones: for each sentence in the system-produced summary, a sentence is considered to be correct if at least k of the n human-annotated summaries contain the sentence. The precision increases with smaller k. If $k=1$, it is sufficient for any judge to sanction a sentence selection. If $k=n$, the sentence must be shared by all human-annotated summaries. Given k, the precision for each system-produced summary is calculated and then the values are averaged across all summaries. So a precision rate can be given under any chosen (n, k) setting under the *nk-blind* method. This result can be plotted as an n-k curve which is similar to p-r curve. We can compare two summarizers via their n-k curves.

In the experiments, those system-produced five-sentence summaries are compared with the human-annotated five-sentence summaries. We use an in-house tool for

Chinese word segmentation. The baseline system is a lead baseline system, which takes the first five sentences in the document as the summary.

All results reported in Figure 1 give the precision values for n=8 judges with all values of k between 1 and n. "w/o re-ranking" means that the system selects top five sentences in the candidate sentence set generated in the first step and produces the summary without the second step. "w/ re-ranking (MMR)" means that the traditional MMR re-ranking method with the Cosine metric is taken to re-rank the candidate sentences and then the summary is produced. "w/ re-ranking (EMD-MMR)" means that the EMD-MMR re-ranking method is taken to re-rank the candidate sentences. Seen from Figure 1, the lead baseline method performs worst. The re-ranking step does benefit the summarization performance in that it can remove redundancy in the summary. The EMD-MMR re-ranking method outperform the traditional MMR re-ranking method, which proves that the EMD-based similarity metric has a better ability to measure semantic similarity between texts than the Cosine metric. The many-to-many matching between words plays the key role for the performance improvement. From human's perspective, someone judges whether two texts are similar enough not by the word occurrences but by the semantic similarity between the texts.

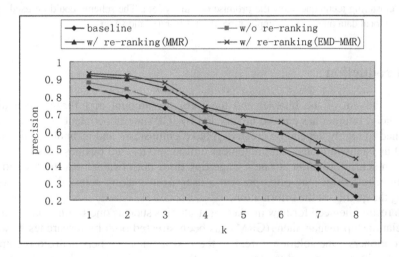

Fig. 1. Comparison of *nk-blind* precisions

References

1. Carbonell, J., Goldstein, J.: The Use of MMR, Diversity-based Reranking for Reordering Documents and Producing Summaries. In Proceedings of SIGIR'98 (1998)
2. Rubner, Y., Tomasi, C. and Guibas, L.: The Earth Mover's Distance as a Metric for Image Retrieval. *Int.* Journal of Computer Vision **40-2** (2000) 99-121
3. Wu, D., Fung, P.: Improving Chinese Tokenization With Linguistic Filters On Statistical Lexical Acquisition. In Proceedings of ANLP'94 (1994) 180-181

A User Classification for Internet Content Provider Based Modified Fuzzy Neural Network

Yunfeng Li and Yukun Cao

Department of Computer Science, Chongqing University, Chongqing, 400044 P.R. China
lyf129@126.com, marilyn_cao@163.com

Abstract. With the explosive growth of the Internet, it has entered the age led by ICP (internet content provider). Helping users to locate relevant information in an efficient manner is very important both do the person and to the ICPs. As such, it is highly desired to have a systematic system for extracting user features effectively, and subsequently, analyzing user orientations quantitatively. The experimental results of this clustering technique show the promise of our system. This paper presents a new approach that employs a modified fuzzy neural network based on adaptive resonance theory to group users dynamically based on their Web access patterns. Such a user clustering method should be performed prior to ICPs as the basis to provide personalized service. The experimental results of this clustering technique show the promise of our system. The scheme could be used in local data management application, digital library, and so on.

1 Introduction

With the advent of the Internet and the web, the amount of information available grows daily. Internet has entered the age led by ICP (internet content provider), which is defined to highly depend on creativity, have enthusiasm and technological capacity as well as bandwidth, and can implement online service and business. However, having too much information at one's fingertips does not always mean high quality information, in fact, it may often prevent a user from making sound decisions, by degrading the quality of the information.

As a result, the need for new marketing strategies such as one-to-one marketing and user relationship management (CRM) has been stressed both by researches as well as by practitioners. One solution to realize these strategies is a personalized recommendation that helps users find the information they would interest in by producing a list of recommended information for each given user. Such understanding of users can be applied to transform user information into quality services or products. However, with the great number of users, how do ICPs identify their interests? The answer to this question is to build personalized Internet services. Personalization, a special form of differentiation, when applied in market fragmentation can transform a standard product or service into a specialized solution for an individual. The user's satisfaction and loyalty can thus be enhanced, and the increase in each user's visiting frequency can further create more transaction opportunities and benefit the ICPs. The purpose of our approach is to group users on the basis of their interests using neural network, what is one of the most important means to build personalized Internet services.

E.A. Fox et al. (Eds.): ICADL 2005, LNCS 3815, pp. 176–185, 2005.
© Springer-Verlag Berlin Heidelberg 2005

In the approach, we presents a framework that dynamically groups users according to their Web access, which consist of the users' behavior on web site. The proposed approach is developed on the basis of neural network, and involves two sequential modules including: (1) trace users' behavior on web site and generate user profiles, (2) classify users according user profile using neural network. In second module, we employ a modified fuzzy ART, that is a kind of adaptive resonance theory neural network. The remainder of the paper is organized as follows. In Section 2, the framework to automatically extract user preference and recommend personalized information is expatiated in detail. Section 3 presents three classifier used in our experiments briefly. Implementation issues and the results of empirical studies are presented in Section 4. Finally, the conclusion can be found in Section 5.

2   A User Cluster Framework

In this section, an on-line user cluster framework is presented, which is performed prior to an Internet bookstore in our experiment. The framework includes three modules: user behavior recording, user profile generating and user grouping.

2.1   User Behavior Recording

Most personalization systems gather user preference through asking visitors a series of questions or needing visitors rating those browsed web pages. Although relevance feedback obtained directly from users may make sense, it is troublesome to users and seldom done. In the paper, we present a user behavior recording module to collect the training data without user intervention through tracking the users behavior on a e-commerce web site. The user behavior includes the browsing time, the view frequency, saving, booking, clicking hyperlinks, scrolling and so on.

According to some relate works, visiting duration of a product pages or images is a good candidate to measure the preference. Hence, in our work, each product page or image, whose visiting time is longer than a preset threshold (e.g. 30 seconds), is analyzed and rated. Periodically (e.g. every day), the module analyzes the activities of the previous period, whose algorithm is shown as follows:

```
BEGIN
If (page category P_i doesn't exist in user log file)
{favorite(P_i)=0;}
For each page a user browsed in page category P_i
   { if (page browsing time) > threshold
       { switch (happened operation)
           { case  (saving, booking operation happened):
                 favorite(P_i)= favorite(P_i)+0.03;break;
             case  (page-view frequency>threshold):
                 favorite(P_i)= favorite(P_i)+0.02;break;
```

```
            case   (clicking, scrolling operation hap-
   pened):
                     favorite(P_i)= favorite(P_i)+0.01;break;  }
      }

   }
   updating favorite(P_i) in User Log file;
   END
```

where the function *favorite(P_i)* measures the favorite degree of a certain page category in a ICP web site, and the record in user log file is shown as follows: *page-id,
category, favorite*. The *category* element is the category path of a resource, what is a
path from the root to the assigned category according the hierarchical structure of
Internet bookstore. For example, in a Internet bookstore, "JavaBean" category is a
subclass of "Java" category, "Java" category is a subclass of "Programming" category, and "Programming" category is a subclass of "Computer & Internet" category,
then the category path of the pages or images belonging to "JavaBean" is
"/JavaBean/Java/Programming/Computer&Internet".

2.2 User Profile Generate (Generator)

In this approach, we employ a tree-structured scheme to represent user profile, with
which users specify their preference. Generator could organize user preference in a
hierarchical structure according the result of Recorder and adjust the structure to the
changes of user interests. User profile is a category hierarchy where each category
represents the knowledge of a domain of user interests, which could easily and precisely express user's preference. The profile enhances the semantic of user interests
and is much closer to a human conception. The logical structure of the preference tree
is shown as follows:

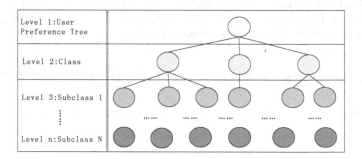

Fig. 1. The Logical Structure of User profile

User profile is established according the hierarchical structure of a certain
e-commerce web site. It means the number of levels and the categories in the profile
are similar with the web site. Each node in the tree, representing a category might be
interested in, is described by an energy value E_i what indicates the favorableness of a

page category. E_i controls the life cycle of a category in a profile. The energy increases when users show interest in the page category, and it decreases for a constant value for a period of time. Relatively, categories that receive few interest will be abstracted gradually and finally die out. Based on the energy values of categories, the structure of user profile can be modulated as users interests change. The algorithm is shown as follows:

```
BEGIN
  for each (page cagetory P_i in user log file f)
  { inserting(P_i);
    if ( Energy E_i of P_i) >1 { E_i =1; }
  }
  if (the days from the last updating) > threshold {up-
dating(f)}
  END
```

To construct user profile, we employ two Functions: *inserting* and *updating*. The inserting operation is utilized to insert new categories into a profile and adjust the energy values of existing categories. The updating operation is utilized to remove those categories users don't interest anymore. The two operation just like planting a new kind flower and pruning for a plant in a garden. And we must keep the energy value from 0 to 1, what is expected by A MODIFIED FUZZY ART neural network.

2.2.1 Inserting

The User Log File mentioned in section 3.1 is considered as the basis of inserting operation to construct the user profile. For each page in a log file, we first check if the category of the product exists in the preference tree. If the category exists, the *energy* value of the category should be refreshed. If the category does not exist, we will create the category in user profile, whose *energy* is the value of *favorite*. Then the *energy* value of the new node should be calculated. The following method is used to calculate the new energy value of each category:

$$E_i = \frac{\sum_{p \in P_i^{new}} W_{p,i}}{|P_i^{new}|} + \lambda \times E_i \tag{1}$$

where E_i is the energy value of page category C_i, P_i^{new} is the set of the pages assigned to the category C_i in user log file , the absolute value $|P_i^{new}|$ is the number of products in P_i^{new}, and $W_{p,i}$ is the *favorite* of the product p. The parameter λ, called *decaying factor*, is set from 0 to 1, hence the older records have less effects to the representation of category. In our experiment, λ is assigned to 0.98.

2.2.2 Updating

Since user interests often change, it is important to adjust the user profile incrementally, in order to represent user interests accurately. In discussion of the changes of user interests, it is found that there are two types of the user interests. One is the long-term interest and the other is the short-term interest. The long-term interest often reflects a real user interest. Relatively, the short-term interest is usually caused by a hot products event and vanishes quickly. The updating operation is designed to adjust the part reflecting user short-term interests.

In contrast to the inserting operation that adds the new interesting categories into user profile, the updating operation is the mechanism to remove the out-of-favor categories. Categories with a continual attention can continuously live, otherwise, they will become weak and finally die out. In user preference, every category's energy value should be reduced a predefined value ψ periodically (e.g. 15 days). The parameter ψ, called *aging factor*, is used to control the reduction rate. In the experiment, ψ is assigned to 0.90.

When no or few products browsed in a category, its energy value will decline gradually. If a category's energy value is less than (or equal to) a pre-defined threshold, we remove the category from user preference tree. To keep a personal view on part to the trend of user interest, categories with low energy value are removed.

2.3 User Cluster (Cluster)

User cluster could group users into different teams according their profiles using adaptive neural network. Nowadays, there are various approaches to cluster analysis, including multivariate statistical method, artificial neural network, and other algorithms. However, some of the methods like self-organizing map algorithm implies some constraints: the need to choose the number of clusters a priori, heavier computational complexity and merging the groups representing the same cluster, because the SOM, by approximating the distribution patterns, finds more than one group representing the same cluster. Moreover, successive SOM results depend on the training phase and this implies the choice of representative training examples. For this reason, we employ a modified fuzzy ART, one of the clustering methods using neural network, for cluster analysis.

The Fuzzy ART [9] network is an unsupervised neural network with ART architecture for performing both continuous-valued vectors and binary-valued vectors. It is a pure winner-takes-all architecture able to instance output nodes whenever necessary and to handle both binary and analog patterns. Using a 'Vigilance parameter' as a threshold of similarity, Fuzzy ART can determine when to form a new cluster. This algorithm uses an unsupervised learning and feedback network. It accepts and input vector and classifies it into one of a number of clusters depending upon which it best resembles. The single recognition layer that fires indicates its classification decision. It the input vector does not match any stored pattern, it creates a pattern that is like the input vector as a new category. Once a stored pattern is found that matches the input vector within a specified threshold (the vigilance $\rho \in [0,1]$), that pattern is adjusted to make it accommodate the new input vector. The adjective fuzzy derives from the functions it uses, although it is not actually fuzzy. To perform data clustering, fuzzy ART instances the first cluster coinciding with the first input and allocating new groups when necessary (in particular, each output node represents a cluster from a group). In the paper, we employ a modified Fuzzy ART proposed by Cinque al. [10] to solve some problems of traditional Fuzzy ART [10,11]. The algorithm is shown as follows:

```
BEGIN
For each (input vector V_i)
 { for each (exist cluster C_i) {C*=argmax(choice(C_i,V_i));}
   if match(C*,V_i)⩾ρ {adaptation(C*,V_i);}
   else { Instance a new cluster; }
 }
END
```

Function *choice* used in the algorithm is the following:

$$choice\ (C_j, V_i) = \frac{(|C_j \wedge V_i|)^2}{|C_j| \cdot |V_i|} = \frac{(\sum_{r=1}^{n} z_r)^2}{\sum_{r=1}^{n} c_r \cdot \sum_{r=1}^{n} v_r} \tag{2}$$

It computes the compatibility between a cluster and an input to find a cluster with greatest compatibility. The input pattern V_i is an n-elements vector transposed, C_j is the weight vector of cluster J (both are n-dimensional vectors). "$\wedge$" is fuzzy set intersection operator, which is defined by:

$$x \wedge y = \min\{x, y\}$$
$$X \wedge Y = (x_1 \wedge y_1, \cdots, x_n \wedge y_n) = (z_1, z_2, \cdots, z_n) \tag{3}$$

Function *match* is the following:

$$match\ (C^*, V_i) = \frac{|C^* \wedge V_i|}{|C^*|} = \frac{\sum_{r=1}^{n} z_r}{\sum_{r=1}^{n} c_r^*} \tag{4}$$

This computes the similarity between the input and the selected cluster. The *match* process is passed if this value is greater than, or equal to, the vigilance parameter $\rho \in [0,1]$. Intuitively, ρ indicates how similar the input has to be to the selected cluster to allow it to be associated with the user group the cluster represents. As a consequence, a greater value of ρ implies smaller clusters, a lower value means wider clusters.

Function *adaptation* is the selected cluster adjusting function, which algorithm is shown as following:

$$adaptation\ (C^*, V_i) = C_{new}^* = \beta(C_{old}^* \wedge V_i) + (1 - \beta)C_{old}^* \tag{5}$$

Where the learning parameter $\beta \in [0,1]$, weights the new and old knowledge respectively. It is worth observing that this function is not increasing, that is $C_{new}^* < C_{old}^*$.

In the study, the energy values of all leaf nodes in a user profile consist an *n-elements* vector representing a user pattern. Each element of the vector represents a product category. If a certain product category doesn't include in user profile, the corresponding element in the vector is assigned to 0. Pre-processing is required to ensure the pattern values in the space [0,1], as expected by the fuzzy ART.

3 Other Classifiers Used in Our Experiments

To verify our proposed system, we built traditional fuzzy ART, k-means, and SOM classifier. In this section, these classifiers are briefly described.

3.1 Traditional Fuzzy ART

Adaptive resonance theory (ART) describes a family of self-organizing neural networks, capable of clustering arbitrary sequences of input patterns into stable recognition codes. Many different types of ART networks have been developed to improve clustering capabilities, including ART1, ART2, ART2A, and fuzzy ART etc. The modified fuzzy ART presented in the paper is similar with traditional fuzzy ART, but employs different *choice* function. The choice function utilized in traditional fuzzy ART is as following:

$$choice \ (C_j, V_i) = \frac{|C_j \wedge V_i|}{\alpha + |V_i|} = \frac{(\sum_{r=1}^{n} z_r)}{\alpha + \sum_{r=1}^{n} v_r} \tag{6}$$

Where α is choice parameter providing a floating point overflow. Simulations in this paper are performed with a value of $\alpha \approx 0$.

3.2 K-Means Algorithm

K-means is one of the simplest unsupervised learning algorithms that solve the well known clustering problem. The main idea is to define k centroids, one for each cluster. These centroids shoud be placed in a cunning way because of different location causes different result. So, the better choice is to place them as much as possible far away from each other. The next step is to take each point belonging to a given data set and associate it to the nearest centroid. When no point is pending, the first step is completed and an early groupage is done. At this point we need to re-calculate k new centroids as barycenters of the clusters resulting from the previous step. After we have these k new centroids, a new binding has to be done between the same data set points and the nearest new centroid. A loop has been generated. As a result of this loop we may notice that the k centroids change their location step by step until no more changes are done. In other words centroids do not move any more. Finally, this algorithm aims at minimizing an *objective function*, in this case a squared error function. The objective function is given by:

$$J = \sum_{j=1}^{k} \sum_{i=1}^{n} \left\| x_i^{(j)} - c_j \right\|^2 \tag{7}$$

where $\left\| x_i^{(j)} - c_j \right\|^2$ is a chosen distance measure between a data point $x_i^{(j)}$ and the cluster centre c_j, is an indicator of the distance of the n data points from their respective cluster centres.

3.3 Self-organizing Maps

The self-organizing maps or Kohonen's feature maps are feedforward, competitive ANN that employ a layer of input neurons and a single computational layer. Let us denote by y the set of vector-valued observations, $y = [y_1, y_2, ..., y_m]^T$, the weight vector of the neuron j in SOM is $w_j = [w_{j1}, w_{j2}, ..., w_{jm}]^T$. Due to its competitive nature, the SOM algorithm identifies the best-matching, winning reference vector w_i (or winner for short), to a specific feature vector y with respect to a certain distance metric. The index i of the winning reference vector is given by:

$$i(y) = \arg \min_j \{ \| y - w_j \| \}, \quad j = 1, 2, ..., \quad n \tag{8}$$

where n is the number of neurons in the SOM, $\|\cdot\|$ denotes the Euclidean distance.

The reference vector of the winner as well as the reference vectors of the neurons in its neighborhood are modified using:

$$w_i(t+1) = w_i(n) + \Lambda_{i,j}(t)[x(t) - w_i(t)], \quad t = 1,2,3,... \tag{9}$$

Where $\Lambda_{i,j}(t)$ is a neighourhood function, t is a discrete time constant. The extent of the neighbourhood is the radius and learning rate contribution, which should both decrease monotonically with time to allow convergence. The radius is simply the maximum distance at which the nodes from the winner are affected. A typical smooth Gaussian neighbourhood kernel is given bellow in equation (10).

$$\Lambda_{i,j}(t) = \alpha(t) \cdot \exp \left(- \frac{\| r_i - r_j \|^2}{2\sigma(t)} \right) \tag{10}$$

where $\alpha(t)$ is the learning rate function, $\sigma(t)$ is the kernel width function, $\| r_i - r_j \|^2$ is the distance of BMU i unit to current unit j. For further details about the SOM please refer to [12] and [13].

4 Experiment

In the experiment, we construct an experimental web site and the proposed framework utilizing Java servlet and Java bean. The trial simulated 45 users behavior on an experiment Internet bookstore over a 30-day period, and they were pre-grouped 15 groups. The experimental web site is organized in a 4-level hierarchy that consists of 4 classes and 50 subclasses, including 5847 book pages and images obtained from www. Amazon.com. As performance measures, we employed the standard information retrieval measures of recall (r), precision (p), and F1($F1=2rp/(r+p)$). Traditional fuzzy ART was simulated by an original implementation. It was used in the fast learning asset (with $\beta =1$) with α set to zero. Values for the vigilance parameter ρ were found by trials. In the simulation of k-means, parameter K representing the number of clusters is assigned to 7 by trials. In particular, we used a rectangular map with two training stages: the first was made in 750 steps, with 0.93 as a learning parameter and a half map as a neighborhood, and the second in 300 steps, with 0.011 as a learning parameter and three units as a neighborhood. Map size was chosen by experiments. In the proposed system, decaying factor λ is assigned to 0.95, aging factor ψ is set to 0.03, β is set to 1, and vigilance parameter ρ is assigned to 0.96 by trials. With the growth of vigilance parameter, the amount of clusters is increased too.

Figure 2 illustrates the comparisons of three algorithms mentioned before, including precision, recall and F1. The average for precision, recall and F1 measures using the SOM classifier are 81.7%, 78.3%, 79.9%, respectively. The average for precision, recall and F1 measures using the traditional fuzzy ART classifier are 87.3%, 84.8%, 86%, respectively. And the average for precision, recall and F1 measures using the k-means classifier are81.6%, 76.9%, 79.2%, respectively. In comparison with the proposed system, the precision, recall, and F1 measures are 92.3%, 88.1%, 90.15%, respectively. This indicates that if the parameters are selected carefully, the proposed framework could group users pattern accurately.

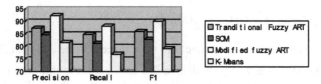

Fig. 2. The comparison of SOM, tranditional ART and modified fuzzy ART algorithm

5 Conclusions

In this paper, we have presented a new framework to automatically track user access patterns on an Internet commerce web site and group users using an adaptive neural network. Our approach, essentially based on neural network computation, i.e., learning capacity, satisfies some of its main requirements: fast results, fault and noise tolerance. A pattern grouping module totally independent of the application was also proposed. The cluster system made up of the modified fuzzy ART and the user pattern track module, was very simple to use. As such system does not use specific knowledge, by adopting the most proper operators, it becomes possible to customize it to different scenarios.

References

1. Brooks C.: Linear and non-Linear forecastability of high-frequency exchange rates, J Forecast, Vol. 16 (1997), pp. 125-145
2. Chen CH, Khoo LP: Multicultural factors evaluation on elicited user requirements for product concept development, Proceedings of 16th Interneational Conference for Production Research (ICPR-16), July 29-August 3 2001, pp. 15-23
3. Yan W, Chen CH: A radial basis function neural network multicultural factors evaluation engine for product concept development, Expert System, Vol. 18(5), (2001), pp.219-232
4. Cotrell M, Girard B: Forcasting of curves using a Kohonen classification. J Forecast, Vol. 17, (1998), pp. 429-439

5. Curry B, Davies F: The Kohonen self-organizing map: an application to the study of strategic groups in the UK hotel industry, Expert System, Vol. 18(1), (2002), pp. 19-30
6. Sang Chul Lee, Yung Ho Suh: A cross-national market segmentation of online game industry using SOM, Expert Systems with Application, Vol. 27, (2004), pp. 559-570
7. Santosb K. Rangarajan, Vir V. Pboba: Adaptive Neural Network Clustering of Web Users, Computer, Vol. 4, (2004), pp.34-40
8. Tung-Lai Hu, Jiuh-Biing Sheu: A fuzzy-based user classification method for demand-responsive logistical distribution operations, Fuzzy Sets and System, Vol. 139, (2003), pp. 431-450
9. G.A. Carpenter: Fuzzy ART: fast stable learning and categorization of analog patterns by an adaptive resonance system, Neural Networks, Vol. 4, (1991), 759-771
10. L. Cinque, G. Foresti: A clustering fuzzy approach for image segmentation, Pattern Recognition, Vol. 37, (2004), pp.1797-1807
11. A. Baraldi, E. Alpaydm: Simplified ART: a new class of ART algorithms, International Computer Science Institute, Berkeley CA,1998
12. Teuvo Kohonen: Self-Organizing Maps, Second Extended Edition. Springer Series in Information Sciences, Vol. 30, Berlin, Heidelberg, New York, (1997)
13. S. Haykin: Neural Networks: A Comprehensive Foundation (2nd Edition). Prentice Hall, (1999)

Eyes of a Wiki: Automated Navigation Map

Hee-Seop Han and Hyeoncheol Kim

Korea University,
Dept. of Computer Science Education, College of Education,
Anam-dong Sungbuk-ku, Seoul 136-701, Korea
anemon@korea.com, hkim@comedu.korea.ac.kr

Abstract. There are many potential uses of a Wiki within a community-based digital library. Users share individual ideas to build up community knowledge by efficient and effective collaborative authoring and communications that a Wiki provides. In our study, we investigated how the community knowledge is organized into a knowledge structure that users can access and modify efficiently. Since a Wiki provides users with freedom of editing any pages, a Wiki site increases and changes dynamically. We also developed a tool that helps users to navigate easily in the dynamically changing link structure. In our experiment, it is shown that the navigation tool fosters Wiki users to figure out the complex site structure more easily and thus to build up more well-structured community knowledge base. We also show that a Wiki with the navigation tool improves collaborative learning in a web-based e-learning environment.

1   Introduction

There have been discussions on potential uses of a Wiki within a digital library, such as a knowledge base system, a web site content editing tool and a content management system [3]. The Wikipedia is a good example that shows how users can build up a community-based digital library efficiently and effectively[http://en.wikipedia.org/wiki/Wiki]. Wiki is a simple yet powerful web-based collaboration platform where users can edit any existing pages and add new pages[1][2]. Since it provides a transparent way for users to publish and exchange their ideas with others over the web and fosters information flows within an organization, it has been used for collaborative e-learning environment as well as collaborative works.

In this article, we address how a Wiki way of knowledge management approach fosters collaborative learning experience for learners on distributed e-learning environment. The first impression of Wiki to learners is, however, usually of chaos [6]. Since every participants in the wiki can edit pages and make new links asynchronously and independently, complexity of the hypertext structure increases and thus it might turn out to be chaos to learners. We developed an automated navigation tool embedded in the Wiki which lets you know where you are and recommends you where to go. The navigation map changes dynamically as you hop the hyper-linked pages. It would let you navigate the

E.A. Fox et al. (Eds.): ICADL 2005, LNCS 3815, pp. 186–193, 2005.
© Springer-Verlag Berlin Heidelberg 2005

hyper-link forest with ease and fun, instead of being lost in the chaos. This paper describes architecture of the automated navigation embedded in Wiki and its effectiveness for collaborative learning. To evaluate the effectiveness, we experimented controlled tests between a Wiki with the navigation tool and a Wiki without it.

2 A Wiki-Based Community Knowledge Base

Mutual interaction among community users creates a community knowledge. A Wiki fosters a community knowledge construction by its two features: freedom to edit any existing pages and freedom to create new pages linked to existing pages. Therefore users can contribute their knowledge to a community knowledge construction in two different ways: by editing existing pages and by creating new pages linked to existing pages.

- Knowledge of a user A is represented in a page. By a user B editing the page, knowledge of user A and B is mixed and represented in the page. By a number of users editing the same page, their knowledge interacts each other resulting in a community knowledge agreed. Thus a Wiki's function of user editing of existing pages plays an important role in construction of a community knowledge.
- Users can contribute their knowledge by creating new pages. By linking the new pages to existing page structure, the user knowledge can be incorporated into a community knowledge structure.

In our previous studies, we investigated how community users interact their ideas with others in a Wiki page. In an experiment of a team-based foreign language translation project, it was shown that the knowledge of team members interacts heavily for agreement of translated terms and context [4]. Final output showed a well-translated article agreed by all users participated, which is a team knowledge. Another experiment of writing relay novel was performed to see how the interactivity in a Wiki improves individual user knowledge [5]. Range of imagination and vocabulary was enriched by the interactivity.

In this paper, we investigate how the creation of new pages contribute a community knowledge structure. In a Wiki, any users can create new pages by linking them to existing pages. It generates different level of knowledge interaction from editing pages. Users create a new page when they want to add their knowledge associated to an existing one. The linked structure of a Wiki site represents a community knowledge base. The link is made by individual users independently. In order to creating new pages, users need to figure out existing linked structure of community knowledge before he add new pages to it. However, the linked structure of a Wiki is very complex and changing dynamically. Thus, we developed an automated navigation tool embedded in a Wiki so that users can figure out the linked structure easily. In this paper, we experimented to see whether the Wiki with navigation tools encourages community users to build up community knowledge structure more effectively and efficiently.

3   Navigation Map in a Wiki

3.1   Link Structure and Page Types

Front page is the entry point in a Wiki that users access. From the front page, pages are created non-linearly by hyperlinks. Users access any page to modify knowledge or create new linked pages from the page. Since all the users are free to create and modify the linked pages, the structure gets more complex and users have difficulty to access or organize the knowledge structure. From the

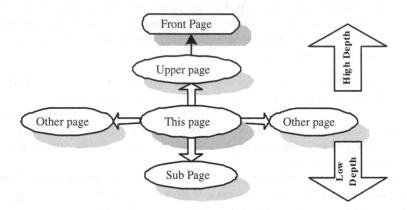

Fig. 1. Three types of browsing

current page that users work on, we defined three types of Wiki pages: *Upper, This&Others* and *Sub.* Users at *This* page can move to one of the three directions as illustrated in Figure 1. *Upper* pages contain more general (i.e., super) topic associated to current page topic, and *This&Others* page are associated to the same super topic, but contain different information. *Sub* pages provide more detailed information on current page topic. Navigation interface is shown in Figure 2 where Wiki pages belong to one of the three types. The number next to page name represents its relevance value to current page, which plays as a clue for users to decide where to navigate. We call it as a relevance score. Figure 3 illustrates an example of linked structure. A Line with arrow represents hyperlink with two types: a dotted line and a solid line. The solid lines are related to three page types: *UpperPage, This&OtherPage* and *SubPage. Upper* pages are the pages with links to *This* page like the black circle number 1 and 2. *Other* pages are the pages with links from the *Upper* pages like the number 5 and 6. Both *This* page and *Other* page have links from same *Upper* pages. The sub pages of *Other* page like the number 7 and 8 are not shown in our navigation map, but they are used to calculate the relevance score of *Other* page. *Sub* pages are just pages that are connected from *ThisPage* like the number 3. The links like number 4 are used to calculate the relevance score of *Sub* page.

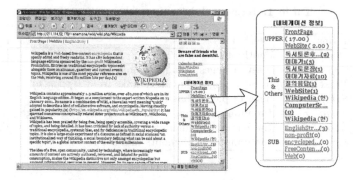

Fig. 2. Navigation Interface in Wiki Page

3.2   Relevance Scores

Our navigation map provides the three types of pages in separate boxes as in Figure 2. For each type, pages in the type are listed descending order according to their relevance scores. The idea of relevance score is based on the assumption that users want to move to the pages with more information related to the current page. Users navigate *Upper* pages to find different information but similar topic category. Notice that all the *Upper* pages have links to current page. Any *Upper* page with more linked-pages might provide users with more information related to current page. Users want to navigate to *Other* pages to find more information related to current page or new information with same depth level. In the similar manner, Users want to find more detailed information from *Sub* pages. Thus, we give more score to the pages with more links among the pages of a same type. From a viewpoint of a current page c in the browser, $Score(p_k)$, relevance score of a page p_k, is defined as follows:

$$
Score(p_k) = \begin{cases} \dfrac{\sum_{i=1}^{Size(Upper(c))} Npage(p_i)}{Depth(p_k)} + Npage(p_k), & \text{if } p_{i,k} \in Upper(c), \\[3ex] \dfrac{Nlink(p_k)}{\sum_{i=1}^{Size(ThisOther(c))} Nlink(p_i)}, & \text{if } p_{i,k} \in ThisOther(c), \\[3ex] \dfrac{Nlink(p_k)}{\sum_{i=1}^{Size(Sub(c))} Nlink(p_i)}, & \text{if } p_{i,k} \in Sub(c). \end{cases}
$$

The terms used in the equation are defined in Table 1.

4   Observation and Result

4.1   Experiment Design

We expected the navigation map to assist students to figure out complex structure of wiki-based site and to organize their collaborative knowledge better. In our experiments, hypertext structures of a Wiki that students had worked on were analyzed.

Table 1. Terms and definitions used in $Score(p)$

Terms	Definitions
$Depth(p)$	depth of page p
$Upper(p)$	a set of pages that have links to the page p
$ThisOther(p)$	a set of pages that have links from $Upper(p)$
$Sub(p)$	a set of pages that have links from page p
$Npage(p)$	the number of pages that have links from page p
$Nlink(p)$	the number of links in page p
$Size(A)$	the number of elements in a set A

Two groups of undergraduate students participated in our experiments. Group I of 37 students (male:12, female:25) used the Wiki with navigation map, and group II of 38 students (male:13, female:25) used the normal Wiki. A team-based activity was assigned to each team composed of three or four students. Goal of the activity is to develop a team-based Wiki site (i.e., a group knowledge base) on computer science subjects. Participants had never learned the topic before. The activity consists of two tasks as follows:

1. Each student collects related contents from internet and publish three or more pages in a Wiki.
2. They construct a knowledge map of the collected materials in just one public page.

Process of the activity is illustrated in Figure 4.

The activity lasted three weeks and we tracked all the navigation pathes of every participants to observe knowledge changes and user navigation patterns. We estimated participants' comprehension of knowledge map by letting them draw the map individually.

4.2   Experimental Results

As a result of the activities, group I and II generated 214 pages and 254 pages, respectively. The difference is actually not meaningful because it comes from just typing of related URL or uploading of related files instead of creating new pages. Results of tracking participants' event-reading, modification and creation were stored 15308 rows for group I, and 15331 rows for group II into DB. Which tells that participation degree is very similar each other. We also investigated the participation degree of each individual student and the individual participation was good enough. However, the two groups shows differences in several factors as shown in Table 2. We summarize the experimental results with two viewpoints as follows:

Complexity of the Group Knowledge Structure. Even though the number of pages are similar, a normal Wiki has simpler structure than the one with a navigation map. For example, depth of the linked structure in normal Wiki is 3 while it is 6 in the Wiki with a navigation map. It is because normal Wiki

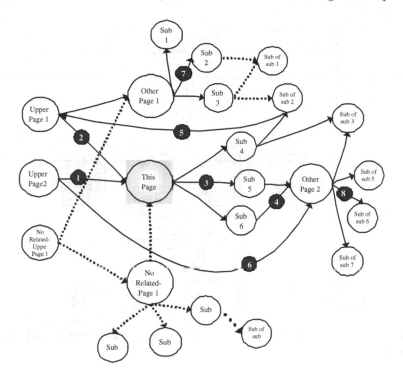

Fig. 3. Example of Linked Structure

users feel uncomfortable to construct a more complex structure. They also tried to gather links in just one page whenever it is possible, and therefore they tend to express the structure of knowledge not by links, but by paragraph in one page. The number of crosslinks in the Wiki with a navigation map is obviously larger than the one in the normal Wiki. Thus, similar number of pages are organized quite differently with different complexity of linked structures. We can conclude that the group knowledge structure with the navigation map is more well organized with necessary complexity.

Understandability of the Group Knowledge Structure. Crosslink can be another clue that shows how well users understand the linked structure of their Wiki site. In a normal Wiki, most of the crosslinks are just simple links

Table 2. Summary of experimental results

Factors	Wiki with navigation map	Normal Wiki
Depth starting from Front Page	6	3
The Number of Cross-Links	A lot(74/328)	Little(7/296)
User Response	Interesting	Difficulty(path finding)

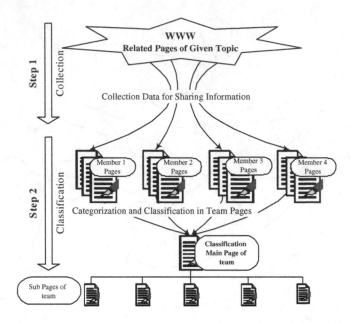

Fig. 4. Experimental activities. Four students in a team collect contents and construct a team Wiki site.

to the front pages or members' pages where users visit frequently. In a Wiki with navigation map, however, many meaningful crosslinks between inner pages have been found, which indicates that users in the Wiki have good understanding about the pages in the whole linked structure. From the difference of the number of crosslinks in Table 2, it is obvious that navigation map helps users to grasp the linked structure with ease. Responses from normal Wiki users tell that it was difficult for them to find pathes and to navigate in the complex unlinear link structure, while navigation map users tells that the tool was very useful during the team-based activity.

5   Conclusion

A Wiki has great potential for collaborative learning in distributed environment. Community knowledge linked in non-linear hypertext is changed as anyone can create, edit and modify the knowledge and links. To make the Wiki to be a more effective learning tool, we developed the navigation map which guides learners not to get lost in the Wiki's structural chaos. The navigation map shows learners where they are and where they can find more information associated to the current page in the complex structure of a Wiki. Experimental results show that it helped learners to understand linked structures of pages, and thus to access pages more easily and to organize group knowledge more efficiently. Wiki with the automated navigation map makes wiki-based collaborative learning more easy and effective for learners. The wiki site implemented with the experimental navigation map is open at http://ini.korea.ac.kr/~anemone/wiki01/wiki.php.

References

1. A. L. Burrow. Negotiating access within wiki. *Proceedings of the fifteenth ACM conference*, pages 77–86, August 2004.
2. W. Cunningham. Wiki design principles. *Portland Pattern Repository*, November 2003.
3. J. Frumkin. The wiki and the digital library. *OCLC Systems & Services*, 21(1):18–22, 2005.
4. J.-J. Kim and H. Kim. Interactivity in the wiki-based learning environment. In *Proceedings of the 14th KACE Winter conference*, pages 236–241. Korean Association of Computer Education, 2005.
5. Y.-J. Kim and H. Kim. Wiki can develop creative imagination -case of relay writing-. In *Proceedings of the 14th KACE Winter conference*, pages 78–84. Korean Association of Computer Education, 2005.
6. R. E. Raygan and D. G. Green. Internet collaboration: Twiki. In *Proceedings IEEE SoutheastCon 2002*, pages 137–141. IEEE, 2002.

A Collaborative Filtering Based Re-ranking Strategy for Search in Digital Libraries

U. Rohini[1] and Vamshi Ambati[2]

[1] International Institute of Information Technology,
Hyderabad, India
rohini@research.iiit.ac.in
[2] Institute for Software Research International, Carnegie Mellon University
Forbes Avenue, PA, USA
vamshi@cmu.edu

Abstract. Users of a digital book library system typically interact with the system to search for books by querying on the meta data describing the books or to search for information in the pages of a book by querying using one or more keywords. In either cases, a large volume of results are returned of which, the results relevant to the user are not often among the top few. Re-ranking of the search results according to the user's interest based on his relevance feedback, has received wide attention in information retrieval. Also, recent work in collaborative filtering and information retrieval has shown that sharing of search experiences among users having similar interests, typically called a community, reduces the effort put in by any given user in retrieving the exact information of interest. In this paper, we propose a collaborative filtering based re-ranking strategy for the search processes in a digital library system. Our approach is to learn a user profile representing user's interests using Machine Learning techniques and to re-rank the search results based on collaborative filtering techniques. In particular, we investigate the use of Support Vector Machines(SVMs) and k-Nearest Neighbour methods (kNN) for the task of classification. We also apply this approach to a large scale online Digital Library System and present the results of our evaluation.

1 Introduction

Digital Libraries(DLs) have received wide attention in the recent years allowing access of digital information from anywhere across the world, providing additional services typically not available in a traditional digital library. Examples include alerting services and recommendation, search facilities, [4] [13] and others. Earlier work on DLs has focused more on making digital content available to a generic user. With the tremendous progress achieved, DLs should now move from serving a generic user to customizing and adapting to a specific user's interests [8][2][6].

In practice, users in a information resource, use the same resource over and over to gather the required information. But, the time consuming effort put in

E.A. Fox et al. (Eds.): ICADL 2005, LNCS 3815, pp. 194–203, 2005.
© Springer-Verlag Berlin Heidelberg 2005

searching the resource is often forgotten and lost. Hence it requires a repetition of the manual labor of searching and browsing, every time the information is accessed. This can be avoided if the system learns the user's needs from his interactions with the system and adapts to his requirements. Though the complete set of interests of a user usually differs from any other user, there is a great possibility of overlap of interests among the users if the information in the information source matches their requirements, expectations and motivation. Hence, users benefit by sharing information, experiences and awareness eventually evolving into a community, a group of people who share common interests. Such sharing of information has been widely used in collaborative filtering methods. These methods became popular for recommending news [14], audio CDs[18], movies [1] music, research papers [11] etc. Recommendations to a particular user are typically computed using the feedback namely in the form of item ratings taken from the other users in the communit y. It is advantageous if the users in a DL can collaborate in a similar way and share the information. This could save the laborious effort put by a user in finding the book to a great extent.

Users in a digital library search for books by querying on the meta data of the book, called 'Meta data Search' or search for information in the pages of the book by querying using keywords, called 'Content Search'. Due to the myriad of information available, search engines in a digital library that perform the afore mentioned searches, often return a huge list of results. Though these results might contain the query terms, the results are not necessarily relevant to the user and are often not presented in the order of relevance to the user. Re-ranking the results to contain the most relevant documents on the top is useful and is a well known problem in the area of information retrieval. We aim to improve the relevance of the results to a given user by re-ranking them using the profiles of the given user and other users in the community he belongs to. A user profile is a representation of the interests of the user. It is learned from the user's interactions with the digital library system. In the case of meta data search it is built from the ratings of the books that the user provides explicitly. While in the case of content search, it is built from the content of the pages that have been judged as relevant by the user.

The rest of the paper is organized as follows. Section 2 discusses the related work on digital libraries, Section 3 discusses the system and the proposed re-ranking strategy in detail, Section 4 discusses our Experimental Setup and presents our preliminary Evaluation Results. Section5 presents the Conclusions on our work also briefing our future work.

2   Related Work

Earlier work on collaboration in DL concentrated on providing alerting services [4], customizable and personalized arrangement of folders in which the Digital library Objects(DLOs) are stored, sharing of these folders and group recommendations based on organization of the DLOs in folders [13], additionally recommending users [19]. PASS[2] provided personalized service in a Digital Library by

---

[1] http://movielens.umn.edu/

computing similarity between user profiles and documents in a pre-classified research domain. The system described in [6] emphasized collaborative functions of DLs by grouping users based on their profiles. [15] discusses a number of hybrid approaches combining collaborative and content based methods for recommending research papers to users in a digital library of research papers like CiteSeer[2]. [10] describes an approach for personalized search exclusively for a medical digital library by re-ranking the search results using modified cosine similarity.

The objective of this work is to reduce the user's effort in two search processes in a digital library namely the meta data search and the content search. We believe that this will greatly improve the user's search experience in a DL. We approach this by providing customized results to the user by filtering and re-arranging the search results. We investigate the use of collaborative filtering based methods and machine learning techniques for the same. In particular we apply techniques like K-Nearest Neighbor (kNN) and Support Vector machines (SVMs). kNN methods has been very popular in collaborative filtering [3] for finding user and item similarities. SVMs are a popular classification technique backing in statistical theory[20]. It has been applied with great success in various text applications like text classification[21][9], web pages classification and others. Recently, they have been used for Text Retrieval[5] and achieved performance comparable and even better than the traditional approaches [16][7][17].

3   The Proposed Approach

In this section we describe the re-ranking approach and also show how it is applied to an online digital library system to enhance the search process in it. Re-ranking of search results typically involves calculating and assigning a score to the search results returned by a search engine, using the profile of the particular user built from his feedback. However due to the large multitude of data present in today's DLs, it is not possible for a user to provide feedback to at least a significant proportion of them. Hence usage of a community to share across the relevance feedback becomes crucial and useful. The interests of a user regarding the books is learned in a phase called profile learning through the ratings of the books provided by the user. We apply this approach to digital libraries. As mentioned earlier, users of a digital library search for books by querying on the meta data of the book, or search for information in the pages of the book by querying using keywords. The meta data search in a digital library returns books which the user could then provide feedback by rating them. This profile is the user's MS-Profile. However, the same profile can not be used to decide the relevance of information on a page during a content search. Because, search results in the case of meta data search are books and in content search it is a page in the book. The relevance of a page merely talks about interest of some facts or pieces of information in the page and does not necessarily correspond to the whole book. Hence separate user profile is learned for content search using the relevance judgments of the pages given by the user. This profile is called the

---

[2] http://citeseer.ist.psu.edu/

user's CS-profile. To summarize, the approach consists of learning user profile and using the particular user profile along with the profiles of other users in the community to re-rank the search results initiated by the particular user.

In sub sections 3.1 and 3.2 we discuss how profile learning and re-ranking of search results takes place in in the meta data search and content search respectively, and in 3.3 we describe the architecture of the search process in a digital library that is enhanced by the proposed approach.

3.1   Collaboration Based Re-ranking in Meta Data Search

Learning the user's MS-profile. Users in a DL search for books using the meta data search and read them online. The user then rates the book on a scale of 1-5. These ratings reflect how much the book has been interesting to him. For each user, the system records these ratings in a database. This constitutes the user's MS-profile, essentially a vector of ratings of all the books given by him. Similarly, profiles are learned for all the users. In the current work, only explicit feedback is assumed.

Re-ranking of Search Results. Re-ranking of results is done reflecting the user's interests of the books. Ranking in done in descending order based on the ratings of the book if present in the given user's MS-profile. Otherwise, a prediction of the given user's rating of the book is computed using the particular user's MS-profile and the profile of other users in the community. The predicted rating is a weighted combination of prediction using only the particular user's MS-profile and prediction using the MS-profiles of other users in the community. For computing prediction of a book in the former case, kNN is used to pick the k most similar books to a given book among all the books rated by the user.

To describe the computation of these predictions in detail, we first introduce commonly used notation. Books in the DL are typically described by meta data information like 'Title of the Book','author' etc. Let a be a user in the DL, then the rating of the book b given by the user is denoted by $r_{a,b}$ and $p_{a,b}$ denotes the prediction of the book computed by the system. Then the predicted rating of a book b is computed as

$$p_{a,b} = \alpha p1_{a,b} + (1 - \alpha)p2_{a,b}$$

where $p1_{a,b}$ is the prediction calculated using on the user a's MS-profile and is computed as

$$p1_{a,b} = \frac{\sum_{k_b} r_{a,B_i} * Sim_{B_i,b}}{\sum_{k_b} Sim_{B_i,b}}$$

where k_b denotes the k most similar books to the book b. The similarity of the books is based on the meta data content of the book. For the particular books B_i B_j, the similarity is calculated as

$$Sim_{B_i,B_j} = \sum_{f \epsilon F} g(B_i(f), B_j(f))$$

where g is an appropriate scoring function and F is a set containing the meta data features of the book. These similarities are computed offline. Hence they do not add any overheard to the computation of prediction of rating of a book. $p2_{a,b}$ is the prediction calculated using the MS-profiles of the other users in the community and is computed similar to other works in collaborative filtering.

$$p2_{a,i} = \overline{r_a} + \frac{\sum_{u=1}^{U}(r_{u,i} - \overline{r_u})X S_{a,u}}{\sum_{u=1}^{U} S_{a,u}}$$

and

$$S_{a,u} = \frac{\sum_{i=1}^{B}(r_{a,i} - \overline{r_a})X(r_{u,i} - \overline{r_u})}{\sum_{i=1}^{B}(r_{a,i} - \overline{r_a})^2 X(r_{u,i} - \overline{r_u})^2}$$

U is the set of users in the community that the user belongs to, $S_{a,u}$ denote the similarity between the active user a and the user u in the community. B is the total number of books considered in the DL. To summarize, the rank of a book is computed as follows

$$Rank_{b,a} = \begin{cases} r_{a,b} & \text{if the book has already been rated by the user a} \\ p_{a,b} & \text{otherwise.} \end{cases}$$

The book results of the meta data search are then arranged in descending order of the ranks calculated as above.

3.2   Collaboration Based Re-ranking in Content Search

Learning the User's CS-profile. A user in a DL searches for information in the books using the content search and also gives relevance judgment of the page. As mentioned earlier, CS-profile represents the facts or information inside the book that are of interest to the user. In the current work, user's CS-profile learning involves training a classifier on the pages using their relevance judgments given by the user as the class labels. The relevance judgments of the pages are gathered through interactions from the user which are boolean values consisting of a 1 which symbolizes relevant class or -1 which symbolizes irrelevant class. We investigated the use of SVMs in this work. Training an SVM on the pages and their feedback results in a model which consists of two sets of hyperplanes , one hyperplane going through one or more examples of the non-relevant class and one hyperplane going through one or more examples of the relevant class. This model forms the user's CS profile and is now capable of classifying a page of a book into a relevant class or non relevant class. In this section, we use the terms documents and pages interchangeably.

For training the SVM, each document is represented as a vector with tf(Term Frequency) representations of the words in the pages of the books as features. After eliminating stop words and words not occurring in at least 5 pages, we obtained about 3000000 dimensions. There were a total of 36,000 books and 14 million pages. We use libsvm [1] in our work for experiments on SVM and Lucene[3] is the search engine.

---

[3] http://jakarta.apache.org/lucene

Re-ranking of search results. For re-ranking of search results of a given query posed by the particular user a, we first get all the documents matching the query using the search engine. Let U represent the set of all the users in the community that the user belongs to. Relevance factors for the documents are calculated using the CS-profile of the user a and the CS-profiles of U. The Relevance factors represent the systems predictions of how much the page is of interest to the user. These factors are essentially the probability estimates of the membership of the document in the relevant class given by the SVM. Given the user a's CS-profile ,the CS-profiles of U, the search engine's $TFIDF - rank$ and the rating of the book $r_{a,B}$ new rank of the document to the user a is computed as

$$Rank_{a,d} = \alpha(\mathcal{P}_{a,d} + r_{a,B}) + \beta(\rho_{C,d}) + \gamma TFIDF - rank$$

where d is a page in a Book B, $\mathcal{P}_{a,d}$ is the probability estimate given by the the user a's profile. The values α, β, γ are chosen based on experiments. However, they can be reset by the user reflecting the relative importance given to the predicted rank of the page, the TFIDF rank etc.

3.3 Architecture

We test our approach by applying the re-ranking strategy to an online digital library. The digital library consists of a meta data database and the data servers where the actual content of the books is stored. A web based interface for the meta data search engine helps the user query for books using meta data. Also the content servers are indexed and search engine with a web interface is provided which queries for pages based on keywords. Both the search engines are enabled to gather feedback from the users. The re-ranking strategy is defined in the following two main components-

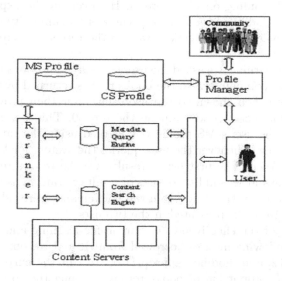

Fig. 1. Architecture of the enhanced retrieval process

1. Profile Manager: The Profile Manager receives the feedback from the user and creates or edits the corresponding profile for the user. The profiles are saved in the corresponding profile database for the search.
2. Reranker: The Reranker uses the profile database created by the profile manager and executes the ranking strategy. The search engines pass the result sets of a search to the re-ranker, which then re orders the results and returns them.

4   Experimental Results

We have conducted preliminary experiments evaluating the proposed approach by applying it to the search process in **The Digital Library of India Project**. The project aims at digitizing books and enabling them online for the easy access to information for everyone around the world. The library currently contains about one tenth of a million books with close to 25 million pages. To ease the computations and processing we have used only a quarter portion of these books in our experiments. However we believe that the strategy and the algorithm scales and holds good for any number of books and pages. In this section, we describe the experimental setup used in evaluating the proposed approach, metrics used for evaluation, and the evaluation results.

4.1   Experimental Setup

The first step in the evaluation involves discovering the communities. In this work, we have assumed static and pre-defined communities. For example, economy of India, religion, rocket science etc. The user joins the communities of interest to him of which he then becomes a member. A user can join more than one community depending on his interests. However, in the experiments that follow, we assume that the user explicitly chooses a community of interest before initiating a query. In this section, we use the terms participants and user interchangeably.

For user profile learning, we asked the users to search for books using the meta data specifying the community. All the books results returned by the meta data search engine were then shown to the user. The user then provides feedback on a significant number of books among the top 30. This was repeated for a few searches and the user's MS profile was learned using the ratings provided. After profile learning, whenever the user queries the system for books, two sets of results are returned. The first list of results are the results returned by the meta search engine and second list consists of results re-ranked using our ranking strategy described in Section 3.1. Again the participants were asked to rate the books in the top 10 books presented in the two lists.

For evaluation of the effectiveness of our profile learning and ranking strategy, we use the following metrics borrowed from IR and Recommendation Systems literature [12] and modified appropriately to suit the current scenario. 1. RelevanceRatio-N: proportion of books relevant among the top N. 2. Novelty Ratio-N: proportion of relevant books retrieved that have not yet been rated by the user in top N. RelevanceRatio-N describes the number of results relevant to the user out of the top N results. The Novelty Ratio-N symbolizes the number of new relevant books discovered by the system for which the user has not yet given feedback. A high RelevanceRatio-N value indicates that a good proportion of the results are relevant to the user. A high Novelty Ratio-N indicates that the system is able to learn and generalize the user's interests. Both of these measures combined determine the effectiveness of our ranking strategy. We followed similar procedure and experimental set up for evaluating the effectiveness of CS-profile learning and ranking strategy in content search. The user gives relevance judgments of the pages in this case instead of ratings. User profile learning and re-ranking of the search results is done as described in Section 3.2.

4.2   Evaluation Results

The Tables 1 and 2 show the averaged RelevanceRatio-N value over all the users. For simplicity of comparison, we showed the RelevanceRatio-N values for 5 users in the graph. For each user, the RelevanceRatio values shown in the graph are the values averaged over all the queries issued by the user in the experiments conducted. The NoveltyRatio-N helps us to assess the improvement of the search due to the re-ranking strategy and the evaluations proved it to be useful. In all

Table 1. Evaluation of Metadata Search

Method	Average RelevanceRatio-10
Without re-ranking	0.2
Proposed re-ranking	**0.404**

Table 2. Evaluation of Content Search

Method	Average RelevanceRatio-10
Without re-ranking	0.318
Proposed re-ranking	**0.767**

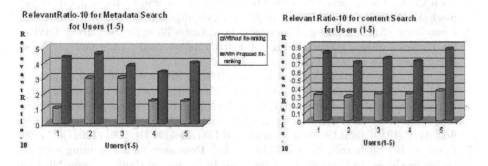

Fig. 2. RelevanceRatio-10 of Metadata search and Content Search

these experiments, we considered $N = 10$, ie only the top 10 search results were considered. As it can be seen from the tables, our ranking approach showed significant improvement in the RelevanceRatio-10. With the number of users in the community increase and the feedback increases, the results would show constant improvement.

5   Conclusions and Future Work

In this paper we have identified two types of searches performed in a digital library and have shown that by providing relevance feedback and by sharing of user experiences in a user community, the relevance of the results returned by these search could be improved. In particular we have experimented machine learning techniques like SVM for learning user profile models. We have also applied the techniques to **The Digital Library of India Project** which is an evolving digital library consisting of about one tenth of a million books and also presented the results of evaluation. In future we would like to experiment other machine learning techniques and compare the results. Also the success of the system discussed above depends largely upon the user and the community that he belongs to. We would like to define the communities based on user behaviour studies and also discover the similar users dynamically instead of requiring the user to pre define it.

Acknowledgments

We would like to acknowledge the pioneering effort of Dr. Raj Reddy and his vision for a 'Universal Digital Library'. We also thank Dr.Raj Reddy and Dr.Rajeev Sangal for their supporting the work done. We would like to extend our thanks to the student teams involved in the project for developing the user interface and participation in the user studies for evaluation.

References

1. Chih-Chung Chang and Chih-Jen Lin: LIBSVM : a library for support vector machines, Software available at http://www.csie.ntu.edu.tw/ cjlin/libsvm (2001)
2. Chun Zeng., Xiaohui Zheng., Chunxiao Xing., Lizhu Zhou : Personalized Services for Digital Library. In Proceedings of Fifth International Conference on Asian Digital Libraries (ICADL) (2002) 252-253
3. Cohen, W., Fan, W. 2000: Web-collaborative ltering: Recommending music by crawling the web. In Proceedings of World Wide Web Conference (WWW2000) (2000)
4. Daniel Faensen., Lukas Faulstich., Heinz Schweppe., Annika Hinze., Alexander Steidinger. Hermes: A notification service for digital libraries. In Proceedings of the first ACM/IEEE Joint Conference on Digital Libraries (JCDL 2001) (2001) 373-380
5. Drucker, H., Shahraray, B. and Gibbon, D.: Relevance feedback using support vector machines. In Proceedings of the 18th International Conference on Machine Learning (2001) 122-129

6. Elena Renda, M., Umberto Straccia : A Personalized Collaborative Digital Library. Environment. In Proceedings of Fifth International Conference on Asian Digital Libraries (ICADL 2002) (2002) 262-274
7. Harman, D. : Relevance feedback revisited. Proceedings of the Fifth International ACM SIGIR Conference on Research and Development in Information Retrieval (SIGIR'92) (1992) 1-10
8. Jamie Callan., Alan Smeaton., : Personalization and Recommender Systems in Digital Libraries. Joint NSF-EU DELOS Working Group Report (2003)
9. Joachims, T. : Text categorization with support vector machines: learning with features. In European Conference on Machine Learning (ECML-98)(1998)
10. Kathleen R. McKeown., Noemie Elhadad., Vasileios Hatzivassiloglou: Leveraging a Common Representation for Personalized Search and Summarization in a Medical Digital Library. In Proceedings of the Third ACM/IEEE Joint Conference on Digital Libraries (JCDL 2003) (2003)
11. McNee, S., I. Albert, D. Cosley, P. Gopalkrishnan, S.K. Lam, A.M. Rashid, J.A. Konstan, and J. Riedl: On the Recommending of Citations for Research Papers. In Proceedings of the ACM 2002 Conference on Computer Supported Cooperative Work (CSCW 2002) (2002) 116-125
12. Nicholas J. Belkin., Gheorghe Muresan: Measuring Web Search Effectiveness: Rutgers at Interactive TREC. WWW2004 Conference Workshop
13. Norbert Fuhr., Norbert Gvert., Claus-Peter Klas: Recommendation in a Collaborative Digital Library Environment. Technical Report, University of Dortmund, Germany (2001)
14. Paul Resnick., Neophytos Iacovou., Mitesh Suchak., Peter Bergstrom., John Riedl. : GroupLens : An Open Architecture for Collaborative Filtering of Netnews. In Proceedings of the ACM 1994 Conference on Computer Supported Collaborative Work (CSCW 94) (1994) 175-186
15. Roberto Torres., Sean M. McNee., Mara Abel., Joseph A. Konstan., John Ried: Enhancing Digital Libraries with TechLens+. In Proceedings of the Fourth ACM/IEEE Joint Conference on Digital Libraries (JCDL 2004) (2004) 228-237
16. Rocchio, J.J. : Relevance feedback in information retrieval, The SMART Retrieval System: Experiments in Automatic Document Processing, ed: Gerald Salton, Prentice Hall (1971) 313-323
17. Salton, G., Buckley, C.: Improving retrieval performance by relevance feedback. Journal of the American Society of Information Science and Technology (JASIST) (1990) 288-297
18. Shardanand, U., P. Maes: Social information Filtering, Algorithms for automating "word of mouth". In Proceedings of the 1995 ACM SIGCHI Conference on Human Factors in Computing Systems (CHI 95) (1995) 210-217
19. Theobald, M., Klas, C. P.: BINGO! and Daffodil: Personalized Exploration of Digital Libraries and Web Sources, In 7th International Conference on Computer-Assisted Information Retrieval (RIAO-2004) (2004)
20. Vladimir N. Vapnik: The Nature of Statistical Learning Theory. Springer, 1995
21. Yang, Y. and Liu, X.: A Re-examination of Text Categorization Methods. In Proceedings of the 22nd Annual International ACM SIGIR Conference on Research and Development in Information Retrieval (SIGIR'99) (1999) 42-49

Harvesting for Full-Text Retrieval

Fabio Simeoni[1], Murat Yakici[1], Steve Neely[2], and Fabio Crestani[1]

[1] University of Strathclyde
[2] University College of Dublin
fabio.simeoni@cis.strath.ac.uk

Abstract. We propose an approach to Distributed Information Retrieval based on the periodic and incremental centralisation of full-text indices of widely dispersed and autonomously managed content sources.

Inspired by the success of the Open Archive Initiative's protocol for *metadata harvesting*, the approach occupies middle ground between: (*i*) the crawling of content, and (*ii*) the distribution of retrieval. As in crawling, some data moves towards the retrieval process, but it is statistics about the content rather than content itself. As in distributed retrieval, some processing is distributed along with the data, but it is indexing rather than retrieval itself. We show that the approach retains the good properties of centralised retrieval without renouncing to cost-effective resource pooling. We discuss the requirements associated with the approach and identify two strategies to deploy it on top of the OAI infrastructure.

1   Introduction

Our interest is in content-based retrieval of widely dispersed and autonomously managed text sources. This is the central problem of Distributed Information Retrieval (DIR) and, over the past ten years, it has been approached by distributing the process along with the data: queries have been 'pushed' towards the content and the results of their local execution have been centrally gathered and presented to the user. While peer-to-peer models of distribution have recently generated some research interest [3], the traditional DIR approach relies on the simple client/server architecture depicted in Fig.1 (cf. [2]).

Rather independently and over a longer period of time, the Digital Library community has also explored the potential of distributed retrieval in the practice of its information services. Here, retrieval has mainly been interpreted as a deterministic process defined against the explicit structure of descriptive and manually authored metadata. Nonetheless, queries and results have still been exchanged within the client/server architecture in Fig.1; the Z39.50 protocol [14], in particular, has standardised the syntax and semantics of such exchange.

Over the past five years, however, the DL community has progressively favoured the complementary approach of iteratively and incrementally centralising metadata as a pre-condition to the retrieval of the associated data: metadata has been 'moved' towards the queries in advance of their execution (see Fig.2).

E.A. Fox et al. (Eds.): ICADL 2005, LNCS 3815, pp. 204–213, 2005.
© Springer-Verlag Berlin Heidelberg 2005

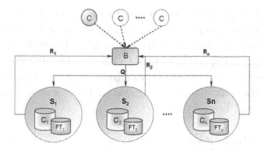

Fig. 1. Client/server distributed retrieval. A search broker B interfaces clients C and dispatches their queries Q to a number of autonomous search engines $S_1, S_2, , S_n$, each of which executes it against an index FT_i of some content C_i before returning results R_i back to B which merges them and relays them to C. Optionally, B optimises query distribution by selecting a subset of the engines based on previously gathered descriptions of their content.

Standardised by the *OAI-PMH*, the Protocol for Metadata Harvesting of the Open Archive initiative (OAI) [9], the *harvesting* model has proved particularly suitable to meet the technical and sociological requirements of retrieval within large-scale Federated Digital Libraries (FDLs)(e.g. [7]). A principled analysis of such success is found in [10] and may be summarised it here as follows.

From a technical perspective, harvesting eliminates the network as a real-time observable of service provision and, with it, a major obstacle to its medium-large scalability within wide-area networks [8]. Bandwidth fluctuations induced by traffic congestions and latency-inducing factors associated with slow, un-available, or particularly distant data sources have no impact on the continuity, reliability, responsiveness, and even effectiveness of service provision. Retrieval, in particular, may regain the simplicity, generality, and QoS guarantees which are normally associated with local computations.

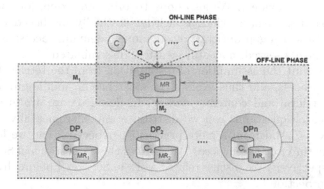

Fig. 2. Metadata harvesting. (a) *off-line phase*: a service provider SP gathers metadata M from data providers $DP_1, DP_2, , DP_n$ and stores it in a metadata repository MR; (b) *on-line phase*: SP interfaces clients C and resolves their queries Q against MR.

From a sociological perspective, the model captures the disparity of strengths and interests which characterises FDLs; in particular, it clearly distinguishes the roles, responsibilities, and costs of *service providers* from those of *data providers*. Data providers may give broad visibility to their data without having to face the complexity of full service provision; service providers also benefits from simplified participation, for the scope and usefulness of their services may scale beyond previously experienced bounds [6].

1.1   Scope and Motivations

In this paper, we investigate the applicability of the harvesting model to full-text retrieval.

The motivation is two-fold. Firstly, we hope to expand the scope of Distributed Information Retrieval beyond the assumptions which have bound it so far. Secondly, we aim to extend the benefits of the harvesting model within the same domains which to date have successfully but only partially adopted it. Within today's FDLs, a reconciliation of harvesting with full-text retrieval would guarantee homogeneous scope and QoS across both metadata-based and content-based services; using the OAI-PMH for the purpose, in particular, would immediately leverage a widely deployed infrastructure of tools and providers.

Under a generic interpretation, of course, the applicability of harvesting to content-based retrieval need not be questioned: any Web search engine stands as a witness of the feasibility and scalability of moving data towards the retrieval process. Here, however, we focus on a stricter but more advantageous interpretation of harvesting in which retrieval remains predicated on the sole movement of metadata. However, we now give to metadata the technical meaning which it normally assumes in Information Retrieval, and thus focus on automatically generated content statistics rather than manually authored descriptive records. In particular, we assume that the content remains distributed and that a full-text index of the union of the distributed sources is instead centralised[1]. By doing so, we expect to make better use of shared bandwidth and to reduce load at both data and service providers. We also hope to promote scope, for the approach may offer visibility to data which is neither statically published nor publicly accessible; data which is proprietary, costs money, demands access control, or is simply dynamically served, may still be safely disseminated.

Overall, we shift the assumption of distribution from the retrieval process to the indexing process, and thus explore the existence of middle ground between distributed retrieval and content crawling. In doing so, we are guided by the following research questions: can we distribute and incrementally execute the indexing process? And from a more practical perspective: can we leverage the OAI infrastructure for the purpose? We address these questions in Section 2 and Section 3, respectively. We discuss related work in Section 4 before drawing some conclusions in Section 5.

---

[1] Interestingly, client-server retrieval already relies on a harvesting approach whenever it centralises collection-level descriptions for the purposes of selective query distribution.

2   The Approach

We use an example to clarify the approach and identify the requirements it raises at both ends of the exchange model.

2.1   Harvesting Scenarios

In the standard harvesting scenario, a service provider relies on the OAI-PMH to periodically centralise descriptive metadata from a number of data providers. Independently from dissemination agreements, the providers maintain their metadata in databases and use it routinely to offer local services to their users, including a structure-based retrieval service; some providers also maintain full-text indices on their file systems and use them to complement the retrieval service with keyword-based queries. Models and languages for metadata, indexing, and retrieval are locally defined and locally maintained. At each provider, a dissemination service implements the server side of the OAI-PMH and resolves protocol requests by: (i) executing a fixed range of queries against the metadata database, and (ii) mapping the results expressed in the local metadata model onto instances of a model agreed upon for exchange, say unqualified Dublin Core (DC) [5]. At the service provider, the DC records are normalised and otherwise enhanced (e.g. duplicates are removed and subjects are automatically inferred), and then added to the input of an interactive retrieval service. The service accepts structure-based as well as content-based queries, but it executes both types of query against the harvested DC records.

We propose an extension of the previous scenario in which the descriptive metadata exposed by data providers is augmented with content statistics (see Fig. 3). The providers obtain this information from pre-existing or dedicated full-text indices, rather than databases, but they still map records onto an exchange model. Similarly, at the service provider, the statistics are extracted and used to update a local full-text index, possibly after having been normalised and enhanced to reflect current content statistics and local indexing requirements, respectively. The index is then used to satisfy full-text queries while the descriptive metadata supports the presentation of results. For flexibility, (subsets of) the same content statistics may be used to support more than one model of retrieval (e.g. a vector space model and a language model).

2.2   Requirements

From a conceptual perspective, the extension is relatively straightforward. Its only requirement is for the service provider to rely on a model of indexing which allows modular representation of content over space and time. More formally:

(**Modular Indexing**) If M is an indexing model, C_0 and C_1 two content sources, and I_0 and I_1 their M-indices, then M is *modular* if the difference $\Delta C = C_1 - C_0$ implies a difference $\Delta I = I_1 - I_0$ such that ΔI is computable from I_0 and ΔC only.

Interpreted along a spatial dimension, modularity guarantees the distributivity of the indexing process across independently maintained content; interpreted along a temporal dimension, it guarantees the incremental nature of such process. In turn, modularity is guaranteed by content properties whose measurement may be distributed over document-grained increments. Common indexing models satisfy this requirement, for they either rely on term-related properties which pertain to individual documents – such as in-document term number, frequency, and location – or else pertain to groups of documents and yet may still be progressively derived, such as inverse document frequency [13].

From a pragmatic perspective, however, the enriched semantics of the exchanged data unavoidably adds development complexity and resource consumption. Most noticeably, it assumes data providers which are: (i) sufficiently sophisticated to offer integrated management of descriptive metadata and full-text indices, and (ii) sufficiently rich to sustain the load on computational resources – from storage to memory and network bandwidth – which is induced by the increased size of (per-document) content statistics over descriptive metadata.

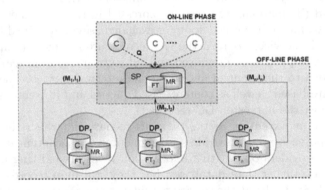

Fig. 3. Full-text index harvesting. (a) *off-line phase*: a service provider SP gathers pairs (M_i, I_i) of metadata and content statistics from data providers $DP_1, DP_2, , DP_n$ and stores them in a metadata repository MR and a full-text index FT, respectively; (b) *on-line phase*: SP interfaces clients C, resolves their queries against FT, and uses the metadata in MR to present the results.

Clearly, issues of data integration and size concern both ends of the exchange scenario. On an absolute scale, problems may seem more acute at the client side of the protocol but the harvesting philosophy indicates that the server side is where adoption and scalability may be more obviously at stake. In particular, data providers must accommodate the cost of generating, maintaining, and serving full-text indices within their resource allocation policies; whenever such costs may not be directly justified in terms of local requirements – i.e. in the assumption of dedicated development – then it may prove too expensive to accommodate the novel dissemination requirements. Cost estimates will vary from case to case and only deployment experience may indicate what level of tool support may help reducing complexity.

As to the issue of size, we expect compression to play an important role at both ends of the protocol. Lossless compression techniques based on optimised representation structures are the first obvious choice, be it for the persistent storage of indices, their in-memory management, or their transfer on the wire[2]. In harvesting, furthermore, compression ratios may be pushed further than they may when decompression is a real-time observable of service provision. Lossy compression techniques may also be conveniently used to complement lossless approaches. Well-known algorithms – ranging from standard case folding, stop-word removal, and stemming algorithms, to static index pruning and document summarisation algorithms (e.g. [4]) – may all grant additional size reductions without excessively compromise the final quality of retrieval.

One last pragmatic question concerns the suitability of the OAI-PMH to support the extended exchange semantics. We dedicate the next Section to a possible answer.

3   Protocol Design

We first summarise the features of the OAI-PMH and then assess two strategies to deploy the extended exchange semantics on top of the existing OAI infrastructure.

3.1   OAI-PMH

At its heart, the OAI-PMH is a client-server protocol for the selective exchange of self-describing data. Six types of requests are available to clients: three to discover capabilities of servers (*auxiliary requests*) and three to solicit data from servers in accordance with their capabilities (*primary requests*). To support incremental harvesting, primary requests may be temporally scoped with a granularity of days or seconds; selective harvesting relies instead on the optional definition of a hierarchy of potentially overlapping datasets. Simple session management mechanisms support large data transfers in the face of transaction failures. For ease of deployment, the overall semantics of exchange – including error semantics – is 'tunnelled' within HTTP's, while XML provides syntax and high-level semantics for response payloads.

The exact semantics of the exchanged data is formally undefined but, by design, it is expected to fall within the domain of content metadata; indeed, all servers are required to produce DC metadata on request. In particular, an exchange model associates servers with repositories of *resources* and resources with one or more metadata descriptions, or *records*; the latter form the basic unit of exchange. The model says little about resources but it offers a layered model of metadata in which records are format-specific instantiations of fully abstract resource descriptions, or *items*. The identification of items and formats is explicit; the protocol suggests an implementation scheme for item identifiers (e.g.

---

[2] Transport-level compression, in particular, is already within the scope of standard OAI-PMH exchange semantics.

`oai:dp:hep-th/9901001`) and defines an extensible lists of format identifiers (e.g. `oai_dc` for the required DC). Individual records are instead implicitly identified by their format and the item they instantiate; they are nonetheless explicitly associated with datestamps and thus may change independently from their items. As an example of OAI-PMH data exchange, the following HTTP GET request:

```
http://www.dp.org/oai?
verb=ListRecords&MetadataPrefix=oai_dc&from=2005-01-01
```

asks a server available at `http://www.dp.org/oai` to return all the DC records which have changed since the beginning of the current year. The following is a sample response[3]:

```
<OAI-PMH>
  <responseDate>2005-01-01T19:20:30Z</responseDate>
  <request verb="ListRecords" from="2005-01-01"
    metadataPrefix="oai_dc">http://www.dp.org/OAI</request>
  <ListRecords>
    ...
    <record>
      <header>
        <identifier>oai:dp:hep-th/9901001</identifier>
        <datestamp>2005-02-18</datestamp>
      </header>
      <metadata>
        <dc>
          <title>Opera Minora</title>
          <creator>Cornelius Tacitus</creator>
          <identifier>http://www.dp.org/res/9901001.html</identifier>
          ...
        </dc>
      </metadata>
    </record>
    ...
  </ListRecords>
</OAI-PMH>
```

3.2   Design Strategies

The increasing popularity of the OAI-PMH has generated some interest in using the protocol beyond its original design assumptions. Building on the generality of the data model, original use has sometimes been predicated on creative instantiations of the modelling primitives [11]. In other cases, the exchange semantics has been extended to accommodate additional functionality (e.g. [12]). Both design routes are available for our protocol: we could conceive it as an *application* or as an *extension* of the OAI-PMH.

The first solution may be simply predicated on: (i) a specialisation of the protocol's data model, and (ii) the definition of a dedicated format for the integrated exchange of descriptive metadata *and* content statistics. The model would simply introduce constraints on the notion of resource, namely: (a) resources have at least one digital and text-based manifestation, and (b) a distinguished manifestation, the *primary manifestation*, satisfies (a) and is designated to represent the content of the resource for harvesting purposes. The format would instead bind descriptive metadata and content statistics of primary manifestations to

---

[3] For clarity, namespace information is omitted in this and following examples.

individual request/response interactions, so as to avoid the synchronisation problems which may arise if each form was harvested independently from the other. The solution is appealing for it proves the concept whilst requiring no change to the protocol and its deployment infrastructure. While it may immediately serve the needs of specific communities, however, its design is rather ad-hoc and requires the definition of dedicated formats for each variation in the shape of descriptive metadata and/or content statistics. This induces a 'combinatorial' approach to standardisation which may unnecessarily compromise interoperability across communities of adoption.

To illustrate the full potential of the approach, we concentrate instead on the definition of a more modular exchange mechanism which may gracefully accommodate arbitrary forms of descriptive metadata and content statistics. Specifically, we retain the data model specialisation defined above, as well as the binding of metadata and content statistics within individual request/response interactions. However, we now identify each form of data independently from the other and thus assume that a record includes both a metadata part and an index part. In particular, we expect requests to specify a format for the metadata part and a format for the index part.

This leads to a protocol extension defined by: (i) the addition of an auxiliary request ListIndexFormats with associated response format; (ii) the addition of an optional parameter indexPrefix to primary requests; and (iii) the addition of an optional index child to the record elements contained in responses to primary requests. ListIndexFormats is used to discover the index formats supported by servers, and as such it extends the semantics of ListMetadataFormats. Similarly, indexPrefix specifies the format of the index part of records and thus mirrors metadataPrefix and its associated error semantics. Finally, index elements contain the index part of records and follow the standard metadata elements.

The extension of the sample request/response pair shown in Sect. 3.1 may then be the following::

```
http://www.dp.org/oai?
verb=ListRecords&metadataPrefix=oai_dc&indexPrefix=tf_basic&from=2005-01-01

<OAI-PMH>
  ...
  <ListRecords>
    ...
    <record>
      ...
      <metadata>
        <dc>...</dc>
      </metadata>
      <index>
        <terms>
          ...
          <term name="opera" freq="26">
          <term name="minora" freq="36">
          ...
        </terms>
      </index>
    </record>
    ...
  </ListRecords>
</OAI-PMH>
```

Here, `tf_basic` is the identifier of a simple format which captures the name
and frequency of occurrence of the terms chosen to represent primary manifestations (possibly after stemming and stop-word removal). The underlying model
serves the purpose of a proof of concept but supports most of the indexing models which may be employed at the client side. Variations are of course possible;
for example, a format which captures only term names and document lengths
would decrease resource consumption and still support simple models of boolean
retrieval. On the other hand, a model which includes positional information for
each term occurrence would increase resource consumption but also support
proximity searches at the client side.

4   Related Work

The relationship between the proposed approach, distributed retrieval, content
crawling, and existing implementations of the harvesting model has been extensively discussed in previous Sections. Here, we concentrate on what - to the best
of our knowledge - is the only work which directly shares some of our motivations.

The Harvest system [1] was initially proposed in the mid-nineties as a sophisticated end-to-end solution for content-based retrieval over the inter-network.
Harvesting is a central component of the system's architecture and its technical contribution to the OAI initiative has been repeatedly acknowledged in the
literature. Unlike the OAI-PMH, however, the system abstracts over the precise semantics of the harvested data, which may range from manually authored,
descriptive metadata, to automatically derived, and type-specific content statistics. Text-based formats, in particular, are processed along lines similar to those
advocated in this paper.

Our work, however, frames the approach within an evolved infrastructural
context, where later developments - particularly XML and the role-based model
OAI-PMH itself - are leveraged towards a more general data exchange mechanism than what may be found buried within a closed system. In particular, we
operate in a context in which interoperability is predicated on protocol-based
solutions, rather than end-to-end implementations. Further, Harvest focuses on
the indexing of type-specific content summaries, which represents just one of
many possible applications of the approach. Overall, our work motivates, con-
textualises, and generalises the good properties of an architectural model which
has been previously implemented and yet has to receive widespread acceptance.

5   Conclusions

A topological separation between the processes of indexing and retrieval suits
DIR systems in which content is widely distributed and autonomously managed.
Indexing is conceptually distributed along with the content and remains the only
responsibility of content providers; located elsewhere on the network, retrieval is
centralised around a periodic and incremental harvest of the indexes produced at

each provider. A protocol-based infrastructure for harvesting descriptive metadata in support of structured retrieval has already been widely and successfully deployed and we have shown how it may be leveraged for full-text retrieval. As a proof-of-concept, we have tested the approach in a prototype for multi-model retrieval of distributed and potentially unmanaged file collections; due to lack of space, however, we leave a report on the implementation to future work.

References

1. Bowman, C.M., Danzig, P.B., Hardy, D.R. et al.: Harvest: A Scalable, Customizable, Discovery and Access System. Technical Report TR CU-CS-732-94, Department of Computer Science, University of Colorado-Boulder, 1994.
2. Callan, J.: Distributed information retrieval. In W.B. Croft, editor, Advances in information retrieval, chapter 5, pages 127-150. Kluwer Academic Publishers, 2000.
3. Callan, J., Fuhr, N., Nejdl, W. (Eds.): Proceedings of the SIGIR Workshop on Peer-to-Peer Information Retrieval, 27th Annual International ACM SIGIR Conference, July 29, 2004.
4. Carmel, D, Cohen, D. et al.: Static Index Pruning for Information Retrieval Systems. In Proceedings of the 24th ACM SIGIR Conference on Research and Development in Information Retrieval, pages 43-50, 2001.
5. The Dublin Core Metadata Initiative: Dublin Core Metadata Element Set, Version 1.1: Reference Description, 2004 (http://dublincore.org/documents/dces/).
6. Lagoze, C., Van de Sompel, H.: The Open Archives Initiative: Building a low-barrier interoperability framework. JCDL '01: Proceedings of the First ACM/IEEE-CS Joint Conference on Digital Libraries, 2001.
7. Lagoze, C., Hoehn, W., Arms, W., Allan, J. et al.: Core Services in the Architecture of the National Digital Library for Science Education (NDSL). Cornell University, Ithaca, arXiv Report, cs.DL/0201025, 2002.
8. Lynch, C.: The Z39.50 Information Retrieval Standard: Part I: A Strategic View of Its Past, Present, and Future. In D-Lib Magazine, April 1997 (http://www.dlib.org/dlib/april97/04lynch.html).
9. The Open Archives Initiative: The Open Archives Initiative Protocol for Metadata Harvesting (2.0), 2003 (http://www.openarchives.org/OAI/openarchivesprotocol.html).
10. Simeoni, F.: Servicing the Federation: the Case for Metadata Harvesting. In ECDL '04: Proceedings of the 8th European Conference on Research and Advanced Technology for Digital Libraries, Lecture Notes in Computer Science 3232, Springer, 2004.
11. Van de Sompel, H., Young, J., Hickey, T.:Using the OAI-PMH...Differently. In D-lib Magazine, July/August 2003.
12. Suleman, H., Fox, E.:Designing Protocols in Support of Digital Library Componentization. In ECDL'02: Proceedings of the 6th European Conference on Research and Advanced Technology for Digital Libraries, pages 568-582, 2002.
13. Witten, I., Moffat, A., Bell, T. Managing Gigabytes: Compressing and indexing documents and images. Van Nostrand Reinhold. 1994.
14. Z39.50 Maintenance Agency: Information Retrieval (Z39.50): Application Service Definition and Protocol Specification, 2003.

Word Extraction from Table Regions
in Document Images

Chang-Bu Jeong[1], Sang-Cheol Park[2], Hwa-Jeong Son[2], and Soo-Hyung Kim[2]

[1] Department of Internet Software, Honam University,
59-1 Sebong-dong, Gwangsan-gu, Gwangju 506-714, Korea
cbjeong@honam.ac.kr
[2] Department of Computer Science, Chonnam National University,
300 YongBong-dong, Buk-Gu, Gwangju 500-757, Korea
{sanchun, sonhj}@iip.chonnam.ac.kr, shkim@chonnam.ac.kr

Abstract. This paper describes a method to extract words from table regions in document images. The proposed approach consists of two stages: cell detection and word extraction. In the cell detection module, a table frame is extracted first by analyzing connected components and then intersection points are detected by a method using masks in the table frame. We correct false intersections, and detect the location of the cells within the table. In the word extraction module, a text region in each cell is located by using the connected components information that was obtained during the cell extraction module, and segmented into text lines by using projection profiles. Finally we divide the segmented lines into words using gap clustering and special symbol detection. The method correctly included character components touching the table frame with words, so experimental results show that more than 99% of words were successfully extracted from table regions.

1 Introduction

With the continuous development of computer technology and the Internet environment, we can efficiently produce, store, process, and transmit document images. However, as more and more documents are stored in the image format for full-text image retrieval services or digital libraries, it is impossible to retrieve information from document images with text-based search engines that do not recognize text from images. The retrieval of relevant documents is usually based on indices (e.g. title, author, keyword, and so on) of pre-catalogued documents in the text format, so that it becomes necessary for the user to download part of or the entire document images and confirm the contents when retrieving relevant documents with information not specified in the indices. Over the past few years, a considerable number of studies have focused on keyword spotting through automatic indexing of document images to compensate for this drawback. Such a keyword spotting approach makes it possible to retrieve relevant word images regardless of the language of the document and character segmentation errors because it uses word image features [1-3].

There are a lot of technologies in the document image processing for keyword spotting, such as skew correction, layout analysis, word extraction, and etc. Jeong et

E.A. Fox et al. (Eds.): ICADL 2005, LNCS 3815, pp. 214–223, 2005.
© Springer-Verlag Berlin Heidelberg 2005

al. [4] presented a document image preprocessing system for keyword spotting, which segments and classifies a document image into text regions and non-text regions (table, figure, etc) and then performs word extraction to decompose words from the text regions. Therefore the system is limited in that words in the non-text regions cannot be extracted. The words in the table regions, however, may be more useful for keyword spotting than words from other non-text regions because they may contain more meaningful words. Thus, it is necessary to decompose words from table regions in this respect.

In this paper, we propose a method to extract words from table regions in document images. The proposed approach consists of two stages: cell detection and word extraction (Fig. 1). In the cell detection module, a table frame is extracted first by analyzing CCs (connected components), and then intersection points are detected by a method using masks in the table frame. We correct false intersections using the correlation between neighboring intersections, and use the information of intersections to extrapolate the location of the cells within the table. In the word extraction module, a text region in each cell is located by using the CCs information that was obtained during the cell extraction module, and segmented into text lines by using projection profiles. Finally we divide the segmented lines into words using gap clustering and special symbol detection.

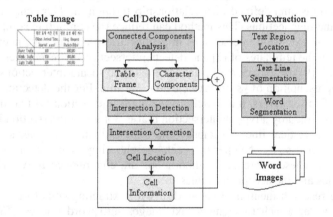

Fig. 1. Block diagram of the proposed method

2   Related Works

Previous research on extracting tables from document images can be divided into two types according to how tables are formed. One method is to analyze or recognize the table images delimited by line-art boundaries, and the other is to recognize the table images formed by the vertical alignment of fixed-width fields without line-art boundaries [5]. The proposed method is related to the former, but most of the previous research has dealt with form document images. Certainly, both tables and forms are sometimes used interchangeably, but a clear distinction exists. Tables are tabular structures, machine-printed for output, and their frame and content are created simultaneously. But, forms are rectilinear structure, machine- or hand-printed for input, and their frames are created prior to creating the content. While the aim of the research on table images is to vectorize the table frame by analyzing the line components comprising the table and to extract character components, the existing research on form images sought to classify unknown input forms by utilizing the extracted structural information from the forms, querying the input to a form types database, selecting matching forms, and extracting content from form types that do not match.

Watanabe et al. [6] described tables by using the upper-left corners of cells. Firstly, the proposed approach detects vertical and horizontal line segments from the binarized document images by using two extraction filters, and then applies two corner detection filters to the edge-extracted document images for the detection of upper-left corners. However, it is difficult to detect the intersection errors because it detects only the upper-left corners and the corner detection filters may not perform well in case line segments are distorted.

Horizontal and vertical lines can intersect each other to form any of the nine structures: ⌐, ¬, ⌐, ∟, ⊢, ⊤, ⊣, ⊥, ✛. Taylor et al. [7] use four 9×9 pixel templates to detect the intersections. Each template finds one of the basic intersections (⌐, ¬, ⌐, ∟), and then the detected corners are combined into an appropriate way for detecting the extensions (⊢, ⊤, ⊣, ⊥, ✛). However, Arias et al. [8] did not use templates but the leg length of the basic and extended intersections in the corresponding horizontal and vertical directions, and defined their relationship through the hierarchical representation of the nine intersections. This method can reduce the computing complexity spent on detecting the extension intersections in [7] because it obviates the need to visit all of the pixels in the templates of [7] and detects intersections by using their relations.

Neves et al. [9] use binary mathematical erosion to locate intersections and the hierarchical representation of [8] to save calculation time. For the detection and correction of identification errors, it also defines the tenth intersection (virtual intersection), which is represented by a type 0 intersection that is not a real intersection but a part of a horizontal or vertical line. To improve the cell extraction, it detects and corrects identification errors by comparing each neighboring intersection to reference neighborhoods. These reference neighborhoods are congregated in two manners, the rejection tables and the acceptance tables.

While the research mentioned above deal with extracting cells from table images, [4] presents an approach to segment text images into word images. This approach separates text regions into text lines by a horizontal projection profile analysis, and then utilizes gaps and special symbols as delimiters between words by a CC analysis in order to separate a text line into word units. As it combines the top-down approach (projection profile analysis) and the bottom-up approach (CC analysis), it is more efficient than other methods using a single approach.

3 Proposed Algorithm

3.1 Cell Detection

In table images, line components, which compose the table frame, and character components coexist. The line with the largest width is determined as a table frame by virtue of the 8-CC analysis. Thus, in order to extract cells from a table image, we deal with only the table frame while excluding character components. The intersection extraction module determines the position and the type of intersections on the table frame.

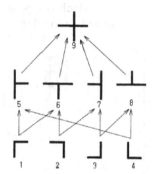

Fig. 2. Hierarchy of intersections

For extracting intersections, we employ the technique in [8] to reduce the extraction time. The intersections can be classified into 9 types: four with two legs, four with three legs, and one with four legs. They can be arranged in a hierarchy as shown in Fig. 2. Each type of intersection is assigned a number from 1 to 9. The proposed approach consists of trying to fit the largest possible intersection type in every black pixel of the table frame and assigning the corresponding label to the pixel. The fit of an intersection consists of finding runs of consecutive black pixels in the corresponding horizontal and vertical directions with the length equal to the leg length of the intersection. The process of labeling the pixels is performed in a hierarchical manner: Corners (⌐, ⌐ , ∟, ⌐) are tried first: if one can be fitted, the corresponding intersections (⊢, ⊤, ⊣ , ⊥) are tried, and so on. While around 30 pixels are checked for each leg in [8], 10 pixels are checked in our work so that the operation of searching for intersections is performed more efficiently. Although the time to check the length of the leg checked is reduced by one-third, there need not be any concern about the number of candidates for intersections amounting to larger than in [8] because character components are excluded from the intersection extraction.

When a vertical line and a horizontal line intersect, one intersection is generated. Two more candidates corresponding to the intersection can be detected according to the thickness of the lines of the table frame so that it becomes necessary to choose from among them by analyzing the information of the candidates. The position of the intersection is located in the center of the candidates, and the type is decided by a majority vote.

Since a cell is generally composed of four intersections, a representation model for extracting cells with intersections can be made with regard to the vertical position of intersections. Fig. 3 shows the representation model, whose elements determine the intersection type and position within a simple table. For example, "1-(3, 5)" corresponding to the element of (1, 1) in Fig. 3 means the intersection of type 1 (⌐) located in (3, 5) of table image. In general, it is possible to extract cells using this representation model with nine types of intersections, but it is necessary to modify the representation model in case two more cells are vertically or horizontally merged into a cell. If the distance between the horizontal positions of intersecting neighborhoods in a vertical direction is larger than the threshold, we consider that there is a merged cell in the table and then add a virtual intersection, which is type 0. In Fig. 3, (b) shows the representation model modified from (a) to add a virtual intersection.

	1	2	3
1	1-(3, 5)	6-(203, 5)	2-(473, 4)
2	5-(3, 139)	9-(203, 138)	7-(474, 138)
3	5-(3, 143)	9-(203, 143)	7-(474, 143)
4	5-(203, 190)	7-(474, 190)	
5	5-(203, 243)	7-(474, 242)	
6	5-(3, 296)	9-(203, 296)	7-(474, 295)
7	4-(2, 300)	8-(202, 300)	3-(473, 300)

	1	2	3
1	1-(3, 5)	6-(203, 5)	6-(473, 4)
2	5-(3,139)	9-(203, 138)	7-(474, 138)
3	5-(3,143)	9-(203, 143)	7-(474, 143)
4	0-(3,190)	5-(203, 190)	7-(474, 190)
5	0-(3,243)	5-(203, 243)	7-(474, 242)
6	5-(3,296)	9-(203, 296)	7-(474, 295)
7	4-(2,300)	5-(202, 300)	5-(473, 300)

(a) Before inserting virtual intersections   (b) After inserting virtual intersections

Fig. 3. Representation model for a cell

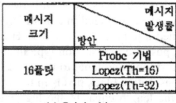
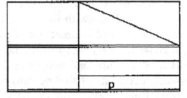

(a) Original image   (b) CC of the table frame

Fig. 4. An example that a character CC touches at a table frame

But when certain line intersections do not appear due to the poor quality of the acquisition, binarization problems, or skew correction, etc, it is difficult to correctly extract intersections with only the method described so far. Since those factors can distort document images and prevent the detection of real intersections, or even detect false intersections, it is necessary to detect and correct the error of intersections. Therefore, we adapt the technique in [9] to detect and correct the error of intersections by comparing each intersection neighborhood with reference neighborhoods. When a character component and the table frame touch as shown in Fig. 4, the character component is recognized as part of the table frame and false intersections can be detected around this area. The false intersections must be modified into virtual intersections by correcting the intersections.

After the intersection correction, each cell is determined with the four adjacent intersections excluding the virtual intersections appropriately chosen from the extracted intersections. But the meaningless cells formed by double lines must be excluded by considering the height and width of cells.

3.2 Word Extraction

The analysis of character components within the cells can be conducted faster and easier than the previous approaches by using the information from the character components that were excluded from the line component analysis. This method reduces or removes the influence of line components that may be located within the cells. Firstly, text regions within cells are determined by examining whether or not the CCs are located inside the appropriate cell. Since the character components touching the table frame are regarded as line components as mentioned above, we use the extracted cell information to separate these character components from the line components and add them to character components.

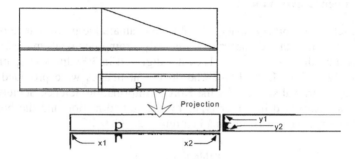

Fig. 5. Processing method for locating the internal region of the cell when character components touch the table frame

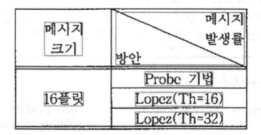

Fig. 6. Result of locating the internal region of the cell when characters components touch the table frame

When the false intersections detected in the intersection correction are located in the table frame, we assume that character components are touching the table frame. We detect the cell in which this contact occurs by analyzing the position and type of the false intersections, and then locate the internal region of the cell from the table frame by using the projection profile of the cell. By comparing with the neighborhood projection profile in the direction of center from both ends, the internal region of the cell (x1, x2, y1, y2) is decided if a current value is less than 10% of the previous value in Fig. 5. We analyze the CCs again for the part of the table frame located in the internal region of the cell and then add it to the character components of the text region in the cell. Fig. 6 shows the result for locating the internal region of the cell when character components touch the table frame.

Basically we employ our algorithm proposed in [4] for separating text regions into words, and additionally perform a post-process because words are not located in a text region but a table. The post-processing for the word segmentation is needed when the characters within a word are segmented into words due to the special spacing of the cell.

4 Experiment

4.1 Experiment Environment

We used a set of 100 binary images of table to evaluate the performance of the proposed method. The data are constructed manually from document images, which are pre-processed by the system in [4]. They are digitized in 300 dpi with spatial resolutions from 849×117 to 1500×1770. The document images were provided from the full-text image retrieval services by the Korean Information Science Society. Table 1 shows the data classified into four types by the cell formation and the boundary of cell, etc. The experiment was run on a Pentium-4 2.0 GHz PC.

Table 1. Test data

Type of table	Number
Normal table	60
Table whose cells are merged	20
Table consisted of a cell	10
Table which all or a part of border lines are missed	10
Total	100

4.2 Experiment Results

The performance results from the proposed method were evaluated in terms of accuracy and speed. The results obtained by the proposed cell extraction were 100% accurate for cell extraction (the total number of cells extracted is 2,313 in 100 table images). There were 7 false intersections in 5 table images due to the contact between character components and a table frame, but our algorithm corrected them and extracted all cells correctly.

Table 2. The result of word segmentation

		Result-1		Result-2	
# of images	# of words	# of successes	# of failures	# of successes	# of failures
100	4,547	4,301 (94.59%)	246 (5.41%)	4,509 (99.16%)	38 (0.84%)

Table 2 shows the results of word segmentation using the extracted cell information: Result-1 was obtained by applying only a gap clustering and Result-2 was obtained by additionally applying the special symbol detection. In the word segmentation module, we obtained an accuracy of 94.59% with only the gap clustering, and improved the performance rate by 4.57% by additionally applying the special symbol detection. Finally, we achieved an accuracy of 99.16% in the word segmentation. Fig. 7 shows the final result of the proposed method.

트래픽 형태 \ 메시지크기	메시지 발생률	0.01	0.1
균등분포	16 플릿	2.202	2.076
	32 플릿	2.391	2.146
	64 플릿	2.564	2.432
perfect-shuffle	16 플릿	1.947	1.95
	32 플릿	1.973	2.181

Fig. 7. The final result of the proposed method

There are several types of errors in the word segmentation and Fig. 8 shows a few examples. The first type is because an underline extends over two or more words and then between-word gaps cannot be computed by using horizontal projection profiles. So the words connected by an underline is segmented into a word as shown in Fig. 8(a). The second one is due to a split in a character. Some character can be split in two because of the image degradation or low quality and then classified as special symbols. Such a split character is used for an additional between-word gap shown in Fig. 8(b). The other is due to miss-classification of special symbols. When a special symbol touches neighbor characters as shown in Fig. 8(c) or has a property of the Italic fonts as shown in Fig. 8(d), our system cannot classifies them into special symbols.

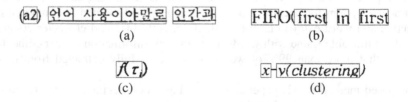

(a2) 언어 사용이야말로 인간과   FIFO(first in first
                (a)   (b)

              f(τ,)   x-y(clustering)
                (c)   (d)

Fig. 8. Examples that the proposed system failed

The average processing time for cell detection and word segmentation was about 1.399 and 0.071 seconds respectively. Since the information of the CCs analyzed in the cell extraction module was repeatedly used in the word segmentation module, the processing time for cell detection was significantly longer than the word segmentation module.

Table 3 shows the result obtained by combining the proposed method into the system in [4]. While the accuracy rate of word extraction was 90.84% for 50 Korean images before the combination, a 2.66% improvement was obtained after the combination. The performance improvement can be mainly attributed to the fact that the proposed method is able to extract words from the table regions, whereas the system in [4] is unable to achieve. For example, the accuracy rates of the 35th and 47th images were less than 70% before the table processing, but they were improved by more than 96% after the table processing.

Table 3. The result of the [4]'s system with the proposed method

Image ID	# of real words				# of extracted words				Accuracy(%)	
	TR	NTR		All	TR	NTR		All	Before table processing	After table processing
		Tab.	Fig.			Tab.	Fig.			
1	474	0	0	474	472	0	0	472	99.58	99.58
2	707	0	0	707	707	0	0	707	100.00	100.00
3	581	0	35	616	581	0	0	581	94.32	94.32
4	570	0	27	597	569	0	0	569	95.31	95.31
...					...					
35	374	208	0	582	353	208	0	561	60.65	96.39
36	546	74	0	620	537	71	0	608	86.61	98.06
...					...					
46	432	43	19	494	420	43	0	463	85.02	93.72
47	400	169	0	569	387	169	0	556	68.01	97.72
48	491	0	10	501	486	0	0	486	97.01	97.01
49	477	0	15	492	470	0	0	470	95.53	95.53
50	402	53	45	500	378	53	0	431	75.60	86.20
									90.84	93.50

5 Conclusion

We have proposed a method to extract words from table images and improve the word extraction system for document images. The proposed method is composed of cell detection and word extraction. The method correctly included character components touching the table frame with words using the cell information, so experimental results show that more than 99% of words were successfully extracted from table regions.

The proposed method in this paper can be used as a core technology for keyword spotting or retrieval systems for digital libraries.

Acknowledgement

This work was supported by grant No. R05-2003-000-10396-0 from the KOSEF.

References

1. Oh, I. S., Choi, Y. S., Yang, J. H., Kim, S. H.: A Keyword Spotting System of Korean Document Images. Lecture Notes in Computer Science, Vol. 2555. Springer-Verlag, Berlin Heidelberg New York (2002) 530
2. Marinai, S., Marino, E., Cesarini, F., Soda, G.: A General System for the Retrieval of Document Images from Digital Libraries. Proceedings of the First International Workshop on Document Image Analysis for Libraries (2004) 150-173
3. Lu, Y., Zhang, L., Tan, C. L.: Retrieving Imaged Documents in Digital Libraries Based on Word Image Coding. Proceedings of the First International Workshop on Document Image Analysis for Libraries (2004) 174-187
4. Jeong, C. B., Kim, S. H.: A Document Image Preprocessing System for Keyword Spotting. Lecture Notes in Computer Science, Vol. 3334. Springer-Verlag, Berlin Heidelberg New York (2004) 440-443
5. Lopresti, D., Nagy, G.: A Tabular Survey of Automated Table Processing. Lecture Notes In Computer Science, Vol. 1941. Springer-Verlag, Berlin Heidelberg New York (1999) 93-120
6. Watanabe, T., Luo, Q., Sugie, N.: Layout Recognition of Multi-Kinds of Table-Form Documents. IEEE Transactions on Pattern Analysis and Machine Intelligence, Vol. 17. (1995) 432-445
7. Taylor, S., Fritzson, R., Pastor, J.: Extraction of Data from Pre-printed Forms. Machine Vision and Applications, Vol. 5. No. 3. (1992) 211-222
8. Arias, J. F., Kasturi, R.: Efficient Extraction of Primitives from Line Drawings Composed of Horizontal and Vertical Lines. Machine Vision and Applications archive, Vol. 10. (1997) 214-221
9. Neves, L. A. P., Facon, J.: Methodology of Automatic Extraction of Table-Form Cells. XIII Brazilian Symposium on Computer Graphics and Image Processing, (2000) 15-21

Where the Speed Matters...
Zero-Response-Time Search Engine for
Small Collections

Ruwan Gamage

School of Information Management, Wuhan University, China
and
Library, University of Moratuwa, Sri Lanka
ruwan@lib.mrt.ac.lk

Abstract. Users with slow internet connections experience slow retrieval of results in web catalogues. JavaScript search engines can be used to enable client side search, reducing the load on the server, and increasing the response time. However, it is not a popular method until now, because of various reasons including limitation of number of data objects and lengthier response time for the first search. Here the author suggests negotiating the issue of response delay with the user. This would enable high speed basic search in small catalogues, usually with less than 300 data objects. Larger catalogues can be divided into smaller ones. Special or rare collections, multimedia artifacts and subject (web) directories are prospective candidates for this type of search systems. A prototype catalogue of 'Sri Lankan Web Sites' was tested in www.srilankasupersearch.com. Users' behavior and response to the system is yet to be studied.

Keywords: JavaScript; search engines; response time; negotiation; OPAC; models.

1 Introduction

Web based digital libraries and web catalogues offer search tools for users to mine information from databases. Most of these databases offer server side handling of search queries. In this type of systems, users experience a delay in retrieval of results. This delay is termed as response time, latency or lag time. Technically, response time refers to the amount of time it takes for input from a keyboard to reach the application and a response returned.

Length of 'response times' depends on various factors. Response time in a network is usually proportional to the number of users currently using the network, the location of the network components, and the complexity of the network.

Higher the response time, it is more embarrassing for the user. Previous research suggests that user productivity is dramatically reduced when response time is significantly longer. Sterbenz [1] states that further productivity gains are realized

E.A. Fox et al. (Eds.): ICADL 2005, LNCS 3815, pp. 224–231, 2005.
© Springer-Verlag Berlin Heidelberg 2005

when the response time decreases to the range of 100 ms. According to him, human factors studies have also indicated that consistent response time is better for users than response with a significant variance, since users alter their behavior based on response time at a relatively slow rate.

Nielsen [2] confirms that 0.1 second (100 ms) threshold is suitable while 1.0 second limit is acceptable. Within this limit users' flow of thought will be uninterrupted. Ten seconds is the limit the user can focus his attention.

These observations were used to create a model for enabling high speed client side search for a very small data set.

1.1 Client Side Processing

In contrast to client-server systems, client side search strategies mainly depend on the performance of the client computer and browser. Therefore it is quite fast to handle a search request, rather than transforming the load on to the server.

JavaScripts use this strategy efficiently. A JavaScript search engine can be used to imitate OPACs with comparatively smaller collections. Data objects for search can be arranged in an array within the JavaScript. The JavaScript then creates cookies on client machine. However the time needed to create cookies depend on the number of elements in the array. If the number of elements in the array is more, the JavaScript becomes heavy, taking a lot of time to create cookies on the client machine. A suggestion for negotiating this time lag with user is described here.

1.2 Other Attempts to Increase Response Time or Negotiating with the User

Most of the other attempts described here are meant for large databases. Though these can not be compared with this model, it will give an idea on the quest for reducing response time.

Chan and Ueda [3] focused on using cached objects with enough information to connect back to the server to request more information. However, such solutions require resources to be held open on the server, waiting for client responses. Long [4] introduces a query slicing technique which would display data in sets, not as a whole.

One other approach for searches is to build web agents. Web agents will search for information on behalf of the user, according to his preferences. Such preferences are stored in a user profile database. It has a learning function and can learn the users' likes and dislikes when the user searches the web with keyword searching thus reducing the response time for the next search [5].

Sterbenz [1] advices the programmer to display the reason for the delay, which the user can read while he waits for the result/expected page. He further proposes on running the more complex operation in a new window. That leaves the user the original page for working with, until he gets the search result.

1.3 Overview of the Search Engine

While JavaScript search engines are easy to write, and there are many predefined ones openly available on the web, the author used JSE Search, an open source Java Script [6].

JSE is platform independent and doesn't require .NET, ASP, CGI or any other technologies on host. JSE circumvents HMTL's inability to pass a value from one page to another by using a session or non-persistent cookie. The cookie expires when the user's session ends.

JSE consists of two scripts (see Appendix). The first writes a cookie containing the search words and then loads the results page. The second script does all the work; reading the cookie, defining the matches and generating the search results. Results set is a single page numbered list with links to detailed pages if available. For users, searching is similar to Google. A preceding minus character excludes a word, while phrases are supported within double-quotes.

The cookie is stored in browser's memory. Therefore subsequent searches experience virtually zero response time compared to the first search.

1.4 Data Array

Data is held as a JavaScript array, within the search.js JavaScript file. Within the array, each line consists of a data object and its description, URL, etc. If the number of data objects is high, size of file becomes larger. This will cause a delay in creating cookies on browser. That results in a delay in the response time of the first search of the session.

2 Search Model

As explained above, using a JavaScript for searching means there is a delay between the first search request and displaying of the first result. Though the delay in the first search is high, the response times of subsequent searches become virtually zero. Therefore there should be a method to negotiate with the user until the first search is carried out. The strategy used here for this is first allowing the user to do a configuration before doing the actual search. This configuration is actually a pseudo search (See fig.1).

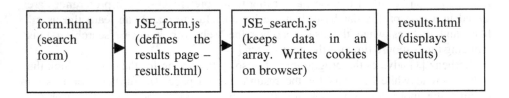

Fig. 1. Existing model for *JSE Search*

In order to achieve the pseudo search, one layer of action (2 files) was added to the existing model (See fig. 2, 3 & 4).

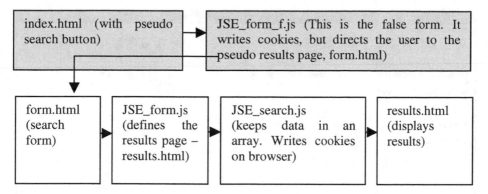

Fig. 2. Proposed model for negotiating with user to stay until *cookies* are created on browser

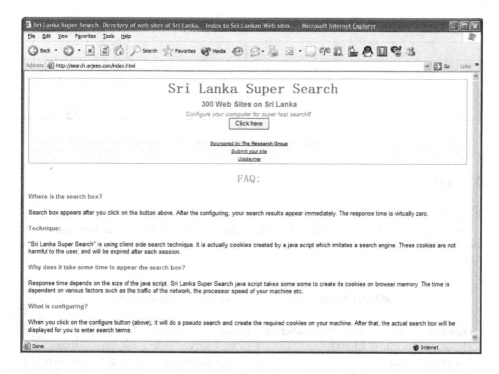

Fig. 3. Home page of *www.srilankasupersearch.com* requesting the user to configure the system before search

When the pseudo search finishes its function, the following page appears where the user can carry out his own search.

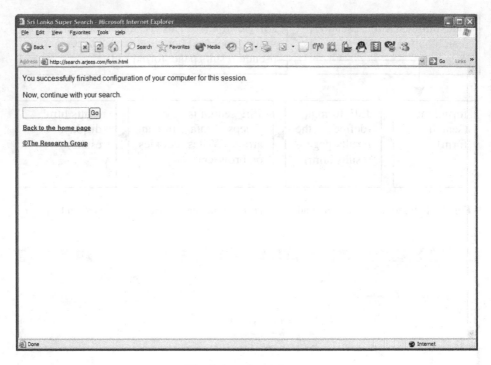

Fig. 4. Actual search page

3   Results

Response times were measured for different sized search.js files. All measures were taken using an Intel Celeron (900 MHz) machine within a half an hour time period to avoid differences in web traffic during different times of day. The results are as follows.

Table 1. Change of response time with size of the JavaScript

Number of data elements in the JavaScript array	Size of JavaScript file (kb)	Initial Response time - server side search (seconds)	Subsequent response times - client side search
1025	350	177	*
500	165	140	*
400	129	103	*
300	105	40	*

* Virtually zero

As this is a negotiated task, an empirical threshold of 40 seconds; 4 times than the limitation of keeping attention stated by Neilson [2], was considered to be acceptable.

Therefore only 300 data objects were considered for the web search. In other words, the service is for searching within a sample of 300 items.

4   Limitations, Improvements, and Uses

4.1   Limitations

Security threats, limitation of size of the file, requirement of expertise and labor to write the JavaScript are shortcomings in the present model. Also, this model can be used only with browsers which support cookies. Also, if the user has disabled script activities, the interface will simply ignore the request of the user.

Also, it should be noted that the above response times can not be standardized because these may change in other situations dependent on various factors including processor speed, internet connection, etc. which are beyond the scope of this article.

There are many disadvantages of the display method and display screen. Inability to prioritize results is a major draw back. However, already there are JavaScript search engines with many advanced features as the one given by Bradenbaugh [7]. He also claims that the JavaScript search engine he presents has carried nearly 10000 data elements without much problem.

OPAC data should be ones which can be made publicly available, because outsiders can easily download the whole JavaScript file with data, from the server. However, linked full text or other source files can be housed in the sever using ASP or other technologies, giving more security.

4.2   Improvements

Whether the user accepts this model or not is yet to be decided based on user behavior studies. If the user agrees to wait for a long time, the number of data objects can be further increased. This will also be based on the importance of the set of data objects for the user.

Writing Javascripts appears troublesome. However this can be automatically written using open source software like WinISIS, one which is familiar to library professionals. Header and footer be the same, while it is only the data objects *(array)* which is added to the script. It is a matter of creating a good *'print format'*.

4.3   Advantages and General Use

One of the benefits against a server side search engine is, this can be tested even on a stand alone computer as it is. Debugging is easy. The same JavaScripts, along with search form and results page can be housed in a real server. Therefore even school and small public libraries can house their OPACs on web. Because higher technologies such as .Net, ASP or CGI are not needed, even a free web server can be used to host the OPAC.

Because the server is made free after the first search of each session (configuration), the server can accommodate more requests from first time users. The server-side traffic is lower than server side search engines.

If the database is so large, it can be separated into well defined categories. Search can be enabled within these categories.

The categories themselves can be identified as data objects. Therefore, an optional primary search can be made available to identify which categories have results related to the user's information need.

5 Conclusion

Using JavaScript search engines for imitating OPACs for very small collections can improve the customer satisfaction by giving speed access to search results. Demanding the user to search in several search spheres is apparently a backward option, but it is worthwhile compared with virtually zero response time in subsequent searches. This would enable catalogues already on web to improve their search options. Also, this model will be helpful to immediately host web OPACs for those who have not yet done so.

This would enable high speed basic search in a very small catalogue, usually with less than 300 data objects. Rare books, dissertations, multimedia artifacts and other special collections are prospective candidates for this type of search systems.

One should not always assume that using a JavaScript search engine means some amount of delay. If the number of data objects is very low, the system may retrieve even the first results set, very quickly.

References

1. Sterbenz, James P. G.: High-Speed Networking: A Systematic Approach to High-Bandwidth Low-Latency Communication. John Wiley & Sons, Incorporated, New York (2001) 441-442.
2. Nielsen, J.: The need for speed at http://www.useit.com/alertbox/9703a.html. 1997. Retrieved June 2005.
3. Chan E. and Ueda K.: Efficient Query Result Retrieval Over the Web. In Proceedings International Conference on Parallel and Distributed Systems. IEEE Computer Society (2000).
4. Long, B. A: Design Pattern for Efficient Retrieval of Large Data Sets from Remote Data Sources in on the Move to Meaningful Internet Systems, LNCS 2519 (2002) 650–660.
5. Quah, Jon T. S., Chen, Y. M., Leow, Winnie C. H.: in Chapter XVIII Networking E-Learning Hosts Using Mobile Agents Leow, Intelligent Agents for Data Mining and Information Retrieval. Idea Group Inc., Hershey (2004). 263-293.
6. JSE Documentation. Downloaded from http://www.JavaScriptkit.com/script/script2/jse/jse10a.zip on 30.05.2005.
7. Bradenbaugh, Jerry. JavaScript Cookbook. 1st Edition October 1999 (est.) O'Reilly.

Appendix: Form.js and Search.js (part) JavaScript Files

form.js

```
// ---------- script properties ----------
var results_location = "results.html";
// ---------- end of script properties ----------
function search_form(jse_Form) {
    if (jse_Form.d.value.length > 0) {
        document.cookie = "d=" + escape(jse_Form.d.value);
        window.location = results_location;
    }
}
```

search.js

```
// ---------- script properties ----------
var include_num = 1;
var bold = 0;
// --------- sites ----------

var s = new Array();

 s[0]                                                            =
"Autosrilanka.com^http://www.autosrilanka.com/^<blockquote><b>ht
tp://www.autosrilanka.com/</b>     >>>     Free     advertisements
(vehicles)</blockquote>^Autosrilanka     Advertising     free
advertisements   promotion   vehicles   auto   cars   vans
automobilespublicity promotions marketing sales";
 s[1]                                                            =
"EeZee2.com^http://www.eezee2.com/^<blockquote><b>http://www.eez
ee2.com/</b>             >>>             Free             Classified
Advertisements.</blockquote>^EeZee2.com     Advertisingpublicity
promotions marketing sales";

 // ---------- sites continue within this array----------

 // ---------- end of script properties and sites ----------

 var cookies = document.cookie;
 var p = cookies.indexOf("d=");

 // ---------- script continues ----------
 --------
 --------
 --------
 end.
```

A Hybrid Information Retrieval Model
Using Metadata and Text

Sung Soo Kim[1], Sung Hyon Myaeng[1], and Jeong-Mok Yoo[2]

[1] Information and Communications University, Korea
{kss, myaeng}@icu.ac.kr
[2] Digital Home Research Division, Electronics and Telecommunications Research Institute,
Daejeon, Korea
jeongmok@gmail.com

Abstract. Information retrieval (IR) with metadata tends to have high precision as long as the user expresses the information need accurately but may suffer from low recall because queries are too exact with the specification of the metadata fields. On the other hand, full-text retrieval tends to suffer more from low precision especially when queries are simple and the number of documents is large. While structured queries targeted at metadata can be quite precise and the retrieval results can be accurate, it is not easy to construct an effective structured query without understanding the characteristics of the metadata. Casual users, however, are usually interested in spending time to understand the meaning of various metadata. In this paper, we propose a hybrid IR model that searches both metadata and text fields of documents. User queries are analyzed and converted into a hybrid query automatically. Experiments show that the hybrid approach outperforms either of the cases, i.e. searching text only or metadata only.

1 Introduction

Metadata are data about data. It means that metadata often describe the property of data or provide information describing the raw data such as video, audio, graphics, and text. Since metadata are succinct and structured with smaller search space, metadata-based retrieval is more efficient than full-text retrieval. When the meanings of the metadata are understood by the users or the retrieval systems, distributed data with heterogeneous characteristics can be searched and their results integrated in a consistent manner.

Despite the clear advantages and needs for metadata, users may have a burden to understand the meanings and the structure of metadata and interrelationships among different sets of metadata, in order to perform effective retrieval. As witnessed by the experiences of using Boolean retrieval systems, casual users would not be familiar with the characteristics of metadata and hence not well versed to constructing effective queries. As a result, users would benefit from a help provided by the system in constructing a structure metadata-based query or translating an information need to such a query.

E.A. Fox et al. (Eds.): ICADL 2005, LNCS 3815, pp. 232–241, 2005.
© Springer-Verlag Berlin Heidelberg 2005

Metadata-based queries have other limitations. Since metadata describe the characteristics of raw data, the information contained in them is necessarily limited compared to that contained in the raw data, although the former may not be available in the latter (i.e. the date of a document was translated). In other words, it is more likely that a metadata-based query finds nothing matched because the value space for the metadata is limited. It is also possible that the user specifies a wrong metadata field to be searched, like specifying the author field for "Elsevier", a publisher name.

Given these problems with metadata-based retrieval, we propose a hybrid retrieval model where both metadata and text fields are searched for a query. For the metadata-based retrieval part, we attempt to select appropriate metadata fields given query terms.

2 Related Work

It has been studied to translate a keyword-based query into a query for structured documents [5, 8]. In [5], they investigated the research question: do structured queries improve effectiveness in Digital Library searching? To answer this question, they empirically compared the use of unstructured queries against the use of structured queries. They then tested the capability of a simple Bayesian network system, built on top of Digital Library retrieval engine, to infer the best structured queries from keywords entered by the user.

In [8], keyword-based queries formulated by the user are given a structure by the use of Bayesian network model. They generated all candidate structured queries based on the user query by taking all combinations of the metadata fields in the document collection. The ranking of the candidates is accomplished through the use of the Bayesian network model. This is somewhat similar to the work of Croft et al. [14], where Boolean queries are derived from a natural language query, and then improved with automatically inferred phrases. Bayesian network models were first used in IR problems by Turtle and Croft [14] and later by Ribeiro and Muntz [12]. Bayesian network model also have been applied to other IR problems besides ranking, for example, relevance feedback [9], query expansion [4], structured document retrieval [10], information filtering [2], classification [3, 16].

3 Definition

Consider a database D accessible through a query interface. We define this database as a collection of documents. Each document d_i consists of metadata (M_i) alone or text (T_i) and metadata together.

$$D = \{d_1, d_2, ..., d_i, ..., d_n\} \quad n \geq 1$$

$$d_i = <M_i, T_i> \text{ where } T_i = \varnothing \text{ Or } T_i = <t_1, ..., t_j>$$

The metadata M_i consists of a set of field name (F_k), and each document has at least one metadata component which is a filed name F_k, and field value v_{ki} pair. If a document has the text field, it has at least one term.

$$M_i =< (F_1, v_{1i}), (F_2, v_{2i}), ..., (F_k, v_{ki}) > \quad k \geq 1.$$
$$\text{IF} T_i \neq \emptyset, \ T_i =< t_1, ..., t_i, ..., t_l > \quad l > 1$$

Given a document d_i, for example, consisting of three fields, title, author, and publication, with their values, "semantic web", "Tim Burners Lee", and "ACM", respectively, tt can be expressed as d_i = <(title, "semantic web"), (author, "Tim Burners Lee"), (publisher, "ACM")>

A query is divided into two parts: one is a unstructured query (UQ) and the other is a structured query (SQ). We define an unstructured query UQ as a set of keywords (or terms)

$$UQ =< t_1, t_2, ..., t_i, ..., t_l > \quad l \geq 1$$

A structured query (SQ) consists of a query for metadata (Q_M) and another for text (Q_T)

$$SQ =< Q_M, Q_T >$$

Q_M is defined as an ordered list of pairs and Q_T is the same as UQ.

$$Q_M =< (F_1, v_{1q}), (F_2, v_{2q}), .., (F_i, v_{iq}), .., (F_m, v_{mq}) > \quad m \geq 1$$
$$Q_T = UQ$$

where each F_i is a field and each v_{iq} is a value belonging to the domain of F_i. Field value v_{iq} has at least one term.

$$v_{iq} =< t_1, t_2, .., t_i, .., t_l > \quad l \geq 1$$

In this paper, metadata fields in a structured query can be divided into two types of fields: one is the field that the user selects (F_{user_select}) and the other is what the system selects (F_{system_select}). If a structured query was given by a user as SQ = <(title, "information retrieval"), (author, "Kim")>, F_{user_select} corresponds to title and author. When unstructured query is entered by the user, the system infers the relevant fields from the collection. The resulting field is F_{system_select}. For example, an unstructured query formulated by the user as UQ = <"information retrieval">, the system can reason out the relevant field to given terms. If "title" is given by the system, F_{system_select} is title.

4   Retrieval Environment

We consider the following assumptions. First, a user may submit an unstructured or structured query. Second, the user is not familiar with creating a structured query. Therefore, there may be another field more relevant to the user query than the field that the user selects. Finally, no relevant document can be found when only a particular metadata field is searched, making it necessary to search other metadata fields as well as text.

Our proposed model consists of the following parts to be executed in sequence:

1. Finding the field that is the most related to user query
   Similarity or relevance of a field with respect to the user query is first calculated so that the fields are ranked based on their relevance for the query. The field with the most relevance value is selected as the metadata field to be searched. For example, when UQ = <"Tim Burners Lee"> and we find the "author" field as the most appropriate for "Tim Burners Lee", SQ becomes <(author, "Tim burners Lee")}>. The way relevance for individual metadata fields is explained later.
2. Retrieving documents based on the selected metadata field
   If SQ is <(author, "Tim Burners Lee")>, the value is searched against the specified field of individual documents.
3. Retrieving documents based on the text
   The following query SQ = <(text, "Tim burners Lee")> is used to search the text.
4. Merging two similarities from the metadata and text fields for ranking documents.

5   Hybrid Information Retrieval Model

5.1   Processing a Structured Query

A structured query is the one with a field designated by the user. Assuming that users may have difficulty formulating a structured query and that there may be another metadata field more relevant to the user's information need than the field the user selected, we should judge whether the field-value pairs in a query are suitable or not. In [8], they used a Bayesian network model to determine the ranking of the candidate queries.

In our approach, we attempt to judge relevance of a metadata field for a query by computing the similarity between the vector based on the terms in the user query and the vector representing the content of a metadata field in the entire collection. This is an indirect way of judging the semantics of a metadata field and the likelihood that the query terms would be found in the field.

More formally, we create an imaginary document C_{field} for a given field by aggregating all the terms occurring in individual fields F_i of the same kind in the collection. Essentially, the terms collected from the same field in all the documents form a vector for a "mega" document. The similarity between C_{field} and the query terms is represented as:

$$Sim(\vec{C}_{field}, \vec{q})$$

which is defined in Section 5.3.

For example, when SQ = <(title, "information retrieval")> is given, appropriateness of the field *title* as the metadata field to be search can be calculated by computing the similarity between a mega document C_{title} and the query vector $\vec{q}$ consisting of "information retrieval." The same computation is done for other fields to select the best fit.

A system selected query is defined as the query that has the highest similarity value:

$$Sim(\vec{C}_{system\_select}, \vec{q}) = \max[Sim(\vec{C}_1, \vec{q}), ..., Sim(\vec{C}_i, \vec{q})] \quad i \neq user\_select$$

There are two possible cases:

1) $Sim(\vec{C}_{system\_select}, \vec{q}) \leq Sim(\vec{C}_{user\_select}, \vec{q})$

2) $Sim(\vec{C}_{system\_select}, \vec{q}) > Sim(\vec{C}_{user\_select}, \vec{q})$

In (1), the user probably has chosen the right field for the query. In (2), however, the user may have selected an inappropriate field although it is important not to ignore the field selected by the user. Instead of replacing the user selected field by the system selected one, we uses both. As a result, when the condition (1) holds, we search two fields, the user selected and the text fields, while we search three fields when the condition (2) holds: user selected, system selected, and text fields.

5.2 Processing an Unstructured Query

An unstructured query is defined as consisting of keywords only without a metadata field designation. In this case, the system needs to translate the query into a structured one by selecting the metadata field that is most related to the original query.

$$Sim(\vec{C}_{system\_select}, \vec{q}) = \max[Sim(\vec{C}_1, \vec{q}), ..., Sim(\vec{C}_i, \vec{q})]$$

The way we calculate pertinence of a field with respect to the query is shown in 5.3.

5.3 Pertinence of a Field to a Query

Pertinence judgment of a field with respect to a query is based on the similarity calculation in the vector space model [1]. A mega document consisting of the terms occurring in a specific field (C_{field}) and a user query (q) are represented as t-dimensional vectors. The similarity between the vectors $\vec{C}_{field}$ and $\vec{q}$ can be measured by the cosine of the angle between these two vectors:

$$Sim(\vec{C}_i, \vec{q}) = \cos(\vec{C}_i, \vec{q}) = \frac{\sum_{t_k \in T_i} w_{ik} g_k(\vec{q})}{\sqrt{\sum_{t_k \in T_i} w_{ik}^2} * \sqrt{\sum_{t_k \in T_i} g_k(\vec{q})^2}}, \quad w_{ik} = ftf_i(k) * fidf(k)$$

where $ftf_i(k)$ is term frequency of term k in the field i, i.e., the number of times term k occurs in the field i, and $fidf(k)$ is the inverse field frequency, i.e., the inverse of the number of fields in which the term k appears. $g_k(\overrightarrow{q})$ gives the value of the *k-th* variable of the vector $\overrightarrow{q}$, and T_i is the set of all the terms in the mega document corresponding to the field F_j.

5.4 Retrieving Documents

Having chosen the best field for the given query, the next step is to calculate the similarity between individual documents and the query. This can be done in the same way documents are retrieved in a conventional vector space model, except that the document vector is defined for the metadata field chosen previously. Hence, we compute the similarity between d_{ij} and $\overrightarrow{q}$ as follows:

$$Sim(\vec{d}_{ij}, \overrightarrow{q}) = \cos(\vec{d}_{ij}, \overrightarrow{q}) = \frac{\sum_{t_k \in T_i} w_{ik} g_k(\overrightarrow{q})}{\sqrt{\sum_{t_k \in T_i} w^2_{ik}} * \sqrt{\sum_{t_k \in T_i} g_k(\overrightarrow{q})^2}}, \quad w_{ik} = ftf_{ij}(k) * idf_i(k)$$

where $ftf_{ij}(k)$ is the term frequency of term k in field i of document j, i.e., the number of times the term k occurs in the field i of document j, and $idf_i(k)$ is the inverse document frequency, i.e., the inverse of the number of documents term k appears in field i. $g_k(\overrightarrow{q})$ gives the value of the *k-th* variable of the vector $\overrightarrow{q}$, and T_i is the set of all terms in the values of field F_j.

5.5 Merging Similarities and Ranking Retrieved Documents

After documents are retrieved based on two or more designated fields, the results should be combined to return a ranked list of documents to the user. Fig. 1 shows how to merge the similarities calculated for multiple fields in document d_1.

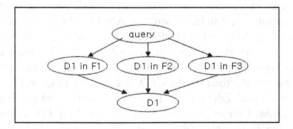

Fig. 1. Merging the retrieved documents

The similarities are calculated with $Sim(\vec{d}_{11}, \overrightarrow{q})$, $Sim(\vec{d}_{21}, \overrightarrow{q})$, and $Sim(\vec{d}_{31}, \overrightarrow{q})$. When they are merged to the final similarity, we reflect the pertinence value between a field and the query such as $Sim(\vec{C}_1, \overrightarrow{q})$, $Sim(\vec{C}_2, \overrightarrow{q})$, and $Sim(\vec{C}_3, \overrightarrow{q})$.

For merging similarities, we adopt the evidence gathering method used in the inference network approach to information retrieval [14]. For example, $Sim(\vec{d}_{11}, \vec{q})$ and $Sim(\vec{d}_{21}, \vec{q})$ should be merged if the document was retrieved based on the two fields chosen with $Sim(\vec{C}_1, \vec{q})$ and $Sim(\vec{C}_2, \vec{q})$. In this case, the belief calculation is done with the following link matrix L_{d1} that specifies the conditional probabilities for different combinations of the fields being used.

$$L_{d1} = \begin{bmatrix} 1 & 1 - Sim(\vec{C}_2, \vec{q}) & 1 - Sim(\vec{C}_1, \vec{q}) & 0 \\ 0 & Sim(\vec{C}_2, \vec{q}) & Sim(\vec{C}_1, \vec{q}) & 1 \end{bmatrix}$$

Here the second row is for the case where the document is retrieved with different fields. The value in the first column represents the probability that the document is retrieved when both fields are not used. The values in the second and third columns are for the cases where the second and third fields are used, respectively. The last column specifies the probability of retrieving the document when both fields are used.

Using the link matrix, the final similarity value for d_i is calculated as follows:

$$Sim(d_1, \vec{q}) = Sim(\vec{C}_2, \vec{q}) * Sim(d_{21}, \vec{q}) * (1 - Sim(d_{11}, \vec{q})) +$$
$$Sim(\vec{C}_2, \vec{q}) * Sim(d_{11}, \vec{q}) * (1 - Sim(d_{21}, \vec{q})) + Sim(d_{11}, \vec{q}) * Sim(d_{21}, \vec{q})$$

6 Experiment

The purpose of our experiment was to demonstrate superiority of the proposed hybrid method compared to other forms of queries: 1) unstructured queries for text retrieval (UG), 2) structured queries specified by the user for metadata retrieval (SQ), and 3) automatically constructed structured queries as proposed in [8] (VQ). The hybrid queries proposed by this research retrieve both metadata and text and the similarity values are combined to rank the documents. The structured part can come from the user or from the system. For SQ, we consider both AND and OR queries where multiple field specifications are combined with an AND or OR quries, respectively. They are referred to as SQ (AND) and SQ (OR). There are two types in VQ: V1 is the case where only one best query is used for retrieval whereas V1-5 is the case for using the best five structured queries for retrieval and merging the five result sets.

Experiments were performed on the CITIDEL (Computing and Information Technology Interactive Digital Educational Library) collection which contains metadata from the ACM Digital Library, the DBLP collection, NDLTD-computing (the computing subset of the Networked Digital Library of Theses and Dissertations), and other sources – totaling more than 440,000 metadata records. Only a subset of the ACM Digital Library, with approximately 98,000 metadata records, was supported by Virginia Tech Digital Library Research Lab. Among these metadata, we used only 39,698 metadata that contain the abstract field. The metadata fields considered in the experiment were title, author, publication, and abstract, where publication means the name of the conference or journal where the paper was published.

All relevant and non-relevant documents returned for each query were used to compute precision and recall, and F1 measures. Precision is the percentage of retrieved documents that are relevant. Recall is the percentage of all the relevant documents in the collection. It indicates if the system is able to retrieve all of the relevant documents. Finally, F1 combines precision and recall with equal weights and is defined as F1=2PR/(P+R).

Table 1. Performance

	UQ	SQ(AND)	SQ (OR)	V1	V1-V5	HQ
Precision	26.05%	55.08%	50.10%	50.52%	51.05%	54.37%
Recall	40.72%	39.55%	79.87%	79.79%	80.62%	86.30%
10-Precision	28.24	65.87	72.50	80.08	82.01	84.12
F1	30.01	46.29	60.17	60.59	62.51	66.71

6.1 Comparison Among UQ, SQ, and V1

As shown in table1, SQ is superior to UQ. This is simply because the queries are more suitable for metadata than text. Besides, SQ was constructed by the actual users, reflecting their information needs more exactly than UQ. The performance values of V1 and SQ are similar because the automatically structured queries in V1 are almost identical to the structured queries constructed manually in SQ [8].

6.2 Comparison Among SQ, VT1, and V1-V5

The performance of the V1-V5 case where the top five automatically generated queries were used is better than that of SQ. This is because SQ or V1 retrieves from only one field that the user selected or the system selected, but V1-V5 retrieves from at least two fields. For example, unstructured queries entered as UQ = <"information retrieval">, SQ or VT1 can be only one structured query among candidate queries such as <(title, "information retrieval")>, <(text, "information retrieval")>, <(publication, "information retrieval")>, <(title, "information") (text, "retrieval")>, or <(text, "information") (title, "retrieval")>.

6.3 Comparison Between V1-V5 and HQ

As in Table 1, the performance of HQ that merges results from the best metadata fields and text is better than that of V1-V5. Our analysis shows that this is due to the shortcomings of the V1-V5 queries and at the same time the strengths of the proposed hybrid methods.

1. Excessively expanded fields in V1-V5
   V1-V5 builds all possible candidate queries and ranks them based on the probability of best representing the user's need. Since the top 5 structured queries are used for retrieval, it is entirely possible that one or more of the fields are totally irrelevant to the terms used in the original query. For example, if the query entered is UQ = <"information retrieval">, <(publication, "information retrieval")> can be included among

the top five structured queries. This may retrieve many irrelevant documents because the publication field is likely to contain the term "information" with a high frequency.

2. Not using the weights of the top 5 structured queries in V1-V5

Even though V1-V5 adopted the Bayesian network model to calculate the probability of generating the top 5 structured queries, the probability values are not used for retrieval. When Q1 is the highest ranked query and Q5 is the lowest, they are treated equally. Even when the results are combined, their relative merits are not considered.

On the other hand, HQ, proposed in this paper, has two fields (system selected and text fields) or three fields (user selected, system selected, and text fields), so that it doesn't suffer so much from the first problem. Moreover, the relative importance of the metadata fields is taken into account when the documents retrieved by different fields are merged.

7 Conclusion and Future Work

We proposed a new retrieval model for documents containing metadata and text, focusing on three ideas: 1) generating automatically structured queries, i.e. choosing the right metadata fields for query terms, by calculating their pertinence with the similarity between a mega documents containing all the terms in the field across all the documents and the query terms, 2) retrieving from both metadata and text fields in a complementary manner, and 3) using the pertinence values for the chose metadata fields when the retrieval results are merged.

The proposed method can provide the user with relevant documents even though the user specified an inappropriate metadata field. The experiments show that the proposed model can provide more relevant items than a previously introduced method because it retrieves not only from metadata field, either specified by the user or the system, but also from the text field.

It is very important to decide what metadata fields are searched when a structured query is generated. Although the efforts in semantic Web and ontology are trying to fill the gap among different metadata, the users do not necessarily understand the meaning of the metadata fields fully and may not have enough ideas about which fields he needs to search, without knowing the data characteristics. While the proposed model attempts to calculate pertinence of metadata fields for given query terms and combine metadata search with text search, more analytic research would be necessary for better understanding of their interplays.

References

1. Baeza-Yates, R., Ribeiro-Neto, B.: Modern Information Retrieval. Addison Wesley, New York, NY (1999)
2. Callan, J, P.: Document filtering with inference networks. In Proceedings of the 19th Annual International ACM SIGIR Conference on Research and Development in Information Retrieval, Zurich Switzerland (1996) 262-269

3. Calado, P., Cristo, M., Moura, E., Ziviani B., Goncalves, M, A.: Combining link-based and content-based methods for web document classification. In Proceedings of the 12ᵗʰ International Conference on Information and Knowledge Management, New Orleans LA USA (2003) 394-401

4. Campos, L, M., Ferenandez-Luna, J, M., Huete, J, F.: Query Expansion in Information Retrieval Systems Using a Bayesian Network-Based Thesaurus. In Proceedings of the 14ᵗʰ Annual Conference on Uncertainty in Artificial Intelligence (UAI-98), San Francisco CA (1998) 53-60

5. Calado, P., Silva, A, S., Vieria, R, C., Laender, A, H, F., Ribeiro-Neto, B, A.: Searching Web Databases by Structuring Keyword-based Queries. In proceedings of the 11ᵗʰ International Conference on Information and Knowledge Management, McLean VA USA (2002) 26-33

6. Dumais, S, T., Platt, P., Hecherman, D., Sahami, M.: Inductive learning algorithms and representations for text categorization. In Proceedings of the 7ᵗʰ International Conference on Information and Knowledge Management CIKM'98, Bethesda Maryland USA (1998) 148-155

7. Deniman, D., Sumner, T., Davis L., Bhushan, S., Jackson · Merging Metadata and Content-Based Retreival. In proceedings of Journal of Digital Information, Volume 4 Issue 3.

8. Goncalves, M, A., Fox, E, A., Krowne, A., Calado, P., Laender, A, H, F., Silva, A, S., Ribeiro-Neto, B, A.: The effectiveness of Automatically Structured Queries in Digital libraries. In proceedings of the 2004 joint ACM/IEEE conference on Digital libraries - Volume 00, Tuscon AZ USA (2004)

9. Haines, D., Croft, W, B.: Relevance feedback and inference networks. In Proceedings of the 16ᵗʰ Annual International ACM SIGIR Conference on Research and Development in Information Retrieval, Pittsburgh, PA, USA, June (1993) 2-11.

10. Myacng, S. II., Jang, D. H., Kim, M. S., Zhoo, J. C.: A Flexible Model for Retrieval of SGML documents." Proc. of the 21st ACM SIGIR International Conference on Research and Development in Information Retrieval, Melbourne, Australia (1998).

11. Passin, T, B.: Explorer's Guide to the Semantic Web, Manning press (2004)

12. Ribeiro-Neto, B., Muntz, R.: A belief network model for IR. In proceedings of the 19ᵗʰ Annual International ACM SIGIR Conference on Research and Development in Information Retrieval, Zurich, Switzerland, August (1996) 253-260

13. Silva, I., Ribeiro-Neto, B., Calado, P., Moura, E., Ziviani, N.: Linked-based and Content-Based Evidential Information in a Belief Network Model. In Proceedings of the 23ʳᵈ Annual International ACM SIGIR Conference on Research and Development in Information Retrieval, Athens Greece (2000) 96-103

14. Turtle, H, R., Croft, W, B.: Inference networks for document retrieval. In Proceedings of the 13ᵗʰ Annual International ACM SIGIR Conference on Research and Development in Information Retrieval, Brussels, Belgium, September (1990) 1-24.

15. Turtle, H, R., Croft, W, B.: Croft. Evaluation of an Inference network-Based Retrieval Model. ACM Transactions on Information Systems 9,3 (1991), 187-222

16. Valle, R, F., Ribeiro-Neto, B, A., Lima, L, R, S., Laender, A, H, F., Junior, H, R , F, F.: Improving text retrieval in medical collections through automatic categorization. In Proceedings of the 10ᵗʰ International Symposium on String Processing and Information Retrieval SPIRE 2003, Manaus Brazil (2003) 197-210.

A Standards-Based Approach for Supporting Dynamic Access Policies for a Federated Digital Library

K. Bhoopalam, K. Maly, F. McCown, R. Mukkamala, and M. Zubair

Department of Computer Science,
Old Dominion University, Norfolk, Virginia 23529 USA
Voice: 1+757+683+3915
{kbhoopal, maly, fmccown, mukka, zubair}@cs.odu.edu

Abstract. With the increasing acceptability of interoperability standards like Open Archives Initiative protocol for metadata harvesting, it is becoming feasible to build federated discovery services which aggregate metadata from different digital libraries (data providers) and provide a unified search interface to users. Content-based access control is one of the primary requirements of data providers. While this concept has been predominant in the research realm, practical systems incorporating this concept are rare. In this paper, we propose a framework that supports and enforces content-based access policies using existing COTS components. We have prototyped the framework by building a system using XACML, and a XACML policy engine. The system can also be generalized to environments other than digital libraries.

Keywords: metadata, access control, content management.

1 Introduction

With the increasing acceptability of interoperability standards like Open Archives Initiative protocol for metadata harvesting, it is becoming feasible to build federated discovery services [9, 10]. These services aggregate metadata from different digital libraries (data providers) and provide a unified search interface to users. One of the primary obstacles that keep data providers from joining the federation is the lack of an infrastructure to support content-based access policies. A data provider is more willing to share its metadata with a service provider if it can provide content-based access control, in addition to the traditional access control (e.g., role-based [14]).

Our earlier works [2, 3] addressed the basic issues in managing access to a federation service that is being accessed by many communities (e.g., educational institutions), each having different contracts with different commercial data providers (e.g., American Physical Society) to the federation and content-based restriction using XACML [12]. In this paper, we propose a framework that supports and enforces content-based restrictions and provisional actions defined by data providers for a federated digital library.

Content-based restrictions restrict access to full text or metadata containing specific phrases. For example, we can restrict any material containing word *nuclear* from being accessed by a specific user group. In addition, we provide another

E.A. Fox et al. (Eds.): ICADL 2005, LNCS 3815, pp. 242–252, 2005.
© Springer-Verlag Berlin Heidelberg 2005

important feature relevant for both government and commercial agencies: *provisional actions*. Provisional actions [7] are directives such as auditing of information access prior to the granting of access privileges to a user. For example, an administrator may require a digital library to send an e-mail prior to providing access to a user from a certain organization. It is possible to combine content-based restrictions with provisional actions such as "send an e-mail to the data provider if a specific user community accesses any of its material containing the word *nuclear*."

This paper elaborates our framework and a prototype implementation to incorporate the above two features into a general access management system. While the framework is flexible in terms of its modularity and ability to incorporate COTS components, the prototype implementation of the framework illustrates how the available technologies such as Shibboleth and XACML can actually be employed to achieve the goals. The paper is organized as follows. Section 2 summarizes previous work in this area. Section 3 describes the proposed framework. In section 4, we provide details of our prototype implementation. Section 5 discusses the frameworks and the prototype implementation challenges. Finally, section 6 summarizes our contributions and discusses future work. In particular, we describe our goals for the framework and the flexible framework for access control models in digital libraries to include provisional actions and content-based restrictions.

2 Previous Work

In this section, we provide background information on Archon a federated digital library on which much of our work is based and also discuss previous work in this area.

2.1 Archon: A Distributed Access Management System for Federated Digital Library

In a federated digital library, the aggregator enforces a custodial contract governing the relationship between contributors and subscribers using an access manager. Archon [11] is an Open Archives Initiative [9] compliant federated digital library with an emphasis on physics for the National Science Digital Library (NSDL) [13]. In our earlier work [3], we developed an authentication and access control architecture for Archon. Archon uses the Dublin Core Metadata standard [5] to store metadata. We have used vocabulary from the Dublin Core standard for representing resources and vocabulary from EduPerson [6] for representing subject attributes in our preliminary '<subject , resource, action>' Access Policies, thereby providing a uniform naming convention for resources and subject attributes. It also provides a technological demonstration of secure federated digital libraries to support authentication at authoritative sources. In [2] we have shown how COTS based policy languages can be used to represent content-based access control.

2.2 Content Labeling vs. Content Restrictions as Obligations

Some of the earlier work on content based authorization models [1] proposes the association of "concepts" with digital library. "Concepts" as the name implies are a set of phrases that accurately capture the relevance of a digital object. The association of concepts is akin to content-based authorization based on a label value. We believe that their approach adds considerable administrative overhead whenever a new digital object is introduced. Additionally, it is not favorable for content-based access on pre-existing digital archives that have not introduced this labeling mechanism. Our approach does not require additional labels, and allows for the specification of content-based restrictions on the values of any of the meta-data fields or labels.

2.3   Embedding Access Control Information Within Digital Objects vs. External Representation

Some systems such as [8] wrap a digital object (e.g., multimedia objects) with authorization information. Although such an association allows for fine-grained access to parts of a digital object, the association remains static. Hence, it is not possible to include content-based access control using this method. Additionally, the model also does not permit provisional actions. In our work, we employ external representation of authorization information to facilitate more flexible authorization as well as accommodate content based restrictions.

3   Proposed Access Enforcement Framework

As mentioned in the introduction, the primary contribution of this paper is a flexible framework for access management in federated digital libraries. In particular, the objectives for the framework are as follows.

1. Provide a modular framework for the enforcement of content-based access control with provisional actions.
2. Facilitate content based access control in digital libraries without any fundamental changes to the submission, dissemination and preservation process of digital collections.

In our framework (figure 1), we enforce content based access restrictions and provisional actions without additional infrastructure or tools, beyond what may be used for access control on metadata fields. We have incorporated content-based restrictions and the provisional actions at two points: the Policy Decision Point (PDP) and Policy Enforcement modules (PEP). The framework is described in terms of interactions (1-15) among different components. The access requestor receives the user's request via the gateway in any (or among a set of) domain dependent formats (1). Upon receiving the request, the access requestor fetches the policies required for access evaluation and the necessary information required for request construction from the resource and access policy directory (2). Then, the access requestor submits the relevant policies and the requests to the PDP (3). The PDP evaluates the requests against the policies, and provides responses to the access decision handler (4). The access decision handler constructs an access token to store the compendium of the access decisions and invokes the pre-query provisional action fulfiller, the query builder, and the post query provisional action fulfiller to implement content independent provisional actions, fetch content from the digital library and implement content based provisional actions (5-13). Finally the access decision handler passes the fetched content and the access token to a user interface filter that renders the content based on the access decisions in the access token (14,15).

Our framework modularizes the Policy Enforcement Point and establishes clear interfaces with the PDP, the resource directories, the information repository (database) and other tools required for provisional actions. This modular architecture allows for changes in the modules and also the exclusion of modules as and when user requirements change with minimum impact. For example, if user's attributes are received in a different format, the access requestor is the only module that needs to be changed. Similarly, if the domain of the resources and the permitted actions change, the Access-Requestor needs only to interact with a different Resource and Access policy Directory. The Pre and Post-Query Provisional Action fulfiller can be excluded if the access control system does not require provisional actions. The Post-Query Provisional action fulfiller can be excluded if there aren't any provisional actions that depend upon the contents of the information fetched from the database. A separate Query Builder isolates data-base connection handling and access in a separate module, hence, allowing for queries to be optimized for various databases (the system uses JDBC to connect to an oracle database, and hence is considered database independent as long the database understand the SQL standard,). Additionally a separate User-Interface handler provides for the separation between access-evaluation, storage mechanism and information presentation.

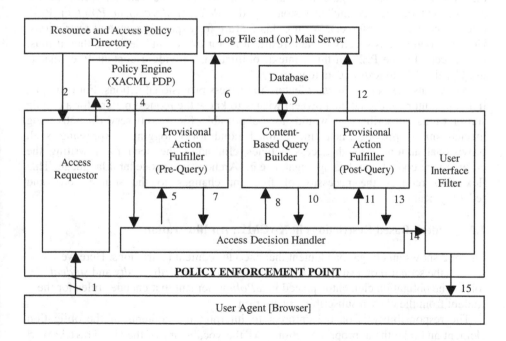

Fig. 1. Access Enforcement Framework

4 Implementation

The current implementation of the proposed framework is primarily based on three components: (a) OAI-PMH based Archon [12] (b) the Shibboleth framework [4] to provide secure remote authentication and transport of authenticated information, and (c) XACML to specify access control rules. In the rest of the section we elaborate on the specification and enforcement of content restrictions and provisional actions (using XACML), the implementation of the access enforcer, and how the adoption of a standards-based tool for specification (e.g., XACML) has influenced our design of the access enforcer.

4.1 Implementing Content-Based Restrictions and Provisional Actions

We have used XACML's *obligation* feature (element) for specifying content restrictions and provisional actions. In the current implementation, we have limited content-based restrictions to metadata fields only. For example, students from a particular subscribing institution are restricted from viewing records with (i) a "description" metadata field containing phrases "nuclear weapon" and/or "anthrax" and (ii) a "subject" field containing the phrase "WMD."

In XACML, obligations are used to provide directives to the enforcer. Each obligation in a *Policy* element can be associated with a "Permit" or "Deny" decision. If an obligation accompanies a "Permit" decision for a particular access request, then the XACML semantics state that all obligations *must* be fulfilled prior to the enforcement of the "Permit" decision (by the *Policy Enforcement Point* or PEP, referred here as the enforcer). We use this feature for expressing content restrictions. Hence, if obligations specify content restrictions for a "Permit" decision, then it must be enforced by the PEP. In this context, obligations provide a content filter that is used by the PEP to restrict data to users.

We can also use the *obligation* feature to express provisional actions. For example, if a contributor (or digital data owner) wishes to know the request pattern for a certain subset of its subscribers, it would not be possible for a web server's native log mechanism to provide such fine grained conditional logging. Expressing such provisional actions through access policies eliminates the need for rewriting the enforcement code at the data aggregator (e.g., Archon) in a procedural language. This flexibility reduces the necessity of frequent changes to the source code and redeployment.

4.2 Content-Based Restrictions in XACML: An Illustration

Figure 2 shows an obligation element that encodes content restrictions. Here we assume the scenario of a subscribing academic institution with *faculty* and *student* roles. The obligation element is placed in a *Policy* element that encodes rules for the student from the chosen subscribing institution.

The responsibility is on the enforcer to interpret the contents of the obligation element and take the appropriate actions. As the vocabulary of the `ObligationId` and `AttributeAssignment` attribute values are not standards based, it is important that people responsible for coding the policy enforcer and the policy editor

```
<Policy>
  ...
  <Obligations>
    <Obligation ObligationId="content_restrictions"
    FulfillOn="Permit">
    <AttributeAssignment AttributeId="description"
            DataType="http://www.w3.org/2001/XMLSchema#string">
            nuclear:anthrax</AttributeAssignment></Obligation>
  </Obligations>
</Policy>
```

Fig. 2. Content Restrictions in XACML

agree upon the syntax and the semantics of the various directives listed in the obligations. In the absence of such cooperation, the enforcer would not understand the obligation(s) and hence would not be able to provide any access privileges (based on XACML guidelines) to the user. It should be noted that this example can lead to "false positives," for example, a content restriction string If multiple phrases need to be specified for content restrictions in each metadata field, they are separated by a colon (e.g., nuclear:anthrax). As this obligation is encoded to be fulfilled on a permit decision, the policy engine returns the entire obligation *as is* to the enforcer (PEP). This obligation is translated into a SQL statement below to ensure that only the required information is fetched from the database. XACML snippets are agreed upon by the enforcer and the policy specifier. In the example, the obligation with obligationId "content-restrictions" states the following: "Whenever a (student role) user's request is permitted (e.g., permission to read metadata), the user may not see records that contain *nuclear* or *anthrax* in the description field.

> SELECT <permitted column list indicating metadata names>
> FROM <database table>
> WHERE (description NOT LIKE (%nuclear%)
> OR description NOT LIKE (%anthrax%))

However, this method may have unintended consequences of excluding valid material. If the phrase "nuclear" was intended to hide digital objects that contain "nuclear bomb" or "nuclear device" may also hide digital objects that contain phrases like "nuclear family". We are currently working towards a method that allows for the specification of regular expressions, so that a trained security administrator, using a visual editor, can accurately define content-restriction phrases thereby reducing the occurrence of such false positives.

4.3 Provisional Actions: An Example

In the XACML implementation for our system, all content based provisional actions are characterized as either "pre-query" or "post-query" using the obligationId.

The snippet in Figure 3 encodes a pre-query provisional "pre_query_audit", which mandates that the policy enforcer log the *time* and the *role,* or *identity* if available of the requesting user, and a "post_query_email" which mandates that an e-mail be sent to dlib-admin@cs.odu.edu if the "description" metadata field of contents fetched from the database have the phrase "particle physics" in them. The policy evaluator responds with the obligations only if the request is permitted. This requirement is stated in the FulfillOn attribute of the obligation.

```
<Policy>
   ....
   <Obligations>
      <Obligation ObligationId="pre_query_audit" FulfillOn="Permit">
      <AttributeAssignment AttributeId="time"
                   DataType="http://www.w3.org/2001/XMLSchema#string">

                   CURRENT_TIMESTAMP</AttributeAssignment>
      <AttributeAssignment AttributeId="subject"
                   DataType="http://www.w3.org/2001/XMLSchema#string">
                   role:identity</AttributeAssignment></Obligation>
      <Obligation ObligationId="post_query_email" FulfillOn="Permit">
      <AttributeAssignment AttributeId="content_description"
                   DataType="http://www.w3.org/2001/XMLSchema#string">
                   particle physics</AttributeAssignment>
      <AttributeAssignment AttributeId="emailto"
                   DataType="http://www.w3.org/2001/XMLSchema#string">
                   dlib-admin@cs.odu.edu</AttributeAssignment>
      <AttributeAssignment AttributeId="static body"
                   DataType="http://www.w3.org/2001/XMLSchema#string">
                   Accessing flagged records.</AttributeAssignment>
               </Obligation>
      </Obligations>
   </Policy>
```

Fig. 3. Content-based Provisional actions in XACML

4.4 Formal Specification of Content-Based Access Control with Provisional Actions

Content restrictions have the effect of hiding the entire digital object for which the content restriction rule satisfies. Label or metadata based restrictions have the effect of hiding only the label or metadata, and applies to all digital objects being retrieved.

Content based access control: (credentials, labels$_1$, privilege, +) ^ Σ(credentials, label$_2$, restriction-phrase, -)

A user with attributes 'credentials' is granted the privilege (currently a read permission) on the labels$_1$ of those digital objects which do not have the phrases specified as 'restriction-phase' in label$_2$. The 'Σ' indicates that content-restrictions can be specified on different labels of a digital object.

Content based provisional actions: (credentials, labels$_1$, privilege, [+ or -]) ^ Σ(credentials, label$_2$, restriction-phrase, pa)

A user with attributes 'credentials' is granted or denied the privilege (currently a read permission) on the labels$_1$ of digital objects, and if the digital objects contain the phrases specified in 'restriction-phase' for label$_2$, the provisional actions 'pa' must be implemented. The 'Σ' indicates that content-restrictions can be specified on different labels of a digital object. Although most previous instances of the "credentials" in this paper refer to user's role in his home (also subscribing) organization, the XACML specification allows any number of attributes of the user including user ID, age, time or location of access, etc. Using XACML provides our implementation with the capability to easily extend the complexity of the access rules. In our system, the XACML policy specifies the role-privilege mapping. The user-role mapping is performed at the home organization of the user and the mapping is honored by the policy enforcer at the aggregator.

4.5   Management of Access Policies

As specified earlier, a contributor has a contractual agreement with subscribers, thereby enabling selected personnel from the subscribing institutions to have access to the contributor's content (hosted by Archon). Archon provides the contributor with a "Policy Editor" tool to manage access policies for end-user roles of its subscribing institutions. The matrix format [15] shown in figure 4 is among the most widely used access models and visual representation method to specify access control as it allows for only consistent rules to be specified. XACML per se does allow inconsistent rules to be formulated. As we have demonstrated already in [3], this form of policy specification can be automatically translated into XACML and is extremely easy to use by non-technical people.

Figure 4 is a scaled-down version (contains fewer services and metadata, and end user roles than the test bed) of the policy editor we have developed for our system. Figure 4 shows the access policy of the contributor APS for faculty of the subscribing institution ODU. A selected check box indicates the metadata or the services is permitted for the specific end user role. The checked items are listed as resources in

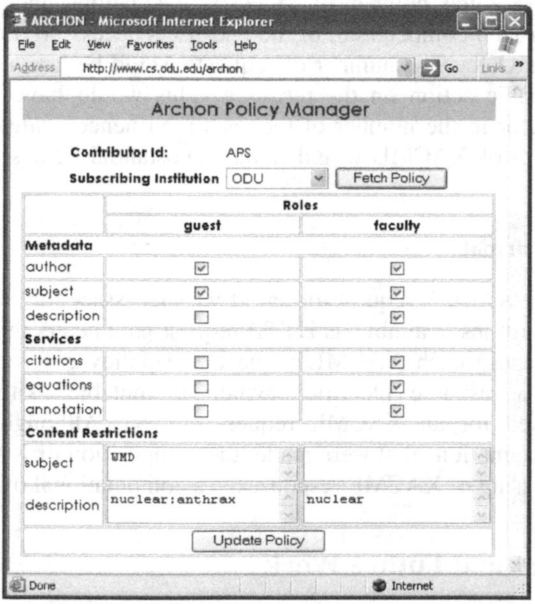

Fig. 4. Access Policy Editor

an XACML rule and each permitted resource is accessed from the database by including the corresponding column name in the SQL query shown earlier. The content restrictions are applied to the description and subject metadata fields and are specified as colon separated phrases. The content administrator manages XACML access policies through this simple point-and-click editor that enforces the specification of consistent access policies.

5 Discussion

As we have adopted a standards-based approach to implement access control, we have been limited by several constraints of the standards. This section describes some of the complexities of our implementation due to our choice of XACML for access specification. XACML specifies a schema for specifying requests to the policy decision point and for responses when the policy decision point responds with its decision. The schema of the request format constrains each XACML request to encapsulate only one `resource` element and only one `action` element. The schema of the response context contains a single `decision` element that specifies whether the request was permitted or denied. This request specification format introduced several limitations in our system.

5.1 Number of Interactions Between Policy Enforcer and Policy Decision Point

End users can have different sets of permissions on the resources provided by different contributors; hence, multiple requests are required to compose the compendium of access privileges. If the number of resources provided by a contributor is $O(K)$, the number of requests, evaluations and responses that are required to construct a compendium of the end-users access privilege on resources of one contributor is $O(K)$. The number of requests would be larger if there were more than one permissible action on the resource. This would have introduced another multiplicative factor in the number of requests (and hence evaluations). We believe that this constraint of XACML would induce substantial delays in high-transaction digital libraries.

5.2 Changing Formats

Due to the current XACML request format, it was necessary for the policy enforcer to translate user assertions available as HTTP request parameters into XACML context requests. To compose each XACML request, the policy enforcer embeds the user credentials and a resource identifier, which is mutable, within the immutable constructs required for an XACML request context. Although simple in design because of the assumptions that were made, the composition of XACML requests and subsequent processing of XACML responses is a computational overhead.

6 Conclusions and Future Work

Access control for digital libraries currently is rather primitive due to the fact that most large digital libraries are solitary, proprietary systems that do not interoperate and are only available to the user community managed by each digital library. To provide a seamless access to many digital libraries simultaneously, a more sophisticated security model is needed. We have provided in this paper a framework that we have implemented that provides a sophisticated access paradigm to distributed user groups for distributed digital libraries at no noticeable cost to the user in terms of response time. By using declarative languages such as XACML we can make changes in policies effective immediately and minimize the cost of changing enforcement code at the resource (typically a federation service). Enforcement actions that need to be written into the source code of the resource are restricted to two places: the presentation layer and the query construction modules. All decision making as to access permissions are made by a standard XACML policy engine.

Currently, we are investigating the possibility of incorporating the role-based access control on hierarchical roles and subjects using declarative languages like XACML. We are also investigating the usage of a canonical set of subject attributes in government and commercial organizations to broaden the usage of our work.

Acknowledgements

The work has been partially funded by IBM University Research Fellowship Program.

References

1. Adam N.R., Atluri V., Bertino E., and E. Ferrari. A content-based authorization model for digital libraries. IEEE Trans. on Knowledge and Data Engineering, 14(2):296–315, March 2002.
2. Bhoopalam, K., Maly, K., Mukkamala, R., Zubair, M. A Flexible Framework for Content Based Access Management for Federated Digital Libraries. Proceedings of IADIS, Madrid, October 6-9, 2004.
3. Bhoopalam, K., Maly, K., Mukkamala, R., Zubair, M. Access Management in Federated Digital Libraries. Proceedings of IADIS, Madrid, October 6-9, 2004.
4. Cantor, S., Erdos, M. Shibboleth-Architecture DRAFT v05, http://shibboleth.internet2.edu/docs/draft-internet2-shibboleth-arch-v05.pdf (21 April 2004).
5. DCMI Metadata Terms, Dublin Core Metadata Initiative, http://dublincore.org/documents/dcmi-terms/
6. EduPerson Specification, http://www.nmi-edit.org/eduPerson/internet2-mace-dir-eduperson200312.html
7. Hada, S. and Kudo, M. XML Access Control Language: Provisional Authorization for XML Documents. (Tokyo Research Laboratory, IBM Research). October 16, 2000.
8. Kodali N., Farkas C., Wijesekera D. An Authorization Model for Multimedia Digital Libraries. The Int. Journal of Digital Libraries, Vol 4, 139 -155., 2004.
9. Lagoze, C.,and H, Sompel, V., Nelson, M., Warner, S. The Open Archives Initiative Protocol for Metadata Harvesting, Open Archives Initiative. http://www.openarchives.org/OAI/openarchivesprotocol.htm (21 October 2004).
10. Liu, X., Maly, K., Zubair, M., and Nelson, M. 2001. Arc -- An OAI Service Provider for Cross Archiving Searching. Proceedings of the ACM/IEEE Joint Conference on Digital Libraries, Roanoke, VA, June 24-28, 2001, pp. 65-66.

11. Maly, K., Anan, H., Tang, J., Nelson, M., Zubair, M. and Yang, Z. Challenges in Building Federation Services over Harvested Metadata. Proceedings of ICADL2003. pp.602-614, Kuala Lumpur, Malaysia, Dec 2003.
12. Moses, T. (eds.). OASIS eXtensible Access Control Management Language (XACML). Version 2.0, OASIS Standard, http://docs.oasis-open.org/xacml/2.0/access_control-xacml-2.0-core-spec-os.pdf (1 February 2005).
13. National Science Digital Library. http://www.nsdl.org/, (05 November 2004).
14. Sandhu, R., et al. Role-Based Access Control Models. IEEE Computer 29(2): 38-47, IEEE Press, 1996.
15. Sandhu, R. The typed access matrix model. In Proc. of the 11th IEEE Symp. on Security and Privacy, pp. 122-136, 1992.

Exploiting Lexical Knowledge in Learning User Profiles for Intelligent Information Access to Digital Collections

G. Semeraro[1], P. Lops[1], M. Degemmis[1], C. Niederée[2], and A. Stewart[2]

[1] Dipartimento di Informatica,
Università di Bari, Bari 70126, Italy
[2] Fraunhofer IPSI, Darmstadt 64293, Germany
{semeraro, lops, degemmis}@di.uniba.it,
{niederee, stewart}@ipsi.fhg.de

Abstract. Algorithms designed to support users in retrieving relevant information base their relevance computations on *user profiles*, in which representations of the users interests are maintained. This paper focuses on the use of *supervised machine learning* techniques to induce user profiles for Intelligent Information Access. The access must be *personalized* by profiles allowing users to retrieve information on the basis of *conceptual content*. To address this issue, we propose a method to learn sense-based user profiles based on WordNet, a lexical database.

Keywords: personalization, information retrieval, text categorization, word sense disambiguation, WordNet.

1 Introduction

Personalization is an important method for digital libraries to take a more active role in dynamically tailoring its information and service offer to individuals [2]. Novel solutions for *personalized information access* exploit machine learning algorithms to induce a structured model of a user's interests, referred to as *user profile*, from text documents. These methods require users to label documents by assigning a relevance score and automatically infer profiles exploited in the filtering/retrieval process. A crucial issue is that keywords are rarely an appropriate way of locating the information a user is interested into due to the well-known problems of *polysemy* and *synonymy*. Due to synonymy, relevant information might be missed if the profile does not contain the exact keywords occurring in the documents, while wrong documents might be deemed as relevant because of the occurrence of words with multiple meanings. These problems call for methods able to learn *semantic* profiles that capture concepts representing user interests from relevant documents. In semantic profiles, keywords will be replaced with their meanings, defined in lexicons or ontologies. We propose a strategy to induce *semantic* user profiles from documents represented by features generated using WordNet [9] as a reference lexicon. The paper is organized as

E.A. Fox et al. (Eds.): ICADL 2005, LNCS 3815, pp. 253–262, 2005.
© Springer-Verlag Berlin Heidelberg 2005

follows: after introducing in Section 2 the task of learning user profiles as a text categorization problem, in Section 3 we present the probabilistic approach we adopted to accomplish this task. Section 4 proposes a WordNet-based document representation and describes how this representation could be exploited to learn semantic user profiles, whose effectiveness is evaluated in Section 5 through some experiments. Conclusions and future work are drawn in Section 6.

2 Learning User Profiles as a Text Categorization Problem

The content-based approach to Information Filtering [5] generally involves the application of Machine Learning techniques able to generate a user profile, based on information that has been previously labeled by the user. As domains in Information Filtering are primarily textual in nature, the Machine Learning techniques generally used are those well-suited for text categorization (TC) [15]. These approaches automatically build a text classifier by learning, from a set of *training documents* - documents labeled with the categories they belongs to - the features of the categories. We consider the problem of learning user profiles as a binary TC task: each document has to be classified as interesting or not with respect to the user preferences:the set of categories is restricted to c_+, that represents the positive class (user-likes), and c_- the negative one (user-dislikes). In this paper, we present a content-based profiling system named ITem Recommender (ITR), able to induce user profiles as naïve Bayesian classifiers [10].

2.1 Document Representation

The representation that dominates the text classification literature is known as *bag of words* (BOW). In this approach each feature corresponds to a single word found in the training set. In the experiments conducted with ITR, items to be suggested to users are movies. Each information item (a movie description) is represented by a set of *slots*, where each slot is a textual field corresponding to a specific feature of the item. The slots that represent a movie are: *title*, *cast*, *director*, *summary*, a short text that presents the main points of the narration; *keywords*, a list of words describing the main topics of the movie. Each instance, i.e. a document used in the training set or a new document to be classified, is represented by five BOWs, one for each slot, by taking into account the occurrences of words in the original text. This strategy, that considers separately the occurrences of a word in the slots in which it appears, was adopted in an attempt to catch, in a more effective way, the informative power of a word in a document. The BOWs of the items have been obtained by applying common preprocessing steps to the original documents: tokenization, elimination of common English stop words, stemming [12]. In section 4, we extend the classical BOW model to a model in which the senses corresponding to the words in the documents are considered as features. This sense-based model will be exploited by the learning algorithm in an attempt to produce user profiles able to catch topics users are really interested into.

2.2   Related Work

Syskill & Webert [11] is an agent that learns a user profile used to identify interesting Web pages. The learning process is conducted by using algorithms like Bayesian classifiers, a nearest neighbor algorithm and a decision tree learner. In *ifWeb* [1], that supports users in document searching, user profiles are stored in form of weighted semantic network, that represents terms and their context by linking nodes (words) with arcs representing co-occurrences in some documents. *SiteIF* [6] exploits a sense-based representation to build a user profile as a semantic network whose nodes represent senses of the words in documents requested by the user. Several methods have been proposed for integrating lexical information to training documents for text categorization. In [13], WordNet is used to enhance neural network learning algorithms. This approach only made use of synonymy and involved a manual word sense disambiguation step, whereas our approach uses synonymy and hypernymy and is completely automatic. Scott and Matwin [14] proposed to include WordNet information at the feature level, by expanding each word in the training set with *all* the synonyms extracted from WordNet for it, including those available for each sense in order to avoid a word sense disambiguation process. This approach has shown a decrease of effectiveness in the classifier obtained, mostly due to the word ambiguity problem.

3   A Naïve Bayes Method for User Profiling

Naïve Bayes is a probabilistic approach to inductive learning. The learned probabilistic model estimates the *a posteriori* probability, $P(c_j|d_i)$, of document d_i belonging to class c_j. This estimation is based on the a priori probability, $P(c_j)$, i.e. the probability of observing a document in class c_j, $P(d_i|c_j)$, that is the probability of observing document d_i given c_j, and $P(d_i)$, the probability of observing the instance d_i at all. Using these probabilities, Bayesian classifiers apply Bayes theorem to calculate $P(c_j|d_i)$. To classify a document d_i, the class with the highest probability is selected. As a working model for the naïve Bayes classifier, we use the multinomial event model [8]:

$$P(c_j|d_i) = P(c_j) \prod_{w \in V_{d_i}} P(t_k|c_j)^{N(d_i, t_k)} \tag{1}$$

where $N(d_i, t_k)$ is defined as the number of times word or token t_k appeared in document d_i. Notice that rather than getting the product of all distinct words in the corpus, V, we only use the subset of the vocabulary, V_{d_i}, containing the words that appear in the document d_i. A key step in implementing naïve Bayes is estimating the word probabilities $P(t_k|c_j)$. We use Witten-Bell smoothing [16] that sets $P(t_k|c_j)$ as follows:

$$P(t_k|c_j) = \begin{cases} \frac{N(t_k, c_j)}{V_{c_j} + \sum_i N(t_i, c_j)} & \text{if } N(t_k, c_j) \neq 0 \\ \frac{V}{V_{c_j} + \sum_i N(t_i, c_j)} \frac{1}{V - V_{c_j}} & \text{if } N(t_k, c_j) = 0 \end{cases} \tag{2}$$

where $N(t_k, c_j)$ is the count of the number of times t_k occurs in the training data for class c_j, and $|V_{c_j}|$ is the total number of unique words in class c_j. ITR implements the above described method to classify documents as interesting or uninteresting for a particular user.

The documents used to train the system belong to a collection of movie descriptions. Ratings on these documents were obtained from the EachMovie dataset, in which ratings from 72,916 users were recorded on a discrete scale from 0 to 5 (see Section 5 for a detailed description of the dataset). An instance labeled with a rating r, $0 \leq r \leq 2$, belongs to class c_- (user-dislikes); if $3 \leq r \leq 5$ then the instance belongs to class c_+ (user-likes). Each rating r was normalized to obtain values ranging between 0 and 1:

$$w_+^i = \frac{r-1}{MAX-1}; \qquad w_-^i = 1 - w_+^i \qquad (3)$$

where MAX is the maximum rating that can be assigned to an instance. In order to apply equations in (3), the rating scale has been shifted in the range 1-6.

In the collection, movies are grouped by genre (categories). ITR learns a profile of the movies preferred by a user in a specific category. Thus, given a user u and a set of rated movies in a specific category of interest, the system learns a profile able to recognize movies liked by u in that category. Since each instance is encoded as a vector of documents, one for each BOW, Equation (1) becomes:

$$P(c_j|d_i) = \frac{P(c_j)}{P(d_i)} \prod_{m=1}^{|S|} \prod_{k=1}^{|b_{im}|} P(t_k|c_j, s_m)^{n_{kim}} \qquad (4)$$

where $S = \{s_1, s_2, \ldots, s_{|S|}\}$ is the set of slots, b_{im} is the BOW in the slot s_m of the instance d_i, n_{kim} is the number of occurrences of the token t_k in b_{im}. To calculate (4), we only need to estimate $P(c_j)$ and $P(t_k|c_j, s_m)$. The weights in (3) are used for weighting the occurrences of a word in a document and to estimate the probability terms from the training set TR. The prior probabilities of the classes are computed according to the following equation:

$$\hat{P}(c_j) = \frac{\sum_{i=1}^{|TR|} w_j^i + 1}{|TR| + 2} \qquad (5)$$

Witten-Bell estimates in (2) have been modified by taking into account that documents are structured into slots and that word occurrences are weighted using weights in equation (3):

$$P(t_k|c_j, s_m) = \begin{cases} \frac{N(t_k, c_j, s_m)}{V_{c_j} + \sum_i N(t_i, c_j, s_m)} & \text{if } N(t_k, c_j, s_m) \neq 0 \\ \frac{V}{V_{c_j} + \sum_i N(t_i, c_j, s_m)} \frac{1}{V - V_{c_j}} & \text{if } N(t_k, c_j, s_m) = 0 \end{cases} \qquad (6)$$

where $N(t_k, c_j, s_m)$ is the count of the weighted occurrences of the word t_k in the training data for class c_j in the slot s_m, V_{c_j} is the total number of unique words in class c_j, and V is the total number of unique words across all classes. $N(t_k, c_j, s_m)$ is computed as follows:

$$N(t_k, c_j, s_m) = \sum_{i=1}^{|TR|} w_j^i n_{kim} \tag{7}$$

In (7), n_{kim} is the number of occurrences of the term t_k in the slot s_m of the ith instance. The sum of all $N(t_k, c_j, s_m)$ in the denominator of equation (6) denotes the total weighted length of the slot s_m in the class c_j. In other words, $\hat{P}(t_k|c_j, s_m)$ is estimated as a ratio between the weighted occurrences of the term t_k in slot s_m of class c_j and the total weighted length of the slot. The final outcome of the learning process is a probabilistic model used to classify a new instance in the class c_+ or c_-. The model can be used to build a personal profile that includes those words that turn out to be most indicative of the user's preferences, according to the value of the conditional probabilities in (6).

4 WordNet-Based User Profiles

In the classical *bag of words* (BOW) model, each feature corresponds to a single word in the training set. We propose a *bag of synsets* model (BOS) in which a synset vector corresponds to a document instead of a word vector. This model is used as a starting point to build *semantic user profiles* taking into account the senses of the words contained in the training documents. The task of word sense disambiguation (WSD) consists in determining which of the senses of an ambiguous word is invoked in a particular use of the word [7]. As for sense repository we have adopted WordNet (version 1.7.1), a large freely available lexical database for English, commonly used within the computational linguistics community. Nouns, verbs, adjectives and adverbs are organized into *synsets* (*synonym sets*), each representing one underlying lexical concept. Synsets are linked by different semantic relations and organized in hierarchies. The main advantage of the BOS model is that synonym words can contribute to the user profile definition by referring to the same concept. Moreover, the use of a WSD procedure reduces classification errors due to ambiguous words, and consequently allows a better precision in the user model construction.

4.1 A WordNet-Based Strategy for Word Sense Disambiguation

We propose a WSD strategy based on the idea that semantic similarity between synsets a and b is inversely proportional to the distance between them in the WordNet IS-A hierarchy, measured by the number of nodes in the path from a to b [4]. The path length similarity, computed by the function SINSIM(a,b) is used to associate the proper synset to a polysemous word w. SINSIM(a,b)$= -log(N_p/2D)$, where N_p is the number of nodes in path p from a to b, D is the maximum depth of the taxonomy (in WordNet 1.7.1 $D = 16$) [4]. Measures based on path length suffer from the differences in depth found in various parts of the taxonomy, but it was difficult to adopt other measures, like those based on corpus frequencies because of the reduced dimensions of training data. This is an inherent problem in learning user profiles. Thus, we adopted an approach exclusively based on the knowledge coming from WordNet. Let S be the set of all candidate synsets for w and C the context of w, that is the window of all words that surround w with a fixed radius. The strategy first builds T, the set of all synsets of the word forms in C with the same part-of-speech as w, and then computes the semantic similarity $score_{ih}$ between each synset s_i in S and each synset s_h in T. The synset s associated to w is the s_i with the highest similarity $score_{ih}$. Each document is mapped into a list of WordNet synsets following three steps: 1) each monosemous word w in a slot of a document d is mapped into the corresponding WordNet synset; 2) for each couple of words $\langle noun, noun \rangle$ or $\langle adjective, noun \rangle$, a search in WordNet is made to verify if at least one synset exists for the bigram $\langle w_1, w_2 \rangle$. In the positive case, algorithm 1 is applied on the bigram, otherwise it is applied separately on w_1 and w_2, using all words in the

---

Algorithm 1. The WordNet-based WSD algorithm

1: **procedure** WSD(w, d)   ▷ find the proper synset of a polysemous word w in d
2:      $C \leftarrow \{w_1, ..., w_n\}$ ▷ C is the context of w. For example,
         $C = \{w_1, w_2, w_3, w_4\}$ is a window with radius=2, if the sequence of words
         $\{w_1, w_2, w, w_3, w_4\}$ appears in d
3:      $S \leftarrow \{s_1, ...s_k\}$ ▷ S is the set of all candidate synsets for w
4:      $s \leftarrow null$ ▷ s is the synset to be returned
5:      $score \leftarrow 0$ ▷ $score$ is a similarity score assigned to s
6:      $T \leftarrow \emptyset$ ▷ T is the set of all candidate synsets for all words in C
7:      **for** $j \leftarrow 1, n$ **do**
8:          **if** $POS(w_j) = POS(w)$ **then**   ▷ $POS(x)$ is the part-of-speech of x
9:              $S_j \leftarrow \{s_{j1}, ...s_{jm}\}$ ▷ S_j is the set of m possible senses for w_j
10:             $T \leftarrow T \cup S_j$
11:         **end if**
12:     **end for**
13:     **for** $i \leftarrow 1, k$ **do**
14:         **for all** $s_h \in T$ **do**
15:             $score_{ih} \leftarrow$ SINSIM(s_i, s_h)   ▷ computing similarity scores between s_i
                 and every synset $s_h \in T$
16:             **if** $score_{ih} \geq score$ **then**
17:                 $score \leftarrow score_{ih}$
18:                 $s \leftarrow s_i$ ▷ s is the synset $s_i \in S$ with the highest similarity score
                     with the synsets in T
19:             **end if**
20:         **end for**
21:     **end for**
22:     **return** s
23: **end procedure**
24: **function** SINSIM(a, b)   ▷ The similarity of the synsets a and b
25:     $N_p \leftarrow$ the number of nodes in path p from a to b
26:     $D \leftarrow$ maximum depth of the taxonomy   ▷ In WordNet 1.7.1 $D = 16$
27:     $r \leftarrow -log(N_p/2D)$
28:     **return** r
29: **end function**

---

slot as the context C of w; 3) each polysemous unigram w is disambiguated by algorithm 1, using all words in the slot as the context C of w.

4.2   Using Synsets to Represent Documents and Profiles

Algorithm 1 was used to represent documents in the EachMovie dataset[1] according to the new model, that we call "bag-of-synsets" (BOS): the final representation of a document consists of a list of WordNet synsets recognized from the words in the document. As reported in section 2.1, a movie description is composed of 5 slots. Each slot is processed separately and the occurrences of the synsets (instead of words) are computed. For example, if the words "artificial" and "intelligence" occur in the same slot of a document, in the corresponding BOW we count one occurrence for each word; in the BOS, we count only one occurrence of the synset "{05766061} ARTIFICIAL INTELLIGENCE, AI − (THE BRANCH OF COMPUTER SCIENCE THAT DEAL WITH...)". A clear advantage of BOS regards synonyms. For example, if the words "processor" and "CPU" appear in the same slot of a document, in the corresponding BOW we count *one* occurrence for each word, even if they refer to the same concept; in the BOS, we count *two* occurrences of the synset "{02888449} CENTRAL PROCESSING UNIT, CPU, C.P.U., CENTRAL PROCESSOR, PROCESSOR, MAINFRAME − ((COMPUTER SCIENCE) THE PART OF A COMPUTER (A MICROPROCESSOR CHIP) THAT DOES MOST OF THE DATA PROCESSING...)". ITR has been adapted in order to deal with the BOS document representation model; however, the learning method has not been modified. The final goal of our investigation is to compare the results of word-based and synset-based user profiles, then we do not modify the structure of the profiles and the learning mechanisms proposed in section 3: the estimates of the probabilities are the same as in the word-based version of the system. The difference with respect to word-based profiles is that synset unique identifiers are used instead of words.

5   Experimental Sessions

The goal of the evaluation is to estimate if the BOS version of ITR improves the performance with respect to the BOW one. Experiments were carried out on a collection of $1,628$ textual descriptions of movies rated by $72,916$ real users, the EachMovie dataset. Movies are rated on a 6-point scale mapped linearly to the interval [0,1]. The content of each movie was collected from the Internet Movie Database [2] by a crawler. Tokenization, stopword elimination and stemming have been applied to obtain the BOW. Documents indexed by the BOS model have been processed by tokenization, stopword elimination, lemmatization and WSD. Movies are categorized into different genres. For each genre or category, a set of 100 users was randomly selected among users that rated n items, $30 \leq n \leq 100$ in that movie category (only for genre 'animation', the number of users that

---

[1] http://www.research.compaq.com/SRC/
[2] IMDb, http://www.imdb.com

Table 1. 10 'Genre' datasets obtained from the original EachMovie dataset

Id Genre	Genre	Rated Movies	% POS	% NEG
1	Action	4,474	72.05	27.95
2	Animation	1,103	56.67	43.33
3	Art_Foreign	4,246	76.21	23.79
4	Classic	5,026	91.73	8.27
5	Comedy	4,714	63.46	36.54
6	Drama	4,880	76.24	23.76
7	Family	3,808	63.71	36.29
8	Horror	3,631	59.89	40.11
9	Romance	3,707	72.97	27.03
10	Thriller	3,709	71.94	28.06
		39,298	71.84	28.16

rated n movies was 33, due to the low number of movies if that genre). For each category, a dataset of at least 3000 triples (user,movie,rating) was obtained (at least 990 for 'animation'). Table 1 summarizes the data used for experiments. Documents have been disambiguated using Algorithm 1, obtaining a feature reduction of 38% (172, 296 words vs. 107, 990 synsets). This is mainly due to the fact that bigrams are represented using only one synset and that synonym words are represented by the same synset. Classification effectiveness was evaluated by the classical measures *precision, recall* and *F-measure* [15]. We adopted the Normalized Distance-based Performance Measure (NDPM) [17] to measure the distance between the ranking imposed on items by the user ratings and the ranking predicted by ITR, that ranks items according to the a-posteriori probability of the class *likes*. Values range from 0 (agreement) to 1 (disagreement). In the experiments, a movie is considered as *relevant* by a user if the rating is greater or equal than 3, while ITR considers an item as relevant if $P(c_+|d_i) \geq 0.5$, calculated as in equation (4). We executed one experiment for each user. Each

Table 2. Performance of the two versions of ITR on 10 different datasets

Id Genre	Precision		Recall		F1		NDPM	
	ITR BOW	ITR BOS	ITR BOW	ITR BOS	ITR BOW	ITR BOS	ITR BOW	ITR BOS
1	0.70	0.74	0.83	0.89	0.76	0.80	0.45	0.45
2	0.51	0.57	0.62	0.70	0.54	0.61	0.41	0.39
3	0.76	0.86	0.84	0.96	0.79	0.91	0.45	0.45
4	0.92	0.93	0.99	0.99	0.96	0.96	0.48	0.48
5	0.56	0.67	0.66	0.80	0.59	0.72	0.46	0.46
6	0.75	0.78	0.89	0.92	0.81	0.84	0.46	0.45
7	0.58	0.73	0.67	0.83	0.71	0.79	0.42	0.42
8	0.53	0.72	0.65	0.89	0.58	0.79	0.41	0.43
9	0.70	0.77	0.83	0.91	0.75	0.83	0.49	0.49
10	0.71	0.75	0.86	0.91	0.77	0.81	0.48	0.48
Mean	0.67	0.75	0.78	0.88	0.73	0.81	0.45	0.45

experiment consisted in 1) selecting the ratings of the user and the content of the movies rated by that user; 2) splitting the selected data into a training set Tr and a test set Ts; 3) using Tr for learning the corresponding user profile; 4) evaluating the predictive accuracy of the induced profile on Ts, using the afore-mentioned measures. The methodology adopted for obtaining Tr and Ts was the 10-fold cross validation. [10]. The results of the comparison between the profiles obtained from documents represented using the two indexing approaches, namely BOW and BOS, are reported in Table 2. We can notice a significant improvement both in precision (+8%) and recall (+10%). The BOS model out-performs the BOW model specifically on datasets 5 (+11% of precision, +14% of recall), 7 (+15% of precision, +16% of recall), 8 (+19% of precision, +24% of recall). Only on dataset 4 (Classic) we have not observed any improvement. This could be an indication that the improved results depend on the balanced distri-bution of positive and negative examples in the dataset (see Table 1). NDPM has not been improved, but it remains acceptable. A Wilcoxon signed ranked test, requiring a significance level $p < 0.05$, has been performed in order to validate these results. We considered each dataset as a single trial for the test. Thus, 10 trials have been executed. The test confirmed that there is a statistically signif-icant difference in favor of the BOS model with respect to the BOS model as regards precision, recall and F-measure, and that the two models are equivalent in defining the ranking of the preferred movies with respect to the score for the class "likes".

6   Conclusions

We presented a system exploiting a Bayesian learning method to induce *semantic* user profiles from documents represented using WordNet synsets. Our hypothesis is that replacing words with synsets in the indexing phase produces a more accurate document representation that could be successfully used by learning algorithms to infer more accurate user profiles. This hypothesis is confirmed by the experiments and can be explained by the fact that synset-based classification allows the preference of documents with a high degree of semantic coherence, not guaranteed in case of word-based classification. As a future work, we plan to exploit the WordNet hierarchy to introduce generalization in the learning process not only in the document indexing process. We plan also to compare the classification accuracy of synset-based profiles with that of other methods such as support vector machines and techniques that replace words by "topics" [3].

Acknowledgments

This research was partially founded by the European Commission under the DE-LOS Network of Excellence on Digital Libraries - Priority: Technology-enhanced Learning and Access to Cultural Heritage - Contract n. G038-507618.[3]

---

[3] `http://delos.info`

References

[1] F. Asnicar and C. Tasso. ifweb: a prototype of user model-based intelligent agent for documentation filtering and navigation in the word wide web. In *Proc. of 1st Int. Workshop on adaptive systems and user modeling on the WWW*, 1997.

[2] J. Callan and A. Smeaton. Personalization and recommender systems in digital libraries. Technical report, NSF-EU DELOS Working Group Report, 2003.

[3] S. T. Dumais, G. W. Furnas, T. K. Landauer, S. Deerwester, and R. Harshman. Using latent semantic analysis to improve access to textual information. In *Proc. of the Conf. on Human Factors in Computing Systems CHI'88*, 1988.

[4] C. Fellbaum. *WordNet: An Electronic Lexical Database*. MIT Press, 1998.

[5] U. Hanani, B. Shapira, and P. Shoval. Information filtering: Overview of issues, research and systems. *User Modeling and User-Adapted Interaction*, 11(3):203–259, 2001.

[6] B. Magnini and C. Strapparava. Improving user modelling with content-based techniques. In *Proc. of 8th Int. Conf. on User Modeling*, pages 74–83. Springer Verlag, 2001.

[7] C. D. Manning and H. Schutze. *Foundations of Statistical Natural Language Processing*. The MIT Press, Cambridge, US, 1984.

[8] A. McCallum and K. Nigam. A comparison of event models for naive bayes text classification. In *Proceedings of the AAAI/ICML-98 Workshop on Learning for Text Categorization*, pages 41–48. AAAI Press, 1998.

[9] G. A. Miller. Wordnet: an on-line lexical database. *International Journal of Lexicography*, 3(4):235–244, 1990.

[10] T. Mitchell. *Machine Learning*. McGraw-Hill, New York, 1997.

[11] M. Pazzani and D. Billsus. Learning and revising user profiles: The identification of interesting web sites. *Machine Learning*, 27(3):313–331, 1997.

[12] M. F. Porter. An algorithm for suffix stripping. *Program*, 14(3):130–137, 1980.

[13] M. d. B. Rodriguez, J. M. Gomez-Hidalgo, and B. Diaz-Agudo. Using wordnet to complement training information in text categorization. In *2nd Int. Conf. on Recent Advances in NLP*, pages 150–157, 1997.

[14] S. Scott and S. Matwin. Text classification using wordnet hypernyms. In *COLING-ACL Workshop on usage of WordNet for in NLP Systems*, pages 45–51, 1998.

[15] F. Sebastiani. Machine learning in automated text categorization. *ACM Computing Surveys*, 34(1), 2002.

[16] I. Witten and T. Bell. The zero-frequency problem: Estimating the probabilities of novel events in adaptive text compression. *IEEE Transactions on Information Theory*, 37(4), 1991.

[17] Y. Y. Yao. Measuring retrieval effectiveness based on user preference of documents. *Journal of the American Society for Information Science*, 46(2):133–145, 1995.

Government Ontology and Thesaurus Construction: A Taiwanese Experience

Chao-chen Chen[1], Jian-hua Yeh[2], and Shun-hong Sie[3]

[1] Graduate Institute of Library and Information Studies,
National Taiwan Normal University
cc4073@cc.ntnu.edu.tw
[2] Depart of Computer and Information Science,
Aletheia University
au4290@email.au.edu.tw
[3] Department of Library and Information Science,
Fu Jen Catholic University
modify@ms37.hinet.net

Abstract. Due to the quantity and the diversity involved in e-government presentations and operations, traditional approaches to web site information management have been found to be rather inefficient in time and cost. Consequently, the necessity of establishing a government knowledge management system, so as to speed up information lookups, sharing, and linkups, naturally arises. Moreover, this knowledge management system would in turn enhance e-government effectiveness as it helps to store and transmit information, be it explicit or implicit in nature. The first step in creating this knowledge management system is to build up the government ontology and thesaurus. Upon the completion of the ontology and thesaurus needed, semantic searching can be conducted, which in turn kickstarts other mechanisms required for effective information management.

Our research team has been commissioned by the Executive Yuan of Taiwan to establish the draft of government ontology and thesaurus and to design a framework for multiple-layered information management systems upon which the ontology and thesaurus can be constructed. The goal of this paper is to present the government ontology and thesaurus which our research team has come up with as well as the related infrastructure and function of the multiple-layered information management system.

Keywords: government ontology; government thesaurus; ontology editor; semantic interoperability; knowledge management.

1 Introduction

The number of web sites of Taiwan government increased quickly in recent years, which made Taiwan a popular e-government country. Due to the quantity and the diversity involved in e-government presentations and operations, traditional approaches to web sites information management have been found to be rather inefficient in time and cost. Consequently, the desire to speed up information lookup, sharing, and linkup created a need to establish a government knowledge management

E.A. Fox et al. (Eds.): ICADL 2005, LNCS 3815, pp. 263–272, 2005.
© Springer-Verlag Berlin Heidelberg 2005

system. Moreover, a knowledge management system would in turn enhance e-government effectiveness as it helps to store and transmit information, be it explicit or implicit in nature. The first step in creating this knowledge management system is building up the government ontology and thesaurus. Upon the completion of the ontology and thesaurus needed, semantic searching can begin to function properly, which in turn would kickstart mechanisms required for effective information management. Three major issues in creating the ontology and thesaurus were analyzed and are as follows:

1. Extend construction and processing level of government web site information

Most government information is presented in the form of web pages, with one web page devoted to each topic. However, the high number of web pages complicates management of pages and maintenance of topic crosslinking. A better way to efficiently manage government information is to use a database for data storage, a high performance search engine for query processing, and a dynamic catalog system for subject browsing.

2. Enhance classification efficiency by using ontology and thesaurus information

Automatic information classification plays an important role in both information retrieval systems and subject catalog systems. A high-quality web site should provide multiple ways for information retrieval and browsing while not requiring tedious manual data classification. Thus the automatic classification function is critical for government knowledge management. Currently, due to the limitations of automatic classification technology, it is common practice to use ontology with thesaurus information to do automatic classification work.

3. Define a semantic exchange standard for government information

Ontology and thesaurus information are the bases for efficient information retrieval and knowledge management of government information. With well-formed subject terms and knowledge hierarchy, the government information can be processed and categorized into a systematic structure, thus becoming a useful knowledge and semantic exchange standard.

2   Related Work

Having a common semantic expression among government departments is becoming more and more important in recent years because of the increase in information exchange among departments. The construction of government ontology and thesaurus information becomes a critical mission in many countries. For example, the Portal Thesaurus Project of New Zealand government, which creates the New Zealand Government Locator Service (NZLGS) Thesaurus; the Australian Governments' Interactive Functions Thesaurus (AGIFT), which provides Australian Government Locator Service (AGLS) a standard thesaurus terms for metadata; others such as UK Pan-Government Thesaurus (PGT), Government of Canada (GoC) Core Subject Thesaurus (CST), ETB Thesaurus for European Schoolnet (EUN), and so forth. These projects have a common feature: to provide a united semantic expression for information exchange, making possible efficient information processing and retrieval.

3   The Proposed Method

The goal of this research is to create a management system for government ontology and thesaurus information. Besides the construction of the system, the government ontology and thesaurus are also specified in this research. The processing steps of this research are shown below:

1. Content analysis
   The content analysis process contains several major steps, including subject term extraction, synonym construction, thesaurus construction, and ontology creation. The subject term extraction process in this research contains both manual and automatic term extraction. The manual term extraction utilizes existing subject category, thesaurus, and related web sites as references to create a basic subject term set. The automatic term extraction applies phrase segmentation and statistical methods to related government web sites to generate candidate terms. After these terms are generated, the synonyms for these terms are created by using Google to search for related information. These terms generated from manual and automatic term extraction are then revised by domain experts to generate final versions of subject terms.
2. System construction
   To support ontology creation from subject term generated previously, the research team creates an ontology management system which contains both ontology and thesaurus maintenance features. This system is able to maintain and present government ontology along with related thesaurus information. The ontology created by this system can be further rendered into RDF-based ontology and XTM-based topic maps.

The entire processing sequence is shown in Fig. 1.

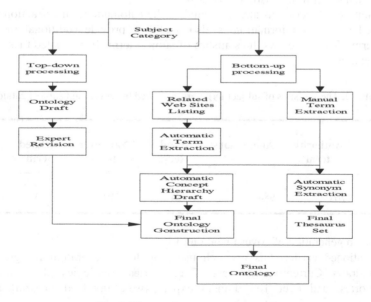

Fig. 1. The ontology processing steps

4 Creation of Government Ontology and Thesaurus

It is quite difficult to generate government ontologies and thesaurus information in a short time. But it is also difficult for government to refine these information without a draft. During the course of this research, we generated an ontology and thesaurus draft in a short time for the government and experts to refine. The achievements of this research are described in the following section.

1. Automatic term extraction

The related information from various web pages was fetched for later use. A web robot fetched more than 1,000 related web sites and generated over six million possible term fragments. Table 1 shows the automatic term extraction result of this research.

Table 1. Automatic term extraction result

Sites fetched	Possible term fragments	Useful term selected	Usefulness ratio
1,107	6,851,165	40,531	0.592%

1. Association build-up of terms

This research adopts a statistical approach along with document feature to generate term associations. The associations suggested by this approach are for human references only.

2. Additional terms from existing thesaurus

Discounting subject terms already found in the automatic term extraction process, the related thesaurus information is also useful to provide additional meaningful subject terms. Table 2 shows the statistics of subject terms from related thesaurus and subject catalog.

Table 2. The statistics of subject terms from related thesaurus and subject catalog

Category	Authority term	Anonymous	Broader term	Narrower term	Related term	Scope note
Count	16,073	984	1,401	2,210	6,389	404

3. Top-down generation of government ontology

As mentioned earlier, this research uses top-down generation for government ontology drafts. Currently, there are 27 categories (ontologies) drafts and 8,135 sub-categories, and over 100 domain experts were involved in draft revision.

4. Association creation between government ontology and thesaurus information

The ontology and thesaurus are both tools for concept or subject presentation, but they traditionally are used separately. Since the features of ontology and thesaurus are in different layers, it is suitable to combine ontology and thesaurus to create more powerful concept representation. The ontology is able to express subject hierarchies, with each node contained in the hierarchy represents a single concept, but only one representation for one concept. The thesaurus contains a set of small term hierarchies, which expresses only one level of term relationship at a time, but the related terms and synonym shows the multiple representation possibilities of a concept. So it is clear that the ontology and thesaurus are complements in our scenario, as shown in Fig. 2.

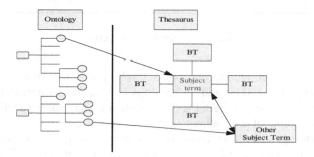

Fig. 2. The role and relationship of ontology and thesaurus in this research

Except for the relationships between ontology and thesaurus information, the concepts contained in ontologies can have associations also. In this research, we define two relationships: interlinks for concept associations across different ontologies, and intralinks for concept associations inside the same ontology. Fig. 3 shows the intralinks and interlinks in this research.

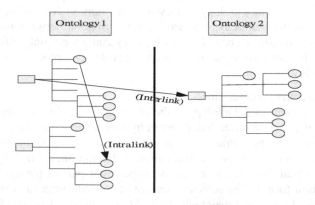

Fig. 3. Intralinks and interlinks

5. Ontology maintenance system

In order to manage the ontology and thesaurus that we constructed, we designed the X-ontology system. The service architecture of this research is shown in Fig. 4:

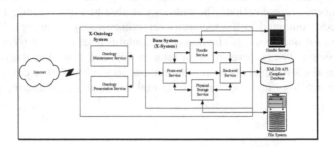

Fig. 4. The service architecture

In Fig. 4, the service architecture of X-Ontology system contains a base system called X-System (Yeh, 2003) and an ontology application extension (X-Ontology); the base system provides all digital archive content management functions while the X-Ontology is capable of processing knowledge network contents.

Since X-Ontology is built on top of the X-System, it certainly uses the functions of the base system to provide advanced ontology related features. In X-Ontology, the ontology structure can be stored to and retrieved from the base system. X-Ontology provides the user a working area for ontology maintenance, association maintenance, and additional thesaurus information. There is also a user interface for ontology content authoring in X-Ontology. These facilities will be discussed in the next section.

6. Ontology contents processing

As we mentioned earlier, the ontology contents created in X-Ontology are stored and retrieved through the base system, implying that the ontology contents are stored in native XML format. The ontology processing functions in X-Ontology support not only a single concept hierarchy, but also links information between ontologies. The result is that the ontologies created by X-Ontology contain not only information on a single concept but also associations between concepts. The processing functions are discussed as below:

6.1 Ontology hierarchy maintenance

The major component in X-Ontology is the ontology hierarchy maintenance service. The X-Ontology provides a tree-based hierarchy maintenance interface for the user to manipulate one concept hierarchy at a time. In addition, associations between hierarchies (ontologies) can also be maintained in this interface. Fig.5 shows the tree-based hierarchy maintenance applet. In the upper-right part of the applet shows the basic information form of the selected concept along with inter- and intralinks. The lower-right part of the applet maintains the additional information, which comes from the thesaurus saved in the system. These features will be discussed in the next paragraph.

Fig. 5. The tree-based ontology maintenance interface in X-Ontology

6.2 Concept associations and additional information maintenance

The goal of concept associations in X-Ontology is to describe the relationships of two concepts "within" or "between" concept hierarchies. These "links" show a number of possibilities of semantics: it can be explained as a related relationship, or it can be treated as an "equal" relationship. However, the semantics of association is provided and used by the user, which will not affect the system implementation. Besides the association maintenance feature, X-Ontology also provides a way to enrich the concept created by the user: the thesaurus information. Fig.6 shows the maintenance interface, the lower-right part if the interface contains a list of additional information selected from thesaurus by user. The thesaurus contents can be picked from a query window (see Fig.7) and then attached to the current editing concept node, this feature gives the user a way to select additional information to enrich the target concept, which will be useful in future applications, such as document classification.

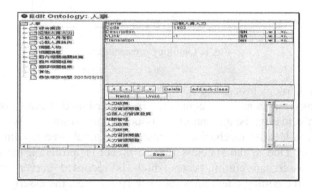

Fig. 6. The hierarchy maintenance interface with association and thesaurus information

6.3 Ontology presentation

The ontology presentation service in X-Onotology is quite straight-forward: information about the selected concept is presented. Fig. 8 shows a tree-based web

Fig. 7. Thesaurus query window for concept hierarchy maintenance interface

page for ontology presentation in X-Ontology. The ontology presentation uses a javascript-based component to perform tree presentation. When a concept is chosen to be displayed, additional information, including thesaurus and association information created by ontology maintenance interface, is also presented. The user can interactively traverse the hierarchy, check the thesaurus information, and jump to other concepts through the associations created by ontology maintenance interface.

Fig. 8. Ontology presentation

6.4 Distributed ontology processing

Since ontology maintenance is conducted in a distributed manner, version control of ontology information is an important issue in our research. We introduced a dynamic resource locking mechanism to ensure that a sub-tree is edited by a single person at a time. Due to the stateless feature of HTTP protocol, the edit ontology action should assert an editing state which is recorded server-side. To avoid deadlocks, once the editing client idles for over 10 minutes, the assertion is dismissed and the lock no longer exists. The lock process flow is shown in the following Fig.9.

Another concern relates to authorization. In this research, different users are able to maintain different sub-tree structure in a specific ontology. Each node contained in an ontology contains read, write, and delete privileges, and these privileges are granted to different users for different maintenance goals. The ontology privilege sample is shown in Fig. 10.

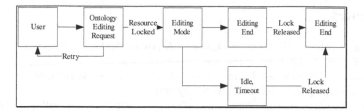

Fig. 9. Resource lock processing

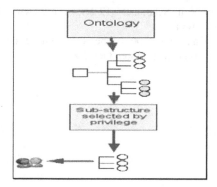

Fig. 10. Ontology sub-structure filtering by privilege

Besides the lock processing and sub-structure selection, our system also provides undo and redo actions to facilitate user maintenance efficiency. User activity logs are also kept for exceptional processing and error recovery. These features are all essential to asserting version control in this system.

5 Conclusion

This paper describes the experience of government ontology and thesaurus construction in Taiwan, and also describes the design of a framework for multiple-layered information management systems. This research produced not only a large amount of ontology and thesaurus content, but also tools which make use of the web to enable wide access and provide users with the ability to publish, browse, create, and edit government ontologies. Both automatic and manual term extraction for ontology creation are adopted, and our experience shows that the automatic process results in low extraction rate for qualified concept terms. In this research, we combine both concept hierarchy and thesaurus information to present a rich information ontology structure. This information will be useful in future applications such as document classification and portal subject browsing. In order to meet the challenges and needs of the e-government providers and users as well as to understand their demands and capabilities on dealing with government knowledge, our research team will continue to maintain Taiwan's government ontology and thesaurus contents as well as develop more supporting infrastructure.

References

The New Zealand Government Locator Service (NZLGS) Thesaurus, http://www.e-government.govt.nz/docs/interim-thesaurus/index.html

The Australian Governments' Interactive Functions Thesaurus (AGIFT), http://www.naa gov.au/recordkeeping/gov_online/agift/summary.html

The UK Pan-Government Thesaurus (PGT), http://www.govtalk.gov.uk/documents/UK%20Metadata%20Framework%20v1%202001- 05.pdf

Government of Canada (GoC) Core Subject Thesaurus (CST), http://en.thesaurus.gc.ca/intro_e.html

ETB Thesaurus for European Schoolnet (EUN), http://www.eun.org/eun.org2/eun/en/etb/sub_area.cfm?sa=440&row=1

Yeh, Jian-hua and Chen, Chao-chen,(2003), The X-System: Design and Implementation of a Digital Archive System, Technical Report, Oct. 2003

Concept Expansion Using Semantic Fisheye Views

Paul Janecek[1], Vincent Schickel[2], and Pearl Pu[2]

[1] Computer Science and Information Management, School of Advanced Technologies,
Asian Institute of Technology (AIT),
P.O. Box 4, Klong Luang,
Pathumthani 12120, Thailand
paul@cs.ait.ac.th
[2] Human Computer Interaction Group, Faculty of Computer and Communication Sciences,
Swiss Federal Institute of Technology in Lausanne (EPFL),
CH-1015 Lausanne, Switzerland
{vincent.schickel-zuber, pearl.pu}@epfl.ch

Abstract. Exploratory search over a collection often requires users to iteratively apply a variety of strategies, such as searching for more general or more specific concepts in reaction to the information they encounter. Rich semantic models, such as WordNet, are potentially valuable aids for making sense of this information. However, these large complex models often contain specialized vocabularies and a detailed level of granularity that makes them difficult to use for opportunistic search. In this paper, we describe how Semantic Fisheye Views (SFEV) can be designed to transparently integrate rich semantic models into the search process, allowing users to effectively explore a diverse range of related concepts without explicitly navigating over the underlying model. The SFEV combines semantic guided search with interactive visualization techniques, creating a search tool that we have found to be significantly more effective for exploratory tasks than those based on keyword-similarity alone.

1 Introduction

Similarity-based search models (such as the vector space model and relevance-feedback algorithms) are often very effective for precise queries, but less effective when search goals are not easily defined, such as a search to learn about an unfamiliar domain of knowledge or to discover the diversity of "interesting" information in a collection. This type of search is not simply a series of independent iterative queries, each of which is progressively refined towards more relevant information. On the contrary, it is an interactive, opportunistic process that evolves in response to the information found, the users' knowledge, and their search strategies [1]. An important component of this process is "sensemaking," where users construct and refine their mental schemas of the concepts and relationships they encounter in the documents of a collection [2]. In this paper, we describe the implementation details of Semantic Fisheye View (SFEV) [3], a *focus + context* technique that interactively guides a user's attention over a potentially dense visualization of information to the objects that are the most *semantically* related to their current focus.

E.A. Fox et al. (Eds.): ICADL 2005, LNCS 3815, pp. 273–282, 2005.
© Springer-Verlag Berlin Heidelberg 2005

Bates described the following characteristics that distinguish opportunistic (or "berry-picking") search from a series of separate queries [1]:

1. *Nature of the query.* Queries are not static, but rather evolve as the user analyzes the result sets. It is important to note that this evolution is not an increase in precision, but rather a change of focus (e.g., exploratory, explanatory, exhaustive).
2. *Nature of the overall search process.* Information is gathered in bits and pieces instead of in a single set of results (e.g., lists of keywords, an author, documents).
3. *Range of search techniques used.* Users employ a wide variety of search strategies during the search process (e.g., keyword matching, concept expansion) [4].
4. *Information domain where the search is conducted.* More than one type of information is consulted during the search process (e.g., text, figures, cross-references).

Bates' model inspired us to develop a prototype, VisAmp, which implements several information sensemaking strategies as *interest metrics* in the SFEV framework [5]. We described the architecture of SFEV in [5], focusing on the strategies used to support real time display of semantic fisheye views and how interaction can be rapidly and smoothly handled. In a related paper [3], we described an experimental evaluation where users were significantly more effective at sensemaking tasks with an interface that revealed semantically related information rather than one that revealed keyword co-occurrence. The results of the experiment do not discount the usefulness of keyword-similarity or imply that semantic models are more effective in all cases. However, the results do suggest that users greatly appreciate the opportunity to access information using semantic models. Our research explores how to integrate the increasingly available semantic models (alongside other similarity models) into highly interactive visual interfaces for information retrieval.

The contribution of this research to the domain of information retrieval is in the integration of semantic models into a highly interactive visual tool for strategically exploring, accessing, and understanding collections of information. The contribution of this paper over our previous work is a detailed description of how *degree of interest* functions combine multiple concept similarity metrics at the keyword and document levels to guide exploration over a collection. In this paper we describe these functions at a sufficient level of detail for other researchers to implement the SFEV algorithms.

In the following sections, we first examine related work in several domains. We describe the general framework of SFEV, including the interest metrics, the concept expansion and goal refinement mechanisms, and the visualization component of SFEV. We then illustrate our framework with a user scenario of information sensemaking within a large professionally annotated image collection. Finally, we conclude this paper with a short summary of the work achieved.

2 Related Work

This work can be compared with others on three themes: alternative search paradigms, visual information retrieval interfaces (VIRI), and fisheye view visualization techniques.

As metadata and ontologies become increasingly available, a growing number of researchers are investigating how to integrate this information into search tools. For example, some researchers have focused on tools for semantically organizing gathered information with annotations [6] or concept maps [7]. Our research, on the other hand, focuses primarily on the problem of *encountering* relevant information. This is particularly difficult with image collections, which typically have few keyword annotations. In this domain, researchers have utilized semantic models, such as WordNet [8], to improve the effectiveness of keyword-based queries [9][6] and interactive browsing [10] over image collections. More recent research has used similar techniques with large ontologies [11] and combinations of ontologies [12].

However, there are several unresolved problems with these approaches. First, general solutions have had limited success in large, complex image collections and ontologies, which are often inconsistent in their level of detail and incomplete in their coverage. This amplifies the difficult problem of matching the annotations in the image collection to the relevant concepts in an ontology (i.e., lexical/semantic disambiguation). Second, most of these interfaces do not allow users to interactively adjust the matching algorithms between the collection, the ontology, and the query, which limits the users' ability to adapt in response to the results they find [1].

A third problem is that they are not visual. Furnas identified a number of advantages of Visual Information Retrieval Interfaces (VIRI) over more traditional query/result-list interfaces [13]. One of the most significant was the synergy between search and browsing. Displaying results in a persistent and meaningful location allows users to accumulate knowledge through navigation.

One significant obstacle for effective visualizations is how to handle visual complexity as the amount of information in a representation increases. Furnas [14] first described the fisheye view as a technique for selectively reducing the information in a display to show only the most interesting items, where interest was calculated as a tradeoff between *a priori* importance (in a global context), and relevance to the user's current task. Furnas suggested that this general technique could be used to create compact views in a variety of domains by redefining the function that calculates the degree of interest. Researchers have developed a wide range of fisheye view or *focus + context* techniques. Many of these use geometric distortions to magnify objects near the focus [15]. SFEVs, on the other hand [3], calculate conceptual distance from the focus within one or more data models, and are therefore independent of a particular visual representation [5].

Our research combines the main strengths of semantic-guided search, VIRIs, and *focus + context* visualization techniques in one framework. This combination allows users to visually explore the semantic relationships between documents as they refine their search goals.

3   The Semantic Fisheye View Framework

Fisheye views are based on the observation that, from the user's perspective, the importance or utility of information at any given moment is a function of two general components: *a priori* interest (*API*), and interest metrics. *API* reflects the importance of an object within a particular structure, task, or domain, and is independent of the user's current focus. Interest metrics determine the relative interest of every object in the collection with respect to the user's current focus and task. In a semantic fisheye view, both *API* and interest metrics can be generally described and combined [5]. When using SFEVs to implement search strategies, we model a user's current search goal as a focus, and the system's reaction in terms of *degree of interest* (*DOI*) and emphasis. The *DOI* is the relative importance of every object in the information space, and emphasis is a mapping between the *DOI* of an object to a visual property used to display that object, such as size.

We use the following general function to calculate the *DOI* in a particular context of an object *x*, given the focus f_p:

$$DOI_{context}(x \mid f_i = y) = f\left(API_i(x), \sum_{j=1}^{n} w_j dist_j(x,y)\right). \tag{1}$$

This general function highlights an important characteristic of this framework: both *API* and the conceptual distance between objects may be derived from one or more distance metrics (*dist_j*). The weight, w_i, is the weight associated with the distance metric being used and *n* is the number of metrics being used. We define a focus f_i, as a tuple of one or more weighted objects:

$$f_i = \left\langle Q_i^*, K_i^*, I_i^*, L_i^*, C_i^*, F_{n<i}^* \right\rangle. \tag{2}$$

The focus may include objects from different domains: the history of queries (*Q*); the keywords (*K*) and images (*I*) extracted from the Corbis annotated image collection as a result of these queries; the Lemmas (*L*) and Concepts (*C*) extracted from WordNet that correspond to these keywords; and the history of previous foci (*F*).

The way in which these distance metrics are combined depends on the context being modeled. By orienting the framework to support multiple metrics, it is able to support richer models of user interest that may span multiple domains, such as related concepts and history of interaction. The prototype, which we have developed for exploring image collections, uses multiple *API* and distance metrics to model relative interest. The focus transitions between objects in the domains of queries, keywords, images and concepts.

3.1 *A Priori* Interest

Conceptually, the *API* establishes the global context in which the user searches. In our framework, the *API* is used to model the information that should remain stable as the focus changes. For example, when the user moves their focus over the images and keywords in the collection, the system will continuously recalculate the *DOI* of objects. However, when there is no current focus, the *DOI* of each object will always return to its *API* value. In this way, objects with a high *API* will remain prominent and serve as visual landmarks.

The prototype allows the user to set the *API* interactively in two different ways. First, the *API* may be defined by the result of a query (3.a). In this case, we model the user's focus as a lexical or semantic query (*Q*), and the *DOI* of the objects in the workspace reflect their relevance to the query. The prototype calculates the relevance of the keywords as a function of their frequency in the results of the query. By default we use relative frequency, which emphasizes common themes in the collection. Alternatively, using the inverse document frequency (*idf*) emphasizes infrequent keywords, which is effective for highlighting unique words such as names.

The user may also define the *API* from the *DOI* calculated using a previous foci (3.b). In this case, the *API* is utilized to accumulate important objects in the workspace (like Bates' berry-picking strategy, or relevance-feedback algorithms).

$$API_i(x) = \begin{cases} DOI_{context}(x \mid f_j) & 0 \le j < i \quad (a) \\ DOI_{context}(x \mid f_{i-1}) & (b) \end{cases} . \tag{3}$$

In this case, we use *API* to model information that the user would like to remain persistent, such as a selection. For example, this would allow a user to compare multiple foci by selecting one object and then brushing over another.

3.2 Distance Metrics

The SFEV models semantic queries for complex combinations of concepts as a distance metric between concepts within one or more related semantic models. The approach we used for semantic queries calculates the minimum distance between collections of concepts, based on research by [16]:

$$sim(c_1, c_2) = \frac{depth(c_a)}{depth_{max}} . \tag{4}$$

In this equation, c_1, c_2, and c_a are concepts in WordNet, *depth* is measured in one of the WordNet hierarchies, and c_a is the lowest common ancestor between c_1 and c_2. This metric calculates the distance between concepts based on the generalization structure of WordNet. We precalculated the similarity between all concepts in the subset of WordNet that is related to the keywords in the image collection. The result of this time-consuming calculation is stored in a concept similarity table. To build this table, we first extracted the subset of concepts that have an exact or inexact match to keywords in the image collection. We then iteratively calculated the similarity of all combinations of concepts in the *kind-of*, *part-of*, and *member-of* hierarchies in WordNet using equation 4. Finally, we normalized the similarity values to the range [0,1].

We calculate the similarity between a query, Q, and the collection of keywords annotating an image, A, using equation (5), proposed by [17] and also used by [16]:

$$sim(Q, A) = \frac{\sum_{i=1}^{n} \max_{j=1,...,m_i} \{ sim(q_i, a_j) \cdot w_{q_1} \cdot w_{a_i} \}}{n} . \tag{5}$$

In this equation, $sim(q_i, a_j)$ is the precalculated similarity described in (4), w is the weight of the concept in $Q=\{<q_1, w_{q1}>, ..., < q_n, w_{qn}>\}$ or $A=\{<a_1, w_{a1}>, ..., < a_m, w_{am}>\}$, and n is used to normalize the similarity measure. Essentially, this equation sums the similarities of the closest matching concepts between a query and an image.

The images and keywords that are found as the result of lexical and semantic queries are loaded into the local workspace of the prototype.

Concept Expansion. In addition to searching for images by similarity over its concepts, we have also developed a method for concept expansion that interactively reveals the semantic neighborhood of a concept using several of the search tactics identified by Bates [4]: SUPER (finding more general concepts), SUB (finding more specific concepts) and SIBLING (finding concepts from the same parent, which Bates referred to as RELATE). Each concept expansion command encapsulates an algorithm for iterating over the WordNet structure and generating queries for related concepts. The information seeker is only presented with related concepts that have instances in the collection (i.e., images and keywords), and therefore is not required to navigate over the complex structure and vocabulary of WordNet. This approach allows the user to direct the search process at the tactical and strategic level, as suggested by Bates [18].

3.3 SFEV Supporting Information Sensemaking

We now describe the interest metrics we have developed to support the sensemaking process. Figure 1 traces the flow of information from the user's interaction on the bottom right through the composite metric that calculates semantic similarity and back to the updated view on the top right.

The model is divided into three vertical regions, from left to right: WordNet, the Image Collection, and the View. The WordNet model is the subgraph of WordNet

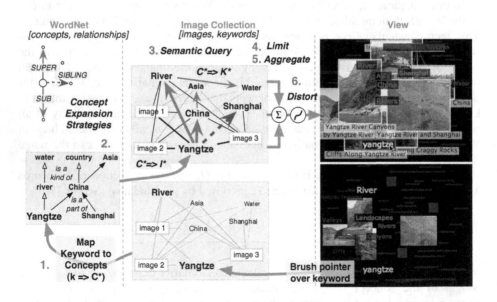

Fig. 1. SUPER, SUB and SIBLING strategies implemented using a composite semantic metric

that is related to the keywords in the image collection. The image collection is modeled as a graph, where images and keywords are nodes and the links between them are edges. The output of an interest metric is a table that assigns a new DOI to each object in the related collection.

When a user brushes over a keyword in the graphical model, the associated keyword object is passed as a focus to an interest metric that calculates the DOI for related images and keywords as follows:

1. *Map keyword to different senses (k=>C*)*: A semantic disambiguation metric maps the keyword to one or more related concepts from WordNet and assigns a confidence to each based on a precalculated keyword/concept mapping.
2. *Concept expansion*: These concepts are passed to metrics implementing the SUPER, SUB, and SIBLING strategies. Each metric traverses the WordNet graph in parallel, gathering a collection of relevant concepts weighted by proximity.
3. *Semantic query*: The concepts from each strategy are then passed to metrics that find the most relevant keywords/images $(C=>K/I)$:
- $C* => K*$: the similarity between a concept and a keyword is a combination of the term usage ordering encoded in WordNet and the lexical match.
- $C* => I*$: the similarity between a concept and an image is found by calculating the sum of the similarities to the keywords annotating the image.
4. *Limits within strategies*: The number of keywords and images, as well as the distribution of interest values may vary enormously depending on the structure of WordNet (e.g., branching factor), the strategy (e.g., most concepts have a single parent but potentially hundreds of children), and the annotation vocabulary. Limits are used both to maintain a relatively constant visual complexity and to avoid having one strategy dominate the others (i.e., each strategy is perceivable).
5. *Combine results of strategies:* The results of the different strategies are aggregated.
6. *Distort DOI distribution:* The distribution of interest for the sets of images and keywords are scaled to the range of 0.1 and 1.0 and distorted to increase the contrast between min and max values.

Emphasis Techniques. Visualizations often attempt to show as much information as possible within the constraints of the available space. However, Pirolli et al. [19] point out that "squeezing" more information into the display does not necessarily "squeeze" more information into the mind, but that strong information scent cues and *focus + context* techniques can enable users to navigate and search through information at more than twice the rate of the user of a normal browser.

VisAmp uses several emphasis techniques to align the visual weight of objects with their semantic importance in a particular context so that the "most interesting" objects are immediately apparent (i.e., "pop out"), and "less interesting" objects fade to the background (e.g., through dimming, shrinking in size and detail, or filtering) [3]. The relative contrast creates a visual ordering that allows a user to rapidly and opportunistically access the most important contextual information, i.e., visual emphasis corresponds to information "scent".

Goal Refinement. As the user's focus changes, the interface calculates the DOI of all objects in the workspace and smoothly animates changes in their representation. The DOI is computed based on equation 1, and the interest metric is based on conceptual similarity. Thus, the new DOI will be computed as follows:

$$DOI_{context}(x \mid f_i = y) = API_i(x) + \sum_{j=1}^{n} w_j sim_j(x,y) \cdot \tag{6}$$

In this equation, the results of a number of different similarity metrics, n, are combined to determine DOI within a particular context. By exploring the information revealed by the SFEV, users learn the vocabulary and conceptual relationships within the collection and are able to interactively refine their search goals.

4 An Image Retrieval Example

We demonstrate the prototype with a scenario where a student uses the prototype to learn about China before attending a conference there. The user starts with an initial query for "China" to see what kinds of images are available. The system populates the workspace with several hundred pictures matching the query, positions them (and their keywords) using a spring layout, and resizes them to reflect their relevance as shown in Fig. 2a. The layout organizes images so that similarly annotated images are near each other, such as the images of flags clustered at the bottom.

As he brushes the cursor over different images, they smoothly grow in size so he can read the captions and then fade slowly back to their original size as he moves to another. Pausing over an image reveals related keywords, and moving the cursor over a keyword reveals related images and concepts. For example, in Fig. 2b he pauses the cursor over *China*, which reveals subconcepts (in cyan) such as the *Great Wall* and the *Yangtze*, superconcepts (in red) such as *Asia*, and siblings (in magenta) such as *Nepal* and New *Zealand*.

Brushing over a general concept, such as *Building* (Fig. 2c), expands to reveal a diverse range of subconcepts, such as *cafes*, *courtyards*, *skyscrapers*, *temples* and *ruins*. Brushing over an unfamiliar term, such as *Yangtze* (Fig. 2d), provides a context that helps interpretation, such as *River* and *China*. The responsiveness of the prototype allows him to rapidly transition between overview and detailed inspection, and the underlying semantic interest metrics allow him to access the information in an opportunistic but well structured manner. Although the overlapping images and keywords in the figure may appear too dense to be usable, the animated transitions, limitations on visual complexity, and visual ordering allow the user to rapidly perceive promising directions for exploration.

This simple example describes how the prototype uses the underlying semantic model and several search strategies to interactively guide the user towards related concepts and images. The formal evaluation described in [3] investigated differences in exploratory search behavior and sensmaking tasks between VisAmp prototypes using keyword- or concept-based similarity metrics. Users performed significantly better with the semantic metrics, and commented that they strongly appreciated the semantic structure for exploring and making sense of the unstructured collection.

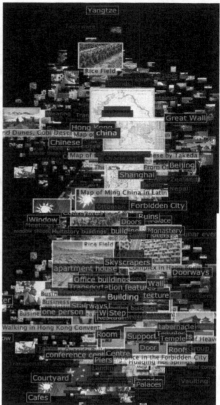

Fig. 2. Exploring images of China using VisAmp (clockwise from top left): (*a*) overview of search results; (*b*) brushing over the keyword *China* reveals subconcepts such as *Yangtze* and *Beijing*, superconcepts such as *Asia*, and siblings such as *Nepal*; (*c*) brushing over *Building* reveals diversity in the collection; (*d*) focusing on *Yangtze* gives context for an unfamiliar word

5 Conclusions

In this paper we described the interest metrics that allow SFEVs to support concept expansion and goal refinement by integrating one or more semantic models into the interface. Users are able to rapidly and interactively discover new concepts and refine their current search goals by simply brushing over objects in the interface without having to create queries or navigate through an explicit representation of the related semantic model. In many cases, large semantic models such as WordNet are too detailed, inconsistent, or confusing for users to navigate over explicitly. An experimental evaluation described in [3] found that users significantly prefer this semantic guided approach over keyword-similarity alone. Future work includes supporting multiple foci and refining the interest metrics to take into account multiple connections between concepts, as discussed by Andreasen in [20].

References

1. Bates, M. J., The Design of Browsing and Berrypicking techniques for the online search interface, *Online Review*, 13(5):407-424, 1989.
2. Russell, D., et al. The cost structure of sensemaking, in *Proc. of the ACM Conf. on Human Factors in Computing Systems (INTERCHI '93)*, 269–276, 1993.
3. Janecek, P., and Pu, P., An Evaluation of Semantic Fisheye Views for Opportunistic Search in an Annotated Image Collection. *Intl. Journal of Digital Libraries*, 4(4). Special Issue on "Information Visualization Interfaces for Retrieval and Analysis." 2004.
4. Bates, M., J., Information Search Tactics, *Journal of the American Society for Information Science*, 30:205-214, 1979.
5. Janecek, P., and Pu, P., A Framework for Designing Fisheye Views to Support Multiple Semantic Contexts, in *Proc. of Intl. Conf. on Advanced Visual Interface (AVI02)*, Trento, Italy, ACM Press, 51-58, 2002.
6. Sereno, B., Buckingham Shum, S., Motta, E., ClaimSpotter: An environment to support sensemaking with knowledge triples. In *Proc. of the ACM Conf. on Intelligent User Interfaces (IUI'05)*, San Diego, CA, USA, January 2005.
7. Leake, D. B., et al., Aiding Knowledge Capture by Searching for Extensions of Knowledge Models. In *Proc. of the ACM Intl. Conf. on Knowledge Capture (KCAP)*, 2003.
8. Miller, G. A., WordNet: A Lexical Database for English. *Com. of the ACM,* 38(11), 1995.
9. Yee, K.-P., et al., Faceted Metadata for Image Search and Browsing, in *Proc. of the ACM Conf. on Human factors in computing systems (CHI '03)*, 401-408, 2003.
10. Aslandogan, Y.A., et al., Using Semantic Contents and WordNet in Image Retrieval, in *Proc. of the 20th Annual Intl. ACM SIGIR Conf. on Research and Development in Information Retrieval.* p. 286-295, 1997
11. Liu, H., and Lieberman, H., Robust Photo Retrieval Using World Semantics, in *Proc. of the LREC 2002 Workshop on Creating and Using Semantics for Information Retrieval and Filtering: State-of-the-art and Future Research*, 15-20, 2002.
12. Hollink, L., et al., Semantic Annotation of Image Collections, in *Proc. of the ACM Workshop on Knowledge Capture and Semantic Annotation (KCAP'03). 2003.*
13. Furnas, G., W., and. Rauch, S. J, Consideration for Information Environments and the NaviQue Workspace, in *DL'98: Proc. of ACM Intl. Conf. on Digital Libraries*, 79-88, 1998.
14. Furnas, G., W., Generalized Fisheye Views, in *Proc. of the SIGCHI Conf. on Human factors in computing systems*, ACM Press, 16-23, 1986.
15. Leung, Y., and Apperley, M., A Review and Taxonomy of Distortion-Oriented Presentation Techniques, *ACM Transactions on Computer-Human Interaction*, 1(2): 126-160, 1994.
16. Yang, J., et al., Thesaurus-Aided Approach for Image Browsing and Retrieval, in *Proc. of 2nd IEEE Intl. Conf. on Multimedia and Expo (ICME 2001)*, 313-316, 2001.
17. Smeaton, A. F., & Quigley, I., Experiments on Using Semantic Distances between Words in Image Caption Retrieval, in *Proc. of the 19th Annual Intl. ACM SIGIR Conf. on Research and Development in Information Retrieval*, pp. 174-180, 1996.
18. Bates, M., J., Where Should the Person Stop and the Information Search Interface Start?, Information Processing and Management, 26(5), 575-591, 1990.
19. Pirolli, P., Card, S., and Van Der Wege, M, The Effects of Information Scent on Visual Search in the Hyperbolic Tree Browser, *ACM Transactions on Computer-Human Interaction*, 10(1), 20-53, 2003.
20. Andreasen, T., Bulskov, H., and Knappe, R., From Ontology over Similarity to Query Evaluation, in *Proc. of 2nd Intl. Conf. on Ontologies, Databases, and Applications of Semantics for Large Scale Information Systems (ODBASE)* (Catania, Sicily, Italy, 2003).

Development and Evaluation of a Multi-document Summarization Method Focusing on Research Concepts and Their Research Relationships

Shiyan Ou, Christopher S.G. Khoo, and Dion H. Goh

Division of Information Studies,
School of Communication & Information,
Nanyang Technological University,
Singapore, 637718
{pg00096125, assgkhoo, ashlgoh}@ntu.edu.sg

Abstract. This paper reports the design and evaluation of a method for summarizing a set of related research abstracts. This summarization method extracts research concepts and their research relationships from different abstracts, integrates the extracted information across abstracts, and presents the integrated information in a Web-based interface to generate a multi-document summary. This study focused on sociology dissertation abstracts, but can be extended to other research abstracts. The summarization method was evaluated in a user study to assess the quality and usefulness of the generated summaries in comparison to a sentence extraction method used in MEAD and a method that extracts only research objective sentences. The evaluation results indicated that the majority of sociology researchers preferred our variable-based summary generated with the use of a taxonomy.

1 Introduction

Multi-document summarization has begun to attract more and more attention in the last few years [6]. Different from single-document summarization, multi-document summarization is capable of condensing a set of related documents into one summary. It is more useful in digital libraries and Web search engines. A multi-document summary has several advantages over the single-document summary. It provides an overview of a topic indicating common information across many documents, unique information in each document, and cross-document relationships (relationships between pieces of information in different documents), and can allow users to zoom in for more details on aspects of interest.

The purpose of this study was to develop an automatic method to summarize a set of related sociology dissertation abstracts that may be retrieved by a digital library system or search engine in response to a user query. Recently, many digital libraries have begun to provide online dissertation abstract services, since dissertation abstracts contain a wealth of high-quality information by specifying research objectives, research methods and research results of dissertation projects. However, a dissertation abstract is relatively long, about 300~400 words, and browsing too many of such

E.A. Fox et al. (Eds.): ICADL 2005, LNCS 3815, pp. 283–292, 2005.
© Springer-Verlag Berlin Heidelberg 2005

abstracts can result in information overload. Therefore, it would be helpful to summarize a set of dissertation abstracts to assist users in grasping the main ideas on a specific topic.

The sociology domain was selected for the study because much of sociology research adopts the traditional quantitative research paradigm of looking for relationships between research concepts often operationalized as research variables. Sociology dissertation abstracts are also well-structured and have the classical research report structure with five standard sections - *background*, *research objectives*, *research methods*, *research results* and *concluding remarks* [9]. Many other domains such as psychology and medicine adopt this research paradigm and report structure.

The summarization method used in this study focuses on research concepts and their research relationships. Concepts are often operationalized as variables whose values vary. A relationship refers to the correspondence between two variables. A variable-based framework was developed to integrate research concepts and their research relationships extracted from different abstracts and thus summarize a set of dissertation abstracts on a specific topic [8]. The framework has a hierarchical structure in which the summarized information is in the top level and the more detailed information is found in lower levels. Based on the framework, an automatic summarization method for sociology dissertation abstracts was developed. The method extracts research concepts and their research relationships from different documents, integrates the extracted information across documents, and presents the integrated information using the variable-based framework. Although the summarization method was developed based on sociology dissertation abstracts, it also can be applied to other domains which adopt the same research paradigm of seeking to investigate research concepts and their relationships, and use a similar research report structure.

2 Review of Multi-document Summarization Approaches

In previous studies, the main approaches used for multi-document summarization include sentence extraction, template-based information extraction, and identification of similarities and differences between documents. With sentence extraction, documents or sentences across all the documents are clustered, following which, a small number of sentences are selected from each cluster and concatenated into a summary [1, 7, 13]. In order to generate more coherent summaries, lexical chains are sometimes considered for extracting internally linked sentences instead of separate sentences [2]. Some multi-document summarizers, such as SUMMONS [5], RIPTIDES [14] and GITEXTER [3], use information extraction techniques to extract pieces of information to fill in one or more pre-defined templates. Another important approach for multi-document summarization is to extract information that is common or repeated in several documents plus selected unique information in individual documents to generate the summaries [4]. In addition, cross-document rhetorical relationships are used to create multi-document summaries by extracting the sentences which have some specific rhetorical relations (e.g. *equivalence* or *contradiction*) among them [12, 15]. However, these existing summarization approaches focus more on physical granularities (words, phrases, sentences and paragraphs) and rhetorical relations based on shallow analysis, without paying much attention to higher-level semantic content and semantic relations expressed within and across documents. Another problem is that different users have different information needs. Thus, an ideal multi-document summarization should provide different levels of detail for different aspects of the topic according to the user's interest. But these approaches usually construct fixed multi-document summaries.

Like most of previous multi-document summarization approaches, the method used in this study summarizes a set of related documents by identifying the similarities and differences among them. However, in the study, the identification of the similarities and differences is based more on semantic-level research concepts and their research relationships expressed in the text, instead of words, phrases or sentences themselves used in previous studies. To do that, the summarization method analyzes the macro-level (between sentences and segments) discourse structure peculiar to sociology dissertation abstracts to identify which segments of the text contain the more important information, and analyzes the micro-level (within sentences) to identify the specific kind of information to be extracted from specific segments, as well as analyze the cross-document structure to identify similar information, unique information, and relationships between pieces of information across documents and integrate them together using a variable-based framework.

3 The Summarization Method

The summarization method comprises five main steps: *data preprocessing, macro-level discourse parsing, information extraction, information integration,* and *information presentation.*

3.1 Data Preprocessing

The input files are a set of related dissertation abstracts on a specific topic retrieved from the Dissertation Abstracts International database indexed under *sociology* subject and *PhD* degree. Each file contains one dissertation abstract in HTML format. Each dissertation abstract was segmented into sentences using a simple algorithm. Then each sentence was parsed into a sequence of word tokens using the Conexor parser [11]. For each word token, its lemma (base form) and part-of-speech tag were indicated.

3.2 Macro-Level Discourse Parsing

In the macro-level discourse analysis, dissertation abstracts were parsed into five sections or categories - *background, research objectives, research methods, research results,* and *concluding remarks.* Each section comprises one or more sentences and contains a specific kind of information. *Research objectives* and *research results* sections are hypothesized to contain the more important information relating to the main ideas of the dissertation study. To parse the macro-level discourse structure automatically, a decision tree classifier was developed to assign each sentence in a dissertation abstract to one of the five categories or sections according to the sentence position in the document and the presence of indicator words in the sentence [9]. The categorization was improved using more reliable indicator phrases, such as "*The purpose of the study was to ...*" found at the beginning of the sentences in the *research objectives* section, while "*The results indicate that ...*" found at the beginning of the sentences in the *research results* section.

3.3 Information Extraction from the Micro-Level Discourse Structure

In the micro-level discourse analysis, four kinds of information were extracted within sentences - *research concepts* and *their research relationships*, *research methods* and *contextual relations*.

At the linguistic level, research concepts, research methods and contextual relations appear as noun or noun phrases. A list of syntactic rules, specifying the possible sequences of part-of-speech tags in a noun phrase, was defined and used to identify sequences of contiguous words that are potential noun phrases. The terms relating to research methods and contextual relations were identified using indicator phrases. The terms relating to research concepts were selected from the *research objectives* and *research results* sections. To extract relationships between variables, linguistic patterns were constructed that a relationship pattern contains two or three slots and the concepts that match with the slots in the pattern represent the research variables connected by the relationship. Pattern matching was performed to identify the text segments in the sentences that match with each relationship pattern.

3.4 Information Integration Across Documents

In a set of related dissertation abstracts, the similarities and differences across different abstracts are mainly reflected through research concepts and their research relationships. Similar concepts were identified and clustered according to their syntactic structure. The terms of different word lengths which follow specific syntactic variation rules were considered term variants and represented similar concepts at different generalization levels, for example, "*abuse* -> sexual *abuse* -> childhood *sexual abuse* -> survivor of *childhood sexual abuse* -> woman *survivor of childhood sexual abuse* -> adult *woman survivor of childhood sexual abuse*". An automatic integration method links shorter term variants to longer term variants from the single head word to a specific full term to from a hierarchical chain, and thus a group of similar concepts was obtained from the nodes of the chain. Concepts at the lower level can be generalized by the broader concepts at the higher level. The chains sharing the same root node are combined to form a hierarchical cluster tree which represented a cluster of similar concepts sharing the same cluster label. The concepts at the higher level in a cluster were selected and integrated together using a new sentence.

Research methods and contextual relations were identified using pre-defined indicator phrases and normalized using uniform terms. For example, "*qualitative design*" and "*qualitative study*" were normalized as "*qualitative research*".

For a cluster of similar concepts, their relationships with other concepts were integrated together to provide an overview of all associated concepts connected by various types of relationships. Each type of relationship (e.g. correlation or cause-effect relationship) was identified using a group of patterns. For the same type of relationships, linguistic normalization was carried out to normalize different surface expressions using a standard expression and to conflate them. For example, "*school size is not significantly related with school crime rate*" and "*there is no relationship not significantly related with* school crime rate" and "*there is no relationship between* school size *and* school dropout rate" were transformed and conflated into "*school size is not related with* school crime rate and school dropout rate".

3.5 Information Presentation

The four kinds of information - *research concepts* and *their research relationships*, *research methods* and *contextual relations*, were combined and reformulated for presentation in a Web-based interface to generate an interactive summary viewable through a Web browser. The interface presents the combined information at three hierarchical levels which are connected through hyperlinks: (1) the summarized information at the top level; (2) the specific information extracted from individual dissertation abstracts at the second level; and (3) the original dissertation abstract at the third level. The hierarchical structure of the interface allows users to explore details of interest by clicking on hyperlinks rather than viewing traditional plain text summaries.

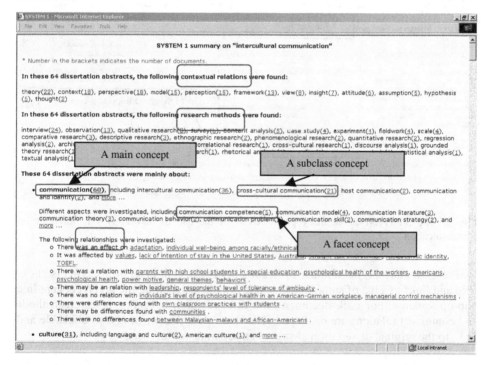

Fig. 1. The SYSTEM 1 summary generated without the use of taxonomy on "intercultural communication"

The summarized information is displayed in the main window as the main summary while the other two hierarchies are displayed separately in pop-up windows. In the main window, the clustered and summarized research methods, contextual relations, research concepts and their research relationships extracted from different documents, are combined based on the variable-based framework. There are two types of main summaries – (1) SYSTEM 1 generated without the use of the taxonomy (see Figure 1); and (2) SYSTEM 2 generated with the use of the taxonomy (see Figure 2). The function of the taxonomy is to remove non-concept terms, highlight the important sociology concepts, and categorize main concepts into different subjects.

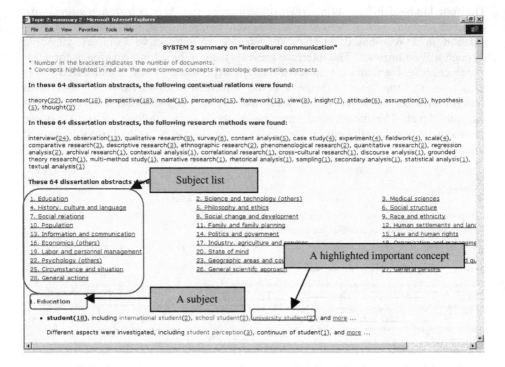

Fig. 2. The SYSTEM 2 summary generated with the use of taxonomy on "intercultural communication"

For each concept, the number of documents is given in parenthesis. This is clickable and links to a list of summarized single documents sharing the given concept in a pop-up window. For each document, the title, research concepts, research methods and contextual relations are displayed. The title of the document is also clickable and links to the original dissertation abstract in a separate pop-up window.

4   Evaluation of the Summarization Method

The overall quality and usefulness of the final summaries were assessed intrinsically in a user study. The users were asked to subjectively judge the quality of the summaries and their usefulness for research-related purposes, by comparing the summaries generated using our summarization method with or without the use of the taxonomy against a summary generated by MEAD using a sentence extraction method and a summary generated by extracting research objective sentences only.

4.1 Evaluation Design

20 research topics were obtained from 20 researchers in the field of sociology, who were Master's or PhD research students or faculty members at Nanyang Technological University, Singapore, and National University of Singapore. Each researcher was asked to submit one research topic that he/she was working on or had worked on. For each topic, a set of PhD sociology dissertation abstracts were retrieved from the Dissertation Abstracts International database using the topic as the search query, but at most 200 abstracts were retained. The set of dissertation abstracts retrieved for each topic was condensed into a summary. Four different summaries were provided for each topic with two kinds of structures – (1) variable-based summaries, and (2) sentence-based summaries. The four types of summaries were:

- *A variable-based summary generated without the use of the taxonomy.* It focuses on research concepts and their research relationships, as well as research methods and context relations. This type of summary was labeled *SYSTEM 1* (see Figure 1).
- *A variable-based summary generated with the use of the taxonomy.* It also focuses on research concepts and their research relationships, as well as research methods and contextual relations. Furthermore, based on the taxonomy, non-concept terms were filtered out, important sociology concepts were highlighted in red, and concept clusters were categorized into different subjects. This type of summary was labeled *SYSTEM 2* (see Figure 2).
- *A sentence-based summary generated by extracting research objectives of each abstract.* It consists of sentences that are research objectives extracted from each dissertation abstract. The type of summary was labeled *OBJECTIVES*.
- *A sentence-based summary generated by a peer system.* It consists of sentences that were ranked as important, according to certain sentence features, in the set of dissertation abstracts. It was created by a multi-document summarization system MEAD 3.08, which uses a centroid-based sentence extraction method [13]. This type of summary was labeled *MEAD*.

The four types of summaries were constructed using the same compression rate of 20% in terms of the number of the words. For each topic, the four types of summaries were compared by human subjects on two aspects: (1) quality of the summaries including readability and comprehensibility; (2) usefulness of the summaries for research-related purposes.

4.2 Evaluation Results

The overall quality (readability and comprehensibility) and usefulness of the four types of summaries were scored by the human subjects on a 7-point scale. The average scores for the four types of summaries from 20 researchers are shown in Table 1.

(1) Quality (readability and comprehensibility)
SYSTEM 2 obtained the second highest readability and comprehensibility score (5.2 and 5.1) among the four types of summaries. It was rated better than SYSTEM 1 (4.4

Table 1. Average scores for the overall quality (readability and comprehensibility) and usefulness of the four types of summaries

		SYSTEM 1	SYSTEM 2	OBJECTIVES	MEAD
Qual-ity	Readability	4.40	5.20	**5.70**	5.00
	Comprehensibility	4.75	5.10	**5.60**	4.95
Usefulness		5.00	**5.70**	5.65	4.9

and 4.75), indicating that with the use of a taxonomy for information filtering and organization, the quality of the variable-based summary was substantially improved. SYSTEM 2 was rated better than the set of important sentences in MEAD (5.0 and 4.95), but still worse than the research objective sentences in OBJECTIVES (5.7 and 5.6). There was a significant difference in the average readability score between SYSTEM 1 and SYSTEM 2 (p=0.008).

For readability, the researchers indicated that SYSTEM 1 & 2 were more concise and contain less vacuous or general information than OBJECTIVES and MEAD. This is because SYSTEM 1 & 2 consist of important concepts and simple relationship sentences whereas OBJECTIVES and MEAD consist of complete sentences. On the other hand, the researchers indicated that SYSTEM 1 & 2 contain more duplicate information and dangling anaphors, and are less fluent than OBJECTIVES and MEAD. This is because a concept can be assigned to more than one cluster from difference perspectives. Moreover, separate concepts are less fluent than complete sentences.

For comprehensibility, the researchers indicated that OBJECTVIES and MEAD are a little easier to understand than SYSTEM 1 & 2. This is because complete sentences are easier to understand than separate concepts. Furthermore, the researchers indicated that the research objective sentences in OBJECTIVES can indicate the main ideas of the topic very well.

(2) Usefulness
For research-related purposes, SYSTEM 2 obtained similar usefulness score (5.7) as the research objective sentences in OBJECTIVES (5.65), but was rated much better than the set of the general important sentences in MEAD (4.9) and SYSTEM 2 (5.0). This indicates that with the use of the taxonomy for information organization, the usefulness of the variable-based summary was improved. In addition, the research objective sentences was rated much better than the set of the general importance sentences, indicating that the researchers were more concerned about research objectives than other kinds of information in a dissertation.

The researchers indicated that SYSTEM 1 & 2 were more useful in indicating similarities among previous studies, important concepts and research methods used in the area. OBJECTIVES and MEAD were more useful in identifying the documents of interest easily and indicating important theories, views or ideas in the area.

The four types of summaries were ranked by 20 researchers. A weighted rank score was calculated for each summary: a weight of 4 was assigned to the first rank, 3 for the second rank, 2 for the third rank, and 1 for the fourth rank. The researchers were also asked to select one or more summaries that they preferred to use for their

Table 2. Ranking and preference for the four types of summaries

Rank	SYSTEM 1	SYSTEM 2	OBJECTIVES	MEAD
No.1 (weight=4)	3 (15%)	11 (55%)	6 (30%)	0
No.2 (weight=3)	5 (25%)	2 (10%)	7 (35%)	6 (30%)
No.3 (weight=2)	5 (25%)	6 (30%)	5 (25%)	4 (20%)
No.4 (weight=1)	7 (35%)	1 (5%)	2 (10%)	10 (50%)
Weighted rank score	2.15	**3.15**	2.85	1.8
Preference	6 (30%)	**14 (70%)**	11 (55%)	5 (25%)

research-related work. The ranking and the researchers' preference for the four types of summaries are summarized in Table 2.

According to the weighted rank scores, the final ranking of the four types of summaries is: (1) SYSTEM 2, (2) OBJECTIVES, (3) SYSTEM 1 and (4) MEAD. SYSTEM 2 obtained the first rank among the four types of summaries. The highest percentage of the researchers (70%) indicated preference for SYSTEM 2 for their research-related work, and 55% of the researchers indicated preference for OBJECTIVES.

The researchers indicated that the variable-based summaries were more effective in providing an overview of a topic and can help researchers find similar information easily. However, they were too brief to provide accurate information and sometimes confused the users. On the other hand, the sentence-based summaries can provide more direct information and were easy to understand. But it was time-consuming to read them and hard to locate the relevant information.

5 Conclusion and Future Work

This paper has reported the development and evaluation of an automatic method for summarizing a set of sociology dissertation abstracts. Our system focuses on extracting research concepts and their research relationships from each document, integrating the extracted information across documents, and presenting the integrated information in an interactive Web interface.

A user study was carried out to evaluate the quality (readability and comprehensibility) and usefulness of the summaries using a questionnaire. In the variable-based summary generated with the use of a taxonomy, non-concept terms were filtered out, concepts were categorized into different subjects, and important sociology concepts were highlighted. The evaluation results demonstrated that this kind of summary was more readable, comprehensible, and useful than the one generated without the use of the taxonomy. It ranked higher than the research objective summary and the MEAD summary. The majority of the sociology researchers in the study (70%) indicated preference for the variable-based summary generated with the use of a taxonomy, and 55% indicated preference for the research objective summary.

References

1. Boros, E., Kanto, P.B., & Neu, D.J.: A clustering based approach to creating multi-document summaries. *Document Understanding Conferences* (2002). Available at http://www-nlpir.nist.gov/projects/duc/pubs/2001papers/rutgers_final.pdf
2. Brunn, M., Chali, Y., & Dufour, B. (2002). The University of Lethbridge text summarizer at DUC 2002. Document Understanding Conferences. Retrieved May 19, 2003 from http://www-nlpir.nist.gov/projects/duc/pubs/2002papers/lethbridge_chali.pdf.
3. Harabagiu, S.M., & Lacatusu, F.: Generating single and multi-document summaries with GISTEXTER. *Document Understanding Conferences* (2002). Available at http://www-nlpir.nist.gov/projects/duc/pubs/2002papers/utdallas_sanda.pdf
4. Mani, I., & Bloedorn, E.: Summarization similarities and differences among related documents. Information Retrieval, 1(1) (1999) 1-23
5. Mckeown, K., & Radev, D.: Generating summaries of multiple news articles. In *Proceedings of the 18th Annual International ACM Conference on Research and Development in Information Retrieval (ACM SIGIR)*. Seattle, WA (1995) 74-82
6. National Institute of Standards and Technology. : *Document Understanding Conferences* (2002). Available at http://www-nlpir.nist.gov/projects/duc/index.html
7. Otterbacher, J.C., Winkel, A.J., & Radev, D.R.: The Michigan single and multi-document summarizer for DUC 2002. *Document Understanding Conferences* (2002) Available at http://www-nlpir.nist.gov/projects/duc/pubs/2002papers/umich_otter.pdf
8. Ou, S., Khoo, C., & Goh, D.: Multi-document summarization of dissertation abstracts using a variable-based framework. In *Proceedings of the 66th Annual Meeting of the American Society for Information Science and Technology (ASIST)*. Long Beach, CA, 19-23 October (2003) 230-239
9. Ou, S., Khoo, C., Goh, D., & Heng, Hui-Hing. : Automatic discourse parsing of sociology dissertation abstracts as sentence categorization. In *Proceedings of the 8th International ISKO Conference*. London, UK, 13-16 July (2004) 345-350
10. Ou, S., Khoo, C., & Goh, D.: A multi-document summarization system for sociology dissertation abstracts: design, implementation and evaluation. In *Proceedings of the 9th Conference on Research and Advanced Technology for Digital Libraries (ECDL)*. Vienna, Austria, 18-23 September (2005) in press
11. Pasi, J. & Timo, J.: A non-projective dependency parser. In *Proceedings of the 5th Conference on Applied Natural Language Processing*. Washington, DD: Association for Computational Linguistics(1997) 64-71
12. Radev, D.: A common theory of information fusion from multiple text sources step one: cross-document structure. In *Proceedings of the 1st SIGdial Workshop on Discourse and Dialogue* (2000). Available at http://www.sigdial.org/sigdialworkshop/proceedings/radev.pdf
13. Radev, D., Jing, H., & Budzikowska, M.: Centroid-based summarization of multiple documents: sentence extraction, utility-based evaluation and user studies. In *Workshop held with Applied Natural Language Processing Conference / Conference of the North American Chapter of the Association for Computational Linguistics (ANLP/ANNCL)* (2000) 21-29
14. White, M., Korelsky, T., Cardie, C., Ng, V., Pierce, D., & Wagstaff, K.: Multi-document summarization via information extraction. In *Proceedings of the 1st International Conference on Human Language Technology Research (HLT-01)* (2001)
15. Zhang, Z., Blair-Goldensohn, S., & Radev, D.: Towards CST-enhanced summarization. *In Proceedings of the 18th National Conference on Artificial Intelligence (AAAI-2002)*. Edmonton , Canada, August (2002)

Automatic Classification of Western Music in Digital Library

Won-Jung Yoon, Kang-Kue Lee, Kyu-Sik Park, and Hae-Young Yoo

Dankook University,
Division of Information and Computer Science,
San 8, Hannam-Dong, Yongsan-Ku, Seoul Korea, 140-714
{helloril, fitz, kspark, yoohy}@dankook.ac.kr

Abstract. In this paper, we propose a new robust content-based western music genre classification algorithm using multi-feature clustering (MFC) method combined with feature selection procedure. This paper focuses on the dependency problems of the classification result to different query patterns and query lengths which causes serious uncertainty of the system performance. In order to solve these problems, a new approach called MFC-SFSS based on k-means clustering is proposed. To verify the performance of the proposed method, several excerpts with variable duration were extracted from every other position in a same queried music file. Effectiveness of the system with MFC –SFSS and without MFC-SFSS is compared in terms of the classification results with k-NN decision rule. It is demonstrated that the use of MFC-SFSS significantly improves the system stability of musical genre classification with better accuracy.

1 Introduction

Musical genre classification based on music content has been a growing area of research in the last few years. All content-based classification methods have three common stages of a pattern recognition problem: feature extraction, training of the classifier based on the sample music, and classification. Depending on different combinations of these stages, several strategies are employed in these studies. Tzanetakis and Perry [1] combined standard timbral features with representations of rhythm and pitch content and they achieved classification performance in the rage of 60% for ten musical genres. The classification accuracy based on just rhythm and pitch content was quite poor such as 23%~28%. In Ref. [2], Li performed extensive comparative study on the selection of features between Daubechies wavelet coefficient and the ones used in [1], and they conclude that the timbral feature is more suitable than rhythmic or pitch content for musical genre classification. Burred et al., [3] suggested hierarchical classification approach and genre dependent feature sets. In 13 musical genres, they can achieve 57.8% classification accuracy. Other methods regarding feature extraction and classification performance for music and general audio information are described in [4-8]. Although many combinations of music features and classifiers have been evaluated in those works, little attention has been paid to the following two practical issues: Firstly, the classification results corresponding to

E.A. Fox et al. (Eds.): ICADL 2005, LNCS 3815, pp. 293–300, 2005.
© Springer-Verlag Berlin Heidelberg 2005

different query patterns (or portions) within the same music file may be much different. Secondly, the classification performance is also quite dependent to the lengths of the test query. A system dependency problem on different query portions and query lengths may cause remarkable uncertainty of the system performance.

In this paper, a new robust feature extraction method called multi-feature clustering (MFC) combined with SFFS feature selection is proposed to overcome the system uncertainty problem. This paper is organized as follows. Section 2 describes feature extraction and. feature selection procedure. Proposed multi-feature clustering method is introduced in section 3. Section 4 shows extensive experimental results of the proposed method. Finally, section 5 gives the conclusion.

2   Proposed Method- Feature Extraction, Selection and Clustering

2.1   Feature Extraction

Feature extraction can be thought of as representation conversion, taking low-level representation and identifying higher level features [9]. Before classification, the music signals are normalized to have zero mean and unit variance in order to avoid numerical problems caused by small variances of the feature values. At the sampling rate of 22 kHz, the music signals are divided into 23ms frames with 50% overlapped hamming window at the two adjacent frames. Two types of features are computed from each frame: One is the timbral features such as spectral centroid, spectral roll off, spectral flux and zero crossing rates. The other is coefficient domain features such as thirteen mel-frequency cepstral coefficients (MFCC) and ten linear predictive coefficients (LPC). The means and standard deviations of these six original features are computed over each frame for each music file to form a total of 54-dimensional feature vector. Since these features are well-known in the literature, detail description of each feature is omitted in this paper.

2.2   Feature Selection

Not all the 54-dimensional features are used for musical genre classification purpose. Some features are highly correlated among themselves and some feature dimension reduction can be achieved using the feature redundancy. In order to reduce the computational burden and so speed up the search process, an efficient feature selection method is desired. As described in paper [10], two different types of feature selection procedures are widely used in the literature. These are the sequential forward selection (SFS) and the sequential floating forward selection (SFFS). In this paper, these two methods are tested and compared in terms of the classification success rate. They allow not only choosing best feature sets that maximize the classification success rate, but also it helps to keep reasonable size of trained database in multi-feature clustering (MFC) algorithm in next subsection.

2.3   Multi-feature Clustering (MFC)

As pointed out earlier, the classification results corresponding to different query patterns and query lengths within the same music file or same class may be much different. It may cause serious uncertainty of the system performance. In order to overcome these problems, a new robust feature extraction method called multi-feature clustering (MFC) with feature selection is implemented based on k-means clustering algorithm. Basic idea is to extract features over the full-length music signal in a step of 20 sec large window using SFS or SFFS method and then cluster these features in a number of disjoint subsets. This allows feature set to characterize whole intervals of music signal while maintaining a reasonable size of database.

The performance of k-means clustering algorithm is well known to depend on the number of clusters and there is currently no apparent practical or theoretical literature on the determination of the optimal size of clusters. For this reason, the number of clusters or centroids was determined as four experimentally. Fig. 1 outlines the proposed MFC with feature selection method.

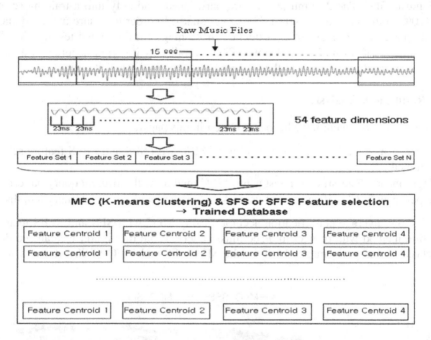

Fig. 1. Proposed MFC with feature selection for trained DB

After the proposed MFC with defined feature selection in the trained database, the system then ready to classify the genre of the queried music using well-known k-NN pattern classification algorithm. We recall that the proposed MFC method has four sets of features vector for each music signal in trained database instead of one as in usual content-based system. Because of this difference in building up the trained database, the k-NN algorithm is slightly modified as follows. In modified k-NN, a query to be classified is compared to each one of the four feature sets in training data vectors from different classes and classification is performed according to the distance to the k nearest feature points with Euclidean distance measure. Finally, the classification is done by picking the k points nearest to the current test query point, and the class most often picked is chosen as classification result. The implementation of modified k-NN is quite straightforward.

3 Experiments on Music Classification

3.1 Experimental Setup

The proposed algorithm has been implemented and used to classify music data from a database of about 240 music files. 60 music samples were collected for each of the four genres in Classical, Hiphop, Jazz, and Rock, resulting in 240 music files in database. The experts of the dataset were taken from radio, compact disks, and internet MP3 music files. The 240 music files are partitioned randomly into a training set of 168 (70%) sounds and a test set of 72 (30%) sounds. In order to ensure unbiased classification accuracy because of a particular partitioning of training and testing, this division was iterated one hundred times. The overall classification accuracy was obtained as the arithmetic mean of the success rate of the individual iterations.

3.2 Results and Analysis

Three sets of experiment have been conducted in this paper.

- Experiment 1: Performance verification of MFC with SFS and SFSS feature selection method
- Experiment 2: Classification test using MFC method with different query patterns
- Experiment 3: Classification test using MFC method with different query lengths

Fig. 2 shows average classification accuracy using MFC with SFS and SFFS feature selection method with respect to 5 sec music query. From the figure, we can see that the classification performance both for the MFC-SFS and MFC-SFSS increases with

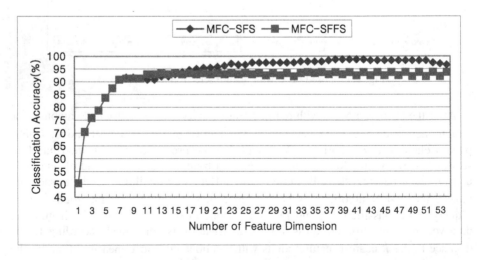

Fig. 2. Feature selection procedure for MFC-SFS and MFC-SFFS method

the increase of features up to certain number of features, while it remains almost constant or smoothly increased after that. Thus based on the observation of these boundaries in figure 2, we can select first few features up to the boundary and ignore the rest of them. As we intuitively know, the less number of feature set is always desirable.

As seen on the table 1, MFC-SFSS achieves little higher classification accuracy than MFC-SFS when using first 10 feature set. We note that, in ref. [8], they end up with 20 features which are twice of our feature dimension.

Table 1. Classification statistics for SFS and SFFS feature slection method

Feature selection method	SFS	SFFS
Classification Accuracy	91.3	93.7
Number of Selected Features	10	10

Table 2 shows detailed MFC-SFFS performance in musical genre classification in a form of a confusion matrix. As a comparison purpose, the classification results using 54 dimensional feature vector is included in the table. The numbers of correct classification with MFC-SFFS lie in the diagonal of the confusion matrix. The numbers shown in parenthesis represent statistics with all 54 dimensional features. From table 2, we see at least 7% improvement of classification performance using only 10 dimensional features derived from MFC-SFFS feature selection method. The MFC-SFFS method works fairly well over the genre of Classical, Hiphop, and Jazz while the average rate of correct classification is little lower in Rock genre.

Table 2. Genre confusion matrix with MFC-SFFS feature optimization (%)

Query / Result	Classic	Jazz	Hiphop	Rock
Classic	95 (98)	1. 7(12)	0(0)	5(7)
Jazz	1. 7(0)	96.7 (72)	3.3(0)	3. 3(2)
Hiphop	0(0)	0(5)	96.7 (97)	5(13)
Rock	3.3(2)	1.7(12)	0(3)	86.7 (78)
Average classification accuracy 93.75% (86.25 %)				

As pointed out earlier, the classification results corresponding to different query patterns (or portions) may be much different. It may cause serious uncertainty of the system performance. In order to overcome this problem, MFC-SFFS is used as explained in section 2. To verify the performance of the proposed method, seven excerpts with fixed duration of 5 sec were extracted from every other position in same query music- at music beginning and 10%, 20%, 30%, 40%, 50%, and 80% position after the beginning of music signal. Fig. 3 shows the classification results with seven excerpts at the prescribed query position.

As we expected, the classification results without MFC-SFFS greatly depends on the query positions and it's performance is getting worse as query portion towards to two extreme cases of beginning and ending position of the music signal. This is no wonder because, in general, the musical characteristics are not rich enough at those extreme intervals of music signal. On the other hand, we can find quite stable classification performance with MFC-SFSS method and it yields higher accuracy rate in the range of 72% ~ 94%. Even at two extreme cases of beginning and ending position, the system with MFC-SFSS can achieves classification accuracy as high as 72% which is

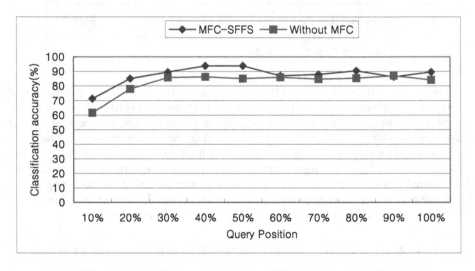

Fig. 3 Genre classification results at different query portions with MFC-SFFS

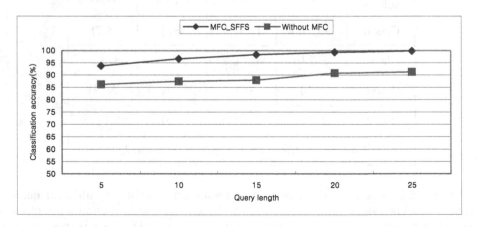

Fig. 4. Genre classification results at different query lengths with MFC-SFFS

more than 10% improvement over the system without MFC-SFSS. This is a consequence of good MFC property which helps the system to build robust musical feature set over the full-length music signal.

Fig. 4 explains an importance of the query length to the overall system performance. Five excerpts with duration of 5sec, 10sec, 15 sec, 20sec and 25sec are used as a test query positioned at 20% after the music beginning. Again, we see the desirable characteristics of MFC-SFFS with stable classification performance and more than 20% improvement over the one without MFC-SFSS

5 Conclusion

In this paper, we propose a new content-based music genre classification algorithm using multi-feature clustering (MFC) combined with SFFS feature selection method. It can prevent unstable classification problems due to the different query patterns and query lengths. For the implementation of the proposed algorithm, SFFS feature selection method is first applied to the 54 dimensional feature set to reduce the feature dimension in the order of one-fifth and then multi-feature clustering (MFC) is adopted to build a robust feature vectors in trained DB. The system then compares the query pattern to each one of the four feature sets of music file in trained database, and it classifies the musical genre based on the k-NN decision rule. Experimental comparisons for music genre classification with several query excerpts with variable duration from every other position are presented and it demonstrates the superiority of MFC-SFSS method in terms of the classification stability and accuracy. Future work will involve the development of new features, further analysis of classification and retrieval system for practical implementation, and the incorporation of more music classes.

Acknowledgment

This work was supported by grant No. R01-2004-000-10122-0 from the Basic Research Program of the Korea Science & Engineering Foundation.

References

1. G. Tzanetakis and P. Cook, "Musical genre classification of audio signals," *IEEE Trans. on Speech and Audio Processing*, vol. 10, no. 5, pp. 293-302, July 2002.
2. T. Li, M. Ogihara and Q. Li, "A comparative study on content-based music genre classification," in *Proc. of the 26th annual internal ACM SIGIR*, pp. 282-289, ACM Press, July 2003.
3. J. J. Burred and A. Lerch, "A hierarchical approach to automatic musical genre classification," in *Proc. DAFx03*, 2003, pp. 308-311.
4. E. Wold, T. Blum, D. Keislar, and J. Wheaton, "Content-based classification, search, and retrieval of audio," *IEEE Multimedia*, vol.3, no. 2, 1996.

5. J. Foote, "Content-based retrieval of music and audio," in *Proc. SPIE Multimedia Storage Archiving Systems II*, vol. 3229, C.C.J. Kuo *et al.*, Eds., 1997, pp. 138-147.
6. J. Foote *et al*, "An overview of audio information retrieval," *ACM-Springer Multimedia Systems*, vol. 7, no. 1, pp. 2-11, Jan. 1999.
7. Y. Wang, Z. Liu and J. Huang, "Multimedia content analysis: using both audio and visual clues," *IEEE Signal Proc. Mag.*, Nov. 20000
8. S. Blackburn, "Content based retrieval and navigation of music, 1999, Mini-thesis, University of Southampton.
9. M. Liu and C. Wan, "A study on content-based classification retrieval of audio database," *Proc. of the International Database Engineering & Applications Symposium*, pp. 339 - 345. 2001.
10. Anil K. Jin, Robert P.W. Duin, Jianchang Mai, "Statistical Pattern Recognition: A Review" IEEE Trans. Pattern Analysis and Machine Intelligence, vol. 22, no. 1, Jan. 2000.

Finding Pertinent Page-Pairs
from Web Search Results

Takayuki Yumoto and Katsumi Tanaka

Dept. of Social Informatics, Graduate School of Informatics, Kyoto University,
Yoshida Honmachi Sakyo-ku Kyoto 606-8501, Japan
{yumoto, tanaka}@dl.kuis.kyoto-u.ac.jp

Abstract. Conventional Web search engines evaluate each single page
as a ranking unit. When the information a user wishes to have is distributed on multiple Web pages, it is difficult to find pertinent search
results with these conventional engines. Furthermore, search result lists
are hard to check and they do not tell us anything about the relationships between the searched Web pages. We often have to collect Web
pages that reflect different viewpoints. Here, a collection of pages may
be more pertinent as a search result item than a single Web page. In this
paper, we propose the idea to realize the notion of "multiple viewpoint
retrieval" in Web searches. Multiple viewpoint retrieval means searching Web pages that have been described from different viewpoints for a
specific topic, gathering multiple collections of Web pages, ranking each
collection as a search result and returning them as results. In this paper,
we consider the case of page-pairs. We describe a feature-vector based
approach to finding pertinent page-pairs. We also analyze the characteristics of page-pairs.

1 Introduction

Web search engines can find pertinent pages, and lead us to them. However,
there are some cases when they cannot find pertinent answers. We consider
two of them here. The first case is where information a user wishes to have is
distributed on multiple Web pages. Conventional search engines do not suggest
the misleading results but they do not tell us which pages include which part of
the information we want. The second case is where we have to collect Web pages
that reflect different viewpoints. For example, suppose that we wish to obtain
information about "wind power generation" and "nuclear power generation".
Some pages are described from the viewpoint of "wind power generation" and
others are described from the viewpoint of "nuclear power generation". A single
page with one viewpoint will not provide enough answers. Also, a conventional
search engine will not tell us anything about the relationships between searched
Web pages.

This is due to the same reason, i.e. conventional Web search engines evaluate
each single page as a ranking unit. In both cases, a collection of pages may be
more pertinent as an item for a search result than a single Web page.

E.A. Fox et al. (Eds.): ICADL 2005, LNCS 3815, pp. 301–310, 2005.
© Springer-Verlag Berlin Heidelberg 2005

In this paper, we propose the new concept of "multiple viewpoint retrieval", which means searching Web pages described from different viewpoints for a specific topic, gathering multiple collections of Web pages, ranking each collection as a search result and returning them as results. We also describe a simple approach to achieve multiple viewpoint retrieval and analyze the characteristics of page-pairs.

This paper is organized follows. Section 2 explains our motivation and the concept behind multiple viewpoint retrieval. Section 3 describes our approach to achieve multiple viewpoint retrieval, which we evaluate in Section 4. Section 5 is the conclusion and discusses future work.

2   Multiple Viewpoint Retrieval

2.1   Motivation

Although Web search engines can find pertinent pages, there are two cases conventional search engines cannot find these. This is where

- Information, the user wishes to have is distributed on multiple Web pages and where
- We have to collect web pages that reflect different viewpoints.

These cases have common problems. There are that conventional search engines do not reflect on the relationships between search results and search result lists output by conventional search engines give us no information about the relationships between Web pages.

2.2   Concept

To solve these problems, we propose "multiple viewpoint retrieval", which means searching Web pages described from different viewpoints for a specific topic, gathering multiple collections of Web pages, ranking each collection as a search result, and returning them as results. When pages described from different viewpoints include the same topics, their content is different and the points they focus on are also different. To achieve multiple viewpoint retrieval, we need to establish the following:

1. Collecting Web pages: What Web pages should be collected?
2. Gathering multiple collection: What Web pages should compose each collection and what relationships they satisfy?
3. Ranking the each collection: What collection is pertinent?

2.3   Our Approach

We focused on gathering multiple collections and ranking each collection and took the approach re-ranking search results with conventional search engines[1].

---

[1] In this paper, we used Google[1].

This was because conventional search engines can find good results as a single page. To achieve "multiple viewpoint retrieval" simply, we considered page-pairs as ranking units.

The multiple viewpoint retrieval was executed in three steps:

1. Submit a query to a conventional search engine, and collect the Web pages,
2. Collect page-pairs taking the relationship between pages into consideration, and
3. Calculate the evaluation function for page-pairs and rank them.

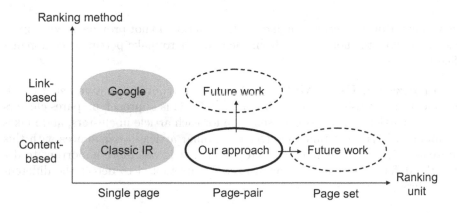

Fig. 1. The relationship between our approach and other research

Conventional Web search engines compute ranking scores for searched pages by the content-analysis approach (computation of page similarity to a query) or the link-analysis approach (such as Google's PageRank). In this paper, we also use the content-analysis approach like classic information retrieval. The major differences of our work from conventional work is that the information unit for ranking is not a single page, but a page-pair. Extensions of our approach to the link-analysis method and to the arbitrary collection of pages are remained as future work.

2.4   Related Work

Retrieval with Clustering. Cutting *et al.* proposed document clustering for efficient browsing [2], and some search engines take this approach. They prepare clusters from search results and display each page[3]. These are different approaches to ours. Clusters are collections that consist of similar pages. Our "multiple viewpoint search" prepares a collection from pages that are similar but have some different parts. Web pages in different clusters, which are prepared by search engines with clustering, are sometimes described from different

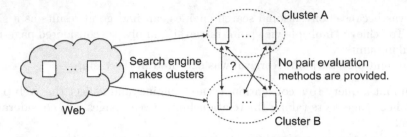

Fig. 2. Search engine with clustering

viewpoints. However, search engines with clustering do not provide us with information on how to choose pages from each cluster to make pertinent page-pairs. (See Figure 2.)

Summarization Using Multiple Documents. Summarization using multiple documents is used to summarize news [4, 5]. This approach prepares clusters from news articles, matches each sentence for each article in clusters, and makes a summary. It is important to detect the similar articles or sentences with this approach. Our goal was more challenging in that it was more important to detect the differences than the similarities. We attempted to detect the different viewpoints.

3   Multiple Viewpoint Retrieval for Page-Pairs

3.1   Model

We used a vector-space model to describe Web pages, page-pairs, and queries. Term Frequency Inverse Document Frequency (TFIDF)[6] word weight was used for the feature-vector. TF is the number of times words appeared in each document, and IDF of keyword kw was calculate as follows:

$$IDF(kw) = log\frac{N}{df(kw)} + 1 \tag{1}$$

N is the number of searched results and $df(k)$ is the number of documents with keyword "kw". IDF scores were calculated from collections of search results and also page-pairs. (p_1, p_2) denotes page-pair consisting of pages p_1 and p_2. Even if $p_1 \neq p_2$, $(p_1, p_2) = (p_2, p_1)$. In the feature-vector of page-pairs, the TF values are the summation of the TF values of p_1 and p_2, and the IDF values are calculated from all of page-pairs.

The feature-vector of query v_q is :

$$v_q = (v_q^{(1)}, v_q^{(2)}, \cdots, v_q^{(n)}) \tag{2}$$

$$v_q^{(i)} = \begin{cases} 1 \text{ if term } t_i \text{ in query} \\ 0 \text{ if otherwise.} \end{cases}$$

3.2   Feature Values

We defined three feature values to analyze characteristics of page-pairs:

- *Inter-page similarity* : $sim(v_{p_1}, v_{p_2})$,
- *Page-pair relevance* : $sim(v_{(p_1,p_2)}, v_q)$, and
- *Page relevance* : $sim(v_p, v_q)$

We adopted a cosine correlation value for similarity. Similarity in feature vector v_1 and v_2 was calculated as:

$$sim(v_1, v_2) = \frac{v_1 \cdot v_2}{|v_1||v_2|} \tag{3}$$

Inter-page similarity indicates how much duplication there is between pages composing page-pairs. Page-pair relevance indicates how pertinent a page-pair is for given query. Higher values are best. We adopted it as evalua tion value for page-pairs. Figure 3 shows the relationship between the feature vectors of pages p1 and p2 (denoted as v_{p1}, v_{p2}), and page-pair (p1,p2) (denoted as $v_{(p1,p2)}$). v_q is feature vector of query q. Each bar corresponds to each element of a feature vector. Three bars from the left-most one correspond to the keyword included in query (k1,k2,k3). If $sim(v_{(p1,p2)}, v_q)$ has a high value, the following conditions are required:

- The values of elements, which corresponds to a query, complement each other in $v_{(p1,p2)}$ and reach a high value.
- The values of other elements are set off against each other in $v_{(p1,p2)}$ and stay low.

When pages are described from the different viewpoints, the above conditions are satisfied. (Duplication in query terms occurs many times, but occurs little in other terms.)

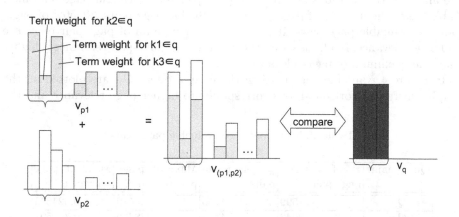

Fig. 3. Feature vector for pertinent page-pair

Page relevance indicates how pertinent a single page is for given query.

We defined valuable page-pair as page-pair which has higher page-pair relevance than page relevance of both pages consisting of it. In other words, valuable page-pairs satisfy following equation.

$$sim(v_{(v_{p1}, v_{p2})}, v_q) > max(sim(v_{p1}, v_q), sim(v_{p2}, v_q)) \qquad (4)$$

The valuable page-pair is more pertinent than the single pages which compose it.

4   Analysis for Page-Pairs

We analyzed characteristics of page-pairs. We first analyzed the relationship between page-pair relevance and page relevance. We then analyzed the relationship between page-pair relevance and inter-page similarity. We also analyzed the relationship between page-pair relevance and Google's ranking. We used following four queries in Table 1. We obtained 100 URLs for each query by Google[1], and made page-pairs from the available pages.

Table 1. Queries used for the experiments

Query name	Query terms	# of page-pairs
Q_A	"wind power generation", "nuclear power generation"	4656
Q_B	"America", "Iraq"	4753
Q_C	"Nobunaga Oda", "Mitsuhide Akechi" (They were Japanese feudal warlords in the 16th century.)	4656
Q_D	"Hong Kong", "gourmet"	4095

4.1   Page-Pair Relevance and Page Relevance

We analyzed the relationships between page-pair relevance and page relevance. Table 2 lists the number of page-pairs and valuable page-pairs. 30–50% of page-pairs are valuable page-pairs. It also lists the maximum of page-pair relevance and page relevance. In all the cases, the maximum of page-pair relevance is higher than the maximum of page-relevance.

In Figure 4, valuable page-pairs in the case of query Q_A are plotted on the graph, where the horizontal axis corresponds to higher page relevance and the

Table 2. The numbers of valuable page-pairs

Query name	# of valuable page-pairs	# of page-pairs	Max. of page-pair relevance	Max. of page relevance
Q_A	1599	4656	0.631579	0.624543
Q_B	2042	4753	0.428426	0.378591
Q_C	2102	4656	0.467308	0.436177
Q_D	2002	4095	0.443854	0.407625

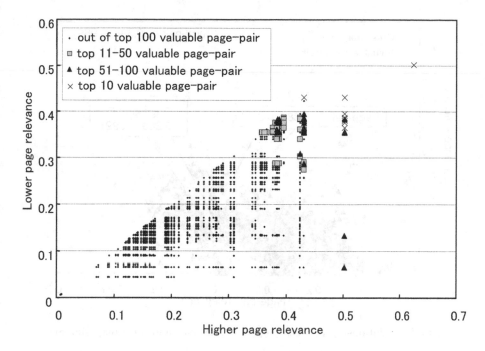

Fig. 4. The distribution of valuable page-pairs

vertical axis corresponds to lower page relevance for each page-pair. In this graph, the shapes of points are classified by the page-pair relevance ranking of valuable page-pairs. We found that many of highly-ranked valuable page-pairs appear in upper-right corner of the graph. It should be noted that some valuable page-pairs, having a page whose page relevance is low, has a high rank score of page-pair relevance. It means that there are the pages which have low page relevance but are valuable as the members of page-pair.

4.2   Page-Pair Relevance and Inter-page Similarity

We analyzed the relationship between page-pair relevance and inter-page similarity. Figure 5 shows the relationship between page-pair relevance and inter-page similarity in the case of query Q_A. Each point in the graph corresponds to a valuable page-pair or other page-pair, where the horizontal axis corresponds to the page-pair relevance and the vertical axis corresponds to the inter-page similarity.

Page-pair A and B in Figure 5 are valuable page-pairs and have the same page-pair relevance. Their inter-page similarity values are different. Page-pair A has a high inter-page similarity, and page-pair B has a low inter-page similarity. The both pages which compose Page-pair A describe about electric power circumstance, including both of "wind power generation" and "nuclear power generation". On the other hand, page-pair B consists of the page which mainly describes "wind power generation" and the other which mainly describes "nuclear power generation".

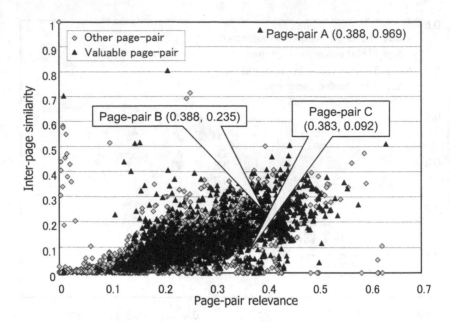

Fig. 5. The relationship between page-pair relevance and inter-page similarity

Page-pair C in Figure 5 is also a valuable page-pair but has very low inter-page similarity. It includes the pages which are much larger than the other. In such page-pairs, the characteristics of smaller pages are ignored. They are regarded as 'noise'.

Considering this, we can say,

- When inter-page similarity is too high, two pages are described from the same viewpoints, and
- When inter-page similarity is too low, page-pair depends on only one page.

Therefore, pages are regarded to be described from different viewpoints when the inter-page similarity satisfies the following for appropriate thresholds θ_1 and θ_2,

$$\theta_1 < sim(v_{p_1}, v_{p_2}) < \theta_2 \tag{5}$$

4.3   Page-Pair Relevance and Google's Ranking

We analyzed the relationship between page-pair relevance and Google's ranking of pages composing page-pairs. We classified page-pairs into four groups, i.e.,

- Group A : Page-pairs composed by the pages in the top 20 for Google's ranking.
- Group B : Page-pairs composed by the pages in the top 50 for Google's ranking, which are not in group A.
- Group C : Page-pairs composed by the pages in the top 100 for Google's ranking and which were not in groups A or B or D.

Table 3. Distribution of top 10 and 50 pertinent page-pairs

Query name		# of page-pairs			
		Group A	Group B	Group C	Group D
Q_A	top 10	0	3	7	0
	top 50	3	26	21	0
	all	190	1035	2350	1081
Q_B	top 10	2	1	6	1
	top 50	6	12	24	8
	all	190	1035	2400	1128
Q_C	top 10	2	4	4	0
	top 50	19	13	18	0
	all	190	1035	2350	1081
Q_D	top 10	0	8	2	0
	top 50	2	28	20	0
	all	190	1035	2050	820

- Group D : Page-pairs composed by the pages from the top 50 to 100 for Google's ranking.

We prepared page-pairs from 100 search results by using several queries and ranked them with their page-pair relevance. Table 3 lists the distribution of the top 10 page-pairs and the top 50 of pertinent page-pairs. As a result, we found that:

1. At least about 60% of top ranking page-pairs were in groups B and C,
2. At most only about 40% were in gourp A, and
3. There were very few in group D.

When we browsed Web pages with Google's ranking, we noticed page-pairs in group A. However, there are few good pertinent page-pairs in group A. Considering 1 and 3 above, most good pertinent page-pairs consists of pages with a high and a low Google's ranking. When we browsed Web pages with Google's ranking, such page-pairs were difficult to find. Therefore, our approach was better than browsing Web pages with Google's ranking.

5   Conclusions

We proposed the new concept, multiple viewpoint retrieval and explained our simple approach to achieve it. We analyzed the characteristics of page-pairs. We found that

- There are the pages which have low page relevance but are valuable as the members of page-pair.
- Page-pairs consisting of the pages which are described from different viewpoints has a high page-pair relavance and a low inter-page.

- Pertinent page-pairs are difficult to find by browsing with Google's ranking but multiple viewpoint retrieval can find them easily.

Future work is as follows:

- The development of the algorithm for finding pertinent page-pairs quickly, and
- The extensions to the link-analysis method and arbitary collection of pages.

Acknowledgements

This work was supported in part by the Japanese Ministry of Education, Culture, Sports, Science and Technology under a Grant-in-Aid for Software Technologies for Search and Integration across Heterogeneous-Media Archives, and the Informatics Research Center for Development of Knowledge Society Infrastructure (COE program by Japan's Ministry of Education, Culture, Sports, Science and Technology).

References

1. Google, http://www.google.com/.
2. D. R. Cutting, J. O. Pedersen, D. Karger and John W. Tukey. Scatter/Gather: A Cluster-based Approach to Browsing Large Document Collections, Proceedings of the Fifteenth Annual International ACM SIGIR Conference on Research and Development in Information Retrieval, pp.318–329, 1992.
3. Clusty the Clustering Engine, http://clusty.com/.
4. NewsInEssence, http://lada.si.umich.edu:8080/clair/nie1/nie.cgi .
5. Columbia NewsBlaster, http://www1.cs.columbia.edu/nlp/newsblaster/ .
6. G. Salton. Developments in automatic text retrieval. Science, (253):pp.974–979, 1991.

A Relevant Score Normalization Method Using Shannon's Information Measure*

Yu Suzuki[1], Kenji Hatano[2], Masatoshi Yoshikawa[3],
Shunsuke Uemura[2], and Kyoji Kawagoe[1]

[1] Ritsumeikan University, 1-1-1 Noji-Higashi, Kusatsu, Shiga 525-8577, Japan
[2] Nara Institute of Science and Technology,
8916-5 Takayama, Ikoma, Nara 630-0192, Japan
[3] Nagoya University, Furo, Chikusa, Nagoya, Aichi 464-8601, Japan

Abstract. Given the ranked lists of images with relevance scores returned by multiple image retrieval subsystems in response to a given query, the problem of combined retrieval system is how to combine these lists equivalently. In this paper, we propose a novel relevance score normalization method based on Shannon's information measure. Generally, the number of relevant images is exceedingly smaller than that of the entire retrieval targets. Therefore, we suppose that if the subsystems can clearly identify which retrieval targets are relevant, the subsystems should calculate high relevance scores to a few retrieval targets. In short, we can calculate the sureness of the IR subsystem using the distribution of the relevance scores. Then, we calculate the sureness of the IR subsystems using Shannon's information measure, and calculate the normalized relevance scores using the sureness of the IR subsystems and the raw relevant scores. In our experiment, our normalization method outperformed the others.

1 Introduction

In Web metasearch engine research field, researchers have been discussed how to deal with multiple retrieval results, whereas the researchers in image retrieval research field have discussed rarely. For example, Montague et al. [1, 2] premise an Web IR system that combines multiple retrieval results of some Web IR subsystems. When that Web IR system combines relevance scores, the similarity values between the retrieval targets and the users' queries, the IR system does not combines the raw relevance scores directly, but combines the normalized relevance scores. Because, the relevance scores calculated by different IR subsystems are not always equivalent with each other.

We should note that the high relevance scores calculated by subsystems do not always indicate high relevances. Because, if we have a poor subsystem, this subsystem cannot identify which retrieval targets are relevant to the users' queries. In this case, the subsystem may calculates high relevance scores to many retrieval targets even if these retrieval targets are irrelevant. However, these high relevance scores actually do not indicate the high relevances.

---

* This work is partially supported by the Ministry of Education, Culture, Sports, Science and Technology, Japan under grants 16700103.

E.A. Fox et al. (Eds.): ICADL 2005, LNCS 3815, pp. 311–316, 2005.
© Springer-Verlag Berlin Heidelberg 2005

In this paper, we propose a novel relevance score normalization method using the sureness of the IR subsystem. We assume that the sureness depends on the distribution of the relevance scores calculated by the IR subsystem. For example, when the IR system calculates a few high relevance scores, the IR system has a high sureness. From this assumption, we measure the sureness of the IR systems using Shannon's information measure [3]. And then, the IR system combines this measure and the raw relevance scores.

2   Basic Issues

In this section, we introduce the following two issues; 1) why we decide that the IR system combines relevance scores instead of combines feature vectors, and 2) why we decide that the IR system uses the relevance scores instead of ranks.

First, we introduce two typical types of approaches about the IR systems that can deal with multiple features. One approach is a method of combining multiple feature values, which is mainly used in the content-based image retrieval research field [4]. In this method, the IR systems merge multiple feature values into one feature vector per one retrieval target. Therefore, using this combined feature vectors, the IR systems can calculate similarity values between the users' queries and the retrieval targets. Nevertheless, the IR systems do not always deal with the feature values equally. For instance, we suppose that an IR system extracts two kinds of feature vectors a and b from each retrieval target, and the numbers of dimensions of a and b are 1 and 10000, respectively. Of course, the number of dimensions in the merged feature vector c is 10001. In this case, the elements of two vectors, such as b and c, are almost the same. Accordingly, the IR systems do not deal with a when the IR systems merge these two feature vectors. In this way, using a merging approach, the IR systems may ignore some feature values.

Here, we are interested in how to equivalently deal with the multiple feature values. We suppose that if the IR systems use better approach, a method of merging multiple retrieval results, the method will be able to improve the accuracies of the IR systems. Before explaining this approach, we show the overview of the image IR system using this method in Figure 1. Our image IR system retrieves the retrieval targets using the following three steps; (1) Our IR system inputs the users' queries to these three IR subsystems, (2) each IR subsystem outputs the retrieval result using one kind of feature value, and (3) the IR system integrates these three retrieval results and outputs one integrated retrieval result. In this case, we suppose that if the IR system equally integrates the retrieval results, the IR system can equivalently deal with the multiple feature values. In this paper, we suppose that step (3) of the IR system is the most important step, then we consider how to integrate multiple retrieval results equivalently.

As mentioned earlier, the goal of this research is to find a retrieval method that can deal with multiple feature values equivalently. To this end, we use the relevance scores instead of the ranks, because the ranks do not always express the exact similarities between the retrieval targets and the users' queries. This means that when we have the two ranks, that are calculated by different IR subsystems, and that are calculated for the two different retrieval targets, are the same, we suppose that the similarities between the two retrieval targets are different in many cases. The reason of this is that the rank

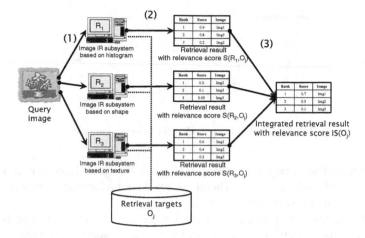

Fig. 1. An architecture of the IR system that uses multiple feature values

of a retrieval target depends on not only the exact similarity value between the retrieval target and the user's query but also the similarity values of the other retrieval targets. Because of the above discussion, we use the relevance scores to calculate the integrated retrieval results.

3   Relevance Score Normalization Method

In this section, we explain a requirement of normalized relevance scores. We also explain our proposed method that fulfill such the requirement.

The basic concept of our idea is that the sureness of the IR subsystems should depend on the distributions of the relevance scores. This means that when an IR subsystem calculates high relevance scores to many retrieval targets, these relevance scores do not necessarily to indicate high relevances, then the IR subsystem should have low sureness. In this section, we explain our normalization concepts in detail, and we also explain how to normalize the relevance scores using the sureness of the IR subsystems.

A Requirement for Relevance Score Normalization Method. Before describe our proposed normalization method, we should discuss which method is the best. To determine the effectiveness of normalization methods, we define that if two normalized relevance scores calculated by any two retrieval targets are the same, users judge that the relevance of one retrieval target is as much as that of another retrieval target.

For example, if two relevance scores, $S(R_1, O_1)$ and $S(R_2, O_2)$, are the same value, users judge whether both two retrieval targets and are relevant or irrelevant to the query. Therefore, when a user judge that O_1 is relevant and O_2 is irrelevant when the IR system uses a normalization method, this method is the best.

When a normalization method fulfill this requirement, the normalization method must determine which two raw relevance scores should be normalized to the same value. Therefore, we suppose that the relevance feedback method is the most suitable method for normalization. This is because, unless the users' judgements, the IR system cannot

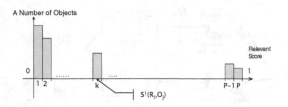

Fig. 2. Calculation method of the information values

identify which retrieval targets are really relevant to the users. However, users cannot judge numbers of retrieval targets. Therefore, we do not adopt the relevance feedback method to normalize raw relevance scores.

To fulfill the above requirement, we need a normalization method that fulfill this requirement without users' judgements. In the following sections, we discuss several normalization methods from the point of view of whether it meets the above requirement.

The idea behind our method. To make our method that fulfill the requirement for normalization, we focus on the distribution of the raw relevance scores. That is, if an IR subsystem calculates many high relevance scores, this IR subsystem has a low sureness. We use Shannon's information measure to scale the difficulty of getting high relevance scores. That is, if a retrieval system calculates many high relevance scores, the information value is low, and the normalized relevance scores are also low.

Calculation of the Information Value of Relevance Scores. Using the pre-normalized relevance scores, the IR system calculates the information values of all retrieval targets. First, we divide the ranges $[0, 1]$ into the p-th sections shown in Figure 2, where p is an integer parameter. We should note that the length of each section L is $1/p$. Next, the IR system set the values of $F(k)$ which expresses a distribution of the relevance scores. Here, the IR system sets the value of $F(k)$, the ranges $[\frac{k}{p}, \frac{k+1}{p}]$, to the number of the retrieval targets which relevance scores are on the range $[0, \frac{k+1}{p}]$. Finally, the IR system calculates the information value $I(R_i, O_j)$ using the following function:

$$I(R_i, O_j) = -\log_2 \frac{F(k)}{M} \tag{1}$$

This function is based on Shannon's information measure [3]. Here, Shannon's information measure is based on the probability of the phenomenon. Therefore, we cannot use this measure directly. Then, we use the ratio of the number of retrieval targets in k-th section to the amount of all retrieval targets instead of the probability of the phenomenon.

Integration of Relevance Scores and the Information Value of Relevance Scores. Finally, the IR system calculates the normalized relevance score using the raw relevance score $S^*(R_i, O_j)$ and the information value $I(R_i, O_j)$ as follows:

$$S'(R_i, O_j) = S^*(R_i, O_j) \cdot I(R_i, O_j) \tag{2}$$

Using these steps, the IR systems can normalize relevance scores using Shannon's information measure.

4   Experimental Evaluation

We compare the accuracy of the IR systems which use our proposed method with that which uses the other normalization methods. We made image retrieval systems which deals with three image features, such as color histogram, shape of objects in the image, and texture of objects.

In our experiment, we compared our proposed normalization methods with the other normalization methods proposed by Montague et al. [1], such as Standard, Sum, and ZMUV. After we normalize, we used two integration functions, CombSUM and CombMNZ, to integrate relevance scores of histogram, shape, and texture. In short, we compared 11 patterns of retrieval systems. Three patterns of systems use one of three image features. Eight patterns of systems use one of four normalization methods, such as Standard, Sum, ZMUV, and our proposed methods. These eight patterns of systems also use one of two integration functions, such as CombSUM and CombMNZ.

In Fig. 3, we show the average precision ratio of all IR systems. From this figure, we find out that the accuracy of the IR system which use our proposed method with CombMNZ gives better accuracy than the other normalization system, such as Standard, Sum, and ZMUV. However, the IR system which uses our proposed method with CombSUM has worth accuracy than that which uses Standard with CombSUM. From this result, our proposed method does not always gives the best accuracy. We suppose that when the IR system uses the integration function CombSUM, the IR system ignores the information measure.

From this result, we can conclude that the compatibility of integration function and normalization method is important. This is because, the method of CombMNZ is based on the entropy of integrated relevance scores, which are very similar to our proposed method. On the contrary, CombSUM is based on average value of integrated relevance scores. This reason is why our proposed method makes better accuracy with CombMNZ

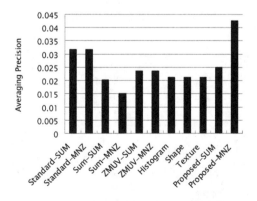

Fig. 3. The 11pt averaging precision of retrieval results using the normalization methods

than with CombSUM, and why the normalization method "SUM" makes better accuracy with CombSUM than with CombMNZ.

5   Conclusion

In this paper, in order to improve the accuracy of the IR system, we introduce a relevance score normalization method. In our method, we expect the sureness of the IR subsystems from the distribution of the relevance scores of the IR subsystems. That is, when the IR subsystems calculates high relevance scores to many retrieval targets, we suppose that these retrieval targets are not always relevant. Based on the sureness of IR subsystems and the raw relevance scores, we calculate the normalized relevance scores. Using our proposed normalization method, the accuracy of the IR system improves without complicated interactions between the IR system and the users. We suppose the reason of the improvement is that we can correctly assume the sureness of the IR system using the distribution of the raw relevance scores and Shannon's information measure.

References

1. Montague, M., Aslam, J.:   Relevance Score Normalization for Metasearch.   In: Proceedings of the 10th ACM International Conference on Information and Knowledge Management (CIKM01). (2001) 427 – 433
2. Montague, M., Aslam, J.:   Conduct fusion for improved retrieval.   In: Proceedings of the 11th ACM International Conference on Information and Knowledge Management (CIKM02). (2002) 538 – 548
3. Shannon, C.E.: A mathematical theory of communication. Bell System Technical Journal **27** (1948) 379 – 423
4. Veltkamp, R.C., Tanase, M., Sent, D.:   5.   In: State-of-the-art in Content-Based Image and Video Retrieval. Kluwer Academic Publishers (2001) 97 – 124

Configurable Meta-search for Integrating Web Public Access Catalogs

Hou Ieong Ho and Jieh Hsiang

Department of Computer Science and Information Engineering,
National Taiwan University,
Taipei, Taiwan
brent@turing.csie.ntu.edu.tw, jhsiang@ntu.edu.tw

Abstract. A Web Public Access Catalog (WebPAC) is an important feature of modern libraries. In this paper we propose a meta-search method to provide users with simultaneous access to WebPACs of different libraries. Our method gives a librarian full freedom to select WebPACs to be incorporated in the service but requires no programming effort from the librarian's side. At the core of our method is a meta-search engine which sends a query to incorporated WebPACs, receives results, and post-processes the query results into a uniform presentation format. To incorporate an existing WebPAC into our system, one needs to analyze the query interaction behavior between the WebPAC and the browser. This can be done by extracting the query parameters from a query and the subsequent query result web pages. We modeled and abstracted these interactions and defined the corresponding XML formats to capture the needed parameters from these web pages. The resulting XML pages will then be fed to the search engine which will automatically incorporate the designated WebPAC as part of its search.

The advantage of our method is that the search engine does not need to be modified when new WebPACs are added. When adding a new WebPAC, the librarian only needs to analyze a few web pages to decide the parameters. Even this step can mostly be done automatically. To illustrate the effectiveness of our method, we have built a system, called MetaCat, that has incorporated the WebPACs of 26 major libraries in Taiwan. MetaCat can be accessed at http://MetaCat.ntu.edu.tw.

This research is supported in part by the National Science Council of the Republic of China under grant numbers NSC-94-2422-H-002-008 and NSC-93-2213-E-002-039.

1 Introduction

The most important common service provided by modern libraries is the Web Public Access Catalog (WebPAC). By using WebPAC, users can search a library's catalog quickly via internet. However, try to find books from several libraries can be a painful experience. The user needs to visit the WebPAC of every intended library and issues the same query to each of them separately. If the user does not have a clear idea of the books that she is looking for, it can be another time-consuming experience to go

E.A. Fox et al. (Eds.): ICADL 2005, LNCS 3815, pp. 317–322, 2005.
© Springer-Verlag Berlin Heidelberg 2005

through the search results from those WebPACs. It is therefore reasonable to design an integrated search that can access several WebPACs simultaneously. This service can be achieved by either building a centralized union catalog (such as WorldCat of OCLC), establishing standard data exchange protocols (such as Z39.50 [1] or OAI-PMH [2]), or using meta-search (see [3] as an example).

In this paper we propose a new meta-search methodology that allows a librarian to build her library's cross-WebPAC service without *any* programming effort. Our method involves a core search facility and an XML format that allows the incorporation of a WebPAC service by simply identifying parameters involved in queries. To demonstrate the effectiveness of our method, we have implemented such a service, called MetaCat, for the National Taiwan University Library. MetaCat currently incorporates the WebPACs of 26 major libraries of Taiwan. It is also a popular search tool provided by the NTU Library.

In Section 2 of the paper we give the methodology of our configurable meta-search method. Section 3 describes the implementation of MetaCat. We conclude the paper with some discussion and future directions.

2 Methodology

Meta-search for WebPACs is a mechanism that allows the users to access and search, via Web, WebPACs of different libraries from a single webpage in a uniform way. In a typical (single) WebPAC service of a library, a user issues a query such as a title or author, the system then searches through the catalog of the library and returns a list of books (if any) that match the query. If we treat the inner working of a WebPAC as a black box, then the query session described above can be regarded as a series of web-page exchanges through the http protocol. The query issued by the user is sent as a sequence of parameters, usually wrapped inside the control elements (buttons, check-boxes, radio buttons, menus, text input, file select, hidden controls, object controls, etc) [9] of the <form> tag of an html page. The query results, once retrieved from the data base, are embedded in another html page and presented to the user's browser. This *http interaction model* between the browser and the WebPAC is quite simple, and can be summarized as the following states:

1. Send request, as an html page, to WebPAC
2. Receive an html page from WebPAC
3. Identify the html template of received html page
4. Extract data from the html page
5. Stop, or use the extracted data and go to State 1

As far as the Web interface is concerned, the only differences between two Web-PACs are the configurations (parameters) of the queries that the WebPAC interfaces send to their respective search engines, and the configurations of the query results that the interfaces get back from the WebPAC search engines and present to the user. Among the five states of the above http interaction model, all except State 2 (the *receive* state) have their own configurations.

2.1 Consolidate WebPAC Services Through Meta-search

For integrating several WebPACs, a conventional meta-search solution would analyze the interface of each WebPAC and incorporate them through programming. This process can be rather laborious and requires programming skills beyond the capability of an average librarian. Furthermore, if a WebPAC changes its interface or if a new WebPAC is to be added, then the program needs to be modified.

Our method uses a modular approach. WebPACs, due to their public-service nature, usually employ interfaces that are much simpler than commercial Web-accessed data bases. Therefore instead of using programming to incorporate each WebPAC, we propose general *XML configuration formats* to capture the parameters embedded in the http interaction. To include a WebPAC into our meta-search facility, then, all that need to be done is to transform its http interactions into their respective XML formats and incorporate them in the meta-search mechanism. This action only requires knowledge of Web query parameters and XML, and can be done by any experienced librarian with some training. Furthermore, this framework is general enough that a library can choose the WebPACs that it wants to incorporate in its own meta-search service and builds its own system. Adding a new WebPAC service or modifying an existing one can also be done easily.

Note that four of the five states in the WebPAC http interaction model given above involve webpages with parameters containing information related to the WebPAC transaction. They are captured in our framework through four classes of *XML configuration formats*. They are the *Request configuration format*, *Verify configuration format*, *Extract configuration format* and *Flow configuration format*. They correspond, respectively, to State 1 through 5 (except State 2, which does not need a corresponding configuration). The *Request* configuration format deals with the parameters of the *queries* of a WebPAC. *Verify* and *Extract* have to do with those of the *query results*. *Flow* analyzes whether the WebPAC has any session control features. Due to space limit, we only briefly outline these formats. Detail information can be found in a longer version of this paper upon request.

Request Configuration. The most basic operation in a WebPAC is to issue a query. *Request configuration* is the XML format that captures all the information involved in the query-sending process. They include the host URL, the connection method (GET or POST), proxy information, query parameters, and user agent information such as accept content type, accept-language, and accept-encoding. If a WebPAC has been incorporated in the meta-search service, the meta-search engine will use that Web-PAC's Request configuration to simulate a user query to that particular WebPAC. We remark that the process of extracting the necessary query information and incorporating them into the Request format can be done almost automatically. The only human effort required is to issue sample queries to each of the query fields (such as title, author, etc). The parameters associated with each query will be extracted and embedded into the corresponding configuration.

Verify Configuration. Several outcomes may happen when a WebPAC returns the query results. It may find *no record*, *one record*, or *several records*. The *Verify configuration format* includes three XML forms, each for the template of "no record", "brief listed records", and "detailed information". Identifying which form that a web-page corresponds to can be done by identifying specific key phrases that are pertinent to that particular template. Determining which verify configuration forms are needed in a specific WebPAC requires the assistance of a librarian. An experienced librarian needs to indicate to the system the types of query result webpages that her WebPAC may produce, and for each template, identify a key phrase that is unique for that template.

Extraction Configuration Format. After identifying the templates of the query result webpages, we need to extract the parameters, such as title, author, and hyperlink to a page with detailed information from each of the templates. This is the purpose of the *Extraction configuration format*, which is an XML format that locates the bibliographic information embedded in html. Similar to the Verification configuration format, there are also several Extract configuration forms; each corresponds to a possible query result webpage.

To locate bibliographic information in a query result html page, we define four elements needed for the *Extraction configuration*: "Single tag" element, "Range tags" element, "Nested single tag" element, and "Nested range tags" element. "Single tag" element is used to locate a particular html tag using the tag's name and its order of appearance in an html page. "Range Tags" element is used to locate the range enclosed within an html tag, such as "<tr>...</tr>". It can also be used to specify repeated ranges within the same tag name. "Nested single tag" and "Nested range tags" are used when the located content need further utilized by the extraction elements.

Flow Configuration Format. In order to control query sessions, some WebPAC systems generate a *transaction key* when a user enters, and the key may expire after a time out. This key is hidden in the webpages and is either for giving better services (by remembering previous queries in the same session) or for preventing abuse from external agents. The *Flow configuration format* is, then, an XML format that analyzes the flow of the http interactions of a WebPAC so that this type of *session control* can be handled.

To check whether a WebPAC has this type of session control is quite simple. One simply needs to enter the library's query system from two different computers, issues the same query, then compares the parameters sent from the two browsers.

2.2 How to Incorporate a WebPAC

Using the four configurations mentioned above, a librarian can add a WebPAC to meta-search engine easily and without any programming effort. With the help of aiding tools, most of the needed configurations can be generated automatically. The librarian only needs to provide minimum help (such as identifying the parameter name if a key is needed in a WebPAC with session control and the key phrases associated with Verify configurations) by highlighting the related terms.

3   MetaCat – An Implementation

To demonstrate how our method works, we have built a meta-search service, Meta-Cat, for the National Taiwan University Library. MetaCat currently incorporates the

WebPAC services of 26 major libraries in Taiwan. To provide better services to all users in Taiwan, we have grouped them (not mutually exclusively) into 7 categories, according to geographic locations (four different areas covering northern, central, southern, and eastern Taiwan), size (a group that contains only libraries with over half a million books), and specialties (medical and educational). This arrangement makes it easier for a user with special interest or from a specific locality to find what she wants. The user can also select the libraries of her choice from the list of 26 by clicking buttons. MetaCat provides a query field with 6 query modes (title, author, subject, ISBN, ISSN, and keywords) on its query interface.

Although the 26 WebPACs are from 3 vendors, Innovative (Innopac), Transtech (TOTAL II) and Dynix (iPAC), each has its own variations in query interface and query result presentation and needs to be dealt with individually.

Querying multiple WebPACs and gathering their results may take a while, especially when the network is slow. To expedite the query outcome, MetaCat (1) simultaneously dispatches query to the involved WebPACs, (2) displays query results in an incremental, first-arrive-first-present way, and (3) waits a maximum of 30 seconds, to compensate for possible site failure or a congested network.

Another important feature of MetaCat is that it groups the same books into a single result, with links to the different libraries from which the book records are retrieved. MetaCat does this by checking for similarities in bibliographic information from query results and aggregating the similar ones together. This feature can significantly reduce the number of items in the list of results and make the system much easier to use. We have also implemented a tool bar plug-in that can be installed on an IE browser.

MetaCat is quite popular among users in NTU. It is also gaining acceptance among librarians because it is much more up-to-date than the Taiwanese union catalog NBInet.

4   Discussion

In this paper we introduced an approach to building configurable meta-search services for WebPACs. In addition to providing the core search facilities, we introduced four general XML configuration formats, with which one can incorporate the parameters from a WebPAC's query process and query result presentations. In our method, new WebPACs can be added to the meta-search service without any programming effort or modification of the programming code. To demonstrate the effectiveness of our method, we have built such a service, called MetaCat, for the NTU Library. In addition to having incorporated the WebPAC of all major libraries in Taiwan (26 in total), MetaCat also provides six query modes, seven categories of libraries for the ease of use, and post-processing features that make query results much easier to use than other similar services.

We have designed tools to help librarians analyze the configurations. We are also studying the possibility of fully automating this process. There are methods for extracting content from webpages (see, e.g., [4] [5] [6]). They need to be tailored for WebPAC applications. The DeepSpot Agent Tool Box [7] provides ways to extract information based on pattern discovery [8]. But the rules generated from that approach are not human-readable and may be hard for librarians to check for accuracy.

References

[1] National Information Standard Organization (NISO).ANSI Z39.50: Information Retrieval Service and Protocol, 1992.

[2] The Open Archives Initiative Protocol for Metadata Harvesting protocol version 2.0 http://www.openarchives.org/OAI/2.0/openarchivesprotocol.htm

[3] Lin Fang, Library of Central China Normal University. A Developing Search Service - Heterogeneous Resources Integration and Retrieval System. D-Lib Magazine, Volume 10 Number 3, March 2004

[4] N. Kushmerick, D. Weld and R. Doorenbos. Wrapper induction for information extraction, IJCAI-97, 1997. http://sherry.ifi.unizh.ch/kushmerick97wrapper.html

[5] Hongkun Zhao, Weiyi Meng, Zonghuan Wu, Vijay Raghavan, and Clement Yu. Fully Automatic Wrapper Generation for Search Engines. Proc. of 14th International World Wide Web Conference (WWW14), pp.66-75, Chiba, Japan, May 2005

[6] Benjamin Habegger. Multi-pattern wrappers for relation extraction from the Web. In Proceedings of the European Conference on Artificial Intelligence, 2002

[7] Chia-Hui Chang, Harianto Siek, Jiann-Jyh Lu, Chun-Nan Hsu, Jen-Jie Chiou. "Reconfigurable Web Wrapper Agents," IEEE Intelligent Systems, vol. 18, no. 5, pp. 34-40, September/October 2003.

[8] Chia-Hui Chang and Shao-Chen Lui. IEPAD: information extraction based on pattern discovery. In Proceedings of the Tenth International Conference on the World Wide Web, pages 681–688, Hong Kong, China, 2001.

[9] Forms - User-input Forms: Text Fields, Buttons, Menus, and more HTML 4.01 Specification W3C Recommendation 24 December 1999 http://www.w3.org/TR/REC-html40/interact/forms.html#h-17.10

Annotating Text Segments Using a Web-Based Categorization Approach

Hsin-Chen Chiao[1], Hsiao-Tieh Pu[2], and Lee-Feng Chien[1]

[1] Institute of Information Science, Academia Sinica, Taipei, Taiwan 115
{hcchiao, lfchien}@iis.sinica.edu.tw
[2] Graduate Institute of Library & Information Studies, National Taiwan Normal University,
Taipei, Taiwan 106
htpu@ntnu.edu.tw

Abstract. Conventional automatic text annotation tools mostly extract named entities from texts and annotate them with information about persons, locations, and dates, etc. Such kind of entity type information, however, is insufficient for machines to understand the context or facts contained in the texts. This paper presents a general text categorization approach to categorize text segments into broader subject categories, such as categorizing a text string into a category of paper title in Mathematics or a category of conference name in Computer Science. Experimental results confirm its wide applicability to various digital library applications.

1 Introduction

Text mining can be used to add value to unstructured data, like documents in digital library collections. [1] In general, current tools for automatic text annotation mostly extract named entities from texts and annotate them with information about persons, locations, dates and so on. [2] However, this kind of entity type information is often insufficient for machines to understand the facts contained in the texts, thus preventing them from implementing more advanced or intelligent applications, such as text mining. [3] In this paper, we try to remedy this problem by presenting a more generalized text categorization approach which is pursued to categorize text segments, i.e., meaningful word strings including named entities and other important text patterns such as paper titles and conference names, into broader subject categories.

Named Entity Recognition (NER) is an important technique used in many intelligent applications such as information extraction, question answering and text mining. The NER task consists in identifying phrases in text, which are often short in length, e.g., single words or word bigrams, into certain types such as organizations, persons and locations. To deal with such task, effective techniques are required to delimit phrases and exploit various evidences of the candidate strings to classify entities. Fewer investigations or research were found to recognize longer strings, such as paper titles and conference names, and classifying them into broader subject categories of concern. Examples include categorizing a paper title into Mathematics category or a conference name into Computer Science category. This paper addresses the problem

E.A. Fox et al. (Eds.): ICADL 2005, LNCS 3815, pp. 323–331, 2005.
© Springer-Verlag Berlin Heidelberg 2005

of text segment categorization and presents a feasible approach using the Web as an additional knowledge source.

In this paper, a text segment is defined as a meaningful word string that is often short in length and represents specific concept in a certain subject domain, such as a keyword in a document set and a natural language query from a user. Text segments are of many types, including word, phrase, named entity, natural language query, news event, product name, paper or book title, etc. Categorizing short text segments is a difficult problem given that, unlike long documents, short text segments typically don't contain enough information to extract reliable features. For longer documents, their subject information can be represented based on the composed words and the similarities to a classifier can be estimated based on the common composed words. However, for text segments, their subject information cannot be simply judged by using the same way due to the fact that text segments are usually short and don't contain enough information in the composed words. Thus, the most challenging task is to acquire proper features to characterize the text segments. For those text segments extracted from documents, e.g., key terms from documents, the source documents can be used to characterize the text segments. However, in real-world cases, such as in dealing with search engine query strings, there may not exist sufficient relevant documents to represent the target segments. In other words, the lack of domain-specific corpora to describe text segments is usually the case in reality.

Fortunately, the Web, as the largest and most accessible data repository in the world, provides rich resources to supplement the insufficiency of information suffered by various text segments. Many search engines constantly crawls Web resources and provides relevant Web pages for large amounts of free text queries consisted of single terms and longer word strings. The major idea of the proposed approach is to use the Web search result snippets to extract related contextual information as the source of features for text segments. In other words, the proposed approach incorporates the search result snippets returned from search engines into the process of acquiring features for text segments. Often there are some text segments too specific to obtain adequate search results using current keyword-matching-based search engines. This motivates our exploration of a better query processing technique, named query relaxation, which is designed to acquire more relevant feature information for long text segments through a bootstrapping process of search requests to search engines. Initial experiments on categorizing paper titles into Yahoo!'s Computer Science hierarchy has been conduced and the experimental results show the potential and wide adaptability of the proposed approach to various applications.

2 Related Work

2.1 Named Entity Recognition

Effective techniques are required in NER to delimit phrases and exploit various evidences of the candidate strings to classify entities. It has been a well-accepted principle that two different types of evidences, i.e., internal and external evidences, are keys in clarifying the ambiguities and improving the robustness and portability. For example, the internal evidences, such as capitalization, are features found within the candidate string itself; while the external evidences, such as neighboring words associations, are derived by gathering the local context into which the string appears. A number of approaches have been developed for utilizing external evidences to find functional-similar words and identifying named entities. Usually these approaches rely on analysis of the considered objects' contextual information obtained from tagged corpus. [4] Instead of using tagged corpus for categorizing word- or phrasal-level objects, the proposed approach exploits Web resources as a feature source to categorize text segments, which might be longer in length, into broader subject categories. Our research assumes that the text segments are formed with a simple syntactic structure containing some domains-specific or unknown words. Either conventional syntactic sentence analysis or complete grammatical sentence analysis may not be appropriate to this case.

2.2 Text Categorization

Text categorization techniques are often used to analyze relationships among documents. [5] However, as previously mentioned, there is a great difference between document categorization and text segment categorization. Documents normally contain more information than text segments do. The similarity between a document and a target category can be estimated based on the difference in the distribution of the words contained in document itself and the training set of the category; whereas the similarity between a short text segment and a target category cannot be estimated in this way. Further, conventional text categorization techniques assume manually-labeled corpora are ready and can be used for training process. In reality, labeling the corpus is laborious and may suffer from the problem of subjectivity. Using the Web as a corpus source proves a better alternative. Our previous work has proposed an approach to train classifiers through Web corpora to build user-defined topic hierarchies. [6] The proposed approach in this paper extends the previous work, and focuses on the text segment categorization problem.

2.3 Text Mining and Web Corpora

Our research is also related to the work concerning with the knowledge discovery in huge amounts of unstructured textual data from the Web. [7] To name a few related research here, such as automatic extraction of terms or phrases, [8] the discovery of rules for the extraction of specific information patterns, [9] and ontology construction based on semi-structured data. [10] Different from previous works, the proposed approach is to categorize text segments via mining search result pages.

3   The Approach

This section first defines the problem, and then introduces the proposed approach. Given a set of subject categories, $C = \{c_1, c_2, ..., c_n\}$, a collection of text segments $T = \{t_1, t_2, ..., t_m\}$, and also a mapping $M : T \rightarrow C$ that describes the correct category a text segment is supposed to be assigned with. The major concern is to design a one-to-one mapping scheme $M': T \rightarrow C$ that the maximal size of the correct result set is $CRS = \{t_i \,|t_i \text{ in } T, M'(t_i) = M(t_i)\}$. The approach is essentially composed of two computational modules: feature extraction and text segment categorization. The approach exploits highly ranked search result snippets retrieved from search engines as the feature sources. The feature extraction module collects features for the text segment of concern. The text segment categorization module decides appropriate categories for the text segment. Detailed discussion of each module is presented in the following subsections.

3.1 Feature Extraction and Representation

To decide the similarity between a text segment and a target subject category, a representation model is necessary to describe it characteristics. As previously mentioned, a text segment cannot offer sufficient feature terms by itself. In other words, calculating the distance between the text segment and a target category directly is not possible. To overcome this problem, the approach sends the text segment as a query to search engines and use the returned pages as its feature source. Note that, instead of the whole page, only the snippets were used as the sources to save a large number of page accesses. The approach adopts the vector space model to describe the features of both text segments and thematic categories. Suppose that, for each query q (in fact a text segment or some Boolean expressions of category names), the approach collects up to N_{max} search result snippets, denoted as SRS_q. Each query can be then converted into a bag of feature terms by applying normal text processing techniques, e.g., removing stop words and increasing stemming, to the contents of SRS_q. Let T be the feature term vocabulary, and t_i be the i-th term in T. With a simple processing, a query q can be represented as a term vector v_q in a $|T|$-dimensional space, where v_{qi} is the weight t_i in v_q. The term weights in this work were determined according to one of the conventional tf-idf term weighting schemes, in which each term weight v_{qi} is defined as:

$$v_{q,i} = (1 + \log_2 f_{q,i}) \times \log_2(n / n_i),$$

where f_{qi} is the frequency of t_i occurring in v_q's corresponding feature term bag, n is the total number of category objects, and n_i is the number of category objects that contain t_i in their corresponding bags of feature terms. The similarity between a text segment and a category object is computed as the cosine of the angle between the corresponding vectors, i.e.,

$$sim(v_a, v_b) = cos(v_a, v_b),$$

3.2 Text Segment Categorization

Given a new text segment t, the approach determines a set of categories C_t that are considered as t's most related categories. As discussed in previous section, the candidate text segment t is represented as a feature vector v_t. For this categorization task, a kNN approach was used. kNN has been found to be an effective classification approach to a broad range of pattern recognition and text classification problems. Using the kNN approach, a relevance score between t and candidate category object C_i is determined by the following formula:

$$r_{kNN}(t, C_i) = \sum_{v_j \in R_k(t) \cap C_i} sim(v_t, v_j)$$

where $R_k(t)$ represents t's k most-similar category objects, measured by a *sim* function, in the whole collection. The categories a text segment being assigned with are determined by either a predefined number of most-relevant clusters or a threshold used to pick those clusters having scores higher than that of the specified threshold value. The performance evaluation of the proposed approach was mainly based on the extraction of five most-relevant categories as candidates.

3.3 Query Relaxation

Sometimes there exist text segments that are too specific to obtain adequate search results using current keyword-matching-based search engines. Insufficient snippets may cause the obtained information sparse and not so unreliable, and may even decrease the relevance measurement among text segments. The case of retrieving inadequate search results mostly occurs when dealing with long text segments, e.g., paper titles and natural language queries. Compared with a short text segment, a long segment contains more information, i.e., with more terms, and it's rather difficult to obtain documents exactly matching all of the terms. However, as a long text segment contains more information, not all terms in the segment are equally informative to its intended topic(s). This motivates our invention of a query processing technique, named query relaxation, to acquire more relevant feature information for long text segments through a bootstrapping process of search requests to search engines.

```
q=Polynomial-Time Reinforcement Learning of Near-Optimal Policies
    q¹=Reinforcement Learning Near-Optimal Policies
    q²=Reinforcement Learning Policies
q=Named Entity Recognition using an HMM-based Chunck Tagger
    q¹=Named Entity Recognition HMM-based Tagger
    q²=Named Entity Recognition Tagger
q=A digital library of conversational expressions: helping profoundly disabled users
    communicate
    q¹=digital library conversational expressions helping disabled users communicate
    q²=digital library conversational expressions helping users communicate
```

Fig. 1. Examples of paper title and their relaxed versions

To clarify the idea of query relaxation, let's take the title of this paper as an example of long text segment: "Annotating Text Segments Using A Web-based Categorization Approach." Suppose that one needs to select a subset of terms as the query that can mostly represent the topical concept of this segment, one most probably selects those of "Annotating Text Segments." If one needs to further reduce the sub-segment "Annotating Text Segments," "Annotating Text" seems a better choice. Though this selection process may not be always feasible and may depend on the decisions made, the idea shows that the textual part of a long text segment can be effectively reduced or relaxed. The reduced segment represents a concept that is still close to (or usually it is broader than) the main topical concept of the original segment, and it usually can retrieve more search results due to the reduced segment holds fewer terms. The above example suggests a possible approach in an inclusion manner, i.e., to select a subset of terms that are most informative from the given text segment. Instead of following such inclusion manner, our approach was designed in an exclusion manner. In other words, when the search results of the given text segment are not adequate, a single term is removed from the segment, and the rest form a new query to search engines. The newly retrieved search results are then augmented into the set of the original search results. For those overlapping entries, they will be deleted and not added. This relaxation process is repeated until the obtained information is considered enough. For illustration, figure 1 shows several examples of paper titles with their relaxed versions obtained using the proposed query relaxation technique.

4 Experiments

To assess the performance of the proposed approach, some initial experiments have been conducted. We used the Yahoo! Computer Science hierarchy as the subject categories of concern. In the hierarchy, there are totally 36 second-level, 177 third-level, and 278 fourth-level categories, all rooted at the category of "Computer Science". A data set consisting of the academic paper titles were collected from six computer science conferences held in 2002. The experiment tried to categorize them into the 36 first-level categories, such as "Artificial Intelligence" and "Operating Systems". Table 1 lists the relevant information of this paper data set. For each category, we created a text classifier using a training corpus obtained via taking the category name itself and each of its subcategory names as a query to retrieve search result snippets respectively, which is a process similar to that of extracting feature sources for text segments.

To evaluate the categorization accuracy, each conference was assigned to the Yahoo! categories to which the conference was considered to belong, e.g., AAAI'02 was assigned to "Artificial Intelligence", and all the papers from that conference were unconditionally assigned to that category. Notice that this might not be absolutely correct categorization strategy as some papers in a conference may be more related to other domains than the ones assigned. To make the experiment easier to implement, we made this straightforward assumption.

Tables 2 shows the results of the achieved top 1-5 inclusion rates, where the top n inclusion rate is the rate of the test text segments (paper titles) whose highly ranked n

Table 1. The information of the paper data set

Conference	# Papers	Assigned Category
AAAI'02	29	CS: Artificial Intelligence
ACL'02	65	CS: Linguistics
ICML'02	87	CS: Artificial Intelligence
JCL'02	69	CS: Lib. & Info. Sci.
SIGCOMM'02	25	CS: Networks
SIGGRAPH'02	67	CS: Graphics

candidates contain the correct category. This experiment was conducted without using the query relaxation technique. From Table 2, it shows that the achieved accuracy was promising.

Table 2. Top 1-5 inclusion rates for categorizing paper titles

Conference	Top-1	Top-2	Top-3	Top-4	Top-5
AAAI'02	.6897	.7586	.8621	.8966	.9301
ACL'02	.5321	.7077	.7692	.8	.8153
ICML'02	.5172	.6437	.7701	.8161	.8391
JCDL'02	.2753	.4493	.4927	.5072	.5217
SIGCOMM'02	.88	1.0	1.0	1.0	1.0
SIGGRAPH'02	.8599	.9552	.9552	.9701	.9701
AVG	.5965	.7193	.7690	.7953	.8187

Table 3 further lists some wrongly categorized examples and it can be observed that not all of the miss-categorized papers might be incorrect. In some cases, they were more related to the result subject categories than those we assigned to them. This experiment reveals a great potential of using the proposed approach to categorizing paper titles and organizing academic papers on the Web.

Table 3. Selected examples of miss-categorized paper titles.

Paper Title	Conference	Target Cat.	Top-1	2	3	4	5
A New Algorithm for Optimal Bin Packing	AAAI	AI	ALG	AI	MOD	COLT	DNA
(Im)possibility of Safe Exchange Mechanism Design	AAAI	AI	NET	SC	LG	DB	MD
Performance Issues and Error Analysis in an Open-Domain Question Answering System	ACL	LG	AI	LG	ALG	DC	SC
Active Learning for Statistical Natural Language Parsing	ACL	LG	AI	LG	NN	COLT	ALG
Improving Machine Learning Approaches to Coreference Resolution	ACL	LG	AI	LG	ALG	FM	NN
A Language Modelling Approach to Relevance Profiling for Document Browsing	JCDL	LIS	AI	UI	LG	LIS	ALG
Structuring Keyword-based Queries for Web Databases	JCDL	LIS	AI	LIS	DB	ALG	ARC
A Multilingual, Multimodal Digital Video Library System	JCDL	LIS	LG	UI	LIS	ECAD	NET
SOS: Secure Overlay Services	SIGCOMM	NET	SC	NET	MC	OS	DC

Abbreviation List:	AI :Artificial Intelligence	DNA :DNA-Based Computing	MOD:Modeling
	ALG :Algorithms	ECAD:Electronic Computer Aided Design	NET :Networks
	ARC :Architecture	FM :Formal Methods	NN :Neural Network
	COLT:Computational Learning Theory	LG :Linguistics	OS :Operating Systems
	DB :Databases	LIS :Library and Information Science	SC :Security
	DC :Distributed Computing	MC :Mobile Computing	UI :User Interface

It was also observed in the experiment that many paper titles were too long and the search engine did not provide a sufficient number of Web pages, which undoubtedly lowered the accuracy rate. Our study was thus interested in whether the query relaxation technique could overcome this problem. We adjusted the values of N_{min} and N_{max}, i.e., the minimal and maximal number of Web pages to describe the text segments, and conducted the same experiment again. Table 4 lists the archived result. Note that the result achieved without using the query relaxation technique can be taken as applying query relaxation vacuously, i.e., $N_{max} = 100$, $N_{min} = 0$. From this table, it can be observed the query relaxation technique did help to boost the accuracy rate, though the extent of the improvement is limited. Another interesting observation can be made from the table is that the size of the training data to describe text segments doest not necessarily bear a positive influence on the performance of our approach. Fewer pages sometimes describe a text segment more precisely – a possible conclusion considering that the more pages, the more noises may occur.

Table 4. Top 1 inclusion rate applying the proposed query relaxation technique

#Snippets	$N_{min} = 0$	= 25	= 50	= 75
Nmax = 25	.6550	N/A	N/A	N/A
50	.6199	.6374	N/A	N/A
75	.6082	.6082	.6140	N/A
100	.5965	.5965	.5965	.6082

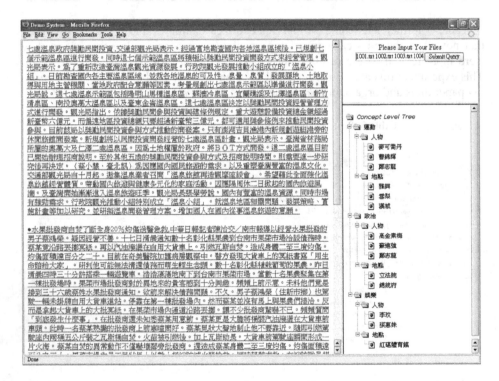

Fig. 2. A prototype information summarization system allowing users to browse documents with the categorized key terms and user-defined categories

The proposed approach is independent of language differences. Currently, the approach has been applied to developing a system called LiveSum, which allows users to browse Chinese documents through the categorized key terms and user-defined categories. As shown in Figure 2, the system extracts key terms from documents (a set of documents collected in a digital library or retrieved from a search engine), and classifies them into user-defined categories. The corresponding classifiers can be developed using the Web mining approach proposed by Huang, Chuang & Chien (2004). As noted, the system accepts a list of file names as given at the upper-right corner. These documents are displayed at the left part of the browser, and some key terms are extracted and classified into user-defined categories as at the lower-right corner. This provides a new way of information summarization. As the authors observed, it can benefit a lot when a user wants to quickly browse the important concepts embedded in a set of documents.

5 Conclusion

In this paper, we have addressed the problem of text segment categorization and presented a feasible approach dealing with the problem by using the Web as an additional knowledge source. The proposed approach is able to categorize text segments into broader subject categories and is more generalized than conventional named entity recognition approaches. Some initial experiments on categorizing paper titles into Yahoo!'s Computer Science hierarchy has been conducted and the achieved experimental results confirm the potential and its wide adaptability to various digital library applications.

References

1. Witten, I.H., et al.: Text Mining in a Digital Library. *International Journal on Digital Libraries* 4:1 (2004) 56-59.
2. Zhou, G.D., Su, J.: Named Entity Recognition Using an HMM-based Chunk Tagger. *Proceedings of the 40th Annual Meeting of the ACL* (2000) 473-480.
3. Hearst, M.: Untangling Text Data Mining. *Proceedings of the 37th Annual Meeting of the Association for Computational Linguistics* (1999).
4. Banko, M., Brill, E.: Scaling to Very Large Corpora for Natural Language Disambiguation. *Proceedings of the 39th Annual Meeting of the Association for Computational Linguistics* (2001) 26-33.
5. Cohen, W., Singer, Y.: Context-sensitive Learning Methods for Text Categorization. *Proceedings of the 19th Annual International ACM SIGIR Conference on Research and Development in Information Retrieval* (2001) 307-315.
6. Huang, C.C., Chuang, S.L., Chien, L.F.: LiveClassifier: Creating Hierarchical Text Classifiers through Web Corpora. *Proceedings of the 2004 World Wide Web Conference (WWW'04)* (2004).
7. Kosala, R., Blockeel, H.: Web Mining Research: A Survey. *ACM SIGKDD Explorations*, 2:1 (2000) 1-15.
8. Feldman, R., et al.: Maximal Association Rules: A New Tool for Mining for Keyword Co-occurrences in Document Collections. *Proceedings of the Third International Conference on Knowledge Discovery and Data Mining* (1997) 167-170.
9. Soderland, S.: Learning Text Analysis Rules for Domain-specific Natural Language Processing. Ph.D. thesis, technical report UM-CS-1996-087 University of Massachusetts, Amherst (1997).
10. Agirre, E., Ansa, O., Hovy, E., Martinez, D.: Enriching Very Large Ontology Using the WWW. *Proceedings of ECAI 2000 Workshop on Ontology Learning* (2000).

iQA: An Intelligent Question Answering System

Zhiguo Gong[1] and Mei Pou Chan[1,2]

[1] Faculty of Science and Technology,
University of Macau,
Macao, PRC
[2] Macao Polytechnic Institute,
Macao, PRC
zggong@umac.mo, calanachan@ipm.edu.mo

Abstract. Question answering (QA) is the study on the methodology that returns exact answers to natural language questions. This paper attempts to increase the coverage and accuracy of QA systems by narrowing the semantics gap between questions with terms written in abbreviations and their potential answers. To achieve this objective, the processing includes (1) identifying terms that might be abbreviations from the user's natural language question; (2) retrieving documents relevant to that abbreviation term; (3) filtering noun phrases that are considered to be potential long forms for that abbreviation within the returned result.

1 Introduction

Question answering (QA) is the study on the methodology that returns exact answers to natural language questions, rather than a list of potentially relevant documents, which users have to scan through in order to dig out the necessary information. In other words, question answering is a step closer to information retrieval rather than document retrieval.

The challenge with QA system is how to return answers to user's natural language questions. The whole process is quite complicated as it involves quite a number of different techniques to work closely together in order to achieve the goal, including query rewrites and formulations, question classification, information retrieval, passage retrieval, answer extraction, answer ranking and justification. The end-to-end performance of a complete QA system hence depends on each of these independent factors. Over the past few years, individual research groups have been continuing to refine each of these steps with the intention to increase the coverage and accuracy of QA systems.

Several question answering systems have been made available for use on the Web. However, these QA systems have not taken questions with terms written in abbreviations into consideration. They can present the relevant information among the returned answers in response to the question *"Where is University of Macau?"*. However, when the abbreviation for "University of Macau" is used instead, that is, when *"Where is Umac?"* is submitted, though the returned result set contains information related to "umac", it has nothing to do with "University of Macau" because

E.A. Fox et al. (Eds.): ICADL 2005, LNCS 3815, pp. 332–341, 2005.
© Springer-Verlag Berlin Heidelberg 2005

the abbreviation "umac" can stand for many different things besides "University of Macau". In other words, system-wise speaking, these answers are justified to be correct. Only that in this case, it so happens that the semantics of the returned answers does not meet the expectation need of the user.

This work addresses this problem by attempting to reduce the semantics gap between questions with terms written in abbreviations and the potential answers. WordNet[1] is used here to help solve this problem. The terms in the user's natural language question will be sent to WordNet. Due to the large coverage of WordNet on English-language word, terms that cannot be found in WordNet will be considered as abbreviations, though there are cases when this is not true. A query solely consisting of that term will be sent to a search engine, and the retrieved relevant documents will be processed to obtain the possible long forms for that term to be used in feedback loop for the user's original question. The details of this process will be discussed in the later sections.

The rest of the paper is organized as follows: section 2 briefly talks about the motivation of this work; section 3 details the implementation of the proposed QA system—iQA, including the solution to reduce the semantics gap between questions with terms written in abbreviations and the potential answers, and section 4 is the evaluation and conclusion of this work.

2 Motivations

Question answering systems have their history dated back to the 1960's, using highly edited knowledge bases, edited list of FAQ, sets of newspaper articles and encyclopedia as knowledge base. Given the limited size of these corpora, it is necessary to have a deep understanding on the language in order to find an answer to a question because the chance of finding strings/sentences that closely match the question string within a relatively small textual collection is small. Thus, many complex natural language processing (NLP) techniques have to be used because syntactic information about how a question is phrased and how sentences in documents are structured potentially provides important clues for the matching of the question and answer candidates in the sentences, e.g. in discovering the sentence *"Columbus Day celebrates the Italian navigator who first landed in the New World on Oct 12, 1492."* to be the answer to the question *"Who discovered America?"*.

However, the emergence of the Web has made way for a brand new perspective for question answering systems. Given the Web's huge data size, it is highly possible that an answer string that occurs in a simple relation to the question exists in the Web. Hence, the degree of difficulty of question answering systems does not primarily depend on the question per se, but rather on how closely a given corpus matches the question. Taking an example given by Hermjakob et al. [1] as a demonstration,

      Q: Who discovered America?
      S1: Columbus discovered America.

---

[1] WordNet is an online lexical reference system developed at Princeton University's Cognitive Science Laboratory by Psychology Professor George Miller. It is an extensive English-language word database developed over the last thirty years.

S2: Columbus Day celebrates the Italian navigator who first landed in the New World on Oct 12, 1492.

The question above can be answered more easily from sentence S1 than sentence S2 because the string Q is "closer" to string S1 than string S2. Since the Web's size dwarfs any human-collected corpora by orders of magnitude, it is not uncommon to have the same piece of information written and expressed in various ways. This property can be exploited to eliminate the need to understand both the structure and meaning of natural language, yet, be able to extract the answer. The greater the redundancy in the source, the more likely an answer can occur in a simple relation to the question, without the need to solve the difficulties with NLP systems.

In fact, several studies [2, 3] have shown that by consulting the Web as the knowledge base, QA systems can still achieve a satisfactory level of performance without the need to solve the difficulties with NLP systems. The trick is to take advantage of the redundancy of data present in the Web and use simple pattern matching techniques.

The possibility of finding an answer to a factoid question without the need for a deep understanding of the language forms the launching pad for this work. Driven by the stimulation of TREC QA track[2], individual research groups have worked on refining each of the various components that make up a complete QA system, with the intention to increase the coverage and accuracy of QA systems.

Sharing the common goal as to increase the coverage and accuracy of QA systems, the driving force behind this work is to develop a QA system that can precisely answer users' factoid questions stated in the form of natural language, using the Web as the knowledge base. In particular, the system should handle questions with terms written in abbreviations, thus narrowing the semantics gap between the questions and the potential answers.

Everyone agrees that an abbreviation term can stand for many different things depending on the context used. For instance, taking the term ATM as an example. For the general public, the first concept that comes to their mind might be "automatic teller machine", from which they enjoy convenient money withdrawal service from time to time. Nevertheless, for people working in the computer network area, ATM implies "asynchronous transfer mode" in their day-to-day work conversation.

Hence, if a QA system does not keep this in mind, though the returned answers are related to ATM, which is considered to be correct system-wise speaking, might yet be considered to be an incorrect answer by the user because the user has a different expectation on the context of the abbreviation term.

In order to reduce this semantics difference, iQA includes questions with terms written in abbreviations into consideration. The proposed procedures for attacking this particular challenge are as follows: (1) identifying terms that might be abbreviations from the user's natural language question; (2) retrieving documents relevant to that abbreviation term; (3) filtering noun phrases that are considered to be potential long forms for that abbreviation within the returned result.

---

[2] TREC (the Text REtrieval Conferences)[2] is a series of workshops co-sponsored by the National Institute of Standards and Technology (NIST) and DARPA (Defense Advanced Research Projects Agency).

A complete QA system, iQA, will be developed incorporating the proposed solution for questions with terms in abbreviations into it so as to increase the coverage of the system. iQA will use shallow parsing techniques to obtain the necessary information for answer extraction. Shallow parsing, also called partial parsing or chunking, is the task of identifying phrases, possibly of several types, in natural language sentences based purely on part-of-speech tags and without a deeper understanding of the content. It is simpler, conceptually and computationally, than full parsing, but still provides fundamental sentence structure information such as noun phrases and verb phrases. The following sections will detail the steps needed to build such a system.

3 Methodologies in Implementing iQA

The overall architecture of our proposed system, iQA, can be divided into four main modules: (1) question analysis module, (2) document analysis module, (3) answer extraction module, and (4) abbreviation analysis module. Figure 1 shows the system architecture of iQA. The functions performed by each of these modules are discussed below.

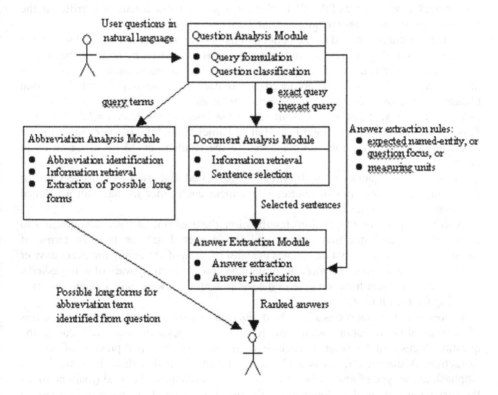

Fig. 1. System architecture of iQA

3.1   Question Analysis Module

Question analysis module is mainly consisted of two operations: query formulation, and question classification. As the name suggests, query formulation handles the formulation of queries to be used in the document analysis module. The query formulation process of iQA involves the generation of two types of queries, exact queries and inexact queries, similar to the idea proposed by [4].

An exact query is composed by simply removing the question stem from the factoid question, and re-arranging the position of the verb if necessary, based on the idea from [5]. The syntactic structure of the question has to be analyzed in order to re-position the verb accordingly. For example, the exact query for *"What are pennies made of?"* is *"pennies are made of"*.

Brill et al. [2] has proposed a much more exhaustive rewrite approach. Given a query such as "Who is $w_1 w_2 \ldots w_n$", where each of the w_i is a word, a rewrite is generated for each possible position the verb could be moved to (e.g. "w_1 is $w_2 \ldots w_n$", "$w_1 w_2$ is $\ldots w_n$", etc). This approach guarantees that the proper movement position is found.

Exact query has a low recall but a high precision rate because if the retrieved documents contain sentences that match with the exact query, it is highly possible that a potential answer can be located within it. In fact, this is an attempt to fully exploit the data redundancy property of the Web where it is possible that a sentence written in the form that closely matches the question can be found.

An inexact query is based on the belief that an answer is likely to be found within the vicinity of a set of query terms. An inexact query is composed by treating the natural language question as a bag of query terms. Given a factoid question, a query in a form of $q^{(0)} = [q_1^{(0)}, q_2^{(0)}, \ldots q_k^{(0)}]$ is produced, where each query term $q_i^{(0)}$ might be a noun phrase, a verb, an adjective, or any other content words present in the question. For example, the inexact query for *"What city is the home to the Rock and Roll Hall of Fame?"* is [city, home, Rock and Roll Hall of Fame]. Such kind of query has a higher recall but a lower precision rate compared to the result returned by using an exact query.

In our system, queries of both types are generated and used to retrieve data for processing. The two types of queries supplement each other to maintain a balance between recall and precision.

As for the operation of question classification, the goal is to analyze the questions to derive the detailed question classes and the expected answer type in terms of named-entity. This information enables the later process of extracting the exact answer from the candidate sentences more accurately. When a system is aware of being asked a when-question, it can focus on time or date as potential answers, and a where-question is asking for location, etc.

However, not all questions allow the derivation of an expected answer type in terms of named-entity, including what, which, and how questions. For such cases, the question focus can be taken advantage of in guiding the later process of answer extraction. A question focus is a phrase in the question that disambiguates it and emphasizes the type of answer being expected. In most cases, the head (main noun) of the first noun phrase of the question is the question focus. For instance, in question *"What book did Rachel Carson write in 1962?"*, the question focus *"book"* can be used to provide supporting clues to locate the answer in the later process, by looking for phrases containing the question focus.

Question classification, i.e., putting the questions into several semantic categories, can significantly reduce the search space of plausible answers. The accuracy of question classification is very important to the overall performance of a question answering system.

3.2 Document Analysis Module

After the question analysis module, the next step is document analysis module. The main objective of this module is to retrieve data from the Web based on the exact and inexact queries generated from the question analysis module, and then select sentences likely to contain an answer from the returned data for further processing.

iQA uses Google, an existing generic search engine, as information retrieval back-end, and effort can be mainly driven to answer extraction and justification process. In this case, post-processing procedures to extract the potential answers have to be implemented.

The returned snippets and summaries are split into separate sentences. In iQA, sentences that contain either the exact query, or the query terms of the inexact query are selected to be passed to the answer extraction module.

3.3 Answer Extraction Module

With the clues derived from question classification of the question analysis module, and the candidate sentences retained by the document analysis module, the answer extraction module is ready to start. The main objective of this module is extraction of simple potential answers, and answer justification.

If an expected answer type in terms of named-entity can be derived during the question analysis module, the candidate sentences retrieved from the document analysis module are first processed by a named-entity tagger in order to obtain phrases of expected answer type, which become the candidate answers. Otherwise, the answer extraction depends on the recognition of question focus or any other clues derived during the question analysis module.

These candidate answers are then scored based on the frequency each of them appears within the potential candidate answers retrieved. Clustering will then be done to group the similar candidate answers together so that shorter answers are used as evidence to boost the score of longer answers. Voting based on the number of scores will determine the rank of the potential candidate answers [3, 6]. That is, to use data redundancy to validate the accuracy of answer. The multiple occurrences of the same answer in different documents lend credibility to the proposed answer.

3.4 Abbreviation Analysis Module

After all the previous processing, the answers are now ready to be displayed. However, what if the user question contains terms written in abbreviations? The answers in hand are relevant to that abbreviation term. However, there are so many different interpretations to each abbreviation term, will the answers lie in the same context as expected by the users? This uncertainty drives the inclusion of the abbreviation analysis module to increase the coverage of QA systems. The work mainly includes (1) identifying terms that might be abbreviations from the user's natural language question; (2) retrieving documents relevant to that abbreviation term; (3) filtering noun phrases that are considered to be potential long forms for that abbreviation within the returned result.

3.4.1 Which are Abbreviation Terms?

Given a user's natural language question, how can the system automatically identify the abbreviation term? WordNet is used here to help solve this problem. Query terms consisting of one word only will be sent to WordNet. That is, if the user question is *"Where is umac?"*, the term "umac" will be sent to WordNet , whereas the term "University of Macau" in *"Where is University of Macau?"* will not be sent. This is based on the observation that terms consisting of more than one word are seldom abbreviations. Due to the large coverage of WordNet on English-language word, terms that cannot be found in WordNet will be considered as abbreviations, though there might be cases when this is not true.

When the thought-to-be abbreviation term has been filtered out, a separate query consisting solely of that abbreviation term will be sent to a search engine to retrieve documents relevant to that abbreviation term.

3.4.2 Filter Corresponding Potential Long Forms

In this step, the returned result from the search engine will be processed to obtain the possible long forms for that term to be used in feedback loop for the user's original question. Two approaches are adopted to filter the possible long forms.

The first approach is to retrieve all noun phrases that have the first character matches with the first character of the term being considered as abbreviation. Subsequent character matching is not necessary as in the case of "umac" for "University for Macau". The three characters together, "mac", represent the word "Macau".

However, this approach alone is not sufficient to solve the problem. There are cases where the first character of the abbreviation is not the same as the first character of the long form, as in the case of "CPTTM" for "Macau Productivity and Technology Transfer Center". Hence, the second approach is to take advantage of the patterns

<A; parenthesis; X; parenthesis> and
<X; parenthesis; A; parenthesis> and
<A; dash; X>

Example: "IFT (Institute for Tourism Studies)"

where A denotes the abbreviation and X denotes the possible long form. The pattern elements are divided by a semicolon. The idea of this pattern is based on the work of M.M. Soubbotin et al. [7]. Presence of such patterns in the noun phrase serves as an indication of the presence of an acronym.

Those noun phrases that are retained by these two approaches are then listed for users to choose as feedback loop to the original question, to return answers falling into the same semantics expectation of the users, hence, significantly boosting up the performance of QA systems.

3.4.3 Work in Action

The difference between iQA and the other available search engines in the Web is the consideration of questions with terms written in abbreviations. Taking the question *"Where is ift?"* as an example. After user inputs the question and presses the "Find Answer" button, the preliminary answers are displayed, as shown in the following figure. In addition, since the term "ift" is not included in WordNet, the possible long forms for "ift" will be retrieved and listed as well.

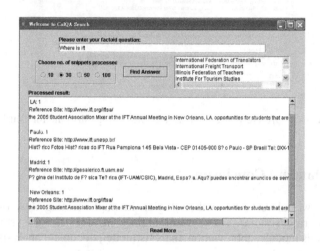

Fig. 2. Screen shot of iQA's response to *"Where is ift?"*

As seen from figure 2, the answers include LA, Paulo, Madrid, New Orleans. System-wise speaking, all these answers are relevant to the question *"Where is ift?"*. This is a good example showing that one abbreviation term can have more than one interpretation.

However, in fact, "ift" stands for many other things in addition to those answers listed above. But, in order not to overload the users with too much information, which is exactly the goal of QA systems, only those answers within the top 5 rankings are displayed in iQA. This means that the "ift" users have in mind might not be taken into consideration within the answers displayed. To supplement this shortage, in addition to the answers displayed, the possible long forms that are available for the term "ift" are simultaneously listed for users to choose as feedback loop into the original question, as shown in figure 2.

For instance, if the user wants to know the location of "Institute for Tourism Studies" instead, the user can choose that option from the list and press "Find Answer" button again. In this case, "ift" will be substituted by "Institute for Tourism Studies" in the query sent to the search engine. The corresponding answers for *"Where is Institute for Tourism Studies?"* will then be displayed, as shown is figure 3.

Hence, with such an implementation, the coverage and accuracy of QA systems is increased, through narrowing the semantics difference between questions with terms written in abbreviations and the potential answers.

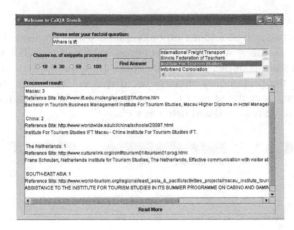

Fig. 3. Screen shot of iQA's response to "*Where is ift?*" using "Institute for Tourism Studies" in the feedback loop

4   Evaluation and Conclusion

In this paper, we address our methodologies in implementing iQA (an intelligent question answering system). Our system mainly includes 4 sub-systems, namely, question analysis module, abbreviation analysis model, document analysis module and answer extraction module.

Question analysis module takes users' natural language questions as input, and tries to classify the original questions into several groups. By consulting corresponding patterns or rules in the knowledge base of the system, the original questions are transformed into native queries to general-purpose search engines. Google is used as our only backend search engine in our current implementation. In order to handle the problems caused by abbreviation in user's questions, we develop abbreviation analysis module for this sake. As a matter of the fact, this sub-system uses WordNet firstly to learn if the terms in the questions are possible abbreviations. To expand the abbreviation to some potential phrases or concepts, this module tries to retrieve from Google by matching some patterns. Then, the abbreviation terms will be replaced in the original question with users' feedbacks. The document analysis module takes charge of document access through general-purpose search engine. And finally, the answer extraction module will try to mine out potential answers in response to the original question.

In order to evaluate the general performance of iQA, the first 100 TREC 2003 questions are sent to iQA, and the MRR is 0.49. Borrowing the idea used by TREC, the answer accuracy of the system is measured by the mean reciprocal rank (MRR) which assigns a number equal to 1/R where R is the rank of the correct answer. If none of the answers returned are correct, or if the system does not return any answers, the precision score for that question will be zero. The system's overall score is calculated as the MRR across all the 100 questions.

Since iQA has a particular function to handle questions with abbreviation terms, besides using the TREC questions as a general evaluation basis, questions with abbreviation terms present in the Macao local region are also used to test the performance of iQA. The evaluation result is displayed in table 1.

Table 1. Evaluation result on questions with abbreviation terms

Questions with abbreviation terms	Answers correct?	Remark – local context for Macao region
Where is Umac?	Yes	Umac – University of Macau
Where is IFT?	Yes	IFT – Institute for Tourism Studies
Where is IIUM?	Yes	IIUM – Inter-University Institute of Macau
Where is AIOU?	Yes	AIOU – Asia International Open University
Where is UNU-IIST?	Yes	UNU/IIST – United Nations University
Where is CPTTM?	Yes	CPTTM – Macau Productivity and Technology Transfer Center

References

1. U. Hermjakob, A.E., D. Marcu. *Natural Language Based Reformulation Resource and Web Exploitation for Question Answering.* in *TREC 2002.* 2002.
2. E. Brill, J.L., M. Banko, S. Dumais, A. Ng. *Data-Intensive Question Answering.* in *TREC-2001.* 2001.
3. Charles L. A. Clarke, G.V.C., Thomas R. Lynam, *Exploiting Redundancy in QA.* Proceedings of the 24th annual international ACM SIGIR conference on Research and development in information retrieval, 2001: p. 358-381.
4. J. Lin, A.F., B. Katz, G. Marton, S. Tellex. *Extracting Answers from the Web Using Data Annotation and Knowledge Mining Techniques.* in *TREC 2002.* 2002.
5. Dell Zhang, W.S.L., *Web based pattern mining and matching approach to question answering.*
6. Cody Kwok, O.E., Daniel S. Weld, *Scaling QA to the Web.* ACM transactions on Information Systems, 2001. **19**(3): p. 242-262.
7. M.M. Soubbotin, S.M.S. *Patterns of Potential Answer Expressions as Clues to the Right Answers.* in *TREC-2001.* 2001.

Evaluating the Effectiveness of a Collaborative Querying Environment

Lin Fu, Dion Hoe-Lian Goh, and Schubert Shou-Boon Foo

Division of Information Studies,
School of Communication and Information,
Nanyang Technological University,
Singapore 637718
{p148934363, ashlgoh, assfoo}@ntu.edu.sg

Abstract. Collaborative querying seeks to help users formulate queries by sharing expert knowledge or other users' search experiences. In previous work, a collaborative query environment (CQE) was developed for a digital library. The system operates by clustering and recommending related queries to users using a hybrid query similarity identification approach. Users can explore the query clusters using a graph-based visualization system known as the Query Graph Visualizer (QGV). The purpose of this paper is to evaluate the CQE with goal of informing the usefulness and usability of such a system. Our results show that compared with traditional information retrieval systems, collaborative querying can lead to faster information seeking when users perform unspecified tasks.

1 Introduction

The study of information seeking behavior reveals that interaction and collaboration with other people is an important part in the process of information seeking and use [1, 6]. Given this idea, collaborative querying aims to assist users in formulating queries to meet their information needs by harnessing other users' expert knowledge or search experience [2]. A common approach in collaborative querying is to cluster similar queries issued by other users. Such queries are typically found in web user logs, which are then extracted and clustered to obtain recommended queries to users. In this way, there is an opportunity for a user to take advantage of previous queries used by previous users and use the appropriate ones to meet his/her information need.

In our previous work, a set of collaborative querying techniques was developed for a digital library [3, 4]. The system operates by clustering and recommending related queries to users using a hybrid query similarity identification approach. Users can explore the query clusters using a graph-based visualization system known as the Query Graph Visualizer (QGV). The QGV is designed as a Java applet and is an independent and reusable software component that can be incorporated into existing information systems to provide enhanced information retrieval services.

With the completion of the QGV, there is a need to assess its usefulness and usability with the goal of guiding future research in this area. A collaborative querying environment (CQE) was therefore developed by incorporating these

E.A. Fox et al. (Eds.): ICADL 2005, LNCS 3815, pp. 342–351, 2005.
© Springer-Verlag Berlin Heidelberg 2005

collaborative querying techniques and the QGV into an existing OPAC system. A pilot study was then conducted with participants using the CQE to perform two categories of tasks. The remainder of this paper reports on the CQE, QGV, evaluation design and the results of this evaluation.

2 The Collaborative Querying Environment

Figure 1 shows the CQE that is built upon the OPAC system at Nanyang Technological University (NTU), Singapore. The system offers typical functions found in current information retrieval systems. Users submit their searches in the query area and view retrieved documents in the results list area. The results contain information about a document's title, author, call number and location of the information entity of physical format (e.g., the book is located in Library 2, Level B4). The details of each result item include this information together with the publisher and the subject heading, displayed in a separate popup window when selected from the results listing (Figure 2). In addition, the CQE shows recommended queries next to the search results list in HTML format. Users can click on the recommended queries to carry out further rounds of searches.

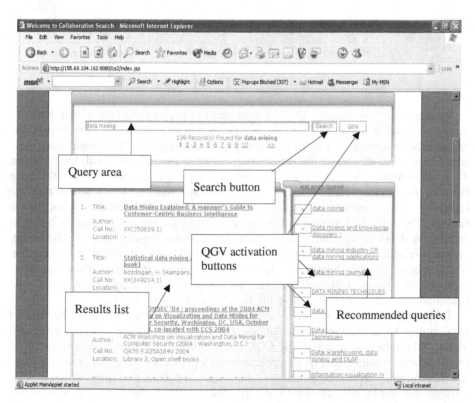

Fig. 1. The Collaborative Querying Environment

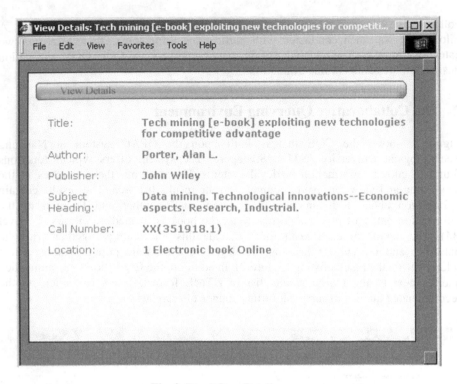

Fig. 2. Result Item Details

Further, users can trigger the QGV (Figure 3) to explore the relationship between the recommended queries in a graph format by clicking on the button next to the recommended queries in Figure 1. Each graph node represents a single query and edges between nodes show the relationship between two queries, with the value on the edge indicating the strength of the relationship. For example, 0.3 on the edge between the nodes "data mining" and "knowledge discovery" indicates that the similarity weight between these two nodes is 0.3. Figure 3 shows a network for the submitted query "data mining". This query is directly related to queries such as "predictive data mining" and "data warehousing, data mining and OLAP". The former in turn is related to "spss", a commonly used software tool in the field, indicating that "data mining" is also related to "spss". This approach therefore allows users to explore new query formulations that are diverse, sometimes unexpected, and potentially useful. More information on the QGV can be found in [6].

In a typical scenario of use, we consider a user who is interested in the field of data mining. He is a novice in this domain and would like to learn and explore related topics. When the user accesses the CQE, he first submits a query "data mining". A moment later, results of the query are displayed together with a list of queries related to "data mining" as recommendations (see Figure 1 for an example). After looking through the results list, the user feels that the results do not adequately meet his information need and he consults the list of recommended queries on the right column of the CQE interface. Due to a lack of domain knowledge in data mining, the user decides to peruse the relationships between the recommended queries before making use of them and thus decides to generate a query graph using "data mining" as the root node. The user therefore triggers the QGV which launches in a separate pop up window (see Figure 3 for an example).

While browsing the graph, the user becomes interested in the node "knowledge discovery". It is a new phrase to him but seems related to his search topic. Wanting to peruse the queries related to "knowledge discovery", he zooms into this node and examines queries related to it by using the graph navigation options of the QGV. After examining the graph carefully, the user is prepared to carry out another around of information retrieval by using the node "knowledge discovery". He thus right clicks on the node and chooses "Display result in a separate browser". The query "knowledge discovery" will be executed and the results displayed in the search page (see Figure 1 for example). The user may repeat this process of query reformulation and graph exploration until he finds the desired information.

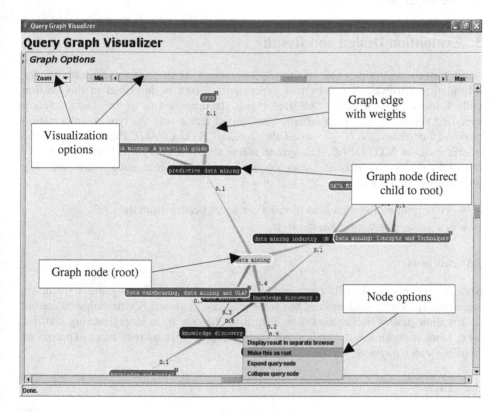

Fig. 3. The Query Graph Visualizer

A typical mode of interaction with the CQE can thus be summarized as follows:

- Formulate an initial query. The user will express the information need in a format understandable by the information retrieval system.

- Evaluate the results list: After the system returns the results from the initial query, the user will determine if the results contain the desired information. If not, a new query can be issued. Alternatively, the user can make use of the recommended queries generated by the CQE outlined in the next two steps.
- Examine the recommended queries in HTML format. The user will decide whether the recommended queries are appropriate in helping explore the domain of interest for query reformulation. If so, the recommended queries are activated by directly clicking on them.
- Explore query graph. The user might want to peruse the entire network belonging to a certain recommended query. He can thus trigger the QGV to examine the structure of the query graph and manipulate the visualization area by using options such as "zoom", "rotate", etc. The user can make use of a selected query by causing the QGV to post it to the OPAC. The results will then be displayed in the CQE.

3 Evaluation Design and Results

A pilot study was conducted on the CQE to assess its usefulness and usability for information retrieval. A two-by-two experiment design is described in this section with 4 users in each cell. One factor was the complexity of the tasks (clearly specified versus unclearly specified). The second factor was the type of information retrieval interface used (CQE versus the standard NTU OPAC). Figure 4 shows the interface of the NTU OPAC. The system offers standard query functions available in most OPAC systems including searching by keyword, subject, author, title, etc. The objectives of this study are:

- To determine for what kind of tasks can users benefit from the CQE.
- To assess the usability of the CQE.

3.1 Subjects

Sixteen students from NTU participated in this evaluation. Among the sixteen, six were undergraduate students and ten were graduate students. Six participants had an information studies background, five were from various areas in engineering and five were from communication studies. All participants confirmed they were experienced in using search engines.

3.2 Tasks

In line with the first objective of determining the types of tasks users could benefit from when using the CQE, two categories of tasks were created: clearly specified tasks and unclearly specified tasks [8]. Each category contained two tasks. The clearly specified tasks required specific and explicit information, e.g. "Find the book with the title 'Managing data mining technologies in organizations' and record the bibliographic information of this book". In this case, the information need for clearly specified tasks are straightforward and precise which in turn can be expressed by a simple query on a certain field or attribute of the information source. For the previous example, the user could obtain the desired information by simply using the title of the book as a query. Unclearly specified tasks on the other hand, have requirements that cannot be stated precisely [8], e.g. "Find 5 relevant journals related to information seeking behavior". Put differently, the information needs for unclearly specified tasks are vague and usually involve iterative query reformulation. Table 1 shows the tasks designed for the study.

Fig. 4. The NTU OPAC System

Table 1. Tasks Used in the Study

	Clearly Specified Tasks	**Unclearly Specified Tasks**
1	Find the proceedings of the Third International Semantic Web Conference. Record bibliographic information of this book.	Determine whether Singapore citizens are satisfied with the quality of traditional Chinese pharmacy available in the market.
2	Find the document with the name "Developing a common set of agents for E-commerce". Record bibliographic information of this document.	Find 10 international journals related to information retrieval and record the editors' names of these journals.

3.3 Experiment Design

The 16 participants were randomly divided into four groups of four participants each (Table 1). Groups A and B used the CQE to complete the clearly specified and the unclearly specified tasks respectively. Participants in Groups C and D used the existing OPAC system to complete the clearly specified and the unclearly specified tasks respectively. Participants in Group A and B were given a 10 minute introduction of the CQE followed by a practice session before carrying out the tasks. Participants in Groups C and D were introduced to the CQE after they had completed the tasks using the OPAC, and then asked to try the system. The time taken to accomplish the tasks successfully was recorded and used to measure the usefulness of the CQE, which is similar to that done in [8]

At the end of the study, all participants were asked to complete a preference questionnaire about the CQE. We adopted Nielsen's heuristic evaluation approach [7] to assess the usability of the system. This technique is used to find usability problems by getting a small number of evaluators to examine an interface and judge its compliance with ten recognized usability principles. The goal is to obtain the most useful information for guiding re-design with the least cost. Here, each heuristic is reflected by one or more questions concerning the design of the system. Each question is rated along a five-point scale – "strongly disagree", "disagree", "neutral", "agree" and "strongly agree".

3.4 Results and Discussion

Table 2 shows the average time needed for each group to finish the tasks. Compared with Group D, participants in Group B exhibited a major reduction in terms of average time to complete the unclearly specified tasks. This suggests that the CQE helped participants find the desired information more quickly than using the OPAC system alone for unclearly specified tasks. In other words, it appears that collaborative querying can help users formulate better queries by harnessing other information seekers' knowledge and reduce the time needed to sift through search results documents in search of relevant content when the information needs are vague and difficult to express. The reason is that most users cannot formulate a precise query to represent their information need in the first round of search. This leads the participants in Group D having to spend more time sifting through the results listings and reformulating their queries. However, for the participants in Group B, they were able to formulate better queries by either harnessing the recommended queries or exploring the QGV which in turn reduced the time in examining the results listings.

On the other hand, there is no noticeable difference between Groups A and C in the time required to complete the clearly specified tasks accurately. This suggests that collaborative querying has no time advantage in the process of information seeking for clearly specified tasks. The reason here is that all users could formulate an accurate query to express their information need and retrieve the target information in the first iteration of search. Further, the target information was easily found in the search results listings and typically occurred on the first results page returned by both the CQE and the NTU OPAC.

Table 2. Average Task Completion Time for Each Group

	Clearly Specified	Unclearly Specified
CQE	3 min (Group A)	12.5 min (Group C)
OPAC	3 min (Group B)	22 min (Group D)

As for usability, the CQE satisfies most of Nielsen's 10 heuristics according to our 16 participants (see Table 3). Due to space limitations, we show the results as numeric values (1-5) and only report the average value obtained for each heuristic. Here, higher values represent a greater level of agreement that the CQE adhered to the corresponding heuristic. As shown in Table 3, users agreed that the CQE adhered to most of Nielsen's 10 heuristics, with scores of four ("agree") or higher. For example, in "visibility of system status", 14 participants rated 4 or 5 (average value of 4.1) which indicated that they agreed or strongly agreed that the CQE provided enough information to reflect the action status of the system. As far as "consistency and standards" was concerned, 12 participants rated 4 or 5 (average of 3.8) which implies that they were comfortable with the layout and graphic design of the CQE and agreed that the font size, color, buttons, text box and popup menus were consistent with existing user interface standards. The results thus indicate that the CQE performs well in terms of usability issues.

In addition, qualitative remarks about the CQE confirmed the usability and usefulness of the system. Here, positive features included the recommended query lists being able to give users more ideas on what query terms to use, and the

Table 3. Heuristic Evaluation Summary of the CQE

Heuristic	Average value
Visibility of system status	4.1
Match between system and real world	3.3
User control and freedom	4.5
Consistency and standards	3.8
Error prevention	4.8
Recognition rather than recall	4.4
Flexibility and efficiency of use	4.8
Aesthetic and minimalist design	4.8
Help user recognize, diagnose and recover from errors	4
Help and documentation	2.3

usefulness of the graph visualization scheme which specifies the relationships between queries with varying weights. For example, one participant commented that:
"it was a helpful system to better understand the domain I am searching. Based on the recommended queries, I know how other people search for documents of my interests. The relationships between the recommended queries are clearly shown. By using the recommended terms to construct my queries, I get the relevant documents quickly".
Participants also commented that the system made searching more "fun" due to the graph visualization approach and the ability to explore the query nodes.

Negative comments go to the lack of detailed documentation which was needed to support the successful use of the system and was reflected in the low score of the "help and documentation" heuristic (average of 2.3). This low score could be attributed to the fact that some technical terms were used in the system, such as "nodes" and "weights". Despite this, 13 of the 16 participants expressed a strong interest in the system, and indicated that they would use the CQE if it became publicly available in the future.

4 Conclusion

This paper presents the CQE and reports on its evaluation. The CQE is a collaborative querying system and operates by harnessing the collective knowledge embedded in query logs to assist users in query formulation. Harvested queries can be used directly as recommendations for query reformulation or visualized in a graph format for exploration.

A few systems bear some relevance to the CQE in their support for collaborative querying. For example, Glance [5] developed an agent known as the Community Search Assistant. However the system does not employ a graph-based visualization scheme for users to explore and interact with the recommended queries. Further, the CQE adopts an alternative query clustering approach to detect related queries that has been demonstrated to be more effective [3]. Eurekster (www.eureskster.com) is another system which adopts a community-based approach to collaborative querying through search groups of users who share similar interests. However Eureskster requires more effort by users in building the search group before the benefits of collaborative querying can be realized. In contrast, the CQE is non-intrusive and operates by comparing the user's current query and existing clusters in the query repository in the background and sharing the related queries automatically [4].

Our study shows that users can benefit from the CQE for unclearly specified tasks and that the system does not adversely affect searching performance for clearly specified tasks. This therefore suggests the viability of the collaborative querying concept. Nevertheless, our evaluation also highlighted several areas for further improvement. For example, because the graph-based mode of interaction is unfamiliar to many users, online help will need to be incorporated. However, due to the small sample size of this initial evaluation, our findings cannot be generalized. Instead, a comprehensive evaluation will be conducted to further assess the performance and effectiveness of the CQE involving more users and a greater variety of task types.

Acknowledgements

This project is partially supported by NTU with the research grant number: RCC2/2003/SCI. Further we would like to express our thanks to the NTU library and the Centre for Information Technology Services at NTU for providing access to the queries.

References

[1] N. J. Belkin, (2000). Helping people find what they don't know. *Communications of the ACM, 43*(8), 58-61.

[2] E.F. Churchill, J.W. Sullivan & D. Snowdon. (1999) Collaborative and co-operative information seeking, *CSCW'98 Workshop Report 20*(1), 56-59.

[3] L. Fu, D. Goh & S. Foo. (2003) Collaborative querying through a hybrid query clustering approach. *Proceedings of the 6th International Conference of Asian Digital Libraries*, 111-122.

[4] L. Fu, D. Goh, S. Foo & Y. Supangat (2004) Collaborative querying for enhanced information retrieval. *Proceedings of the 8th European Conference on Digital Libraries*, 378-388.

[5] N. S. Glance, (2001). Community search assistant. In *Proceedings of 6th ACM International Conference on Intelligent User Interfaces*, 91-96.

[6] G.N. Marchionini, (1995) *Information seeking in electronic environments* (Cambridge University Press, Cambridge, 1995).

[7] J. Nielsen. (1992). Finding usability problems through heuristic evaluation. *Proceedings of the ACM CHI'92 Conference,* 373-380.

[8] C. Plaisant, B. Shneiderman, K. Doan, & T. Bruns. (1999) Interface and data architecture for query preview in networked information systems. *ACM Transactions on Information Systems, 17*(3), 320-341.

Opinion Leader Based Filtering

Hyeonjae Cheon[1] and Hongchul Lee[1]

Department of Industrial Systems and Information Engineering,
Korea University, 136-701 Seoul, South Korea
{slash, hclee}@korea.ac.kr

Abstract. Recommendation systems are helping users find the information, products, and other people they most want to find, therefore many on-line stores provide recommending services e.g. Amazon, CDNOW, etc. Most recommendation systems use collaborative filtering, content-based filtering, and hybrid techniques to predict user preferences. We discuss the strengths and weaknesses of the techniques and present a unique recommendation system that automatically selects opinion leaders by category or genre to improve the performance of recommendation. Finally, our approach will help to solve the cold-start problem in collaborative filtering.

1 Introduction

According as online services become various and grow, recommendation systems are used by E-commerce sites to suggest products to their users and to provide users with information to help them decide which products to purchase. Recommendation systems can be broadly categorized into content-based filtering [17], collaborative filtering [11], and hybrid systems. Content-based systems provide recommendations by comparing representations of content contained in an item to representations of content that interests the user. On the other hand, collaborative filtering systems work by collecting user feedback in the form of ratings for items in a given domain and exploit similarities and differences among profiles of several users in determining how to recommend an item. Content-based filtering requires correct user profiles and it is difficult for a computer to analyze the profiles to matching an item. Also, content-based filtering cannot account for community endorsements; For example, in the case of movie recommendation systems using content-based filtering, if a user likes an actor, the system will always recommend movies in which the actor appears to the user regardless of other peoples opinion [9]. Collaborative filtering has been very successful in both research and practice [14]. However, collaborative filtering also has two fundamental problems:

Sparsity: In practice, most users do not rate most items and hence the user-item rating matrix is typically very sparse. Therefore the probability of finding a set of users with significantly similar ratings is usually low and the accuracy of recommendations may be poor [13], [6].

E.A. Fox et al. (Eds.): ICADL 2005, LNCS 3815, pp. 352–359, 2005.
© Springer-Verlag Berlin Heidelberg 2005

Cold-start problem (new-user cold-start problem): Another difficult problem commonly faced by recommendation systems is the cold-start problem, where recommendations are required for new users for whom little or no information has yet been acquired. Therefore, an item cannot be recommended unless a user has rated it before [7]. The focus of this paper is to solve the cold-start problem in collaborative filtering.

Hybrid systems have tried to overcome shortcomings of the content-based and collaborative filtering recommendation systems. An example of a hybrid system is Fab [1], which recommends web pages. Fab still needs a few early ratings from each user in order to create a training set and mandates that the content-based techniques to build the user profile be extremely accurate. Claypool *et al.* [3] provided an approach to combining content-based and collaborative filtering by basing a prediction on a weighted average of the content-based prediction, but it was not easy that the system timely changed weights. Polcicova [8] proposed a method for content-based and collaborative filtering combination, where content-based filtering estimates were used to fill up some missing ratings for collaborative filtering. However, the method also requires early ratings from new user. To make things worse, incorrectly estimated ratings can cause negative impact to collaborative filtering.

In this paper, we present a unique approach that the recommendation system automatically selects opinion leaders by category or genre to solve the cold-start problem in collaborative filtering and the opinion leaders directly recommend items to new users or users who changed their preferences.

2 Collaborative Filtering

In this section, we briefly describe the pure collaborative filtering that computes similarities between users using a Pearson correlation coefficient. Predictions for an item are then computed as the weighted average of the ratings for the items from those users that are similar, where the weight is the computed coefficient. The numerical formula for a prediction for an item for user u is (1):

$$prediction = \bar{u} + \frac{\sum_{i=1}^{n} (corr_i) \times (rating_i - \bar{i})}{\sum_{i=1}^{n} (corr_i)} \tag{1}$$

where $\bar{u}$ is the mean rating for the user in question, $corr_i$ is the Pearson's correlation coefficient of user i with the user for whom the prediction is being computed, $rating_i$ represents the rating submitted by user i for the article for which the prediction is being computed, $\bar{i}$ is the average rating for user i, and n is the total number of users in the system that have some correlation with the user and have rated the item [11].

3 Opinion Leader Based Filtering

We designed a new algorithm for our recommendation system that automatically selects opinion leaders to solve the cold-start problem in collaborative filtering and the opinion leaders directly recommend items to new users or users who changed their preferences.

3.1 Opinion Leader

An opinion leader [16] is recognized that he has professionalism and knowledge about specific subject from other people. If an opinion leader adopts a trend, many members of the same social group are likely to follow. Hence one useful way to judge the potential impact of a trend is to follow the diffusion path; if it is adopted by opinion leaders it will likely be widely adopted; if opinion leaders ignore it, other people probably will, too. The following is opinion leader's characteristics [12]:

1. Opinion leaders meet more often than other people with the mass media connected with the area of the item. For example, women's clothing fashion opinion leaders will more often read fashion magazines.
2. Opinion leaders have more interest in information for the item than other people.
3. Opinion leaders are more social than other people.
4. Opinion leaders are more innovative than other people.

The opinion leadership theory has many implications for advertising and marketing. We applied the opinion leadership theory to our recommendation system for solving cold-start problem in collaborative filtering. In this paper, the opinion leader is regarded as a person who has qualifications for a recommender.

3.2 RFM (Recency, Frequency, Monetary)

We propose a method based on RFM to identify opinion leaders in various user groups. The value of RFM [4] analysis as a method to identify high-response customers in marketing promotions, and to improve overall response rates is well known and is widely applied today. The following describes the RFM:

Recency is the time that has elapsed since the customer made his most recent purchase.
Frequency is the total number of purchases that a customer has made within a designated period of time.
Monetary is each customer's average purchase amount.

Customers will be scored on each of the three variables mentioned above, therefore high scored customers may be more valuable, confidential than low scored customers.

$$RFM = Recency + Frequency + Monetary \qquad (2)$$

Opinion leader based filtering is partly based on RFM and is used to select opinion leaders in our research.

3.3   Fuzzy Logic Based RFM (FLRFM+)

Opinion leader should be selected by other opinion leaders and users but original RFM has some lack of ability to reflect it, therefore we designed the fuzzy logic based RFM (FLRFM+) that is modified from the original RFM. The following describes the FLRFM+:

1. The original RFM is redefined.
   - "purchase" is replaced by "rating".
2. **Accuracy** is added to the original RFM to reflect user feedback.
   - **Accuracy** is the total number of cases that the user rating and recommender's rating are same or almost same.
3. All is converted into fuzzy inference model.

The FLRFM+ is computed by sugeno-type fuzzy inference system [15]. The input variables are the three variables of RFM (*recency, frequency, monetary*) and *accuracy*. The output variable is the score of FLRFM+. The rule-base is presented as (3).

$\Re_i$: if *recency* is A_1^i and *frequency* is A_2^i and *monetary* is A_3^i and *accuracy* is A_4^i

then $z_i = a_1^i \times recency + a_2^i \times frequency + a_3^i \times monetary + a_4^i \times accuracy$ (3)

where $\Re_i(i = 1, 2, \ldots, n)$ denotes the i-th rule, n is the number of fuzzy rules, z_i is the output from the i-th rule, $a_k^i(k=1, 2, \ldots, l)$ are consequent parameters, l is the number of input variables, *recency, frequency, monetary* and *accuracy* are the input variables, and A_k^i are fuzzy sets whose membership functions are denoted by the same symbols as the fuzzy values. If there are n rules in this rule-base then the crisp control action is computed as

$$z_0 = \frac{\sum_{i=1}^n \alpha_i z_i}{\sum_{i=1}^n \alpha_i} \qquad (4)$$

where $\alpha_i(i=1, 2, \ldots, n)$ denotes the firing level of the i-th rule, z_0 is the score of FLRFM+.

FLRFM+ has the following features:

1. FLRFM+ is able to reflect user feedback.
2. FLRFM+ is flexible.
   - With any given system, it is easy to handle it or modify it without starting again.
3. FLRFM+ is able to embed ambiguousness in it.
   - **Monetary** is always not important to selecting the opinion leader.

3.4   Selecting Opinion Leaders

Our approach uses the FLRFM+ to select opinion leaders. Kim et al. [5] used dynamic expert groups which were automatically formed to recommend domain specific documents for unspecified users. Their method only tends to recommend familiar or popular items because of emphasizing the accuracy of expert, but our method considers not only the accuracy but also customer loyalty [10]. Opinion leader based filtering algorithm to select opinion leaders can be summarized in the following steps:

1. Compute the FLRFM+ to find candidates for the opinion leader.
   - If a user has high FLRFM+, he will be candidate for the opinion leader.
2. Find candidates in each category.
   - Candidates have rated items in each category are sorted by FLRFM+ in descending order.
3. Select Top-N opinion leaders in each category.
   - The size of opinion leaders (N) is determined by our experiments in section 5.
4. Select Top-M items from opinion leaders.
   - The number of recommended items (M) is also determined by our experiments in section 5.
5. Recommend items to new user.

4   Recommendation

The overview of our system is shown in Fig. 1. If a new user selects an interested category, he is offered a voting list recommended by opinion leaders in the category. That is to say, the new user is recommended items provided by the opinion leader based filtering. In contrast, established users that have enough user ratings are recommended items provided by the collaborative filtering. The new or established user is determined by the number of ratings (r) which is proposed by our experiments in section 5.

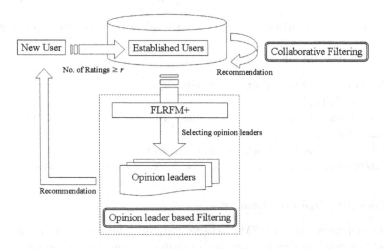

Fig. 1. Overview of the recommendation system

5   Performance Evaluation

In order to evaluate the performances of our opinion leader based filtering (OLBF), we simulated the proposed system using data from MovieLens [13], [14]. The data set consists of 100,000 ratings (1-5) from 943 users on 1682 movies and is divided into 80% training set and 20% test set. Also, we used Mean Absolute Error (MAE) as a metric for evaluating our OLBF algorithm and the traditional CF algorithm because it is most commonly used and easiest to interpret directly. MAE between ratings and predictions evaluate the accuracy of a system by comparing the numerical recommendation scores against the actual user ratings for the user-item pairs in the test data set. First, we evaluated with training set and test set to determine the relevant number of recommended items (M, see section 3.4) and size of opinion leaders (N, see section 3.4). Fig. 2

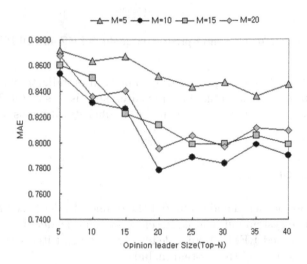

Fig. 2. Sensitivity of the opinion leader size on OLBF

shows the MAE according to the number of recommended items (M). In this each experiment, we varied the size of opinion leaders from 5 to 40 with step 5 for OLBF algorithm. When the number of recommended items is 10, M=10 is better than other cases on the whole. Especially, when the size of opinion leaders is between 20 and 30, the related value of MAE is somewhat smaller than others. We determined the size of opinion leaders as N = 20 and used these values for the rest of our experiments. Next, we also evaluated the number of user ratings that is an important factor of the cold-start problem. In this each experiment, we varied the number of user ratings from 10 to 80 with step 10 for both algorithms. Fig. 3 shows the comparison of CF and OLBF in terms of MAE. The size of the neighborhood for CF was specified as Neighborhood size = 30 that had been proposed by Sarwar[14]. When the number of rating is increased, the MAE of each algorithm is changed. Especially, the MAE of CF goes down the

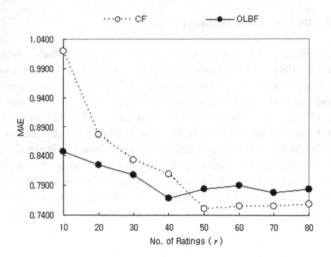

Fig. 3. Comparison of prediction quality of CF and OLBF

MAE of OLBF at $r = 45$ approximately. The results indicate which algorithm will be used to recommend items in some case. That is to say, OLBF is used for our recommendation system only when the number of ratings is smaller than $r = 45$.

6   Conclusion

In this paper, we proposed and evaluated the opinion leader based recommendation system. The system automatically selects opinion leaders by category using the fuzzy logic based RFM. Opinion leaders recommend items to new user. In summary, the features of this system include:

1. Opinion leader based filtering is a method that can help to solve the cold-start problem.
   - Opinion leader based filtering does not require new user to rate items.
   - New user can be recommended for items by rigorously selected opinion leaders.
2. A user who changed his preference has no need to reset his profile and to wait for the system to adapt itself to the new preference.

References

1. Balabanovi, M., Shoham, Y.: Fab: content-based, collaborative recommendation. Communications of the ACM, Vol. 40. No. 3 (1997) 66–72
2. Baudisch, P.: Joining Collaborative and Content-based Filtering. Online Proceedings of the CHI '99 Workshop Interacting with Recommender Systems (1999)

3. Claypool, M., Gokhale, A., Miranda, T.: Combining content-based and collaborative filters in an online newspaper. Proceedings of the ACM SIGIR Workshop on Recommender Systems: Implementation and Evaluation (1999)
4. Cullinan, G.: Picking them by their batting averages recency-frequency-monetary method of controlling circulation. Manual release 2103, Direct Mail/Marketing Association, N. Y. (1977)
5. Kim, D., Kim, S.: Dynamic Expert Group Models for Recommender Systems. Web Intelligence: Research and Development, Lecture Notes in Artificial Intelligence, Vol. 2198. Springer-Verlag (2001) 136–140
6. Melville, P., Mooney, R. J., Nagarajan, R.: Content-boosted collaborative ?ltering. In Proceedings of the SIGIR2001 Workshop on Recommender Systems, New Orleans (2001)
7. Middleton, S., Alani, H., Shadbolt, N., De Roure, D.: Exploiting synergy between ontologies and recommender systems. In Proceedings of the WWW2002 International Workshop on the Semantic Web, Hawaii (2002)
8. Polcicova, G., Navrat, P.: Combining Content-Based and Collaborative Filtering. ADBIS-DASFAA Symposium (2000) 118–127
9. Popescul, A., Ungar, L., Pennock, D., Lawrence, S.: Probabilistic models for unified collaborative and content-based recommendation in sparse-data environments. In 17th Conference on Uncertainty in Artificial Intelligence, Seattle, Washington (2001) 437–444
10. Reichheld, F., Sasser, W.: Zero defections: Quality comes to services. Harvard Business Review, Vol. 68. (1990) 105–111
11. Resnick, P., Iacovou, N., Suchak, M., Bergstrom., Riedl, J.: GroupLens: an open architecture for collaborative filtering of netnews. Proceedings of CSCW 94. ACM Press (1990) 175–186
12. Rogers, E.: Diffusion of Innovations. Fourth Edition. The Free Press (1995)
13. Sarwar, B. M., Karypis, G., Konstan, J. A., Riedl, J.: Analysis of Recommendation Algorithms for E-Commerce. In Proceedings of the ACM EC'00 Conference, Minneapolis (2000) 158–167
14. Sarwar, B. M., Karypis, G., Konstan, J. A., Riedl, J.: Item-based Collaborative Filtering Recommender Algorithms. In Proc. of the 10th International World Wide Web Conference (WWW10), Hong Kong (2001) 285–295
15. Sugeno, M.:Industrial applications of fuzzy control. Elsevier Science Pub. Co. (1985)
16. Summers, J.: The identity of women's clothing fashion opinion leaders. Journal of Marketing Research, Vol. 7. (1970) 178–185
17. Yates, R., Neto, B., Yates, R.: Modern Information Retrieval. Addison-Wesley (1999)

Comparison and Analysis of the Citedness Scores in Web of Science and Google Scholar

Peter Jacso

University of Hawaii, Department of Information and Computer Sciences,
2550 The Mall, Honolulu, HI 96882
jacso@hawaii.edu

Abstract. An increasing number of online information services calculate and report the citedness score of the source documents and provide a link to the group of records of the citing documents. The citedness score depends on the breadth of source coverage, and the ability of the software to identify the cited documents correctly. The citedness score may be a good indicator of the influence of the documents retrieved. Google Scholar gives the most prominence to the citedness score by using it in ranking the search results. Tests have been conducted to compare the individual and aggregate citedness scores of items in the results list of various known-item and subject searches in Web of Science (WoS) and Google Scholar (GS). This paper presents the findings of the comparison and analysis of the individual and aggregate citation scores calculated by WoS and GS for the papers published in 22 volumes of the *Asian Pacific Journal of Allergy and Immunology* (APJAI). The aggregate citedness score was 1,355 for the 675 papers retrieved by WoS, and 595 for 680 papers found in GS. The findings of the analysis and comparison of tests, and the reasons for the significant limitations of Google Scholar in calculating and reporting the citedness scores are presented.

1 Introduction

The Institute for Scientific Information (ISI) has been the only abstracting/indexing (I/A) service for decades which included the name of the authors, journals and the chronological and numerical designations of the documents (articles, books, book chapters, dissertations) cited by the source articles. ISI has processed more than 8,000 periodical publications (20) for its three citation databases which form the backbone of the WoS database and service (19).

This value added information has provided a powerful complementary option to the traditional searching based on titles, abstracts and descriptors of the records in indexing and abstracting databases - as envisioned by Eugene Garfield (5,6,7). Still, for 40 years there was no competition because the cost of adding and processing cited references has been prohibitive. Various research projects were the first to demonstrate the advantages of citation-based searching through open access scholarly databases (3,10).

Apart from the short-lived e-psyche database, the widely used PsycINFO database of the American Psychological Association was the first commercial I/A database to

E.A. Fox et al. (Eds.): ICADL 2005, LNCS 3815, pp. 360–369, 2005.
© Springer-Verlag Berlin Heidelberg 2005

add about 1.2 million cited references to more than 300,000 records - selectively from 1988, and to all the records (where applicable) from 2001. CSA followed suit on a smaller scale in some of it's A/I databases (13).

Many journal publishers have made available their full text article archives on the web (mostly for print subscribers, although there are hundreds of open access, full-text journal archives). These -by definition - include the cited references, usually as a clearly identified and distinguished set of data elements.

The introduction of the multidisciplinary, Scopus database (1) of Elsevier in the summer of 2004 represented the first challenge to the Web of Science database of ISI (4). Scopus processes 14,000 scholarly and professional journals enhancing by cited references records of articles published from the mid-1990s.

Google introduced in November, 2004 its free Google Scholar (GS) service (2) based primarily on the full-text archives of some of the largest scholarly publishers (combined with some of the open access A/I databases, preprint and reprint repositories, and pages of presumably academic Web sites). Google has not disclosed any quantitative information about the breadth of the database, the number of partner publishers, the scope of journals and other sources, the size and the time span of the database.

Some of the online services provide not only a link to the cited and citing articles, but also calculate and report the citedness score of articles. WoS, Scopus and GS also offer to sort the results by citedness score. WoS curremtly limits the set to be sorted to 300 records, while GS makes the citedness score the primary ranking criteria in presenting the search results. Scopus offers the most flexibility by not limiting the set to be sorted by the citedness score or any of the other sort criteria. Sorting by citedness score can be a useful option by bringing to the top the most cited (and presumably the most important) documents on a subject, in a journal and/or by an author - if the score is based on an appropriate set of scholarly and professional publications, and it is calculated correctly. For level playing field it would be better to calculate the per year citedness score as an option because older articles have more time to accumulate citations and increase their citedness scores (14).

The appropriateness of the source coverage depends on the number and quality of the potentially citing sources processed for a database, and the retrospective extent of inclusion of cited references in the records. The correct calculation of the citedness score assumes that the references are precisely identified by the software in spite of their differences in spelling, punctuation and abbreviation. WoS and Scopus also offer very good or adequate tools and options to look up, search for and collocate the variant formats of the cited references. Google has limited search capabilities and no browsing and consolidating options. Numerous comparison tests by title, author, journal names and publication year alone or in combination have shown poor results by both the original and the updated versions of GS in comparison with the WoS and Scopus (11, 16). GS has remained in beta status since its release.

A series of tests using all the papers published in 22 volumes of the *Asian Pacific Journal of Allergy and Immunology* (APJAI) was conducted in order to trace down the reasons for the prevalent and obvious underreporting and the occasional and more subtle over-reporting of the citedness scores by GS in comparison with WoS.

2 Methods

APJAI is a quarterly journal published by Mahidol University's Department of Microbiology and Immunology for the Allergy and Immunology Society of Thailand. None of its articles is yet available digitally. It has been published since 1983, and is covered by many databases - although to different extent, such as CAB Abstracts (137 items), CSA Life Science Collection (204), Global Health (225), HealthStar (308), EMBASE (552), BIOSIS Previews (573). Medline has the most comprehensive coverage of APJAI, with a total of 698 records (18 of which had an in-process status), from the first issue to the last issue (at the time of the testing) of December, 2004 By the time of this writing in June, 2005 WoS has added 10 records in May for articles published in the first 2005 issue of APJAI, in addition to the 675 records found during the test period, making it the second database with the most comprehensive coverage of the target journal.

All the records were downloaded from Medline and imported into a spreadsheet to serve as a master list of 698 records. The records found in WoS for all the articles published in APJAI before 2005 were also downloaded and merged into the spreadsheet for an item by item comparison of unique items, covered by one but not the other database. WoS made it easy to search for records of APJAI articles because it has a standard abbreviated format for each journal names, and also allows the browsing and searching of the source journal name index in a flexible way, to see if any record with non-standard format may have slipped through authority control. ISI also makes efforts to correct the erroneous citations so prevalent even in the best scholarly journals, but this is a Sisyphean task.

WoS also makes it easy to import records by offering the saving of records in a tab delimited format which in turn can be directly imported into a spreadsheet. The content of the records to be export may be defined by the users who may include not only the bibliographic records, but also the number of references (NR field), and the citedness score (the number of times the paper was cited by articles processed for the Science, Social Science, and Arts & Humanities Index databases of ISI.

Downloading the TC (times cited by) data element is a very important and currently unique feature of WoS. Scopus has this feature for its native download option, but not for the tab delimited option offered through RefWorks since June 2005. CSA which is not merely a producer of datafiles but also a host for its own databases and those of third parties, as well as the developer of the RefWorks software may reconsider its earlier decision to exclude the downloading of the citedness score along with traditional bibliographic data elements. .

Finding and exporting the records for articles published in APJAI from Google Scholar was a daunting task. GS does not offer browsing the source journal index, and its capabilities for searching by journal names are very limited. There is no exact phrase searching for the journal name field. This makes it impossible to search for journals whose title is part of the longer titles of other journals, such as Immunology which appears in the title of many journals, such as *Immunology & Cell Biology, Immunology Letters, Immunology Today*. Although for this test this problem was not an issue, it is a serious limitation in many other cases. So is the lack of truncation option, which would have been needed to find the incorrect variations (*Asia Pacific Journal* instead of *Asian Pacific Journal*) and the inconsistent and often irrational abbreviations of journal title words (Allerg, Aller, even All) in GS. It was a painstakingly long and recursive process to find all the reasonable and many of the unreasonable journal name variants in GS. These strange and redundant abbreviations are generated by GS even when its source (which happens to be Medline for this and many other journals), has already a consistently applied abbreviated journal name: Asian Pac J Allergy Immunol. This is a well-known fact among programmers who deal with metadata-enriched bibliographic records not just with unstructured masses of Web pages.

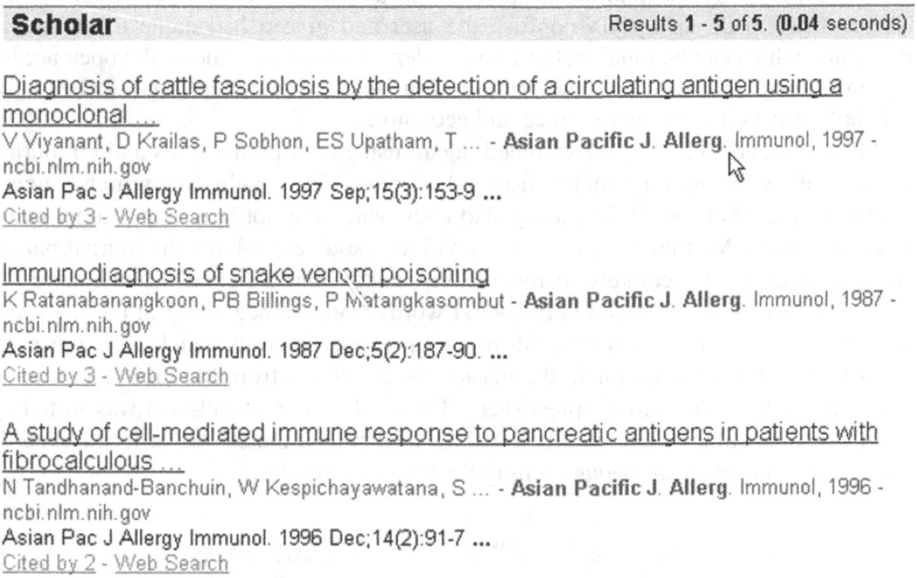

Scholar   Results **1 - 5** of **5**. (**0.04** seconds)

Diagnosis of cattle fasciolosis by the detection of a circulating antigen using a monoclonal ...
V Viyanant, D Krailas, P Sobhon, ES Upatham, T ... - **Asian Pacific J**. **Allerg**. Immunol, 1997 -
ncbi.nlm.nih.gov
Asian Pac J Allergy Immunol. 1997 Sep;15(3):153-9 ...
Cited by 3 - Web Search

Immunodiagnosis of snake venom poisoning
K Ratanabanangkoon, PB Billings, P Matangkasombut - **Asian Pacific J**. **Allerg**. Immunol, 1987 -
ncbi.nlm.nih.gov
Asian Pac J Allergy Immunol. 1987 Dec;5(2):187-90. ...
Cited by 3 - Web Search

A study of cell-mediated immune response to pancreatic antigens in patients with fibrocalculous ...
N Tandhanand-Banchuin, W Kespichayawatana, S ... - **Asian Pacific J**. **Allerg**. Immunol, 1996 -
ncbi.nlm.nih.gov
Asian Pac J Allergy Immunol. 1996 Dec;14(2):91-7 ...
Cited by 2 - Web Search

Fig. 1. Strange journal abbreviation variant in GS

GS does not offer any options for exporting, let alone for format alternatives. Results were saved as HTML files and manually converted into a tab delimited format for importing and merging into the spreadsheet of the master list of records for APJAI articles.

The merged records were sorted by various sort key combinations (author-title, publication-year-author, etc.) to facilitate the determination of unique records which occur in WoS but not in GS, in GS but not in WoS, and in Medline but not in GS. This latter was needed because about 10% of the Medline records for APJAI articles did not show up in GS when searching for the most common format Asian Pac J Allergy Immunol. Some of the searches for variant and erroneous journal names yielded "only" 3-5 matches for each, the search term Asian Pacific J Allergy Immunol found 19 hits in addition to the 615 hits by the most commonly used journal name variant.

Merging and pairing of twin records was not a simple process because the transliterated Asian names sometimes use the first name for the last name, and the transliteration is not consistent among the sources either. There are also spelling variations which scatter two or more records for the same article. For example, the title found in WoS as "A 1st Report on Pediatric Sarcoidosis in Thailand" appears as "A first report of pediatric sarcoidosis in Thailand" in GS which correctly followed the spelling in the article. While the uppercase and lowercase differences do not matter, the 1st and First, pediatric and paediatric variations separated twin records in the spreadsheet of merged records which should have appeared adjacent to each other. In GS it adds to the problem of titles (or what GS presents as titles), that sometimes they are preceded by section titles, such as Original article, or Short communication, and/or display only the end of the actual title as illustrated by this extract below. These titles made up by GS confuse the user and give a bad name to automatic extraction which can be much better done as demonstrated in some of the open access systems using autonomous citation indexing such as CiteSeer and RePEC for scholarly papers in computer science and economics.

Missing records in GS were searched again using only partial titles and no journal name to allow fishing for matches from a larger set. These additional searches found additional records from GS including also ones which did not have any journal name even though the Medline records used by GS as a source did have the journal names in the correct field accurately. It remains enigmatic how GS could leave behind the journal names, why did it chop off several words from the beginning of the titles and how many records are effected in GS by this practice. Records which were retrieved from WoS but did not appear in the master list generated from Medline (and thus in GS) were added to the master spreadsheet. The final master spreadsheet was sorted by year, title, and "times cited by" (TC) values to facilitate the efforts to locate records with variant and even erroneous spelling for the same article,

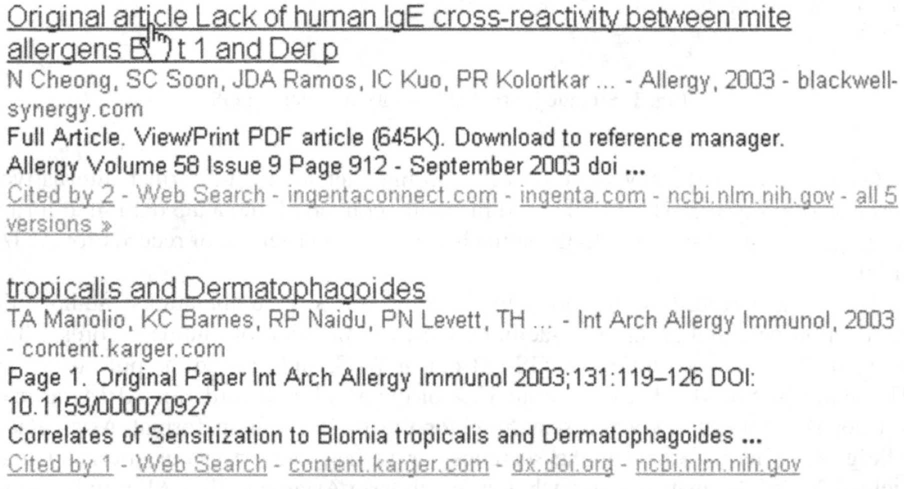

Original article Lack of human IgE cross-reactivity between mite allergens B t 1 and Der p

N Cheong, SC Soon, JDA Ramos, IC Kuo, PR Kolortkar ... - Allergy, 2003 - blackwell-synergy.com
Full Article. View/Print PDF article (645K). Download to reference manager.
Allergy Volume 58 Issue 9 Page 912 - September 2003 doi ...
Cited by 2 - Web Search - ingentaconnect.com - ingenta.com - ncbi.nlm.nih.gov - all 5 versions »

tropicalis and Dermatophagoides

TA Manolio, KC Barnes, RP Naidu, PN Levett, TH ... - Int Arch Allergy Immunol, 2003 - content.karger.com
Page 1. Original Paper Int Arch Allergy Immunol 2003;131:119-126 DOI: 10.1159/000070927
Correlates of Sensitization to Blomia tropicalis and Dermatophagoides ...
Cited by 1 - Web Search - content.karger.com - dx.doi.org - ncbi.nlm.nih.gov

Fig. 2. "Enhanced" and chopped off titles in GS

3 Findings

Medline had 698 source records, WoS had 675 and GS returned after many recursive searches a total of 680 source records. GS includes in its results not only source records but also mini records extracted from the bibliographies of full text articles published in journals whose publishers offered unfettered access for Google's crawlers. These are identified with the [CITATION} prefix in the result list. These must be consolidated when counting the number of hits reported by GS for a search, and also when judging the citedness score of articles. The inability of GS to match and consolidate source and citing items is detrimental also for the end-users In the above case the two entries are not close enough when searching about Blomia tropicalis without limiting to journal name. The first with 8 citing articles is ranked (listed) as item #21 in the result list, and the second with 5 citing articles as item #30. With the aggregate citedness score of 13 the article would be listed as item #12. More poignantly, with the aggregate citedness score this item turns out to be the most cited article in the entire run of APJAI in GS. Such discrepancies are difficult to identify for articles with much higher citedness scores scattered into several entries.

WoS did not have records for any of the 35 documents published in 1983 in APJAI. Records for 4 additional papers on the master list created from Medline were not found in WoS. On the other hand, Wos had 15 records which were not present in Medline (and thus in GS). These are mostly bibliographic citations about collections of abstracts of the meetings of the Hong Kong Society for Immunology, and the Allergy and Immunology Society of Thailand.

From WoS and Medline combined a total of 713 records could be retrieved for APJAI. Google had no unique source records for APJAI. Beyond the 15 documents GS also missed some records from Medline. In addition GS did not have records for the articles in the last issue of APJAI, presumably because the crawlers of GS did not visit the Medline database after records were added to it about those articles. The year by year break-down of the number of records for APJAI illustrates these minor discrepancies between WoS and GS for the target journal.

Culture of Blomia tropicalis and IgE immunoblot characterization of its allergenicity
FC Yi, FT Chew, S Jimenez, KY Chua, BW Lee - Asian Pac J Allergy Immunol, 1999
- ncbi.nlm.nih.gov
Culture of Blomia tropicalis and IgE immunoblot characterization of its allergenicity. Yi FC, Chew FT, Jimenez S, Chua KY, Lee BW. ...
Cited by 8 - Web Search

[CITATION] **Culture of Blomia tropicalis** and IgE immunoblot of its allergenicity
FC Yi, FT Chew, S Jimenez, KY Chua, BW Lee - Asian Pac J Allergy Immunol, 1999
Cited by 5 - Web Search

Fig. 3. Split citedness scores for the same article in two records (juxtaposed for illustration by exact title phrase searching)

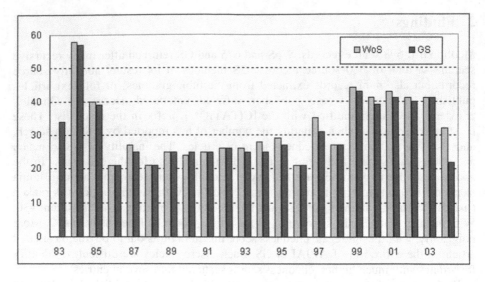

Fig. 4. Comparable number of records in every year (except for 1983 and 2004) in WoS and GS

After consolidating the scattered entries and scores for each item in GS the normalized scores were compared with the scores reported by WoS. The differences in the aggregate year-by year citedness scores are significant. The total citedness score for the 675 articles in WoS was 1,355, and for the 680 articles in GS it was 595. WoS reported 275 records which were not cited, GS had 422 such records.

The item-by item comparison and analysis showed that in 45 records GS had a higher citedness score than WoS, mostly by one citation (28 records) or two citations only (12 records). In three records GS had three more citations from a Chinese, a Kuwaiti and a Turkish journal not covered by WoS. In one record GS had 5 more citing documents, most from some procedural manuals.

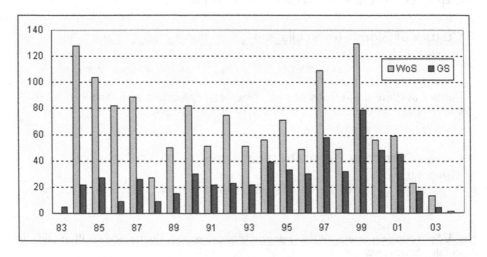

Fig. 5. Significant differences in the aggregated citedness scores

WoS had 302 articles for which it had more citing documents than GS. The largest difference was for an 1986 article cited by 28 articles in WoS, and by 3 articles in GS. The second largest discrepancy of 31 vs 10 citing documents was for the article shown below.

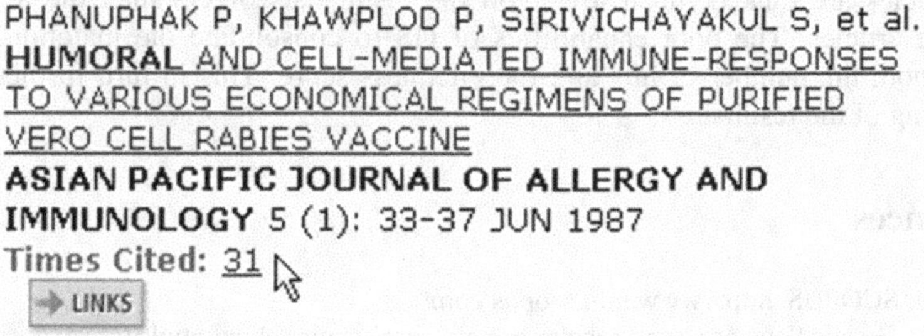

PHANUPHAK P, KHAWPLOD P, SIRIVICHAYAKUL S, et al.
HUMORAL AND CELL-MEDIATED IMMUNE-RESPONSES
TO VARIOUS ECONOMICAL REGIMENS OF PURIFIED
VERO CELL RABIES VACCINE
**ASIAN PACIFIC JOURNAL OF ALLERGY AND
IMMUNOLOGY** 5 (1): 33-37 JUN 1987
Times Cited: 31

➡ LINKS

Fig. 6. Article reported as cited by 31 papers in journals processed by WoS

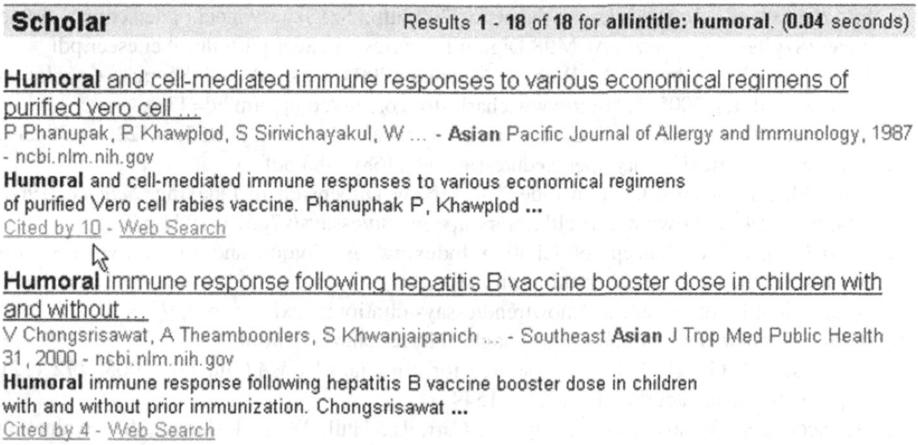

Scholar   Results 1 - 18 of 18 for **allintitle: humoral**. (0.04 seconds)

Humoral and cell-mediated immune responses to various economical regimens of
purified vero cell ...
P Phanupak, P Khawplod, S Sirivichayakul, W ... - **Asian** Pacific Journal of Allergy and Immunology, 1987
- ncbi.nlm.nih.gov
Humoral and cell-mediated immune responses to various economical regimens
of purified Vero cell rabies vaccine. Phanuphak P, Khawplod ...
Cited by 10 - Web Search

Humoral immune response following hepatitis B vaccine booster dose in children with
and without ...
V Chongsrisawat, A Theamboonlers, S Khwanjaipanich ... - Southeast **Asian** J Trop Med Public Health
31, 2000 - ncbi.nlm.nih.gov
Humoral immune response following hepatitis B vaccine booster dose in children
with and without prior immunization. Chongsrisawat ...
Cited by 4 - Web Search

Fig. 7. Same article reported as cited by 10 documents processed by GS

4 Conclusions

WoS identifies far more citing sources per source documents than GS. WoS sources are limited to serial publications, but most of them are among the most prestigious journals in their respective disciplines. WoS makes available the list of journals (20) processed for its citation indexes (19). ISI's competence and experience in the theory and practice of citation indexing is apparent from the test.

The main virtue of GS is that currently it is free for anyone. It is certainly an asset for those who cannot afford the professional multidisciplinary citation-enhanced databases or who need only a few good scholarly articles on a subject. GS is limited to the sources made available for its crawlers by publishers, and to open access sources with widely differing qualities. Thousands of scholarly journals and millions of articles are ignored by GS, or are underreported in terms of citedness. Many of them are top ranked ones in their respective categories such as *Vaccine* and the *Journal of Allergy and Clinical Immunology* in this test where many articles from these journals citing papers in APJAI were ignored by GS and thus not counted for the citedness score. For the scholarly users it can be detrimental as many of the most cited articles are ranked much lower on the result lists of GS than the average or mediocre articles. The poor capabilities of GS to consolidate the matching records inflates both the number of hits and the citedness score. This in turn further distorts the ranking of the results.

References

1. About SCOPUS. http://www.info.scopus.com/
2. About Google Scholar. http://scholar.google.com/scholar/about.html
3. Bollacker, K. D., Lawrence, S. and Lee, C., CiteSeer: An Autonomous Web Agent for Automatic Retrieval and Identification of Interesting Publications. in: *Proceedings of 2nd International ACM Conference on Autonomous Agents*, ACM Press, 1998, pp. 116-123. http://citeseer.csail.mit.edu/cache/papers/cs/209/http:zSzzSzwww.neci.nj.nec.comzSzhome pageszSzgileszSzpaperszSzACM98.Digital.Libraries.CiteSeer.pdf/giles98citeseer.pdf
4. Deis, L. and Goodman, D., Web of Science (2004 version) and Scopus. *Charleston Advisor* [online], 2005, 6. http://www.charlestonco.com/comp.cfm?id=43
5. Garfield, E., Citation Indexes for Science. *Science*, 1955, 122, 108-111. http://www.garfield.library.upenn.edu/essays/v6p468y1983.pdf
6. Garfield, E., "Science Citation Index" – A New Dimension in Indexing. *Science*, 1964, 144, 649-654. http://www.garfield.library.upenn.edu/essays/v7p525y1984.pdf
7. Garfield, E., The Concept of Citation Indexing: A Unique and Innovative Tool for Navigating the Research Literature. [online]
   http://scientific.thomson.com/knowtrend/essays/citationindexing/concept/
8. Google Scholar Help. http://scholar.google.com/scholar/help.html
9. Henderson, J. Google Scholar: A source for clinicians? *CMAJ* June 7, 2005; 172 (12). http://www.cmaj.ca/cgi/reprint/172/12/1549 .
10. Hitchcock, S., Woukeu, A., Brody, T., Carr, L., Hall, W. and Harnad, S., Evaluating Citebase, an Open Access Web-based Citation-ranked Search and Impact Discovery Service. [online], 2003. http://opcit.eprints.org/evaluation/Citebase-evaluation/evaluation-report.html
11. Jacsó, P., Google Scholar Redux. *Gale — Reference Reviews* [online] (June 2005). http://googlescholar2.notlong.com
12. Jacsó, P., Google Scholar: the Pros and the Cons. *Online Information Review*, 2005, 29, 208-214. http://dx.doi.org/10.1108/14684520510598066
13. Jacsó, P., Citation Enhanced Indexing/Abstracting Databases. *Online Information Review*, 2004, 28, 235 238. http://dx.doi.org/10.1108/14684520410543689
14. Jacsó, P., Citedness Scores for Filtering Information and Ranking Search Results. *Online Information Review*, 2004, 28, 371-376. http://dx.doi.org/10.1108/14684520410564307
15. Jacsó, P., Browsing Indexes of Cited References. *Online Information Review*, 2005, 29, 107-112. http://dx.doi.org/10.1108/14684520510583972
16. Jacsó, P., As We May Search: Comparison of Major Features of Citation-based and Citation-enhanced Databases (Web of Science, Scopus, and Google Scholar). *Current Science*, 2005, 88 [in press]

17. Kennedy, S. and   Price, G. Big News: "Google Scholar" is Born. *Resourceshelf*, 2004
    http://www.resourceshelf.com/2004/11/wow-its-google-scholar.html
18. Myhill, M., Google Scholar review. *Charleston Advisor* [online], 2005, 6.
    http://www.charlestonco.com/review.cfm?id=225
19. Thomson — ISI Citation Products. http://www.isinet.com/cit/
20. Thomson — ISI Journal List. http://www.isinet.com/journals/

Enhancing Services in a Digital Age – 10 Years of Experience from the Systems Librarians' Perspective

Edward F. Spodick and Ki-Tat Lam

The Hong Kong University of Science and Technology Library,
Clear Water Bay, Kowloon, Hong Kong
{lbspodic, lblkt}@ust.hk

Abstract. This paper is an attempt by the authors to share their experiences in equipping a young academic library with the information technologies needed to enhance services in a digital environment. After discussing the advent of *digital libraries*, the paper explores a progression of projects which make use of advancing technologies, from Web interfaces to XML metadata, and their effectiveness in a non-English (CJK) environment. These digital initiatives have become a core component of the Hong Kong University of Science and Technology (HKUST) Library's service infrastructure, in addition to enhancing its traditional roles. The past ten years' accelerating pace of technological change has had a tremendous impact on the provision of library services. Through this paper, the authors have provided one institution's experiences both in benefiting from and contributing to these changes.

1 Introduction

The Hong Kong University of Science and Technology is a very young institution, having its first student intake in 1991. The early years of the University coincided with several streams of radical change and optimism – from an incredibly accelerated expansion of information technology to the economic and political progression of Asia, including a peaceful and mostly welcomed change of sovereignty for Hong Kong. Locally, the University was established and funded to serve as a leader in research and development, and was positioned as the leading edge of an expansion in tertiary education for Hong Kong. In a few short years the University has become ranked in the top tier in Hong Kong, and in many fields it holds such a place globally.

All of this was a major factor in the Library's ability to innovate and to embrace new techniques and technologies during what has been perhaps the most tumultuous upheaval in librarianship and the provision of library services in the history of our profession. From the Library's founding, it embraced new technologies in an effort to enhance information access and services. In 1991, the Library rolled out one of the first fully Chinese-capable multilingual integrated library systems in the world and the first large-scale campus-wide CD-ROM network in Asian academic libraries; 1992 saw the installation of the largest networked full text database system in Asia, followed in 1993 by an early Course Reserve Image System. And 1995 saw the first academic library Web server in Hong Kong. In subsequent years the Library established a mirror site for

E.A. Fox et al. (Eds.): ICADL 2005, LNCS 3815, pp. 370–374, 2005.
© Springer-Verlag Berlin Heidelberg 2005

some subscription databases, a wide-scale implementation of native XML-based database development projects, and a host of other innovations [1].

Upheaval, change and challenge have been our constant companions, and we believe they have been a significant factor driving the Library and University's achievements.

2   From Traditional to Digital

The past few decades have seen a remarkable alteration in the technology available for information processing. Coupled with the ability to obtain ever more powerful equipment and more capable software for an ever-decreasing investment, this has allowed more smaller or less well funded libraries to participate in the exploration and integration of technology for the improvement of operations, collections and services.

Initially the advances promised since the development of a standard for MAchine Readable Catalog records were available only to the largest institutions. Even the smallest school library has the option to do far more than merely replace their card catalog with an electronic version. And thus the concept of a "Digital Library" began to be more than just a theoretical exercise – it became a topic of increasingly common discussion and experimentation. This was especially relevant to a small library in a brand new university – one that had the option of "going digital" from its creation.

While there may continue to be discussion of the differences between definitions used for "digital", "electronic" and "virtual" libraries, the authors agree with Roy Tennant when he states that while the term "electronic library" may be more inclusive it is "digital library" which has become the accepted terminology [2].

There are three basic ways of defining what is meant by the term "digital library":

1. Libraries providing a) access to digital information using a variety of networks, including the Internet, and b) services in an automated environment
2. The result of projects to digitize library materials for network access
3. A discipline which refers to research on the theories and technologies for the building of digital libraries

The first definition most fits the ongoing efforts of the authors and their colleagues. As part of these efforts, the second definition is representative of attempts to provide access and improve services in relation to materials that exist in the print collection.

The third definition comes into play as part of the ongoing efforts of the authors and others to learn how to incorporate new technologies and methodologies into the services and collections, as well as in their work to enhance collaborative efforts and to contribute new ideas to the profession as a whole.

One of the most important points the authors wish to stress is that the term "digital library" simply reflects a fundamental shift in **how** libraries do what they do, rather than in **what** they do. Since their initial establishment, libraries have provided access to information and services to assist their patrons in obtaining this access and utilizing the information acquired through it. None of this is new. Improvements in information technology have allowed a much greater degree of flexibility in all stages of these processes. But the basic mission of a library to support its user community through enhanced access and services remains the same.

3 Digital Libraries in Practice

The HKUST Library began testing the Lynx and NCSA Mosaic Web browsers, for connection to Gopher, WAIS and Web sites, in 1994. In view of its potential capability for becoming the library's gateway to information, serving not just plain-text but multi-media documents, approval was obtained to set up a Library Web Server. Officially released in May 1995, it was the first such server in Hong Kong and the region.

Once the web infrastructure and technology were in place, a progression of digital library projects began to take place. The following sections discuss a selected number of issues and lessons learned during the implementation of these projects.

3.1 Content Digitization and Web-Based Document Management System

In 1998, after more than four years of experience in digitizing course reserve materials in TIFF format for access from dedicated workstations, the authors began to base future digitization projects on Adobe's PDF document format with a Web interface. Although PDF is now a popular format for content delivery, it was not an easy decision seven years ago. PDF was selected because it was more portable and smaller than TIFF, with a free viewer which seamlessly launched as a web browser plug-in. The documents were digitized into PDF and hyperlinked to the bibliographic metadata. Text was extracted using Acrobat Capture and some Chinese OCR software.

Three digital library databases were created during that time, serving up HKUST Theses, the Digital University Archives and HKUST-related News Clippings.

It was also not an easy task at that time to identify a web-based document management system that could handle full-text searching and display of text in both English and Chinese. With much localization, the databases were created on a commercial document management system called BASIS, which was later replaced by native XML database systems, although the basic design concepts remained unchanged.

3.2 Interchange of XML Metadata with the Library Catalog

The HKUST Library uses INNOPAC, an integrated library system, to host the Library Catalog and to provide automated library functions such as circulation, cataloging and acquisitions. The Library Catalog contains bibliographic metadata for all print, multimedia and electronic resources.

When building digital library databases, the authors frequently must export metadata from the Library Catalog to the database for indexing and displaying purposes. A pioneering attempt at HKUST to deploy XML technologies to extract the metadata from the Catalog in real-time began in 2000, using the INNOPAC's built-in *xrecord* command and XSL style sheets. These technologies were then adopted for most of HKUST's digital library projects, including an Electronic Journals database system rolled out in 2001.

XML is a very flexible format – being able to extract data in XML is critical to a Digital Library project's success. If your catalog or database does not have this capability yet, push the vendor hard or switch to something else.

3.3 CJK and Unicode

The HKUST Library has been working very actively with the INNOPAC vendor to enhance support for CJK (Chinese, Japanese, Korean) characters in the Library Catalog, which ensured that CJK bibliographic metadata can be seamlessly stored, indexed, searched, sorted and displayed.

With advances in computer hardware and operating system software, the past decade saw many critical CJK issues resolved [3]. However, Web technology, together with its increasing adoption of Unicode, has brought another layer of problems.

The CJK-using library communities have traditionally used a legacy character set known as EACC (East Asian Character Code). It is used in MARC 21, an international bibliographic metadata content description standard, for cataloging CJK materials. Both MARC 21 and EACC are maintained by the Library of Congress (LC) and are widely adopted by bibliographic metadata suppliers and systems vendors. The cross-walk problem of mapping between EACC and Unicode began to emerge when suppliers and vendors began to develop Web- and Unicode-based applications. A failure in mapping usually results in various types of display and searching problems.

In early 2003, Library staff conducted an analysis of the EACC-Unicode mapping of CJK characters in the HKUST Catalog and concluded that Hong Kong users of the INNOPAC system should work more closely with the vendor to clean up the mappings. A Hong Kong Innovative Users Group (HKIUG) working group made up of members from the HKUST, City University of Hong Kong, Chinese University of Hong Kong and University of Hong Kong libraries was then established to develop an HKIUG version of the EACC-Unicode mapping table. The table was subsequently adopted by the vendor for implementation at its customer sites, with the first implementation being at HKUST in late 2003.

3.4 Global Name Access Control

In 2002, the HKUST Library began the development of an XML Name Access Control Repository [4] to address the problems experienced by catalogers and catalog users in identifying personal authors whose names are in non-Latin scripts [5].

In cataloging, the use of names in bibliographic records is controlled by authority records, and the process involved is called Authority Control. The main purpose of name authority control is to authorize a form of a name (known as the established form) to be used in bibliographic records as an access point. The concept of Access Control as proposed by Barnhart [6] expands on the role of an authority record by enriching into a central place for looking up various forms of a name, allowing the linking of variant forms without declaring any of them to be the authorized form.

It was concluded from this research project that distributed repositories of metadata for describing various forms of an author's name, with encoding in original scripts and their Latin forms, can be built globally by various bibliographic utilities, national libraries and library consortia to form a virtual name access control platform. To achieve this, there must be a mutually agreed-upon metadata schema for data interchange between repositories. The XML Name Access Control Repository is an initiative to promote the establishment of such a standard.

3.5 Open Source Software and Open Access

Thanks to the open source software movement the authors have been extensively using such tools for library applications. Two of our projects were based on the open source software *DSpace*. *EPrints* and *DSpace* were then the only options, and *EPrints* did not support Unicode, making it useless when CJK characters are required.

The HKUST Institutional Repository was established in early 2003 [7] to create a permanent record of the University's research and scholarly output. It was the first such initiative in Asia. By allowing the content of the Repository to be globally and openly accessible, we are contributing to the international open access effort that campaigns for free and unrestricted online access to research literature.

The Digital University Archives on DSpace was released in late 2004. In contrast to open access, the Archives requires authorization. The DSpace source code was modified to search and display only authorized documents based on LDAP authentication, so different user groups would access different document sets. This kind of localization would not have been feasible if DSpace were not open source.

4 Conclusion

These are exciting times to be a Librarian. The expansions in information technology discussed in this paper have opened up many new vistas of information and service provision. The possibilities continue to be enormous, limited more by the inability to find time to explore them than by fiscal constraints. The authors urge all Librarians to set aside some time on a periodic basis to simply **think** about new options and technologies they see in their readings and explorations, and **ponder** how to relate them to solving identified local needs for the traditional library roles of providing access to needed information and services both to support that access and to improve users' ability to utilize the information obtained.

References

1. Library's First Ten Years. (http://library.ust.hk/info/exhibit/sep2001/)
2. Digital v. Electronic v. Virtual Libraries. (http://sunsite.berkeley.edu/mydefinitions.html)
3. K.T. Lam. Chinese Information Access and Retrieval: Issues Facing Libraries. Presentation at the Seminar on Chinese Information Processing in Libraries, January 1998, The HKUST Library. (http://hdl.handle.net/1783.1/1924)
4. XML Name Access Control Repository. (http://library.ust.hk/info/nac/)
5. K.T. Lam. XML and global name access control, OCLC Systems & Services, vol. 18, no. 2, 2002, p.88-96. (http://hdl.handle.net/1783.1/443)
6. Barnhart, L. Access control records: prospects and challenges. Authority Control in the 21st Century: An Invitational Conference, March 31-April 1, 1996. (http://www.oclc.org/oclc/man/authconf/)
7. K.T. Lam. DSpace in action: implementing the HKUST Institutional Repository system. International Conference on Developing Digital Institutional Repositories : Experiences and Challenges, December 9-10, 2004, Hong Kong. (http://hdl.handle.net/1783.1/2023)

Constructing a Wrapper-Based DRM System for Digital Content Protection in Digital Libraries

Jen-Hao Hsiao[1,2], Jenq-Haur Wang[1], Ming-Syan Chen[2], Chu-Song Chen[1], and Lee-Feng Chien[1]

[1] Institute of Information Science, Academia Sinica, Taiwan
{jenhao, jhwang, song, lfchien}@iis.sinica.edu.tw
[2] Department of Electrical Engineering, Nation Taiwan University, Taiwan
mschen@cc.ee.ntu.edu.tw

Abstract. Conventional digital libraries utilize access control and digital watermarking techniques to protect their digital content. These methods, however, have drawbacks. First, after passing the identity authentication process, authorized users can easily redistribute the digital assets. Second, it is impractical to expect a digital watermarking scheme to prevent all kinds of attack. Thus, how to enforce property rights after digital content has been released to authorized users is a crucial and challenging issue. In this paper, we propose a wrapper-based approach to digital content protection that integrates digital watermarking, cryptography, information protection technology, and a rights model. In this rights enforcement environment, the behavior of all content players is monitored and digital content can only be accessed after certain usage rules have been satisfied. Furthermore, the proposed architecture can be easily integrated into any digital content player, or even existing DRM systems in digital libraries. With the protection of the proposed DRM system, the abuse of digital content can be drastically reduced.

Keywords: Digital rights management, digital watermark, content protection, intellectual property, access control.

1 Introduction

With rapid development of the Internet and computer technology, digital content, including digital images, video, and music, can be distributed instantaneously across the Internet. However, digital content in digital world differs from objects in real world, since it can be easily copied, altered, and distributed to a large number of recipients. This almost certainly causes copyright infringement and revenue losses to content owners. The National Digital Archives Program (NDAP) in Taiwan has amassed a rich collection of cultural and historical artifacts. These assets have been digitized to enhance their preservation, and make them more accessible to users. The metadata and digital content storage systems are called archival systems, and – like other types of digital content – they too face the problem of piracy. Thus, content holders are sometimes unwilling to release digital content, because their intellectual property rights could be infringed. To protect high-value digital content and avoid

E.A. Fox et al. (Eds.): ICADL 2005, LNCS 3815, pp. 375–379, 2005.
© Springer-Verlag Berlin Heidelberg 2005

digital piracy, we need a system that prevents unauthorized access and manages content usage rights.

In this paper, we propose a wrapper-based DRM system that enhances the protection of digital content and drastically reduces piracy. The remainder of the paper is organized as follows. In the next section, some previous works are discussed. The architecture of proposed DRM system is described in Section 3. We then present a brief discussion in Section 4, followed by our conclusions in Section 5.

2 Related Work

To prevent the abuse of digital content, most digital libraries and museums adopt digital watermarking [8] techniques to guard their digital images. Though useful, watermark-based image protection systems are still not robust enough to resist a variety of image attacks. Digital Rights Management (DRM) is a protocol of hardware and software services and technologies governing the authorized use of digital content and managing any consequences of that use throughout the entire life-cycle of the content (as defined by IDC). DRM is a new concept that can be used to protect high-value digital assets and control their distribution and usage. The design of a DRM system must address the following key issues: (1) a digital rights enforcement (DRE) environment, (2) digital rights, and (3) standardization for interoperability. In [9], the author proposed a typical DRM system architecture, including several essential components. Then, in 2004, Pramod et al. [7] proposed that DRM should be adopted as a layered framework, whereby various services are offered to users of the digital content at each layer. In addition, Bogdan et al.[1] proposed a security architecture that enables digital rights management of home networks. The concept of an "authorized domain" is used to authenticate compliant devices, instead of relying on expensive public key cryptographic operations. Although the above works suggest novel architectures for a DRM system, they do not fully address the three issues mentioned earlier. For example, in the area of rights enforcement, authorized users could still distribute digital assets easily after they pass the identity authentication process. To overcome this problem, Nicolakis et al. [6] developed a DRM system called MediaRights that protects digital images. However, although this kind of architecture solves the rights management problem, a customized image viewer is not convenient for users. Furthermore, the circulation of digital assets is seriously impaired. Hence, how to enforce the usage rules and protect content owners' property rights after images have been released are the major challenges in DRM research. Several commercial DRM solutions, such as InterTrust, Alpha-Tec, Digimarc, and LTU, are available. But the requirements of digital libraries vary enormously and differ from those of industry. It is very unlikely that existing commercial systems can meet the demands of digital libraries. Building a DRM system for digital libraries based on existing commercial solutions without any modification is therefore impractical.

3 A Wrapper-Based DRM System

Multimedia Center (MMC) [2], the core of the archival systems in NDAP, provides an integrated tool that helps content managers store and manage multimedia files efficiently. It also enables users to access digital content in a convenient manner. To protect digital images in MMC, we use the proposed DRM techniques to attach specific restriction on the use of digital content, which effectively reduces illegal copying. The security in MMC could be improved substantially to protect precious digital assets from illegal use.

3.1 System Architecture

The majority of multimedia files in MMC are digital images, classified as low, middle, and high-resolution images. Fig. 1 gives an overview of the wrapper-based DRM system, which consists of two building blocks: the server side preprocessing module and the client side protection module. To facilitate player-independent encapsulation of rights and encryption information, we propose the following wrapper-based approach.

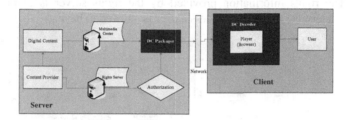

Fig. 1. Overview of the Wrapper-based DRM System

3.2 Rights Model

There are several existing rights models and rights expression languages (RELs), such as XrML and ODRL. XrML is a general purpose REL with good expressive power. For content protection in digital libraries, it is only necessary to consider the following restrictions: play/view, print, save, valid date, and compliant player. A user can only play, print, or save digital images when he authorized to do so. The valid date limits the time that digital images are accessible, while the compliant player ensures that digital images can only be accessed by specific machines.

3.3 DC Packager

The DC Packager envelops digital images in a protected file. An invisible digital watermark representing the copyright of NDAP is then embedded into images prior to release. The usage rules derived from the rights server are then combined with the watermarked image to form a new content package, which is then encrypted for security. The resulting file is called a "protected digital content" file, meaning that the digital image is ready for distribution, and that the usage rules can be enforced with certainty.

3.4 DC Wrapper

DC Wrapper enforces the rules related to the use of digital images. As shown in Fig. 2, after a user downloads a protected file from the network and views it on a player (e.g., a browser), DC Wrapper launches automatically and monitors the user's behavior. Furthermore, the digital images are released with specific restrictions on their usage. If these rules are violated, or a user refuses to view images under monitoring by DC Wrapper, the content is rendered unavailable. DC Wrapper is implemented with a binary instrumentation technique called a Detours tool [3][4], which intercepts OS functions by re-writing target function images. Note that the wrapper-based design allows more flexibility in the choice of an underlying content player that is independent of the DRM modules. DC Wrapper's mechanisms decode encrypted digital content based on predefined rules, and transform the content into a readable format for the content player. Note that DC Wrapper monitors the behavior of the player rather than acting as a multimedia player itself. Hence, there is no need to use a customized player to play digital content. The rights information provided by the rights server is employed by DC Wrapper to determine the kind of access a user is allowed to have.

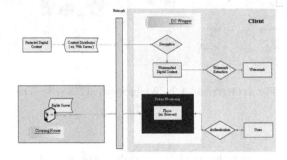

Fig. 2. An operational view of the DC Wrapper

4 Discussions

Our proposed architecture has three major advantages. First, the wrapper-based approach can be a stand-alone system, or it can be integrated into existing content players, even commercial DRM systems. Second, the difficult problem of enforcing usage rules when digital content is playing is addressed by DC Wrapper. It monitors the behavior of the content player, and prevents illegal access to digital content. Third, the proposed architecture enables two or more intellectual property rights protection systems to cooperate and complement each other.

Since the DC Wrapper is implemented using a binary interceptor approach, it is kind of OS dependent. This is a trade-off between better control and platform independence when considering the integration with various existing DRM systems. After all, intercepting the message in the OS level is more robust and compatible than in the un-standardized application level. Just like any other system security tools, there is no 100% secure DRM system which can always survive all kinds of attacks.

For example, a malicious media player could possibly bypass all the usage rules. However, the development of such a malicious player is so complicated and time-consuming that is not technically feasible for an average user. It is also what we try to do to raise the barrier for the abuse of digital content.

5 Conclusions

The distribution of digital content requires content protection and rights management in order to engender trust between the parties involved. Trusted computing platforms and the integration of DRM components into the digital libraries would probably encourage content providers to release precious digital assets. In this paper, we have proposed a novel rights enforcement environment that provides stronger protection for digital images, and thereby drastically reduces the piracy of digital content.

Acknowledgements

This work was partially supported by the following grants: NSC 94-2422-H-001-006, 94-2422-H-001-007, and 94-2422-H-001-008. The authors would like to thank Dr. L. F. Chien and various professional parties in NDAP Research & Development of Technology Division for their contributions to this paper.

References

1. Bogdan C. Popescu, Frank L.A.J. Kamperman, "A DRM security architecture for home net-works", Proceedings of the 4th ACM workshop on Digital rights management, 2004. pp 1 – 10
2. Chen, Hsin Yu, Ho, Jan-Ming, "Multimedia Center: A Novel Multimedia File Management System in NDAP", The Second Workshop on Digital Archives Technologies, 22-23 July 2002. Pages:89-96
3. G. Hunt and D. Brubacher. "Detours: Binary interception of win32 functions". Proceed-ings of the 3rd USENIX Windows NT Symposium, July 1999 , pages 135-143
4. Lin, Tzung-Bo, Huang, Shih-Kun, "OpenDReaMS: A Generic DRM Wrapper for COTS Readers, The Third Workshop on Digital Archives Technologies", 5-6 Aug 2004, Pages: 289-295
5. Liu, Qiong; Reihaneh, Safavi-Naini; Sheppard, Nicholas Paul, "Digital rights management for content distribution", Proceedings of the Australasian information security workshop conference on ACSW frontiers 2003
6. Nicolakis, Theo; Pizano, Carlos E.; Prumo, Bianca; Webb, Mitchell, "Protecting Digital Archives at the Greek Orthodox Archdiocese of America", Proceedings of the 2003 ACM workshop on Digital rights management, October 2003
7. Pramod A. Jamkhedkar, Gregory L. Heileman, "DRM as a layered system", Proceedings of the 4th ACM workshop on Digital rights management, 2004, Pages: 11 - 21.
8. Serrao, C. Marques, J., "DIGIPIPE - a pipeline methodology for digital image production and protection", 4th EURASIP-IEEE Region 8 International Symposium on VIPromCom, 16-19 June 2002
9. Susanne Guth, A Sample DRM System, Lecture Notes in Computer Science, Volume 2770, November 2003, pp. 150 - 161

Digital Preservation Lifecycle Management for Multi-media Collections

Arcot Rajasekar[1], Reagan Moore[1], Fran Berman[1], and Brian Schottlaender[2]

[1] San Diego Supercomputer Center,
University of California at San Diego, California, USA
{sekar, moore, berman}@sdsc.edu
http://www.sdsc.edu
[2] UCSD Libraries,
University of California at San Diego, California, USA
becs@ucsd.edu

Abstract. Increasingly, intellectual content is "born digital." In order to make it as easy as possible for content creators to preserve their content for the long-term, preservation processes should be integrated into the content production lifecycle. Our project takes an existing video production workflow and integrates it with a digital preservation life-cycle management process that will enable the digital content to be archived for long-term preservation. The collection, "Conversations with History," is produced at the University of California, Berkeley, edited by University of California, San Diego–TV (UCSD-TV), and broadcast and Web-cast through UCTV. The proposed system will demonstrate an effective preservation methodology by demonstrating a standard reference model for digital preservation lifecycle management that can be integrated into active production workflows.

1 Introduction

In August 2003, the National Science Foundation and the Library of Congress sponsored a compelling report [3] that described the gap between the growing body of digital collections and the ability to capture, manage and preserve them: "... *from a long-term preservation perspective, there is a dark side to the rapid growth in digital information. The technologies, strategies, methodologies, and resources needed to manage digital information for the long term have not kept pace with innovations in the creation and capture of digital information.*" The report described the importance of working *now* to preserve the digital assets that represent the cultural history and intellectual capital of education, science and government institutions. These assets are threatened by lack of adequate infrastructure, lack of adequate resources, and technology evolution within access mechanisms, encoding formats, and storage systems. Over the last 10 years, a considerable body of literature has been generated by scientific and library communities enumerating the complex issues in digital preservation that need to be solved. [1,2,10].

In this paper, we outline a life-cycle management methodology for multi-media film/video digital collections that we are currently developing. We describe the

E.A. Fox et al. (Eds.): ICADL 2005, LNCS 3815, pp. 380–384, 2005.
© Springer-Verlag Berlin Heidelberg 2005

design, and automation of preservation processes that comprehend the accession, description, organization, and preservation of film/video collections and associated digital content.   The automation of these processes requires the integration of workflow systems that are used in active production with preservation systems, and the tracking of the execution of the preservation processes for completion and error recovery.   The inherent challenges include the extraction of relevant metadata to support long-term preservation and access, and retention and preservation of the video file itself and the derived products that are used to augment the video, together with the associated resource material all with minimal impact on the production workflow process.   We plan to explore how the process can be abstracted into a set of generic procedures for preserving other multi-media collections as well.

1.1 Exemplar Collection: "Conversations with History"

The exemplar video collection in our project is the video-taped interviews collection called the   "Conversations with History" [16], conducted by Harry Kreisler, a broadcast series taped at the University of California at Berkeley. The "Conversations with History" collection is produced in a distributed workflow environment, with a) the original presentation filmed at UCB, b) the video edited at the University of California, San Diego by the UCSD-TV [17] facility, c) the final broadcast and webcast performed by UCTV [18] and then d) the presentation published in a Web portal.   The multi-media assets for this collection includes video, audio, text transcripts, Web-based material, databases of administrative and descriptive metadata, derived video segments, copyrights, attributions, credits, and contains diverse types of data, created at multiple stages within the content production. The ability to incorporate and integrate preservation procedures within such a complex generation environments while minimizing the impact on production, represents a substantial challenge that we address in our project.

2   Preservation Dataflow

The application of archival processes requires the use of software automation technology to minimize the impact on the production processes.   In particular, the level of granularity for interaction with the production workflow needs to be quantified and optimized. As part of our integration process we have identified several processing steps that are part of this preservation lifecycle management. The multiple sources of the material, along with the processes that support capture of the material, the processes that organize the material into Archival Information Packages (AIPs), and the preservation processes that manage the AIPs within an archive are shown in Figure 1 that presents a workflow diagram of the preservation lifecycle management system using the Kepler workflow management system [13].

The preservation of the collection requires the application of traditional preservation processes of appraisal, accession, arrangement, description, preservation, and access. For each process, workflow modules are constructed to extract associated metadata, generate the AIPs, and register the material into the preservation environment.

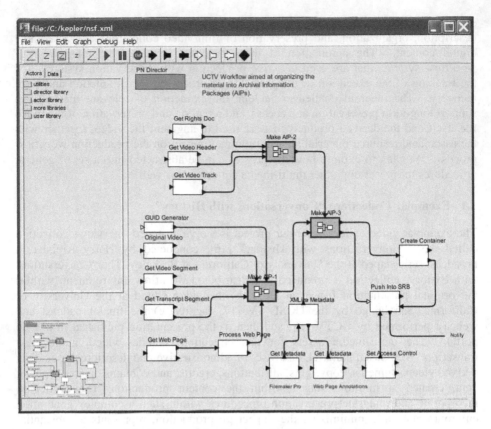

Fig. 1. Preservation Lifecycle Workflow in Kepler

Appraisal – the determination of which presentations within the "Conversations with History" collection are appropriate for preservation;

Accession – the controlled process by which the videos are imported and evaluated for completeness and correspondence to a preservation agreement;

Description– the process of assembling the context that will be used to describe provenance, integrity, and structural and behavioral characteristics of the video;

Arrangement – the process of structuring the metadata into a collection hierarchy, and aggregating digital entities into containers for storage management;

Storage – the storage of the material within a data grid to facilitate creation of replicas for disaster recovery, access controls to minimize risk of corruptions, and audit trails.

Preservation – the process of managing technology evolution and maintaining integrity by migrating to new media, new encoding formats, new information syntax, and new storage technologies as more cost effective systems become available; and

Access – the process of supporting discovery, manipulation, individual and bulk retrieval, and display of the videos.

3 Integration of Video Collection Workflow with Preservation Lifecycle

Our design of the integration environment is based on generic modules that can be used in a plug-and-play manner with other production workflows and hence will be applicable to other collections with similar characteristics. To achieve this level of abstraction, we use the following methodologies:

XML Interfaces for Inter-Module Communication: Our design modules are based on strong input-output characteristic definitions. We use XML to define the interfaces or 'ports' between the modules..

Push and Pull Interactions: Since our goal is to have minimal impact on the production workflow, the preservation dataflow should not impose any requirements on changes to the workflow. Using the strongly typed ports, one can custom-design push and pull versions of the modules, so that one can have them interact with the production workflow in an active (push) or passive (pull) modes of access.

Workflow Systems: Our design uses Kepler [13], a open source workflow system, to interconnect the modules into a customizable data flow architecture.

Data Grid Systems for Preservation: The Storage Resource Broker (SRB) [6,11,12] based data grid technology [5] is used to provide the preservation mechanisms needed to control and track the integrity of the archived collections [7,9]. The SRB supports organization of digital entities into collection hierarchies, making it possible to manage independently each preserved collection. The SRB toolkit also has provisions for crawling Web sites and registering the retrieved material into an SRB collection after re-linking URLs into SRB logical names. SRB is currently being used as a preservation environment for multiple federally funded projects, including the NARA [15] prototype persistent archive, the NHPRC Persistent Archive Testbed [8], and others [14]. In addition, the NSF National Science Digital Library persistent archive [4] is built on the SRB framework.

4 Conclusion

Independence between the production workflow and the preservation life-cycle management is a corner stone of our design. This requirement is mandated not only because preservation should not intrude on the production process but also to make the preservation life-cycle management to be easily portable and applicable to a wide range of production frameworks. The merits of our system will be seen in not only preserving the chosen exemplar collection, but also in its usage in preserving other video production pipelines. The project is currently underway and we plan to make a first release of the framework in the next few months.

Acknowledgement

The infrastructure that is being used in the project has been supported in part by the NSF and the Library of Congress under NSF Grant IIS-0456055, in part by the NSF Grant ACI-9619020 (National Archives and Records Administration supplement), in part by NSF ITR Grant IIS-0427196, in part by the NSF NSDL grant under sub-award S02-36645. The views and conclusions contained in this document are those of the authors and should not be interpreted as representing official policies, either expressed or implied, of the NSF, NARA or the LoC.

References

1. *Science and Engineering Through Cyberinfrastructure: Report of the National Science Foundation Blue-Ribbon Advisory Panel on Cyberinfrastructure.* Washington, D.C.: National Science Foundation, January 2003.
2. National Research Council. *Building an Electronic Records Archive at the National Archives and Records Administration*, National Academy Press, 2003.
3. Hedstrom, M., et. al. *It's About Time: Final Report of the Workshop on Research Challenges in Digital Archiving and Long-term Preservation, April 12-13, 2002*
4. NSDL, National Science Digital Library, http://www.nsdl.nsf.gov/indexl.html.
5. Moore, R. "Evolution of Data Grid Concepts", Global Grid Forum Data Area Workshop, January 2004.
6. SRB, Storage Resource Broker, Version 3.1, http://www.sdsc.edu/dice/srb, 2004.
7. Moore, R., et. al., "Collection-Based Persistent Digital Archives – Parts 1& 2", *D-Lib Magazine*, April/March 2000, http://www.dlib.org/
8. PAT, Persistent Archive Testbed, http://www.sdsc.edu/PAT.
9. Moore, R., "Preservation of Data, Information, and Knowledge," *Proceedings of the World Library Summit, Singapore, April 2002.*
10. OAIS Reference Model, http://ssdoo.gsfc.nasa.gov/nost/isoas/
11. Rajasekar, M. Wan, R. Moore, "mySRB and SRB, Components of a Data Grid", 11th High Performance Distributed Computing, Edinburgh, Scotland, 2002.
12. Rajasekar, A., M. Wan, R. Moore, A. Jagatheesan, G. Kremenek, "Real Experiences with Data Grids - Case studies in using the SRB," *Proc. International Conference on High Performance Computing, 2002.*
13. Kepler: A System for Scientific Workflows, http://kepler-project.org/
14. Marciano, R, Preserving the Electronic Records Stored in a Records Management Application, ICA2004,Vienna Austria, 2004.
15. NARA: National Archives and Records Agency, //http:www.nara.gov
16. Kreisler, H. "Conversations With History", UC Berkeley, Institue of International Studies, http://globetrotter.berkeley.edu/conversations/
17. UCSD-TV, http://www.ucsd.tv/
18. UCTV, http://www.uctv.tv/

DRMS: Massive Digital Resource Management System Based on OSS*

Chunxiao Xing[1], Fengrong Gao[1], and Lizhu Zhou[2]

[1] Research Institute of Information Technology, Tsinghua University, Beijing 100084
[2] Department of Computer Science and Technology, Tsinghua University, Beijing 100084
{xingcx, gaofengrong, dcszlz}@mail.tsinghua.edu.cn

Abstract. We discuss challenging issues and technologies in managing massive digital resources, and review the related works. We design a massive digital resource management system(DRMS) based on an open source system (OSS) and Web service, and implement the key components and core services. The virtual collection of DRMS is built for configuring and managing related service components. The DRMS has shown three important characteristics -- universality, extensibility, and interoperability.

1 Introduction

The explosive growth of information in digital forms has posed challenges not only to traditional archives and their information providers, but also to organizations in the government, commercial and non-profit sectors. The latest report by Peter Lyman and Hal Varian, Berkeley [1], the world's total yearly production of print, film, optical, and magnetic content would require roughly 1.5 billion gigabytes of storage which is roughly 250 megabytes for every man, woman, and child on the earth. Printed documents of all kinds comprise only .003% of the total. They include digital texts, documents, scientific data, images, animation, video, audio etc. The applications of the digital resources are quite broad, including Digital Library, Movie/Video center, other public media (television, broadcast, newspaper, etc.), museum, and national or cooperative information center.

These massive digital resources present many challenging issues in data management technology area: data model, system architecture, massive information storage, organization and interoperation, and query processing. The problems mentioned above will remain as a major goal to researchers in next few years. To fulfill this end, we present a universal digital library management system (DRMS) in this paper. The DRMS is intended to meet the requirements of managing digital resources characterized by universality, extensibility, and interoperability.

The other parts of this paper are organized as follows: In Section 2 we review related works on open source system for digital library. In Section 3, we design a universal architecture of DRMS for digital resource management, and describe its key functional components, service components, and implemental environment of DRMS briefly. The conclusion and the future work are given in Section 4.

---

* Supported by the National Natural Science Foundation of China under Grant No. 60473078.

E.A. Fox et al. (Eds.): ICADL 2005, LNCS 3815, pp. 385–389, 2005.
© Springer-Verlag Berlin Heidelberg 2005

2   The Related Works

DSpace [3] provides a sustainable solution for institutional research materials and publications in a professionally maintained repository that captures, stores, indexes, preserves, and redistributes the intellectual output of a university's research faculty in digital formats. Developed jointly by MIT Libraries and Hewlett-Packard (HP), DSpace is freely available to research institutions worldwide as an open source system that can be customized and extended. DSpace is designed for ease-of-use, with a web-based user interface that can be customized for institutions and individual departments. DSpace runs on any UNIX or LINUX operating system. DSpace is an open source software system that enables institutions to: 1)Capture and describe digital works using a custom workflow process; 2) Distribute an institution's digital works over the web, so users can search and retrieve items in the collection; 3) Preserve digital works over the long term.

The OCLC SiteSearch [4] provides a comprehensive solution for managing distributed library information resources in a World Wide Web environment, and consists of two software programs -- Database Builder and WebZ. Database Builder software 1) provides a complete set of software tools to build and maintain local databases; 2) facilitates Web-based record creation for easy information capture; 3) provides specialized templates that take advantage of multiple metadata standards and formats; 4) permits online record updates, so databases are always available; 5) makes local resources such as archives, special collections and reserve room materials Web accessible; 6) supports load a full range of databases, regardless of size or complexity; 7) offers flexible indexing options so users can find information quickly. WebZ software includes three basic starter interfaces (above, from left to right): a virtual catalog that supports resource sharing, an integrated reference solution with a frame version for high-level access, and a non-frame version that meets the requirements of the Americans with Disabilities Act.

Fedora (Flexible Extensible Digital Object and Repository Architecture) [5] system is sponsored by Andrew W. Mellon funding, which is an open-source system developed by Virginia and Cornell University. It implements the digital object architecture and is a universal digital object management system. Fedora can be used in many fields, such as digital library, content management, digital asset management and resource preservation. The Fedora System consists of two fundamental entities: the underlying Fedora digital object architecture and the Fedora repository.

Until recently, there has been no common approach and system architecture for large-scale digital libraries construction. All kinds of libraries, research institutions and universities traditionally developed their digital library system using techniques, vocabularies, and presentation schemes that suited their unique needs and purposes.

3   DRMS: Digital Resource Management System

In this section, we propose a universal architecture of DRMS based on analyzing and researching the related works. We design and implement the DRMS by complying with related standards and making use of enabling technologies and OSS [7,8]. The

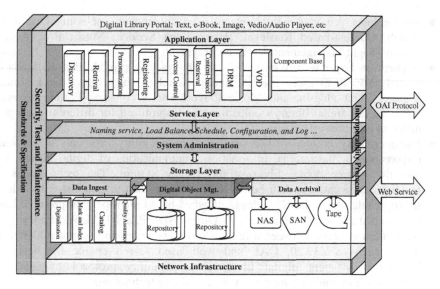

Fig. 1. The Architecture of DRMS

motivation is providing a common framework and software platform for constructing the large-scale digital library.

3.1 System Architecture of DRMS

The architecture is more OSI-like reference model, but it focus on the massive information service, management, and archival. All kinds of functional components lie in the different layers (as shown in Fig. 1). Meanwhile interoperability protocols will provide the way to bridge other remote digital libraries and legacy systems. Security, Test and maintenance will ensure that the architecture is robust and reliable framework. All layers will comply with related standards and specifications for making the architecture reusable, open, and interoperable.

- Network Infrastructure provides the fundamental interconnecting and communicating services and functions.
- Storage layer consists of Data Ingest, Data Management, Knowledge Management, and Data Archival. The component provides the services and functions for storing, maintaining, and accessing both metadata repositories and virtual collections. It includes administering the metadata database, multimedia databases and file systems. It will maintain schema and view definitions, and referential integrity, and perform database updates (loading new descriptive information or administrative data).
- System Administration layer provides the services and functions for the overall operation of the digital library system. Administration functions include Naming service, Load Balance, Schedule policy, and Configuration management of system hardware and software. It also provides system engineering functions to monitor and improve system operations and performance. It is also responsible for establishing and maintaining each layer's standards and policies.

- Service layer provides major service-based components including Discovery, Search, Content-based Retrieval, Personalized Service, Notification, Access Control, Right Management, VOD and Payment.
- Application Layer uses Web-based user interface to provide that all kinds of related services to users friendly and personalized by using E-book, Image Viewer, VOD Plug-in, and Music Player. The Web-based Portals provides access to the digital library's collections and optimized for different users and different purposes effectively.
- Interoperability Protocols: The vertical Interoperability Protocols is not only responsible for the internal information communication of digital library, but also the remote digital libraries and legacy system. The technologies of middleware, agent, and distributed object will be used to establish all kinds of interoperable protocols. Nowadays, metadata-based interoperable protocol have be designed and used such as Z39.50, Dienst, SDLIP, and OAI. We are trying to reach a compromise between a full-scale, all encompassing search middleware design such as Z39.50, OAI, and web-based search engine for design a lightweight efficient digital library interoperability protocol by analyzed previous search middleware designs and enabling technologies.
- Security, Test, and Maintenance: ensure that the architecture is open, robust, maintainable and testable. It will reduce overall software costs; improve system performance and quality.
- Standards and Specifications: In order to ensure system openness, scalability, and interoperability, we will comply with all kinds of related standards and specifications to design the system architecture.

3.2 Implementation of DRMS

We have implemented the function modules of DRMS. We use the DOA as the basis of digital object management and implement the digital object management architecture by reference to the SiteSearch and Fedora system. In our system, each digital resource is encapsulated into a digital object, stored in a fedora repository, identified by a unique persistent identifier (PID). A repository is a physical concept which is a storage unit with different access interface in Fedora. We extend the original definition of virtual collection. DRMS is composed of a set of collections. Each collection might consist of one or many repositories, or parts of repository. Virtual collection just likes the "view" concept in DBMS. As the key component, the virtual collection of DRMS provides an efficient and effective way to integrate digital objects across repositories. The Digital objects stored in Fedora repository physically can belong to one or more virtual collection logically. When these digital objects are collected in a collection, some special services can be provided, such as full-text or content-based image retrieval across repositories or digital libraries, we can create various virtual collections according to different types of digital objects. The virtual collection provides flexible integration of all kinds of digital resource across repositories or digital libraries. In DRMS, each digital resource is encapsulated into a digital object, encoded by extended METS. The digital object includes DataStream and Disseminator and is identified by a unique digital object identifier (DOI). The digital objects with the same attributes are stored into a repository, which is a physical management unit. There is an important data structure---External Index, designed for improving the search services for DRMS resources. We build the external index to support different metadata formats search and provide corresponding retrieval service.

Based on prior works on Tsinghua University Architecture Digital Library (THADL) project [2], we implement DRMS system based on OSS in following environment: OS: Linux Redhat 9.2 or Window 2000 Server; Web Server: Tomcat 4.1.27; Java Runtime Environment: J2SDK 1.4.2; Web-based MVC framework: Struts 1.1; Digital object Manager: based on Fedora 1.2; DBMS: MySQL 4.0; Open source SAN (Storage Area Networking): 10 TB; Digital Objects types: text, XML document, e-Book, image page, image, audio, and video.

4 Conclusion

In this paper, firstly we discuss challenging issues and technologies in managing very large digital contents and collections, and give some related works based on OSS. We design a universal architecture of DRMS, and describe the key components and services. In the future, we will study and develop software middleware for massive storage management, XML based search engine, and multilingual full-text search. We will apply the DRMS to more practical digital library projects.

References

1. http://www.sims.berkeley.edu/research/projects/how-much-info-2003/
2. XING Chun-Xiao, ZENG Chun, LI Chao, ZHOU Li-Zhu. A Study on Architecture of Massive Information Management for Digital Library. Journal of Software. 15 (1):76-85 ,2004
3. http://dspace.org/introduction/index.html
4. http://opensitesearch.sourceforge.net/docs/helpzone/main.html
5. Sandra Payette, Carl Lagoze. Flexible and Extensible Digital Object and Repository Architecture (FEDORA). Second European Conference on Research and Advanced Technology for Digital Libraries, September 21-23, 1998
6. Arms, W. Y., et al, "An Architecture for Information in Digital Libraries", D-Lib Magazine, 1997
7. ZENG Chun, XING Chun-Xiao, ZHOU Li-Zhu. A Personalized Search Algorithm by Using Content-Based Filtering. . Journal of Software. 14 (5):999-1004 ,2003
8. XING Chun-xiao, ZENG Chun, LI Chao, ZHOU Li-zhu. A Study on Architecture of Massive Information Management for Digital Library. Journal of Software. 15 (1):76-85, 2004

Developing Communities and Collections with New Media and Information Literacy

Jerry Watkins and Angelina Russo

Senior Research Associates,
Australian Research Council Centre of Excellence for Creative Industries and Innovation,
Queensland University of Technology,
Tel/fax +61 7 3105 7353
jj.watkins@qut.edu.au

Abstract. As part of its many functions, the reference library is charged with developing both its collection and its user community. These two functions are sometimes pursued as separate initiatives (with separate funding) by library managers. In Australia, the State Library of Queensland (SLQ) is committed to an exciting policy of simultaneous collection development and community engagement by integrating new media technologies with public programs. SLQ's Mobile Multimedia Laboratory is a purpose-designed portable digital creativity workshop which is made available to communities as a powerful platform to capture and disseminate local digital culture, and also to promote and train community members in information literacy. The Mobile Multimedia Laboratory facility operates in conjunction with SLQ's Queensland Stories project, an innovative portal for the display and promotion of community co-created multimedia. Together, the Mobile Multimedia Laboratory and the Queensland Stories initiatives allow SLQ to directly engage with existing and new communities, and also to increase its digital collection with community created content. Not only are both initiatives relatively cost-effective, they have a positive impact upon information literacy within the state.

1 Information Literacy and the Role of the Library

The skills required to engage in digital consumption have been termed the information literacies. Literacy has historically been a field of study most notably discussed in education, but media and cultural studies have recently focused on the information - or "new" - literacies and what skills are demanded of audiences as they negotiate the potential of expanding digital services. For example, Nixon proposes that forces such as the global cultural economy and public policies regarding information and communication technologies (ICTs) are now so deeply embedded in daily life - at home, work and school - that in many places they are shaping a 'new landscape of communication' and 'new learning environments' [1]. Leu *et al* suggest that "The new literacies of the Internet and other ICTs include the skills, strategies, and dispositions necessary to successfully use and adapt to the rapidly changing information and communication technologies and contexts that continuously emerge in our world and influence all areas of our personal and professional lives" [2].

E.A. Fox et al. (Eds.): ICADL 2005, LNCS 3815, pp. 390–394, 2005.
© Springer-Verlag Berlin Heidelberg 2005

Through ICT the types and quantities of information in which an individual requires literacy are changing. No longer is it adequate to think of textual and visual modes of literacy separately, nor envision the internet as only a vast catalogue and receptacle of information. Through their pervasiveness and global nature the internet and ICT challenge traditional roles of producers and consumers in culture, narrowing the distance between them. Shedroff suggests that "the most important skills for almost everyone to have in the next decade and beyond will be those that allow us to create valuable, compelling, and empowering information and experiences for others. To do this, we must learn existing ways of organizing and presenting data and information and develop new ones" [3].

The information literacies are a readily recognizable phenomenon: the impact of technology on cultural communication should be well-known to anyone familiar with the history of the printing press, radio, telephone and television. Indeed, interaction design research and practice have dealt quite successfully with some of the usability design issues raised by the information literacies. Furthermore, ICTs offer an opportunity for regional and remote communities to partner with cultural institutions in the representation of cultural identity. This research is formed around interaction design principles which foreground 'human' rather than 'technical' determinants of ICT usage. While this is not a new approach, the focus is on audience-centered outcomes which are facilitated by design and curation: audience experience drives technology and not vice versa.

The historic position of the library as a repository of community knowledge positions it well as a candidate for the focus of information literacy within the community. Indeed, the role of new media provider may provide an answer to Darke's plea for a more user-focused library: "We must find ways of bringing the public back to the library. Tomorrow's libraries must become the movie-theatres of today. What does the public want? How can we help them? Do we know? If not, we had better get out there and find out. We have to make libraries fun places to visit, an entertainment experience where people can get answers for their questions, and have a good time while they are doing it" [4].

As ICTs become further embedded in our daily lives, they have the potential to create new platforms for community engagement. This paper argues that the discussions ranging around literacy can be considered integral to the further development of meaningful services for communities. As theories and practices in media/ cultural studies, education and Information Technology converge to contend with institutional access and community participation in production, all find themselves in relatively new territory. What seems to be consistent in each of these arguments is that literacy will be the key to the making of meaning. Literacy which enables cultural production can be developed by drawing together the discrete practices of a number of fields towards the empowerment of audiences and the development of the cultural consumer/ producer. In doing so, not only are the processes of cultural production demystified, but the audience's ability to effectively engage in the civic opportunities afforded by new media can also be realized.

2 Developing User Communities Via Co-creation

Community content creation is not a new field of study. Since the 1960s, cultural institutions in the USA and UK have broadened their public programs to include audience interaction with content through education [5]. However, whilst audiences have come to interact with the institution, the artefacts they create are not usually collected, registered and archived within an institution's collection. Therefore audience interaction has been restricted to entertaining ways of "making meaning" from existing content without providing an avenue for the collection and distribution of artefacts created through this interaction - thus limiting the long-term value of community interaction with content. Only recently have the ICTs familiar to higher-end metropolitan users started to become available to regional communities. When such technologies are married to traditional forms such as community narratives, they present an opportunity for individuals and communities to preserve their stories and distribute this knowledge to a wider audience.

Schuler argued that communities were distinguished by lively interaction and engagement on issues of mutual concern and that their well-being contributes to the well-being of the state as a whole. He proposed that ICT could play a role in community life by improving communication, economic opportunity, civic participation and education. His position extended to community-oriented electronic communication where community networks have a local focus. Schuler fails to provide a credible economic blueprint of how to deliver universal online access for communities, although he does make a case for how institutions can provide greater community access to ICT by providing no-/low-cost public access points [6]. But the relationship between institution and community has a far greater potential than the one-way provision of access and facilities. The newly literate community not only has the tools to consume digital culture, it can also work with the institution to create its own digital cultural artefacts. This relationship underpins the process of community co-creation.

3 Community Co-creation and Collection Development

Livingstone suggests that information literacy has limited value to communities if they cannot access technologies, nor have reason to [7]. The State Library of Queensland's Mobile Multimedia Laboratory (MML) project is designed to widen and deepen the sharing of cultural knowledge by creating a channel for cultural knowledge distribution from community to audience via the State Library. The MML is a fully portable media workshop designed and specified by the authors which allows SLQ trainers to travel anywhere within the enormous state of Queensland in order to provide communities with the skills and equipment to create their own digital media. The MML will be used to continue the Library's existing program of information literacy workshops. These regional sessions include community training in use of internet, and skills upgrade workshops for regional library staff in scanning etc. Importantly, the MML also provides the creative technical platform for SLQ's flagship community co-creation and collection development project, Queensland Stories. This is an ambitious new program whereby the State Library empowers communities to tell their own stories about life in Queensland. These stories will become part of SLQ's collection, accessible by a wider online audience. SLQ provides the Mobile Multimedia Laboratory and its own trainers to communities who have particular events or histories to record. During a three- to four -day workshop, SLQ's trainers introduce community participants to the techniques required to prepare a short multimedia narrative, including scanning, digital imaging, storyboarding and scriptwriting. Participants are encouraged to follow a loose format established by The Center for Digital Storytelling [8], which consists of approximately 10 stills images accompanied by a 3 minute scripted voiceover of about 250 words, narrated by the creator. By using this consistent format, the State Library is able to use its growing digital story collection to build its own valuable community snapshot of people, places and attitudes in Queensland – a snapshot taken by the community itself, rather than interpreted by a curator. The finished stories are reviewed for inclusion on SLQ's Queensland Stories website [9].

4 Application and Lessons Learned

The first application of the Mobile Multimedia Laboratory in April 2005 was to facilitate training of the State Library of Queensland's core group of digital storytelling facilitators for the Queensland Stories project. This training program was designed and delivered by the authors to be compatible with the Australian National Training Authority's framework for nationally transferable vocational qualifications so that successful completion of the training program would lead to basic multimedia qualifications for the participant.

The eight participants were all SLQ staff members or associates, many of whom had been involved in the Library's ongoing regional information literacy outreach training program. Technical competence ranged from advanced through to basic PC familiarity. Each workshop was designed to be delivered over an intensive four-day period, but lack of participant availability meant that each workshop was delivered in three days. This unavoidable compression meant that the time available for participants to experiment with the first person narrative form that distinguishes digital storytelling was very restricted. Nonetheless, a good compilation of stories was produced by the group, and can be seen on the Queensland Stories website.

Perhaps the most interesting findings of the workshops were related to policy issues, rather than storytelling. For example, SLQ must observe all due copyright, privacy and intellectual property issues and has therefore decided not to allow the use of any commercial music as part of any digital stories hosted on its website. Another interesting issue to arise from the workshops was that of identity privacy. Due to the risk of web-based invasion of privacy or pedophilia, published stories are only labeled with the creator's first name or nick name so that they cannot be identified.

5 Conclusion

The State Library of Queensland's community-focused digital initiatives aim to give more Queenslanders the opportunity of further realizing their own creative potential, and the excitement of publishing this work on the Internet for a wider audience to enjoy. SLQ hopes to use the Mobile Multimedia Laboratory to reach regional, rural and remote communities with information literacy and community co-creation programs in order to include wider audiences in its public programs and collections. Unlike print-based literacy, information literacies draw together texts, contexts and social practices across a number of media and create artifacts which afford communities the ability to both create and to broadcast community narratives, histories and content within an online environment. This greater online presence of community knowledge can be ably supported and enabled by cultural institutions such as libraries, which can provide training and technologies for information literacy. In this way, the library can position itself at the centre of a cost-effective community co-creative hub.

References

1. Nixon, H.: Textual diversity: who needs it? In: Proceedings of International Federation for the Teaching of English Conference, July 2003, Melbourne
2. Leu, D., Kinzer, C., Coiro, J., Cammack, D. Toward a Theory of New Literacies Emerging From the Internet and Other Information and Communication Technologies. In: Ruddell, R., Unrau, N., (eds.): Theoretical Models and Processes of Reading, 5th edn. International Reading Association (2004)
3. Shedroff, N.: Information Interaction Design: A Unified Field Theory of Design. In: Jacobson, R. (ed.): Information Design. Mass., MIT Press (1999)
4. Darke, A. M.: Surviving and Thriving in the Age of the Internet: Libraries – coming soon to a theatre near you? http://www.slq.qld.gov.au/__data/assets/file/11001/ Darke99.doc (1999)
5. Vergo, P. (ed.): *The New Museology*. London: Reaktion Books Ltd. (1993)
6. Schuler, D.: Community networks: Building a new participatory medium. In: Association for Computing Machinery. Communications of the ACM, 37 [1], 38 (2002)
7. Livingstone, S.: The changing nature and uses of media literacy. In: Media@lse Electronic Working Papers, London School of Economics, 4 (2003)
8. Center for Digital Storytelling. http://www.storycenter.org
9. State Library of Queensland, Queensland Stories. http://www.qldstories.slq.qld.gov.au

Discovering Patterns from Ontology-Derived Texts*

Ki Chan and Wai Lam

Department of Systems Engineering and Engineering Management,
The Chinese University of Hong Kong,
Shatin, Hong Kong
{kchan, wlam}@se.cuhk.edu.hk

Abstract. We propose a framework for constructing semantic features for textual documents from tackling the problem of abstracting information in document representation. Semantic patterns are discovered from ontology-derived texts which provide rich contextual information regarding the concepts. The patterns represent the syntactic and semantic relationships implied in the textual documents which can help in extracting and representing the underlying concepts in texts. We also investigate the significance of using the patterns in automatic summarization of biomedical articles.

Keywords: semantic feature extraction, pattern discovery, text mining, information mining.

1   Introduction

Currently, extracting the syntactic or semantic relations requires huge amount of manual and domain specific preprocessing works, such as tagging the relations within the texts, and constructing extracting rules. We propose using domain-ontology related texts for automatic discovery of semantic features. It can be achieved by using world knowledge, which exists around us, that is ontology. about terms or concepts. Many ontologies also provide definitional texts associated with each concept. Rich contextual information can be derived from such kind of texts in the ontology. These ontology-derived texts have the advantage of being more readily available than the tagged corpus. For example, the Gene Ontology, a controlled vocabulary provided by the Gene Ontology Consortium, contains the definitions of each gene ontology term which can be openly accessed.

Research on automatic pattern acquisition from natural language text have been carried out in different domains and using different techniques. Pattern extraction is particularly useful for natural language understanding [1]. To reduce

---

* The work described in this paper was substantially supported by grants from the Research Grant Council of the Hong Kong Special Administrative Region, China (Project Nos: CUHK 4179/03E and CUHK 4193/04E) and CUHK Strategic Grant (No: 4410001).

E.A. Fox et al. (Eds.): ICADL 2005, LNCS 3815, pp. 395–399, 2005.
© Springer-Verlag Berlin Heidelberg 2005

the human effort in preparing the training data or extraction patterns, unsupervised methods for identifying extraction patterns have been proposed [2, 3]. For the biomedical domains, many researchers have investigated automatic annotation [4] and extracting information such as protein-protein interactions and relations using different kinds of extraction patterns or rules [5, 6].

Our approach differs from the above existing works in that we not only reduce the amount of manual efforts but also the amount of manually reviewing and tagging the sentences and preparing the extraction rules. Unsupervised learning method is adopted for extracting relations within documents using a set of domain ontology related text fragments or sentences. We also investigate the significance of using the extracted pattern in automatic text summarization.

2   Our Approach

Our approach proposes the use of ontology-derived texts for assisting the text information processing. Informative texts can be derived from ontologies of a particular domain, for example, from the definitions of terms or concepts in the domain. By discovering and constructing linguistic patterns from these ontology-derived text, automatically, we can study the semantic relations conveyed in the domain concerned. No additional human efforts are required for filtering or tagging the relations. The system can automatically construct domain-specific linguistic-oriented patterns with much less effort.

To capture the characteristics in ontologically-derived unstructured format texts, pattern extraction is adopted. Meant for discovering semantic relations in text, we utilize semantic patterns for acquiring and representing the semantic information. The semantic pattern generation process aims at capturing the similarities between similar concepts with different variations of expressing a concept in sentence.

In our approach, patterns are discovered by parsing every sentence to generate all interactions within and identify the similarities between the interactions within sentences through a generalization process. A clustering-based pattern generalization approach with heterogeneous distance evaluation is presented.

Link Path Generation. Domain-related sentences are collected from textual information regarding an ontology, as an example, the definitions of the ontological terms. These ontology-derived sentences or sentence fragments contain rich information. It can be observed that complex semantic structures are also present in phrase fragments.

Since words presented in a sentence can have different roles and interact differently between words in a sentence, the study of the interactions helps the identification of semantic features. To facilitate the study of interactions between words, we employ the Link Grammar Parser [7], which can provide not only the roles of the words but also the interactions of the words. It takes into consideration the relationship between words in a sentence. Example of a parsed sentence by the Link Grammar parser is shown in Fig. 1. The definitions of major concepts in link grammar are given below:

- **Connectors:** Connectors connect the words together, they represent the relation types. It describes how the words are used. For example, an "S" and "PP" represent "subject" and past-participle relationship respectively.
- **Links:** For each sentence, words are inter-connected by some kinds of connectors, which are referred as links. The "Os" link connects between the left connected word "enables" and the right connected word "movement". It represents an object relation, which connects "enables" to its object, "movement".
- **Linkage:** A linkage of the sentences includes all the possible links between the words. A complete linkage represents one of the means for connecting all the words together.

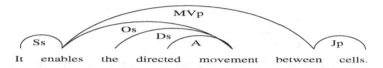

Fig. 1. Example of a linkage generated for the sentence "It enables the directed movement between cells"

For each sentence, we parse it using the Link Grammar Parser. We identify the possible sequence of links with the capability matching over sentence fragments. Hence, instead of processing the whole linkage for pattern generations, we identify each and every path of links, which we referred as link paths. The complete definitions of link path and link level are given below:

- **Link Path:** A link path represent an ordered sequence of links between two words in a sentence. It can be obtained by tracing through the links from a word to another. It describes the relations necessarily existed between two concepts.
- **Link Level:** A word can be connected to or from more than one link. To differentiate the links connected to the same word, the links are associated with a number called link level.

Pattern Generation. We design a clustering-based generalization process between link paths or patterns to form a set of candidate patterns. We search for similar link paths to discover the semantic patterns. Our approach measures the similarity between two link paths from four aspects, namely, the word contents, the link types, the level of the links, and the proximity of the links. We are able to identify link paths with similar complexity even without processing the whole linkage, or complete structure of the sentence. For the link types and word contents, they are treated as nominal, whereas the proximity and level of the links are treated as continuous. Equation 1 depicts how the similarity between two links is computed. l_1, l_2 are two links in the link paths while $lw(l_1)$ is the left connected word of the link, and $rw(l_1)$ is the right connected word of the link k. $v_1 = (p_{11}, p_{12}, p_{13})$ represent the proximity and level information of a link, where p_{11} and p_{12} represent the position of the left and right connected word of the link l_1, and p_{13} is the level of the link l_1. $t(l_1)$ is the link type of the link, such as "Os", "Ds", etc. α is the controlling factor on the relative importance of the words and the link types in a link.

Equation 1 considers the extent of how similar the two links are, where $word\_overlap(w_1, w_2)$ and $link\_overlap(w_1, w_2)$ equals to 1 if their connected words and link types are identical respectively. Equation 2 considers the Euclidean distance between two links by using their proximity and level information.

$$s(l_1, k_2) = \{\alpha * [word\_overlap(lw(l_1), lw(l_2)) + word\_overlap(rw(l_1), lw(l_2))] \\ + (1 - \alpha) * link\_overlap(t(l_1), t(l_2))\} * \frac{1}{d(l_1, l_2) + 1}$$

(1)

$$d(l_1, l_2) = d(v_1, v_2) \\ = \sqrt{(p_{11} - p_{21})^2 + (p_{12} - p_{22})^2 + (p_{13} - p_{23})^2}$$

(2)

The total similarity of two link paths or patterns are computed using a longest common subsequence based approach. A dynamic programming approach depicted in Equation 3 is used for calculating the score, where L_1 and L_2 represent two link paths, and each link path is a sequence of links l, $L_1 = (l_{10}, l_{11}, l_{12}, ...l_{1i})$ $S(l_{1i}, l_{2j})$ represents the similarity score obtained for the best alignment up to position i of link path 1 and position j of link path 2. $\delta(i, j)$ represents the replacement score for link i by link j. $\delta(i, -)$ is the replacement score of link i with a null link. The total similarity score of positions i and j depends on the score of the previous alignments. It compares the score of aligning the links l_{1i} and l_{2j}, or skipping the link i, or skipping the link j.

$$S(l_{1i}, l_{1j}) = max \begin{cases} S(l_{1i-1}, l_{2j-1}) + s(l_{1i}, l_{2j}) \\ S(l_{1i-1}, l_{2j}) + \delta(i, -) \\ S(l_{1i}, l_{2j-1}) + \delta(-, j) \end{cases}$$

$$where\ S(l_{1i}, 0) = i * \delta(i, -)\ and\ S(0, l_{1j}) = j * \delta(-, j) \\ and\ S(l_{2i}, 0) = i * \delta(i, -)\ and\ S(0, l_{2j}) = j * \delta(-, j)$$

(3)

A clustering based generalization approach is adopted. The generalization of patterns is considered as identifying clusters of similar links. Hence, an agglomerative algorithm is designed for identifying similar links and generalizing pairs of links. The patterns retain the link path format. By iteratively generalizing the link paths and patterns, we obtain a list of candidate patterns, which can then be applied for feature engineering.

3   Experiments and Discussion

In our experiments, we applied the patterns discovered on summarizing textual documents. We employed the patterns discovered from the ontology-derived texts for identifying relevant sentences from biomedical documents. We made use of the Gene Ontology definitions as the ontology-derived texts for pattern discovery.

For using scientific ontology definitions, expressions which are not in phrasal or sentence forms are filtered out. Patterns are discovered through our pattern generation approach. The parameter α mentioned in Section 2 controlling the importance of link types towards the associated words is set to 0.5 and the threshold on pattern generalization is 0.8. The significance of patterns are then investigated through an summarization application of the patterns on biomedical documents.

The identified sentences for each of the randomly selected documents from MGI databse are evaluated for their correctness. The sentences are judged manually for their relevancy. The accuracy of the sentences identified by the patterns are shown in Table 1.

Table 1. Accuracy on sentences identified by patterns generated

Number of sentences for processing	5,283
Number of sentences identified	761
Number of sentences correctly identified	535
Accuracy	70.30%

The results show that the generated patterns contain rich contextual information regarding the biological process, cellular component, and molecular function concepts. Their abilities for identifying the relevant sentences imply that they can be precious semantic features for text processing.

References

1. Chan, K., Lam, W.: Extracting causation knowledge from natural language texts. International Journal of Intelligent Systems **20** (2005) 327–358
2. Riloff, E.: Automatically generating extraction patterns from untagged text. In: The Thirteenth National Conference on Artificial Intelligence. (1996) 1044–1049
3. Yangarber, R.: Counter-training in discovery of semantic patterns. In: 41th Annual Meeting of the Association for Computational Linguistics 2003, ACL 2003, Sapporo, Japan (2003) 343–350
4. Chan, K., Lam, W.: Gene ontology classification of biomedical literatures using context association. In: Asia Information Retrieval Symposium, Jeju, Korea (2005)
5. Bunescu, R., Ge, R., Kate, R., Mooney, R., Wong, Y.: Learning to extract proteins and their interactions from medline abstracts. In: ICML-2003 Workshop on Machine Learning in Bioinformatics, Washington DC (Aug 2003) 46–53
6. Yakushiji, A., Tateisi, Y., Miyau, Y.: Event extraction from biomedical papers using a full parser. In: The sixth Pacific Symposium on Biocomputing, Hawaii, USA (2001) 408–419
7. Sleator, D., Temperley, D.: Parsing English with a Link Grammar. In: Third International Workshop on Parsing Technologies. (1993)

Multimedia Retrieval Using Time Series Representation and Relevance Feedback

Chotirat Ann Ratanamahatana[1] and Eamonn Keogh[2]

[1] Dept. of Computer Engineering, Chulalongkorn University, Bangkok 10330 Thailand
ann@cp.eng.chula.ac.th
[2] Dept. of Computer Science & Engineering, Univ. of California, Riverside, CA 92521 USA
eamonn@cs.ucr.edu

Abstract. Multimedia data is ubiquitous and is involved in almost every aspect of our lives. Likewise, much of the world's data is in the form of time series, and as will be shown, many other types of data, such as video, image, and handwriting, can be transformed into time series. This fact has fueled enormous interest in time series retrieval in the database and data mining community. However, much of this work's narrow focus on efficiency and scalability has come at the cost of usability and effectiveness. In this work, we explore the utility of the multimedia data transformation into a much simpler one-dimensional time series representation. With this time series data, we can exploit the capability of Dynamic Time Warping, which results in a more accurate retrieval. We can also use a general framework that learns a distance measure with arbitrary constraints on the warping path of the Dynamic Time Warping calculation for both classification and query retrieval tasks. In addition, incorporating a relevance feedback system and query refinement into the retrieval task can further improve the precision/recall to a great extent.

1 Introduction

A time series database can be defined as any database that consists of sequences of ordered events, with or without concrete notions of time. With this definition, some of the multimedia data or the less-intuitive domains can be transformed into one or two dimensional time series data. Most of previous work on time series retrieval has utilized the Euclidean distance as the similarity metric because it is very amenable to indexing [1], [2]. However, there is increasing evidence that the Euclidean metric's sensitivity to discrepancies in the time axis makes it unsuitable for most real world problems. In this work, we introduce a distance measure based on the well-known Dynamic Time Warping (DTW), and show its utility with comprehensive experiments. Despite its potential weakness that it requires some training to achieve its superior results, we can use the relevance feedback technique to reach this end.

2 Time Series Representation of Multimedia Data

We wish to expand the readers' appreciation for the ubiquity of time series data. We will consider some less obvious applications that can benefit from efficient and effective retrieval; sometimes, multimedia data may also best be thought of as time series.

E.A. Fox et al. (Eds.): ICADL 2005, LNCS 3815, pp. 400–405, 2005.
© Springer-Verlag Berlin Heidelberg 2005

Video Retrieval. Video retrieval is one of the most important areas in multimedia database management systems. Generally, research on content-based video retrieval represents the content of the video as a set of frames, leaving out the temporal features of frames in the shot. However, for some domains, including motion capture editing, gait analysis, and video surveillance, it may be fruitful to extract time series from the video, and index just the time series (with pointers back to the original video). Fig. 1 shows an example of a video sequence transformed into a time series by tracking the centroid of the right hand (our object of interest) in both the X- and Y-axes.

Fig. 1. Stills from a video sequence; the right hand is tracked, and converted into a time series (only X-axis values are shown here)

There are several reasons why using the time series representation may be better than working with the original video sequence data. One obvious point is the massive reduction in dimensionality, which enhances the ease of storage, transmission, analysis, and indexing. In addition, it is much easier to make the time series representation invariant to distortions in the data, such as time scaling and time warping.

Image Retrieval. Image Retrieval has become increasingly crucial in the information-based community. Large and distributed collections of scientific, artistic, technical, and commercial images have become more prevalent, thus requiring more sophisticated and precise methods to perform similarity or semantic based queries. For some specialized domains, it can be useful to convert images into "pseudo time series." For example, consider Fig. 2; an image of a maple leaf is converted into a time series by measuring local angles of a trace of its perimeter (edge). The utility of such a transform is similar to that for video retrieval; working in the time domain also makes scale, offset, and rotation invariance trivial to handle. A different image size (zooming in/out) is also trivial to handle by interpolating time series to the same length.

Fig. 2. Many image indexing/classification tasks can be solved more effectively and efficiently after converting the image into a "pseudo time series"

Handwriting Retrieval. While the recognition of online handwriting [4] may be largely regarded as a solved problem, the problem of transcribing and indexing existing historical archives remains a challenge. The problem of indexing historical archives is difficult, because unlike the online handwriting problem, there is no pen-acceleration information, and the handwriting typically has to be treated as an image.

In addition, the archives may be degraded or stained, and while humans learn to adapt their handwriting to make online handwriting recognition easier, archival handwriting is often highly stylized and written only with the intent of being legible to the writer. Many off-line handwritten document image-processing algorithms have recently been proposed in the interest of word recognition and indexing [5]. While handwriting is not a time series, there exist several techniques to convert handwriting to time series; many of these transformations were pioneered by Manmatha and students [6], as shown in Figure 3. Recent work suggests this representation may still allow the high precision in indexing historical archives while simplifying the problem from 2- to 1-dimensional domain [6].

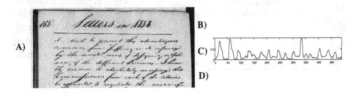

Fig. 3. A)George Washington's handwritten text. B) A zoom-in on the word "Alexandria." C) A projection profile. D) Upper and Lower profiles.

3 The Ratanamahatana-Keogh Band (*R-K Band*)

Despite the explosion of interest in time series indexing in the last decade, the majority of the work has focused on the Euclidean distance, which assumes linear mappings between the query and the candidate time series. However, recent work has demonstrated that this similarity model generally does not work well for many real-world problems, where variability in the time axis is always present. This problem of distortion in the time axis can be addressed by Dynamic Time Warping (DTW) [7]. This method allows non-linear alignments between the two time series to accommodate sequences that are similar but out of phase. Our approach takes this recent work on DTW as its starting point, then fine-tune the algorithm, for a particular domain, and even a particular query, by selectively limiting the amount of warping we allow along various parts of the query, using a new representation, the *Ratanamahatana-Keogh Band (R-K Band)*. As will be shown, by selectively limiting the amount of warping allowed, we can actually improve the accuracy of DTW and its indexing performance. The 'global constraint' of DTW has been almost universally applied to DTW, primarily to prevent unreasonable warping and to speed up its computation. We recently proposed a new representation, the *Ratanamahatana-Keogh Band (R-K Band)* [8], which can represent arbitrary shaped constraints, and proven to improve accuracy and precision/recall. Due to space limitations, please refer to [9] for more details on DTW.

We can exploit the *R-K Bands* for both classification and indexing/query retrieval problems, depending on the task at hand, by using a heuristic search. Due to space limitations, only learning an *R-K Band* for indexing or query retrieval is included here. The full details of *R-K Bands* have been extensively shown in [9].

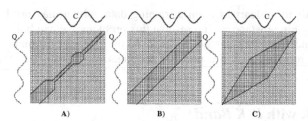

Fig. 4. With R-K Band, we can create arbitrary global constraints.   A) We can specify all existing global constraints, including the Sakoe-Chiba Band B) and the Itakura Parallelogram C).

A)   B)   C)

3.1 Learning an *R-K Band* for Indexing (Query by Content)

In addition to creating R-K_c *Bands* for classification, we can learn one single *R-K Band* for indexing or query retrieval using generic heuristic hill-climbing search techniques, except that we only maintain one single band representing the whole problem and that we measure the precision/recall instead of the accuracy. This approach is re-illustrated by the following experiment, measuring precision and recall for indexing. Ten examples are taken from Gun dataset and placed in a database containing another 10,000 sequences that are similar in shape but do not belong in the class. Another thirty (disjoint) examples from Gun dataset with other 970 other sequences are used in the *R-K Band* training process. Then, another ten different (disjoint) examples from the Gun dataset are used to make ten iterations of k-nearest neighbor queries, using various distance measures   The precision from 1-object to 10-object recall levels and the time taken are measured. The results are shown in Fig. 5. The resultant precision improves to 0.46 using only 3.24 seconds.

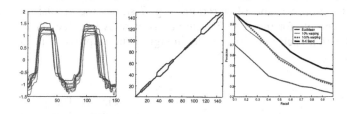

Fig. 5. (left) Some examples from the Gun dataset. (mid) The resulting single R-K Band learned and the precision/recall plots comparing among various distance measure (right)

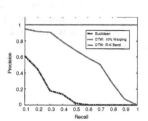

Fig. 6. The Precision/Recall curves from 10% to 100% recall levels for various distance measures: Euclidean, DTW with 10% window size, and the proposed method – R-K Band that gives perfect precision for all recall levels

Fig. 6 shows another experiment result, querying the *Cylinder* data [10] from a collection 10,000 *random-walk* sequences.

It is apparent that utilizing an *R-K Band* in this problem significantly improves both precision and recall, compared to Euclidean and DTW with 10% warping.

However, an *R-K Band* needs to be learned from a training data, which may not be practical or available in many circumstances. To resolve this problem, we can build a training data through relevance feedback system to improve the query performance, with some help from a user in identifying the positive and negative examples to the system.

4   Relevance Feedback with *R-K Band*

Relevance feedback methods attempt to improve performance for a particular informational need by refining the query, based on the user's reaction to the initial retrieved documents/objects. In this time series retrieval system, a user will provide a sample image or video as an initial query. The system then converts the query image/video into time series, using the method discussed earlier. The converted time series is then used for querying the 10 nearest neighbor from the multimedia time series database. The user is then asked to rank each image result in a 4-point scale, which will then be converted into appropriate weights in query refinement processes (averaging the positive results with current query). Once the user ranks each of the results, a query refinement is performed such that a better-quality query is produced for the next retrieval round. However, averaging a collection of time series that are not perfectly time-aligned is non-trivial and DTW is needed [11]. In our experiments, we consider 3 multimedia datasets using our relevance feedback technique (complete datasets details are available in [9]). To evaluate our framework, we measure the precision and recall for each round of the relevance feedback retrieval. We then measure the performance of our relevance feedback system with the precision-recall plot from each round of iteration. Fig. 7 shows the precision-recall curves of the three datasets for the first five iterations of relevance feedback. Our experiments illustrates that each iteration results in significant improvement in both precision and recall.

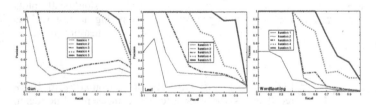

Fig. 7. The precision-recall plot for the 3 datasets with 5 iterations of relevance feedback

5   Conclusion

We have shown an alternative way of representing the multimedia data as time series. We then introduced a framework for both classification and time series retrieval. The *R-K Band* allows for any arbitrary shape of the warping window in DTW calculation. With our extensive evaluation, we have shown that our framework incorporated into relevance feedback can reduce the error rate in classification, and improve the precision at all recall levels in video and image retrieval.

References

1. Agrawal, R., Lin, K. I., Sawhney, H. S., & Shim, K. (1995). Fast similarity search in the presence of noise, scaling, and translation in times-series databases. VLDB, pp. 490-501.
2. Faloutsos, C., Ranganathan, M., & Manolopoulos, Y. (1994). Fast subsequence matching in time-series databases. In Proc. ACM SIGMOD Conf., Minneapolis. pp. 419-429.
3. Keogh, E. and Kasetty, S. (2002). On the Need for Time Series Data Mining Benchmarks: A Survey and Empirical Demonstration. In the 8th ACM SIGKDD. pp. 102-111.
4. Jain, A.K. & Namboodiri, A.M. (2003). Indexing and Retrie-val of On-line Handwritten Documents. ICDAR: 655-659.
5. Kavallieratou, E., Dromazou, N., Fakotakis, N., & Kokkinakis, G. (2003). An Integrated System for Handwritten Document Image Processing. IJPRAI, (17)4, pp. 617-36.
6. Rath, T. & Manmatha, R. (2003). Word image matching using dynamic time warping. CVPR: II, 521-27.
7. Sakoe, H. & Chiba, S. (1978). Dynamic programming algorithm optimization for spoken word recognition. IEEE Trans. Acous., Speech, and Signal Proc., ASSP-26: 43-49.
8. Ratanamahatana, C.A. & Keogh, E. (2004). Making time-series Classification More Accurate Using Learned Constraints. SDM International Conference, pp. 11-22.
9. Ratanamahatana, C.A. (2005). Improving Efficiency and Effectiveness of Dynamic Time Warping in Large Time Series Databases. Ph.D. Dissertation, Univ. of Calif., Riverside.
10. Kadous, M. W. (1999). Learning comprehensible descriptions of multivariate time series. In Proc. of 16th International Machine Learning Conference, pp. 454-463.
11. Gupta, L., Molfese, D., Tammana, R., and Simos, P. (1996). Nonlinear Alignment and Averaging for Estimating the Evoked Potential. IEEE Trans. on Biomed Eng(43)4.

WebArc: Website Archival Using a Structured Approach

Ee-Peng Lim and Maria Marissa

School of Computer Engineering,
Nanyang Technological University,
Block N4, Nanyang Avenue, Singapore 639798

Abstract. Website archival refers to the task of monitoring and storing snapshots of website(s) for future retrieval and analysis. This task is particularly important for websites that have content changing over time with older information constantly overwritten by newer one. In this paper, we propose WebArc as a set of software tools to allow users to construct a logical structure for a website to be archived. Classifiers are trained to determine relevant web pages and their categories, and subsequently used in website downloading. The archival schedule can be specified and executed by a scheduler. A website viewer is also developed to browse one or more versions of archived web pages.

1 Introduction

Websites are often archived for various reasons ranging from backups, website design, content analysis, web data extraction, etc.. For websites that have content changing over time (e.g., online news, product sales, etc.)[2], their archival will have to be performed at intervals in order to capture the dynamic changing web content. To reduce the manual efforts and time in website archival, a number of of web archival software tools have been developed and commercialized. With these tools, the web archival task is very much simplified. Nevertheless, there are still a few issues that remain to be addressed:

– Most archival tools do not distinguish the semantic types of web objects. They are designed to simply download all web pages and other objects from the specified websites and store them for further processing.
– As the existing archival tools assume that the normal web browsers will be used to the archived web content, they normally do not provide special browsing or visualization capabilities.

In this paper, we present a structured approach to model a website to be archived. We believe that by identifying the website structure, one can then specify the relevant website content by identifying the corresponding website sub-structures. The archival task can therefore be defined to download a subset of website content instead of the entire website. This is especially important as there can often be many objects that are not really required by the archival

E.A. Fox et al. (Eds.): ICADL 2005, LNCS 3815, pp. 406–410, 2005.
© Springer-Verlag Berlin Heidelberg 2005

task, e.g., advertisement web pages, mirror web pages, etc.. With this focused and structured archival, the archival overheads can be reduced and the archived information can be more relevant.

2   Construction of Logical Website Structure

In WEBARC, we model a website by a *logical website structure* defined as a tree. Each logical node in the tree represents a class of web pages sharing the same type of content, and the edge between a parent node and a child node represents the set of links from the web pages of parent class to the web pages of the child class. The root class of the logical website structure usually has only one web page belonging to it, i.e., the home page of the website. On the other hand, a logical website structure does not necessary include node classes to cover all web pages of a website.

It is noted that more than one logical website structure can be constructed for a website due to different archival needs. Each leaf node in the logical website structure represents a class of web pages that are the targets for future viewing and processing. The root and internal nodes represent classes of web pages that link the the website's home page to the target pages.

For example, suppose we would like to define a logical website structure for archiving the campus announcements, conferences, seminars, and talks of our university's website. A logical website structure can be constructed as shown in Figure 1. The structure consists of a root node, under which there is the "Event and Notification" class. There are two logical nodes in the next level, "Campus Announcement Directory" and "Conferences, Seminars, and Talks Directory". Each node contains a set of of web pages related to announcements on campus and conferences/seminars/talks respectively. The leaf nodes represent the sets of web pages of interest.

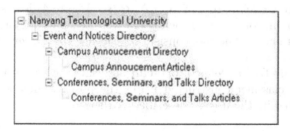

Fig. 1. Example of logical website structure for NTU website

Once defined, the same logical website structure can be reused multiple times in the future. However, the structure itself does not provide the rules to extract the members of each page class.

Given a logical website structure node, there may be only a single web page belonging to it. The URL of the single web page will then be associated with the node. For example, the root node is always associated with a complete URL. When there are multiple web pages belonging to a node, we associate with the node a classifier that determines those web pages belonging to the node. Since web pages of the same node often share some common URL pattern, the classifier is therefore designed to exploit this URL pattern and build a decision tree for that.

We assume that the user will provide some sample web pages of the node as positive training examples and other web pages as negative training examples. We partition each URL into multiple components known as *URL sections* determined by the '/' delimiters. For example, the URL http://www.ntu.edu.sg/oad/home/renewed_perspective.htm is partitioned into sections as shown in the Figure 2.

Fig. 2. Partitioning URL Into URL Sections

A decision tree classifier is then constructed using the ID3 algorithm to classify the positive and negative training examples into mutually exclusive and exhaustive subsets[1]. Each internal node of the decision tree denotes a URL section to be tested, and a branch from the internal node is defined for each value of the section. Each leaf node of the decision tree is finally assigned a class label. For example, the decision tree in Figure 3 determines that URLs with "Grad+student" as their 3rd level sections do not belong to the "Academic Staff" node, while thoses with "staffcsc", "staffis", or "staffacad" as their 3rd level sections do.

The structure modeling tool of WEBARC (see Figure 4) is designed to facilitate expert users in constructing the logical website structure and the classifiers of each structure node. The tool consists of a *logical tree editor* to edit the node tree as shown in Figure 4.

After the node tree is defined, one can associate with each node a URL or a decision tree classifier constructed using the positive and negative training examples selected by the user as described earlier.

3   Website Downloading and Scheduler Tools

Using a logical website structure, WEBARC's downloading tool can conduct website downloading by navigating from the home page of the website. Note that the URL of home page is associated with the the root node of the logical website structure. The downloading tool then examines the URLs of those links embedded in the home page. If the URLs meet the conditions of any of the child nodes of the logical website structure, the corresponding web pages will be saved

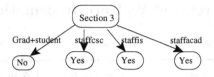

Fig. 3. A decision tree example for a logical node "Academic Staff"

and further navigated. Otherwise, the corresponding web pages will not be navigated at all. The process continues in a recursive manner until the leaf level of the logical website structure is reached.

The downloaded web pages are saved in a project folder designated for all archived web pages using the same logical website structure. To distinguish the different versions of downloaded web pages, a sub-folder labelled with the downloading date is created for each version of downloaded web pages.

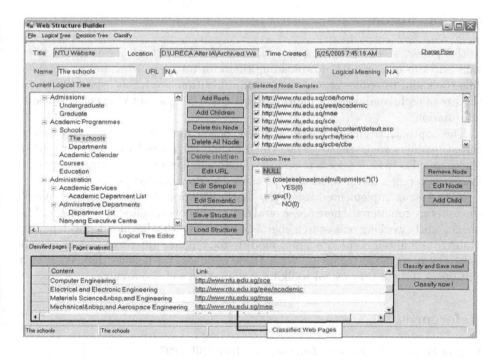

Fig. 4. Structure Modeling Tool

The downloading task can be manually invoked or scheduled. The scheduler tool of WEBARC allows a user to specify the logical website structure to be used for scheduled downloading and the downloading schedule consisting of start date, end date, and downloading interval. The schedule will then be stored and read by a background scheduler program for execution. The status of schedule execution is recorded in a log file for user reference.

4   Viewing of Archived Website Information

In the WEBARC approach, a structure viewer tool is used to browse the different versions of archived web pages with the help of logical website structure. The structure viewer tool consists of a browser component which functions very much like a normal web browser. However, this browser component is able to browse web pages according to the logical website structure. When a node in the logical website structure is selected, the list of web pages belonging to the node is shown under the "Classified Pages" panel. User can also select the versions to be viewed when there are multiple downloaded versions. As the user browses downloaded web pages within the structure viewer, the external URLs in the web pages will be converted to the local ones if the web pages have been downloaded earlier. Otherwise, the corresponding web pages will be fetched from the Web if they are available.

5   Conclusion

In this paper, we describe WEBARC as a set of software tools for archiving relevant portions of a website, downloading them for future viewing and processing. The tools aim to reduce storage and communication overheads especially when the size of useful and relevant information is small compared to the entire website information.

The approach begins with the modeling of website using a logical tree structure. Classifiers are learnt to extract the relevant web pages based on their URLs. There are also tools for users to specify downloading schedule, saving the downloaded web pages in versions, and browsing the downloaded pages.

WEBARC is implemented using C# in the Window XP environment. While the tools are functional, there are several enhancements remained to be made. We are currently working on a search engine for querying the downloaded web pages. WebArc will also incorporate a new module to compare different versions of web pages so as to detect changes. With these changes, we believe that WEBARC will prove to be a very useful toolkit for managing website archives.

References

1. Tom M. Mitchell. *Machine Learning*. McGraw Hill, 1997.
2. Sriram Raghavan and Hector Garcia-Molina. Crawling the hidden web. In *Proceedings of the 27th International Conference on Very Large Data Bases*, pages 129–138, 2001.

Interactive Causal Schematics for Qualitative Scientific Explanations

Robert B. Allen[1], Yejun Wu[2], and Jun Luo[2]

[1] College of Information Science and Technology, Drexel University,
Philadelphia, PA 19104, U.S.A.
allen@acm.org
[2] College of Information Studies, University of Maryland,
College Park, MD 20742 U.S.A.
{wuyj, jun}@glue.umd.edu

Abstract. We present a simple model for describing causal processes. We apply it to generate schematics of complex scientific processes. Our interface allows users to select among causal threads and then to follow the state transitions of those explanations. Moreover, these schematics can provide a framework for interacting with texts.

1 Modeling Events and Causation

Here, we extend our ongoing investigation on helping people to understand the relationship of events using timelines [1–3]. We turn from focusing on chronological order to showing causal relationships among the events in the timelines. There is evidence that much human reasoning about physical processes is qualitative (e.g., [6, 9]). Thus, we have developed a qualitative model for describing causal relationships. Specifically, events are described as simple state transitions, causes are the factors which make state changes, Fig. 1, and a state change is a change in one or more attributes.

For instance, a change in the mayor of a town (a state change) could be caused by an election. The entity "Mayor" is changed from one person to another. Or, if we said that "Jill gave the book to John", the "possessed-by" attribute of the book has been changed from Jill to John and that was caused by Jill's action. Furthermore, we can chain events together. If we said that Jane took the book from Tim and gave it to John, there would be three states for the book (possession by Tim, by Jill, and by John).

We use this model to describe the contents of a science text and build a browser to explore the network of events and causes described in the text. Thus, we show the network of causal links as a type of interactive hypertext map; we call it an interactive causal schematic.

Such a system should be useful for a student trying to understand the associated text. It will be a interactive cognitive organizer which extends Franks and Bransford's original notion of cognitive organizers [7].

E.A. Fox et al. (Eds.): ICADL 2005, LNCS 3815, pp. 411–415, 2005.
© Springer-Verlag Berlin Heidelberg 2005

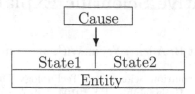

Fig. 1. A cause creates a change of state in an entity

2   Implementation

2.1   Overview

We analyzed texts about the relatively complex scientific processes of the "Snowball Earth" theory as described in [8]. This theory proposes that the earth froze over and the freeze finally ended with the accumulation of greenhouse gasses. We also developed a much simpler causal schematic to describe the failure of the immune system in AIDS. We developed a Java applet for displaying the causal schematics developed from these analyses.

2.2   Interactive Causal Schematics

We initially tried to develop rigid timeline-like grids in which each event was a discrete point or interval. However, that model rapidly became overly tangled as more events and links were introduced. Therefore, we adopted a model with fragments of timelines that illustrates state changes qualitatively (Fig. 2).

In this view, time moves left to right. These interval markers are relative and not exact values since the article does not provide exact values and they may not even be knowable.

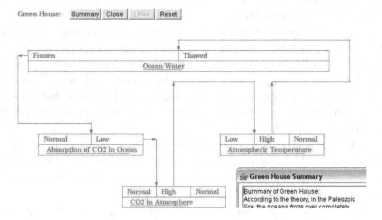

Fig. 2. One thread of the Snowball Earth explanation is shown which describes the subsystem of atmospheric CO_2 and temperature by which the theory claims the frozen earth was thawed. The user follows the steps by clicking the "Links" buttons at the top of the screen.

The links between states are presented one at a time as the user follows the explanation. For instance, the description shown in the figure starts with a causal link from the frozen-ocean-water state to the reduction in the absorption of CO_2. The theory is complex involving the impact of that freeze on ocean sediments and on evolution. We identified three argument threads in the theory: Atmospheric CO_2, Mineral Deposits, and Biological Abundance. The Atmospheric CO_2 cycle (illustrated in the figure) restores the earth to its thawed state and it is the primary scientific hypothesis being presented. The other threads suggest processes that are confirmed by other evidence and contribute to the richness and believability of the entire model.

The user can view all the threads or select among them. For Ocean Water Temperature within the Atmospheric CO_2 thread (Fig. 2) there was a transition from Frozen to Thawed. That is, there was a state transition. That transition can be decomposed and explained by a sequence of other transitions as shown in the figure.

2.3   Associating the Text with the Schematics

The causal schematics should be both informative in themselves and an interactive cognitive organizer to help users to understand and navigate the texts from which they are drawn (Fig. 3). Cognitive organizers, such as a descriptive a schematic, or a concept map, can facilitate understanding complex material such as a text [7]. A cognitive organizer helps a reader either instantiate a previously existing conceptual cognitive schema or develop an entirely new cognitive schema. Cognitive organizers are generally static, but interactive cognitive organizers have the potential to be better focused on the user's interests and needs. For example, an interactive table of contents is both a navigation aid and a cognitive organizer. Beyond simply illustrating the process, like SuperBook [5], the interface would point back into the text of the document. Thus, when the

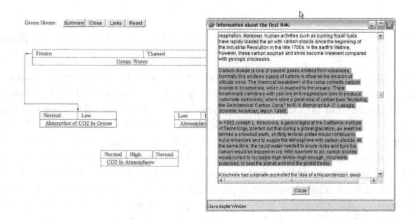

Fig. 3. Highlighting the text corresponding to the schematic display. The text in the widget on the right scrolls to the passage associated with the causal link.

links are shown in the graphic, the corresponding section of text is displayed and highlighted.

3   Conclusions and Future Work

We have extended the basic model of causation in Fig. 1 into cascaded sets of causes and states to provide visualization of scientific explanations. The current implementation is a prototype to which several features should be added; for instance, there should be an automatic layout manager.

While the simplicity of this model is a virtue, the interface could be enhanced by extending it with multimedia and even animation. Moreover, there could be a smooth transition from these schematic interfaces to ones which provide more detailed temporal order.

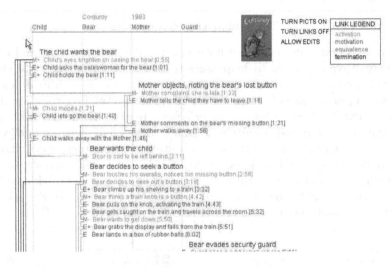

Fig. 4. A Java interface showing a narrative path through a children's story (from [4])

It would also be helpful for the interface to include conditionals, non-causal relationships and the many different senses of "causality" [11]. For instance, much of the article on the Snowball Earth hypothesis [8] discusses alternative hypotheses and the collection of evidence relevant to them. Similarly, a full browser for discourse structure (e.g., [10, 12]) would be useful. For example, recent research has modified the theory to describe the earth as more "slush-ball" than snowball and the debate could be captured by such a browser. It would be helpful to have a mechanism for replicating a process across several instances. For instance, the Snowball Earth freeze was postulated to have occurred four times. This mechanism might be generalized by introducing some processes (e.g., chemical reactions) as templates or macros that apply to a large number of specific instances.

Earlier we developed a browser for the plots of narratives [4] (Fig. 4). Plots often describe how a goal is reached or a problem is resolved by following a causal chain. However, narratives are more complex than many scientific processes because they may involve human personality and emotional reactions. In comparison to narratives that are based on complex human motivation, explanations of physical processes such as geologic history can generally be reduced to objective processes. In the present work, this reduction in complexity was used to advantage to simplify the interface options. We intend to revisit the representation of human agency with the current model. We are working to apply these approaches to much more complex material such as describing historical events in the context of browsing collections such as digitized historical newspapers (e.g., [3]).

Acknowledgments

This work is funded in part by NSF grant #0329111 for "Interacting with Threaded Event Scenarios" and was completed at the University of Maryland. We thank Joshua Raditz and Craig Murray who worked on earlier versions of this project.

References

1. ALLEN, R. B. Timelines as information system interfaces. In *Proceedings International Symposium on Digital Libraries* (1995), pp. 175–180. http://www.cis.-drexel.edu/faculty/ballcn/PAPERS/TL/isdl.pdf.
2. ALLEN, R. B. Developing a query interface for an event gazetteer. In *Proceedings Joint ACM/IEEE Digital Libraries Conference* (2004), pp. 72–73.
3. ALLEN, R. B. A focus-context timeline interface for browsing historical newspapers. In *Proceedings Joint ACM/IEEE Digital Libraries Conference* (2005), pp. 260–261.
4. ALLEN, R. B., AND ACHESON, J. A. Browsing structured multimedia stories. In *Proceedings ACM Digital Libraries Conference* (2000), pp. 11–18.
5. EGAN, D. E., REMDE, J. R., GOMEZ, L. M., LANDAUER, T. K., EBERHARDT, J., AND LOCHBAUM, C. C. Formative design evaluation of SuperBook. *ACM Transactions on Information Systems 7*, 1 (1989), 30–57.
6. FORBUS, K. Qualitative reasoning. In *CRC Handbook of Computer Science and Engineering*, A. Tucker, Ed. CRC Press, 1996.
7. FRANKS, J. J., AND BRANSFORD, J. D. The acquisition of abstract ideas. *Journal of Verbal Learning and Verbal Behavior 11* (1972), 451–454.
8. HOFFMAN, P. F., AND SCHRAG, D. P. Snowball earth. *Scientific American* (Jan. 2000). http://www.scientificamerican.com/2000/0100issue/0100hoffman.html.
9. HOLLAN, J. D., HUTCHINS, E. L., AND WEITZMAN, L. STEAMER: An interactive inspectable simulation-based training system. *AI Magazine 5*, 2 (1984), 15–27.
10. MANN, W., AND THOMPSON, S. Rhetorical Structure Theory: Toward a functional theory of text organization. *Text 8*, 3 (1988), 243–281.
11. WIKIPEDIA. http://en.wikipedia.org/wiki/causation#stanford_encyclopedia_of_philosophy:.
12. WOLF, F., AND GIBSON, E. Representing discourse coherence: A corpus-based analysis. *Computational Linguistics 31* (2005), 249–287.

Automatic Conversion System for Mobile Cartoon Contents

Eunjung Han, Sungkuk Chun, Anjin Park, and Keechul Jung[*]

HCI Lab., School of Media, Soongsil University, Seoul, South Korea
{hanej, k612051, anjin, kcjung}@ssu.ac.kr
http://hci.ssu.ac.kr

Abstract. As the production of mobile contents is increasing and many people are using it, the existing mobile contents providers manually split cartoons into frame images fitted to the screen of mobile devices. It needs much time and is very expensive. This paper proposes an Automatic Conversion System (ACS) for mobile cartoon contents. It converts automatically the existing cartoon contents into mobile cartoon contents using an image processing technology as follows: 1) A scanned cartoon image is segmented into frames by structure layout analysis. 2) The frames are split at the region that does not include the semantic structure of the original image 3) Texts are extracted from the splitting frames, and located at the bottom of the screen. Our experiment shows that the proposed ACS is more efficient than the existing methods in providing mobile cartoon contents.

Keyword: mobile content, cartoon, comic content, mobile browser, text extraction.

1 Introduction

The mobile industry is increasing and developing gradually by means of the infrastructure for ubiquitous computing age. According to this environment, a lot of on-offline contents are being converted into mobile contents. The cartoon contents are one of the most popular and profitable mobile contents.

However, the existing mobile cartoon contents have many problems owing to the small screen of mobile devices. The providers of mobile cartoon contents provide mobile cartoon contents to users as follows: First the provider gets a page of cartoon using a scanner. If this page is shown directly on the screen of mobile device, it is impossible that cartoon contents are delivered efficiently to users due to the small screen. It means that the existing providers have to manually split cartoons into the proper images fitted to the screen size of mobile devices. Therefore, this work needs much time and is very expensive.

Recently, to overcome these problems, the cartoon contents on mobile devices occasionally are produced by the computer software such as Photoshop. However, it is

---

[*] Corresponding author: kcjung@ssu.ac.kr

E.A. Fox et al. (Eds.): ICADL 2005, LNCS 3815, pp. 416–423, 2005.
© Springer-Verlag Berlin Heidelberg 2005

difficult to create suitable contents with computers, since the cartoonists are accustomed to drawing the cartoon by hands for a long time.

To solve previously mentioned problems and provide automatically mobile cartoon contents, we need two processes: cartoon splitting and text extraction. Cartoon splitting is necessary to show the cartoon on the small screen of mobile devices. Text extraction is necessary to prevent the text from excessive minimizing, when the cartoon contents is shown on the small screen of mobile devices.

We propose an Automatic Conversion System (ACS) for providing efficiently and quickly mobile cartoon contents. The ACS cuts tentatively the page into the frames using X-Y recursive cut algorithm[1]. Then, to customize the cartoon contents in mobile devices, ACS splits definitely the frame into the frame images fitted to the screen size of mobile devices. Especially, we also consider a semantic structure of a frame since it includes important contexts of cartoon. When the fitted image is provided on mobile devices, it can be scale-downed if it is bigger than the size of mobile screen. Therefore, the ACS extracts the text using connected component analysis[2] before the image is minimized since users can not understand the excessively minimized text. Lastly, the ACS provides fitted frame images without texts on mobile devices, and locates the extracted text at the bottom of the screen. Hereby, it can convert automatically offline cartoon contents to mobile cartoon contents (Fig.1).

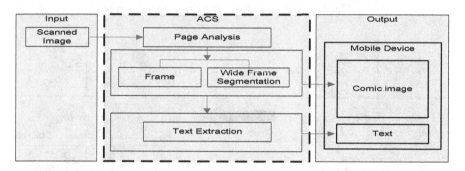

Fig. 1. Structure of ACS

2   Page Analysis

2.1   Cutting the Page into the Frames

We consider two characteristics about cutting the page into the frames as follows: 1) a screen of mobile device is smaller than the one of cartoon page, 2) the semantic structure of a cartoon page is divided into the frames. If the page is excessively minimized to show it at once, users may not understand exactly the provided cartoon contents. And the meaning of the cartoon page is constituted by the meanings of each frame, therefore we cut the cartoon page into the frames. Based on this, the ACS cuts the

---

[1] Cartoons consist of the frames.
[2] The text is located in the balloon, and the regions of the figure in the frame are connected to each other.

page into the frames using X-Y recursive cut(Fig. 2). It is a top-down recursive partitioning algorithm which divides the binary image into the several pieces by repeated formation of blocks. To make the fitting frame image the screen size of mobile devices, the ACS cuts tentatively the page into the frames (Fig. 3).

```
function Split_By_Projection(direction, region)
{
    if(direction is X)        Projection_on_X_Axis(region);
    else      Projection_on_Y_Axis(region);

    Find_Valleys_in_Projection;

    if(valley satisfy threshold)
    {
        Split_Regions_at_Valley;
        For (each sub_region from splitting)
        {
            if(direction is X)        Split_By_Projection(Y, sub_region);
            else      Split_By_Projection(X, sub_region);
        }
    }
}
```

Fig. 2. Algorithm to divide the page into the frames

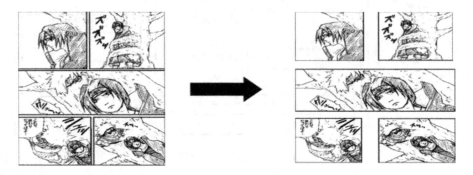

Fig. 3. Cutting the cartoon page into the frame

2.2 Splitting the Wide Frame

When the wide frame is minimized excessively to show it at once, the user can not understand exactly the provided cartoon contents. Therefore, the wide frame has to be split into the fitted frame images. We split the wide frame at the column which has the largest number of white pixels based on the assumption that the white pixel does not include an important context of cartoon. When we split the wide frame at the center column, an important object of the frame may be partitioned (Fig. 4(b)). As this result, the users can not understand the provided cartoon contents. Therefore, splitting the wide frame has to consider an important context of the frame (Fig. 4(c)). As such, we find the splitting line near center line with considering the context of frame images by counting white pixels.

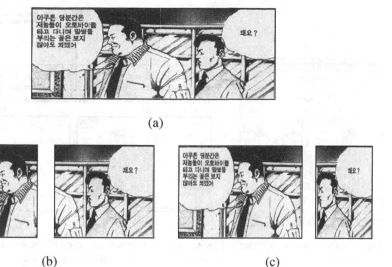

Fig. 4. Two methods to split the wide frame: (a) original frame, (b) splitting at the center of the wide frame, (c) splitting the wide frame through considering an important context of the frame

To split this wide frame, the ACS uses the vertical projection profile. So our work is to find the splitting column l that is defined as:

$$l = \arg\max_{c \in R} \{S_c\}. \tag{1}$$

where S_c is the sum of the luminosity of pixels in column c and R is the observation range in horizontal direction. S_c is defined as :

$$S_c = \sum_{i=1}^{h} P_{ic} \tag{2}$$

where h is frame's height and P_{ic} is the luminosity of pixel at position (c, i).

2.3 Text Extraction

The readability of cartoon contents may decreases due to the rescaling of an image. Therefore, we extract the text before the image is minimized. Fig. 5 shows the scale-downed image and text when we do not perform the text extraction on the fitted frame image.

Based on the assumption that the text is located at the center of the balloon on white background, we extract the text using a connected components algorithm. First, to extract the text efficiently, we convert the split image into the binary image using thresholding (Fig 6). Then we extract the text from the binary image using connected component analysis. We locate the extracted text to the bottom of the screen. Through this process, we endow the consistency to each cartoon contents, and can support the readability of cartoon contents.

Fig. 5. The cartoon without text extraction

Fig. 6. Text extraction: (a) original image, (b) binary image, (c) image without the text, (d) extracted text

3   Experimental Results

We used a PDA POZX301 model based on Pocket-PC 2003. It consists of 400MHz XScale Processor, 62MB SDRAM and 160MB Flash Rom.

To compare with the ACS and the existing methods, we produced mobile cartoon contents using the existing method which scans a cartoon image and manually produces the frame images using Photoshop. The existing method needs much time and is very expensive, since each processing is manually performed. However, our method automatically produces the frame images fitted to the mobile screen (Fig. 7).

Fig. 7. Processes of the existing method and the ACS

We perform to convert the 30-cartoon pages into mobile cartoon contents using each method. Table 1 is the executing times for converting the 30 cartoon pages using each method. Especially, it takes over 10 minutes to convert the comic book using the existing methods because a comic book usually has over 100 pages. On the other hand, it takes about 1.5 minutes to convert the comic book using the automatic conversion system.

Table 1. Executing times for converting the 30 cartoon pages using each method

	Manual Method	Automatic Conversion System
Executing Times	10 (min)	1.5 (sec)

To make the frame images fitted to the screen size of mobile devices, the ACS cuts tentatively the page into the frames. We expect that if a cartoon page consists of 5 frames, the 30 cartoon pages will divide into over the 150 pieces. However, we knew that the 30 cartoon pages were divided into 120 pieces using the ACS through the experiment. The rest of 30 pages were not divided as shown in Fig. 8. If the frame overlaps other frames (Fig 8(a)) or an image exists on the outline of frame (Fig 8(b)), they were not divided.

(a)   (b)

Fig. 8. Cartoon pages, which can not be split into the frames: (a) the frame, which exists in the other frame, (b) the frame of which outline is cut by the image

The ACS splits the frame into fitted frame image to the screen size of mobile devices, considering the semantic structure of the frame. Therefore, it split the frame at the most meaningless column of frame (Fig. 9).

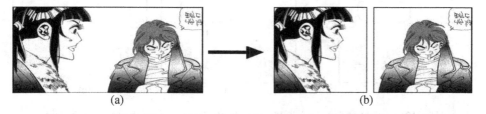

(a)   (b)

Fig. 9. Splitting the frame: (a) input image, (b) split frames

If a background is black and the meaningful object is white, the ACS has an illusion that the column in the object most meaningless column in the frame. According to this, it can occur that wide frame is split at the object (Fig. 10).

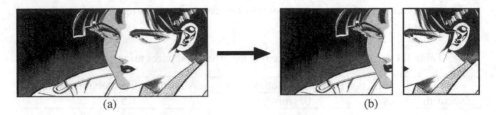

Fig. 10. Failing in efficient splitting: (a) input image, (b) split frames

If the text is excessively minimized, the users can not understand it. To augment the readability of cartoon contents, the ACS extracts the text, shows it at the bottom of screen without scale-down. Therefore the users can be provided efficiently mobile cartoon contents. Fig. 11 shows the result of text extraction.

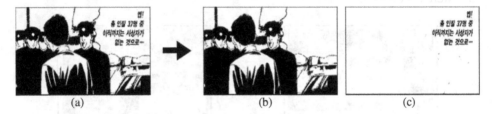

Fig. 11. Text extraction: (a) input image, (b) the image except the text, (c) the text

We consider two assumptions about the text extraction: 1) the text is located in the center of the balloon, 2) the pixels of the background are 255. Namely, it means that the other region except the text is able to be extracted, if it is suited to the two assumptions. For example, region of eye is suited to the two assumptions, it exists in the face, and the pixels of background are a white color. According to this, it can occur that the other region except the text is extracted by the ACS. Moreover, after the text is extracted, the region the text has existed remains the meaningless region, like Fig. 12.

Fig. 12. Text extraction: (a) input image, (b) the image except the text, (c) the text

4 Conclusions

The main difficulties in manual conversion from offline cartoon images into mobile cartoon contents are that it needs much time and is very expensive. To solve the problems, this paper proposed automatic conversion method of the existing cartoon contents into mobile cartoon contents.

As future works, we will go forward to solve the problems of this system. For accurate segmentation on the unstructured environment, we will cut the page into the frames using a vanishing point. And, to minutely extract the text, we will extract the text using a geometric alignment. In addition to this, we will research about provision of mobile cartoon contents to provide efficiently and cheaply through to develop continuous the automatic conversion system.

Acknowledgement. This work was supported by the Soongsil University Research Fund.

References

1. Baldonado, L.L., Junjie C., Hantao S.: The research of Web mining. In Proceedings of the 4th World Congress on Intelligent Control and Automation, Vol. 3, (2002) 2333-23337
2. Buyukkokten, O., Garcia-M., Hector, Paepcke,: Andreas Seeing the Whole in Parts: Text Summarization for Web Browsing on Handheld Devices. In Proceedings International WWW Conference (10), Hong-Kong (2001)
3. Jung K.: Neural network-based text location in color images. Pattern Recognition Lett, 22 (14) (2001) 1503-1515
4. Li H., Doerman D.: A video text detect system based on automated training. In: Internet Conf. on Pattern Recognition (2000) 223-226
5. Strouthopoulos C., Papamarkos N.: Text identification for document image analysis using a neural network. Image Vision Computer, 16, (1998) 879-896,
6. Wernicle A., Lienhart R.: On the segmentation of text in videos. In: IEEE Internet. Conf. on Multimedia and Expo, Vol. 3 (2000) 1511-1514
7. Y..Chen, W.Y.Ma, H.J.Zhang,: Detecting Web Page Structure for Adaptive Viewing on Small Form Factor Devices. In Proceedings International WWW Conference,Budapest, Hungary. ACM 1-58113-680-3/03/0005 (2003) 225–233

Subjective Relevance: Implications on Interface Design for Information Retrieval Systems

Shu-Shing Lee, Yin-Leng Theng, Dion Hoe-Lian Goh, and
Schubert Shou-Boon Foo

Division of Information Studies,
School of Communication and Information,
Nanyang Technological University,
Singapore 637718
{ps7918592b, tyltheng, ashlgoh, assfoo}@ntu.edu.sg

Abstract. Information retrieval (IR) systems are traditionally developed using the objective relevance approach based on the "best match" principle assuming that users can specify their needs in queries and that the documents retrieved are relevant to them. This paper advocates a subjective relevance (SR) approach to value-add objective relevance and address its limitations by considering relevance in terms of users' needs and contexts. A pilot study was conducted to elicit features on SR from experts and novices. Elicited features were then analyzed using characteristics of SR types and stages in information seeking to inform the design of an IR interface supporting SR. The paper presents initial work towards the design and development of user-centered IR systems that prompt features supporting the four main types of SR.

1 Introduction

Traditional information retrieval (IR) systems are developed using the "best match" principle assuming that users can specify needs in queries [2]. Using this principle, the system retrieves documents "matching closely" to the query and regards these documents as relevant. Relevance is computed using a similarity measure between query terms and terms in documents without considering users' contexts [3, 14].

Hence, this objective relevance is limited somewhat as it does not consider users' needs, in particular, the possible distinction between experts' and novices' needs, and the contexts in which queries are submitted [3]. In other words, experts and novices have varying needs as experts have experience with IR systems and domain knowledge which allow them to search and judge relevance more effectively [4].

Subjective relevance (SR), alternatively, considers relevance from the perspective of users' knowledge and needs [8]. SR is defined as the usefulness of information objects for fulfillment of user's tasks [8]. Hence, one approach of addressing experts' and novices' needs is to possibly enhance objective relevance and tackle its limitations by considering relevance from the perspective of users' knowledge and contexts, an emerging research area in SR [8].

This paper presents initial work towards designing user-centered IR systems by investigating features prompting SR and exploring its implications towards interface

E.A. Fox et al. (Eds.): ICADL 2005, LNCS 3815, pp. 424–434, 2005.
© Springer-Verlag Berlin Heidelberg 2005

design for experts' and novices' needs. The paper uses theories from SR and information seeking to provide rationale for designing an IR interface so that users are guided to find more relevant documents during their information seeking processes.

2 Related Studies

Different approaches have attempted to enhance objective relevance and address its limitations. Works by Chen and Kuo [5] and Gilbert and Zhong [7] have looked at facilitating query formulations by capturing users' personal interpretations of query terms and by accepting queries in natural language respectively. Another research area looks at collaborative browsing where users interact with each other to facilitate their browsing processes and retrieve more relevant documents. An example of this application is *Let's Browse* [9]. A third research area is collaborative filtering. This technique helps users retrieve documents for their needs by recommending documents based on users' past behaviors and behaviors of other users with similar profiles. Examples of such applications are *Fab* [1] and *GroupLens* [12].

The approach described in this paper differs from those described above. Firstly, a user-centered approach is employed by eliciting SR features from experts and novices. Secondly, concepts from SR [6] and information seeking [10] are used to provide theoretical underpinnings for understanding elicited features and informing interface design so that the designed IR interface supports experts' and novices' SR judgments during their information seeking processes.

3 Our Approach

In order to design a user-centered IR system with features supporting SR, we turn to two previous works on SR [6] and information seeking in electronic environments [10]. These works are described briefly in Sections 3.1 and 3.2 to provide theoretical underpinnings for investigating what features experts and novices need to support SR in information seeking. We then design a pilot study to elicit SR features from experts and novices. Methodology and findings of this study are presented in Sections 3.3 and 3.4 respectively. Elicited features are next analyzed using characteristics of SR [6] and stages in information seeking [10] to ensure features elicited and designed support users' SR evaluations and information seeking tasks. These analyses are presented in Sections 4 and 5 respectively. In Section 6, we present how analyses of elicited features in Sections 4 and 5 are used to inform interface design for an IR system supporting SR.

3.1 Subjective Relevance Types

Relevance is a relation between the user and an information object [13]. Since objective relevance using recall and precision measures does not consider users' needs, we examine SR which considers relevance from the perspective of users' changing knowledge and information needs [8]. Four SR types are discussed in [6] and are briefly described in this section. This work is selected because it describes characteristics of the four SR types in a comprehensive manner.

- Topical relevance: This relevance is achieved if the topic covered by the assessed information object is "about" the topic specified in the query.
- Pertinence relevance: This relevance is measured based on a relation between a user's knowledge state and retrieved information objects as interpreted by the user.
- Situational relevance: This relevance is determined based on whether the user can use retrieved information objects to address a particular situation/task.
- Motivational relevance: This relevance is assessed based on whether the user can use retrieved information objects in ways that are accepted by the community.

The discussion on SR seems to indicate two important components: 1) user's information seeking behavior and skills and 2) user's domain knowledge. User's information seeking behavior and skills are important because they provide a means for the user to retrieve information objects and SR evaluations to occur. User's domain knowledge is also important in SR because it may affect how the user evaluates a document. For example, a document may be appropriate for a user's task but due to a lack of domain knowledge, the document may be deemed as irrelevant. Since user's information seeking behavior is a key component for evaluating documents towards task completion, we will next review an established information seeking model and discuss how information seeking may support task completion.

3.2   Information Seeking in Electronic Environments

Here, we examine a well-established model for information seeking in electronic environments [10]. This model is selected because it explicitly describes the information seeking stages users may go through while using an IR system.

Machionini's [10] model describes eight stages in information seeking and its transitions. The eight stages are: 1) recognizing and accepting an information problem; 2) defining and understanding the problem; 3) choosing a search system; 4) formulating a query; 5) executing search; 6) examining results; 7) extracting information; and 8) reflection/iteration/stopping. Transitions between these stages (depicted as 1-8) are presented in Figure 1. The default and high probability transitions are presented as solid arrows and dotted arrows respectively.

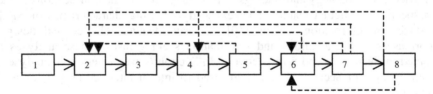

Fig. 1. Transitions and Stages in Information Seeking

To further understand how users may carry out different information seeking stages in an IR system to complete tasks, the eight information seeking stages in Marchionini's [10] model are viewed using Norman's [11] generic model of user interaction in interactive systems. Norman's [11] model describes seven activities that users go through while interacting with a system to complete tasks. Using this model, it may be inferred that Marchionini's [10] information seeking stages can be divided into three phases in terms of user-system interactions proposed by Norman: 1) before execution of an action; 2) during execution of an action; and 3) evaluation of action. Marchionini's Stages 1-4 in information seeking can be mapped to Norman's Phase 1, with Stage 5 in information seeking referring to Phase 2, and Stages 6-8 in information seeking referring to Phase 3.

3.3 Pilot Study

Theoretical frameworks for SR and information seeking, described briefly in Sections 3.1 and 3.2 respectively, seemed to indicate that one possible way to value-add objective relevance and address its limitations could be to design a user-centered IR system supporting users' SR evaluations in information seeking. Hence, a pilot study was carried out to elicit SR features from experts and novices.

Selected Groups: Profiles of Subjects
Eight students (6 Masters and 2 PhD students) from the School of Communication and Information, Nanyang Technological University, were selected as subjects. They were divided into four groups, namely Groups A-D, with 2 subjects in each group. Subjects' level of domain knowledge was determined based on the nature of the task while level of information seeking skills was determined based on whether they had taken a module on "information sources and searching" in their postgraduate studies. Profiles of subjects are shown in Figure 2. In this figure, domain knowledge is depicted as DK and information seeking skills is depicted as IS.

	DK Expert	DK Novice
IS Expert	Group D (2 subjects)	Group B (2 subjects)
IS Novice	Group A (2 subjects)	Group C (2 subjects)

Fig. 2. Profile of Subjects

Methodology
The study was conducted in two sessions, Session 1 for Groups A and B and Session 2 for Groups C and D. This was done because different tasks were used in each session to distinguish subjects' levels of domain knowledge. In each session, subjects were first briefed on the study's objective and the different types of SR. After that, they were given 20 minutes to complete a task. The purpose of this task was to set a context to get subjects thinking about what design features could help them assess a document's relevance. A form was constructed for subjects to note down features that were useful for their tasks, and if not, how these features could be improved.

   In Session 1, subjects' task was to gather information for a discussion on "The social impact of the Internet" using two IR systems: Communication Abstracts (a subscription-based database); and ACM Digital Library (a digital library).

   In Session 2, subjects' task was to gather information for a discussion on "The different types of information seeking models" using three IR systems: Emerald

Fulltext (a subscription-based database); Library and Information Science Abstracts (a subscription-based database); and ACM Digital library (a digital library). These IR systems were selected as they were commonly used by the subjects.

After completing the task in each session, subjects brainstormed features that they thought were useful for assessing a document's relevance. They were also asked to indicate which features were most important amongst the suggested ones.

3.4 Findings

The study elicited a list of features supporting SR from experts and novices grouped according to their domain knowledge and information seeking skills. A total of 23 and 33 features were elicited from Sessions 1 and 2 respectively. To facilitate analysis, elicited features from both sessions were consolidated by removing duplicates to arrive at a final list of 52 features. To illustrate, we present some features from this list in Table 1. Features elicited from Session 1, Groups A and B were coded with symbols, S1A and S1B, respectively. Features elicited from Session 2, Groups C and D were coded with symbols, S2C and S2D, respectively. Symbols, (++) and (+), were coded next to each feature to indicate whether it was "very important" (++) or "nice to have" (+) to support SR judgments respectively.

Table 1. Example of SR features elicited from the pilot study

Features	Example of SR features elicited from the pilot study
1	Provide recommendations of documents and related topics based on queries users submitted (S2D/++)
2	Rank retrieved documents by relevance (S1B/+)
3	Provide tutorials / search examples (S1A/++; S1B/++)
4	Provide search options, for example, search by title, author, abstract, etc. (S1A/++; S1B/++; S2D/++)
5	Provide abstract of documents retrieved in results list (S1B/++; S2D/++)
6	Provide direct download of documents in PDF format (S1A/++)
7	Provide selected references used in documents (S1A/++; S1B/+)
8	Provide collaborative features (S1B/+)

4 Analyzing Features Using Characteristics of SR

In this section, we describe how we verified if elicited features (see Table 1) supported the four SR types. To achieve this, features elicited from the study were coded to characteristics of the four SR types as described in [6]. Analysis was done based on whether an elicited feature helped users achieve characteristics of a particular SR type. If the feature supported characteristics of a particular SR type, it was coded to that SR type. The coding process was done for all 52 features elicited.

Due to space constraints, we are unable to show coding and rationale for all 52 elicited features. As an illustration, we will describe how elicited features from Table 1 were coded to the four SR types. This coding is presented in Table 2.

- Features in Table 2, Rows 1 and 2, were coded to *topical relevance* as they might provide users with access to other documents and topics that could be similar to topics specified in the query. Moreover, ranking of retrieved documents might also provide an indication of similarity between topics in retrieved documents and topics specified in the query.

- Features in Table 2, Rows 3 and 4, were coded to *pertinence relevance* as they might guide users in query formulations which could be useful for novices.
- Features in Table 2, Rows 5 and 6, were coded to *situational relevance* as document's abstract and full text might provide users with access to document's contents for evaluation towards task completion.
- Features in Table 2, Rows 7 and 8, were coded to *motivational relevance* as references might provide an indication of whether reputable sources had been used to develop document's contents. Moreover, collaborative features might also facilitate discussions to help determine if a document is favored by the community.

5   Analyzing Features Using an Information Seeking Model

In order to understand how elicited features might support SR in users' information seeking processes, we turned to an established model of information seeking by Marchionini [10] to code elicited features to stages in information seeking.

Coding of elicited features to stages in Machionini's [10] model was done by analyzing whether elicited features supported characteristics of a particular stage. If an elicited feature supported characteristics of a stage, it was coded to that particular stage. The coding was done for all 52 features elicited from the pilot study.

To illustrate, we will describe how elicited features from Table 1 were coded to stages in Marchionini's [10] model. Features in Table 2, Rows 3 and 4, were coded to

Table 2. Coding of features elicited from the pilot study

Row	Example of features elicited from the pilot study	SR type	Information seeking stages	Phases in task completion
1	Provide recommendations of documents and related topics based on queries users submitted (S2D/++)	Topical relevance	Stage 6	Evaluating action
2	Rank retrieved documents by relevance (S1B/+)	Topical relevance	Stage 6	Evaluating action
3	Provide tutorials / search examples (S1A/++; S1B/++)	Pertinence relevance	Stage 4	Before executing action
4	Provide search options, for example, search by title, author, abstract, etc. (S1A/++; S1B/++; S2D/++)	Pertinence relevance	Stage 4	Before and during execution
5	Provide abstract of documents retrieved in results list (S1B/++; S2D/++)	Situational relevance	Stage 6	Evaluating action
6	Provide direct download of documents in PDF format (S1A/++)	Situational relevance	Stage 7	Evaluating action
7	Provide selected references used in documents (S1A/++; S1B/+)	Motivational relevance	Stage 6	Evaluating action
8	Provide collaborative features (S1B/+)	Motivational relevance	Stage 6	Evaluating action

Stage 4 (formulate a query) as they might guide users in query formulation. Features in Table 2, Rows 1, 2, 5, 7, and 8, were coded to Stage 6 (examine results) as they provided users with information about documents retrieved to facilitate relevance evaluation. Table 2, Row 6, was coded to Stage 7 (extract information) because it allowed users to access document full text for information extraction.

To further ensure that features helped users complete information seeking tasks, elicited features in Table 2 were viewed from the perspective of interaction phases described in Norman's model of interaction [11] (see Section 3.2). Using this perspective, elicited features in Table 2 seemed to support all three phases, hence, indicating that these features might be useful for task completion.

6   Interactive Interfaces for Supporting SR

We next describe how analyses of elicited features using characteristics of SR types (see Section 4) and information seeking stages (see Section 5) were used to inform the design of an IR system that might support users' SR evaluations during information seeking. As an example, we will use elicited SR features and coding in Table 2.

Coding of SR features in Table 2 was used to inform the design of three interactive interfaces: 1) basic search page supporting "before execution" phase; and 2) results list page with 3) document record page supporting "after execution" phase. The overall design aimed to enhance objective relevance and support users' contexts by explicitly supporting user's SR judgments during information seeking. This was achieved by designing a user interaction flow and tips section in each of the three interactive interfaces (see Figures 2-4) to respectively indicate different stages that users had gone through in the system and to show users how to use features to support their SR evaluations.

Users' level of information seeking skills and domain knowledge were also considered in the overall design. The search interface selection page had remarks next to selection options for basic and advanced search pages to help users choose the right interface for their needs. Moreover, users had to indicate their level of domain knowledge in the search page so that retrieved documents in the results list page were appropriate for their contexts.

The subsequent paragraphs in this section describe in detail how elicited SR features and coding in Table 2 were used to inform the design of three interactive interfaces (basic search page, results list page, and document record page).

Elicited SR features in Table 2 coded to Stage 4 in information seeking included: 1) provide tutorials / search examples and 2) provide search options, for example, search by title, author, abstract, etc. SR features, mentioned in this paragraph, might be designed in a search page to possibly support retrieval of documents for relevance evaluation. These features were gathered from experts and novices in information seeking skills. Thus, it was inferred that SR features elicited from experts (information seeking skills) could be designed in an advanced search page while SR features elicited from novices (information seeking skills) could be designed in a basic search page. In this example, we took SR features as those elicited from novices to design a basic search page for query formulation and execution.

Marchionini's [10] information seeking model suggested that query execution led to the results list page (see Section 3.2). Similarly, executing a query in the designed basic search page led to the results list page. Figure 3 shows the designed basic search page for novices and its features.

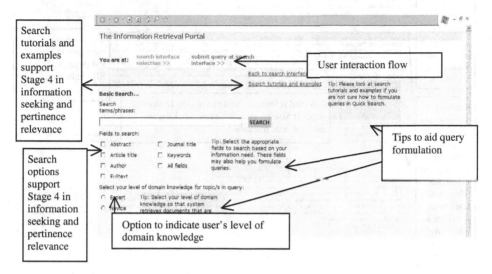

Fig. 3. Basic Search Page for Novices ("Before Execution" Phase)

Elicited SR features in Table 2 coded to Stage 6 in information seeking could be designed in the results list page to possibly support evaluation of documents retrieved. The designed SR features included: 1) provide recommendations of documents and related topics based on queries users submitted; 2) rank retrieved documents by relevance; 3) provide abstract of documents retrieved in results list; 4) provide selected references used in documents; and 5) provide collaborative features. These SR features were elicited from experts and novices in domain knowledge. Thus, it was inferred that SR features elicited from domain experts might be designed in a results list page for domain experts while SR features elicited from domain novices might be designed in a results list page for domain novices. Designed SR features 1, 3, and 4 (mentioned in this paragraph) were elicited from domain experts while designed SR features 2 and 5 (mentioned in this paragraph) were elicited from domain novices. Thus, it was inferred that the designed results list page was for domain experts as most of the designed features were elicited from experts. Although designed SR features 2 and 5 were elicited from domain novices, they were also designed in the results list page. This was because the designed SR feature 2 provided ranking of retrieved documents which was inferred as a common feature in IR systems while the designed SR feature 5 allowed users to discuss issues with other users so that characteristics of motivational relevance could be supported.

Marchionini's [10] information seeking model indicated that Stage 6 in information seeking led to Stages 4 and 7 (see Section 3.2). Hence, it was inferred

Recommendations of topics and documents related to the query support Stage 6 in information seeking and topical relevance

User interaction flow

Link to search page

Tips on how elements in results list page facilitate SR evaluation

Ranking of documents supports Stage 6 in information seeking and situational relevance. Each title provides a link to the document record page

Selected references and discussion forums support Stage 6 in information seeking and motivational relevance

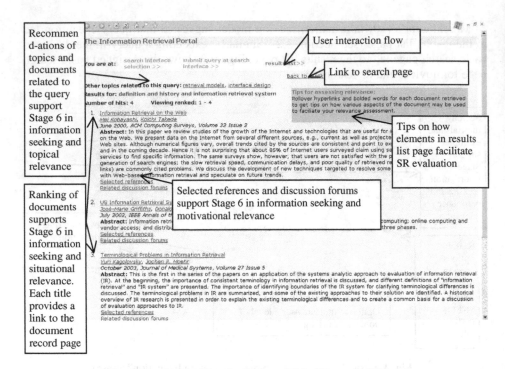

Fig. 4. Results List Page for Experts ("After Execution" Phase)

Direct download of document full text supports Stage 7 in information seeking and situational relevance

User interaction flow

Links to results list and search page

Tips on how elements in document record might facilitate SR evaluation

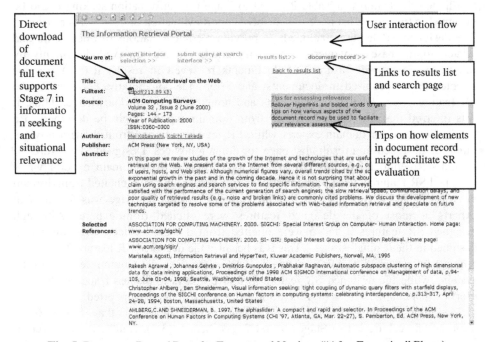

Fig. 5. Document Record Page for Experts and Novices ("After Execution" Phase)

that the designed results list page could have a link back to the basic search page and each document title in the results list page could lead to a document record page providing users with more details about the document. Figure 4 highlights some features implemented in the designed results list page for experts.

The SR feature in Table 2 coded to Stage 7 in information seeking was: provide direct download of documents in PDF format. This feature could be designed in the document record page as it helped experts and novices (information seeking skills and domain knowledge) accessed document full text for information extraction to occur. Detailed document information was also designed in the document record page so users could cite document's source when its contents were used for task completion.

Marchionini's [10] information seeking model indicated transitions to Stages 4 and 6 from Stage 7 (see Section 3.2). Hence, links back to the basic search page and results list page were designed in the document record page. Figure 5 presents the designed document record page for experts and novices.

This is only an illustration of how elicited SR features from Table 2 could inform interface design. Certainly, designing the initial interface for an IR system supporting SR would involve using all SR features elicited from the pilot study.

7 Conclusion and On-Going Work

In this paper, we have described an approach using concepts from SR and information seeking to design a user-centered IR interface supporting SR. A pilot study was conducted to gather features to support experts' and novices' SR judgments. Elicited features were then analyzed using characteristics of SR types and stages in information seeking to inform the design of an IR interface supporting SR.

The designed IR interface presented here seemed to include existing features in current IR systems. Reasons for this included: 1) the small number of participating subjects and 2) subjects brainstormed SR features after they had completed a task, hence, causing them to suggest features that they had found useful whilst using example IR systems. This is an initial study and certainly more subjects should be recruited in future studies to brainstorm novel SR features.

In contrast to other studies addressing limitations in objective relevance [e.g. 1, 5], our approach described in this paper is unique in several aspects. Firstly, a user-centered approach incorporating theoretical frameworks from SR [6] and information seeking [10] were used to elicit and validate features supporting experts' and novices' SR judgments in information seeking. Secondly, the designed IR system explicitly addressed experts' and novices' needs by guiding users select the appropriate search page for their information seeking skills. Moreover, users' level of domain knowledge were also considered as they had to specify their level of domain knowledge in the search page so that the results list page included appropriate details to support their SR judgments. Thirdly, the designed IR system explicitly embraced users' SR judgments in information seeking by providing a user interaction flow to indicate pages that users' had gone through in the system. In addition, tips were designed to explicitly indicate how designed features could be used to support SR and help users find relevant documents for their tasks.

Findings presented here are preliminary and part of on-going research to elicit features and explore a framework using concepts from SR and information seeking to inform the design of an IR system that supports users in finding relevant documents for their needs. Elicited SR features and the approach used to inform interface design need to be further refined and tested before they can emerge as principles for designing user-centered IR systems. Future work could focus on validating elicited SR features through a quantitative study to ensure that the designed IR interface meets experts' and novices' needs.

References

1. Balabanovic, M. and Shoham, Y. (1997). Fab: Content-based, collaborative recommendation. *Communications of the ACM, 40*(3), 66-72.
2. Belkin, N. J., Oddy, R. N., & Brooks, H. (1982). ASK for information retrieval: Part I. background and theory. *The Journal of Documentation, 38*(2), 61-71.
3. Case, D. O. (2002). Looking for information: A survey of research on information seeking, needs, and behaviour. California, USA: Elsevier Science.
4. Chen, H., Houston, A. L., Sewell, R. R., & Schatz, B. R. (1998). Internet browsing and searching: Use evaluations of category map and concept space techniques. *Journal of the American Society for Information Science, 49*(7), 582-603.
5. Chen, P.-M. and Kuo, F.-C. (2000). An information retrieval system based on a user profile. *The Journal of Systems and Software, 54*, 3-8.
6. Cosijin, E., and Ingwersen, P. (2000). Dimensions of relevance. *Information Processing and Management, 63*, 533-550.
7. Gibert, J. E. and Zhong, Y. (2003). Speech user interfaces for information retrieval. *Proceedings of the 12th International Conference on Information and Knowledge Management*, New Orleans, USA, 77-82.
8. Ingwersen, P. and Borlund, P. (1996). Information transfer viewed as interactive cognitive processes. In Ingwersen, P. and Pors, N. O. (Eds.). *Information Science: Integration in Perspective* (pp. 219-232). Copenhagen, Denmark: Royal School of Librarianship.
9. Lieberman, H. (1995). An agent for web browsing. *Proceedings of the International Joint Conference on Artifical intelligence*, Montreal, 924-929.
10. Marchionini, G. (1995). *Information seeking in electronic environments* .Cambridge, U.K.: Cambridge University Press.
11. Norman, D. A. (1988). *The psychology of everyday things*. New York: Basic Books.
12. Resnick, P., Iacovou, N., Mitesh, S., Bergstron, P., and Riedl, J. (1994). GroupLens: an open architecture for collaborative filtering of Netnews. *Proceedings of the ACM Conference on Computer Supported Cooperative Work*, Chapel Hill, USA, 175-186.
13. Saracevic, T. (1996). Relevance reconsidered '96. In Ingwersen, P. and Pors, N. O. (Eds.). *Information Science: Integration in Perspective* (pp. 201-218). Copenhagen, Denmark: Royal School of Librarianship.
14. Tang, R. and Soloman, P. (1998). Toward an understanding of the dynamics of relevance judgment: An analysis of one person's search behavior. *Information Process and Management, 34*, 237-256.

Scalability of Databases for Digital Libraries[*]

John Chmura, Nattakarn Ratprasartporn, and Gultekin Ozsoyoglu

Department of Electrical Engineering and Computer Science,
Case Western Reserve University, Cleveland, Ohio 44106
{jlc18, nxr27, tekin}@case.edu

Abstract. Search engines of main-stream literature digital libraries such as ACM Digital Library, Google Scholar, and PubMed employ file-based systems, and provide users with a basic boolean keyword search functionalities. As a result, new and powerful querying capabilities are not easy to implement on top of such systems, and not provided. In comparison, query languages of database systems traditionally have high expressive power. This paper evaluates the scalability of the approach of deploying relational databases as backend systems to digital libraries, and, thus, making use of the query languages and the query processing capabilities of database query engines for literature digital libraries.

To evaluate our approach, we built a scalable prototype digital library built on top of a relational database management system, and its advanced query interface which allows users to specify dynamic text and path queries in an intuitive, hierarchical manner. This paper evaluates the scalability of two search query processing approaches, namely, ad-hoc queries, pre-compiled queries (stored-procedures). We demonstrate that, with reasonably priced hardware, we are able to build an RDBMS-based digital library search engine that can scale to handle millions of queries per day.

Keywords: Scalability, Database, Metadata, Path Query, Query Interface.

1 Introduction

Main-stream literature digital libraries such as ACM Digital Library [12], CiteSeer [13], and PubMed [14] traditionally employ file-based systems with indexes, and provide users with a basic Boolean keyword search functionality. As more and more researchers find themselves dependent on these digital libraries, there is a need for more advanced query capabilities. Consider the query *"find papers of authors who published in ACM SIGMOD conferences and wrote papers whose titles are similar to 'data mining' with a score of above 0.7"* or the query *"find papers on "web data mining" and on a citation path of distance of length at least 3 starting with paper P"*. Presently, there are no main-stream search systems that allow users to specify such queries. New and powerful querying capabilities, such as path queries and dynamic text queries with approximate similarity predicates and text joins, are not easy to implement on top of file-based systems. At the other end, database systems traditionally provide query languages with high expressive power. In this paper, we evaluate the hypothesis that relational database query engines have now become efficient and effective, and that they can scale for use as backends to literature digital libraries.

---

[*] This research is supported by the US National Science Foundation grant ITR-0312200.

E.A. Fox et al. (Eds.): ICADL 2005, LNCS 3815, pp. 435–445, 2005.
© Springer-Verlag Berlin Heidelberg 2005

To evaluate our hypothesis, we have built Case (Anthology) Explorer [1, 10], a scalable prototype digital library built on top of a relational database management system (RDBMS). Case Explorer is populated with metadata from approximately 15,000 papers from the ACM SIGMOD Anthology [2] and 415,000 paper titles from DBLP bibliography [3]. To specify powerful new queries dynamically, we have designed the advanced query interface (AQI) of Case Explorer, which is browser-based, and allows users to specify dynamic text and path queries in an intuitive and hierarchical manner.

To execute queries generated by AQI, we propose (and evaluate (a) and (b)) five approaches: (a) *ad-hoc queries*, (b) *pre-compiled queries* (stored-procedures) (c) *divide-and-conquer approach*, (d) *user-defined functions*, and (e) an *adaptive-dynamic query interface*. Each approach has performance or flexibility implications.

Finally, we present experiments that test the scalability of Case Explorer from several aspects. By executing queries of increasing complexity and under increasing load conditions, we are able to test the overall performance of the system in high load situations. Our experiments also test system performance in the absence of database indexes and caching. Overall, our experiments demonstrate that, with reasonably priced hardware, we are able to build an RDBMS-based digital library search engine that can scale to handle millions of queries per day.

Section 2 presents the design and implementation of the Case Explorer interface. In section 3, we discuss text-similarity search design considerations. Section 4 lists several query execution methods for achieving balanced scalability and flexibility. In section 5, we evaluate two of the proposed query optimization methods as well as the overall performance of Case Explorer. Section 6 concludes.

2   Advanced Query Interface (AQI) and Path Queries

Case Explorer database [10] is designed to store metadata extracted from papers and research articles. The database contains information about papers both in text form, TF-IDF vectors, and Microsoft Full text Search (MSFT) [7] form. Similarity of two papers is measured [4] based on different sections of a paper:

$$RelatedToPapers(A, B) = \sum_{\forall c \in Comp} w_c \bullet Sim(A_c, B_c) \tag{1}$$

Where *A, B* are papers, *Comp* is the set of paper components {Title, Authors, Abstract, Index Terms, Body, References}, and w_c is the component's weight. Indices are built on the metadata [10].

Case Explorer provides a basic search screen that allows users to search by keyword, author name, paper year, and publication venue. The results of a search and query statistics are displayed on the "results screen" (Fig. 1).

In addition to basic search, the advanced query interface (AQI), whose design is inspired by the Pathway Explorer [16], allows users to specify and expand a given query dynamically. Due to the inherent hierarchical relationships, the AQI is able to provide multiple different hierarchical views to represent nested predicate types. Different types of predicates, as added to the AQI, form a tree structure. Fig. 2 illustrates one of the possible hierarchical views.

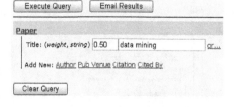

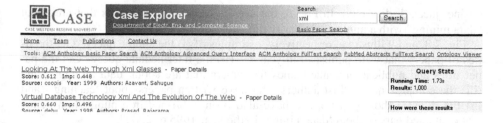

Fig. 1. Search Results Screen

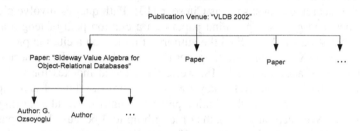

Fig. 2. Example Hierarchy of Anthology Explorer Data

From the initial state (Fig. 3), queries are designed by selecting one of the three main *predicate types* (publication venue, author, or paper) and creating its instances. The user then selects which relations to display in the output (by clicking to any entity type, and the AQI coloring the entity), and executes the query. In Fig. 4, the *Publication Venue* relation has been selected for inclusion into the output.

Fig. 3. AQI Initial State

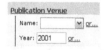

Fig. 4. Designating an Output Relation

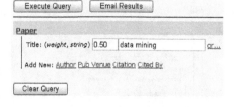

Fig. 5. Multiple Constraints

Fig. 6. Minimal Similarity Threshold in AQI

Each relation in the AQI has one or more search fields available (Fig. 5). When left blank, no constraints are placed on the query. The AQI also allows the user to specify a *minimal similarity threshold* (with respect to a pre-specified similarity measure, e.g., cosine, jaccard, dice etc.). In Fig. 6, the user is searching for papers that are about "data mining" with a minimal similarity threshold of 0.5.

Fig. 7,8, and 9 illustrate, respectively, examples of (i) the simple query "Get the titles of papers that were published in year x", (ii) the intermediate query "Get the paper titles and publication venue names for papers that are about 'data mining'", and (iii) the complex query "List authors who have written papers about 'caching' (and list the titles of those papers), and have also been published in a publication venue that contained papers about 'data mining' in the year 1995 or 2002".

Path queries of Case Explorer allow users to locate papers using predefined path queries. This is a highly useful feature that is expensive to offer by conventional research paper search engines, such as Citeseer [13]. Path queries involve citation relationships between papers, e.g., "Find papers on a citation path of length at least (X) starting with the paper (Y)", "Find the authors of papers on a citation path of distance of length at least (X) ending with the paper (Y)", etc. Because these queries are recursive by nature, in addition to DBMS, we use file-based indexes for scalability. The index file is a hash file where the key for each record in a bucket is a paper-id, and values stored are all papers in the citation paths of length 1, 2, and 3 starting or ending with each key. We keep only the paths of length up to 3 because longer paths usually loose context and become less relevant. Fig. 10 illustrates the query "find papers that are about 'caching', and cite a paper in SIGMOD 1997 within length 2".

To answer a path query, the index file is used to retrieve all papers in the citation path of a specified length starting or ending with a given paper. The results are then

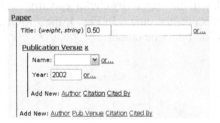

Fig. 7. Simple Query (Q_S) Design in AQI

Fig. 8. Intermediate Query (Q_I) in AQI

Fig. 9. Complex Query (Q_C) Design in AQI

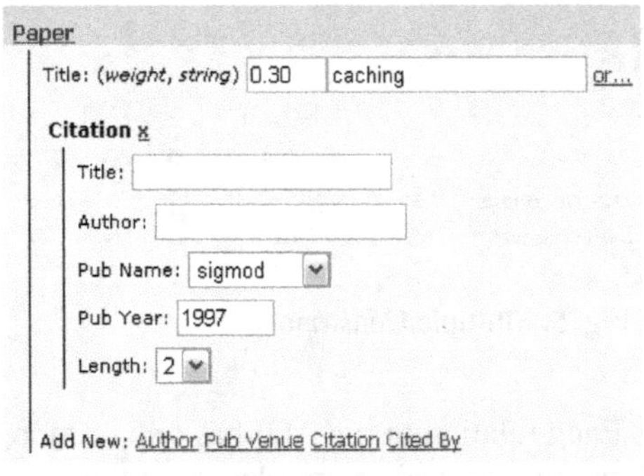

Fig. 10. Example of Path Query in AQI

transferred to the DBMS to retrieve paper contents, such as full title, publication, and year, and details are output.

Path queries are integrated with the Paper Details page and the AQI. From the Paper Details page (of paper Y), users can choose to view citation paths of length 1, 2, or 3 starting or ending with the paper Y. From the AQI, path queries (citation or cited by) are added to the tree structure (but not as the root of the tree).

3 Text-Similarity Search Design Considerations

In the experiments of this paper, to perform the text-similarity search in both the Basic Search and the AQI, we have used the Jaccard similarity measure provided by the Microsoft Full-Text Search component *as opposed to* TF-IDF-based similarity measures implemented as user-defined functions (UDF). The reason is the present nonscalability of the UDF function, which we refer to as *sva_selection* [6, 15]. In earlier work, we have advocated [6, 15] the integration of *"sva operators"* into DBMS query engines for highly powerful and efficient computations of text-based similarity measures, and ranking query outputs, which we believe, when implemented, will outperform the presently employed "SQL optimization+MSFT processing" approach. However, in the absence of such an integrated approach, when we implemented the *sva_selection* UDF through a series of selections from the database relations as well as insertions and updates of temporary tables, *sva_selection* did not scale, and we had to abandon it.

The Microsoft Full-Text Search (MSFT) [7] component is an external full-text search service included with SQL Server that is specifically designed to provide text-search capabilities from within SQL queries. After scanning database relations to index the content, MSFT stores its vector data in the form of a compressed, inverted index structure. When performing a text-search, MSFT computes the paper scores using this vector data and a version of the Jaccard measure [8]. In addition, MSFT caches its indexes in the main memory providing fast search results. The disadvantage to this approach is that flexibility is reduced as we can not customize and integrate the indexing methods, scores, or query formulas for our implementation.

4 Form Query Optimization

Ad-hoc SQL queries can be easily generated by the AQI. However, they incur additional overhead as the database engine creates and compiles the query execution plan each time they are executed.

Pre-compiled queries as stored procedures have several advantages over ad-hoc queries. First, stored procedures do not incur the query plan preparation and compilation expense with each execution. Second, to execute the ad-hoc query, the entire SQL Text must be transferred to the DBMS. The stored procedure version however, only needs to transfer the EXEC command; a much smaller amount of text to transfer. However, stored procedures cannot easily provide the dynamic query capabilities that the AQI requires without placing constraints on the interface.

The third option is a *divide-and-conquer approach*, breaking each entity in the query into separate stored procedures which will insert their results into a temporary relation. An ad-hoc query will then be executed to select all the data from this temporary relation. While the DBMS still must compile a query plan for this ad-hoc query, it will be simple as it will only contain a few joins. The negatives here are the overhead associated with the temporary relation. The DBMS can potentially write the contents to the disk. Furthermore, using a global temporary relation across multiple stored procedures will cause the DMBS to recompile the stored procedure more often [11]. Therefore, temporary relations are not a suitable solution for a high-load situation.

The fourth approach is to use the *User Defined Functions (UDF)*. Continuing with the divide-and-conquer approach, the query for each entity in the AQI can be pre-compiled into a user defined function (UDF) that returns a table value, allowing it to be used in a query by joining it to other relations. Again, a dynamic query will be used to join the proper UDFs and project the output. Similar to stored procedures, UDFs provide the benefits of being compiled. However, in order to return its contents in the form of a table that can be used in a join operation, UDFs use table variables. A table variable still can potentially write to disk in a low-memory situation. Moreover, when performing the natural joins on the table outputs, the DBMS can not take advantage of the indexes already on the original relations. The drawbacks of UDFs therefore outweigh the performance gains of being pre-compiled.

Finally, the AQI can be turned into an *adaptive-dynamic query interface*. When a query structure is seen for the first time, the interface will execute the query as if it is an ad-hoc query while it asynchronously creates a stored procedure for the query. Information about the structure, cost estimates, age information, parameters, and the stored procedure name will then be stored in a central repository. A daemon would be

Table 1. Proposed Query Execution Methods

Method	Advantages	Disadvantages
Ad-Hoc Queries	Flexibility. No constraints need to be placed on the AQI.	Incurs query compilation overhead.
Stored Procedures	Compiled queries reduce execution overhead. RPC call reduces network bandwidth.	Requires constraints to be placed on AQI so that all combinations of queries can be enumerated and code generated.
Stored Procedures with Temporary Relations (not evaluated in this paper)	Retains AQI flexibility. Breaks queries into smaller, more manageable stored procedures.	Temporary Relations will incur creation/drop overhead. Most likely to write to disk, drastically reducing performance.
Ad-Hoc using Table-Valued User-Defined Functions (not evaluated in this paper)	Precompiled Queries gives advantages of stored procedures, while retaining AQI flexibility.	Table-Valued UDFs creates table variables in main memory that can potentially write to disk. Can not utilize the main relations' indexes when performing natural joins.
Adaptive-Dynamic (not evaluated in this paper)	Compiled queries provide benefits of Stored Procedure. Retains full AQI flexibility by allowing the system to generate code.	First execution of a new query will be ad-hoc, incurring extra expense. Additional expense to create the stored procedure. Can potentially produce an extremely large number of stored procedures.

responsible for monitoring the stored procedures, the statistics, and the age information, cleaning up infrequently-used queries or alerting system administrators to overly expensive ones. Subsequent queries of similar structure will then use the compiled stored procedures to execute. While in the end this would potentially enumerate every possible combination of queries, there is an advantage over pre-compiling every combination. First, the system builds the code itself, so generating and managing the stored-procedures is not necessary. In addition, queries can still be executed in an ad-hoc fashion. For most queries, it is likely that users will execute a similarly-structured query more than once, thus benefiting from the dynamically created stored procedure. This method, while incurring slight overhead, offers the most flexibility with the least amount of constraints placed on the AQI.

Table 1 provides an overview of the proposed query execution methods.

5 Experiments

In all of the experiments, Case Explorer is run on a Dell PowerEdge 2850 server with two Intel Xeon 3.2GHz processors and 6.0 GB of main memory. The Enterprise Edition of Windows 2003 Server is used as the operating system. Each experiment is run using Microsoft Application Test Center (MATC) [9]. The MATC opens multiple connections to the server and automatically generates HTTP requests, simulating the behavior of an actual user. The *time-to-last-byte* is used as a measure for the amount of delay from a user's point of view. The bandwidth utilization is measured in kilobytes per second per HTTP response.

To measure the performance of the AQI and path queries, we have created queries of increasing complexity and ran an increasing number of these queries simultaneously to emulate multiple users accessing the system concurrently. A summary of all queries used in our experiments is given in table 2.

Table 2. List of queries used in the experiments

Query Name	Description
Simple Q_S	Selection with one join
Simple with No Cache Q_S^{NC}	Simple query with no relations cached in main memory.
Simple with No Index Q_S^{NI}	Simple query with no indexes
Intermediate Q_I	Selection with one join, one projection, and full-text search
Complex Q_C	Selection with four joins, two full-text searches, and one projection
Simple Path Query P_S	Path query that starts with a paper
Complex Path Query P_C	Path query that starts with an author or a publication venue

Queries that are used in the experiments are as follows.

1. Q_S: "Get titles of papers that were published in year x"
   SELECT paper.title FROM paper
   INNER JOIN publication_venue ON paper.pub_id = publication_venue.pub_id
   WHERE publication_venue.year = x

2. Q_I: "Get paper titles and publication venue names for papers that are about 'data mining' "
   SELECT paper.title, publication_venue.name FROM paper
   INNER JOIN publication_venue ON paper.pub_id = publication_venue.pub_id
   WHERE CONTAINS(paper.title, 'data mining')
3. Q_C: "List authors with papers about 'caching' (and list the titles of those papers), and published in a publication venue with papers about 'data mining' in years y_1 or y_2."
   SELECT author.name, paper1.title FROM author
   INNER JOIN AuthorToPaper AtP on author.author_id = AtP.author_id
   INNER JOIN Paper Paper1 on AtP.paper_id = Paper1.paper_id
   INNER JOIN AuthorToPubVenue AtPub on author.author_id=AtPub.author_id
   INNER JOIN Paper Paper2 on AtoPub.pub_id = Paper2.pub_id
   WHERE CONTAINS(Paper1.title, 'caching') AND CONTAINS(Paper2.title, 'data
   mining') AND (Paper2.pub_year = year or Paper2.pub_year = year)
4. P_S: "List papers in the citation path of length at least 1, 2, and 3 starting with paper x"
5. P_C: "List papers that cite a paper written by author x within length 1, 2, and 3"

The *paper* relation used in experiments currently holds approximately 430,000 tuples. Case Explorer will eventually contain over 7.0 million papers (presently, it is being populated with freely-available PubMed papers from biomedical sciences). Therefore, to more accurately simulate the amount of disk IO required to scan the *paper* relation, we have padded each tuple with extra 48 bytes. The extra 48 bytes increases the total amount of space to approximately 26.2 MB; a closer representation of the final dataset. Also, the size of the hash file used in the path query experiments is increased to 500 MB (the actual size is 2MB for the current database).

Each test run is defined by the number c of *concurrent* connections. The experiments begin by running one connection to establish a baseline of a query's running time. The no. of concurrent connections is then increased to 5, 10, 25, 50, and 100.

Simple Query Experiments (Fig. 11a, 11b):
These queries involve simple query Q_S, Q_S^{NI} (no indexing), and Q_S^{NC} (no caching).

By default, the DBMS caches as much data into main memory as possible. However, in the future, it may become necessary to run queries against live data that is very large, and will not fit into the main memory. The first experiment tests how much load, and at what level of performance, our system can handle without caching any data in the main memory. To run this experiment, the DBMS is forced to clear all buffer pages after each query is run. Although overall performance of Q_S^{NC} is poor, the system can fulfill at least 775,000 queries per day with little noticeable delay.

In the Q_S^{NI} experiments, the *pub_id* and *paper_id* indexes are removed from the *paper* relation to force the database engine to scan the entire relation. We use the Q_S^{NI} query to measure performance in a worst case scenario. The amount of time required to perform a full scan reduces performance beyond that of the Q_S^{NC} query. The maximum practical number of requests handled by this experiment is approximately 5 per second, or 432,000 per day.

The Q_S experiment fulfilled 25 requests per second, or 1.9 million per day with a response time of less than one second. We also run the Q_S query from an offsite location to test the effects of internet latency on the query response times. From our remote location, with a single connection, the remote client received the full response from the Case Explorer server in 176.04 milliseconds compared to the 84.29 millisecond response time when run directly from the server. We attribute approximately 90 milliseconds of transfer time to internet latency.

All of the above experiments were executed through an ad-hoc approach. With a simple query experiment, the pre-compiled approach can not be show a significant gain in performance over the ad-hoc approach (19% gain in requests per second, but only 1% gain in performance with respect to response time).

Observation: 1) Although the Q_S experiment demonstrates a 51.4% gain in performance over Q_S^{NC} and 74.3% gain over Q_S^{NI}, the system can fulfill 775,000 and 432,000 queries per day for Q_S^{NC} and Q_S^{NI}. 2) Internet latency adds an average of 90 milliseconds to the server's response. 3) Overall, the gain in performance from pre-compiled queries over the ad-hoc queries is negligible.

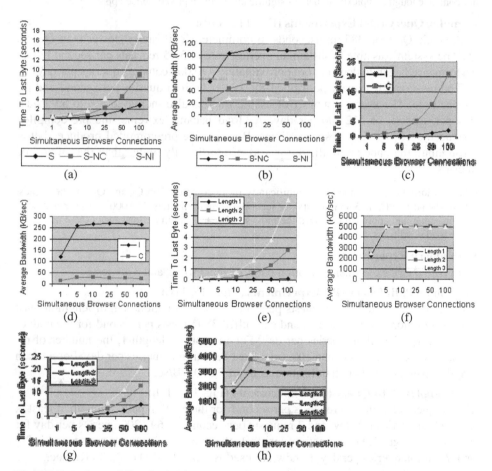

Fig. 11. Experimental Results (ad-hoc approach): (a, c, e, g) are response times and (b, d, f, h) are bandwidth utilizations for Q_S, Q_I and Q_C, P_S, and P_C experiments, respectively

Intermediate Query (Q_I) Experiments (Fig. 11c, 11d):

The response times of this query were fast. A single connection of this ad-hoc query provided a 48.7% gain in response time over the simple ad-hoc query. At a maximum usable rate of 47.4 requests per second, the ad-hoc Q_I can fulfill 4 million queries per day. One side effect of this type of query is that the increased number of connection runs per second greatly increase the bandwidth used. Running at its peak of 47.4 requests per second, the server was transferring data at a speed of 267 KB/sec, a significant increase over other experiments.

Similar to simple queries, the gain in performance from the pre-compiled over the ad-hoc approach is not significant. Below we summarize the results.

Observation: 1) The added predicates in Q_I reduce the amount of data to be processed, and significantly increase the response time (a 53% gain in performance over Q_S). 2) At a maximum usable rate of 47.4 requests per second, the ad-hoc Q_I can fulfill 4 million queries per day. 3) Q_I does not contain enough complexity to benefit significantly from a pre-compiled approach.

Complex Query (Q_C) Experiments (Fig. 11c, 11d):

A single Q_C took 385 milliseconds to complete, significantly slower than Q_S and Q_I. The system was able to sustain an average rate of 5.45 requests per second before performance began to degrade, or approximately 470,000 complex queries per day.

The pre-compiled query performed 8% better both in queries per second and response time. The average number of usable queries also increased 8% to 5.93 queries per second, or 512,000 per day. As load became extreme, the pre-compiled produced a 16% gain in response times. Because the pre-compiled produces better throughput, the bandwidth utilization was proportionally higher than that of ad-hoc queries.

Observation: 1) The ad-hoc Q_C is significantly more complex than Q_S and Q_I. 2) The request rate of the ad-hoc Q_C is 5.45 requests per second, or approximately 470,000 queries per day. 3) The pre-compiled approach produced the most significant gain in performance (16%) under extreme load conditions.

Path Query Experiments:

In path query experiments, citation paths of length 1, 2, and 3 are tested.

a) Simple Path Query (P_S) Experiments (Fig. 11e, 11f):

The P_S query can fulfill 15 requests per second for the citation path of length at least 3, or 1.3 million queries per day, and can fulfill 38 requests per second for the path of length 2, or 3.2 million queries per day. For the path of length 1, the number of requests per second is more than 100, or at least 8.6 million queries per day. For all path lengths, average bandwidth utilization is about 5,000 KB/sec.

b) Complex Path Query (P_C) Experiments (Fig. 11g, 11h):

The P_C query can fulfill 6 requests per second for the citation path of length at least 3, or 259,200 queries per day, and 8 requests per second, or 691,200 queries per day for the path of length 2. For the path of length 1, the number of requests per second is 20, or 1.7 million queries per day. Bandwidth used is around 3,000 to 3,500 KB/sec.

Observation: 1) Path query experiments can fulfill from 259,200 to 8.6 millions queries per day depending on its complexity. 2) The bandwidth utilizations of both experiments (about 4,000 KB/sec) are high when compared to those of regular query experiments because of a larger amount of text transferred to DBMS.

6 Conclusions

In order to provide the AQI functionality and remain scalable, we have devised several strategies for implementing the queries behind the AQI. Ad-hoc queries allow the greatest flexibility while suffering a performance hit. Pre-compiled queries offer greater performance, however limit flexibility. We have discussed benefits and disadvantages of each of these options in detail. We evaluated the scalability of our system using both ad-hoc and pre-compiled queries. Through our experiments, we established that Case Explorer could sufficiently support user's queries in a high-load environment. In addition, pre-compiled queries perform only slightly better than ad-hoc queries. Our tests demonstrate that Case Explorer will be able to fulfill from 200 thousand to about four million queries per day based on the complexity of queries.

References

1. Case Explorer, http://nashua.cwru.edu/CaseExplorer.htm
2. ACM SIGMOD Anthology, http://www.acm.org/sigmod/dblp/db/anthology.html
3. DBLP bibliography, http://www.informatik.uni-trier.de/~ley/db
4. Li, L., "Metadata Extraction: RelatedToPapers and its Use in Web Resource Querying", MS Thesis, EECS Dept, CWRU, 2003.
5. Al-Hamdani, A., "Querying web resources with metadata in a database", PhD Thesis, EECS Dept., CWRU, 2004.
6. Ozsoyoglu G., Al-Hamdani, A., Altingovde, I. S., Ozel, S. A., Ulusoy, O., and Ozsoyoglu, Z. M., "Sideway Value Algebra for Object-Relational Databases". In Proc. of VLDB 2002, Hong Kong, August 2002.
7. Microsoft Full Text Search, http://msdn.microsoft.com/library/en-us/dnsql90/html/sql2005ftsearch.asp
8. Kowalski, G., "Information retrieval systems: theory and implementation", Kluwer Academic Publishers, 1997.
9. Microsoft Application Center Test, http://msdn.microsoft.com/library/en-us/act/htm/actml_main.asp
10. Chmura, J., "Scalable Web Data Source Search Engine Using an RDBMS", MS Thesis, EECS Dept, CWRU, 2005.
11. http://msdn.microsoft.com/library/en-us/dnsql2k/html/sql_queryrecompilation.asp
12. ACM Digital Library, http://portal.acm.org/portal.cfm
13. CiteSeer, http://citeseer.ist.psu.edu
14. Pubmed, http://www.ncbi.nlm.nih.gov/entrez/query.fcgi
15. Ozsoyoglu, G., Altingovde, I.S., Al-Hamdani, A., Ozel, S.A., Ulusoy, O., Ozsoyoglu, Z.M., "Querying Web metadata: Native Score Management and Text Support in Databases", ACM Transactions on Database Systems, Dec. 2004.
16. Newman, S., Ozsoyoglu M., "A Tree-Structured Query Interface for Querying Semi-Structured Data". SSDBM 2004.

GMA-PSMH: A Semantic Metadata Publish-Harvest Protocol for Dynamic Metadata Management Under Grid Environment

Yaping Zhu, Ming Zhang, Kewei Wei, and Dongqing Yang

School of Electronics Engineering and Computer Science, Peking University, 100871, Beijing, China
{zhuyaping, mzhang, wkw, ydq}@db.pku.edu.cn

Abstract. The imperative demand on the description of semantic metadata and the processing of real-time data presents unique challenge to Grid Metadata Service. Grid Monitoring Architecture (GMA), which is a framework for dynamic data management, is limited by its conventional interface of relational database and therefore fails to address the problem of interoperability. Faced with the problem of metadata publishing in GMA, we present a new publish-harvest protocol for semantic metadata called GMA-PSMH (Grid Monitoring Architecture-Protocol for Semantic Metadata Harvesting) by modifying the OAI-PMH metadata harvest framework. As part of the Semantic Metadata Service Project in Peking University, the associated dynamic metadata management framework is then implemented according to the above protocol. At the end, we make the conclusion and overview the future work.

1 Introduction

The imperative demand on scientific distributed processing, cross-domain cooperative computing and resources sharing has greatly accelerated the development of Grid Computing. Grid Computing is an integrated environment of resource and service[1]. Its major objective is to solve the complex scientific and engineering problems by sharing resource and services under a distributed and heterogeneous environment. To achieve this goal, two prerequisites are required:

- The cross-domain resource used in modern scientific activities is characterized by its diversity, so a simple, standard and extensible description mechanism is required.
- In modern scientific cooperation, massive data and resource are processed in real-time, thus an effective retrieval method and dynamic, synchronous update mechanism is on demand in resource management.

Under such environment, resource turns into the core of the whole grid architecture. It is only by effective description of resource that the above goals could be achieved. Metadata and metadata service has consequently become the key to solve the above two problems[2][3].

E.A. Fox et al. (Eds.): ICADL 2005, LNCS 3815, pp. 446–456, 2005.
© Springer-Verlag Berlin Heidelberg 2005

Meanwhile, research on semantic resource description and intelligent information retrieval is developing rapidly in the domain of the Semantic Web[4]. The Semantic Web Activity statement of the World Wide Web Consortium (W3C) describes the Semantic Web as "an extension of the current Web in which information is given well-defined meaning. It is the idea of having data on the Web defined and linked in a way that it can be used for more effective discovery, automation, integration, and reuse across various applications."[5]

Therefore, semantic metadata service will necessarily become the trend of general metadata service. By making full use of the Ontology to describe the semantic relationship between concepts, semantic metadata service could enhance the conventional metadata description in Grid to a knowledge level, and establish a solid foundation for effective resource description and sharing[6].

As part of the "Grid Computing Resource Service Middleware" Project in Peking University, the Semantic Metadata Service Project is supported by the National Science Foundation (NSF) in China under grant No. 90412010 and ChinaGrid project of the Ministry of Education in China.

Per the demand of scientific activities in Grid Computing, the objective of the Semantic Metadata Service Project is to establish the metadata model and classification in a semantic and extensible way, and build the associated semantic metadata services such as resource sharing, discovery, and dynamic management.

To meet the need of metadata publishing in Grid Monitoring Architecture, we designed a new semantic metadata publish-harvest protocol called GMA-PSMH by expanding the OAI-PMH metadata harvest framework. A new dynamic semantic metadata management system is then developed according to the above protocol.

The rest of the paper is structured as follows. Section 2 and 3 describes related work and the architecture of the Semantic Metadata Service Project in Peking University. Section 4 describes the design of GMA-PSMH protocol. In Section 5 and 6, we describe the dynamic semantic metadata management framework and its implementation. The paper concludes with a summary and outlines future research.

2   Related Work

2.1   GMA

Grid Monitoring Architecture (GMA) is defined within the Global Grid Forum (GGF)[7]. Its major purpose is to monitor the real-time data and information under Grid environment. The architecture consists of three components (shown in Figure 1): Consumers, Producers, and a Registry.

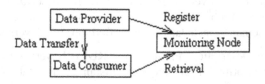

Fig. 1. Grid Monitoring Architecture

- Producers: register its URL and the type of data available with the Registry;
- Consumers: query the Registry to find out the desired type of information and to locate the corresponding Producer. Then the Consumer could get the real-time data by contacting a specific Producer directly with its URL;
- Registry: provides registry service Producers and information retrieval for Consumers[8].

As part of the European Data Grid Project, the Relational Grid Monitoring Architecture (R-GMA) is an implementation of the above-mentioned Grid Monitoring Architecture[9]. It is based on the traditional relational data model, and users could insert and retrieve data from the repository by issuing SQL queries such as SQL INSERT and SQL SELECT statements.

Nevertheless, limited by its interface of relational databases, R-GMA fails to address the problem of interoperability. Nor could it make any support to data publishing and harvesting.

2.2 OAI-PMH

Open Archive Initiative□Protocol for Metadata Harvesting (OAI-PMH) is a framework designed for metadata interoperability in the domain of Digital Library[10]. The framework logically has two kinds of collaborators (shown in Figure 2). Data Provider provides its general repository information, metadata formats and metadata records in response to OAI requests. Service Provider then uses the harvested metadata as a foundation for providing value-added services[11].

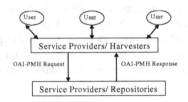

Fig. 2. OAI-PMH

However, OAI-PMH is designed for traditional metadata publishing, and there exists no standard currently for semantic metadata publishing and harvesting.

3 Semantic Metadata Service Project

Berners-Lee proposed a seven-layer architecture for describing different layers of resource in Semantic Web[9]. According to the need of resource description in Grid environment, the semantic metadata are classified into two layers in our project.

- Resource Description Framework (RDF) Layer: describes the detailed semantic information of objects or instances. It establishes the relationship about single object, property and property value and saves them in files formatted in RDF standard[12];

- Ontology Layer: defines the abstract structure of a semantic class and the relationship between different classes. Ontology is defined as the formalized specification of shared conceptual model and OWL is one of the most widely used descriptive languages for Ontology[13]. OWL mainly describes resources by two types of building block: concept and property. It uses semantic relationship such as hierarchical structure, synonymy, logical component, and relational constraint to establish the relationship between resources and saves the model in files formatted in OWL standard.

The Semantic Metadata Service Project uses the above-mentioned two layers to describe the semantic data and metadata. Features of the project include:

First, in metadata service, metadata itself undoubtedly becomes the core data model. Associated core metadata services include the registry, deletion, update and retrieval of metadata. Moreover, extensible description mechanism must be provided for metadata definition management.

Second, we also define the concepts of collection and view to facilitate personalized logical organizing of metadata. Corresponding metadata services include the creation, deletion and update of views and collections.

Last, resource in the Grid is characterized by its changeability. Under such circumstance, traditional metadata service interface could no longer satisfy the need. A new dynamic, semantic metadata management framework is presented in our project to support the registry, synchronous update and retrieval of dynamic metadata.

The whole architecture could be layered in four layers, as shown in Figure 3.

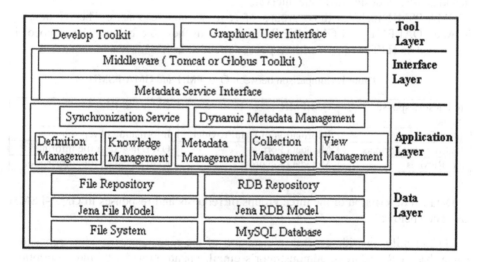

Fig. 3. Semantic Metadata Service Project in Peking University

- Tool Layer: provides develop toolkit and graphical user interface for semantic metadata services;
- Interface Layer: deals with the definition of service interface and the parsing of communication protocol (such as SOAP) and XML documents;

- Application Layer: provides implementation of seven types of semantic metadata service interfaces, including metadata definition management, metadata instance management, collection management, view management, knowledge management and dynamic metadata management and synchronous update;
- Data Layer: stores data objects used for metadata services, including metadata definition, metadata instances, collections, views and knowledge.

In this paper, we mainly focuses on the Dynamic Metadata Management Framework in application layer. In the following section, the paper will describes the design of the Semantic Metadata Publish-Harvest Protocol (GMA-PSMH).

4 Semantic Metadata Publish-Harvest Protocol Design

As stated above, OAI-PMH is designed for traditional metadata publish-harvest[10]. A new Semantic Metadata Publish-Harvest Protocol (GMA-PSMH) is consequently required to solve the problem of dynamic semantic metadata management in Grid.

First, the semantic metadata in the project are classified into two categories, formatted in RDF and OWL individually. Therefore, the protocol should support the publishing of the above two kinds of metadata files. Moreover, according to the need of dynamic metadata management, the protocol must also provide the URL address and average update frequency of metadata files to facilitate synchronous update of metadata files at designated time interval.

GMA-PSMH includes three groups of requests and responses. The relationship between OAI-PMH and GMA-PSMH is shown in the table below. The protocol is also based on HTTP request, with responses encoded in XML streams.

Table 1. Comparison between OAI-PMH and GMA-PSMH

Request/Response Name	OAI-PMH	GMA-PSMH
Identify	Information of DataProvider	Information of repository
ListMetadataFormats	Metadata Format	OWL metadata file information
ListRecords	Metadata Records	RDF metadata file information

Detailed description of the three groups of requests and responses in GMA-PSMH are stated below:

1) Identify: provide general information of the repository, including repository name, base URL address, administrator's email, update granularity and description, similar to OAI-PMH.

2) ListMetadataFormats: describe the formats of semantic metadata, or say, the general information of OWL metadata files, including filename, URL address, average update granularity, last update time, version, copyright and detailed description. Detailed protocol examples is shown below:

```
<?xml version="1.0" encoding="UTF-8" ?>
<GMA-PMHxmlns=http://www.openarchives.org/OAI/2.0/
xmlns:xsi="http://www.w3.org/2001/XMLSchema-instance"
xsi:schemaLocation="http://www.openarchives.org/OAI/2.0/
http://www.openarchives.org/OAI/2.0/OAI-PMH.xsd">
<responseDate>2005-05-17T21:45:33Z</responseDate>
<request verb="ListMetadataFormats" />
<ListMetadataFormats>
<metadataFormat>
<fileName>filesystem.owl</fileName>
       <URL>localhost://filesystem.owl</URL>
       <granularity>2 months</granularity>
       <lastUpdated>2005-05-01T</lastUpdated>
       <version>1.0</version>
       <copyright>pku</copyright>
       <description>file system</description>
</metadataFormat>
</ListMetadataFormats>
</GMA-PMH>
```

3) ListMetadataFiles: describe semantic metadata, or say, the general information of RDF metadata files, including filename, URL address, URI, average update granularity, last update time, version, copyright and detailed description. Detailed protocol examples is shown below:

```
<?xml version="1.0" encoding="UTF-8" ?>
<GMA-PMHxmlns=http://www.openarchives.org/OAI/2.0/
  xmlns:xsi="http://www.w3.org/2001/XMLSchema-
  instance"xsi:schemaLocation="http://www.openarchives.org/
  OAI/2.0/http://www.openarchives.org/OAI/2.0/OAI-PMH.xsd">
<responseDate>2005-05-17T21:45:33Z</responseDate>
<request verb="ListMetadataFiles" />
<ListMetadataFiles>
<metadataFile>
       <fileName>network1.rdf</fileName>
       <URL>localhost://network/network1.rdf</URL>
       <granularity>1 minute</granularity>
 <lastUpdated>2005-05-01T</lastUpdated>
       <version>1.0</version>
       <copyright>pku</copyright>
       <metadataFormat>network.owl</metadataFormat>
       <description>null</description>
    </metadataFile>
   </ListMetadataFiles>
</GMA-PMH>
```

5 Dynamic Metadata Management Framework

In accordance with the demand on dynamic metadata synchronization and management under Grid environment, we designed a new dynamic, semantic metadata management framework by referring to Grid Monitoring Architecture.

452   Y. Zhu et al.

In this framework, three kinds of participators are defined first, namely resource provider, resource consumer and metadata service. Detailed function of each kind of participator is described below:

- Resource Providers: monitor the status of Grid resource and publish the status formatted in semantic metadata according to GMA-PSMH protocol;
- Metadata Service: is in charge of resource provider registration and metadata retrieval. It stores the update address and average update frequency of dynamic metadata, and harvests synchronous metadata to its local repository by parsing the GMA-PSMH protocol at designated time interval;
- Resource Consumers: users of application programs.

Next, different kinds of dynamic metadata in this framework must be classified:

- Real-time Metadata: the metadata provided and published by resource providers to describe the real-time status of resource in Grid;
- Historical Metadata: the metadata harvested from resource providers in the past. Since the resource status in Grid may change rapidly, absolute real-time metadata could not be achieved. So the only way is to set different update frequencies in accordance with the changing features of diverse resources. Historical metadata still shows its significance in metadata retrieval;
- Cached Metadata: the historical metadata stored at metadata service, which is used as a base for information retrieval.

The whole workflow of the Dynamic Metadata Management Framework consists of the following five processes, as shown in Figure 4, with active application processes marked in dark color.

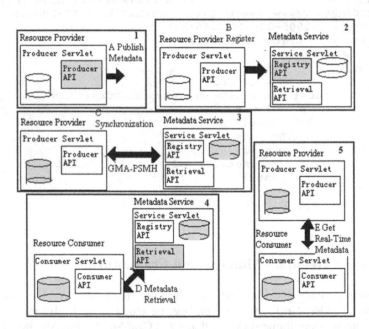

Fig. 4. Dynamic Metadata Management Framework

1)   Resource Provider publishes its dynamic, semantic metadata formatted in RDF and OWL according to GMA-PSMH protocol;

2)   Resource provider registers itself at metadata service;

3)   After registration, metadata service harvests the semantic metadata synchronously at designated time interval, and stores the harvested metadata at its repository as cached metadata;

4)   When resource consumer requests at metadata service, the metadata service returns several matched metadata and the approach to get the real-time metadata;

5)   The resource consumer could choose to use the cached metadata directly or harvest real-time metadata from resource producers.

6 Implementation

6.1 Resource Provider Implementation

As part of the Dynamic Metadata Management Framework, resource provider accepts HTTP requests (Get or Post method) from metadata service or resource consumer, and responses XML streams according to GMA-PSMH protocol. The whole sub-system of the resource provider consists of three functional modules, as shown in Figure 5.

1)   JSP Page Management Module: accepts HTTP requests and parameters, calls the corresponding function in JavaBean, and displays the result page via Apache Tomcat Server.

2)   Database Management Module: Descriptive information of RDF and OWL semantic files is saved in MySQL database in our system. The main purpose of the database management module is to generate appropriate SQL query statements, retrieve the database, and return the result to application program. Also, three tables named GeneralInfo, OWLFiles and RDFFiles are established in our database, saving general information, metadata formats and metadata individually;

3)   XML Format Generator: generators XML stream according to GMA-PSMH.

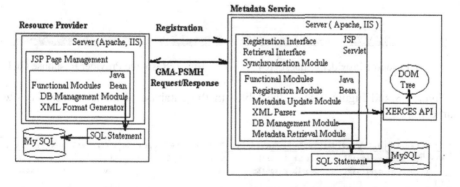

Fig. 5. Resource Provider and Metadata Service Implementation

6.2 Metadata Service Implementation

The primary function of metadata service is to provide resource provider registration and metadata retrieval. Moreover, metadata service has to start up system thread timely, and harvests real-time metadata to update its local repository. The whole sub-system composes five parts, also shown in Figure 5.

1) Resource Provider Registration Module: provides interface for resource providers to register its base URL address. Then, a system thread is started up sending HTTP requests to get general information and metadata of the resource provider.

2) Metadata Update Module: metadata service starts up system thread timely according to the average update frequency provided by resource provider, sends HTTP requests (verb=ListMetadataFormats or verb=ListMetadataFiles), parses XML streams and updates its database.

3) XML Parser: parses GMA-PSMH protocol stream to a DOM tree by making use of the XERCES java package.

4) Database Management Module: generator SQL INSERT or UPDATE statements to update its local repository.

5) Metadata Retrieval Module: returns several matched metadata and provides approaches for resource consumer to get real-time metadata from the provider.

6.3 Graphical User Interface

Resource provider accepts HTTP requests from user and responses in XML streams in accordance with GMA-PSMH protocol, as shown in Figure 6 and Figure 7.

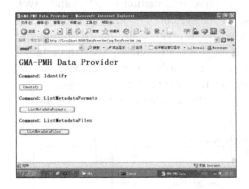 

Fig. 6. Resource Provider Request GUI   **Fig. 7.** Resource Provider Response GUI

Figures 8 and Figure 9 show the tables in the database of metadata service after harvesting.

	filename	dataprovider	url	granularity	lastupdated	version	copyright	description
▶	network.owl	myFirstDP	localh	1 month	2005-05-01T00:	1.0	pku	network eleme
	filesystem.	myFirstDP	localh	2 months	2005-05-01T00:	1.0	pku	file system
✳								

Fig. 8. Table OWLFiles in Metadata Service

filename	dataprovider	url	granularity	lastupdated	version	copyright	metadataformat	description
network1.r	myFirstDP	localh	1 minute	2005-05-01T00	1.0	pku	network.owl	null
network2.r	myFirstDP	localh	30 seconds	2005-05-01T00	2.0	pku	network.owl	null
filesystem	myFirstDP	localh	6 hours	2005-05-01T00	1.0	pku	filesystem.owl	null
network1.r	myFirstDP	localh	1 minute	2005-05-01T00	1.0	pku	network.owl	null
network2.r	myFirstDP	localh	30 seconds	2005-05-01T00	2.0	pku	network.owl	null
filesystem	myFirstDP	localh	6 hours	2005-05-01T00	1.0	pku	filesystem.owl	null

Fig. 9. Table RDFFiles in Metadata Service

The metadata retrieval page and collection view of metadata is shown in Figure 10 and 11.

Fig. 10. Metadata Retrieval Page   **Fig.11.** Collection View of Metadata

7 Conclusion and Future Work

As part of the Semantic Metadata Service Project in Peking University, the paper designed and implemented the Dynamic Metadata Management Framework. Primary features of the system are listed below:

- The system promotes the interoperability of current Grid Monitoring Architecture effectively by publishing and harvesting metadata;
- The system supports semantic metadata publish-harvest by modifying the OAI-PMH in Digital Library domain;

Our future work will focus on the utilization of Web Service[14] [15]. The interoperability of the metadata service system does not only includes metadata publishing, but also web service of current functional modules. As the middleware of Internet, Web Service is a distributed computing technique based on object/ component modules. Based on Web Service, the Internet could become an open component platform, which would facilitate function extension and combination to meet the diverse need of users. Therefore, Web Service will undoubtedly become the trend of next generation Grid Computing.

References

1. Ian Foster, Carl Kesselman, and Steven Tuecke, The Anatomy of the Grid: Enabling Scalable Virtual Organizations, International J. Supercomputer Applications, 15(3), 2001
2. http://www.w3.org/Metadata/
3. Ewa Deelman, et al, Grid-Based Metadata Services, 16th International Conference on Scientific and Statistical Database Management (SSDBM04), 21-23 June 2004 Santorini Island Greece
4. David De Roure, Nicholas R. Jennings and Nigel R. Shadbolt, The Semantic Grid: A Future e-Science Infrastructure, 2004
5. W3C Semantic Web Activity Statement, http://www.w3.org/2001/sw/Activity/
6. Semantic Web, www.w3.org/2001/sw/
7. R-GMA: Relational Grid Monitoring Architecture, www.r-gma.org/
8. Rajesh Ramon, MATCHMAKING FRAMEWORKS FOR DISTRIBUTED RESOURCE MANAGEMENT, 2001
9. European DataGrid Project, http://www.edg.org/
10. OAI, www.openarchives.org/
11. Shuan Wang, Meng Wang, and Ming Zhang, the Design and Implementation of a Metadata Interoperability Architecture based on OAI-PMH, Computer Engineering and Application, 2003.39(20)
12. RDF, http://www.w3.org/RDF/
13. OWL, http://www.w3.org/2001/sw/WebOnt/
14. http://www.w3.org/TR/ws-arch
15. Web Service Architecture: Technology Overview, 2004(4)

Choosing Appropriate Peer-to-Peer Infrastructure for Your Digital Libraries

Hao Ding and Ingeborg Sølvberg

Dept. of Computer and Information System, Norwegian Univ. of Sci. &Tech.,
Sem Sælands vei 7-9, NO-7491, Trondheim, Norway
{hao.ding, ingeborg}@idi.ntnu.no

Abstract. Peer-to-Peer (P2P) overlay network aims to be a feasible platform for building federated but autonomous digital libraries. However, due to a plethora number of P2P infrastructures and corresponding functionalities, it is often not easy to choose appropriate candidates for specific applications. This paper is devoted for this issue by comparing some typcial P2P systems widely used in digtal library or databbase communities and extending an open discussion on how to determine proper infrastructures according to specific system requirements.

1   Introduction

Peer-to-Peer (P2P) overlay network becomes a substantial research topic in recent digital libraries applications. One fact is that a special working group has been settled in DELOS [1] focusing on constructing highly scalable, customizable and adaptive digital libraries, where building digital libraries over P2P overlay network is a major research activity. However, due to a plethora number of P2P infrastructures available, a core requirement exists in determing appropriate P2P infrastructure for specific digital library applications. In this paper, we study some representative P2P infrastructures by comparing several key features which are critical for system functionalities and performances. Section 2 presents a comparsion on selected P2P systems or infrastructures, followed by discussions concerning key issues in deciding appropriate P2P solutions. Conclusions and recommended future work are in Section 3.

2   P2P Systems Summary and Discussion

2.1   Comparing P2P Systems

Although many criteria must be taken into consideration in comparing P2P systems, we believe that information searching will be one of the most significant factors. Hence, the comparison will be centered mainly on this issue. Table 1 illustrates the comparisons over selected systems in aspects of markup schema, hash table usage, semantic routing style, query forwarding support, semantic query support and system topology.

Gnutella (http://www.limewire.com/), Napster (http://www.napster.com), and Freenet [2] are ancestors in P2P computing. They all support keyword-based search. Gnutella is a representative instance for query flooding which can not scale well. Napster goes

E.A. Fox et al. (Eds.): ICADL 2005, LNCS 3815, pp. 457–462, 2005.
© Springer-Verlag Berlin Heidelberg 2005

in the opposite direction and adopts central servers to maintain a centralized directory from which connected peers can register their profiles/expertises and also retrieve a list of peers of user's interest. In Freenet, each file/document is identified by a binary key which is generated using some hash function; each peer maintains a local routing table which keeps information about neighbouring peers and the keys are a sequence of *(file key, node address)* pairs used for retrieval.

Table 1. Typical P2P Systems Summary

System	Markup-Scheme	Hash Table /Usage	Semantic Routing	Query Forwarding	Semantic Query
Gnutella	Keyword	No	No	Yes	No
Naspter	Keyword	No	No	No	No
Freenet	Keyword	Yes(binary)	Serial	Yes	No
Routing Indices	Keyword	No	Serial	Yes	No
Chord	Keyword	Yes	Parallel	Yes	No
CAN	Keyword	Yes	Parallel	Yes	No
pSearch	Keyword	Yes	No	Yes[1]	No
Piazza	Database	No	No	Yes	relational+XML
HyperCup	Keyword	Yes	Separate HyperCube	Yes	Yes
JXTA Search	XML	No	Parallel	Yes	No
Edutella	RDF	No	Parallel	Yes	Yes (regional)
Bibster	RDF/DAML+OIL	No	Parallel	Yes	Yes (global)
OAI-P2P(ongoing)	RDF	No	Parallel	Yes	Yes (regional)
RDFPeers	RDF	Yes	Parallel	Yes	Yes (global)
P-Grid	Keyword	Dist. Search Tree	Serial	Yes	No

Crespo [3] uses Routing Indices (RIs), created and maintained by each peer, to forward queries to neighbours that are more likely to have answers. Any peer's joining or leaving can lead to a cascade of updates in RIs. And this is the overhead generated for the sake of efficient query forwarding in RIs instead of random flooding.

Distributed Hash Table (DHT) is probably the most widely used algorithm in P2P computing. Generally, DHT systems assign each entity (e.g. file names) a key generated by a hashing algorithm, then map the key to the node which also has an ID (e.g. hashed IP address). Normally this ID is the one closest to the key. In consequence, the storage and lookups of keys are distributed among multiple hosts. The performance of all DHT algorithms has been justified pretty good [4]. For instances, each node maintains information only about $O(logN)$ other nodes, and a lookup requires $O(logN)$ messages. Chord [5], CAN [6] and pSearch [7] are representative DHT systems. One requirement in applying DHT is that all participating libraries (peers) must be highly coupled, and moreover, an uneven distribution of document pointers may be expected over the peers and the global state is required beforehand as a support for the algorithm.

Piazza [8] is a peer data management system that enables sharing heterogeneous data in a distributed and scalable way. The assumption in this system is that the participants have similar content to share within other peers. Then, pair-wise mappings are defined between their schemas and users can formulate queries over their preferred schema. Piazza also creates a query answering system for expanding recursively any mappings relevant to the query, retrieving data from other peers.

JXTA [9] is a P2P interoperability framework created by Sun Microsystems. All peers can publish their profiles (i.e., content summary) in way of 'advertising'. One peer in JXTA can thus discover other peers by discovering posted 'advertisements' and then join favorite peer groups. Communications between peers are conducted by 'pipes' specifically generated by them. Typical systems include Edutella [10] and Bibster [11]. Both of them support metadata search within P2P networks while the former focuses on educational domain and the latter on bibliographic records respectively. JXTA itself can be regarded as a super-peer network consisted of many 'rendezvous' peers [9]

HyperCup [12] proposes a graph topology which allows very efficient broadcast and search which intend to reach all peers in the network with the minimum number of messages possible. The number of messages generated when peers leave and join the network is $O(log_b N)$ (b is the base of the hypercube), which can be more efficient than DHT algorithm. Moreover, a global ontology is proposed to determine the organization of peers in the graph topology, allowing for efficient concept-based search.

The ongoing OAI-P2P project [13] aims to design a P2P network for open archives, where data providers form a P2P network which supports distributed search over all connected metadata repositories. In this scenario service providers can be removed from this network and make the data repositories more up-to-date.

RDFPeers [14] is a very interesting approach by extending DHT to support searches over RDF triples. Basically, RDFPeers becomes a scalable distributed RDF repository that stores each triple at three places in a multi-attribute addressable network by applying globally known hash functions to its subject, predicate, and object. Such an approach is very suitable to search through highly distributed RDF repositories.

P-Grid [15] is a kind of Semantic Overlay Network (SON) [16], which differs from other approaches such as Chord, CAN, etc. in terms of practical applicability (especially in respect to dynamic network environments), algorithmic foundations (randomized algorithms with probabilistic guarantees), robustness, and flexibility. The most important properties of P-Grid are: complete decentralization;self-organization;decentralized load balancing; data management functionalities (update);management of dynamic IP addresses and identities; efficient search[15].

2.2   Discussion

In constructing specific P2P-based digital libraries, different institutes may have different requirements in constructing P2P networks. Some critical requirements demanding special considerations are listed as follows:

- Degree of autonomy: does your library accept arbitrary incoming queries? Or can you support a common shared schema? It will force you to convert queries before sending them to connected P2P system.
- Keyword-based search or metadata/ontology-based search;
- Multiple (heterogeneous) metadata schemas support: e.g., LOM, DC, etc.
- Metadata records harvesting: if it is not necessary to keep data up-to-date, consistency issue must be considered.
- Authentication: must the library users be authenticated?
- Peer Selection/Discovery: do you need to locate specific libraries or just let system to find them dynamically?

As to applications quering few metadata fields, such as music file sharing which may request only file names, keyword-based searching over a query flooding P2P environment (e.g., Gnutella) or a centralized server-based P2P network(e.g., Napster) is sufficient. Moreover, if libraries can be highly coupled, DHT-based solutions can be used to achieve more efficient and effective performance. One issue which needs further clarification here is that DHT-based solution can only release the impact of frequent requests for some information. It can not release the impact of data hotspots due to key collisions which may be caused by too much entities/data being associated with one key. Recent approaches in super-peer based topology [17] or SON can be considered as alternatives to improve query efficiency. These approaches can be contributed for requirements when many digital library systems take *autonomy* as a central value since these approaches can support a more flexible mechanism for loosely coupling among peers. It is dissimilar with the rigid infrastructure as in DHT, although the latter makes it easier to locate content later on.

The rest discussion is devoted to the issues which shall be taken into consideration in applying different information searching methods, namely traditional information retrieval (IR)-based and metadata-based (semantic) search. Basically, either search method may be found more suitable than the other in some application scenarios. On one hand, many collections in participating libraries may have various metadata schemas which involve multiple fields, such as title, author, publication, etc. That is, searching over collections can be roughly regared as a matchmaking procedure on related fields recursively. However, when more and complex metadata elements get involved, such as Bibtex metadata with up to 100 metadata entries [11], an advance mechanism for supporting more complex queries is then required. Edutella and Bibster, in this concern, demonstrate the possibility to conduct complex queries over metadata records, by using RQL [18] alike query language and RDF-based database management systems - Sesame [19]. One weakness here is that few approaches have been conducted to support queries across heterogeneous but semantically related metadata records. However, approaches are being conducted in this direction [20–22] and we can foresee more researches to come. On the other hand, if the textual parts, such as description and abstract, take up a large proportion in metadata records, or just simply, any textual documents are available, we may need a conventional full-text IR method to conduct search. However, it becomes complicated in context of P2P overlay network. For example, when using Space Vector Model (SVM) (c.f. [23]), inverted document frequencies (IDF) may not be easy to maintain simply because of the dynamic nature of P2P systems. In order to keep such global statistic information, a huge index may then be maintained which will correspondingly take up a large bandwidth. So as long as there are thousands of peers in a P2P system, it would be problematic to collect the intact information about all the document collections on all peers. Additionally, even if it is possible to get the global statistic parameters by gathering information from all the peers involved, we are still faced with a problem that a peer would join or leave the system at any time. In this case, the collected global statistic information would be out of date and must be updated when new peers joins and old peers leaves. An alternative solution is routing indices (RI) which can avoid the overhead of constant index updates, but due to its local nature, it is in turn difficult to obtain necessary global information. Fortunately, substantial approaches are conducted in this direction [24, 25]. Shen et.al [25] combines Latent Semantic Index (LSI) (c.f. [23]) model to search semantic relevant documents in P2P network, by comparing users query and documents at the concept level, not just matching the keywords. Balke et.al [24] still uses SVM method, but create a novel indexing technique that allows to query using collection-wide information with respect to different classifications.

As a summary, Table 2 illustrates a preliminary result of our discussion. It is not a complete one but can be served as a stepping stone for P2P infrastructures selection.

Table 2. Preliminary Results

Scale	metadata elements	Semantic support	Autonomy	Adaptable P2P Network	Info. Srching Technique
small	few	No	high	pure P2P, RI	Information retrieval (IR)
small	few	No	low	pure P2P, Central server-based P2P, DHT	IR
small	many	No	high	pure P2P, RI	XML-based IR, RDF database
small	many	Yes	high	pure P2P, RI	RDF database
small	many	No	low	pure P2P, Central server-based P2P	XML-based IR, database
large	few	No	high	Super-Peer, SON	IR
large	few	No	low	DHT, Central server-based P2P	IR
large	many	No	high/low	Super-Peer, SON	XML-based IR, database
large	many	Yes	high	Super-Peer, SON	RDF database + RQL
large	many	Yes	low	Super-Peer, SON, DHT + logical layer	RDF database + RQL

3 Conclusion and Future Work

In summary, determining appropriate infrastructures for P2P-based digital libraries needs a consolidated guideline. This paper compares some representative P2P systems and aims to clarify advantages and weaknesses in applying different topologies. A discussion based on information searching is conducted and leads to preliminary results which are highly necessary for the future research. The paper can serve as a stepping stone for deciding architectures and techniques in the context of P2P-based digital library applications.

References

1. DELOS Digital library architecture (WP1)- Cluster Objectives. http://www.delos.info/WP1.html (2004)
2. Clarke, I., Sandberg, O., Wiley, B., Hong, T.W.: Freenet: A distributed anonymous information storage and retrieval system. In: InternationalWorkshop on Design Issues in Anonymity and Unobservability, LNCS 2009. Volume 2009 of Lecture Notes in Computer Science., Berkeley, CA, USA, Springer (2000) 46-66
3. Crespo, A., Garcia-Molina, H.: Routing indices for peer-to-peer systems. In: Proceedings of the 22 nd International Conference on Distributed Computing Systems (ICDCS'02). (2002)
4. Jain, S., Mahajan, R., Wetherall, D.: A Study of the Performance Potential of DHT-based Overlays. In: USENIX Symposium on Internet Technologies and Systems 2003, Seattle, Washington, USA (2003)
5. Ion Stoica, Robert Morris, D.K., Kaashoek, F., Balakrishnan, H.: Chold:A scalable peer-topeer lookup service for internet applications. In: SIGCOMM, California, USA (2001)
6. Ratnasamy, S., Francis, P., Handley, M., Karp1, R., Shenker, S.: A scalable contentaddressable network. In: SIGCOMM, San Diego, California, USA (2001)

7. Tang, C., Xu, Z., Mahalingam, M.: psearch: Information retrieval in structured overlays. In: Proceedings of HotNetsI02, Princeton, New Jersey, USA (2002)

8. Halevy, A.Y., Ives, Z.G., Mork, P., Tatarinov, I.: Piazza: data management infrastructure for semantic web applications. In:WWW. (2003) 556-567

9. Oaks, S., Traversat, B., Gong, L.: JXTA in a Nutshell. OReilly & Associates, Inc. (September, 2002)

10. Nejdl, W., Wolf, B., Qu, C., Decker, S., Sintek, M., Naeve, A., Nilsson, M., Palmer, M., Risch, T.: EDUTELLA: a P2P networking infrastructure based on RDF. In: International WorldWide Web Conferences (WWW). (2002) 604-615

11. Haase1, P., Broekstra3, J., Ehrig, M., Menken, M., et.al.: Bibster:a semantics-based bibliographic peer-to-peer system. In: The 3rd International Semantic Web Conference (ISWC2004), Japan (2004)

12. Schlosser, M.T., Sintek, M., Decker, S., Nejdl, W.: Hypercup - hypercubes, ontologies, and efficient search on peer-to-peer networks. In: AP2PC. Volume 2530 of Lecture Notes in Computer Science., Springer (2002) 112-124

13. Ahlborn, B., Nejdl,W., Siberski,W.: OAI-P2P:A Peer-to-Peer Network for Open Archives. In: 2002 International Conference on Parallel ProcessingWorkshops (ICPPW02), Vancouver, B.C., Canada (2002)

14. Cai, M., Frank, M.: Rdfpeers: A scalable distributed rdf repository based on a structured peer-to-peer network. In:WWW. (2004) 17-22

15. Aberer, K., Cudre-Mauroux, P., Datta, A., Despotovic, Z., Hauswirth, M., Punceva, M., Schmidt, R.: P-grid: a self-organizing structured p2p system. SIGMOD Record 32 (2003) 29-33

16. Crespo, A., Garcia-Molina, H.: Semantic overlay networks for p2p systems. Technical report, Computer Science Department, Stanford University (2002)

17. Yang, B., Garcia-Molina, H.: Designing a super-peer network. In: IEEE International Conference on Data Engineering, 2003. (2003) http://dbpubs.stanford.edu:8090/pub/showDoc.Fulltext?lang=en&doc=2003- 33&format=pdf&compression=. (Available: 2004.07).

18. Greg Karvounarakis, e.: The RDF Query Language (RQL). http://139.91.183.30:9090/RDF/RQL/ (2003)

19. : Sesame: Rdf schema querying and storage. http://www.openrdf.org (2005)

20. Calvanese, D., Damaggio, E., Giacomo, G.D., Lenzerini, M., Rosati, R.: Semantic data integration in p2p systems. In: DBISP2P. (2003) 77 90 http://springerlink.metapress.com/openurl.asp?genre=article&issn=0302- 9743&volume=2944&spage=77.

21. Ding, H., Solvberg, I.: Towards the schema heterogeneity in distributed digital libraries. In: 6th International Conference on Enterprise Information System (ICEIS), Portugal (2004)

22. Olmedilla, D., Palm0er, M.: Interoperability for peer-to-peer networks: Opening p2p to the rest of the world. In: WWW05, Chiba, Japan (2005)

23. Baeza-Yates, R., Ribeiro-Neto, B.: Modern Information Retrieval. Addison-Wesley, USA (1999)

24. Balke, W.T., Nejdl, W., Siberski, W., Thaden, U.: Dl meets p2p - distributed document retrieval based on classification and content. In Rauber, A., Christodoulakis, S., Tjoa, A.M., eds.: ECDL. Volume 3652 of Lecture Notes in Computer Science., Springer (2005) 379390

25. Shen, H.T., Shu, Y., Yu, B.: Efficient semantic-based content search in p2p network. IEEE Trans. Knowl. Data Eng. 16 (2004) 813-826

XML Document Retrieval for Digital Museum[*]

Jae-Woo Chang and Yeon-Jung Kim

Dept. of Computer Engineering,
Chonbuk National University, Chonju, Chonbuk 561-756, South Korea
jwchang@chonbuk.ac.kr, yjkim@dblab.chonbuk.ac.kr

Abstract. In this paper, we design an XML document retrieval system used for a digital museum. The system can retrieve XML documents based on both document structure and content. In order to support retrieval based on document structure, we perform the indexing of XML documents based on their basic unit of elements. For supporting retrieval based on content, we design a high-dimensional index structure using the CBF [1] method. Finally, we provide a similarity measure for retrieval on a composite query, based on both document structure and content.

1 XML Document Retrieval System

Recently, there have been a lot of researches on indexing structured documents. One major approach is to use an element tree for indexing a structured document [2][3]. Another approach is to use a structural summary for a graph structured document [4]. We design an XML document retrieval system for a digital museum, which is mainly consists of four parts, such as an indexing part, a storage part, a retrieval part and a user interface part. When an XML document is given, we can parse it and can index its document structure being composed of element units. The index information used for a document structure can be stored into its structure-based index structure. Using the index information extracted from a set of XML documents, documents can be retrieved by the retrieval part so that we may obtain a result to answer user queries. Finally, the document result is given to users through a user interface part using a Web browser.

2 Indexing and Retrieval

Because an element is a basic unit for retrieving an XML document, it is necessary to support a query based on logical inclusion between elements as well as based on the characteristic value of elements. To achieve it, we construct a document structure tree for XML documents after analyzing XML documents based on DTD. To build a document structure tree for XML documents, we parse the XML documents by using

---

[*] This work is financially supported by the Ministry of Education and Human Resources Development(MOE), the Ministry of Commerce, Industry and Energy(MOCIE) and the Ministry of Labor(MOLAB) though the fostering project of the Lab of Excellency.

E.A. Fox et al. (Eds.): ICADL 2005, LNCS 3815, pp. 463–464, 2005.
© Springer-Verlag Berlin Heidelberg 2005

sp-1.3 parser [5]. Finally, we store the document structure information extracted from the tree into the K-ary complete tree structure [6].

Using the stored index information extracted from a set of XML documents, some documents are retrieved by the retrieval part in order to obtain a result to answer user queries. There is little research on retrieval models for integrating structure- and content-based information retrieval. This can be achieved by dealing with MPEG-7 compliant XML documents [7]. To answer a query for retrieval based on document structure, a similarity measure (S_w) between two elements, say q and t, is computed as the similarity between the term vector of node q and that of node t by using a cosine measure. Supposed that a document can be represented as $D = \{ E_0, E_1, \ldots, E_{n-1} \}$ where E_i is an element i in a document D. Thus, a similarity measure (D_w) between an element q and a document D is computed as follows.

$$D_w = \text{MAX} \; \{ \; COSINE \; (NODE_q, NODE_{E_i}), 0 \le i \le n - 1\}$$

3 Conclusions

In this paper, we developed an XML document retrieval system for a digital museum. It can support efficient retrieval on XML documents for both structure- and content-based queries. In order to support structure-based queries, we performed the indexing of XML documents based on their basic unit of element. For supporting retrieval based on content, we implemented a high-dimensional index structure. We finally provided a similarity measure for retrieval on a composite query, based on both document structure and content.

References

[1] S.G. Han and J.W. Chang, "A New High-Dimensional Index Structure using a Cell-based Filtering Technique," Lecture Notes in Computer Science, Vol., pp 79-92, 2000.

[2] C. Zhang, J. Naughton, D. DeWitt, Q. Luo, and G. Lohman, "On Supporting Containment Queries in Relational Database Management Systems," In Proc. ACM SIGMOD. pp 425-436, 2001.

[3] H. Wang, S. Park, W. Fan, and P.S. Yu, "ViST: A Dynamic Index Method for Querying XML Data by Tree Structures," In Proc. ACM SIGMOD. pp 110-121, 2003.

[4] Q. Chen, A. Lim, and K.W. Ong, "D(k)-Index: An Adaptive Structural Summary for Graph-structured Data," In Proc. ACM SIGMOD. pp 134-144, 2003.

[5] http://www.jclark.com/sp.

[6] S.G. Han, J. Son, J.W. Chang and Z. Zhoo, "Design and Implementation of a Structured Information Retrieval System for SGML Document," In Proc. DASFAA, pp81-88, 1999.

[7] U. Westermann and W. Klas, "An Analysis of XML Database Solutions for the Management of MPEG-7 Media Descriptions," ACM Computing Surveys. Vol. 35, No. 4, pp 331-373, 2003.

Design and Implementation of the IMS-IPMP System in Convergence Home-Network Environment

Jong-Hyuk Park[1], Sang-Jin Lee[1], Yeog Kim[1], and Byoung-Soo Koh[2]

[1] CIST, Korea University, 5-Ka, Anam-Dong, Sungbuk-Gu, Seoul, Korea
{hyuks00, sangjin, yeog}@korea.ac.kr
[2] Digicaps Co., Ltd., Jinjoo Bldg. 938-26 Bangbae-Dong, Seocho-Gu, Seoul, Korea
bskoh@digicaps.com

1 Introduction

The traditional contents distribution architecture was fixed pattern, as the distribution subjects - Contents Provider (CP), Contents Distributor (CD), and Contents Consumer (CC) - create, distribute, and consume the digital contents, while in Convergence Home-network Environment (CHE) it would be necessary for each subject to have the distribution system that can be flexibly changed.

In this paper, we designed and implemented the Interactive Multimedia Service-Intellectual Property Management and Protection (IMS-IPMPS) by supplementing and expanding MPEG-21 DID, IPMP, REL, and the mechanism of OMA-DRM. In the proposed system, it is possible for CP to complete the appropriate authentication in CHE, generate the contents, and then register the packaged contents in safety for its distribution. In addition, it is the IMS-IPMP system where one can simultaneously consume the contents that the users from the different home network environments have generated and registered.

2 IMS-IPMP System

IMS-IPMPS in a single-domain was designed so that CPS Module and CCS Module for the supporting the interactive transaction of contents can be supported simultaneously for the flexibility of the distribution subject under the CHE. In addition, Multimedia Streaming Server (MSS) is used for the contents streaming service among multi-domains. User parts of IMS-IPMPS and the principle functions of each module in System Management Center (SMC) are as follows (Refer to Figure 1).

- **CPS (Contents Providing System) Module**: The copyright holder who provides the contents uses this CPS module, and also takes charge of the CDS (Contents Distribution System) module function for its distribution. To take advantage of packager that is embedded in the IMS-IPMPS, it creates digital items by adding the contents-related meta-data and the usage rule setting the usage rights.

---

[1] This research was supported by the MIC(Ministry of Information and Communication), Korea, under the ITRC(Information Technology Research Center) support program supervised by the IITA(Institute of Information Technology Assessment).

E.A. Fox et al. (Eds.): ICADL 2005, LNCS 3815, pp. 465–466, 2005.
© Springer-Verlag Berlin Heidelberg 2005

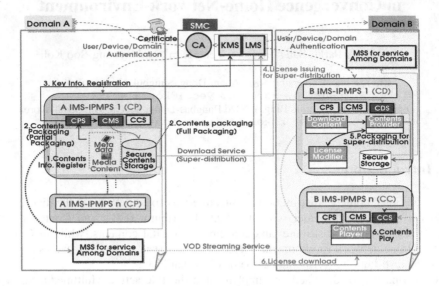

Fig. 1. IMS-IPMP System Architecture

- *CMS (Contents Management System) Module*: It manages the meta-data information that is created when it is packaged with the streaming server for the service of contents streaming within a single domain.
- *CCS (Contents Consumption System) Module*: It is the module for play of contents after receiving the issued license from SMC.
- *SMC*: It takes charge of the authentication about the subjects participating in the contents distribution, the issuing and management of the key used when packaging, and the issuing and management of the license to use the contents. Such as above mention, It consists of CA (Certificate Authority) Module, LMS (License Management System) Module, and KMS (Key Management System) Module.

3 Conclusion

In this paper, we have designed and implemented the IMS-IPMP system suitable for CHE. We have complemented weakness of the inflexible contents distribution among fixed subjects of the existing system. To take into account the environment where a single user can be flexibly changed in CHE, it supports interactive contents transaction within an identical domain. Furthermore, it supports contents super-distribution among multi-domains that a CC well known the market characteristic of the specific domain, can be easily changed and transact contents for the 2nd distribution. Moreover, it supports license format which can be flexibly used in multimedia devices under the wire/wireless environment. Finally, the proposed system support security including device spoofing attack prevention, illegal license alteration attack prevention, illegal user's attack against contents prevention, and so on.

Geotechnical Use of WebGIS in Digital Library Projects

Bo Yu [1], Huijuan Zheng [2], and Meng Zhan[3]

[1,2] College of Power and Mechanical Engineering,
Wuhan University, 430072 Wuhan, Hubei, China
boyu@whu.edu.cn, hjzheng@lib.whu.edu.cn
[3] Wuhan University Library, 430072 Wuhan, Hubei, China
mzhan @lib.whu.edu.cn

Abstract. This paper briefly introduces GIS, how the technology can be applied, and discusses the benefits of its use in design. To illustrate GIS applications, an actual project utilizing GIS is presented.

1 Geographic Information Systems (GIS)

Geographic Information Systems (GIS), which integrate hardware, software and digital spatial data, are powerful tools for organizing, analyzing, and presenting spatial data.

GIS provide mapping capabilities, databases of geographic and feature information, and spatial analysis. GIS technology can be used for analyzing and demonstrating spatial related data. GIS technology makes data visualization become reality. Compared with other analytical, statistical, or reporting products, its powerful visual display of information allows users to comprehend a vast amount of data more easily and better.

2 Digital Library Projects and GIS

It is the mission of libraries to provide access to recorded knowledge, and help users to make good use of information. Thus libraries are constantly challenged to be aware of all kinds of new services and formats, and always be ready to make effective integration of new programs and services into libraries. And GIS is one such service.

GIS technology plays a vital role in organizing and managing geospatial information well on the Web. With GIS services, it not only makes users feel more convenient and easier to search and browse what they need, but also enables users to take the same kind of digital representation of a geographic area, combines it with statistical or other feature information about that area, and conducts spatial analyses.

3 GIS Application in a Digital Library Project

GIS technology is applied to a digital library project in Wuhan University Library to provide an information system of China's Hydroelectric Power Stations on the Internet.

E.A. Fox et al. (Eds.): ICADL 2005, LNCS 3815, pp. 467–468, 2005.
© Springer-Verlag Berlin Heidelberg 2005

This kind of net service is modeled as a server in a client/server or browser/server relationship. The application softwares are MapInfo Professional, MapXtreme for Windows; The developing language is ASP (Active Server Page).

Step 1: Collecting Data and Forming a Map
In a map, geospatial data has been modeled into three kinds of entities: points, lines and areas. The structure of information in GIS is most commonly organized in layers of maps or sets of data. Each layer may contain information of a different nature. We can think of layers as transparencies that are stacked on top of one another. In this project, we defined layers as follows: a layer of station names (points), a layer of rivers (lines), layers of water boundaries (areas), a layer of background and other layers. Then, added another database about the features into the spatial database, i.e., station database concerning names, location, capacity, design head, output, etc.

Step 2: Layers Display in GeoSet Manager
With Geoset Manager, we created a geoset and built a complete map by stacking the needed layers on top of the other. Then we could customize the way in which the layers display, and add, delete, or recorder them. That is, we set display and label properties, recorded the way in which layers display, removed or added additional layers and set whether layers were visible, contained automatic labels, or were selectable.

Step 3: Website Design and Code Developing
MapXtreme for Windows is a mapping application server. The MapXtreme Application Wizard provides a quicker, easier way to develop a simple MapXtreme application, or prototype sample applications and demos. First, we used the Application Wizard to create a sample application. Then, we customized the MapXtreme Application, using the code libraries to modify the sample applications to fit needs. Finally, we added cross-database search function to this system.

Users can acquire the visualized map of these stations in China by clicking and dragging easily. From the map displayed, they can get the brief location of the station, and the detail information about the stations they are searching, or search for station's location by typing the name of it. Also map's download and print are available.

4   Conclusion

GIS is still not applied enough to aid the management of libraries and the research of libraries' collections. User's expectations are growing rapidly in areas relating to GIS. Thus, libraries must develop capabilities to work with spatial data and devise ways of collecting and sharing a vast amount of data to provide a more efficient and friendly information environment.

Establishment of " The Multiple Thesaurus of Chinese Classification" and Using Its Application to Improve the Retrieval Efficiency in the Chinese Bibliographic Databases*

Meng Zhan

Wuhan University Library, 430072 Wuhan, China
Mzhan@lib.whu.edu.cn

1 An analysis of Common Problems in Bibliographic Databases in China

Due to the limitations of Chinese character set in the windows operating system, homophones, pictographic characters or pinyin are often used to replace the complex traditional Chinese characters or any characters that haven't been designed in the character set of the Computer Operating System; as an investigation shows [1] the item of subject in most bibliographic databases is not complete; there are various kinds of classification schemes co-exiting in the bibliographic database, which is very common in the merged universities and regional union catalogues. These problems have greatly affected the efficiency and sharing of digital service. To improve the retrieval efficiency within the present situation in the bibliographic databases, we can design a "multiple thesaurus" i.e. the "Database of Classification Reference" including two classifications and design new method of retrieval for the computerized management of libraries.

2 The Content and Methods of Setting Up the MTCC

2.1 The Theme in "The Multiple Thesaurus of Chinese Classification"

The Multiple Thesaurus of Classification adopts the form of "a list of synonyms", compiles synonyms among "CLC", "LCASC", "CLSC" and "CCD", i.e., to combine the associated headings of classification, subject headings, and discipline name that are similar in meaning and conception, and forms a list of words for retrieval. It realizes cross-reference and exchange between words and codes, or classification Numbers and Disciplinary codes, for each items to start a retrieval is matched with the other three references.

2.2 The Methods of Setting Up "The Multiple Thesaurus of Classification"

2.2.1 Combine Various Classification Schemes
Take the associated headings in the schemes of CLC as the origin source; compile the associated headings in CLC and LCASC. If the associated headings are the same,

* This work is supported by the fund of National Philosophy and Social Science of China under grant No 4401-2-010.

E.A. Fox et al. (Eds.): ICADL 2005, LNCS 3815, pp. 469–470, 2005.
© Springer-Verlag Berlin Heidelberg 2005

keep the former one, quit the latter one, and match the two classification numbers to the associated heading. If the associated headings are different but shares one same concept, keep the words and link two classification numbers to them. For those associated headings that could not be matched in the two classification schemes, keep its classification number and inherit the up-layer classification number of CLC. In this way, the cross-referential relationships between the up-layer and low-layer in the classification schemes will be established with a semantical base.

2.2.2 Comparison Between the Classification Schemes and Subjects Schemes

Index with the classification number in "DAHC", we can compare the associated headings with the subject headings in the "Thesaurus of Chinese subject heading". Merge the same headings and give each subject heading two classification numbers, than to set up the database of the referential relationships between classification numbers and subject headings, which is a combination of subject heading and classification scheme. In this database, classification numbers, associated headings, and subject headings are cross-referential.

2.2.3 Comparison Between the Subject Retrieval Scheme and Discipline Retrieval Scheme

Take the disciplines in the "CCD" published by the National Education Committee of China as the source and check each of them in databases that are mentioned above. In our experience each discipline will match an associated heading. Compile the disciplines numbers in the database, and match each word with three-code attributes. The introduction of the disciplinary codes into the database helps to complete the cross reference among the associated heading, subject heading, classification number and discipline codes in "CLC", "LCASC", "CLSC" and "CCD" and at last comes out with "The Multiple Thesaurus of Classification", a database of referential relationship among classification, subjects and the disciplines.

3 An analysis of the Application of MTCC to the Computer - Based Bibliographic Retrieval System

- ✧   Increase the Function of Retrieval Schemes Switch
- ✧   Set Up the Tree of Retrieval Schemes
- ✧   Setup of the Meta-Database of the Retrieval Languages Based on the Dublin Core (DC) Pattern

METS Cataloging Tool for Heterogeneous Collections

Li Dong[1,2], Chunxiao Xing[1], Kehong Wang[1], Shixin Peng[1],
Bei Zhang[2], and Airong Jiang[2]

[1] Department of Computer Science and Technology, Tsinghua University,
100084 Beijing, P.R. China
{xingcx, wkh-dcs, psx02}@mail.tsinghua.edu.cn
[2] System Division of Library, Tsinghua University,
100084 Beijing, P.R. China
{dongli, zhangbei, jiangar}@lib.tsinghua.edu.cn

Abstract. This paper describes the implementation of DRMSCata, an XML Schema driven web-base cataloging subsystem, which helps to produce various METS encoded documents.

1 Introduction

Tsinghua University has initiated a series projects for long-term preservation of Chinese Science and Technology History resources, including Architecture, Mathematics, Mechanics, Hydraulics, Arts, and Crafts from early 2001. Fedora was chosen as the supporting platform of our Digital Resource Management System (DRMS). In 2003, we have developed a cataloging tool to record preservation metadata for mathematic resources, which is a Java GUI application, and XML Schema is bounded into Java objects with JAXB [1], so that it's difficult to extend it to other subjects' resources. To support heterogeneous collections of variant subjects, we design and developed a Web-based XML Schema-driven cataloging tool for METS document in 2004.

2 Design and Implement

The general working process of DRMSCata is: 1) XML Schema must be an input of the cataloging system; 2) metadata scheme in XML Schema should be translated into a set of program objects, the element name and attributes should not be hardcoded in program; 3) these objects should be able to present as user editable web forms in web browser; 4) user should edit the metadata and submit the result, XML documents will be marshaled in server-side, and validate with the schema-based tool. Editing existed METS documents is also an important feature of DRMSCata.

It is a special characteristic of DRMSCata that DHTML and JavaScript are invoked as part of the cataloging system. With this dynamic layer embedded in the web browser, it is not need to do additional client-server interactions when user performs add/remove elements actions in web browser; the element will be created/deleted within web browser as an DHTML objects. It reduces the interactivities between the web browser and the server side, and makes the cataloging works more effective.

E.A. Fox et al. (Eds.): ICADL 2005, LNCS 3815, pp. 471–472, 2005.
© Springer-Verlag Berlin Heidelberg 2005

DRMSCata contains 3 different modules: 1) Definition Level: System wide schema configurations file and predefined metadata XSD files. When the system is used for cataloging different subjects, only this part needs to be changed; 2) Logical Level: A set of Java objects which used to present the relationship/rules of XML Schema elements. These objects are created by JDOM parser, and are based on the type of XML element tags. Each XML Schema element was mapped with one Java object, this mechanism makes this level simple, easy to implement, and extensible. These objects exist in Tomcat web application container. When the system is starting, all schema objects are created based on the content of XSD files. 3) Presentation Level: The JavaScript, DOM, and HTML form elements are used to provide a dynamic user interface in the Web browser.

We have implemented an XML Schema-driven cataloging tool for METS document creation and modification. All the descriptive metadata, administrative metadata and structural metadata can be constructed for editing. It is proved to be schema independent and flexible.

Currently, we have tested Mathematics resources with this tool, the result of METS documents can be imported into Fedora system properly. In future, we plan to refine the system in the following aspects: 1) Provide a GUI administrative tool for system configuration; 2) support more W3C XML Schema elements and attributes.

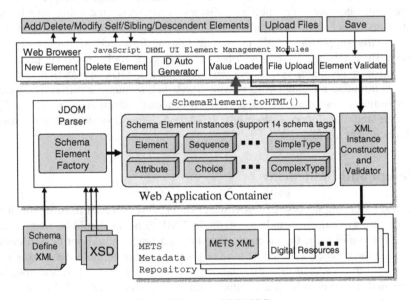

Fig. 1. Diagram of DRMSCata

Reference

1. Li Dong, et al : Cataloging and Preservation Toolkit of a Chinese Mathematics Ancient Books Digital Library. Proceedings of the 7th International Conference on Asian Digital Libraries (ICADL2004). Shanghai, China, December 13~17 2004, pp. 174~183.

A Method for Creating a High Quality Collection of Researchers' Homepages from the Web

Yuxin Wang[1] and Keizo Oyama[2]

[1] School of Multidisciplinary Sciences, The Graduate University for Advanced Studies
[2] National Institute of Informatics,
2-1-2 Hitotsubashi, Chiyoda-ku, Tokyo, 101-8403 Japan
[1] mini_wang@grad.nii.ac.jp
[2] oyama@nii.ac.jp

Extended Abstract. In the web space, information of an entity is often presented by a set of pages that constitutes a logical page group and its proper handling is required. This paper proposes a method for collecting researchers' homepages (or entry pages) by applying new simple and effective page group models for combining page group structure and page content, aiming at narrowing down the candidates for further precise and heavy processes. We mainly focus on high recall but less on precision.

Combined with content-based methods, link/URL information can not only increase the precision but also reduce irrelevant references [1]. Moreover, there several approaches to retrieving the relevant pages in "Information Unit" through search engine with high precision [2] or to collecting pages in "Web Units" from the web directly [3].

Our method is different from other related works in three main issues: (1) Following a heuristic procedure, we manually create property-based keywords on different keyword lists corresponding to researchers' properties; (2) We introduce several page group models (PGMs) considering link structure and URL hierarchy together with the types of the keyword lists (kws) in a consolidated process; (3) The pages are selected on condition if they contain keywords from at least the threshold number of the kws rather than the number of keywords.

In our method, 12 property-based keyword lists that characterize researchers' homepages are first created and grouped into two types: organization-related and non-organization-related keyword lists.

Next, four page group models (PGMs), PGM-Od, PGM-Ou, PGM-I and PGM-U, are introduced, considering out-link to down directories, out-link to upper directories, in-link from upper directories and the site-top/directory-entry pages respectively. The keywords are propagated to a potential entry page of a logical page group from its surrounding pages based on the PGMs to compose a virtual entry page. All keywords for PGM-Od and only organization-related keywords for PGM-Ou, PGM-I and PGM-U are propagated to the entry page. For PGM-Od and PGM-I, the kws are propagated only on condition if the number of out-links and the number of in-links are less than the out-link threshold and the in-link threshold respectively in order to reduce the amount of noise pages.

Finally, the virtual entry pages that contain keywords from at least 4 kws are selected. The threshold value "4" was selected based on our experiment results described below to achieve recall more than 99.0%.

E.A. Fox et al. (Eds.): ICADL 2005, LNCS 3815, pp. 473–474, 2005.
© Springer-Verlag Berlin Heidelberg 2005

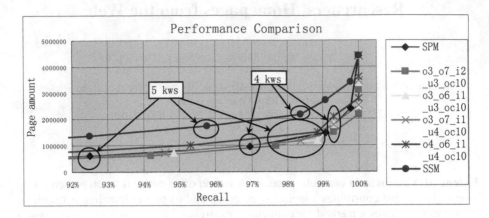

Fig. 1. Performance Comparison of Combinations of PGMs with Different Parameter

For evaluating the effectiveness of the proposed PGMs, we use two other page group models for comparison: SPM that uses only the content in each single page and SSM that uses content in each page and its out-link target pages in the same site. We did experiments first on SPM, SSM and PGMs with various parameters separately, and then on combinations of the four PGMs with different parameters (Figure 1). Compared to that of SPM, the recalls of all the combinations of PGMs that contain at least 4 kws are improved from 96.95% to 99.30%. Meanwhile the recalls even outperform that of SSM by about 1% and the page amounts decreased considerably.

Comparing to SPM and SSM, our method worked effectively since 99.30% of researchers' homepages can be collected within less than 14% of the whole page amount of the corpus. We assessed randomly selected 0.1% of the pages that scored 1, 2, 3 or 4 with SPM but scored at least 5 with one of the combination of PGMs showed in Figure 1 and found 12 entry pages in logical page groups out of 695 pages. It shows the effectiveness of our method for finding researchers' PGM-based entry pages that could not be found with SPM-based method.

Collecting web pages efficiently with high recall is an interesting problem. Our method is simple and effective, and we expect it would also be applicable to other page categories.

References

1. P. Calado, M. Cristo, E. Moura, N. Ziviani, B. Ribeiro-Neto and M. A. Goncalves: Combining Link-Based and Content-based Methods for Web Document Classification, CIKM'03, New Orleans, Louisiana, USA, Nov. 2003.
2. W. Li, K. Candan, Q. Vu and D. Agrawal: Retrieving and Organizing Web Pages by "Information Unit". WWW10. Hongkong (2001)
3. A. Sun and E. Lim: Web Unit Mining- Finding and Classifying Subgraphs of Web Pages. CIKM'03. New Orleans, Louisiana, USA (2003)

Personalized Information Service
Based on Social Bookmarking[*]

Yanfei Xu and Liang Zhang[+]

Department of Computing and Information Technology, Fudan University
{032021154, zhangl}@fudan.edu.cn

Abstract. Social bookmarking is emerging as a new information infrastructure on the web, and has the ability of organizing multicultural metadata for large scale of digital entities. To achieve its potential, we propose a technique to extract the substantial correlation among tags. Based on it, we maintain profiles for users' interests, and recommend items according to them. Experiments against data from del.icio.us reveal the superiority of our method.

1 Introduction

A digital library needs semantic labels or metadata for organizing digital entities. There are generally two ways of attaching metadata to digital entities. One is using elaborated catalogs created by dedicated professionals, but it encounters a severe problem of scalability. Another approach is author provided metadata. It might fail sometimes because it is difficult for authors to master the pre-declared schemas, especially in a multicultural setting of inconsistent vocabularies or taxonomies.

Recently, a new paradigm has been emerged. It is called *folksonomy* [1] which is derived from *social bookmarking* website (e.g. http://del.icio.us). In this paradigm, users mark items they are interested in with their own words (*tags*). Because of the usefulness of bookmarking and the lower barriers of adding tags, people are inclined to use social bookmarking, and it yields a great mass of tags for each item. To turn tags into useful metadata, we need develop new technology to address issues with folksonomy, i.e. to deal with synonyms, polymers, typos, or even deceptions.

In this poster, we report some insights from analyzing tags, and develop a method to distill the inherent knowledge beneath tags. Based on them, we also propose an approach to represent digital entities and users' interests, and recommend items in user's own vocabulary. Experiments against data from del.icio.us reveal the superiority of our approach over two other traditional recommend methods.

2 Turning Tags into Metadata and Making Recommendation

Four insights into social bookmarking help us to get a better understanding of tags' potential to become metadata: (1) there are enough redundant tags for us to explore

[*] This work is partially supported by the National Basic Research Program (973) under grant No. 2005CB321905, the NSFC Key Program under the grant No. 69933010, and the Chinese Hi-tech (863) Projects under the grant No. 2002AA4Z3430, and No. 2002AA231041.
[+] To whom correspondence should be addressed.

E.A. Fox et al. (Eds.): ICADL 2005, LNCS 3815, pp. 475–477, 2005.
© Springer-Verlag Berlin Heidelberg 2005

patterns beneath them; (2) the distribution of tags for an item is stable, so we can represent an item by these tags; (3) the set of frequently used tags is small and stable. 10% most used tags cover 84.3% URLs out of all the URLs that have been marked at least by 3 users. (4) LSA can find related tags effectively, even in complex settings.

We extract inherent correlation of tags as follows. Based on insights (3) and (4), collect the most frequently used tags (denoted as TopTags) and several digital entities (here URLs) for each TopTag, apply LSA on the tag-URL matrix. Thus, get a compact k-dimension representation for each TopTag. As insight (2) suggested, represent a URL by the union of feature vectors of TopTags attached on it, and the result would be stable. Now the tags are turned into more informational metadata. Because of the high coverage of TopTags, most URLs can be marked by them.

A user employs a tag to marks up some URLs in his own way. Most of these URLs have global feature vectors mentioned above. Summing them up will get an average representation for this tag by the specified user. This maps users' language into global metadata without losing individuality. Recommendation is made by calculating the cosine similarity between users' tags and global URLs. The feature vector of a URL will be altered as new tags are added.

Experiments are undertaken with data from *del.icio.us*, including 398 users, 3740 URLs and 1969 tags. We compare our Tag-based method (BTag) with two traditional methods, say content-based recommendation (actually title-based, BTitle) and pure collaborative filtering (PCF). Use $HitRatio = |R \cap C| / \min(N, |C|)$ to evaluate the recommendation quality. Here R is the recommended set of URLs, and C is the set of testing URLs that the user has collected. Experimental results in table 1 demonstrate the superiority of our method.

Table 1. HitRatio for each recommend method with LSA (k=200)

	Top5	Top10	Top15	Top20	Top40
BTitle	0.012	0.016	0.022	0.034	0.057
PCF	0.143	0.289	0.386	0.497	0.535
BTag	**0.173**	**0.339**	**0.589**	**0.700**	**0.735**

In summary, tags provide additional information to digital entities, and the method proposed here is a successful trial of using tags as metadata for recommendation.

Reference

[1] Adam M.: Folksonomies Cooperative Classification and Communication Through Shared Metadata.   http://www.adammathes.com/academic/computer-mediated-communication/ folkson omies.html (2004)

Multi-indexing System for News Stories
Based on XML Documents

Youngrok Song, Kyonam Choo, Yoseop Woo, Hongki Min, and Wonung Lee

Dept. of Information and Telecommunication Engineering, University of Incheon,
177 Dowha-Dong, Nam-Gu, Incheon 402-749 Korea
{youngrok75, kyonam, yswooo, hkmin, wulee}@incheon.ac.kr

Abstract. Indexing is one of the most important key factors in efficient XML information retrieval. Inappropriate indexing may result in improper search results. This paper presents a multi-indexing system that considers not only structure information of documents but also characteristics of pertinent elements in XML documents. The system extracts semantic elements from XML document corpus and identifies characteristics of the elements. By using the characteristics, document structures are classified and a particular indexing method is assigned to each classified structure. Efficiency of our system is confirmed through XML dataset from news stories with relatively accurate formats. The results indicate that the system has significantly high precision in search by element.

1 Introduction

Since XML was proposed in World Wide Web (WWW) in 1996, it has been the standard document form designed to transmit structured documents. XML is intrinsically a hierarchical textual representation of significant data. Because of its simplicity and flexibility, XML is rapidly becoming the most popular format for information representation and data exchange on the web.

In this paper, a multi-index system was constructed which extracts not only structure information of XML documents but also types of meaning of contents entered into each relevant element. In order to implement multi-indexing techniques for XML documents, we designed an indexing system with news stories which have relatively accurate formats

2 Multi-indexing System

In order to embody multi-indexing techniques for XML documents, we designed an indexing system for news stories which have relatively accurate formats. We built a system to convert news stories into XML documents and created a corpus which consists of 1,000 stories. From the corpus, we extract document structures and analyze semantic types of contents in each element.

Figure 1. illustrates the multi-indexing system for XML documents. The system extracts semantic elements for retrieval by using structure information. Because the

E.A. Fox et al. (Eds.): ICADL 2005, LNCS 3815, pp. 477–478, 2005.
© Springer-Verlag Berlin Heidelberg 2005

indexing follows in document structures, we can retrieve news stories in each pertinent element. Moreover, the system gives different weight values to each element according to its importance of document structures, guaranteeing effective results.

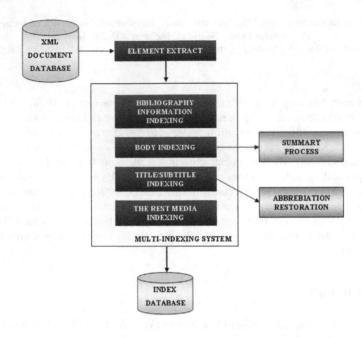

Fig. 1. Multi-Indexing Algorithm

3   Conclusion

Our work has a difference from existing indexing systems which focus only on XML document structure information. To obtain better retrieval results, we proposed a system which is able to extract more meaningful index by applying different indexing techniques according to elements, and also presented methods of creating summaries and restoring abbreviations.

Acknowledgements

This study was supported by research fund from University of Incheon and Multimedia Research Center of the MOCIE and ITEP.

Two-Stage Access Control Model for XML Security

Wei Sun, Da-xin Liu, and Tong Wang

College of Computer Science and Technology, HARBIN Engineering University,
HARBIN Heilongjiang Province, China
sunwei78@hrbeu.edu.cn

1 Summary

As large corporations and organizations increasingly exploit the Internet as a means of improving business-transaction efficiency and productivity, it is increasingly common to find operational data and other business information in XML format. Access control for XML database is non-trivial subjects. A number of recent research efforts have considered access control models for XML data[1-5]. Our first contribution is a novel model for specifying XML security access control. Given an XML document accompanied by a document DTD, we allow a two-stage access control policies to pledge to security access XML document at file-level and element-level respectively. On the element-level access control, our approach for these access control policies is based on the novel notion of *hide-node views*. While the hide-node view DTD is exposed to authorized users, neither the internal XPath annotations nor the full document DTD is visible. Authorized users can only operate data over the hide-node view, making use of the exposed view DTD to access data. Our hide-node view mechanism guarantees that unauthorized user cannot access sensitive data and protects the schema information from access by unauthorized users. We think that the schema information also is sensitive data and should be protected from gain through the data accessing.

2 Two-Stage Access Control Model

Firstly, In order to manage different documents in XML database, an authentication server component, plays an administrator role in XML database. Secondly, another two components are XBLP component for file-level access control and Hide-node views (element-level access control) component for XML document partial access. When a user wants to access to query some XML document, he or she must enter his valid information given by administrator. Then the authentication server component sends authentication information to Security information repository. The next step is that XBLP component handles the request of the user for certain XML document, and determines whether the user can access the XML document. If the user can access the XML document, XBLP component passes the request to Hide-node views component through the message broker. After Hide-node views component receives the information from the broker, it starts to retrieve the data that the user can access. Intuitively, XPath language is used to help *hide-node views* component to specify which region element can be access. The Hide-node views component will rewrite the user

E.A. Fox et al. (Eds.): ICADL 2005, LNCS 3815, pp. 479–480, 2005.
© Springer-Verlag Berlin Heidelberg 2005

requests, and send the rewrite requests to XML database. The file-level access control component and the element-level access control component constitute the XMAC, MAC policy for XML.

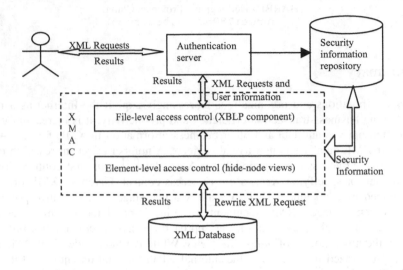

Fig. 1. Two-stage Access Control Model

3 Conclusions

We have proposed a new model for high securing XML data (based on the MAC security policy) and thoroughly studied its algorithm on the Hide-node views. This yields the first XML security model that provides both content access control and schema availability. There are file-level and element-level access controls on the model, implemented by XBLP and Hide-node views respectively. Further, our model can be implemented in query engine for query rewriting and optimization for XML.

References

1. E. Damiani, S. di Vimercati, S. Paraboschi, and P. Samarati. A Fine-Grained Access Control System for XML documents. *TISSEC*, 5(2): 169-202, 2002.
2. S. Hada and M. Kudo. XML access control language: Provisional authorization for XML documents. http://www.trl.ibm.com/projects/xml/xacl/xacl-spec.html.
3. Oasis. eXtensible Access Control Markup Language (XACML). http://www.oasis-open.org/committees/xcaml.
4. Li L, He YZ, Feng DG. A Fine-Grained Mandatory Access Control Model for XML Documents. Journal of software, 2004, 15(10): 1528-1537.
5. R.Sandhu, E.J.Coyne, H.L.Feinstein, Role Based Access Control Models", IEEE Computer, 29, (2): 38-47, 1996.

Optimal Face Classification by Using Nonsingular Discriminant Waveletfaces for a Face Recognition

Jin Ok Kim[1], Kwang Hoon Chung[2], and Chin Hyun Chung[2]

[1] Faculty of Multimedia, Daegu Haany University,
290, Yugok-dong, Gyeongsan-si, Gyeongsangbuk-do,
712-715, Korea
bit@dhu.ac.kr
[2] Department of Information and Control Engineering,
Kwangwoon University, 447-1, Wolgye-dong, Nowon-gu,
Seoul, 139-701, Korea
chung@kw.ac.kr

Abstract. This paper proposes an algorithm on a face classification by using 2D wavelet subband transform and nonsingular fisher discriminant analysis for a face recognition. For a feature extraction, we apply the multiresolution wavelet transform to extract waveletfaces. We also perform the linear discriminant on waveletfaces to reinforce the discriminant power. During classification, the nonsingular fisher discriminant waveletfaces are used. In this study, we found that NDW (Nonsingular Discriminant Waveletface) solves the small sample size matter. Thus, NDW is superior to LDA for an efficient face classification.

1   Introduction

Many effective face recognition and classification algorithms and techniques using Principal Component Analysis (PCA) [1, 2] and Linear Discriminant Analysis (LDA, also known as Fisher Discriminant Analysis-FDA) [1, 2]. PCA has been used in face recognition handprint recognition, human-made object recognition, industrial robotics, and mobile robotics. LDA has also been proposed for genetic object recognition, but results using a large databases of objects have not been reported yet. In this paper, the wavelet transform [3–10] is proposed for facial feature extraction and classification. The most application use the wavelet transform for image compression, edge detection and image fusion. A fundamental reason why the wavelet transform is en excellent tool for feature extraction is its inherent multiresolution [11–13] approach to signal analysis. The dimensionality of a face image is greatly reduced to produce the waveletface. A rapid face recognizer could be achieved. Also, we apply the LDA scheme to linearly transform the waveletface to new feature space with higher separability and lower dimension.

E.A. Fox et al. (Eds.): ICADL 2005, LNCS 3815, pp. 481–482, 2005.
© Springer-Verlag Berlin Heidelberg 2005

2 Conclusion

The proposed algorithm was carried out by two transformations: nonsingular transformation and discriminant transformation. This process was adequate for LDA procedures in cases of either singular or nonsingular scatter matrices. Moreover, when we apply the NDW, the transformed within-class and between-class scatters were unchanged when S_B was nonsingular. However, when S_B was singular, the transformed between-class scatter was unchanged and simultaneously the the transformed within-class was shrunk. The resulting Fisher class separability was increased. This method was different from principal component analysis (PCA) plus LDA, which transformed the features using the eigenvectors of total scatter matrix. In this study, we found that the nonsingular discriminant feature extraction achieves significant face recognition performed compared to the other LDA-related methods for a wide range of sample size and class numbers. Thus, NDW is superior to LDA for an efficient face classification.

References

1. Andrew R. Webb and Qineti Q. Malvern: Statistical Pattern Recognition, 2nd Edition. John Wiley & Sons, LTD, West Sussex PO19 8SQ, England (2002)
2. Richard O. Duda and Peter R. Hart and David G. Stork: Pattern Classification. John Wiley & Sons, LTD, New york, USA (2001)
3. Mallat, S.: A Wavelet Tour of Signal Processing. Academic Press, A Harcount Science and Technology Company Sandiego USA (1998)
4. Burrus, C.S., Gopinath, R.A., Guo, H.: Introduction to Wavelets and Wavelet Transforms. Prentice-Hall International, New Jersey 07458 (1998)
5. Rao, R.M., Bopardikar, A.S.: Wavelet Transforms Introduction to Theory and Applications. Addison-Wesley, Massachusetts 01867 (1998)
6. Vetterli, M., Kovacevic, J.: Wavelets and Subband Coding. Prentice Hall PTR, New Jersey 07632 (1995)
7. Prasad, L., Lyenger, S.S.: Wavelet Anaysis with Applications Image Processing. CRC Press, Boca Raton Boston London Newyork Washington, D.C. (1997)
8. Massopust, P.R.: Fractal Functions, Fractal Surfaces, and Wavelets. Academic Press, California 92101-4495 (1994)
9. Akansu, A.N., Haddad, R.A.: Multiresolution Signal Decomposing, Transforms, Subband, and Wavelets. Academic Press, INC., Harcount Brace Javanovichm, Publishers (1992)
10. Chan, A.K., Peng, C.: Wavelets for sensing Technologies. Arthech House, Inc., Boston (2003)
11. Bai-Ling Zhang and Haihong Zhang and Shuzhi Sam Ge: Face Recognition by applying Wavelet Subband Representation and Kernel Associative Memory. IEEE Transactions on Neural Networks 15 (January 2004) pp. 166–177
12. Regrio Schmidt Feris and Jim Gemmell and Kentaro Toyoma: Hierarchical wavelet Networks for Facial Feature Localization. Proceedings of the Fifth IEEE International Conference on Automatic Face and Gesture Recognition (2002) pp. 1–6
13. Ying Zu and Stuart Schwarts and Micheal Orchard: Fast Face Detection Using Subspace Discriminant Wavelet Features. IEEE (2000)

Evaluating Score and Publication Similarity Functions in Digital Libraries

S. Bani-Ahmad[1], A. Cakmak[1], A. Al-Hamdani[2], and Gultekin Ozsoyoglu[1]

[1] Case Western Reserve Univ, USA
{sulieman, ali.cakmak, tekin}@case.edu
[2] Dept. of Computer Science, Sultan Qaboos University, Oman
abd@squ.edu.om

1 Introduction

Digital libraries do not assign importance/relevance scores to their publications, authors, or publication venues, even though scores are potentially useful for (a) providing comparative assessment, or "importances", of publications, authors, publication venues, (b) ranking publications returned in search outputs, and (c) using scores in locating similar publications. Using social networks and bibliometrics, one can define several score functions.

Existing publication similarity functions, used to locate similar papers to a particular paper, fall into two classes, namely, text-based similarity functions from Information Retrieval, and citation-based similarity functions based on bibliographic coupling and/or co-citation. In this study, we propose a number of publication, author, and publication venue score functions and publication similarity functions, which are then extended and evaluated in terms of accuracy, separability, and independence.

2 Experimental Setup

For each paper in *ACM SIGMOD Anthology (AnthP)*, we extracted titles, authors, publication venues, publication year info, and citations. The experimental dataset includes (a) 106 conferences, journals, and books, (b) 14,891 papers, and (c) 13,208 authors. For more details, see [1].

3 Score and Similarity Functions

Existing citation-based publication score functions are all based on the notion of prestige in social networks [2] and bibliometry [3]. As paper score functions we use (i) the well-known PageRank [4] algorithm, (ii) the *authorities* score of HITS (Hyperlink Induced Topic Search) algorithm [5], and (iii) the normalized citation count which, for paper P that receives C_P citations, is computed as the percentage of papers that receive C_P citation or less[6].

We compute author importances in four different ways. All author importance functions are computed by averaging the scores of selected papers of a given author A. For more details about different scoring functions, see [1].

E.A. Fox et al. (Eds.): ICADL 2005, LNCS 3815, pp. 483–485, 2005.
© Springer-Verlag Berlin Heidelberg 2005

We use bibliographic coupling as a similarity indicator between papers, and propose a number of similarity measures based on (extended)bibliographic coupling similarity and considering the citations iteratively, which we refer to as *reachability analysis*. We also utilize paper scores to explore additional alternatives to compute paper similarities. Finally, we define a number of different co-citation-based similarity functions between papers.

Also, we compute similarity between two papers based on author-coupling (i) directly via the number of common authors between the two papers, and (ii) indirectly via co-authorship in other papers. For more details about different similarity functions, see [1].

4   Major Findings

Our major findings in this study are as follows:

* Among paper scoring functions, the citation-count-based scoring is the best in terms of separability. PageRank-based scoring is the best in terms of accuracy.

* Authorities scores and PageRank scores of papers are highly correlated.

* Separability of PageRank-based paper scores can be enhanced by (a) weighing citations, (b) weighing the *Future Citation Probabilities* represented by the E parameter of PageRank, (c) postprocessing PageRank raw scores by (i) nonlinear normalization, or (ii) linear normalization via a properly selected percentile score or (iii) combining PageRank-based paper scores and publication venue scores.

* Author scores based on author's top K-scored or top-K% scored papers accurately capture author scores.

* Citation-count-based publication venue scores are more accurate than author-score-averaging publication venue scores published in publication venues.

* By evaluating *multiple levels* of paper similarities based on bibliographic-coupling, co-citation and author-coupling, we observe that: (a) similarity value distribution curves are similar within the same group of similarity functions, (b) citation-based and author-coupling based similarity functions are more separable than bibliographic-coupling-based functions, (c) top-K overlapping ratio between paper similarity functions increases as we move to *higher levels* of similarity functions since more papers appear to be similar, (d) text-based similarity function show very low overlapping with citation-based and author-coupling-based functions.

References

1. Bani-Ahmad, S., Cakmak, A., Al-Hamdani, A., Ozsoyoglu, G.: Evaluating score and publication similarity functions in digital libraries. Technical report, CWRU (2005)
2. Wasserman, S., Faust, K.: Social Network Analysis. Cambridge U. Press, Cambridge (1994)
3. Chakrabarti, S.: Mining the Web. Morgan-Kauffman, San Francisco, CA (2003)

4. Page, L., Brin, S., Motwani, R., Winograd, T.: The pagerank citation ranking: Bringing order to the web. Technical report, Stanford DL Technologies Project (1998)
5. Kleinberg, J.: Authoritative sources in hyperlinked environments. In: the 9th ACM-SIAM Symposium on Discrete Mathematics. (1998)
6. Ozsoyoglu, G., Altingovde, I., Al-Hamdani, A., Ozel, S., Ulusoy, O., Ozsoyoglu, Z.: Querying web metadata: Native score management and text support in databases. ACM TODS (2005)

Facilitating Resource Utilization in Union Catalog Systems

Yung-Teng Tsai and I-Chia Chang

Institute of Information Science, Academia Sinica, Nankang, Taipei, Taiwan
{alextsai, eiga}@iis.sinica.edu.tw

1 Introduction

Numerous papers have addressed building Union Catalog (UC) technologies, such as metadata schema, data exchange (e.g., OAI-PMH, Z39.50), and resource classification. In contrast to these approaches, in this article, we focus on UC technologies that leverage resource utilization across digital resources. We take the repositories of Taiwan's National Digital Archives Program (NDAP) in Taiwan as the project content to identify major resource utilization issues. Our solution methodologies include resource unification, information query, information navigation, and unencoded character handling.

2 Background and Issues

The objective of the National Digital Archives Program [2], which is sponsored by the National Science Council (NSC) of Taiwan, is to promote and coordinate the digitization and preservation of content in leading museums, archives, universities, research institutes, and other content holders in Taiwan. Currently, NDAP's digital collections comprise over two million records covering eleven thematic groups. To enhance information sharing among these repositories, we have built a UC prototype to evaluate various building technologies, including OAI-PMH and Dublin Core (DC). However, this consolidation process has raised the following challenging issues:

Resource Unification: NDAP repositories are heterogeneous collections of diverse metadata principles, inconsistent coding systems, as well as assorted and distributed database storage systems. Unifying these heterogeneous repositories is therefore fundamental.

User Needs: UC users range from academic researchers to the general public. Hence, in addition to cross-database and cross-domain search features for researchers, browsing mechanisms are also needed to help general users navigate resources with ease.

Information Exploration: Utilization of NDAP's resources is enhanced by an easy-to-use interface. Access technologies, such as spatial and temporal information browsing, are being developed so that users can view information from different

E.A. Fox et al. (Eds.): ICADL 2005, LNCS 3815, pp. 486–488, 2005.
© Springer-Verlag Berlin Heidelberg 2005

perspectives. Information visibility functions, such as content classification for resource navigation and data grouping for query results, are also being investigated to enhance data clarity.

Unencoded Character Problem: This problem impacts on NDAP resource utilization in the areas of character encoding, text input, font generation, and display. As the UC unifies all NDAP repositories, all unencoded characters are aggregated; thus the problem is magnified. A total solution for the unencoded Chinese character problem is therefore required.

3 Methodologies and Results

We have implemented the following methodologies to facilitate resource utilization in the UC.

Resource Unification: To transform and integrate NDAP's heterogeneous repositories into a uniform resource, we use an extended DC scheme as the unified metadata framework. Two approaches (OAI-PMH and XML file import) have been developed for this purpose.

Information Query and Navigation: By incorporating the Apache Lucene Search Engine, we have implemented full-text query and advanced DC query to consolidate NDAP resource utilization. In addition, four information classifications (participant organizations, content themes, spatial regions, and temporal domains) have been designed to provide comprehensive and intuitive information navigation of the unified NDAP resources. Spatial and temporal browsing are realized through the spatial and temporal data format conversion modules provided by the Academia Sinica Computing Center.

Unencoded Character Handling: The approach developed by the Chinese Document Processing laboratory [1] is used to manage NDAP's unencoded characters in the areas of data representation, storage, retrieval, display, and distribution. This resolves the problem of unencoded Chinese characters by applying a glyph expression model and glyph structure database to manage the characters. A set of tools is built into the data model to support character encoding, font generation, text display and input, and document dissemination functions.

A UC application [3] that incorporates the proposed methodologies has been released to the public. The UC adopts a web-based UI method for exploring information. Furthermore, it categorizes navigated content and query results to enhance data visibility.

Acknowledgements

This work was partially supported by NSC grants 94-2422-H-001-006, 94-2422-H-001-007, 94-2422-H-001-008, and 94-2422-H-001-004. The authors would like to thank Dr. L. F. Chien and various professional parties in the NDAP Research & Development of Technology Division for their contributions to this paper.

References

[1] Chinese Document Processing (CDP) Lab, Institute of Information Science, Academia Sinica. http://www.sinica.edu.tw/~cdp/
[2] National Digital Archives Program. http://www.ndap.org.tw/index_en.php
[3] Union Catalog of National Digital Archives Program. http://catalog.ndap.org.tw/dacs4/System/

Research on Grid-Aware Mechanisms and Issues for CADAL Project[*]

Hong Zhang, Yueting Zhuang, Jiangqin Wu, and Fei Wu

The Institute of Artificial Intelligence, Zhejiang University,
HangZhou, 310027, P.R. China
zhanghong_zju@yahoo.com.cn, {yzhuang, wujq, wufei}@zju.edu.cn

Abstract. CADAL (China America Digital Academic Library) is a cooperated project of universities and institutes in China and America. Regarding the problem that multi-discipline digital libraries are dispersed and isolated without sufficient interconnection, grid technology is introduced for its advantages in large-area resource cooperation and sharing. This paper analyzes how design principles and mechanisms, applied to digital libraries, can be nested within the OGSA paradigm, and further improves multimedia retrieval.

1 Introduction

Digital library projects are developing towards a large-scale cooperation and sharing, while more and more multimedia files are digitized and stored in distributed physical nodes. Traditionally digitized data are connected by web links, and belong to different domains. This forms the so-called information island. And the performance of high-level applications, like multimedia retrieval, is obstructed. Seamless and transparent resource organization and sharing are mostly needed.

Meanwhile, grid emerges as an advanced technology representing "the third internet revolution", and is evolving towards an Open Grid Service Architecture (OGSA). Grid applications gradually extend from scientific computing to E-business, decision support, information retrieval, etc. This paper probes into a set of grid-aware mechanisms and issues for better organization and utilization of digital library resources.

2 Grid Architecture for CADAL

With grid technology, we aim at integrating widespread data and computational resources into super, ubiquitous and transparent aggregation. According to OGSA information service standards, we devise a hierarchical grid architecture, as Fig.1 shows, to meet the infrastructure requirements of CADAL.

Replica Management improves distributed data access. Reliable replica service provides coordinated and fault-tolerant data movement. Replica location service is designed to identify zero or more physical copies of the content specified by a logical

---

[*] This research is supported by the China-US Million Book Digital Library Project (see http://www.cadal.net), and the National Natural Science Foundation of China (No.60272031).

E.A. Fox et al. (Eds.): ICADL 2005, LNCS 3815, pp. 489–490, 2005.
© Springer-Verlag Berlin Heidelberg 2005

file name. With GridFTP protocol, file transfer service is responsible for secure and efficient wide area data transfer between heterogeneous storage systems.

Virtual Organization Management mainly consists of four modules: Resource catalog service manages physical location information and virtual organization topology structure on entire system scale; Multimedia database service provides data services and corresponding resource creation factory based on Resource Description Framework (RDF); Semantic registry maps ontology information to low-level resources; Ontology meta-information is packed as ontology service.

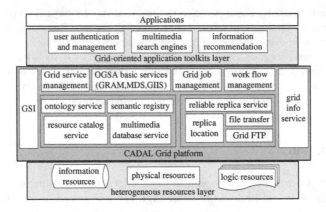

Fig. 1. Grid Architecture for CADAL

3   Grid-Aware Mechanisms for Multimedia Retrieval

Multimedia retrieval is principal service in CADAL. Considering that fourteen member universities in China provide respective multimedia storage and computational capabilities, we propose grid-aware retrieval mechanisms to address the imbalance of resource utilization and improve retrieval performance.

First, CADAL grid portal is developed as the entrance for end users to use grid services. Through grid portal, users can submit jobs, monitor the running process, and inquiry grid resource information. Grid portal provides facilities such as user management and accounting of grid resource usage. Besides, application descriptors, including lists of executable arguments, required environment variables, are organized in grid portal. Grid jobs are automatically created, and then submitted to the chosen Application Server, which is in charge of replica management, multimedia search engine, and application service registry.

Computational resources are delivered by a GRB (Grid Resource Broker), which is realized by a Globus Toolkit installation. Based on a grid job description file and the current status of grid resources, GRB decides where and how to run the application program required by the job.

Data Cleansing and Preparation for Moving Toward Electronic Library Repository

Asanee Kawtrakul

Department of Computer Engineering, Kasetsart University,
Bangkok, Thailand 10900
ak@vivaldi.cpe.ku.ac.th
http://naist.cpe.ku.ac.th

Abstract. Manually annotated metadata usually contains errors from mistyping; however, correcting those metadata manually could be costly and time consuming. This paper proposed a framework to ease metadata correction processed by proposing a system that utilizes OCR and NLP techniques to automatically extract metadata from document image. The system firstly converts images into text using OCR and then extracts metadata from OCR results. After that, the extracted metadata are compared with the data in existing repository to locate error entries. The error entries are then displayed to users whom will correct them using supporting information. Although human decision is required to correct the error manually, this step is necessary with only error entries. The experimental results with 3,712 thesis abstracts show that the proposed solution can automatically extract the relevance information with 91.41% accuracy.

1 Introduction

Like many universities that want to create an online repository of their thesis and dissertations, Kasetsart University faces a problem that most of its documents are available in paper format. To provide a short-term solution to this problem, the Graduate School initiated a project to digitalize the abstract of all documents by using the optical scanner. Unfortunately, the data in existing repository, obtained by manually annotating the document, is inconsistency, incomplete and incorrect.

This paper offers a practical solution to ease the data correction process by utilizing optical character recognition and natural language processing techniques.

2 Methodology

The proposed system [1] consists of three main components: the Optical Character Recognition module for converting abstract images into texts, the Task-oriented Parser module for automatically extracting the relevant information (e.g. thesis title, thesis author, and Supervisor's name) from abstract texts, and the Data Verification module for identifying and correcting error entries of the existing repository by using the extracted information.

E.A. Fox et al. (Eds.): ICADL 2005, LNCS 3815, pp. 491–492, 2005.
© Springer-Verlag Berlin Heidelberg 2005

The input to the system is an image of thesis abstract obtained by scanning an original document. The Character Recognition Module firstly removes the noise from scanned images by using the state of the art techniques [1]. The system then analyses the image to locate the header of the abstract image and recognizes only the header of the image since it contains all the metadata needed to update the existing database. The algorithm for recognizing character images is the one described in [2].

After converted to text, the result is sent to the Task-oriented Parser Module to extract metadata from the text by using context-free grammar (CFG) [3] together with YAPPS2 (Yet Another Python Parser System) which is a LL(1) parser as a parser engine [4] as an internal engine. The underlying property that enables us to automatically extract the relevant information from thesis abstracts is that thesis abstracts have a well-defined structure so that we can easily define a grammar to analyze its structure. By using task-oriented parser together with defined grammar, the relevant information can be directly obtained from parsing results. The extracted information is then used to identify human error entries of the existing repository, since information extracted from paper documents is more up-to-dated and accurate than human entry. After located all error entries, data verification module that display both extracted information and original image is used to ease the data correction process.

3   Conclusion and Result

This paper proposed a framework to ease data correction process by utilizing optical character recognition and natural language processing technology. The proposed system consists of three main components: the OCR Module for converting abstract images into texts, the Task-oriented Parser Module for automatically extracting the metadata from abstract texts, and the Data Verification Module for identifying and correcting the error entries of the existing repository by using the extracted information.

The experimental results with 3,712 thesis abstracts show that the proposed solution can automatically extract the relevant information with 91.41% accuracy which greatly reduces the labors work of data correction process.

References

1. Yingsaeree, C., Kawtrakul, A.: A Unified Framework for Automatic Metadata Extraction from Electronic Document. Proceedings of International Advanced Digital Library Conference (2005).
2. Waewsawangwong, P., Kawtrakul, A.: Multi-Feature Extraction for Printed Thai Character Recognition. Proceedings of 4th Symposium on Natural Language Processing (2000).
3. Wood, D.: Theory of computation. Willey International (1998).
4. Patel, A.: Yapps: Yet Another Python Parser System. 16 June, 2005, from http://theory. stanford.edu/~amitp/Yapps/ (2003).

A Peer-to-Peer Architecture for Web Annotation Sharing*

Cheng-Zen Yang, Shen-Chi Chen, and Ing-Xiang Chen

Department of Computer Science and Engineering,
Yuan Ze University, Taiwan, R.O.C.
{czyang, shenchi, sean}@syslab.cse.yzu.edu.tw

Abstract. In this paper, we present a peer-to-peer (P2P) architecture design called PWAS to share personal Web annotations with a hybrid hierarchical P2P approach. PWAS maintains a user-centric annotation environment in which personal annotations can be flexibly shared with a reduced number of query messages.

1 Introduction

In the research areas of digital libraries, supporting annotation functionalities has been a very interesting issue [1, 2]. Observing the rapid development of peer-to-peer (P2P) technology, we propose a P2P annotation architecture called PWAS (Peer-to-Peer Web Annotation System) to support user information sharing in a digital library environment.

Three major design features are addressed in PWAS. First, PWAS uses a hierarchical architecture model to relieve the single point of failure and the hot-spot problem which can be commonly found in many semi-P2P systems, such as Napster [3], where a centralized server is heavily employed. Second, PWAS adopts a grouping mechanism to reduce the number of broadcasting discovery messages to prevent the flooding problem incurred in many pure P2P systems, such as Gnutella [4]. Third, the establishment of a PWAS environment is straightforward because of its off-the-shelf software components.

2 PWAS Architecture

Figure 1 (a) shows the hierarchical architecture in PWAS. The bottom of the hierarchy consists of groups of PWAS peer nodes. Each peer node has a *local annotation information repository* (LAIR) database to maintain the sharing information of annotations with *group* and *public* permission control. In each group, a peer node is elected as the leader according to its availability to form the middle layer. On the top of the hierarchy, an annotation information provider (AIP) is designated as the global directory server to maintain global annotation information with a *global annotation information repository* (GAIR) database. AIP keeps the GAIR database synchronized with the LAIR databases located at the leader nodes and the PWAS peers. Figure 1 (b) shows the peer node

---

* This work was supported in part by National Science Council of R.O.C. under grant NSC 94-2213-E-155-050.

E.A. Fox et al. (Eds.): ICADL 2005, LNCS 3815, pp. 493–494, 2005.
© Springer-Verlag Berlin Heidelberg 2005

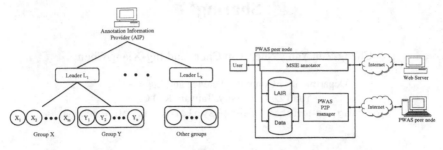

(a) The hierarchical model in PWAS   (b) The architecture of a PWAS peer node

Fig. 1. The system architecture of PWAS

Fig. 2. The PWAS toolbar interface

architecture. Each PWAS peer consists of four components: an MSIE (Microsoft Internet Explorer) annotator, a PWAS P2P manager, a LAIR database, and an annotation database. Figure 2 shows the toolbar interface of the MSIE annotator which provides three functions: *Search*, *Annotate*, and *Option*.

3   Concluding Remarks

This paper presents a P2P architecture design to share personal Web annotations. PWAS has three distinctive features: (1) PWAS is a fully user-centric Web annotation system; (2) the network traffic of annotation sharing is kept low due to its hierarchical structure; (3) annotation searching and sharing is more convenient due to the P2P design. From our experiences with the PWAS prototype, P2P annotation shows its suitableness for an open distributed annotation environment.

References

1. Marshall, C.C.: Annotation: from Paper Books to the Digital Library. Proc. 2nd International Conf. on Digital Libraries, ACM (1997) 131–140.
2. Nichols, D.M., et al.: DEBORA: Developing an Interface to Support Collaboration in a Digital Library. Proc. 4th European Conf. on Research and Advanced Technology for Digital Libraries (ECDL 2000). (2000) 239–248.
3. Napster. http://www.napster.com/.
4. http://www.gnutella.com/.

A Common Grammar for Diverse Vocabularies: The Abstract Model for Dublin Core

Thomas Baker

Göttingen State and University Library,
Papendiek 14, 37073 Göttingen, Germany

Abstract. In its tenth year, the Dublin Core Metadata Initiative has published the "DCMI Abstract Model" (DCAM) as a syntax-independent basis for interoperability of metadata across a diversity of technologies and implementation platforms. Developed since 1997 in parallel with related W3C standards, the DCAM provides a praxis-oriented model for describing resources and for carrying descriptions of multiple resources — i.e., a Dissertation, its Author, and the author's Institution — in exchangeable records. The model associates properties with resources in a way designed to facilitate the creation of mappings and the merging of metadata from a diversity of sources into cross-domain portals and repositories. By design, the model is also compatible with more complex and expressive ontology languages.

Underlying the DCMI approach are several practical insights: The first is that in our complex, multi-lingual world, it is realistic to limit expectations for shared understanding ("semantic interoperability") to a pidgin-like core of generic concepts. The second is that metadata based on complex, hierarchical schemas is difficult to re-use outside a specific application context unless it was pre-designed to be mapped to simpler models.

This approach to interoperability — a focus on core semantics on the basis of a modular, generic model — is of more general use than for describing resources with the well-known, fifteen-element "Dublin Core." The approach is also reflected in standards such as "SKOS Core," an RDF vocabulary for translating existing thesauri (and other Simple Knowledge Organization Systems) into a form usable for intelligent processing. Sharing a model allows implementers to draw on a diversity of vocabularies — DC, SKOS, and vocabularies more specialized or application-specific — as needed, in creating "application profiles" that reflect requirements and content-level agreements ("cataloging rules") within particular implementation communities. Sharing a common model also allows different communities to maintain vocabularies which themselves remain small and manageable, yet when combined in application profiles may be highly expressive.

Having achieved a stable model, DCMI is shifting the emphasis of its activities to that reviewing real-world profiles which can be used as good-practice examples by designers of new applications.

E.A. Fox et al. (Eds.): ICADL 2005, LNCS 3815, p. 495, 2005.
© Springer-Verlag Berlin Heidelberg 2005

Thai's Invaluable Memory Celebrated
Via *Global Memory Net**

Ching-chih Chen

Graduate School of Library and Information Science,
Simmons CollegeBoston, MA 02115, USA
chen@simmons.edu

Abstract. In this digital era, the mode of universal access for information seeking and knowledge acquisition differs greatly from the traditional ways. We have witnessed the exciting convergence of content, technology, and global collaboration in the development of digital libraries, which has offered us unbounded opportunities for dynamic information access and delivery. This author has experienced much of the transformations from analog to digital in the last two decades through her own R&D activities -- from the creation of interactive videodiscs and multimedia CDs on the First Emperor of China's terracotta warriors and horses in the 1980s and 1990s to leading a current international digital library project, Global Memory Net (GMNet), supported by the US National Science Foundation. In presenting her vision for linking world digital resources together for universal access, she will share with the audience the latest development of Global Memory Net In honor of H.R.H. Princess Maha Chakri Sirindhorn at the special occasion of her 50th Birthday. The invaluable images of H.R.H. Princess and the Royal Family, as well as some of the most attractive sites of Thailand, such as the Grand Palace, etc. are included in GMNet as a part of the rare Thai Memory.

I am delighted and deeply honored to be at the ICADL 2005 meeting in Bangkok. Some of you know that I organized the First Pacific Conference on New Information Technology in 1986 in Bangkok, which became the first of a series of twelve International Conferences on New Information Technology (NIT) in different parts of the world from 1986 to 2001. So, Bangkok is very special to me in that very personal sense. It is a great pleasure to see many friends, particularly Prof. Khunying Maenmas Chavalit after 20 years, and many former doctoral graduates of Simmons.

---

* Concepts and systems functionalities presented are modified from an invited talk, entitled "New mode of universal access: Latest development of Global Memory Net," delivered at the *Distinguished Seminar Series* of OCLC, Dublin, OH on September 30, 2005. http://www.oclc.org/research/dss/. This paper follows much of the format of the Invited Speech given at the International Conference on Universal Digital Libraries, Hangzhou, China, Oct. 31-Nov. 2, 2005 [1]. The image contents shown are related to H.R.H. Princess Maha Chakri Sirindhorn, courtesy of the Thai Library Association, and the Royal Family, particularly those related to the late H.R.H. Princess Mother Somdej Phra Srinagarindra Boromarajajonani, and her husband, the late Prince Mahidol of Songkla. These imges are provided by courtesy of the Simmons College Archives.

E.A. Fox et al. (Eds.): ICADL 2005, LNCS 3815, pp. 496–508, 2005.
© Springer-Verlag Berlin Heidelberg 2005

Much more important than these, it is my special privilege and honor to be able to celebrate the 50ᵗʰ Birthday of H.R.H Princess Maha Chakri Sirindhorn, the Patron of the Thai Library Association. In following the theme of this conference, "Implementing Strategies and Sharing Experience," and reflecting on the role of digital libraries, I have chosen to share with you a part of the valuable Thai memory in GMNet when I introduce both the concept and systems functionalities of GMNET.

1 Introduction

In technological terms, it has been a long time since my *PROJECT EMPEROR-I* --a multimedia interactive videodisc project on the First Emperor of China's famous terracotta warriors and horses in 1984. At that time, *PROJECT EMPEROR-I* demonstrated that multimedia technology could change the way we seek, demand, and use information. Two decades later, fueled by enormous progress in science and technology, we have come a very long way from the use of interactive multimedia technology in the workstation environment to the global networked environment... We are truly living in a new period of unprecedented opportunities and challenges! [2] So, in this digital era, we have witnessed the exciting convergence of content, technology, and global collaboration in the development of digital libraries [3] with great potential for providing universal information access.

Thus, today's information seekers, regardless of whether they are the general public, school children, or those from research and higher education communities, seek information for education, research, entertainment, or enrichment in very different ways from before. From the information resources point of views, the old model of "owning" a collection has given way to "sharing," and the new emphases have shifted from possessing large "physical libraries" to "virtual libraries" digitally distributed all over the world.

In the last two decades, I have experienced much of these transformations up-close and personal through my own R&D activities – from the creation of interactive videodiscs and multimedia CDs in the 80s and 90s to leading a current international digital library project, *Global Memory Net,* supported by the International Digital Library Program of the US National Science Foundation [1, 2, 3, 4, 5].

2 Vision for Universal Access

During 1998~2002, I was privileged to serve as a member of the US President's Information Technology Advisory Committee (PITAC), and all members were deeply involved in the drafting of several PITAC Reports to the President. The one related to digital libraries was the 2001 Report of the PITAC Digital Library Panel, entitled Digital Libraries: Universal Access to Human Knowledge [6]. It offers an ambitious vision:

> "All citizens anywhere anytime can use any Internet-connected digital device to search all of human knowledge. Via the Internet, they can access knowledge in digital collections created by traditional libraries,

> *museums, archives, universities, government agencies, specialized organizations, and even individuals around the world. These new libraries offer digital versions of traditional library, museum, and archive holdings, including text, documents, video, sound, and images. ... Very-high-speed networks enable groups of digital library users to work collaboratively, communicate with each other about their findings, and use simulation environments, remote scientific instruments, and streaming audio and video... In this vision, no class-room, group, or person is ever isolated from the world's greatest knowledge resources." [6]*

If we dissect this abbreviated vision statement, and compare the segments with the title and several themes of the ICADL 2005 Meeting, we should be clear on the targets for which we should be aiming. It is clearly stated in the PITAC's vision that one should be able to find any information he/she needs whenever and wherever needed. It is a vision so much easier said than done! It will require sustainable and long-term commitment of many. We should expect many obstacles on the long road to this "elusive" vision, as stated in the Report of the US National Science Foundation's (NSF) Workshop on Research Directions for Digital Libraries, entitled Knowledge Lost in Information [7].

Despite the challenges, in the US, we believe that we have made substantial advances in the technical area in terms of advancing capabilities, through an interagency program of integrated, interdisciplinary, project-oriented research initiatives in the last decade. Now, the convergence of content, technology, and global collaboration in the development of digital libraries should be a natural process. In this digital environment, from a content or information resources point of view, no one institution—no matter how large it is, or one country—no matter how abundant in resources, can possibly have everything. Thus, the old model of "owning" a collection has to give way to "sharing," and the new emphasis has to shift from possessing large "physical libraries" to "virtual libraries" digitally distributed all over the world. If we are talking about content building on a "global" scale, then we must have global collaboration through global community building. Thus, our usual "user community building" has to be of the global scale [1,2,3,4].

3   Components of Digital Library Research

In 2002, I co-chaired the DELOS-NSF Working Group in Digital Imagery for Significant Cultural and Historical Materials [8, 9]. We presented a conceptual model of interdisciplinary digital library research programs with a triangular relationship among people, content, and technology with the center area as "Applications and Use". The scope and parameters set for "users" and "use" are:

- Users: ALL citizens of the world regardless of age, ethnic group, education, social status, religion, etc.
- Uses: For whatever they need.

o Contents - All subject areas, all types of formats, all types of digital collections created by all types of organizations;
o Geographical areas - All parts of the world.

Content is the vast array of significant materials of subject areas throughout the world. Technologies are the enabling research and development in all related technical areas such as information retrieval for multimedia contents, multilingual retrieval, image processing, artificial intelligence, visualization, data mining, etc. In other words, an interdisciplinary digital library research team will develop empowering technologies to enhance the way people can create, disseminate and access the content. Research into application development, presentation and usability will help to focus our R&D work with specific application in mind for the purpose of increasing universal access. [1]

3 New Mode Of Universal Access and Global Memory Net

Effective and collaborative application development in digital libraries will contribute to the eventual realization of the PITAC vision as articulated earlier. Thus, applications and use will be the centerfold of this paper.

To address this, I would like to start by approaching information seeking and use of information from a more conceptual angle. When talking about information seeking to satisfy the users' information needs, organizations like libraries have traditionally followed a linear reference model [1]:

Fine out what one wants? [through Author, Title, Keyword, Terms, Subject, etc.]

→ *Find the book(s) or publication(s) containing the information. Use the keyword(s) etc. to search library card catalog;*
→ *Find the book(s) or publication(s) containing the information.*

Many libraries approach the use of digital resources in the same manner. In other words, taking Web search as an example, one determines the appropriate term(s) [keyword(s), subject(s), etc.], searches the Internet, goes to the located Web site(s), and finds the information in that navigational path. Likewise, many digital libraries are developed with this similar retrieval route in mind using metadata as the sole source of "descriptive" information.

This traditional approach has been very effective for finding needed information for many years and will continue to be, provided one knows what he/she is looking for! Yet, in the current digital environment with the rich and diversified resources available, we should expand our capabilities far beyond the traditional ones. We should realize that "digital libraries offer unparalleled access to information for a far broader range of users than prior physical and organizational arrangement" [4]. In order to benefit from this digital environment, we need to find out whether we have a scalable, interoperable infrastructure that is able to bridge context, culture, and language, and enable us to gather, organize, utilize and share the rich information resources effectively. We need to change the traditional linear reference model to a new one on use and usability, in which information resources actually "talk" to each other. It is a model which stimulates the users' thinking and learning, redefines user experiences, and is geared to much widerranging and broader-based user groups. In this direction, "universal access" is taking on a very different meaning, while data, information, knowledge, users, information services and applications all have much more expanded and different definitions than before [4].

3.1 Role of Global Memory Net in This New Paradigm

Now I shall shift gears to share my own experience during this period of dynamic technological transformations since 1983. The presentation will be quite visual, but for the benefit of the readers, I shall provide some summary descriptions.

In the last two decades, I have experienced these transformations up-close and personal. I have created the interactive videodisc called "First Emperor of China", in the early 1980s; then converted the contents of the analog videodiscs and authored the digital multimedia CD of the same title in the early 1990s. While busy in building up contents, and developing more complete descriptive information (later known as metadata) of the Emperor resources, I proposed the Chinese Memory Net (CMNet) when the US National Science Foundation (NSF) first introduced its International Digital Library Program (NSF/IDLP). CMNet became one of the first NSF/IDLP Projects. Since 2002, CMNet has expanded its scope to Global Memory Net [1].

Although, as the name suggests, Global Memory Net (GMNet) can and should accommodate all types of "memories" therefore all subject areas, but in order to focus our developmental work, for now, GMNet is focusing on topics related to culture, history and heritage; and hopes to be an effective gateway to the world cultural, historical, and heritage image collections from academic educational and research partners in the world. Much of these unique collections of great value to education and research as well as to general public are not currently accessible due to distance, form, and technical barriers. GMNet is to find new ways to enable users to access and exploit these significant research collections via the global network. Each collaborator of this complimentary and synergistic group possesses experience, knowledge, expertise, and capability in different but related research area(s). Each contributes either part of its superb culture and heritage collection, or cutting-edge techniques to facilitate the effective retrieval of multimedia resources.   More background information on the conceptual framework of GMNet as well as the system structure and development of the recent version of GMNet can be found in Zhang and Chen [10], but I shall present the system functional chart in Fig. 1 to show the various systems functionalities of GMNet, as presented to the users as shown in Fig. 3 (the Home Page of GMNet).   Fig. 2 shows how the invaluable images and other multimedia resource of the world's culture, history and heritage are organized, dynamically managed, and intuitively retrieved and delivered to the end users for their uses via both traditional and cutting-edge technologies.

Figures 1-2 also show clearly that GMNet has several major components – such as User, Archives, About Us, News, Policies, etc., but the single most important component, also the most important part of any digital libraries, is "Collections," images or information of which will be displayed at the center of the search screen

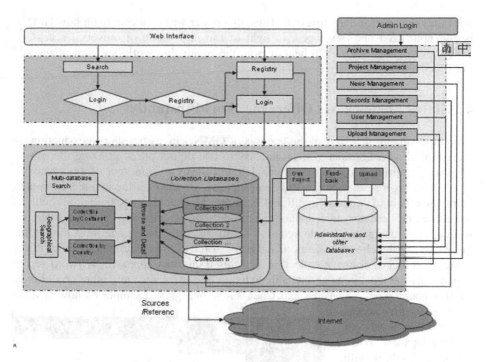

Fig. 1. System functionalities of GMNet (from Zhang & Chen [8])

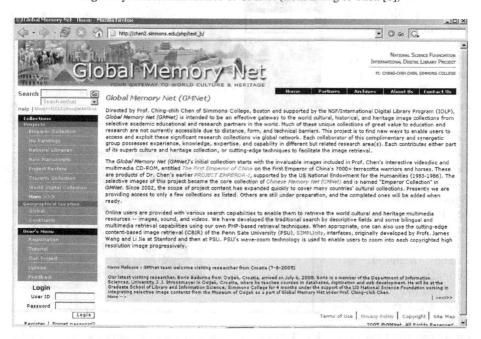

Fig. 2. GMNet's Home Page (Version 3.0)

once they are located and retrieved. Thus, this paper will concentrate on how GMNet is conceptualized and developed, in light of the new mode of universal access, to enable every potential user to benefit from the invaluable world's digital image and multimedia resources.

4 Global Memory Net Offers the World Instantly

It is impossible to describe all the features of GMNet in such a short introduction. In the simplest way, consider GMNet an easy to use digital portal utilizing the cutting edge image retrieval technology to enable one to take a visual tour of any country's culture, heritage, history, and world contributions, all while sitting at one's computer. Here one is able to conduct "traditional" searches by choosing any field or all fields of the metadata - creator, title, location, time period, description, keyword, reference source, etc. - using the Google syntax. To do this effectively, one must have some knowledge of the chosen collection, and know some of the predefined specifics of the contents of a chosen image collection. For this traditional approach, keyword search is generally the most popular one, although one also can search any other or all fields. At this conference, Nagatsuka and Chen show one good example of how GMNet

offers innovative access to the retrieval of ancient Japanese Waka poems and tables with cutting-edge image re-trieval capabilities with supporting contempory Japanese translations and sounds [11]. Here we shall demonstrate with Thai Memory images of H.R.H. Princess Maha Chakri Sirindhorn as well as members of the Royal Family, particularly those of the late H.R.H. Princess Mother Som-dej Phra Srinagarindra Boromarajajonani, and her husband, the late Prince Mahidol of Songkla.

When one enters the Thai Memory Collec-tion, and knows pre-cisely specific topics of interest, he/she can

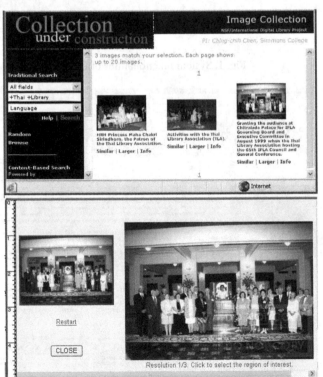

Fig. 3. Results of "traditional search" using one of the metadata fields

simply type the keyword(s) and retrieve. Such is the case of Fig. 3, when one wants to find H.R.H. Princess and the Thai Library Association, for example, he/she can type "Thai Library Association," then three pictures will be found instantly. Then, a chosen picture can be enlarged, such as the one showing the US IFLA Delegation's audience with H.R.H. Princess in 1999 when IFLA met in Bangkok.

However, in most cases, one does not have any idea on what kind of images are available in a given image collection. This is a very important point! Thus, just like a library, we need to provide the users an opportunity to browse the stack, and find what they need and want. In this case, in GMNet, we provide our users the ability to "browse" what is included in a collection in the order of image organization, or to request the random display of images included in the collection by clicking on the "Random" button. This random feature is a significant one because this will provide the user a fast exposure to the scope of coverage as well as some of the specific keywords for pursuing traditional searches as stated above. Yet, what is even better is that once an image strikes the interest of a user, then images of similar color and shape can be instantly displayed by clicking on the "Similar" button. This latter feature utilizes the cutting edge content-based image retrieval technique, SIMPLIcity, developed by Prof. J. Wang of Penn State University (see Zhang and Chen [10]) [12]. The combination of the above mentioned capabilities permit the users to browse,

Fig. 4. Images with both English and Thai titles are shown randomly (Circled one is the chosen image for further information)

retrieve, enjoy, and learn about a chosen subject in just seconds through multiple thousands of digital images accurately and effectively.

If one does not know what kinds of images are included in the collection, how can one be expected to know how to retrieve by keyword and browse by title or subject? Thus, the GMNet's cutting-edge content-based image retrieval technique, as shown in Fig. 4, can enhance both the retrievability and usability of a collection. "Random" search in this case has provided the user an enormous amount of information in a great hurry. It shows images randomly with words in the titles which can be used in traditional searches.

Once a picture of interest is chosen, as shown in Fig. 4, the user has three choices for asking for more information at the click of any of the three choices (Fig.5).

- Similar -- for all the images of similar color and shape. This opens up all possibilities for all related images which are totally unknown to the user earlier;

Fig. 5. Three different approaches to instantly provide more information on a chosen image (note the bilingual capabilities in both retrieval and display of Thai language)

- Larger -- for enlarging the images at multiple levels of zooming depending on the resolution of the image. Once the image is larger than the icon, a digital watermark will be shown dynamically to protect the copyright and intellectual property of the image creator;
- Info -- for textual descriptive information showing all the available metadata fields.

When PDF document, URL address, or sound and video are available, a user can retrieve these instantly. Space limitations do not permit further examples, but it is necessary to mention that the current Thai Memory will have additional images from the Simmons College Archive on H.R.H. Princess' grant-parents, the late H.R.H. Princess Mother Somdej Phra Srinagarindra Boromarajajonani, and the late Prince Mahidol of Songkla, when she was a nursing student at Simmons. Beautiful images of notable sites, like the Grand Palace, will also be included as shown in Fig. 6.

4.1 Linking Images to Bibliographical Resources

Thus, with just a few clicks, a user's knowledge on a subject can have a quantum jump from total ignorance to knowing rather substantially about the subject. At this point, should the user wish to find more information, such as books, journals and additional Web resources on any other related topics, he/she can be linked instantly to these bibliographical and Web sources, such as OCLC's World Cat with the world rich bibliographical resources (about 1 billion records) and Google. With these instant links, a user can truly and seamlessly access the world's invaluable resources in all formats at their fingertips. This is also where the users can benefit from projects like the Million Books when both the quantity and quality of the digital resources grow!

Fig. 6. Images on H.R.H Prince Mother and Prince Mahidol, and Grand Palace

4.2 Linking to World Digital Resources

Since GMNet is intended to be an effective gateway to the world cultural, historical, and heritage image collections from academic educational and research partners in the world, it is important that it can link to the world digital collections for instant access by the users. Considering the enormous cost involved by an institution in developing its digital collection(s), it becomes clear to us that it is not only impossible but also conceptually unsound to consider purely centralized digital collections. For this reason, we have judiciously identified over 2300 digital collections around the world, and all of these are instantly searchable and linked from GMNet. Online users are provided with similar search capabilities to enable them to retrieve these world digital resources -- images, sound, and videos -- with complete backup of textual descriptive information and referral to the world rich bibliographic resources, such as OCLC's World Cat. In GMNet, users also can access all collections include the World Digital Collections by geographical locations. Over 230 countries and geographical areas are also listed for instant retrieval of the available digital resources on and from those areas.

It is impossible to cover all the features of GMNet, but two additional ones are worthy of brief mention:

- *Multi-collection, multilingual and multimedia search capabilities* — Currently users can search all the collections at once or go to each individually. When there are languages other than English present in any of the collections listed, language search selection will be shown for Chinese, Vietnamese, Thai, Croatian and Italian etc.
- *User's own project creation* — When a user finds images of his/her choice and would like to keep them for whatever purposes --report writing, lecture presentation, showing to friends, etc. --they can create up to 3 own projects on any subjects for a selected time period. Upload functions also are possible for them to be a contributor to the system depending on the resolution of security issues.

5 Conclusion

The above is a quick birds' eye view of Global Memory Net and its latest development. Our next steps will consider the development of a simpler system version to enable the involvement of more organizations in the world with lesser technological capabilities, the expansion of subject areas beyond the culture, history and heritage, etc.

When we view our world from a global dimension, it is really much smaller than in the past. To be able to fully leverage the world's rich information resources for the benefit of all citizens in the world, we have shown GMNet's way to seamlessly integrate all types of resources together, and make the use easy and transparent to users. To accomplish our goals, we seek international partnerships and collaboration. As I traveled from country to country with a special "global" lens focused on the potential sharing of cultural and heritage resources in the cyberspace, I was struck with the great potential for meaningful collaborative activities. GMNet has a place for everyone. Instead of building localized digital libraries, let us work on building up large-scale digital contents in multimedia format together beyond national borders, and let us also explore together the fertile future for distributed cross-disciplinary collaboration [13].

Acknowledgment

Global Memory Net is supported by the US National Science Foundation/ International Digital Library Program with Grant Nos. NSF/CISE/IIS-9905833 and NSF/CISE/IIS-0333036.

I am deeply grateful to Boris Badurina for his help in developing the latest Version 3 of Global Memory Net, based on Version 2, developed by Shengqiang Zhang of Sichuan University, China, under my supervision during their stay with GMNet as visiting researchers. I am thankful to another visiting researcher, Hongxia Zhang of the University of Hainan, China, for her assistance in scanning the images included in this paper as well as the preparation of associated metadata information. Pimrumpai Premsmit's effort in providing me with images of H.R.H. Princess Maha Chakri Sirindhorn is very much appreciated. I wish to acknowledge the provision of images from the Simmons College Archive for those of H.R.H. Princess Mother Somdej Phra Srinagarindra Boromarajajonani during her study at Simmons in the early 20s and her continuing association with Simmons. The selection of the images from the Archive by Jason Wood is gratefully acknowledged.

References

1. Chen, Ching-chih, "New mode of universal access and Global Memory Net," Journal of Zhejiang University SCIENCE, 6A (11): to be published, 2005. Invited speech at the Interntional Conference on Universal Digital Libraries, Hangzhou, China, Oct. 31 – Nov. 3, 2005.
2. Chen, Ching-chih, "Global Memory Net offers the world instantly: Potentials for universal access to invaluable Japanese contents," translated by Prof. T. Nagatsuka, Journal of Information Processing and Managment, 47 (11): 751-760. February 2005.
3. Chen, Ching-chih, "*Global Memory Net:* New collaboration, new activities and new potentials," keynote speech in *Proceedings of International Conference on Asian Digital Libraries (ICADL 2004)*, Shanghai, December 14-17, 2004. Shanghai, China: Shanghai Jiao-tong University, 2004.
4. Chen, Ching-chih, "The promise of international digital library collaboration for innovative use of invaluable resources," in *Human Information Behaviour & Competences for Digital Libraries*. Keynote in *Proceedings of the Libraries in the Digital Age*, May 25-29, 2004, Dubrovnik and Mljet, Croatia. pp. 7-15.
5. Chen, Ching-chih, "*Global Memory Net* offers the world instantly: Potentials for universal access to invaluable contents," keynote speech in *Proceedings of CCDL: Digital Library – Advance the Efficiency of Knowledge Utility,* Beijing, September 5-8, 2004. Beijing, China: National Library of China, 2004.
6. PITAC (U.S. President's Information Technology Advisory Committee), 2001. Digital Library Panel. Digital Libraries: Universal Access to Human Knowledge.

7. Larsen, R., Wactlar, H. (eds.), 2004. Knowledge Lost in Information: Report of the NSF Workshop on Research Directions for Digital Libraries. Chatham, MA. School of Information Science, University of Pittsburgh, Pittsburgh, PA. http://www.sis.pitt.edu/%7Edlwkshop/report.pdf.
8. Chen, C.C., Kiernan, K. (eds.), 2002. Report of the DELOS-NSF Working Group on Digital Imagery for Significant Cultural and Historical Materials. http://dli2.nsf.gov/internationalprojects/working_group_reports/.
9. Chen, C.C., Wactlar, H.D., Wang, J.Z., Kiernan, K., 2005. Digital imagery for significant cultural and historical materials: An emerging research field bridging people, culture, and technologies. International Journal on Digital Libraries—Special Issue on EU-NSF Working Group Reports.
10. Zhang, S.Q., Chen, C.C., 2005. Global Memory Net and the development of digital image information management system: Experience and practice. Journal of Zhejiang University SCIENCE, 6A (11): to be published, 2005. Paper presented at the Interntional Conference on Universal Digital Libraries, Hangzhou, China, Oct. 31 – Nov. 3, 2005.
11. Nagatsuka, Takashi, and Ching-chih Chen, "Global Memory Net offers new innovative access to Tsurumi's old Waka poems and tales, and maps," in Proceedings of International Conference on Asia Digital Libraries (ICADL 2005), Bangkok, December 13-15, 2005.
12. Chen, C.C., Wang, J.Z., 2002. Large-scale Emperor Digital Library and Semantics-sensitive Region-based Retrieval. The Proceedings of Digital Library—IT Opportunities and Challenges in the New Millennium, Beijing, China. Beijing Library Press, Beijing, China, p.454-462.
13. Chen, C.C. (ed.), 2001. Global Digital Library Development in the New Millennium: Fertile Ground for Distributed Cross-Disciplinary Collaboration. Tsinghua University Press, Beijing, China.

Digital Library Development in the Asia Pacific

Hsinchun Chen

Artificial Intelligence LabDepartment of Management Information Systems,
Eller College of Management The University of Arizona,
McClelland Hall 430Z, 1130 E. Helen Street, Tucson, Arizona 85721, U.S.A.
hchen@eller.arizona.edu
http://ai.bpa.arizona.edu

Abstract. Over the past decade the development of digital library activities within Asia Pacific has been steadily increasing. Through a meta-analysis of the publications and content within International Conference on Asian Digital Libraries (ICADL) and other major regional digital library conferences over the past few years, we see an increase in the level of activity in Asian digital library research. This reflects high continuous interest among digital library researchers and practitioners internationally. Digital library research in the Asia Pacific is uniquely positioned to help develop digital libraries of significant cultural heritage and indigenous knowledge and advance cross-cultural and cross-lingual digital library research.

1 Introduction

The location and provision of information services has dramatically changed over the last ten years. There is no need to leave the home or office to locate and access information now readily available on-line via digital gateways furnished by a wide variety of information providers, e.g., libraries, electronic publishers, businesses, organizations, individuals. Information access is no longer restricted to what is physically available in the nearest library. It is electronically accessible from a wide variety of globally distributed information repositories.

Digital libraries represent a form of information technology in which social impact matters as much as technological advancement. It is hard to evaluate a new technology in the absence of real users and large collections. The best way to develop effective new technology is in multi-year large-scale research and development projects that use real-world electronic testbeds for actual users and aim at developing new, comprehensive, and user-friendly technologies for digital libraries. Typically, these testbed projects also examine the broad social, economic, legal, ethical, and cross-cultural contexts and impacts of digital library research.

2 The NSF DLI-1, DLI-2 and NSDL Programs

2.1 DLI-1, 1994-1998

The original Digital Library Initiative (DLI or DLI-1), sponsored by the NSF, DARPA, and NASA, was started in 1994. The original program announcement stated:

E.A. Fox et al. (Eds.): ICADL 2005, LNCS 3815, pp. 509–524, 2005.
© Springer-Verlag Berlin Heidelberg 2005

Table 1. Major (Asian) digital library research and development milestones

1994	• NSF Digital Library Initiative Phase 1 (DLI-1) • The First Annual Conference on the Theory and Practice of Digital Libraries, College Station, Texas
1995	• First IEEE Advances in Digital Libraries Conference, McClean, Virginia
1996	• First ACM Conference on Digital Libraries, Bethesda, Maryland
1997	• First European Conference on Research and Advanced Technology for Digital Libraries (ECDL), Pisa, Italy
1998	• The First International Conference on Asian Digital Libraries (ICADL 1998), Hong Kong, China
1999	• President's Information Technology Advisory Committee (PITAC) Report • NSF Digital Library Initiative Phase 2 (DLI-2) • Institute of Museum and Library Services (IMLS) Program • NSF National Science, Mathematics, Engineering, and Technology Digital Library (NSDL) Program • ICADL 1999, Taipei, Taiwan
2000	• ICADL 2000, Seoul, Korea
2001	• ICADL 2001, Bangalore, India • First ACM/IEEE-CS Joint Conference on Digital Libraries (JCDL 2001), Roanoke, Virginia
2002	• ICADL 2002, Singapore • JCDL 2002, Portland, Oregon • China DL Conference, Beijing, China
2003	• ICADL 2003, Kuala Lumpur, Malaysia • JCDL 2003, Houston, Texas
2004	• JCDL 2004, Tucson, Arizona • International Conference on Digital Library, New Delhi, India • ICADL 2004, Shanghai, China
2005	• JCDL 2005, Denver, Colorado • ICADL 2005, Bangkok, Thailand

"The Initiative's focus is to dramatically advance the means to collect, store, and make it available for searching, retrieval, and processing via communica tion networks – all in user-friendly ways. Digital Libraries basically store ma terials in electronic format and manipulate large collections of those materials effectively. Research into digital libraries is research into network information systems, concentrating on how to develop the necessary infrastructure to effec tively mass-manipulate the information on the Net. The key technical issues are how to search and display desired selections from and across large collections."

After a competitive proposal solicitation and review process, six large-scale projects ($4M per project on average) were selected. Most projects were more technical in nature and lead by reputable computer scientists. Each project consisted of a strong team of computer, information and library science researchers, sociologists, and content specialists (http://www.dli2.nsf.gov/dlione/). The DLI projects were extremely successfully and had helped build an international digital library community.

2.2   DLI-2, ITR, IMLS, and NSDL, 1999-

The excitement of Internet-enabled IT developments and e-commerce opportunities in the 1990s prompted the U.S. Government to examine the role of IT research for long-term U.S. interest. A President's Information Technology Advisory Committee (PITAC) was formed, which included many leading U.S. IT researchers and practitioners. Digital library research was identified as one of the successful federal research programs and a target research area.

The success of the original DLI program and the continued IT research interest as stated in the PITAC report allowed the NSF to continue to spearhead the development of the DLI Phase 2 (DLI-2) research program (http://www.dli2.nsf.gov/). DLI-2 funded 29 research projects, with an additional nine projects with an undergraduate emphasis (http://www.dli2/nsf/gov/projects.html).

An additional 15 projects have been funded since 1999 under the Information Technology Research (ITR) program (http://www.dli2.nsf.gov/itrprojects.html). Some address language (e.g., CMU's AVENUE project for adaptive voice translation for minority languages) and 3D modeling topics (e.g., Columbia's project for modeling, visualizing, and analyzing historical and archaeological sites), others research topics in law enforcement information sharing and knowledge management (University of Arizona's COPLINK agent project) and multilingual access to large spoken archives (Survivors of the Shoah Visual History Foundation, a $7.5M project, 20012006).

In addition to the core DLI-2 and related ITR projects, DLI-2 also sponsors 12 international digital library projects (http://www.dli2.nsf.gov/intl.html) involving partners from the U.K. (e.g., University of Liverpool, Southampton University, King's College London), Germany (University Library of Gottingen, University of Trier), China (Tsinghua University, National Taiwan University), Japan (National Institute for Informatics), and Africa (West African Research Center). Most international projects face unique logistics and collaboration challenges.

Several U.S. agencies also began to develop digital library projects that are uniquely tailored to their institution's function. For example, the Institute of Museum and Library Services (IMLS, http://www.imls.gov/about/index.htm), which is an independent federal agency that fosters leadership, innovation, and lifetime learning, supports a series of 130+ smaller-scale digital project grants to libraries and museums for research, digitization, and management of digital resources (http://www. imls.gov/closer/cls_po.asp), from the Brooklyn's Children's Museum to the Chicago Academy of Sciences, and from Duke University's library to the Georgia Department of Archives and History.

Another significant digital library research program was developed concurrently under the NSF National Science, Mathematics, Engineering, and Technology Digital Library Program (NSDL, http://www.nsdl.nsf.gov/indexx.html). The NSDL will offer, via the Internet, high-quality materials for science, mathematics, engineering, and technology education. It will strongly affect education at all levels, including preK-12, undergraduate, graduate, and life-long learning, by providing anytime, anywhere access to a rich array of authoritative and reliable interactive materials and learning environments. More than 60 projects have been funded since 1998 in three areas: the collection track for offering contents (e.g., National Biology Digital Library, Digital Mathematics Library, Experimental Economics Digital Library), the service track for providing technologies and services (e.g., University of Arizona's GetSmart e-learning concept map system), and the core integration track for linking all contents and services under a unified framework.

3 JCDL, ECDL, and ICADL: Building an International Digital Library Community

3.1 JCDL, ECDL, and ICADL, 1995-

Digital Libraries have become far more important nationally and internationally in 2005 than they were in 1996. Many new and significant national digital library initiatives have emerged. In addition, international conferences in digital library have proliferated from their roots of ACM and IEEE Digital Conferences (and then the Joint Conference on Digital Libraries, JCDL) to the European version of ECDL (European Conference on Digital Libraries) and the Asian version of ICADL (International Conference of Asian Digital Libraries).

The ICADL has evolved from its modest inception of about 80 participants in Hong Kong in 1998, to 150+ participants in Taipei, Taiwan in 1999, 300+ participants in Seoul, Korea in 2000, 600+ participants from 12 countries in Bangalore, India in 2001, 400+ participants from 20 countries in Singapore in 2002, 350+ participants from 16 countries in Malaysia in 2003, and 350+ participants from 17 countries in Shanghai, China in 2004. Even regional digital library conferences such as the recent First China Digital Library Conference, hosted by the National Library of China and held in Beijing on July 9-11, 2002, drew 450 participants from 18 countries and 125 exhibitors. Such a high level of activity is due to the continuous interest among digital library researchers and practitioners internationally. This is also partially due to the exponential growth of information content on the Web around the globe, which web searchers are rapidly failing to handle successfully. The 8th ICADL meeting (ICADL 2005) is scheduled to be held in Bangkok, Thailand in December 2005.

4 Digital Library Development in Asia Pacific: Analysis Through ICADL

Over the past decade the development of digital library activities within Asia Pacific has been steadily increasing. Through a meta-analysis of the publications and content within ICADL over the past 7 years, the countries that have contributed and participated in digital library research can be determined. In addition, the various disciplines involved and the research focus of each region can be ascertained. Other major regional digital library conferences held in the past few years are also discussed, following the ICADL analysis.

4.1 Country and Institution Analysis

In August of 1998 the first ICADL was held at the University of Hong Kong. The theme of the conference, "East Meets West," emphasized to the participants the ongoing exchange of ideas between researchers located in the Western and Eastern parts of the globe. Researchers in 7 countries/regions of the world presented twenty-three papers. Of those papers, 18 were from Asian Pacific countries such as mainland China, Hong Kong, Taiwan, Singapore, Korea, and New Zealand.

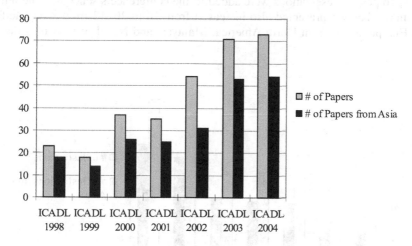

Fig. 1. Number of papers accepted in ICADL

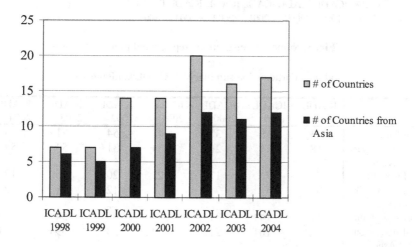

Fig. 2. Number of countries represented in ICADL

The following year the National Taiwan University in Taipei, Taiwan hosted ICADL 1999. Eighteen papers were from 5 Asian and 2 Western countries; 14 being directly from Asia. In 2000, ICADL was held in Seoul, Korea where 37 papers from

14 countries were presented at the conference. This conference saw an increase in interest by countries that were not originally associated with the conference. The number of Asian countries involved in this conference increased from 5 to 7. The fourth ICADL in 2001, held in Bangalore, India, hosted 14 countries: 9 from Asia Pacific, 4 from Europe, and 1 from North America, and a total of 35 papers. Two newcomers from Asia, India and Thailand, were present at the conference. The fifth ICADL conference was held in Singapore in 2002. ICADL 2002 saw a dramatic increase in paper submissions, from 35 in the previous year to 54. In addition to the papers, 16 poster presentations were added to the conference's schedule. The number of countries being represented also increased from 14 to 20: 12 from Asia Pacific, 7 from Europe, and 1 from North America; Malaysia and Nepal were two of the new

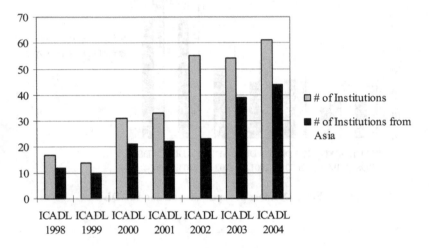

Fig. 3. Number of institutions represented in ICADL

Table 2. Participation summary of ICADL conferences

	ICADL 1998	ICADL 1999	ICADL 2000	ICADL 2001	ICADL 2002	ICADL 2003	ICADL 2004
# of Papers	23	18	37	34	54	71+	73
# of Papers from Asia	18	14	26	25+	31+	53	54
# of Countries	7	7	12	12	20	16	17
# of Countries from Asia	6	5	7	9	12	11	12
# of Institutions	17+	14+	31+	33+	55+	54+	61+
# of Institutions from Asia	12+	10+	21+	22+	23+	39+	44+
# of Academic Departments /Disciplines	6+	6+	8+	8+	11+	17+	18+

Asian Pacific country additions. The sixth ICADL conference was held in Malaysia in 2003. Despite the fact that the Iraq war and SARS affected world travel, ICADL 2003 still recorded 6 invited talks, 68 research paper presentations, and 15 poster presentations from 16 countries: 11 from Asia Pacific, 4 from Europe, and 1 from North America. Iran was the newest country that attended the conference. The most recent ICADL conference was held in Shanghai, China in 2004. ICADL 2004 featured 14 invited speakers, 59 research paper presentations and 37 posters and demonstrations from 17 countries, with 12 from Asia Pacific. Bangladesh was a newcomer from Asia. The number of participant institutions grew from 54 in 2003 to 61 in 2004, among which 14 institutions were from China.

Table 2 summarizes the previous seven ICADL conferences: the number of papers accepted and the number of participating countries, institutions, and departments. Figures 1-3 illustrate the increased number of papers presented at the conferences, as well as the number of countries and institutions attending the conferences.

4.2 Academic Department (Discipline) Analysis

The digital library research and development being conducted within Asian Pacific countries spans many different academic departments and disciplines. Over the past seven ICADL conferences there was an increase from 6+ academic departments to over 18 academic departments being accounted for in technical sciences such as computer science and engineering, as well as within the social science domains. The overwhelming majority of participants came from disciplines such as Information Science (Studies), Library Science, Management Information Systems, Computer Science, Information Engineering, System Engineering, Electrical Engineering, Communication and Information, Education, Anthropology, Geography, Mathematics, Linguistics, and Medical Informatics.

Figure 4 shows the growth in the number of departments (disciplines) that have participated in ICADL.

Aside from popular belief, digital library research is not restricted to those researchers involved in the technical aspects and components of the system; research within digital libraries involves social aspects as well. From a technological

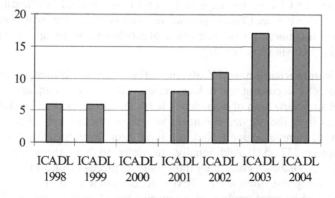

Fig. 4. Number of departments (disciplines) in ICADL

standpoint, digital libraries are a set of electronic resources that are built to help create, search, and use information. From a sociological perspective, digital libraries are constructed by a community of users who use the system to better support their informational needs and applications [6]. In the following sections we analyze the research presented at the ICADL conferences according to these two aspects.

4.3 Topical Analysis: Technical Aspect

Several major technical research areas, including content building and management, text indexing and retrieval, document summarization and categorization, personalization and visualization, interoperability, and multimedia information retrieval, have been reported in the ICADL proceedings over the past 7 years.

Content Building and Management: Digital libraries consist of the collections of digitized resources as well as the links or pointers to other digital sources. Oftentimes they are based on library collections that have been selected by existing library collections or development/archival criteria [30]. The Internet has also been classified as a (somewhat chaotic) digital library by some, where spidering or crawling techniques are needed in order to navigate and create unique content. For example, HelpfulMed, developed at the University of Arizona, provides medical information not only from web pages but also from a variety of online medical databases [13]. A medical spider was designed specifically to collect relevant medical web pages. As a collection building tool, the Greenstone Digital Library Software produced by the New Zealand Digital Library Project has been used to build many digital library collections all over the world [43].

Text Indexing and Retrieval: Indexing is another rapidly growing topic of interest in digital libraries. Indexing is an important task for retrieval. However, while indexing research is on the rise, the ability to correctly index Asian languages such as Chinese and Japanese becomes challenging due to the lack of explicit word boundaries inherent in the language [48]. New research techniques involving the use of n-gram indexing and phrase-extraction algorithms within the Asian digital library community have been used in many research works in order to transcend the word boundary problem. Yang et al. [48] compared n-gram and mutual information-based indexing approaches for the Chinese language and found that a mutual information algorithm could extract more correct Chinese phrases for indexing and retrieval. Ong and Chen [25] presented a Chinese phrase extraction algorithm using an updateable PAT-tree and obtained a precision level of 70%.

Document Summarization and Categorization: Summarization offers a concise representation of a document and reduces its overall size and complexity. In order to automate the summarization of documents, text extraction research has found ways to take sentences from the original document and use them to form coherent summaries [24]. In ICADL summarization techniques have been developed for Asian languages such as Chinese [37, 51]. Additionally, in order to help users identify relevant documents from databases containing thousands of pieces of information, categorization and clustering are often used. Text categorization is the process of assigning documents to one or more predefined categories based on their content [9]. Various categorization techniques have been presented in previous ICADL conferences. Heß and Drobnik [18] proposed a clustering algorithm which analyzed hyperlinks of web pages; Jones and Mahoui [19] described a key phrase-based hierarchical categorization approach; Chan et al. [9] applied a Support Vector Machine algorithm to document categorization. In the recent ICADL, Geng et al. [17], studied Chinese text categorization based on a boosting classifier.

Personalization and Visualization: End users of a system want to be able to organize the information space according to their own subjective perspectives [28]. Personalization provides the ability for users to create their own profiles based on their interests, behaviors, and activities. Chan et al. [9] described a personalized categorization system in which a user could define his/her own category names and refine the categories by providing feedback to the system. Renda and Straccia [28] presented a personalized collaborative digital library system where users could organize the information according to their own interest as well as exchange information with each other. Information visualization is also necessary when designing a human-computer interface to effectively explore information [49]. Several visualization techniques have been studied in ICADL conferences to visualize queries or documents. Yang and Kao [49] considered a 2D presentation of hierarchical information structure called Core Trees. Anderson et al. [2] designed a system which visualizes the frequency of query terms within a document using pie charts and found the pie charts view was preferred by users over a normal text view.

Interoperability: Interoperability in digital library concerns the need for and benefits of integrating distributed collections and systems. Research in this area includes Metadata Encoding and Transmission Standard (METS), Open Archival Information System (OAIS), and Open Archives Initiative (OAI) [7].

Digital libraries typically include content and associated metadata. These metadata provide a description of content, format, ownership, and security as well as links to other versions, source codes, viewers, and related materials [6]. Many different metadata proposals have been presented in ICADL conferences. Existing common metadata schemas such as Dublin Core and Resource Discovery Framework (RDF) were widely adopted in Asian digital library projects [10, 23, 50]. The Open Archives Initiative (OAI) and Open Archival Information System (OAIS) are designed to provide a low barrier for interoperability and are beneficial to collaboration between communities and service providers. Several prototype systems based on OAI protocol were presented in past ICADL conferences [5, 11]. Multimedia data descriptions based on the MPEG-7 standard and other XML-based representations have also been described in various projects [20, 52].

Multimedia Digital Libraries: The contents of a digital library can contain text files, images, audio, and video representations. Because digital libraries are capable of containing multimedia collections, research areas involving the searching and browsing techniques of these content collections have increased. In the ICADL proceedings, Cha and Chung [8] introduced a system for lecture (audio) databases; whereas Rowe et al. [29] described a 3D retrieval system for American ceramic vessels. Ying and Heng [53] introduced the Digital Media Gallery (DMG), a Web-based system that was designed for audio, video, image, and clipart retrieval. It is worth mentioning that digital music libraries have attracted significant interest recently. For example, Bainbridge et al. [4] evaluated different symbolic music matching strategies and explored the effectiveness and efficiency of those strategies under different conditions. In 2004, Li et al. [21] proposed a music theme mining algorithm and content-based music information retrieval algorithm.

4.4 Topical Analysis: Social Aspect

The social aspect of digital libraries emphasizes the activities people engage in when they create, seek, and use information resources. Research within this area focuses on user studies, usage log analysis, multicultural issues, and language-specific issues [6].

User Studies: How end users use and respond to digital libraries is always an important concern of system designers and researchers. User studies provide a glimpse into understanding the users' behavioral patterns when seeking information. Liew et al. [22] conducted an empirical evaluation to study the design of e-journals and how users interacted with them. Their findings showed valuable insights for the designing of e-journals, such as the need for advanced interactivity as compared with their print antecedents.

Usage Log Analysis: Usage log analysis is one of the latest additions to digital library research. This technique analyzes the use of terms, operators, and number of queries per search from usage logs in order to provide a better understanding of digital library usage, user information needs, and system effectiveness [15]. Wolfram and Xie [41] reported on their experience analyzing usage logs and Web-based surveys for end users of the BadgerLink system and drew some conclusions about the behavioral differences between searching and browsing. Cunningham and Mahoui [15] collected usage logs for two digital library systems and compared different searching behaviors in terms of query length, query refinement, and so on when using the two systems. Fu et al. [16] investigated a hybrid method to cluster user queries by utilizing both the query terms and the results returned to queries. By determining and clustering similar queries in query logs, their system could augment the information seeking process by recommending related queries to users.

Multicultural Issues: Digital libraries can help ensure the preservation of collective history and cultural memorabilia [42]. In Asian digital library applications there are countless scenarios that involve creating and distributing locally produced information collections. ICADL publications have included local digital libraries ranging from teachers preparing educational material to medicinal knowledge based on local plants and herbs. For example, the INFLIBNT project aimed at creating a digital library of theses and dissertations from India [40]. SNDT Women's University Library in India developed content for a digital library on Women and Health in South Asia [26]. The Tsinghua University Architecture Digital Library developed a prototype system to provide rich, valuable resources for traditional Chinese architecture research and education [46]. Vaidya and Shrestha [39] produced a study on rural digital library development in Nepal and provided suggestions on technical aspects and cost-effective solutions for digital library development in rural Nepal.

Asian Languages and Cross-lingual Issues: A crucial feature of Asian digital libraries is the ability to work in various local languages [42]. The Chinese language has been widely studied for information retrieval and extraction techniques. In ICADL 1998, Wong and Li [44] and Yang et al. [48] both studied Chinese information retrieval and discussed issues related to Chinese language indexing techniques. In ICADL 1999, Wong et al. [45] presented their method for Chinese news event detection and tracking, where Chinese segmentation was discussed. Ong and Chen [25] studied an updateable PAT-Tree approach to Chinese key phrase extraction. Other Asian languages studied include Japanese, Korean, and Thai. A dictionary-based morphological analysis approach for the Japanese language was proposed by Ando et al. [3]. Theeramunkong et al. [38] investigated using n-gram and HMM approaches for Thai OCR application.

Cross-lingual information retrieval between English and Asian languages has been more widely studied in ICADL conferences than in other Western digital library conferences. Choi et al. [14] proposed a dictionary-based method of Korean-English query translation. Yang and Luk [47] constructed a Chinese-English cross-lingual concept space by utilizing a Hopfield network. In ICADL 2001, Sugimoto [31] presented a multilingual document browsing tool and its metadata creation carried out at ULIS. The application was designed for Japanese, Chinese, Korean, and Arabic languages. Although no query translation was involved in the project, it was the first project of its kind to address the multilingual applications of digital libraries. Recently, in ICADL 2003, Qin et al.[27] presented an English-Chinese cross-lingual Web retrieval system in the business domain. Their system adopted a dictionary-based approach that combines phrasal translation, co-occurrence analysis, and pre-and post-translation query expansion. Sembok et al. [32] implemented a Malay-English scientific terms retrieving software. Several stemming algorithms for the Malay language was discussed and evaluated. More recently, Zhang et al. [54] researched the cross-lingual information problem via ontology alignment.

Many papers have focused on language specific applications in digital libraries. In addition to the ones discussed, several projects and papers were dedicated to looking at collections contained within local languages. For example, Adachi [1] presented NACSIS-ELS, a digital library system of Japanese academic journals. Although the language issue was not the focus in those projects, the experiences were valuable for applying digital library technologies in a multilingual world. Zhou et al. [55] developed a Chinese medical portal, CMedPort, which integrates various techniques such as meta-search, cross-regional search, summarization, and categorization. Their experience provides a good example of adopting information retrieval techniques to non-English languages.

5 Other Related Conferences in Asia Pacific

Several other conferences have been gaining worldwide attention for their efforts within the digital library research domain. Chaired by Ching-chih Chen, the 12th International Conference on New Information Technology was held at Tsinghua University, Beijing, in May, 2001 [12]. She organized twelve International Conferences on New Information Technology (NIT) in various places, including Asian countries such as Thailand, Singapore, Hong Kong, Vietnam, and Taiwan. This series of conferences has helped to encourage international collaboration among information and library professionals.

The International Conference of Digital Library—Opportunities and Challenges in the New Millennium, hosted by the National Library of China, was held in Beijing in July, 2002 [33]. The gathering promoted the development of digital libraries in China as well as other countries. More than 100 papers were published in the proceedings with participants from more than 140 digital libraries and information institutions. The meeting also featured 125 exhibitors ranging from provincial libraries and museums to digital library hardware and software vendors In addition, the International Symposium on Digital Libraries (ISDL) was held in Japan in 1995, 1997, and 1999 [34, 35, 36]. The symposium was hosted by the University of Library and Information Science (ULIS) in Japan and attracted significant Asian and international participation.

6 Conclusions

Digital library researchers in Asia Pacific are facing some challenges in common with researchers in the U.S., Europe, and other parts of the world. However, they are also uniquely positioned to help develop digital libraries of significant cultural heritage and indigenous knowledge and advance cross-cultural and cross-lingual digital library research.

Digital library collections have the widest range of content and media types, ranging from 3D chemical structures to tornado simulation models, from the statue of David to paintings by Van Gogh. A mix of text, audio, and video is common among digital library applications. Collection, organization, indexing, searching, and analysis of such diverse information content continue to create unique technical challenges.

Unlike digital government or e-commerce applications that often generate their own content, digital libraries provide content management and retrieval services to many other content owners. The intellectual property issues (rights and fee collection) surrounding such diverse collections need to be carefully addressed.

Many patrons often would like library services to be "free" or at least extremely affordable. Compounding the issue further is the notion of "free" Internet content. However, for high-quality, credible content to be accessible through digital libraries, cost and sustainability problems needed to be resolved. Different digital library pricing models would need to be developed for different contents and services.

The long history and diversity of the different cultures and peoples in the Asian Pacific region has created a fertile environment for developing digital libraries of cultural heritage and indigenous knowledge. Such content and knowledge could help promote global understanding and collaboration.

Digital library content is often of interest to people all over the world, not just in one region. Many content creation and development processes also require collaboration among researchers and librarians in different parts of the world. Digital library researchers are facing the unique challenge of creating a global service that bridges cultural and language barriers. Researchers in Asia Pacific could significantly contribute to research advancement in cultural and language issues of relevance to the region and to the digital library community as well.

Acknowledgement

This research is supported by: NSF Digital Library Initiative-2, "High-Performance Digital Library Systems: From Information Retrieval to Knowledge Management," IIS-9817473, April 1999-March 2002.

References

1. Adachi, J. (2000). NACSIS-ELS: Digital Library of Japanese Academic Journals. In the Proceedings of the Third International Conference on Asian Digital Library, Seoul, Korea. 15-22.
2. Anderson, T., Hussam, A. Plummer, B. & Jacobs, N. (2002). Pie Charts for Visualizing Query Term Frequency in Search Results. In the Proceedings of the Fifth International Conference on Asian Digital Library, Singapore. 440-451.
3. Ando, K., Lee, T., Shishibori, M. & Aoe, J. (2000). Dictionary Structure for Agglutinative Languages. In the Proceedings of the Third International Conference on Asian Digital Library, Seoul, Korea. 255-260.
4. Bainbridge, D., Dewsnip, M. & Witten, I. (2002). Searching Digital Music Libraries. In the Proceedings of the Fifth International Conference on Asian Digital Library, Singapore. 129 140.
5. Boone, D. & Pennington, S. (2001). Adapting the Open Archival Information System Reference Model for Consumer Initiated Ingestion: A Multi-media Resource Delivery Architecture for the National Gallery of the Spoken Word. In the Proceedings of the Fourth International Conference on Asian Digital Library, Bangalore, India. 258-273.
6. Borgman, C. L. (1998). Social Aspects of Digital Libraries: Making Information Technology Usable and Useful. In the Proceedings of the First Asian Digital Library Workshop, Hong Kong. 6-12.
7. Borgman, C. L. (2002). Challenges in Building Digital Libraries for the 21st Century. In the Proceedings of the Fifth International Conference on Asian Digital Library, Singapore. 113.
8. Cha, G. H. & Chung, C. W. (2000). Modeling and Summarizing Lecture Databases. In the Proceedings of the Third International Conference on Asian Digital Library, Seoul, Korea. 261-266.
9. Chan, C. H., Sun, A. & Lim, E. P. (2001). Automated Online News Classification with Personalization. In the Proceedings of the Fourth International Conference on Asian Digital Library, Bangalore, India. 320-329.
10. Chen, C. C. (ed.) (2001). Proceedings of Global Digital Library Development in the New Millennium—Fertile Ground for Distributed Cross-Disciplinary Collaboration. Tsinghua University Press.
11. Chen, C. C. & Chen, H. H. (2002). Building an OAI-Based Union Catalog for the National Digital Archives Program in Taiwan. In the Proceedings of the Fifth International Conference on Asian Digital Library, Singapore. 425-426.
12. Chen, I. X., Chen, C. M. & Yang, C. Z. (2001). Design of a Search Engine for Cross-library Search Based on Metalogy Metadata. In the Proceedings of the Fourth International Conference on Asian Digital Library, Bangalore, India. 274-282
13. Chen, H. (2001). Medical Text Mining: A DLI-2 Status Report. In the Proceedings of the Fourth International Conference on Asian Digital Library, Bangalore, India. 41-61.

14. Choi, Y. S., Chun, J. & Choi, K. S. (2000). A Study on Dynamic Threshold for Korean English Query Translation. In the Proceedings of the Third International Conference on Asian Digital Library, Seoul, Korea. 201-208.

15. Cunningham, S. J. & Mahoui, M. (2000). Search Behavior in Two Digital Libraries: A Comparative Transaction Log Analysis. In the Proceedings of the Third International Conference on Asian Digital Library, Seoul, Korea. 193-200.

16. Fu, L., Goh, D. H., Foo, S. S. Foo & Na, J. (2003). Collaborative Querying through a Hybrid Query Clustering Approach. In the Proceedings of the Sixth International Conference on Asian Digital Library, Kuala Lumpur, Malaysia. 111-122.

17. Geng, Y., Zhu, G., Qiu, J., Fan, J. & Zhang, J. (2004). An Experimental Study of Boosting Model Classifiers for Chinese Text Categorization. In the Proceedings of the Seventh International Conference on Asian Digital Library, Shanghai, China. 270-279.

18. Heß, M. & Drobnik, O. (1999). Clustering Specialized Web-Databases by Exploiting Hyperlinks. In the Proceedings of the Second Asian Digital Library Workshop, Taipei, Taiwan. 19-29.

19. Jones, S. & Mahoui, M. (2000). Hierarchical Document Clustering Using Automatically Extracted Key Phrases. In the Proceedings of the Third International Conference on Asian Digital Library, Seoul, Korea. 113-120.

20. Joung, Y. S., Hyun, S. J. & Kim, H. B. (2000). A Metadata Repository System for Efficient Description of Multimedia Documents in Digital Libraries. In the Proceedings of the Third International Conference on Asian Digital Library, Seoul, Korea.

21. Li, J., Wang, C. & Shi, S. (2004). A Kind of Index for Content-based Music Information Retrieval and Theme Mining. In the Proceedings of the Seventh International Conference on Asian Digital Library, Shanghai, China. 345-354.

22. Liew, C. L., Foo, S. & Chennupati, K. R. (2000). Enhancing User Interaction with Electronic Journals via Interactivity and Value-adding Features. In the Proceedings of the Third International Conference on Asian Digital Library, Seoul, Korea. 289-294.

23. Lo, S. C. & Chen, H. H. (1999). Resources Organization and Searching Specification: The 'Butterflies of Taiwan' Project. In the Proceedings of the Second Asian Digital Library Workshop, Taipei, Taiwan. 182-201.

24. McDonald, D. & Chen, H. (2002). Using Sentence Selection Heuristics to Rank Text Segments in TXTRACTOR. In Proceedings of JCDL'02, Portland, Oregon. ACM/IEEE-CS. 2835.

25. Ong, T. H. & Chen, H. (1999). Updateable PAT-Tree Approach to Chinese Key Phrase Extraction using Mutual Information: A Linguistic Foundation for Knowledge Management. In the Proceedings of the Second Asian Digital Library Workshop, Taipei, Taiwan. 63-84.

26. Parekh, H. (2001). Library on Women and Health in South Asia: Report of an International Collaboration. In the Proceedings of the Fourth International Conference on Asian Digital Library, Bangalore, India. 367-375.

27. Qin, J., Zhou, Y., Chau, M. & Chen, H. (2003). Supporting Multilingual Information Retrieval in Web Applications: An English-Chinese Web Portal Experiment. In the Proceedings of the Sixth International Conference on Asian Digital Library, Kuala Lumpur, Malaysia. 149-152.

28. Renda, M. E. & Straccia, U. (2002). A Personalized Collaborative Digital Library Environment. In the Proceedings of the Fifth International Conference on Asian Digital Library, Singapore. 262-274.

29. Rowe, J., Razdan, A., Collins, D. & Panchanahan, S. (2001). A 3D Digital Library System: Capture, Analysis, Query, and Display. In the Proceedings of the Fourth International Conference on Asian Digital Library, Bangalore, India. 149-159.

30. Smith, A. G. (1998). Criteria for Evaluation of Internet Resources in a Digital Library Environment. In the Proceedings of the First Asian Digital Library Workshop, Hong Kong. 81-87.
31. Sugimoto, S. (2001). Helping Information Access across Languages Using Simple Tools – Multilingual Projects at ULIS and Lessons Learned. In the Proceedings of the Fourth International Conference on Asian Digital Library, Bangalore, India. 16-29.
32. Sembok, T. M. T., Ali, K. P. N. M., Aidanismah, Y. & Wook, T. S. M. T. (2003). ISTILAH SAINS: A Malay-English Terminology Retrieval System Experiment Using Stemming and N-gram Approach on Malay Words. In the Proceedings of the Sixth International Conference on Asian Digital Library, Kuala Lumpur, Malaysia. 173-177.
33. Sun, J. (ed.). (2002). Proceedings of IT Opportunities and Challenges in the New Millennium, Beijing, China.
34. Tabata, K. & Sugimoto, S. (ed.). (1995). Proceedings of the Third International Symposium on Digital Libraries 1995, Tsukuba, Japan.
35. Tabata, K. & Sugimoto, S. (ed.). (1997) Proceedings of the International Symposium on Research, Development and Practice in Digital Libraries 1997, Tsukuba, Japan.
36. Tabata, K. & Sugimoto, S. (ed.). (1999). Proceedings of International Symposium on Digital Libraries 1999, Tsukuba, Japan.
37. Tang, S., Law, C. & Yen, J. (2000). Summarization for Multi-Document using Concept Space Approach. In the Proceedings of the Third International Conference on Asian Digital Library, Seoul, Korea, 121-130.
38. Theeramunkong, T., Wongtapan, C. & Sinthupinyo, S. (2002). Offline Isolated Handwritten Thai OCR Using Island-Based Projection with N-Gram Models and Hidden Markov Models. In the Proceedings of the Fifth International Conference on Asian Digital Library, Singapore. 340-351.
39. Vaidya, B. & Shrestha, J. N. (2002). Rural Digital Library: Connecting Rural Communities in Nepal. In the Proceedings of the Fifth International Conference on Asian Digital Library, Singapore. 354-365.
40. Vijayakumar, J. K. & Murthy, T. A. V. (2001). Need of a Digital Library of Indian Theses and Dissertations: A Model on Par With the ETD Initiatives at International Level. In the Proceedings of the Fourth International Conference on Asian Digital Library, Bangalore, India. 384-390.
41. Walfram, D. & Xie, H. (2001). State Digital Libraries: Developing Systems for General Audiences. In the Proceedings of the Fourth International Conference on Asian Digital Library, Bangalore, India. 62-74.
42. Witten, I. H. (2001). Visions of the Digital Libraries. In the Proceedings of the Fourth International Conference on Asian Digital Library, Bangalore, India. 3-15.
43. Witten, I. H. (2002). Examples of Practical Digital Libraries: Collections Built Internationally Using Greenstone. In the Proceedings of the Fifth International Conference on Asian Digital Library, Singapore, 67-74.
44. Wong, K. F. & Li, W. (1998). Intelligent Chinese Information Retrieval-Why Is It So Difficult? In the Proceedings of the First Asian Digital Library Workshop, Hong Kong. 47-56.
45. Wong, K. L., Lam, W. and Yen, J. (1999). Interactive Chinese News Event Detection and Tracking. In the Proceedings of the Second Asian Digital Library Workshop, Taipei, Taiwan. 30-46.
46. Xing, C., Zhou, L. Zhang, Z., Zeng, C. & Zhou, X. (2002). Developing Tsinghua University Architecture Digital Library for Chinese Architecture Study and University Education. In the Proceedings of the Fifth International Conference on Asian Digital Library, Singapore. 206-217.

47. Yang, C. C. & Luk, J. (2000). Constructing Chinese-English Concept Space. In the Proceedings of the Third International Conference on Asian Digital Library, Seoul, Korea. 139146.
48. Yang, C. C., Yen, J., Yung, S. K. & Chung, A. K. L. (1998). Chinese Indexing using Mutual Information. In the Proceedings of the First Asian Digital Library Workshop, Hong Kong. 57-64.
49. Yang, C. Z. & Kao, C. H. (1999). Visualizing Large Hierarchical Information Structures in Digital Libraries. In the Proceedings of the Second Asian Digital Library Workshop, Taipei, Taiwan. 243-254.
50. Yang, Y. J., Lee, S. D. & Choi, H. S. (1998). A Metadata Framework for Multimedia Resource Discovery Systems in Digital Library. In the Proceedings of the First Asian Digital Library Workshop, Hong Kong. 216-226.
51. Yeh, J. Y., Ke, H. R. & Yang, W. P. (2002). Chinese Text Summarization Using a Trainable Summarizer and Latent Semantic Analysis. In the Proceedings of the Fifth International Conference on Asian Digital Library, Singapore, 76-87.
52. Yen, J. (2000). From Unstructured HTML to Structured XML: How XML Supports Financial Knowledge Management. In the Proceedings of the Third International Conference on Asian Digital Library, Seoul, Korea. 71-80.
53. Ying, P. M. & Heng, J. S. H. (2002). The NUS Digital Media Gallery – A Dynamic Architecture for Audio, Image, Clipart, and Video Repository Accessible via the Campus Learning Management System and the Digital Library. In the Proceedings of the Fifth International Conference on Asian Digital Library, Singapore. 141-152.
54. Zhang, L., Wu, G., Xu, F., Li, W. & Zhong Y. (2004). Multilingual Collection Retrieving via Ontology Alignment. In the Proceedings of the Seventh International Conference on Asian Digital Library, Shanghai, China. 510-514.
55. Zhou, Y., Qin, J. & Chen, H. (2003). CMedPort: Intelligent Searching for Chinese Medical Information. In the Proceedings of the Sixth International Conference on Asian Digital Library, Kuala Lumpur, Malaysia. 34-45.

From the WWW and Minimal Digital Libraries, to Powerful Digital Libraries: Why and How

Edward A. Fox

Department of Computer Science, Virginia Tech, Blacksburg, VA 24061, USA
fox@vt.edu

Extended Abstract

Digital libraries have emerged since the early 1990s, distinguished in part by their emphasis on useful content, helpful organization, and a range of services that include at least indexing, searching, and browsing. In the 5S (Streams, Structures, Spaces, Scenarios, and Societies) formal model for digital libraries we precisely define key concepts and terms, so the field can move beyond the stage of continually explaining basic ideas and debating definitions. Thus, we define a *minimal digital library* in terms of clear definitions for *repository, metadata catalog, services,* and *societies,* which in turn build upon characterizations of *digital object, collection, hypertext,* etc.

The 5S approach has led to 5SL, an XML-based description language, and 5SGraph, a graphical tool that allows digital librarians to quickly prepare a 5SL description of a digital library suited to their needs. So far, 5SGraph can draw only upon two metamodels (which each include precisely the set of constructs needed for a meaningful class of digital libraries): 1. a minimal digital library whose base layer is of digital objects, and 2. an archaeological digital library that includes as well both real-world artifacts and discipline-specific constructs such as stratigraphic diagrams.

In this work we advance the state-of-the-art in the field by discussing the development of a much richer, third metamodel, for a powerful digital library, which includes most of what is handled by typical commercial, open-source, and research prototype digital libraries, as well as the WWW.

To give a solid grounding to the services part of the new metamodel, we draw upon our development of a taxonomy of digital library services and activities. The top level structure of that taxonomy and some of the key elements is as follows:

- Infrastructure Services
  - Repository Building
    - Creational
      - acquiring, authoring, cataloging, crawling, describing, digitizing, harvesting, submitting
    - Preservational
      - conserving, converting, copying, replicating
  - Adding Value
    - annotating, classifying, clustering, evaluating, extracting, indexing, linking, logging, measuring, rating, reviewing, surveying, training, translating, visualizing
- Information Satisfaction Services
  - browsing, filtering, recommending, searching

E.A. Fox et al. (Eds.): ICADL 2005, LNCS 3815, p. 525, 2005.
© Springer-Verlag Berlin Heidelberg 2005

Metadata Models Toward Community-Oriented Metadata Schemas

Shigeo Sugimoto

Research Center for Knowledge Communities,
Graduate School of Library, Information and Media Studies,
University of Tsukuba,
Tsukuba, Ibaraki, Japan,
sugimoto@slis.tsukuba.ac.jp

Metadata has been widely recognized as an important issue in digital libraries in many aspects. This report briefly describes models and frameworks of metadata schemas developed through metadata-centric research projects at University of Tsukuba, which are a few subject gateways and a few metadata schema projects primarily based on Dublin Core and Web technologies.

From the subject gateway projects, the author has learned that conventional and comprehensive subject vocabularies, e.g., UDC and NDC, are not always useful as a subject classification scheme for a subject gateway, and, on the other hand, subject vocabularies which are reasonably small and tailored in accordance with characteristics of users and application domains are useful to organize information resources and to create navigational user interfaces. Software tools to support development and maintenance of the vocabularies are crucial for the vocabularies oriented to users and their application domains[1][2].

The primary goal of the metadata schema projects is to enhance interoperability of metadata and metadata schemas. The author and his colleagues have been collaborating with the Dublin Core Metadata Initiative (DCMI) for the development of a DCMI metadata schema registry[3]. From the experiences in the schema registry project, we have proposed a simple layered model to help understand a framework of metadata schemas suitable in the Internet environment in order to enhance interoperability and reusability of metadata schemas. Metadata schema registry has potential not only to enhance metadata interoperability but also to support development of software tools to handle metadata, e.g. metadata editor and retrieval tool. We have experimentally developed a software generator attached to our metadata schema registry in order to support development of the software tools.

References

1. Sugimoto, S., et al.: Developing Community-Oriented Metadata Vocabularies: Some Case Studies. Proceedings of DLKC'04. Tsukuba (2004) 128-135
2. Lee, WS., Sugimoto, S.: Developing Community-Oriented Metadata Vocabularies: Some Case Studies. Proceedings of DC-2005. Madrid (2005) 15-24
3. Nagamori, M., Sugimoto, S.: A Framework of Metadata Schema for Functional Extension of Metadata Schema Registry. Proceedings of DC-2004. Shanghai (2004) 3-11

E.A. Fox et al. (Eds.): ICADL 2005, LNCS 3815, p. 526, 2005.
© Springer-Verlag Berlin Heidelberg 2005

Author Index

Lecture Notes in Computer Science

For information about Vols. 1–3727

please contact your bookseller or Springer